C0-AWW-161

HISTORICAL COMMENTARY
ON THE OLD TESTAMENT

* * *

LAMENTATIONS

HISTORICAL COMMENTARY

ON THE OLD TESTAMENT

LAMENTATIONS

by

Johan Renkema

PEETERS - LEUVEN

The translation was made possible in part due to the financial assistance of NWO, the 'Nederlandse organisatie voor wetenschappelijk onderzoek'*.

Translated from the Dutch by Brian Doyle

Dr. Johan Renkema
Lamentations
(Historical Commentary on the Old Testament)
Cover design by Dick Prins
NUGI 632
ISBN 90-429-0677-4
D. 1998/0602/295

* The Dutch Organisation for Scientific Research.

EDITORIAL PREFACE

The Historical Commentary on the Old Testament is a commentary series written by an international team of contributors. The operative word in the title is 'historical', by which the editors mean to convey a specific perspective on the writings of the Old Testament.

In contrast to the ahistorical approach of much of contemporary reader-oriented exegesis, in which it is mainly the interaction between the modern reader and the final text that matters, the editors of the HCOT are committed to an approach which takes seriously the historical embeddedness of the message of the Old Testament. As itself the product of a long and complex process of transmission, and as part of the sacred Scriptures which have been embraced by both Judaism and Christianity, the Hebrew Bible or Old Testament is rooted in the concreteness of human history, and cannot be properly understood apart from that historical rootedness.

The editors are committed to the view that the Old Testament was and is a vehicle of the knowledge of God – a knowledge that was originally imparted at specific times and places within the bounds of human history. In order for people today to recognize and accept the permanent validity of that knowledge, they must realize that the Old Testament originated in a human society which, with respect to the basic realities of the human condition, was not so very different from our own. It was in the context of a fundamentally similar society, in the concreteness of ordinary human history, culture, and language, that the revelation of God was received over the centuries. It is only by concentrating on the specificity of that thoroughly historical revelation (often brought into focus by comparing the traditions of Israel with those of its neighbours), that we can hope to grasp the uniqueness of the faith of ancient Israel.

In connection with this emphasis, the editors aim at producing a commentary on the Old Testament that devotes explicit attention to the history of interpretation, both as this can be discerned within the Hebrew canon itself, and as it has continued subsequent to the close of the Old Testament canon.

As the term 'Old Testament' indicates, the commentary stands in the Christian exegetical tradition. The contributors, representing a wide range of denominational affiliation, will treat the history of both Jewish and

Christian interpretation with due respect, but will also be free to take their own stand on controversial issues.

The commentary will seek to be both up-to-date with respect to contemporary scholarship and in touch with the centuries-long tradition of exegetical reflection on the Old Testament. On the one hand, it is impossible nowadays to present a fully argued exegetical case without referring constantly to the flood of new information which is constantly being made available in such disciplines as archaeology and philology. The wealth of information on any biblical text is so overwhelming that a good commentary nowadays will often need to be more extensive than its predecessors. On the other hand, theological exegesis cannot afford to write off previous scholarship in its field. There is a wealth of largely untapped exegetical wisdom that is available in the history of biblical interpretation.

Since the commentary is intended to serve not only the guild of Old Testament scholars, but also pastors and the educated laity, its format is designed to serve a wide readership. The discussion of every pericope of the biblical text will consist of a new translation of the pericope in question, a relatively brief non-technical section entitled 'Essentials and Perspectives,' and a longer, technical section entitled 'Scholarly Exposition'. The translation will be a new rendering based directly on the Hebrew or Aramaic text. Under the heading Essentials and Perspectives the authors will summarize the results of their exegesis in non-technical language. In this section, a knowledge of the biblical languages will not be assumed, and the exegetical exposition will be based primarily on the final shape of the text. However, if various strata can be discerned in the growth of the present text, it will be appropriate to elucidate the meaning of every stratum in its own historical setting. Related passages elsewhere in the Old Testament may also be adduced in this section, especially those that can be regarded as later applications or actualizations of the text in question. This will also be the place for the treatment of significant exegetical insights from the history of Jewish and Christian interpretation outside of the Old Testament itself, especially those found in the New Testament. Although there is an emphasis in this section on the history of interpretation, the authors are free to bring forward their own insights with respect to the contemporary relevance of the text.

The exegetical summary will constitute an invitation to the reader to consult the subsequent section of Scholarly Exposition, which will contain the more detailed and technical treatment of the exegetical issues.

Here the commentator, though under no editorial constraints with regard to questions of authorship, dating, or method, is expected to deal with the full range of issues raised by modern critical scholarship. However, in accordance with the goal formulated above, the authors are expected to pay due attention to the meaning of every historical stage which they discern in the formation of the text, including its final canonical stage. Tradition-historical and redaction-critical analyses should not become ends in themselves, but should be subservient to an understanding of the inner-canonical history of interpretation.

If the historical context cannot be defined precisely (as is the case with many parts of the book of Proverbs), the historical background of the genre as such (in the case of Proverbs the proverbial wisdom literature of the Ancient Near East) can provide the appropriate historical context in terms of which the text should be understood.

Generally speaking, everything that brings the concrete historical world of the text closer to the modern reader – whether that be specific data regarding climate, geology, geography, minerals, flora and fauna, or whatever – should be treated extensively in the scholarly exposition. Where appropriate, due attention should also be paid to scribal conventions and the physical aspects of the transmission of ancient texts.

The Editors

Cornelis Houtman
Willem S. Prinsloo†
Wilfred G.E. Watson
Al Wolters

Author's Preface

The present volume is a translation of my commentary on *'Klaagliederen'*, published in 1993 in the Dutch series 'Commentaar op het Oude Testament' (COT, Kampen).

For this translation the Dutch text was checked through, minor changes and additions were made, and Hebrew text was vocalized. The bibliography was also revised.

I am most grateful to my translator, drs. Brian Doyle, for his sensitive translation of my original Dutch text and for his obliging cooperation in the final preparation of this volume. Gratitude is also due to the Board of Trustees of the Theological University of Kampen for their generous financial support.

Kampen, February 1998 — Johan Renkema

CONTENTS

ABBREVIATIONS

AB	The Anchor Bible
AJ	Acta Jutlandica
AB	The Anchor Bible
acc.	accusativus
AJ	Acta Jutlandica, Theology Series
AJSL	American Journal of semitic Languages and Literatures
ALUOS	Annual of Leeds University Oriental Society
AOAT	Alter Orient und Altes Testament
AOB	Altorientalische Bilder zum Alten Testament
ANEP	J.B. Pritchard, *The Ancient near East in Pictures Relating to the Old Testament*, Princeton 1969[2]
ANET	*Ancient Near Eastern Texts Relating to the Old Testament.* (Ed.) J.B. Pritchard Princeton 1969[3]
ASOR	American Schools of Oriental Research (Special Volume Series)
ATD	Das Alte Testament Deutsch. Neues Göttinger Bibelwerk
AuS	G. Dalman, *Arbeit und Sitte in Palästina*, 7 Bde, Gütersloh 1928–1942 (reprint: Hildesheim 1964–1971)
BAR	Biblical Archaeology Review
BAT	Die Botschaft des Alten Testaments
BHK	Biblia Hebraica. Edidit Rudolph Kittel. Editio tertia decima emendata typis editionis septimae expressa
BHS	Biblia Hebraica Stuttgartensia
BKAT	Biblischer Kommentar Altes Testament (Neukirchen)
BL	H. Bauer – P. Leander, Historische Grammatik der hebräischen Sprache des Alten Testamentes, Hildesheim 1965 (reprint of 1922)

BOT	De boeken van het Oude Testament (Roermond/Maaseik)
BRL	Biblisches Reallexicon. Hrsg. K. Galling, Tübingen 1977[2]
Brockelmann	C. Brockelmann, Hebräische Syntax, Neukirchen 1956
BS	Bibliotheca Sacra
BWANT	Beiträge zur Wissenschaft vom Alten und Neuen Testament
BZAW	Beihefte zur Zeitschrift für die alttestamentliche Wissenschaft
CB	Coniectanea Biblica
CBQ	Catholic Biblical Quarterly
CI	Complaint of an Individual
COT	Commentaar op het Oude Testament
CP	Complaint of the People
CR	Corpus Reformatorum, ediderunt Baum – Cunitz – Reuss, Brunsvigae 1888
CTA	A. Herdner, Corpus des tablettes en cunéiformes alphabétiques découvertes à Ras Shamra-Ugarit de 1929 à 1939 (Mission de Ras Shamra, 10) 2 tomes, Paris 1963
Debrunner	F. Blass – A. Debrunner, Grammatik des neutestamentlichen Griechisch, Göttingen 1965[12]
dtn	deuteronomic
dtr	deuteronomistic
EdF	Erträge der Forschung
ET	Expository Times
ETL	Ephemerides Theologicae Lovanienses (Leuven)
FRLANT	Forschungen zur Religion und Literatur des Alten und Neuen Testaments
Fs	Festschrift
GES-B	W. Gesenius – F. Buhl, Hebräisches und Aramäisches Handwörterbuch über das Alte Testament, Berlin–Göttingen–Heidelberg 1954[17]

GES-K	W. Gesenius – E. Kautzsch, Hebräische Grammatik, Leipzig 1909[28]
HAL	Hebräisches und Aramäisches Lexikon zum Alten Testament, von L. Koehler und W. Baumgartner, Leiden 1967–1990
HKAT	Handkommentar zum Alten Testament
IB	The Interpreter's Bible, New York
ICC	The International Critical Commentary (Edinburgh)
ITC	International Theological Commentary
JANES	Journal of the Ancient Near Eastern Society
JAOS	Journal of the American Oriental Society
JBL	Journal of Biblical Literature
JNES	Journal of Near Eastern Studies
Joüon	P. Joüon, Grammaire de l'Hébreu Biblique, Rome 1965 (herdruk van 1923)
JR	The Journal of Religion
JSOT	Journal for the Study of the Old Testament
JSS	Journal of Semitic Studies
KAT	Kommentar zum Alten Testament
KBL	L. Koehler – W. Baumgartner, Lexikon in Veteris Testamenti Libros, Leiden 1958
KC	Kamper Cahiers
KD	K. Barth, Kirchliche Dogmatik, I–IV, Zürich 1964[8]–1970
König	E. König, Historisch-Kritisches Lehrgebäude der hebräischen Sprache. Syntax, Leipzig 1897
KTU	M. Dietrich, O. Loretz, J. Samartín, *The Cuneiform Alphabetic Texts from Ugarit, Ras Ibn Hani and Other Places* (KTU: second, enlarged edition), Neukirchen 1976
Lett.	J.P. Lettinga, *Grammatica van het Bijbels Hebreeuws*, Leiden 1976[8]
Luther	M. Luther, Die gantze heilige Schrift Deudsch. Hrsg. H. Volz, Darmstadt 1973[2]

LXX	Septuaginta. Id est Vetus Testamentum graece iuxta LXX interpretes. Edidit Alfred Rahlfs, Stuttgart 1965[8]
MT	Masoretic text
NBG	The Translation of the Dutch Bible Society (1951)
NCBC	The New Century Bible Commentary
NEB	The New English Bible with the Apocrypha, Oxford-Cambridge 1970[2]
OA	Oriens Antiquus
OC	Opera Calvini
OLZ	Orientalistische Literaturzeitung
OR	Orientalia
OTS	Oudtestamentische Studiën (Leiden)
P	Priestercodex
PA	Palaestina Antiqua
PJB	Palästinajahrbuch
POT	De prediking van het Oude Testament
RAC	Reallexikon für Antike und Christentum
RB	Revue Biblique
RGG	Die Religion in Geschichte und Gegenwart, I–IV, Register, Tübingen 1957–1965[3]
SBS	Stuttgarter Biblische Studien, Stuttgart
SEÅ	Svensk Exegetisk Årsbok
STL	Studia Theologica Lundensia
SV	Statenvertaling (Dutch State Translation)
SVT	Supplements to Vetus Testamentum (Leiden)
sv	sub voce
TGI	Textbuch zur Geschichte Israels. Ed. K. Galling, Tübingen 1979[3]
THAT	*Theologisches Handwörterbuch zum Alten Testament, I & II*, E. Jenni – C. Westermann (eds.), München-Zürich 1971–1976

ThB	Theologische Bücherei
TTS	Trierer Theologische Studien
TW	Theologische Wissenschaft, Sammelwerk für Studium und Beruf
TWAT	*Theologisches Wörterbuch zum Alten Testament, I–VIII*, Stuttgart-Berlin-Köln-Mainz, 1970–1989
UF	Ugarit-Forschungen (Neukirchen)
UT	C.H. Gordon, Ugaritic Textbook, Roma 1965
VT	Vetus Testamentum (Leiden)
WMANT	Wissenschaftliche Monographien zum Alten und Neuen Testament
WSB	Wuppertaler Studienbibel
ZAW	Zeitschrift für die alttestamentliche Wissenschaft
ZB	Zürcher Bibelkommentare
ZDPV	Zeitschrift des deutschen Palästina-Vereins
Zorell	F. Zorell – L. Semkowski, *Lexicon Hebraicum et Aramaicum Veteris Testamenti*, Roma 1968
ZthK	Zeitschrift für Theologie und Kirche
√	wortel / radix

COMMENTARIES (chronological)

J. Calvin, *Lamentationes Ieremiae*, in: OC vol. 38, CR vol. 66

B. Blayney, *Jeremiah and Lamentations*, Oxford 1784

O. Thenius, *Die Klagelieder*, Leipzig 1855

H. Ewald, *Die Dichter des Alten Bundes I/2*, Göttingen 1866[3]

C.W.E. Nägelsbach, *Die Klagelieder*, Leipzig 1868

C.F. Keil, *Biblischer Commentar über den Propheten Jeremia und die Klagelieder*, Leipzig 1872

S. Oettli, *Die Klagelieder. Kurzgef. Kommentar zu den Schriften des A.T.*, Nordlingen 1889

K. Budde, *Die Klagelieder*, KHCAT XVII, Freiburg 1898

M. Löhr, *Die Klagelieder des Jeremia*, HKAT III.2.2, Göttingen 1894; 1906[2]

T. Paffrat, *Die Klagelieder*, HSAT VII/3, Bonn 1932

G.Ch. Aalders, *Klaagliederen*, KV, Kampen 1939[2]

M. Haller, *Die Klagelieder*, HAT I 18, Tübingen 1940

L.H. van der Meiden, *De Klaagliederen van Jeremia*, Baarn 1952

N.K. Gottwald, *Studies in the Book of Lamentations*, London 1954

H. Wiesmann, *Die Klagelieder übersetzt und erklärt*, Frankfurt-Main 1954

G.A.F. Knight, *Esther, Song of Songs, Lamentations*, Introduction and Commentary, London 1955

Th.J. Meek, *The Book of Lamentations*, IB VI, New York 1956

B.N. Wambacq, *Klaagliederen*, BOT X, Roermond 1957

H. Lamparter, *Das Buch der Sehnsucht, Ruth Hoheslied Klagelieder*, BAT 16/II, Stuttgart 1962

W. Rudolph, *Die Klagelieder*, KAT XVII/3, Gütersloh 1962

A. Weiser, *Klagelieder*, ATD 16, Göttingen 1967[2]

H.J. Kraus, *Klagelieder*, BKAT XX, Neukirchen 1968[3] (1960[2])

O. Plöger, *Die Klagelieder*, HAT I/18, Tübingen 1969^{2}

R.K. Harrison, *Jeremiah and Lamentations*, London 1973

R. Gordis, *The Song of Songs and Lamentations*, New York 1974

A. van Selms, *Jeremia III en Klaagliederen*, POT, Nijkerk 1974

W.J. Fuerst, *The books of Ruth, Esther, Ecclesiastes, The Song of Songs, Lamentations.* The five Scrolls (CamBC), Cambridge 1975

D.R. Hillers, *Lamentations*, AB 7A, New York 1979^{3}

M. Zlotowitz, מגילת איכה, New York 1979^{6}

O. Kaiser, *Klagelieder*, ATD 16, Göttingen 1981^{3}

R. Brandscheidt, *Gotteszorn und Menschenleid. Die Gerichtsklage des leidenden Gerechten in Klgl 3*, TTS 41, Trier 1983

R. Martin-Achard and S.P. Re'emi, *God's People in Crisis: A Commentary on the Book of Amos; A Commentary on Lamentations*, ITC, Edinburgh / Grand Rapids 1984

H.J. Boecker, *Klagelieder*, ZB AT 21, Zürich 1985

R. Davidson, *Jeremiah 2 and Lamentations*, Philadelphia 1985

H. Groß, *Klagelieder*, Würzburg 1986

C.D. Stoll, *Die Klagelieder*, WSB, Wuppertal 1986

R. Brandscheidt, *Geistliche Schriftlesung. Das Buch der Klagelieder*, Düsseldorf 1988

C. Westermann, *Die Klagelieder, Forschungsgeschichte und Auslegung*, Neukirchen-Vluyn 1990

I.W. Provan, *Lamentations* NCBC, London 1991

O. Kaiser, *Klagelieder*, ATD 16/2, Göttingen 1992

BIBLIOGRAPHY (alfabetical)

Works already mentioned in the list of abbreviations are not included in the bibliography. This includes the much referred to Theologisches Handwörterbuch zum Alten Testament, I & II, E. Jenni – C. Westermann (eds.), München-Zürich 1971–1976 (THAT) and the Theologisches Wörterbuch zum Alten Testament, I–VIII, Stuttgart-Berlin-Köln-Mainz, 1970–1989 (TWAT).

B. Albrektson, *Studies in the Text and Theology of the Book of Lamentations, with a Critical Edition of the Peshitta Text*, Studia Theologica Lundensia 21, Lund 1963

A. Alt, 'Judas Gaue unter Josia', PJB 21 (1925), 100–115

A. Alt, *Kleine Schriften zur Geschichte des Volkes Israël I*, München 1959²

G.A. Anderson, *A Time to Mourn, a Time to Dance. The Expression of Grief and Joy in Israelite Religion*, Pennsylvania, 1991

J.R. Bartlett, *Edom and the Edomites*, JSOT suppl Series 77, Sheffield 1989

H. Bauer – P. Leander, *Historische Grammatik der hebräischen Sprache*, Hildesheim 1965

W. Baumgartner, *Die Klagegedichte des Jeremias*, BZAW 32, 1917

J. Begrich, *Die priesterliche Tora*, BZAW 66, 1936, 63–88; reprint in: J. Begrich, *Gesammelte Studien zum Alten Testament*, ThB 21, München 1964, 232–260

J. Begrich, 'Das priesterliche Heilsorakel', ZAW 52, 1934, 81–92 (= *Gesammelte Studien*, ThB 21, München 1964, 217–231)

I. Beit-Arieh, 'New Light on the Edomites', BAR (1988), 28–41

S. Bergler, 'Threni V – nur ein alphabetisierendes Lied? Versuch einer Deutung', VT XVII (1977), 311–313.

W.A.M Beuken, *Jesaja deel IIIA*, POT, Nijkerk 1989

P.A.H. de Boer, *An Inquiry into the Meaning of the Term* משא, OTS V 1948

J. Böhmer, 'Ein alphabetisch-akrostisches Rätsel', ZAW 28 (1908), 53–57

C. Brockelmann, *Hebräische Syntax*, Neukirchen 1956

H.A. Brongers, 'Der Zornesbecher', OTS 15 (1969), 177–192

G. Brunet, *Les Lamentationes contre Jérémie*, Bibliothèque de l' Ecole des hautes études. Sciences Religieuses 75, Paris 1968

G. Brunet, 'La Cinquième Lamentation', VT XXXIII (1983), 149–170

K. Budde, 'Das hebräische Klagelied', ZAW 2 (1882), 1–52

W.W. Cannon, 'The Authorship of Lamentations', BS 81, Washington 1924, 43–45

H. Christ, *Blutvergießen im Alten Testament*, Basel 1977

W.E. Claburn, 'The Fiscal Basis of Josiah's Reform', JBL 92 (1973)

Ch. Cohen, 'The 'widowed' city', JANES 5 (1973), 75–81

A. Cohen, 'Lamentations 4:9', AJSL 27 (1910/11), 190–191

A. Condamin, *Poèmes de la Bible*, Paris 1933

F.M. Cross, 'Studies in the Structure of Hebrew Verse: The Prosody of Lamentations 1:1–22', in: C.L. Meyers and M. O'Connor (eds.), *The Word of the Lord Shall Go Forth*: Essays in Honor of David Noel Freedman in Celebration of His Sixtieth Birthday, ASOR SVS 1, Winona Lake, Indiana 1983, 129–155

M. Dahood, Review of: B. Albrektson, *Studies in the Text and Theology of the Book of Lamentations, with a critical edition of the Peshitta text.* (Studia Theologica Lundensia 21) 1963; in: Biblica 44 (1963), 547–549

M. Dahood, 'Hebrew-Ugaritic Lexicography VIII', Biblica 51 (1970), 403

M. Dahood, 'Ugaritic Lexicography', Mélanges Eugène Tisserant I (Studi e Testi 231) Vatican City 1964

S. Daiches, 'Lamentations ii 13', ET 28 (1917), 189

G. Dalman, *Arbeit und Sitte in Palästina I–VII*, 1928–42

A. Demsky and M. Kockavi, 'An Alphabet from the Days of the Judges', BAR 1978 IV/3, 23–30

A. van Deursen, *De achtergrond van de Psalmen*, Baarn (undated), 128–135

G.R. Driver, 'Hebrew Notes on "Song of Songs" and "Lamentations" ', Fs. A. Bertholet, Tübingen 1950, 134–146

M. Dijkstra – J.C. de Moor, 'Problematical Passages in the Ugaritic Legend of Aqhatu', UF 7 (1975), 171–215

A.B. Ehrlich, *Randglossen zur hebräischen Bibel VII*, Leipzig 1914

O. Eissfeldt, *Einleitung in das Alte Testament*, 1964^3, 777–781

I. Elbogen, *Der jüdische Gottesdienst in seiner geschichtlichen Entwicklung*, Hildesheim 1967

J.A. Emerton, 'The Meaning of אבני קדש in Lamentations 4,1', ZAW 79 (1967), 233–236

F.C. Fensham, *Exodus*, POT, Nijkerk 1970

G. Fohrer, *Geschichte der israelitischen Religion*, Berlin 1969

G. Fohrer, *Geschichte Israels*, Heidelberg 1977

D.N. Freedman, 'Acrostic Poems in the Hebrew Bible: Alphabetic and Otherwise', CBQ 48 (1986), 408–431

V. Fritz, *Tempel und Zelt*, WMANT 47, Neukirchen 1977

W.J. Fuerst, *The books of Ruth, Esther, Ecclesiastes, The Song of Songs, Lamentations.* The five Scrolls (CamBC), Cambridge 1975

C.J. Gadd, 'The Second Lamentation for Ur', in *Hebrew and Semitic Studies Presented to Godfrey Rolles Driver.* D.W. Thomas & W.D. McHardy (eds.), Oxford, 1963

G. Gerleman, *Ruth. Das Hohelied*, BKAT XVIII, Neukirchen-Vluyn 1965

G. Gerstenberger – W. Schrage, *Leiden*, Stuttgart 1977

N. Glueck, *Das Wort hesed im alttestamentlichen Sprachgebrauch als menschliche und göttliche gemeinschafts-gemäße Verhaltungsweise*, BZAW 47 (1927)

R. Gordis, 'The Asseverative Kaph in Ugaritic and Hebrew', JAOS 63 (1963), 176–178

R. Gordis, 'The Conclusion of the Book of Lamentations', JBL 93 (1974), 298–293

C.J. Goslinga, *Het eerste boek Samuël*, COT, Kampen 1968

H. Gottlieb, *A Study of the Text of Lamentations*, Acta Jutlandica XLVIII, Theology Series 12 Århus 1978

N.K. Gottwald, *Studies in the Book of Lamentations*, London 1954

R. Gradwohl, *Die Farben im Alten Testament*, BZAW 83, Berlin 1963

C. Grave, 'On the use of an Egyptian Idiom in an Amarna Letter from Tyre in a Hymn to the Aten', OA XIX (1980), 205–218

J. Gray, I & II Kings, OTL, London 1970^2

D. Grossberg, *Centripetal and Centrifugal Structures in Biblical Poetry*, Atlanta 1989

A. Guillaume, 'A Note on Lamentations IV 9', ALUOS 4 (1962–63), 47–48

H. Gunkel, *Die Psalmen*, HKAT II/2, Göttingen 1926[4]

H. Gunkel, 'Klagelieder Jeremiae', in: H. Gunkel & L. Zscharnack (eds.), RGG III, Tübingen 1929[2], 1049–1052

H. Gunkel – J. Begrich, *Einleitung in die Psalmen*, Göttingen 1975[3]

A.H.J. Gunneweg, *Vom verstehen des Alten Testaments*, Göttingen 1977

W.C. Gwaltney Jr., 'The Biblical Book of Lamentations in the Context of Near Eastern Lament Literature', in: F.E. Greenspahn (ed.), *Essential Papers on Israël and the Ancient Near East*, New York/London, 1991, 242–265

J.L. Helberg, 'The Incomparable Sorrow of Zion in the Book of Lamentations', in: Studies in Wisdom Literature, W.C. van Wijk (ed.), OTWSA 15 & 16: Old Testament Studies, Papers read at the 15th and 16th Meeting of the OT werkgemeenskap Suid-Afrika 1972 and 1973, 27–36. Edited 1976

J.L. Helberg, 'Land in the Book of Lamentations', ZAW 102, 1990, 372ff

S. Herrmann, *Geschichte Israels*, München 1973

H.W. Hertzberg, *Die Samuelbücher*, ATD 10, Göttingen 1973

C. Houtman, *De hemel in het Oude Testament*, Franeker 1974

A.R. Hulst – C. van Leeuwen, *Bevrijding in het Oude Testament*, Kampen 1981

H. Jagersma, *Numeri deel II*, POT, Nijkerk 1988

H. Jagersma, *Geschiedenis van Israël*, Kampen 1979

H. Jahnow, *Das hebräische Leichenlied im Rahmen der Völkerdichtung*, BZAW 36, Giessen 1923

E. Janssen, *Juda in der Exilszeit*, FRLANT NF 51, Göttingen 1956

J. Jeremias, *Kultprophetie und Gerichtsverkündigung in der späten Königszeit Israels*, Neukirchen 1970

J. Jeremias, *Die Reue Gottes*, Neukirchen 1975

J. Jeremias, *Theophanie*, WMANT 10, Neukirchen 1977[2]

B. Johnson, 'Form and Message in Lamentations', ZAW 97 (1985), 58–73

B.B. Kaiser, 'Poet as "Female Impersonator": The Image of Daughter Zion as Speaker in Biblical Poems of Suffering', JR 67 (1987), 164–182.

O. Kaiser, *Der Königliche Knecht*, FRLANT, NF 52, 1959

O. Kaiser, *Die mythische Bedeutung des Meeres in Ägypten, Ugarit und Israel*, Berlin 1962[2]

O. Kaiser, *Der Prophet Jesaja*, Kapitel 1339, ATD 18, Göttingen 1973

A.S. Kapelrud, 'Guden som sviktet?', SEÅ 41–42 (1976–1977), 138–146

O. Keel, *Die Welt der altorientalischen Bildsymbolik und das Alte Testament*, Zürich-Einsiedeln-Köln-Neukirchen-Vluyn 1977[2]

O. Keel, *JHWH-visionen und Siegelkunst*, SBS 84/85, Stuttgart 1977

O. Keel, *Jahwes Entgegnung an Ijob*, Göttingen 1978

K. Koch, 'Gibt es ein Vergeltungsdogma im AT', ZTHK 52 (1955), 1–42

K. Koch (ed.), *Um das Prinzip der Vergeltung in Religion und Recht des Alten Testaments*, WDF CXXV, Darmstadt 1972, 130–181

K. Koch, 'Die Rolle der hymnischen Abschnitte in der Komposition des Amos-Buches', ZAW 86 (1974), 504–537

L. Köhler, *Theologie des Alten Testaments*, Tübingen 1966[4]

L. Köhler, *Der hebräische Mensch*, Tübingen 1953; herdruk Darmstadt 1976

J.L. Koole, *De tien geboden*, Baarn 1964

J.L. Koole, *Haggaï*, COT, Kampen 1965

J.L. Koole, *Jesaja II, deel I Jesaja 40 tot en met 48*, COT, Kampen 1985

J.L. Koole, *Jesaja II, deel II Jesaja 49 tot en met 55*, COT, Kampen 1990

L. Kopf, 'Arabische Etymologien und Parallelen zum Bibelwörterbuch', VT VIII (1958), 161–215

M.C.A. Korpel – Johannes C. de Moor, 'Fundamentals of Ugaritic and Hebrew Poetry', in: *The Structural Analysis of Biblical and Canaanite Poetry*, (eds. W. van der Meer and J.C. de Moor) JSOT Suppl Series 74, Sheffield 1988

M.C.A. Korpel, *A Rift in the Clouds*, Münster 1990

H.J. Kraus, *Gottesdienst in Israel*, München 1954

H.J. Kraus, *Psalmen, 1–59*, BKAT XV/1, Neukirchen 1978[5]

H.J. Kraus, *Psalmen, 60–150*, BKAT XV/2, Neukirchen 1978[5]

H.J. Kraus, *Theologie der Psalmen*, BKAT XV/3, Neukirchen 1979

E. Kutsch, *«Trauerbrauche» und «Selbstminderungsriten» im Alten Testament*, Theologische Studien 78 (1965) 25–42

C. van Leeuwen, *Hosea*, POT, Nijkerk 1968

C. van Leeuwen, *Amos*, POT, Nijkerk 1985

E. Levine, *The Aramaic Version of Lamentations*, New York 1976

F. Lindström, *God and the Origin of Evil. A Contextual Analysis of Alleged Monistic Evidence in the Old Testament*, Coniectanea Biblica, Old Testament Series 21, Lund 1983

E. Lipiński, 'Etymological and Exegetical Notes on the Mesa Inscription',

Orientalia 40 (1971), 325–340

J.A. Loader, 'De structuuranalytische methoden', in: *Inleiding tot de studie van het Oude Testament*, (ed.) A.S. van der Woude, Kampen 1986, 128–142.

N. Lohfink, 'Enthielten die im Alten Testament bezeugten Klageriten eine Phase des Schweigens?', VT XII (1962), 260–277

P. van der Lugt, *Strofische structuren in de bijbels-hebreeuwse poëzie*, Kampen 1980

H.M. Lutz, Jahwe, *Jerusalem und die Völker*, WMANT 27, Neukirchen–Vluyn 1968

O. Margalith, 'Samson's Foxes', VT XXXV (1985), 227v.

C. McCarthy, *The Tiqqune Sopherim and Other Theological Corrections in the Masoretic Text of the Old Testament*, Göttingen 1981

Th.F. McDaniel, 'Philological Studies in Lamentations I–II', Biblica 49 (1968), 29ff, 199ff

Th.F. McDaniel, 'The alleged Sumerian Influence upon Lamentations', VT XVIII (1968), 198–209

W. McKane, Poison, 'Trial by Ordeal and the Cup of Wrath', VT XXX (1980), 474–492

Z. Meshel, 'Did Yahweh Have a Consort? The New Religious Inscriptions from the Sinai', in: BAR 1979 V/2, 24–35

T.N.D. Mettinger, *King and Messiah, The civil and Sacral Legitimation of the Israelite Kings*, Lund 1976

T.N.D. Mettinger, *The Dethronement of Sabaoth. Studies in the Shem and Kabod Theologies*, Coniectanea Biblica, Old Testament Series 18, Lund 1982

M. Metzger, 'Himmlische und irdische Wohnstatt Jahwes', UF 2 (1970), 139–158

A. Mintz, 'The Rhetoric of Lamentations and the Representation of Catastrophe', Proof 2 (1982) 1–17

K.H. Miskotte, *Als de goden zwijgen. Over de zin van het Oude Testament*, Haarlem 1966

J.C. de Moor, '"O Death, Where Is Thy Sting?"', in: L. Eslinger, G. Taylor (eds.), *Ascribe to the Lord: Biblical and Other Studies in Memory of Peter C. Craigie.* (JSOT suppl Series 67). Sheffield 1988

J.C. de Moor, *De tijd van het heil*, KC 15, Kampen 1970

J.C. de Moor, *The Seasonal pattern in the myth of Ba'lu*, AOAT 16, Neukirchen 1971

J.C. de Moor, *New Year with Canaanites and Israelites*, KC 21, 1972

J.C. de Moor, 'The sacrifice which is an abomination to the LORD', in: *Loven en Geloven*, Fs. Nic. H. Ridderbos, Amsterdam 1975, 211–226

J.C. de Moor, 'Rapi'uma Rephaim', ZAW 88 (1976), 323–345

J.C. de Moor, 'Narrative Poetry in Canaan', in: A. Dearman (Ed.), *Studies in the Mesha Inscription and Moab*, Atlanta 1989, 149–171

J.C. de Moor, *The Rise of YAHWISM*, Leuven 1997[2]

J.C. de Moor, 'The Integrity of Isaiah 40', in: M. Dietrich, O. Loretz (eds.), *Mesopotamica – Ugaritica – Biblica: Festschrift für Kurt Bergerhof zur Vollendung seines 70. Lebensjahres am 7.Mai 1992.* Neukirchen-Vluyn: Neukirchener Verlag 1993, 181-216.

M.S. Moore, 'Human Suffering in Lamentations', RB 83 (1990), 534–555

S. Mowinckel, *Psalmenstudien IV*, reprint Amsterdam 1961

J. Muilenberg, 'A Study in Hebrew Rhetoric: Repetion and Style', VTS I (1953), 97–111

J.M. Myers, 'Edom and Judah in the Sixth-Fifth Centuries B.C.', in: *Near Eastern Studies in Honor of W.F. Albright*, ed. H. Goedicke, Baltimore 1971, 386–392

J. Negenman, *Een geografie van Palestina*, PA 2, Kampen 1982

M. Noth, 'Die Einnahme von Jerusalem im Jahre 597 v. Chr.', ZDPV 74 (1958), 155f

M. Noth, *Die Welt des Alten Testaments*, Berlin 1962

M. Noth, *Geschichte Israels*, Göttingen 1969[7]

M. Noth, *Das vierte Buch Mose*, Numeri, ATD 7, Göttingen 1973[2]

F. Nötscher, 'Zum emphatischen Lamed', VT III (1953), 372–380

A.S. Onderwijzer, *Nederlandsche vertaling van den Pentateuch, benevens eene Nederlandsche verklarende vertaling van Rashie's Pentateuch-Commentaar*, Amsterdam 1977[2]

T.W. Overholt, *The Threat of Falsehood*, London 1970

F. Perles, 'Was bedeutet כמות in Threni 1,20?', OLZ 23 (1920), 157–158

F. Praetorius, 'Threni I,12,14; II,6,13', ZAW 15 (1895), 143–146

H.D. Preuss, *Deuteronomium*, EdF 164, Darmstadt 1982, 153–158

I.W. Provan, 'Past, Present and Future in Lamentations iii 52–66: the Case for a Precative Perfect Re-examined', VT XLI (1991), 164–175

G. von Rad, 'Verheißenes Land und Jahwes Land im Hexateuch', ZDPV (1943), 191–204. Reprint in: *Gesammelte Studien zum Alten Testament*, ThB 8, München 1958, 87–100

G. von Rad, *Theologie des Alten Testaments, Band I, Die Theologie der geschichtlichen Überlieferungen Israels*, München 1966[5]

G. von Rad, *Theologie des Alten Testaments, Band II, Die Theologie der prophetischen Überlieferungen Israels*, München 1968[5]

G. von Rad, *Das fünfte Buch Mose. Deuteronomium*, ATD 8, Göttingen 1968[2]

G.W. Randalf, 'The Qinah: A Study of Poetic Meter, Syntax and Style', ZAW 95 (1983), 54–75

B. Reicke – L. Rost, *Biblisch-Historisches Handwörterbuch*, Göttingen 1962–1979;

J. Renkema, *"Misschien is er hoop...". De theologische vooronderstellingen van het boek Klaagliederen*, Franeker 1983

J. Renkema, 'The Literary Structure of Lamentations (I–IV)', in: *The Structural Analysis of Biblical and Canaanite Poetry*, W. van der Meer & Johannes C. de Moor (eds.) JSOT Suppl Series 74, Sheffield 1988, 294–396

J. Renkema, 'Does Hebrew *ytwm* really mean "fatherless"?', VT XLV (1995), 119–122

J. Renkema, 'The meaning of the parallel acrostics in Lamentations', VT XLV (1995), 379–383

J. Renkema, 'A note on Jeremiah xxviii 5', VT XLVII (1997), 253–255

J. Ridderbos, *De Psalmen I*, COT Kampen 1955

J. Ridderbos, *De Psalmen II*, COT, Kampen 1958

N.H. Ridderbos, *De Psalmen I*, Korte Verklaring, Kampen 1962

N.H. Ridderbos, *Die Psalmen. Stilistische Verfahren und Aufbau mit besondere Berücksichtigung von Ps. 1–41*, BZAW 117, Berlin 1972

N.H. Ridderbos, *De Psalmen II*, Korte Verklaring, Kampen 1973

W.H.P. Römer, *Sumerische 'Königshymnen' der Isin-Zeit*, Leiden 1965

M. Rose, *Der Ausschließlichkeitsanspruch Jahwes*, BWANT 106, Stuttgart-Berlin-Köln-Mainz 1975

K. Roubos, *II Kronieken*, POT, Nijkerk 1972

J. de Savignac, 'Théologie pharaonique et messianisme d'Israel', VT VII (1957), 82

A.M. Schaerlaekens, *De taalontwikkeling van het kind*, Groningen 1985[2]

J. Scharbert, *Der Schmerz im Alten Testament*, Bonn 1955

H. Schmid, *Die Gestalt des Mose. Probleme alttestamentlicher Forschung unter Berücksichtigung der Pentateuchkrise*, EdF 237, Darmstadt 1986

A. van Selms, *Jeremia deel I*, POT, Nijkerk 1972

A. van Selms, *Jeremia deel II*, POT, Nijkerk 1974

A. van Selms, *Jeremia deel III en Klaagliederen*, POT, Nijkerk 1974

A. van Selms, *Job deel II*, POT, Nijkerk 1983

W. Shea, 'The *qinah* Structure of the Book of Lamentations', Biblica 60 (1979), 103–107

P.W. Skehan, 'The Structure of the Song of Moses in Deuteronomy (32:1–43)', in: *Studies in Israelite Poetry and Wisdom*, Washington 1971

R. Smend, *Die Entstehung des Alten Testaments*, TW I, Stuttgart-Berlin-Köln-Mainz 1978

J.A. Soggin, 'Der prophetische Gedanke über den heiligen Krieg als Gericht gegen Israel', VT X (1960), 79–83

J.A. Soggin, 'Der Beitrag des Königtums zur Israelitischen Religion', in: *Studies in the Religion of Ancient Israel*, VTS 23, Leiden 1972

W. Speyer, 'Fluch', RAC 7, col. 1160–1288

H. Spieckermann, *Juda unter Assur in der Sargonidenzeit*, FRLANT 129, Göttingen 1982

H. Spieckermann, *Heilsgegenwart. Eine Theologie der Psalmen*, Göttingen 1989

H. Spieckermann, 'Dies Irae: der alttestamentliche Befund und seine Vorgeschichte', VT XXXIX (1989), 194–208

K. Spronk, *Beatific Afterlife in Ancient Israel and in the Ancient Near East*, AOAT 219, Neukirchen-Vluyn 1986

Th. Struys, *Ziekte en genezing in het Oude Testament*, Kampen 1968

S. Terrien, 'The Omphalos Myth and Hebrew Religion', VT XX (1970), 315–338

W. Thiel, *Die deuteronomistische Redaktion von Jeremia 1–25*, WMANT 41, Neukirchen 1973

W. Thiel, *Die deuteronomistische Redaktion von Jeremia 26–45*, WMANT 52, Neukirchen 1981

J.A. Thompson, 'Israel's "lovers" ', VT XXVII (1977), 475–481

E. Tov, 'De tekst van het Oude Testament', in: *Bijbels Handboek 1*, Kampen 1981, 217–262

E. Tov, *Textual Criticism of the Hebrew Bible*, Assen/Maastricht, 1992

R. de Vaux, *Les Institutions de l'Ancien Testament I*, Paris 1958

R. de Vaux, *Les Institutions de l'Ancien Testament II*, Paris 1960

K.R. Veenhof, 'De geschiedenis van het oude Nabije Oosten', in: *Bijbels Handboek I*, ed. A.S. van der Woude, Kampen 1981, 278–441

Th.C. Vriezen, *Hoofdlijnen der theologie van het Oude Testament*, Wageningen 1966[3]

Th.C. Vriezen & A.S. van der Woude, *Literatuur van Oud-Israël*, Wassenaar 1976[5]

B.K. Waltke - M. O'Conner, *An Introduction to Biblical Hebrew Syntax*, Winona Lake, Indiana 1990

W.G.E. Watson, *Classical Hebrew Poetry. A Guide to its Techniques*, JSOT suppl series 26, Sheffield 1984

W.G.E. Watson, 'Internal or half-line parallelism in Classical Hebrew Poetry', VT XXXIX (1989), 44–66

J. Wellhausen, *Skizzen und Vorarbeiten V*, Berlin 1893[2]

P. Wernberg–Møller, Review of: B. Albrektson, *Studies in the Text and Theology of the Book of Lamentations, with a critical edition of the Peshitta text*, STL 21, 1963; in: JSS X (1955), 103–110

C. Westermann, 'Struktur und Geschichte der Klage im Alten Testament', in: *Forschung am Alten Testament*, ThB 24, München 1964, 266–305

C. Westermann, 'Die Begriffe für Fragen und Suchen im Alten Testament', ThB 55, München 1974, 162–190

C. Westermann, *Genesis 1–11*, BKAT I/1, Neukirchen–Vluyn 1974

C. Westermann, *Theologie des Alten Testaments in Grundzügen*, ATD Ergänzungsreihe 6, Göttingen 1978

G. Widengren, *The King and the Tree of Life in Ancient Near Eastern Religion (King and Saviour IV)*, Uppsala 1951

B. Wielenga, *De Bijbel als boek van schoonheid*, Kampen, 1960[6]

H. Wiesmann, 'Der Verfasser des Büchleins der Klagelieder - ein Augenzeuge der behandelten Ereignisse?', Biblica 17 (1936), 71–84

H. Wildberger, *Jesaja 1–12*, BKAT X/1, Neukirchen 1972

H. Wildberger, *Jesaja 13–27*, BKAT X/2, Neukirchen 1978

H. Wildberger, *Jesaja 28–39*, BKAT X/3, Neukirchen 1982

H. Winitz & O.C. Irwin, 'Infant Speech: Consistency with age', in: Journal of Speech and Hearing Research, 1958(b) I, 245–249

D.J. Wiseman, *The Vassal-Treaties of Esarhaddon*, London 1958

H.W. Wolff, *Dodekapropheton 1, Hosea*, BKAT XIV/1, Neukirchen 1965[2]

H.W. Wolff, *Dodekapropheton 2, Joel und Amos*, BKAT XIV/2, Neukirchen–Vluyn 1969

H.W. Wolff, 'Das Thema "Umkehr" in der alttestamentlichen Prophetie', in: Gesammelte Studien zum AT, ThB 22, München 1973[2], 130–150

H.W. Wolff, *Anthropologie des Alten Testaments*, 1977[3]

H.W. Wolff, *Dodekapropheton 4, Obadja, Jona*, BKAT XIV/3, Neukirchen–Vluyn 1977

H.W. Wolff, *Dodekapropheton 4, Micha*, BKAT XIV/4, Neukirchen-Vluyn 1982

A.S. van der Woude, *Micha*, POT, Nijkerk 1976

A.S. van der Woude, *Jona Nahum*, POT, Nijkerk 1978

A.S. van der Woude, *Habakuk-Sefanja*, POT, Nijkerk 1978

A.S. van der Woude, *Zacharia*, POT, Nijkerk 1984

E. Würthwein, *Der Text des Alten Testaments*, Stuttgart 1973[4]

J. Ziegler, 'Die Hilfe Gottes "am Morgen" ', Fs. F. Nötscher, 1950, 281–288

W. Zimmerli, *Ezechiel 1–24*, BKAT XIII/1, Neukirchen 1979[2]

W. Zimmerli, *Ezechiel 25–48*, BKAT XIII/2, Neukirchen 1969

W. Zimmerli, *Grundriß der alttestamentlichen Theologie*, Stuttgart Berlin Köln Mainz, 1972

A.H. van Zijl, *I Samuël, deel I*, POT, Nijkerk 1988

INTRODUCTION[1]

I Title

The name *'Lamentations'* is a rendering of the Hebrew word קִינוֹת (*qinôt*). The fact that the name was employed by the oldest Jewish traditions for the five songs it designates is evident from its use in the Septuagint (Θρῆνοι), which was followed later by the Vulgate (Lamentationes). The translation 'Lamentations' is incorrect, however, since a קִינָה actually refers to a specific kind of lament: a lament for the dead. The term קִינוֹת, therefore, might be more adequately rendered by the word 'Dirges'. Despite the use of motifs from the dirge genre, however, and the fact that the structure of the five songs is borrowed from the 3 + 2 meter of the dirge (see III.1), one would, nevertheless, search the text in vain for the noun קִינָה. This is due, without doubt, to the fact that the purpose or intention of Lamentations is not the same as that of a dirge.[2] In this sense one might also object to the Masoretic title אֵיכָה ('Ah'), which, although borrowed from the first word of the first song, still leaves one with the impression that Lamentations has something to do with a dirge (see the exegesis of 1_1). If one were to look for a word or phrase in the text itself as an adequate name/title with respect to the content of the songs then one might opt for the core verse 3_{50}: עַד־יַשְׁקִיף וְיֵרֶא יְהוָה, *'until* YHWH *looks down and sees...'*, supplication for YHWH's salvific 'looking down' being the primary intention of the songs (see explanation). The traditional name קִינוֹת, however, was not derived from the songs themselves but rather imposed on them. The reason for this must be sought in the very ancient tradition which ascribed the authorship of the songs to the prophet Jeremiah, most probably on the basis of II Chron 35_{25} where it is said that the prophet sang laments on the occasion of the death of King Josiah. Such an association need not

[1] See also JRenkema, *'Misschien is er hoop...'*, Franeker 1983, 1–4, 43–90. Henceforth this book will be referred to by year only (1983). For the terminology used below (responses, inclusions, cantos and such) see the section dealing with method.

[2] Cf genre (III.2) and 'Sitz im Leben' (III.3).

be surprising given the fact that this prophet had also lived through the events which are treated in the songs and had even predicted them earlier in his prophecies. The fact that this notion was already dominant among the oldest known Jewish traditions is evident from the Septuagint which even mentions Jeremiah by name: "After Israel was taken off into exile and Jerusalem left abandoned, the prophet Jeremiah sat down and wept and uttered this lamentation over Jerusalem saying...".[3] Both the Targum and the Babylonian Talmud (Baba Bathra ['final door'] 15a) understood Jeremiah to be the author of these songs.

At first sight it would appear that the Masoretes have deviated from this tradition. Just like all the other biblical books they labelled the songs – as we mentioned above – according to the initial word of the first song: אֵיכָה. There is no mention of the authorship of Jeremiah and by placing the songs with the *'Writings'* in their canonical ordering they simply disappeared behind their title. All of this need not necessarily imply that in doing what they did the Masoretes distanced themselves from the traditional position. The different ordering of the biblical books in the Masoretic canon does not prove this. No additional material from the Septuagint found its way into the Hebrew text of the Masoretic canon. Furthermore, where Lamentations is concerned, the Greek (interpreting) preamble constitutes nothing less than a disruption of the form of the Hebrew alphabetic acrostic.

While most modern bible translations base themselves on the Masoretic text, they opt, nevertheless, for a translation of the more ancient name קִינוֹת (*qinôt*) as a title.

II Place in the Canon

As far as we know the canonical status of Lamentations has never been in dispute. Where the actual position in the canon is concerned there is once again a difference between the Septuagint and the Masoretic traditions. The former places the songs after the book of Jeremiah, undoubtedly on the basis of his presumed authorship. As we have already noted, the Masoretic deviation from this sequence need not imply a denial of Jeremian authorship; it is simply the consequence of a different ordering of the bib-

[3] Καὶ ἐγένετο μετὰ τὸ αἰχμαλωτισθῆναι τὸν Ισραηλ καὶ Ιερουσαλημ ἐρημωθῆναι ἐκάθισεν Ιερεμιας κλαίων καὶ ἐθρήνησεν τὸν θρῆνον τοῦτον ἐπὶ Ιερουσαλημ καὶ εἶπεν...

lical books. Differences of opinion on the correct order of books in the bible prevailed for quite some time in later Jewish tradition. With respect to the third part of the bible or the 'Writings', variations in sequence continued to exist long into the Christian era.[4] It was not until the sixth century that Song of Songs, Ruth, Lamentations, Qoheleth, and Esther were combined to form the so-called מְגִלּוֹת ('the scrolls'). Even here, however, there were variations in the arrangement of the books. The codex Leningrad (B 19^{A}), for example, placed Lamentations after Qoheleth (because Jeremiah had written after Solomon) and this is the sequence we find in BHK and BHS. The prior order of the 'scrolls' (Song of Songs, Ruth, Lamentations, Qoheleth, Esther) was prompted by the Jewish liturgical year which associated each scroll with a particular feast or commemoration. Lamentations was read (in part) on the 9th of Av which was, among other things, the day of the destruction of the first (and second) temple. This tradition is known from the 6th century CE onwards.[5] The unity of the מְגִלּוֹת, however, cannot be traced any earlier than the 12th century CE. The Christian tradition adopted the Septuagint tradition and continues to place Lamentations after Jeremiah.

III Literary Structure

III.1 Unity

From the perspective of regularity Lamentations manifests a remarkable literary structure. The first two songs are outwardly identical, both being alphabetic acrostics with strophes of equal size each of which beginning with a consecutive letter of the Hebrew alphabet. The two songs differ on only one point: the acrostics are at variance with one another in alphabetic succession.[6] The third song differs from the first two in that the alphabetic acrostic is applied to the beginning of each verse, which is equal three times per strophe. The fourth song is in line with the second, with the exception that it employs two verses instead of three per strophe. The final song is different in every respect. It is not an alphabetic acrostic, it is shorter and it makes use of a different meter.

---

[4] Cf RSmend, *Die Entstehung des Alten Testaments*, TW I, Stuttgart-Berlin-Köln-Mainz 1978, 15f.

[5] Cf IElbogen, *Der jüdische Gottesdienst in seiner geschichtlichen Entwicklung*, Hildesheim 1967, 18ff.

[6] More on this in section III.4.

Given this state of affairs, the fact that even in the most recent research Lamentations has been considered by some to be a collection of disconnected songs will come as no surprise. In literary-critical research this has led to a tendency to focus on each song individually and to examine them, moreover, in the context of the remaining Old Testament literature rather than in context with one another. As a result, there is substantial divergence among scholars with respect to the dating and genre of each song. This opinion and methodical approach can be found in even the most recent publications, evident examples being the commentaries of Kaiser and Westermann.[7]

One of the weaknesses of this approach has always been the fact that while it was easy to point out how the songs differed from one another, no adequate explanation was offered as to why precisely these five songs have always been handed down together. Some have offered the common acrostic structure as the reason for this but one is then left with the stumbling block of the fifth song which does not share this feature.[8] Nevertheless, there have always been exegetes, such as Wiesmann and Plöger, who have maintained the unity of these songs. Their primary reasoning runs as follows: the individual songs cannot be read apart from one another; cf the transition from the second song to the third. Such evident coherence, however, may also have been the work of a redactor.

The redactional character of the unity of Lamentations has recently been energetically defended by Renate Brandscheidt[9] who considers the songs to be independent units and even posits four different authors. She adjudges only Lam III and IV to have the same authorship. Lam II, which describes YHWH's judgement over Zion and the hopelessness which is its outcome, she considers to be the oldest. Lam I came into existence some time thereafter and is a lament over Zion. The long duration of the desperate situation then prompted the writing of Lam V. These three songs were collected by a redactor and Lam IV was added in conscious contrast to Lam II, there being a glimmer of hope for Zion – in her exegesis at least – at the end of the fourth song. Lam III was consciously placed in the centre and is didactic in character teaching how a person ought to behave in the time of judgement. On the basis of the theological reading

[7] More on this question can be found in 1983, 53–58 and in MSMoore, 'Human Suffering in Lamentations', RB 83 (1990), 539–543.

[8] Cf 1983, 59.

[9] RBrandscheidt, *Gotteszorn und Menschenleid*, TTS 41, Trier 1983.

of history evident in the songs – Zion's downfall is YHWH's judgement upon the sins of Israel – she proposes that the author who collected the songs must have belonged to the Deuteronomistic school. Brandscheidt's thesis remains unconvincing. At the level of content, among other things, her argumentation for reduction to a Deuteronomistic redactor is weak and indirect. She uncritically accepts Albrektson's opinion which wrongly presupposes Deuteronomistic influence in Lamentations.[10] Although she rightly points out the influence on the songs of the pre-exilic prophets of doom, she wrongly concludes from the fact that these prophetic traditions had undergone a Deuteronomistic redaction that influence from this redaction must also be present in Lamentations.[11] At the same time, she does not discuss the dating of the relevant Deuteronomistic redaction in relation to the dating of Lamentations. Zion's downfall, however, as YHWH's judgement upon the sins of Israel, might also have been deduced from the unedited preaching of pre-exilic prophets. As far as the literary structure of the songs is concerned her argumentation is equally unconvincing since it is not clear why the author of Lam IV would give a different structure to Lam III which he also had penned. The absence of an alphabetic acrostic in Lam V also remains unexplained as does the absence in the same song of literary indications for the long duration of the distress, such as the prayer-questions one commonly finds at such moments: עַד־אָנָה (cf Hab 1_2; Ps 13_{2f}, 62_4, Job 18_2, 19_2) or עַד־מָה (cf Ps 74_9, 79_5, 89_{47}) as well as עַד־מָתַי (cf Ps 74_{10}, 80_5, 94_3).

An extremely original explanation of the unity and structure of the five songs has been proposed by Shea in his article: 'The *qinah* Structure of the Book of Lamentations'.[12] He argues that the basic pattern of the composition is determined by the structure of the dirge, a structure which possesses a particular meter, the so-called *qinah*-meter, which renders weeping for the dead in a literary form. The *qinah*-meter is characterised by 3 + 2 beats. The first three long beats represent the initial moments of weeping while the final two short beats correspond to the sobs of the dirge.[13] This

---

[10] Cf 1983, 21–32.

[11] More on the subject in 1983, 20–31; 201–213; 260–261; JRenkema, 'The Literary Structure of Lamentations (I–IV)', in: *The Structural Analysis of Biblical and Canaanite Poetry*, WvdMeer & JCdMoor (eds) JSOT supplement series 74, Sheffield 1988, 389. Henceforth this essay will be referred to by year only (1988).

[12] WHShea, 'The *qinah* Structure of the Book of Lamentations', Biblica 60 (1979) 103–107.

[13] Cf KBudde, 'Das hebräische Klagelied', ZAW (1882), 48f and GWRandalf, 'The

special 3 + 2 formation is evidently present in the structure of Lamentations.[14] Shea refers to similar usage of meter as a structuring pattern in II Sam 1 and Ez 26_{17-18}.[15] It is quite remarkable that commentators and researchers writing after 1979 do not refer to Shea's proposal. It is not discussed in Brandscheidt, Kaiser, Groß and Boeker, and is equally left untouched by Moore who presses the question of unity nevertheless.[16] In spite of his 'forschungsgeschichtliche' research Westermann also omits to mention Shea's article. Provan's recent commentary on Lamentations does mention the title of Shea's article but does not discuss his thesis. Provan even writes: "The only explicit evidence of a literary connection between the poems in the book is that found in 3:1", namely in the connection with Lam II which precedes it. This too, however, may be the work of a redactor who brought together five more or less disconnected songs into one group. If Shea's proposal is correct then the presupposition of such a redactional process becomes less and less likely. Excessive restructuring of the form of the already existing songs would have been necessary and it remains a question whether one should continue to consider such activity as redactional.

Shea offers an insightful explanation for the structure of the composition: Lamentations was tailor made to fit this structure. Such an explanation leaves open the possibility that the individual songs possess a relatively significant independence within the unity of the composition. The repetition of the structure of the alphabetic acrostic for four of the songs is evidence that this is true to a certain degree. Each song, furthermore, offers its own elaboration of the themes it shares with the others, a fact which is most evident in the third song with its unique style and content. The final song also has its own character when compared with the four preceding it. In addition, the first two songs differ from one another in terms of the Hebrew alphabetic order. Nevertheless, we were able to demonstrate elsewhere that all five songs are very closely related both from a literary perspective and in terms of content.[17] This relationship can be traced to external parallelisms in the songs which one finds time and again in equivalent parallel letter-strophes or in larger literary units (canticles).

Qinah: A Study of Poetic Meter, Syntax and Style', ZAW 95 (1983), 54–75.

[14] For more on the 3 + 2 formation see DNFreedman, 'Acrostic Poems in the Hebrew Bible: Alphabetic and Otherwise', CBQ 48 (1986), 408f, 429.

[15] For more on this topic see 1983, 72–74 and 1988, 359.

[16] MSMoore, 'Human Suffering in Lamentations', RB 83 (1990), 539–543.

[17] Cf 1988, 361–396.

One can also speak of song-responses. In advance some exemples.

Let us start with the coherence between the א-strophes and include 5_1. In 1_1 Lady Jerusalem is depicted as a widow (כְּאַלְמָנָה). It is well known that widowhood and jewellery are incompatible,[18] a fact which is one of the links with 2_1: the Lord has taken away the jewel of Israel, is equivalent to the temple of Jerusalem. The daughter of Zion has become like a widow because the Lord – 'her husband' – in dark anger has withdrawn his presence from Zion.

The link with 3_1 lies in the darkness which accompanies YHWH's Day of Judgement. The גֶּבֶר complains that the Lord has driven him in darkness and no light, a quotation of Amos' description of the day of the Lord (Amos 5_{18}). The גֶּבֶר, the pious man of 3_1 – who is one of the בְּנֵי צִיּוֹן (4_2) – is an inhabitant of Jerusalem, cf 3_{51}. The misery of Lady Jerusalem – depicted in 1_1 – is the same misery that he is facing. A part of his misery is the destruction of the temple, depicted in 2_1, but also in 4_1. It is caused by the anger of the Lord,[19] and the dimness of the gold of the temple on Zion (4_1) is caused by the darkness of his anger (2_1).

Lam 5_1 shows a strong link with 1_1: the disgrace which is complained about includes the disgrace of Lady Jerusalem, who has become like a widow: כְּאַלְמָנָה (1_1) // חֶרְפָּתֵנוּ (5_1). It also includes the misery of the pious man of 3_1 and the destruction of Zion (2_1, 4_1).

Let us now consider something of the coherence of the ב-strophes. 1_2 points to the tears of Lady Jerusalem caused by the betrayal of her former neighbours who have become her enemies. The effect of their hostile activity is depicted in 2_2 as an act of YHWH, see 2_7. The outcome is the destruction of the strongholds and the kingdom of Judah. This breakdown is contrasted with the building of a prison wall around the pious man (the גֶּבֶר of 3_1): הָרַס contra בָּנָה. There are clear connections with 3, the beginning of the ב-strophe of the third song. Lam 2_2 speaks of the breakdown of the cities and 3_4 speaks of the breakdown of one of their inhabitants, the devout man. As a consequence 4_2 speaks of the children of Zion as broken potsherds. The 'night' of Lady Jerusalem corresponds with the dark places into which the גֶּבֶר has been driven by YHWH. The breakdown of the kingdom and its leaders leaves the population unprotected. 5_2 depicts the result: land, cities and homes have fallen into the hands of the enemies.

One might continue by pointing out the theme of hunger in 1_{11}, 2_{11}, and also in 4_{10} and 5_{10}, or the desperate observation of Lady Jerusalem that the Lord

[18] Cf Jes 61_3, Judith 8_5.
[19] Cf Mi 3_{14}, Lam 4_{11}.

has brought her illness (1_{13c}) and the similarly desperate question of the poets: 'Who will now be able to cure her?' (2_{13c}). We can likewise point to the dismay of the passers-by concerning the brutal fate of Jerusalem (2_{15c}) and the related complaint of the pious man that YHWH has made them as rubbish among the nations (3_{45}), or to the contrasting link between the former sweetness the children of Zion once enjoyed (4_5) and the present bitter food and drink of the גֶּבֶר in 3_{15}; cf Prov 5_{3f}. We can draw attention to the connection between the enemies in the gates of Jerusalem (4_{12}) and the fate of the princes (5_{12}); see also the prayers in 1_{20}, 2_{20}, 3_{58ff}, 5_{19ff}.[20]

For further discussion on these external parallelisms and their particular arrangement as song-responses and inclusions, together with the designation of literary units, consult our description of the method used in the exegesis. Further exegetical research has confirmed our results with regard to the relationship between the songs and has unveiled even more song-responses.[21] The location and meaning of these responses is discussed in the detailed exegesis of each song.

III.2 Genre[22]

The apparent close relationship between the songs made evident by the song-responses has consequences for the traditional manner of approaching the question of genre. The genre of Lamentations as a whole has practically never been discussed. Instead, the most common approach was to seek the genre of each individual song by investigating agreements with well known and appropriate genres such as the dirge or the CI and CP.[23] Westermann was unable to avoid the trap of form-historical research in this regard: he compared the songs with the standard models of the CI and CP – which were nowhere to be found on their own merits – and subsequently considered every deviation to be secondary. According to Westermann, only those sections which most closely represent the (presumed) original forms can have any claim to authenticity. The problem remains, however, that we are not dealing with independent songs which were later cast in the form of alphabetic acrostics and then compiled into a book. The evident cohesion of the songs, therefore, raises the question as

[20] See JRenkema, 'The meaning of the parallel acrostics in Lamentations', VT XLV/3 (1995) 379–382.

[21] The survey on pp 636–641 can be consulted as a supplement to 1988, 392–394.

[22] See also the introduction to each individual song.

[23] Abbreviations of *complaint of an individual* and *complaint of the people.*

to the genre of the whole. Of course, we might be jumping the gun a little in speaking of a genre since we are only justified in doing so when several literary compositions of the same type are available to us. This is not the case. Since there is nothing similar to Lamentations in terms of size in the Old Testament, we are forced to assume that its five closely related songs are a unique literary creation. This takes nothing away from the fact that substantial elements of well-known genres such as CI and CP, together with style-figures from the dirge, have been incorporated into each individual song. Johnson rightly points out with respect to the elements of CI and CP: "but the formal elements are not pure enough to permit an exact qualification. It is rather a *Mischgattung*, where the elements are mixed up instead of following the strict pattern of the classical lament song." [24] One would fail to appreciate the unique literary character of Lamentations if one were to reduce the songs to either a dirge or a CI/CP. Westermann reduces the songs to a CP (Lam III to a CI). As a result he tends to depreciate the alphabetic acrostic as a form for Lamentations, viewing it as a secondary disruption of the structure of the more original form of the CI or CP.[25] One is left, however, without an adequate explanation of the form as it has been transmitted. Something similar might be said with respect to the combination of lament and dirge. For Westermann, the inclusion of elements from the dirge (which he does not always recognise) is nothing more than a further indication of the seriousness of the lament. It is the latter form which dominates. Such an approach does not do justice to the combination of lament with elements from the dirge. The pointed inclusion of style-figures from the dirge (cf, for example, the opening words of 1_1, 2_1, 4_1) suggests the creation of a new mode of expression. More on this topic can be found in VII.2.1. For the difference in alphabetical order between the ע and the פ see III.4.

III.3 'Sitz im Leben'

Westermann's understanding of the genre of the songs is closely related to his vision of their origin and 'Sitz im Leben'. Alone among modern exegetes, he does not consider the songs to be a literary creation from their outset. Their written formation, rather, represents the final stage of an earlier, oral transmission of classical complaints of the people. The de-

[24] BJohnson, 'Form and Message in Lamentations', ZAW 97 (1985), 60.

[25] CWestermann, *Die Klagelieder. Forschungsgeschichte und Auslegung*, Neukirchen 1990, 89–95.

struction of city and land together with the prevailing distress must have quickly led to such complaints.[26] This leads Westermann to a greater appreciation of the similarity, based on themes and motifs, between Lamentations and the Sumarian lament over the destruction of Ur,[27] although he agrees with McDaniel[28] that there can be no question of direct literary dependence. The resemblance between the lament in Sumer and the lament in Israel is due to similarity in experience as well as agreements at the level of content. Parallels can be seen in the inscription, the experience of destruction as an event which includes a religious dimension and the enumeration of all the population groups, from the king down to the children, who are suffering under the situation of distress.

From the form-historical perspective, it is striking that the same connection with elements from the dirge is present in each lament. According to Westermann, the actual experience of the destruction and devastation of a human environment such as a city is a human experience "die auch bestimmte Ausdrucksformen prägte, die an ganz verschiedenen Stellen auftauchen konnten."[29] All of this does not diminish the fact that Lamentations deserves to be interpreted primarily within its own religious and literary context. Westermann complies with this for the most part by relating the songs of Lamentations with the Old Testament complaint of the people which went hand in hand with a specific ritual.[30] In times of great distress the community gathered fasting in the sanctuary. The people dressed in torn clothing, went barefoot and (partially) naked (1_{8b}), in sack-cloth and ashes (2_{10}), covered with dust (2_{10}), lying face down on the ground (2_{10c}, cf explanation), or standing with their hands raised up to heaven (1_{17}; 3_{41}), weeping and wailing (3_{49-50}) and supplicant before YHWH (2_{18-22}). The lament then turned into prayer beginning with the vocative 'YHWH' (cf $1_{9,11,20}$, 2_{20}, 3_{19}, 5_{19}). Westermann sees such complaints of the people, which took place immediately after the destruction of Jerusalem, as the primitive form(s) of Lamentations: "Der Gedanke, daß sie tatsächlich von den Erschütterten, den trauernden Überlebenden gesprochen und sodann von anderen aufgenomen wurden, weitergegeben

[26] Westermann, *Klagelieder*, 92ff.

[27] Text in ANET[3], 611–619.

[28] ThFMcDaniel, 'The alleged Sumerian Influence upon Lamentations', VT XVIII (1968), 198–209.

[29] Westermann, *Klagelieder*, 31.

[30] See for this ritual HGunkel – JBegrich, *Einleitung in die Psalmen*, Göttingen 1975[3], 117–139.

von den Näheren zu den Ferneren, von den Älteren zu den Jüngeren, so daß auf diese Weise eine mündliche Tradition dieser Klagen entstand, ist fast keinem der die Threni Auslegenden gekommen."[31] Westermann's conclusion that the language of Lamentations, together with the comparisons evident therein, suggests that the songs originated with ordinary people fits into this line of thought.[32] The alphabetic acrostic structure was applied when the orally transmitted laments took on written form, although for Westermann this remains secondary with respect to the original shape of the songs. Such a negative evaluation is to be found time and again in Westermann's exegesis. The acrostic is thereby condemned as an unjustified intrusion into the classical structure of the complaint of the people and even seen as the explanation for interrupted thought processes in the songs.[33]

Westermann's approach provides a valuable contribution to the debate on Lamentations because it forces us to reflect on their origin and 'Sitz im Leben'. His arguments are quite convincing at first sight. We have already noted the points of correspondence between Gunkel's description of the event of the complaint of the people and Lamentations (see above). Almost all the elements are to be found and where they are not, a logical explanation can be given for their absence. Fasting, for example, is inappropriate due to the terrible famine and since the temple lay in ruins a meeting in the sanctuary was clearly out of the question.

Important facts remain, however, which show Westermann's reconstruction to be inadequate. He himself, for example, continually refers to the unique character of Lamentations, exhibited in its combination of the complaint of the people and elements from the dirge prompted by the unprecedented catastrophe which had befallen Jerusalem and Judah in 587. Israel had never experienced such disaster hitherto. Given the multiple incidence of this combination in the final written stage of the songs we must assume that it was already present in the oral tradition. This, however, does not lead Westermann to nuance his genre definition of the oral stage. After the fall of Jerusalem a number of the essential prerequisites for organising classic complaints of the people were missing: the sanctuary, the priests, the prophets and the king. Furthermore, as the city of YHWH, the destruction of Jerusalem and particularly the temple must

[31] Westermann, *Klagelieder*, 62.
[32] Westermann, *Klagelieder*, 96.
[33] Cf below the discussion of the genre of Lam I.

have given many the impression that their relationship with YHWH had been shattered once and for all, an idea which is implied by the repetition of 'there is no comforter' in the first song. In light of such extreme circumstances, the usual genre of the complaint of the people was no longer appropriate as a form of expression for Lamentations. The only fitting expressions were those which could appropriate new means to articulate Israel's unprecedented distress. The very multiplicity of the occurrences of the combination of the CP and CI genre with that of the dirge points clearly in this direction. Even the invocation of YHWH is more urgent in the songs of Lamentations than at any other time in Israel's history.[34] The substantial nature of the relationship between the songs remains fatal for Westermann's 'überlieferungsgeschichtliche' reconstruction. His understanding of Lamentations as originally independent oral complaints of the ordinary people which were later adapted, given written form and collated seems, therefore, to be untenable. There can be no doubt about the fact that Lamentations is a written creation, a well-considered compositional unity.

Nevertheless, Westermann's remarks still carry much substance with respect to 'Sitz im Leben'. It is clear that the songs reflect the horror experienced in the city and the land; the tears and lamentation are indeed those of Jerusalem. This, however, constitutes only part of the content of Lamentations. There is an undeniable degree of theological reflection at work also, one which has its roots in the 'Why?' of this catastrophe. Reality and faith do not exist apart from one another. It is apparent from the songs that the poets were in search of an answer. Their harking back to the preaching of those prophets who had announced the fall of Jerusalem and their appropriation of some of their language and motifs[35] shows that they had found an answer therein to the agonising 'Why?' of their downfall.[36] At the same time, they tried to establish for themselves the extent to which they could still acknowledge YHWH and have faith in him. Evidently an element of Psalm theology appears to have survived the disaster.

From previous research we learned that the composers of Lamentations were highly skilled in the language and theology of the Psalms and this led us to the conclusion that they ought to be sought among the temple

[34] Cf the explanation of $1_{9cA,11cA}$, 2_{18-19} and $5_{1B,19A}$.
[35] Cf 1983, 262–267, and passim in this commentary.
[36] See, for example, the explanation of 1_{18a}, 2_{17}, 3_{37ff} etcetera.

singers who had remained in Jerusalem[37] and the present commentary continues to fully endorse such a conclusion. The creation and development of Lamentations, therefore, might be proposed as follows: After the downfall of Jerusalem, the community of YHWH endured terrible distress and spiritual confusion. The priests and the prophets no longer had the power to help.[38] In the midst of the crisis, the temple singers as minor 'clergy' took on a position of leadership. They sought a new way of drawing YHWH's attention to their affliction, a new way of praying and believing in which they could involve their fellow Israelites. Although Westermann, in line with McDaniel, considers a direct connection between Lamentations and the laments over the downfall of Ur implausible, one must also take the possibility into account that the temple singers, who were skilled in matters of literature, might have been familiar with such ancient songs or at least have known of their existence.[39] As far as culture was concerned Israel did not exist in isolation. Comings and goings at the international level had already become common even in our most ancient history and not only for the purpose of exchanging goods and property.[40] One can certainly assume that after the first deportation in 597 there was healthy trade between Babylon and Jerusalem and that the cultural inheritance of Mesopotamia was definitely a topic of conversation in the homeland.[41] Awareness of the existence of songs on the destruction of other cities and their temples may have inspired the temple singers in Jerusalem to give shape to their own thoughts and hopes by writing a similar poem in their own language, adapted to their own situation and, of course, with an *interpretatio israelitica*.

---

[37] Cf 1983, 256–260.

[38] Cf 1_{19}, $2_{9,14}$, 4_{13} and the five times repeated refrain 'there is no comforter' in the first song ($1_{2,9,16,17,21}$).

[39] Cf WCGwaltney Jr, 'The Biblical Book of Lamentations in the Context of Near Eastern Lament Literature', in: FEGreenspahn (ed), *Essential Papers on Israel and the Ancient Near East*, New York/London, 1991, 242–265 with respect to literary-historical lines and agreements and differences at the level of content.

[40] Cf for example, II Kings 16_{10ff} and Keel's remark with respect to the cultural horizon of the temple singers: "Die Pss bewegen sich stärker als andere atl Bücher in einer gemein-altorientalischen Vorstellungs- und Formenwelt."; OKeel, *Die Welt der altorientalischen Bildsymbolik und das Alte Testament*, Zürich-Einsiedeln-Köln-Neukirchen-Vluyn 1977², 78.

[41] Cf CJGadd, 'The Second Lamentation for Ur', in: *Hebrew and Semitic Studies Presented to Godfrey Rolles Driver*. DWThomas & WDMcHardy (eds), Oxford, 1963, 61, as well as the influence on Lamentations of the prophet Ezekiel who resided in Babylon. See, for example, the explanation of 3_{60} and 4_{18}.

It is only natural that their theological interpretation and assessment of the disaster would initially meet with strong resistance.[42] If people still desired to turn to YHWH, however, then it was vital that they be able to envisage the past in a different way and even see themselves with different eyes. It is plausible then that the failure of the prophecy of salvation created the necessary space for the emergence of Jeremiah, Ezekiel and other earlier 'prophets of doom' whose message had been much maligned up to that point. In an effort to justify YHWH's behaviour they proclaimed their prophecy of doom in contrast to the prophecy of salvation being proclaimed by the temple prophets who maintained that because of YHWH's protection Jerusalem could never fall.[43] Before they could speak to their fellow Israelites in this manner, however, they themselves had to find out how to think about YHWH in such a fashion. The downfall of Zion had brought them profound diffidence and distress and had initially left them extremely bitter towards their God. How could He let this happen? was as much their question as anyone else's. In their misfortune, however, they found a way back to their God. They related their spiritual struggle and its heavy costs by utilising the story of the devout man of Lam III, who was to be understood as their embodied representative. More on this topic can be found under the exegesis of 3_{1A} and in section VII below on the theology of Lamentations.

One can adhere in part to Westermann's explanation and accept that the essential contents of Lamentations were uttered in oral form in Jerusalem immediately after the downfall of the city in mutual encounters and exchanges of thought. The initial lack of connection between such more or less incidental questions, complaints, thoughts and responses, however, compelled those who uttered them, almost as a matter of course, towards the creation of a more cohesive, well-considered and structured whole. In such a situation, a plan must have been set afoot – inspired perhaps by ancient Mesopotamian examples – to write Lamentations, a major new poetic form for Israel. The many questions raised by the disastrous situation surrounding the fall of Jerusalem, the destruction of the temple, the failure of Zion's prophets, the profound disappointment, the suffering of small and great, of women and mothers, the unprecedented distress being endured by all, the urgent complaints, the accusations, the bitterness, the hunger, the spiritual crisis and struggle, the alternative prophetic word,

[42] Cf the explanation of $3_{14,33-36}$.
[43] Cf the introduction to Lam 2_{14-15} and see the explanation of 4_{12}.

and above all the deep longing for YHWH their God's saving intervention all had to find their proper place in the cohesive unity of the songs. The arrangement of these related themes and sub-themes into cantos, sub-cantos and canticles together with the response based connections between the songs shows the extent to which the poets laboured to achieve their goal. Their intention in doing so can have been none other than the articulation of their people's experience, the revelation of their own way through the affliction and the inspiration to follow their example. An important element for the 'Sitz im Leben' is thereby provided. We can suppose, therefore, that – after the composition was complete – Lamentations was recited neither in a liturgy nor even less in the ruined temple buildings (cf 2_6) but rather in gatherings of Jerusalemites and Judeans who had remained behind, recited as a means to express and clarify their distress, as a stimulus for reflection and as an appeal for renewed faith in God and prayer to YHWH. At the same time, this analysis makes it clear that the later Jewish liturgical setting of Lamentations as memorial songs on the downfall of the temple was a secondary and even drastic reduction of their original intention which continued to remain valid on another level.[44]

III.4 Different Alphabetical Sequence: ע–פ and פ–ע

If one accepts that Lamentations was recited in gatherings of those who had remained behind – and perhaps later also in Babylon – then it is clear that the written multiplication of the five songs must have become a necessity. It would not be unreasonable to accept that the difference in alphabetical order between Lam I, on the one hand, and Lam II–IV, on the other, might be explained in relation to this fact. Those who do not consider the alphabetical order of Lam I (ע–פ) to be a mistake[45] either saw an argument in the reversed sequence of פ–ע in Lam II–IV for a different origin for the first song over and against the other songs[46] or presumed corruption in the text and endeavoured to reconstruct a hypothetical original sequence.[47]

A different explanation remains possible, however, one which leaves the unity and textual sequence of the songs intact. If one examines the songs in their external form then one will note that apart from Lam I and II, the

---

[44] See for further discussion of this topic the hermeneutical epilogue to Lam III.
[45] Cf many of the older exegetes.
[46] Cf OEissfeldt, *Einleitung in das Alte Testament*, 1964^3, 678.
[47] Cf Wiesmann and Brandscheidt.

remaining songs all differ from one another. Since the final song lacks the form of the alphabetic acrostic it does not require closer examination. Lam IV is striking because of its two-line strophes while it goes without saying that the third song's triple implementation of the alphabetic acrostic is unique and quite eye-catching. Lam I and II, however, can in fact be interchanged! It is imaginable that the songs were written on separate scrolls and were recited one after another by different speakers. In such a scenario it would have been important not to mix the songs up. The same holds for the written multiplication of the songs, certainly where all five were written in the same scroll. In this event, of course, the first song had to be placed at the beginning. By introducing a clear distinction between the first two songs, the poets were able to avoid confusion and interchange. They did this by opting for a different alphabetical order between Lam I and Lam II. That they had the freedom to do such a thing must be put down to the fact that the alphabetical order between the ע and the פ had not yet been fixed. Although a preference for what would later become the normal order of ע and פ must have already existed. The sequence פ – ע can also be found on one of the storage jars from Kuntillet ʻArjud which is inscribed with a quadruple Hebrew alphabet, revealing a certain uniqueness. Cf Meshel: "In these abcedaries the letter פ precedes the ע, rather than the reverse, as is usually the case in the later Hebrew Alphabet. This reversal of letters is also found in four acrostic paragraphs in the Bible (Lam 2–4 and Proverbs 31).[48]

Recently, a Hebrew Alphabet from the 11th century BCE was discovered at Izbet Sartah[49] in which the same letter reversal occurred. Apparently the alphabetic order preserved in the 8th century Kuntillet Arjud Inscription is not an error, but a continuation of a much earlier alphabetic tradition."[50] Demsky and Kockavi also point out that the sequence פ – ע is assumed in the (reconstructed) alphabetic acrostics of Ps 9/10 and Ps 34.[51] The poets chose the usual sequence ע – פ for the introductory first song. At the same time the second song was related to Lam III and IV by way of the פ – ע sequence, since the poets used the identical, but at that time unusual alphabetic order for all three songs. It is simply speculative

[48] More precisely in the LXX of Proverbs 31 (JR!).
[49] See ADemsky and MKockavi, 'An Alphabet from the Days of the Judges', BAR, September/October 1978, 23.
[50] ZMeshel, *Did Yahweh Have a Consort?* The New Religious Inscriptions from the Sinai, in: BAR 1979 V/2, 31.
[51] See Meshel, 30.

to suggest that a deeper significance is attached to the sequence פ–ע, as can be found, for example, in Böhmer who envisages a sort of magic alphabet.[52]

III.5 The Meaning of Alphabetic Acrostics

From the external perspective the form of the Hebrew alphabetic acrostic is certainly the most striking feature of the first four songs. Even the 22 verses of the final song are a conscious echo of the Hebrew alphabet's 22 letters. A variety of explanations for the use of this form have been proposed throughout the history of exegesis. A magical interpretation, for example, suggested that the alphabet in its totality possessed extraordinary power.[53] Mnemonic and pedagogical purposes have also been put forward with some frequency. The majority of modern commentators (Rudolph, Plöger, Gordis, Van Selms, Kaiser; cf Lindström[54]), however, adhere to the notion that the alphabetic acrostic expresses totality itself, in the same way as the expression A – Ω found in the New Testament. The rabbis, furthermore, were aware that the Torah had to be observed from א to ת.[55] In Lamentations the totality in question is that of the great affliction being endured by the people.[56]

Westermann has recently placed a question mark after this explanation and opted instead for an aesthetical understanding: "Die Erklärung als Ganzheit (»von A bis Z«) ist schwierig, weil dann fünf verscheidene Ganzheiten beim gleichen Gegenstand nebeneinanderstehen. Die ästhetische Erklärung reicht aus: Diese Gestaltung der Dichtung wurde als kunstvoll empfunden."[57]

The question remains, however, whether an aesthetic explanation would not be at odds with the situation of Lamentations' composition. Under such dreadful circumstances would it be right to imagine that the poets were still intent on producing a work of poetic beauty? In so do-

[52] JBöhmer, 'Ein alphabetisch-akrostisches Rätsel', ZAW 28 (1908), 53–57.

[53] Cf MLöhr, *Die Klagelieder des Jeremia*, HKAT III.2.2, Göttingen 1906², vii.

[54] FLindström, *God and the Origin of Evil. A Contextual Analysis of Alleged Monistic Evidence in the Old Testament*, Coniectanea Biblica, Old Testament series 21, Lund 1983, 217.

[55] Cf TWNT I 1–3 (Kittel).

[56] For the absence of the alphabetic acrostic form in Lam V see the introduction to that song and the exegesis of Lam 5_{3A}.

[57] Westermann, *Klagelieder*, 91.

ing would they not be placing themselves outside the horrible reality which surrounded them?[58] Although the poets certainly wanted to show off their compositional skills, the purpose of the successive alphabetical acrostics must have been something other than literary beauty. A closer examination of the songs themselves can provide a more adequate solution to our problem.

Since it is unique in the OT to find four alphabetic acrostics in succession followed by an associated fifth song with 22 verses, the poets must have intended to give literary-visual expression to the parallelistic (identical, supplementary, antithetical) character of the content of the songs. In previous study we demonstrated that the five songs are very closely related to one another by song-responses, which means they exhibit both literary and substantial connections at the same level.[59] By placing Lamentations I–IV as alphabetic acrostics and Lam V with its 22 verses next to one another the poets provided a clear literary indication for the mutually respondent character of the songs which they had consciously built in.[60]

III.6 The Meaning of the Triple Alphabetic Acrostic in Lam III

Bearing in mind what we have said so far we have yet to provide an explanation for the triple implementation of the alphabetic acrostic in the third song. Perhaps the most obvious suggestion can be found in the frequently followed aesthetic explanation which proposes that precisely where Lam III is concerned we are dealing with the pinnacle of poetic artistry in which the poets have gone to the limits of their creative ability. In light of what we have noted above, however, such a notion remains open to argument. The inter-responsive character of the five songs calls for greater literary ability than is necessary for the creation of one triple acrostic. For that matter, Ps 119 is an even more complex alphabetic acrostic than Lam III. The same acrostic form is employed in this psalm but with no less than eight times the same initial letter per stanza and without giving the impression that the poet(s) had to do violence to his (their) language in order to achieve it.

[58] Cf Löhr: "Nach unserm Empfinden paßt die Künstelei des alphabetischen Schemas zu den beweglichen Klagen so slecht wie möglich.", *Klagelieder*, VII.

[59] Cf supra III.1 and the exegesis passim. See also 1988, 361–396, and 'Parallel Acrostics', 379–382.

[60] This explanation does not mean that we must drop the explanation from totality which we followed in substance in 1983, 68f. They are not mutually exclusive explanations.

This specific form of the psalm does not appear to be without significance. The explanation for its use can be found in the content of the song itself: in order to declare the – more-than-complete nature of YHWH's Torah – see Ps 119_{96} (in the central ל-strophe![61]) – the poet(s) went one further than seven which was the human number for completeness.[62] Seen against this background, it is not impossible that the triple alphabetic acrostic of Lam III also possessed a special significance. Given the singular form used for Lam I and II, perhaps the triple form of Lam III refers to three songs. A close examination of the literary structure suggests that this is to a certain extent the case. We have already demonstrated the relatively substantial independence of both cantos in this song (3_{1-33} and 3_{34-66}) each of which, in terms of structure and content, already constitutes a reflection of, for example, Lam I and II.[63] It is clear, nevertheless, that the poets also joined both cantos together in the form of a diptych and in so doing created the third song.[64] One might, therefore, characterise Lam III as a literary 'trinity', the triple implementation of the alphabetic acrostic being its literary marker.

III.7 Lam IV

The diptych structure of the fourth song seems to run contrary to our explanation of Lam III. If the triple alphabetic acrostic in Lam III really signifies what we have suggested then why is there no similar explanation for Lam IV which also possess a diptych structure.[65] It is clear, however, that it would be impossible to implement the triple acrostic with the two-line strophes of Lam IV. At the same time this two-line structure leaves one with the impression that the form of the *qinah* for all five songs was of greater significance to the poets than other structuring principles.

Nevertheless, they still provide a clear literary marker for the 'duality' of the fourth song which honours the fact that both of its sub-cantos are more detached from one another than the sub-cantos of Lam III. It is striking to note that Lam I, II and IV all begin with the opening word אֵיכָה which

[61] Cf PWSkehan, 'The Structure of the Song of Moses in Deuteronomy (32:1–43)', in: *Studies in Israelite Poetry and Wisdom*, Washington 1971, 74–75.

[62] Cf Gen $4_{15,24}$, Ps 12_7, 79_{12}, Prov 6_{31}, Isa 30_{26} and TWAT VII 1013 (Otto).

[63] See 1988, 321–334.

[64] For further information on this topic see the translation and explanation of Lam III in the present commentary.

[65] Cf 1988, 334–346 and the translation in the present commentary.

to an important extent sets the tone of the songs. It is equally striking that אֵיכָה is used twice as a marker of inclusion only in the first canticle of Lam IV.[66] This, together with the unity of the alphabetic acrostic might be considered a marker of the dual character of the song.

IV Authorship

We referred above to the results of our previous research concerning the authorial provenance of the songs, namely that the poets of Lamentations should be sought among the temple singers who remained behind in Jerusalem.[67] This was proposed on the basis of their familiarity with and expertise in the manipulation and creation of the language of the Psalms. From the perspective of content, the relationship appears to be based on an earlier adherence to Zion theology[68] and on a subsequent Psalm theology, an essential part of which had survived the crisis which brought on their misfortune.[69] Such knowledge of and preference for Zion must be sought primarily among the temple singers.[70] The exegesis found in the present commentary confirms former discoveries. Time and again a clear preference for Zion and an intense sorrow over her desolation comes to the fore. See, for example, the exegesis of 5_{18}. Our belief that the spiritual struggle for renewed faith in God of the devout one of Lam III is in fact the struggle of the temple singers, is confirmed by the song-responses. Cf the exegesis of 3_{1A}. The song-response of 3_{4-6} with 4_2 presents the גֶּבֶר as one of the children of Zion. The radiance of the גֶּבֶר is that of the sanctuary and the cult.[71]

In the present commentary we will always refer to poets in the plural. It will become clear, however, that our plural usage does not intend to suggest that several poetic redactors worked in succession on the songs. The plural should be understood as entirely synchronic. When dealing with the temple singers we must first realise that we are dealing with guilds. The individual members of such guilds were not in a position to

---

66 See Lam $4_{1aA-2bA}$.

67 Cf 1983, 217–260.

68 Cf for example, the explanation of 2_{15} and 4_{12}.

69 Cf 1983, 32–42.

70 Cf SMowinckel, *Psalmenstudien IV*, reprint Amsterdam 1961, 39. Cf also NHRidderbos, *Die Psalmen. Stilistische Verfahren und Aufbau mit besondere Berücksichtigung von Ps. 1–41*, BZAW 117, Berlin 1972, 114f.

71 See the explanation of $3_{17B,18A}$ etcetera.

create their own songs and insist on their use in the cult under their own authority. Justice has to be done to the different elements of psalm composition. The temple singers certainly possessed a variety of qualities: not only the obvious poetic, musical and vocal skills, but also prophetic and theological gifts.[72] One cannot rule out the possibility that all these skills were in the possession of one individual but it seems more likely that each of the temple singers had a distinct talent or speciality. In this sense one can imagine that they complemented one another in the composition and recitation of their psalms. One can also be sure that songs composed under their supervision were first checked for their theological content and artistic quality before they found their way into liturgical use. It remains implausible that this practice would have been dropped after the downfall. In fact the unique horror of the prevailing circumstances would have led the temple singers into mutual consultation in order to lay out their discoveries in the prophetic tradition together with their own theological interpretations and evaluations of what was going on. The very notion of a poetic work such as Lamentations – originating perhaps with a particular temple singer but elaborated by more than one – would have been presented to the guild members who would then assist in achieving its final form and content through their criticisms, instructions and contributions. In this sense one must consider Lamentations as a collective work of art. The songs were not defined and supported by the authority and skill of an individual temple singer; they must be seen, rather, as the product of the guild, the very collective nature of which must have given the composition even greater authority.

Perhaps it is because of this attitude of the temple singers after the downfall that the same group came to be held in such high esteem after the exile.[73] For more on the subject see also Spieckermann.[74] Cf his interesting thesis: "Ohne großes Wagnis darf man behaupten: Wie die Psalmen in einem gewisssen Grundbestand am besten innerhalb oder in Gefolge des Tempelkultus zu verstehen sind, so stellt sich die Psalmtheologie in einer bis in die frühe Königszeit zurückreichenden Form als Tempeltheologie dar."[75]

[72] Cf II Chron 20_{1-30}; JCdMoor, *De tijd van het heil*, KC 15, Kampen 1970, 18.

[73] For more information on the temple singers as the poets of the Psalms see SMowinckel, *Psalmenstudien IV*, 39, 41–48; NHRidderbos, Psalmen und Kult, in: *Zur neueren Psalmenforschung*, ed PHANeuman, Darmstadt 1976, 264f; cf 1983, 256–260 and the literature referred to therein.

[74] HSpieckermann, *Heilsgegenwart. Eine Theologie der Psalmen.* Göttingen 1989.

V Period and Place of Origin

V.1 Period of Origin

When it comes to dating, commentators differ considerably from one another both on the book of Lamentations as a whole and on the individual songs.[76] The unity of the songs, however, narrows down the complexity of the problem. Indeed, the very synchrony of the composition makes a diachronic analysis redundant. Only the dating of Lamentations as a whole continues to have relevance, therefore, and not that of the individual songs. Information on dating the material can only be derived from the songs themselves. The two extremes are clear, the *terminus a quo* being the fall of Jerusalem in 587 and the *terminus ad quem* being ± 550 or later, the period of Deutero-Isaiah, since the latter was already familiar with the complaints voiced in Lamentations.[77] The *terminus ad quem* of ± 550, however, is certainly too late. The songs leave one with the impression that they were conceived during a period of great misfortune after the fall, when chaos reigned throughout the land. Cf the explanation of $5_{7,20}$. One can be sure then that this does not refer to a period decades after the fall of Jerusalem. The people did not need tens of years to arrive at a kind of *modus vivendi* with the downfall. Rather, the intense emphasis on the dreadful famine points to more recent experience. The devout one of Lam III states that he is an eye witness to the distress of the women of Jerusalem (3_{51}). The very nature of laments, furthermore, implies that they are uttered in close relation to prevailing distress. In fact, the conclusion to Lamentations does not speak of restoration or recovery (cf 5_{19-22}); on the contrary, the people are on the verge of annihilation (cf 3_{54}). Nevertheless, a time for deliberation and theological reflection must have been necessary in conjunction with a prior study of the various prophetic traditions. It remains difficult to say whether this would have taken a substantial amount of time but it is possible that those involved were more familiar with the words of the prophets of judgement than we are willing to permit at first sight (cf Jer 26_{18}). In addition, the words Jeremiah himself prophesied were not considered by all to be heresy (cf Jer 26_{24}). The theological reflection we have suggested may indeed have taken place on the basis of ideas already expressed before the downfall.

[75] Spieckermann, *Heilsgegenwart*, 9f.

[76] See the survey in 1983, 43–59.

[77] Cf 1983, 325–331.

All we have said so far on authorship does not intend to suggest that Lamentations was an occasional composition. Although they were written in response to a specific historical event the significance of the songs transcends that of their particular time and place. The time bound element is implied in analogous human experience. We must return at this point to Westermann's explanation.[78] With reference to analogies and structural correspondences between the laments on the downfall of Ur and Lamentations, Westermann poses the question whether this has any great significance. He himself points to the analogous situation with respect to texts of Gen 1–11, namely those which refer to the deluge of which there are parallel examples to be found the world over. The possibility of world destruction belongs to the primal experience of humanity to which the destruction of a city – a world in itself – constitutes a significant parallel. Such fundamentally analogous experiences elicit similar if not directly dependent reactions, as the correspondences between the various deluge narratives as well as those between the laments on the downfall of Ur and those in Lamentations attest.

It is primarily from the hermeneutical perspective that Westermann's remarks are important, although further specification is necessary with respect to Lamentations. The responsive structure of the songs – within which Lam III holds a central position – makes it clear that Judah's terrible downfall is being conveyed in and through one individual who had lived through it, namely the devout one of Lam III. At the same time, the description of this individual reveals that his experience and the course he follows can have more than individual significance. To have lived through the collapse of one's world was far from the unique experience of this devout individual. His contemporaries also endured the same reality. On one point, however, the course followed by the devout one of Lam III is given surplus value: in the midst of scepticism and disaster he is still able to find a way back to his God. In such a situation of misfortune he is a worthy forerunner because he knows what his contemporaries have had to endure and can speak of it from his own experience.

The poets of Lamentations were not only aware of this potential significance of the devout one they had created but it was with precisely this in mind that they fixed his experience in an appropriate written form. They did so in the first place with their struggling contemporaries in mind, but

[78] Westermann, *Klagelieder*, 31.

it must also have been clear to them that the course followed by their devout one might be significant in future periods of analogous experience.[79]

In considering the time of origin of Lamentations, therefore, we must allow for the possibility of a slightly later date. This does not mean that the distress, famine, lament and spiritual struggle described in the songs is also from a later date. On the contrary, the historical context is none other than that of the downfall of Zion. It is conceivable, however, that the written determination of that downfall in the form of five songs may have taken place at a later period when the poets had become aware of the possible significance of their (faith) experiences and insights for future generations (although the distress of Zion continued for a long time). Such a perspective has the effect of removing the evident discrepancy between the complicated nature of a composition such as Lamentations and the concrete and immediate distress of the period in question. At the same time it has the advantage of leaving the authenticity of the experiences described in the songs unscathed since the poets took care – with respect to the intended purpose of the songs[80] – to mix their experiences with other experiences, insights and perspectives from a later period (of restoration). Indeed, they had the time to express their experiences with better-considered words than a more elementary cry for help would have done. Nevertheless, the complexity of the composition should not be used as an argument to over-stretch the distance in time between the description and the described. The question of complexity is one of very subjective judgement. For those who had first hand familiarity with the language, what appears to us to be ancient and strange poetry was perhaps easier to write and understand than we are tempted to accept.

V.2 Place of Origin

An indirect answer has already been provided to the question of place of origin in the section dealing with authorship. If we accept that the poets were temple singers who had remained behind in Jerusalem then the only possible location for their activity must have been that city. Virtually all modern commentaries follow this line of thought and even the songs themselves provide certain indications in its support, such as the frequent attention paid to Jerusalem/Zion throughout the songs.[81] In addition, the

[79] Cf the hermeneutical epilogue to Lam III.
[80] Cf again the hermeneutical epilogue.

suffering devout one of Lam III is presented as one of the children of Zion (4_2) while in 3_{51} the same individual speaks of the distress of the women of Jerusalem, his city. Finally, the situation of the exile as a whole does not appear to be under discussion in the songs.[82]

VI Religion-Historical Significance

The facts of time and place give a clear indication that Lamentations stems from a period in Israel's history which might somewhat euphemistically be referred to as a cross-roads. The period in question is mostly referred to as that of the exile but where Lamentations is concerned this would be incorrect. The historical context of the songs is not that of the sojourn in Babylon but of the period of the downfall in Judah itself. One can still speak of a cross-roads, however, in the sense that a variety of theological traditions from the time prior to the downfall come together in the five individual songs of Lamentations. The texts reflect the pre-exilic prophetic traditions, for example. One can imagine that by endorsing the content of such traditions the poets both legitimised and canonised them. The same can be said for the element of Psalm theology from the time of Israel's monarchy which is endorsed by Lamentations together with the echoes of Zion theology which have also been preserved therein.[83] The assimilation of these theological traditions was preceded by a time of theological reflection, under pressure from the events of the downfall and the period thereafter, during which a process of selection took place. Thus doubts were raised in prayer as to the absolute character of the prophetic announcements of doom while at the same time distance had to be taken from the notion of Zion's unconditional inviolability. In this context, the insight arose that YHWH had allowed his presence in their midst to be dependent on the purity of their relationship with him.[84] A number of points indicate that Lamentations reveals an understanding of the prevailing prophetic and psalm theology stemming from the period just prior to the downfall,

[81] Cf 1983, 86–89

[82] See the exegesis of 1_{3b}. Even the use and frequency of the names reveals that the authors were exclusively concerned for their native land. Judah is mentioned 5x and Israel and Jacob 3x each, Jerusalem 7x and Zion 15x, thus both together count for twice the frequency.

[83] Cf for example, 2_{14}, $4_{11,20}$; See BAlbrektson, *Studies in the Text and Theology of the Book of Lamentations, with a Critical Edition of the Peshitta Text*, STL 21, 1963, 219–230; see also 1983, 32–39 and 281–294.

[84] Cf 5_{21}; see also under VII (Theology).

thus providing a reasonably secure base for dating the material. The importance of this fact for diachronic research into the prophetic traditions and the theology of the psalms does not require further demonstration. The absence of clear Deuteronomistic influence[85] is also an indication that theological reflection of this sort only got underway at a later date. This concurs with the tendency of the Deuteronomistic texts to interpret the event of Israel's downfall as a warning for future generations, something which would have been absolutely inconceivable in the experience of hopelessness and deathly distress which followed shortly after 587. Compare the connection with elements of the dirge genre, mention of 'the end' in 4_{18} and the hankering for the 'good old days'.[86]

VII Theology

VII.1 Positions

As a matter of fact, by far the majority of exegetes reduce the theological significance of Lamentations to two primary elements. In the first place the songs intended to offer an explanation of the catastrophe which had befallen the people, the origin of which was sought in the fact that YHWH had reacted to their sin and guilt and they were now enduring his judgement. Mettinger concludes from this that YHWH's power was still intact: "Compare the Book of Lamentations, which tries to demonstrate that the catastrophe was a divine punishment for sin; thus the Exile did not imply that the Lord was devoid of power."[87] See also Kapelrud's remark with respect to Lamentations: "De er et gjennemført teologisk dokument som vil gjøre det klart at denne ødeleggelse var ikke noe som bare kom utenfra. Det var Israels egen Gud, Jahve som stod bak det som hendte, det var hans straff over Israels synd."[88] In the second place the songs intended to show a way out of the crisis. In meditation and penance the way had to be found back to God. Nötscher, Meek, Rudolph, Weiser, Plöger and Boecker, among others, tend to follow this line of approach.[89]

A few exegetes offer a more nuanced response to the question of theology, honouring the complaints in the songs as an essential aspect of the

---

85 Cf 1983, 22–32.

86 כְּקֶדֶם; cf the exegesis of 1_{7b} and 5_{21}.

87 TNDMettinger, *The Dethronement of Sabaoth. Studies in the Shem and Kabod Theologies*, Coniectanea Biblica, Old Testament Series 18, Lund 1982, 17.

88 ASKapelrud, *Guden som sviktet?* SEÅ 41–42, 1976/1977, 139.

89 Cf the summary by Westermann, *Klagelieder*, 73f.

prayer to YHWH for deliverance. Among these commentators we can include Hillers, Brunet, Boecker, Mintz and Provan.

VII.1.1 Westermann

Westermann can be singled out in his endorsement of a more nuanced approach to the theology of Lamentations. Once again this is closely related to his understanding of the origin of the songs as initially oral complaints of the people concerning their distress. He stresses thereby that we are not dealing with theological reflection in the complaints in question but with a direct event between God and human persons, "Da die Psalmen Gebete sind, in denen etwas zwischen Mensch und Gott, zwischen Gott und Mensch geschieht, sind sie primär von einer Geschehensfolge bestimmt. (...) Psalmenstruktur meint (...) nicht aneinander gereihte Gedanken, die von einer gedanklichen Logik bestimmt werden."[90] The component parts of the CI and CP genres are component parts of an event. By analogy with the Psalms, Lamentations also possesses this 'Geschehensstruktur', although in an earlier, oral version. It is for this reason that Westermann rejects every hypothesis of theological reflection in the songs which he prefers to see as a product of later consideration of the texts. For Westermann, however, such theological reflection is not implied by the texts themselves. Lam 3_{26-41} constitutes an exception in this regard but in Westermann's judgement these verses are secondary with respect to the original laments. He therefore rejects the studies of the theology of/in Lamentations by Gottwald and Albrektson as well as the opinion of Childs, who considers Lamentations to be the theological victory over a crisis of faith.[91] Rudolph, Weiser and Kaiser follow a similar line to Childs. Westermann detects in such assessments of the purpose of Lamentations a transformation of the 'Existenznot' described therein to a 'Glaubensnot', a religious element of the catastrophe which has been separated from reality, a reduction to a spiritual event going hand in hand with theological reflection which took place at a later time in the awareness of those concerned.[92]

For Westermann, the assessments we have been examining are part and parcel of a theological underestimation of the complaint as a form of prayer. In this context he speaks of a 'Abwertung der Klage'. This has

[90] Westermann, *Klagelieder*, 72; cf idem, *The Role of Lament in the Theology of the Old Testament*, Interpretation 28, 1974, 20–38.

[91] BSChilds, *Introduction to the Old Testament as Scripture*, London 1979, 590–597.

[92] Westermann, *Klagelieder*, 74.

nothing to do with the texts themselves but is based on a presupposition of which virtually all commentators are guilty: "Vor Gott zu klagen is nicht angemessen, es entspricht nicht der richtigen Haltung gegenüber Gott. Die Klage stört oder mindert die fromme Einstellung zu Gott." [93] The Old Testament complaint has disappeared from Christian prayer and is experienced as an inadequate and inappropriate response to God. As examples of this position Westermann points to Haller, Rudolph, Kraus, Plöger and Brandscheidt. The reduction of Lamentations to the treatment of a theological issue or to the recognition therein of God's judgement and the people's confession of guilt, implies much the same underestimation and even negation of the complaint. In contrast to this Westermann makes an appeal for the unique theological value of the complaint. It was not the intention of Lamentations to explain the catastrophe as a judgement. Such a judgement was presumed as a matter of course as was the identity of the one who had brought it about. Both these elements, however, are components of the complaint; complaints have their function in prayer, offering YHWH reasons to deliver the one praying from his or her distress.

Westermann's theological revaluation of the complaint is to be highly commended.[94] Such a revaluation can contribute to a revitalisation of our relationship with God, although the human person must learn acceptance therein. Nevertheless, the proposed explanation remains inaccurate on a number of points. His distinction, for example, between 'Gedankliche und Geschehensstruktur' cannot be left undisputed. At the same time his obsession with the complaint as the primary expression of distress does not leave any room for reflection. The question remains whether complaints can be formulated in a completely spontaneous manner without any element of existing thoughts and ideas. The complaint as prayer presupposes quite a lot: God's listening, the possibility that he can be moved by prayer, his justice, his mercy, his ability to intervene as deliverer etcetera. Although Westermann refers to the first squeal of a child at the moment of birth,[95] the complaints of Hanna and Hezekiah show, nevertheless, how much they make use of pre-conceived and pre-constituted language. Indeed, the older a person becomes the less he or she is able to avoid speaking or thinking in this way. This need not inflict damage on the authenticity

[93] Westermann, *Klagelieder*, 78.

[94] Cf also his further thoughts on the matter in *Theologie des Alten Testaments in Grundzügen*, ATD Ergänzungsreihe 6, Göttingen 1978, 147–153 and *Klagelieder*, 84ff.

[95] Westermann, *Klagelieder*, 84f.

of the complaint as an event, but as such complaints are certainly the product of theological reflection and as such they once again become the possession of the faithful individual via the liturgy. Even if it might still be possible to imagine the individual complaint in terms of individually expressed faith language, the same for the collective lament would be barely thinkable. As is evident from Gunkel's description of the 'Sitz im Leben' of the complaint of the people,[96] such events require organisation. Fixed patterns in the transmitted forms of the CI and CP clearly indicate that a logical structure lies at their foundation. Prayer does not begin with 'amen' and end with an appeal. Distress does not cause one to forget such matters. If one thinks of the temple as the location for such complaints of the people then priests and prophets become involved as mediators.[97] In this event we can begin to speak of liturgy and thus of the ordering of thoughts. At the same time choices and selections are made from the language available to those involved, a language which is itself the product of growth from a process of ongoing exchange between past moments of distress and their associated complaints and the reflection of temple theologians after the event. Spieckermann also disputes Westermann's distinction on the basis of the well-considered theological propositions which are evidently present in the Psalms, the 'Sitz im Leben' of which was the cult: "So ist der Kult in erster Linie Geschehenszusammenhang, in zweiter Linie aber Gedankenzusammenhang, dies sogar ganz entschieden in den das Geschehen leitenden, begleitenden und deutenden Texten, also auch den Psalmen."[98]

A further and more important point is Westermann's faulty assessment of the portrayal of distress found in Lamentations. Not every portrayal of affliction can be placed under the heading 'prayer-complaint' as he in fact does. His mistake here is most clearly demonstrated by his translation of 3_{39} in which he renders the term יִתְאוֹנֵן with 'sich in Klage ergehen'.[99] Kraus – whom Westermann criticises on this point – is much closer to home with his rendering of the term as 'murren'. A distinction needs to be made in Lamentations between complaints intended as an expression of prayer, to be found, for example, in $1_{9c,11c,20-22}$, 2_{20-22}; 3_{55-66}; 5_{1-22}, and complaints which are an expression of dissension and defiance before

[96] See above III.3.
[97] JCdMoor, *De tijd van het heil*, KC 15, Kampen 1970, 14–23.
[98] Spieckermann, *Heilsgegenwart*, 9.
[99] Westermann, *Klagelieder*, 79; cf 159.

YHWH (cf, for example, 3_{1-18}). Such defiance should not be understood as 'lament' but would be more appropriately styled 'murmuring', a translation which is supported by the only other occurrence of the verb in the OT: Num 11_1. It is not a question of providing a date for this text but rather of determining the content of the *hithpa'el* of the root אנן. In Num 11_1 it is quite clear that prayer is not intended, even less a lament with a corresponding function. At the same time, the context is not one of (acute) distress but rather one of dissatisfaction. Even YHWH's reaction – burning wrath (Num 11_{10}) – is a clear indication that the 'murmuring' is not to be understood as prayer, no matter how unfortunate the formulation.

Westermann's obsession with the original form of Lamentations as complaints of the people during the great distress of 587 prevents him from seeing what actually happened: not distress followed by lament-prayer – as was usually the case – but distress followed by disillusionment! From the very outset this disillusionment was theological in nature in the sense that it was the experience of human persons who felt a terrible sense of disappointment in their God. Reality for such people could not be articulated without this element; event and the human incapacity to interpret and explain were inseparably interwoven. What they had undergone was such a contradiction of their faith in and knowledge of God, everything they had been told of him from of old. How in YHWH's name could this happen? [100] How diametrically opposed this was to the visions of their prophets who described Jerusalem as an unassailable fortress! How radical the contrast between former confessions of YHWH's greatness and the present horrors of death and corruption, total collapse of the cult and society! [101] In this equally theological catastrophe, prayer and lament seemed meaningless and even absurd. What was the point in continuing to pray to a God who had abandoned his people in such a dreadful way?! [102]

VII.2 Theological Reflection

Among those who had remained faithful to YHWH in this situation of great distress there must have been a desperate search for theological meaning. There will always be people who refuse to abandon their God, or perhaps better said, refuse to be abandoned by their God no matter what happens to them. In Israel such people were faced with an almost inhuman task.

[100] Cf, for example, the explanation of 2_{20-22} and 3_{34-36}.

[101] Cf $2_{6,7,9}$.

[102] See the explanation of 3_{14}.

It was much more difficult for them than for their fellow Israelites who had severed their ties with YHWH because they felt themselves deceived. They had no comfortable spot to sit down and reflect on what had befallen them; Jerusalem was a ruin and they themselves were emaciated with hunger. In a wrecked and ravaged Zion they stood and wondered in astonishment as to what the relationship might be between God and the horrors they were being forced to undergo. In continuing to hold fast to YHWH, their experience of disillusionment must have been all the more intense. The genuinely devout person who maintains unconditional faith in God is more likely to experience an even deeper sense of disappointment at such moments. Feelings of bitterness and even defiance cannot have been foreign to them. What was the reason for all this? Nevertheless, in the midst of ongoing distress they succeeded in finding a sense of theological direction, albeit an incomplete and controversial one.

VII.2.1 New Language

As is evident from the language, theology and literary skill apparent in the Book of Lamentations it must have been temple singers who remained faithful to YHWH and who charted this faith experience and the way through it they had discovered. Given the circumstances, they could not simply take over the usual forms of the CP and CI in their entirety. They had to find a new mode of expression in order to record their thoughts and experiences and they succeeded in doing so by combining existing genres and motifs. The most striking combination is that of the religious lament with the profane dirge by which the poets were able to demonstrate how life threatening and deadly reality was for them. The combination can be found in all five songs (cf the explanation of 1_1, 2_1, 4_1). Westermann is of the opinion that this connection is absent from the third song[103] and is swallowed up by the lament in the final song[104] but this is incorrect.[105] A new element – certainly in the measure that it can be found in Lamentations – is the use of the lament detached from its prayer context as an expression of self-pity. The experience of an unprecedented reversal in the history of salvation and the accompanying feelings of personal disappointment and bitterness were given expression by the poets in the self-pitying words of the disillusioned devout one of Lam III whose de-

[103] Westermann, *Klagelieder*, 70, 181.

[104] Westermann, *Klagelieder*, 174.

[105] See the explanation of $3_{6,16,53,54}$ and $5_{3,15,18}$.

scription of the suffering being brought upon him by YHWH is unique in its harshness. The devout one's complaints, however, are not directed to YHWH; his self-pitying lament, rather, is intended for those who surround him.[106] By describing their situation from a theological perspective the poets were able to face reality in all seriousness and thereby avoid any pious misjudgement of the misery being endured in Jerusalem and Judah.

VII.2.2 Pre-exilic Prophecy of Doom

In their theological considerations, the poets of Lamentations also sought an answer to the question why all this was happening to them. What had they done that YHWH had turned against them with so much fury? Why had YHWH brought about their downfall and then remained at a distance as their terror unfolded? It goes without saying that a speedy solution to their distress was sought in prayer. Indeed, survival depended on saving intervention, but to whom could they turn for help? The fact remained that YHWH alone could save them, YHWH who had brought and continued to bring this misfortune upon them! It was crystal clear, however, that the relationship between YHWH and his people was seriously damaged if not completely broken. What could they do for their part to bring about repair? The first question, therefore, was the question 'Why?' It is evident in a number of places in the texts that the poets had turned for an answer to those prophetic traditions which had predicted this downfall on the day of YHWH's judgement (יוֹם יְהוָה).[107] In concurring with the accusations of sin and guilt stemming from such prophets, the poets professed YHWH's actions to be justified (cf 1_{18}, 3_{42}, 5_{16}). One should be aware, however, that where 3_{42} is concerned the poets either did not recognise themselves in a portion of the accusations or did not experience that portion to be justified in the context of their (syncretistic) popular piety. It is evident from 2_{14} at least that they did not recognise many of their injustices and blamed their prophets for not pointing out their sins and giving them the chance to repent and change their ways. Nevertheless, even unconsciously committed sin is still sin and the fact of their guilt was apparent from the terrible disaster that had befallen them.

The poets did not only employ this prophetic announcement of doom to concur with the reality of their situation, however. On one essential point

[106] Cf the plural usage in Lam III.

[107] Cf 1983, 262–267; HSpieckermann, 'Dies Irae: der alttestamentliche Befund und seine Vorgeschichte', VT 39 (1989), 194–208 and the exegesis passim.

the prophecy had not (yet) been confirmed. Although the prophets had declared the end for Israel (קֵץ, cf 4_{18}), for the time being that end had not been totally realised in the sense that talk of survival was pointless. Such talk – no matter how marginal – was still a possibility (cf 3_{22}) and was to be considered a sign that YHWH had not (yet) sanctioned a total and definitive end for his people. Was God hesitating? At least there was still time to move YHWH to have mercy.

VII.2.3 Psalm Theology

The acknowledgement of the legitimacy of the prophetic accusations was only a partial answer to the poets' questions. By confessing their guilt they recognised indeed that YHWH was justified, but such a confession did not deliver them from their affliction. Another set of questions arose, therefore, in their process of reflection: To what extent could they still believe in YHWH? What more could they expect from him? Could they still hope in him as before? Such questions must have been extremely difficult to answer since the essential content of pre-exilic Judah's faith appeared to have been rendered worthless by the downfall. They must have considered the fact that as visible signs of YHWH's faithfulness his promised protection of Jerusalem and guarantee of the continuation of the Davidic dynasty had not materialised.[108] If they had been wrong in attaching their faith to such weighty matters, what was there left to believe in?

The people had to learn to think differently with respect to YHWH's promises. Where the protection of Jerusalem was concerned such a change of perspective was perhaps the least problematic. Here too it was possible to subscribe to the proclamations of the prophets of doom who had in fact predicted the downfall of the city as punishment for the sins of its people. This did not mean, however, that the relationship between YHWH and his people was at an end since even prior to their possession of the city YHWH had been Israel's God. Moreover, the pre-exilic prophets of doom had also predicted deliverance and salvation after YHWH's judgement.[109]

The loss of the Davidic king was a much more difficult pill to swallow (cf 2_9, 4_{20}). The prophets had perhaps announced the exile or death of

[108] Cf 1983, 90–145.

[109] Cf, for example, Mi 4_{10} and the exegesis of ASvdWoude, *Micha*, Nijkerk 1976, 129, 154–158.

individual Davidic kings in their prophecies of doom but they had never spoken of a definitive rupture in YHWH's fidelity to the Davidic dynasty. Nevertheless, once again pre-exilic temple theology with regard to the sonship of the Davidic king provided an originally unintended loophole which could now be put to use. The truth was that when one spoke of the Davidic king one spoke of YHWH's representative. In the person of the king YHWH desired to come close to his people with pardon and blessing.[110] At the same time, however, the representative character of the king implied that YHWH's orientation towards his people did not depend on the presence of the king. The period prior to the monarchy offered a precedent for YHWH's immediate closeness and leadership, although the theological problem of the apparent disappearance of YHWH's fidelity to the royal house of David remained to provide the seed ground for later Messianic expectation.

We can indirectly deduce from 5_{21} that the poets had hoped for the return of a Davidic king from Babylon (see the explanation). Such an event might have secured the continuity of the Davidic dynasty but it did not offer any new perspective on the present situation of distress. Judah was now forced to turn to the only one who had the power to save: YHWH. In this sense the poets were thrown back on what they could still confess of him and in their formulation of this confession we can distinguish two different types of expression. The first has to do with YHWH's essence, who he is. The second type has to do with the sort of treatment the people might expect from YHWH. Both types of expression are not distinct or separate from one another: the latter is in fact derived from the former.

VII.2.4 YHWH's Essence

After abandoning his self-pity as leading to nothing and – in spite of everything – giving account of his renewed faith, the devout one of Lam III puts the elementary confession of YHWH's essence into words in the very heart of the songs (3_{22-33}; cf the exegesis). In outline, the first expression refers to YHWH's graciousness (חֶסֶד) which manifests itself in the good things that have happened to him and to his people: the tokens of YHWH's favour (חַסְדֵי יְהוָה, 3_{22}). This favour expresses itself in the fact that the end has not been fully realised as is apparent from their continued and ongoing survival and this in turn can be considered a manifestation of YHWH's

[110] Cf, for example, Pss 2, 21, 72, 110; see Spieckermann, *Heilsgegenwart*, 208–219.

great fidelity (אֱמוּנָה, 3_{23}). In the same canticle (3_{22-27}) the poets speak in response of YHWH's goodness (טוֹב יְהוָה) and mercy (the root רחם, 3_{32}). Moreover, the centrally placed (3_{33}!) connection between YHWH's essence and the prevailing disaster and oppression is extremely important. The connection in question can only be rendered in negative terms: this distress is not what YHWH truly wants (לֹא ... מִלִּבּוֹ)! What is of significance here is the fact that YHWH's acts of judgement (either active or *in absentia*) are alien to him. In dealing thus with his people he is going against his very self. In contrast to this, his people had once come to know and confess him as a God who let mercy count as justice, a God who was moved by human distress whether deserved or undeserved, a God who ultimately could not resist the cry of affliction of the wretched (2_{18f}). At the same time YHWH was a God who could not continue to observe injustice – as they themselves had come to know.[111] The prayers in Lamentations combine both elements: the poets call upon YHWH to observe their distress, brought about by the wickedness of the enemy, in the hope that he will bring it to an end just as he had brought their unjust behaviour to an end.[112] The fact that we are dealing here with a focal moment in the poets' theology is apparent from its relationship with the primary theme of the songs formulated in the central canto verses $3_{17,50}$: their misfortune will only come to an end when YHWH looks down on them once again in deliverance (see explanation of the verses in question). That YHWH had not expressed this aspect of his essence in his actions must have been a source of great tension for him, a tension which the poets insinuate time and again in their laments and prayers.

VII.2.5 YHWH's Deeds; His Kingship

YHWH's essence manifests itself in his deeds. He shows concern for humanity in distress. When people confess their guilt he readily offers forgiveness.[113] In humility[114] and expectation displayed under such conditions of distress the devout one speaks of YHWH's deliverance (תְּשׁוּעַת יְהוָה, 3_{26}), an orientation which is more finely articulated in the parallel sub-canto (3_{55-66}) using familiar expressions of faith from the Psalms which the devout one once again makes his own: YHWH hears and sees his distress; he

---

[111] Cf the explanation of $1_{9c,11c}$.

[112] Cf $1_{18a,20-22}$; 2_{20-22}; 5_1.

[113] Cf 1_{18} and 3_{42}.

[114] Cf 3_{40-42}.

sees the injustice done to him by his enemies; he confesses God as one who is near, as one who whispers *'Fear not... '*.[115] YHWH, who is just and has punished the people for their sins,[116] will now begin litigation and deliver them from their enemy. YHWH will also attend to their hostile offences and hubris – under which not only the devout one is suffering but also the entire land – and his judgement will mean liberation for Israel. The same desire and sense of trust resonates or is elaborated in more detail in the parallel concluding sections of the other songs. In 4_{21-22}, for example, the expectation is expressed that the Edomites will drink the cup of YHWH's judgement in the same way as daughter Zion has been forced to drink it. At the conclusion of the fifth song the devout one's hoped for liberation is transposed to the national level and we hear the people's prayer for deliverance and for the restoration of Zion and the kingdom.

If one were to look for an enduring *theologoumenon* for the acts of salvation we have been discussing then the universal kingship of YHWH would certainly serve the purpose The concluding payer of 5_{19-22}, in which YHWH's royal dominion comes to the fore in the mention of his throne (5_{19}) is significant in this context. YHWH is asked in prayer if he is going to bring an end to the deadly chaos in which the people find themselves. In Lam 2_{13c} the chaos of Israel's downfall is compared to the destructive immensity of the sea. At the same time, however, this baleful comparison breaths something of an unarticulated hope. The ancient Canaanite depiction of Yammu, the sea god who tasted defeat in the struggle against Baal, appears to lie at the base of the comparison[117] In pre-exilic Jerusalemite temple theology this mythological clash is transposed: not Baal but king YHWH (cf Ps 29_{10}) is the One before whom even the mightiest powers of chaos must bow (cf Ps 89_{10}). A similar depiction is evident in the ancient YHWH-King hymn of Ps 93: "More majestic than the thunders of mighty waters, more majestic than the waves of the sea, majestic on high is YHWH" (Ps 93_4). Spieckermann likewise. On the basis of Ps 29, he points to the presence of the notion in pre-exilic Psalm theology that no matter how much YHWH desires to dwell in his sanctuary, he is not definitively bound to it: "Er weiß – sogar mit kanaanäischen Mythenelementen gesagt – seine ihm eigene Unverfügbarkeit zu währen, indem er seinen

---

115 Cf 3_{57}.

116 Cf צַדִּיק הוּא יְהוָה, 1_{18}.

117 Cf JCdMoor, *The Seasonal pattern in the myth of Ba'lu*, AOAT 16, Neukirchen 1971, 36–42.

Ausbruch zu den gewaltigen Wassern und zu den Zedern des Libanon als sein unverbrüchliches Königsrecht proklamiert, nicht zur Erlangung oder Verteidigung seiner Herrschaft, sondern zu ihrem Erweis. Der königliche Tempelthroner Jahwe kann und will seine Herkunft aus der Wüste nicht verleugnen."[118] It almost goes without saying that the ancient notion that YHWH's kingship was not bound to an intact Zion was more than opportune for the temple singers in their moment of crisis. It allowed them to appeal to YHWH as their king in spite of their situation, to YHWH as the Only One who could hold this ravaging chaos in check. Power belonged to YHWH in history and he alone could control the nations (cf 1_{17b}); only YHWH could bring victory or defeat.

All this reveals just how much the other longed for acts of salvation, such as deliverance and redemption, the provision of justice, liberation and retribution came to be understood by the poets as the consequence of YHWH's eternal and universal kingship.[119] Cf also the assimilation of YHWH's kingship in Ps 74_{12} as the foundation for a prayer for deliverance.

VII.3 Tension

The many literal correspondences between Lamentations and the language of the Psalms should not mislead us. There is a fundamental difference between the two: while the context of distress in the Psalms often remains vague and only instinctively perceptible, the dreadful horror of Lamentations is quite clearly related to the downfall of Jerusalem and Judah in 587 and the period following immediately thereafter. In this sense Lamentations is of consequence in itself and not simply a component division of the Psalms. The evident relationship with hard reality also comes quite notably to the fore in Lamentations in the parallelisation of the songs. The faith orientation of the devout one in Lam III is described inclusively, side by side with terrible distress in the other songs. Thus one cannot speak of an already partly realised deliverance on the part of YHWH – as some commentators propose with reference to 3_{55ff} – even less of the end of the exile being in sight.[120]

It would be equally incorrect to absolutise the faith conviction of the devout one of Lam III and isolate it from the rest of the songs as does

118 Spieckermann, *Heilsgegenwart*, 179.

119 Cf $3_{26,58f}$.

120 Cf the explanation of 4_{22A}.

Johnson (1985), for example. He considers the certainty of the coming restoration to be based on 3_{33}: this misfortune is not willingly afflicted by God. Although this does indeed concern a most essential element in Israel's knowledge of God, Johnson does not recognise the fact that in the context of the downfall it did not simply continue unabated as a fixed and undisputed dogma. In Lamentations it is a confession in the form of a personal expression of trust, a renewal of faith in the midst of ongoing affliction in which there is still no sign of YHWH's saving intervention. For precisely this reason, the third song is placed in the midst of the distress presented in the other songs, a distress which it itself includes. This means that the newly recovered faith conviction comes to stand in a particularly tense relationship with hard reality (cf the objections in 3_{34-36}).

In contrast, the poets' are aware that this inhuman reality must be a source of great tension in YHWH and they hope that he will be unable to endure their plight. Their realisation of such a tension is apparent from the central and, for the poets, fundamental expression of the third song which we already mentioned above: ... *for* YHWH *does not willingly afflict or grieve anyone* (3_{33}). In their prayers, this constitutes an enduring thought because they continue to choose to speak of YHWH in such a way that his experience of his punitive actions and his aloofness must be a source of inner conflict.

The poets are also aware of something of God's pain, brought on by the fact that has been forced to do violence to himself in rejecting the people he himself had chosen and by destroying Zion which he himself had built (cf the explanation of $2_{6,7}$, 3_{45}, $4_{10,11}$). With this tension and pain in mind the poets appeal to God against God (see also the explanation of 2_{22}; cf Job 16_{20f}). They endeavour to offset the averted and hidden face of YHWH by calling out to him with outrageous urgency (cf the explanation of $1_{9c,11c}$, 3_{50}, 5_{1}). From a literary perspective, given the structurally rather striking positioning of the imperatives in these verses, this also seems to be a central moment in the songs. With bold insistence the poets plead with YHWH to turn his attention to the affliction they are being forced to endure from day to day. Can he really witness such distress and allow it to continue?

The tension we have been discussing is not resolved in the songs, nor can it be neutralised by human persons no matter how much they humble themselves and put their trust in YHWH. YHWH himself is the one who alone must speak the redemptive word, but his voice is not to be heard in the songs,[121] not even in 3_{57} which is a quotation of YHWH's promise in the context of an expression of trust. Since YHWH himself has not (yet) given answer the songs give the last word to those who are praying: a request of YHWH, but a request indeed which transforms their faith tension into what must ultimately be an unbearable tension for YHWH himself.

[121] Cf WFLahanan, 'The Speaking Voice in the Book of Lamentations', JBL (93), 1974, 49.

METHOD

Before commencing with the exegesis of the text as such, we offer here some summary information on the method used in the present commentary. The reader who has taken the trouble to leaf through the pages of this volume or has already engaged in some random reading will probably have noticed the repeated use of terms such as 'inclusions', 'responses', 'external parallelisms' and ' structural analysis'. The mention of 'structural analysis' might have given some the impression that the author of these pages has weaned himself away from the widely accepted historical-critical method and has become a devotee of one of the modern structure-analytic approaches which frequently go hand in hand with a rejection of the diachronic analysis of texts; cf, for example, the explanation of Loader.[1] Nothing, however, could be further from the truth. Should one seek in vain for a diachronic analysis within the individual exegetical sections of this book this is entirely due to the fact that where the book of Lamentations is concerned there are indications that we are dealing with a unified, 'one-piece' composition. It is evident from our own exegetical research that discrepancies pointed out by other commentators are not rooted in the texts themselves but rather in their explanation of the texts. In our opinion, furthermore, one should be equally sceptical of suggested additions or redactional interventions in the texts of Lamentations which, due to the rigid shape and constant measure of the component strophes, do not tend to lend themselves to such encroachments. The content of the material is similarly unavailing as a source to suggest that the texts have undergone reworking at various stages in their history. The only justified diachronic analysis is one which is oriented towards the period of origin of the songs in which the grounds/occasion of their written creation should be sought.[2]

[1] JALoader, 'De structuuranalytische methoden', in: *Inleiding tot de studie van het Oude Testament*, (ed) ASvdWoude, Kampen 1986, 128–142.

[2] Cf Introduction III.3 *'Sitz im Leben'*.

The fact that a great deal of attention has been paid, nevertheless, to the literary structure of Lamentations is influenced by more recent research into the writing methods of the Old Testament authors together with those in Ugarit.[3] No direct attention was devoted to external structural correspondences with other (world) literature. Research concentrated, rather, on whether the internal literary data point to a conscious structuring of the texts. The results of this research ought to be considered as a welcome complement to the results of already existing synchronic and diachronic approaches. That the latter approach should benefit from the analysis of literary structure might come across as something of a surprise, but the fact remains that purposeful structural analysis can unearth additions as such. We can only offer the briefest survey of the results in question at this point.

The poets of the Old Testament did not write their texts in the same way as they are frequently read and interpreted by modern exegetes, i.e. verse per verse, beginning with 1_1. Not infrequently this has led to a verse-oriented explanation of a text without much reference being made to coherence and unity. Old Testament poetry, however, came into existence in a quite different manner. Having designed a framework, the ancient poets then proceeded to establish divisions and formulate themes and focal points with respect to the material upon which they intended to elaborate. As they fleshed out their work they introduced points of accent by way of repetitions and by way of their use of language they paved the way for the emergence of coherence and division between the various component parts of their composition. Cross draws our attention in Lamentations to: "The recurrence of corresponding words, phrases, cola, and themes at "long range" (...) often in significant cyclic structures." [4] In this sense we can make use of the concept of 'language-architecture', a notion of which Ridderbos speaks when he compares the Psalms to a building in which one portion rests upon the other. Such an approach, however, does not exclude emotion: "No one would want to deny that deeply felt emotions were given expression in the Psalms. The Psalmists, however, did not

---

[3] Cf PvdLugt, *Strofische structuren in de bijbels-hebreeuwse poëzie*, Kampen 1980; *The Structural Analysis of Biblical and Canaanite Poetry*, WvdMeer & JCdMoor (eds) JSOT suppl series 74, Sheffield 1988.

[4] FMCross, 'Studies in the Structure of Hebrew Verse: The Prosody of Lamentations 1:1–22', in: CLMeyers and MO'Connor (eds), *The Word of the Lord Shall Go Forth: Essays in Honor of David Noel Freedman' in Celebration of His Sixtieth Birthday*, ASOR SVS 1, Winona Lake, Indiana 1983, 153.

vent their emotions in an undisciplined and uncontrolled manner. They let themselves be governed by a particular way of composing poetry, by a particular style... Perhaps one can say that the Psalmists' method of writing bore something of an intellectual character; ... The design or structure of the Psalms was under the control of the organising intellect."[5]

A particularly striking tool for the organisation of ancient poet's material came in the form of the now familiar style-figure of parallelism with its inherent and potent eloquence. It is plain to see that parallelism is employed in Hebrew poetry with great variety and imagination. So-called internal parallelism is especially well-known. The classical term *'parallelismus membrorum'* clearly states that parallelism has to do with similarity between the segments of a verse. That one should interpret the 'similarity' in question as broadly as possible is evident from the fact that there are three different types of internal parallelism.[6] If, for example, the second colon in a bicolon is a repetition of the first colon then we are dealing with repetitive or synonymous parallelism. In such cases there is certainly no requirement for the terms involved to be strictly synonymous since the repetition of a thought or a fact using different words can also be considered synonymous parallelism.[7] Another frequent type of parallelism is often referred to as supplementary or synthetic parallelism [8] together with the equally frequent disjunctive or antithetical parallelism.[9] Parallelism in general consists of a forward moving process of thought.[10]

Besides internal parallelism there is also the so-called external parallelism. It is clear from the term itself that in this case the parallel lines are not to be found within the verse but at a greater distance from each other within a text. Such repetitions often serve to underline what lies between them. At the same time, they can also function within the structure of a poem in delimiting literary units. Special forms of external parallelism are used for this purpose, namely: inclusions and responses. Given the fact that

---

[5] NHRidderbos, *De Psalmen I*, KV, Kampen 1962, 44.

[6] Cf, for example, ThCVriezen & ASvdWoude, *Literatuur van Oud-Israël*, Wassenaar 1976[5], 56f.

[7] Cf, for example, Lam 1_{2a}, $2_{6a,7a,10b,16a}$, $3_{4,14,58}$, $4_{3a,7a,11a}$, $5_{5,6,11}$.

[8] See Lam $1_{2c,5a}$, $2_{5a,11a,17a}$, $3_{6,15,10,65}$, $4_{6a,8a,11b}$, $5_{2,4,12}$.

[9] Cf $1_{1bc,2c,19a}$, $2_{2a,8b}$, 3_{37}; $4_{2,5,7,8,20}$, 5_{19-20}. For repetitive and supplementary parallelism we use a double German comma: //; antithetical parallelism is rendered with a double back-slash: \\.

[10] Cf JMuilenberg, *A Study in Hebrew Rhetoric: Repetion and Style*, VTS I (1953), 97.

both terms are used with some frequency in the present commentary a more detailed explanation would seem appropriate at this point.

By the term inclusion we understand an external parallelism at the opposing level within a literary unit. A clear example of this can be found in Psalm 8 which has a similar sounding beginning and end. The psalm also contains other examples of such inclusion, e.g. verse 4 ('the work of your fingers) with verse 7 ('the work of your hands'). An inclusion embraces the text which lies within it and, as it were, closes it in. Lam 2_{12} offers an excellent illustration. In this instance the literary application of inclusion – via the term אִמֹּתָם at the beginning and end of the strophe – gives substance to the enormous suffering of the mothers: they embrace their children who are starving to death. Similar examples can be found in 1_5 and also in 2_{14}. Several inclusions are possible within larger literary units. In such cases they provide that unit with a concentric structure as has already been noted elsewhere.[11] It is not unusual to find the content of such texts thematically formulated or theologically interpreted at the centre of the concentric structure as is the case in verse 5b of Lam 1_{4-6}. Cf also the visual representation given on page 77.

By the term response we mean an external parallelism at the same level within a literary unit. One might think, for example, of a (repeated) refrain at the end of a verse. [12] In Lamentations, responses are to be found at all levels larger than the strophe. A fine illustration would be the second sub-canto (3_{22-33}) of the first canto (3_{1-33}) of Lam III.[13] In this sub-canto the three bicola of the ט-strophe (3_{25-27}) form responses with the כ-strophe (3_{31-33}). The responses in question are supplementary external parallelisms, each having the literary structure: טוֹב (יְהוָה) כִּי....[14]

Although we have already used it on a number of occasions so far the notion of a 'literary unit' continues to be rather vague. For this reason a summary of such units with the terminology we will use to describe them in this commentary would be apropos. The smallest unit is a verse foot, a word with at least one accented syllable. A number of verse feet can constitute a colon, a unit which frequently forms half of a larger section, namely a verse. A verse with two cola (= the plural of colon) is referred to

[11] Cf ACondamin, *Poèmes de la Bible*, Paris 1933, 47–50 and DGrossberg, *Centripetal and Centrifugal Structures in Biblical Poetry*, Atlanta 1989.

[12] Cf Ps 136; cf also Ps $107_{4,10,17,23}$ and Ps $107_{6,13,19,28}$.

[13] For the terms used here see the following paragraph.

[14] Cf Ps 136.

as a bicolon.[15] Several verses together form a strophe.[16] Several strophes together might form what is sometimes referred as a canticle.[17] Several canticles might combine to form an even larger unit: the so-called sub-canto. Sub-cantos in Lamentations are: Lam 1_{1-6} (= 1_{1-3} + 1_{4-6}); 1_{7-11} (= 1_{7-9} + 1_{10-11}). Cf also the introduction to the individual songs. Sub-cantos together can form cantos such as Lam 1_{1-11} which consist of the two sub-cantos: 1_{1-6} and 1_{7-11}. Cantos together can form songs such as Lam 1_{1-22} (= 1_{1-11} + 1_{12-22}) and songs together can even form books, as is the case with Lamentations as a whole. At this level Lam I and V as songs constitute an inclusion, Lam II and IV as songs constitute a response and inclusion at the same time, and Lam III stands in the centre.

In terms of size, the literary unit within which the different types of parallelism might be found can vary considerably. So-called internal parallelism reveals that this can be as small as a bicolon and even inclusions can occur at this level.[18] Examples of inclusions at the level of the strophe can be seen in Lam $2_{12,14}$.[19] Examples of canticle-level inclusions and responses are provided at the introduction to their exegesis. In order to analyse the literary structure of the songs we inquired into the cohesion between their strophes (with Lam V we looked first at the cohesion between the verses) which was established on the basis of binding parallelism together with other literary indications such as key-words, assonance, alliteration and so forth, as well as thematic/substantial unity. At every turn we searched for the most probable level of cohesion.

The unity of Lamentations is made quite evident in the song-responses which consist of external parallel lines at the same level in each of the five songs, that is the strophe-level (cf the same initial letters) but also at the level of parallel canticles. In the latter instance the placing of external parallelism is less critical: it is sufficient for them to be found within the canticle as such. Where there is an uneven number of canticles (Lam V) it is apparent that the verse-level determines the parallelism. Attention should be paid in this context to the correspondence between the 22 verses of the final song with the 22 letters of the preceding alphabetic acrostic. See the survey of the song-responses on pp 635–640. The repetitions heard

15 Cf, for example, Lam 1_{1a}.

16 Cf, for example, Lam 1_{1abc} and Lam $3_{1,2,3}$.

17 Cf, for example, Lam $1_{1-3,4-6,7-9,10-11}$ etcetera.

18 Cf the explanation of Lam 2_{6c}.

19 Cf also the explanation of these verse.

in the responses provide emphasis or supplementation to the theme. The illustration provided in the table below takes external parallelisms in canticles of three or two strophes each of which consist of three verses as its point of departure.

I inclusions		II responses		III resp + incl		IV incl + resp	
1	aaaaaaa	1	nnnnnnn	1	rrrrrrr	1	vvvvvvv
2	sssssss	2		2	sssssss	2	zzzzzzz
3	ccccccc	3	ooooooo	3		3	xxxxxxx
4	eeeeeee	4	nnnnnnn	4	rrrrrrr	4	ccccccc
5		5		5	zzzzzzz	5	zzzzzzz
6	eeeeeee	6	ooooooo	6	uuuuuuu	6	vvvvvvv
7	ccccccc			7	rrrrrrr		
8				8	sssssss		
9	aaaaaaa			9	uuuuuuu		
———		———		———		———	
10	eeeeeee	7	ooooooo	10	aaaaaaa	7	
11		8		11	zzzzzzz	8	
12	eeeeeee	9	nnnnnnn	12		9	ccccccc
13	eeeeeee	10	ooooooo	13		10	xxxxxxx
14	sssssss	11		14	sssssss	11	
15	aaaaaaa	12	nnnnnnn	15	aaaaaaa	12	

Table 1

Explanatory Remarks

The verse constitutes the smallest unit in the above illustration, the numbered blocks under the headings I–IV. The strings of letters stand for words or phrases. In this way we can discover, more or less literally but also at the level of content, if there is a correspondence elsewhere in the poem. In the examples provided in the illustration the verses combine to form strophes: 1–3, 4–6, 7–9, 10–12, 13–15. These strophes in turn combine to form canticles: I$_{1-9}$, II$_{1-6}$, III$_{1-9}$, IV$_{1-6}$. In the second part – beneath horizontal line – the verses also combine to form strophes and the strophes canticles. Equivalent strings of letters represent external parallelisms. Thus verses 4–6 in I not only constitute an inclusion in strophe I_{4-6} but also in canticle I_{1-9}. Verses 3 and 7 constitute an inclusion within I_{1-9}; likewise for verse 1 and 9. Verse 5 holds the central position within this canticle. At the higher level verses 1 and 15, 2 and 14, 4 and 12, 6 and 10 constitute inclusions with the second canticle I_{10-15}. Verse 10 and 13 together constitute a response within the second canticle I_{10-13} in which strofes 10–12 and 13–15 are bound together by means of concatenation, between the bicola of 12 and 13 which form at the same time the most inner inclusion.

In canticle II_{1-6} we find a response between 1 and 4 and between 3 and 6; likewise in canticle II_{7-12} between 7 and 10 and between 9 and 12. If one pays attention to the higher level, however, one can see that the same external parallelisms which constitute responses in the individual canticles II_{1-6} and II_{7-12} also function as inclusions in (sub-canto) II_{1-12}: 1 and 12, 3 and 10, 4 and 9, 6 and 7. Other responses are evident in III_{1-9} between 1, 4 and 7 etcetera. The blank spaces may refer to verses which constitute (particular) external parallelisms on a higher level (in larger units) with other texts.

On occasion responses and inclusions coincide, as is the case in III_{1-9}, for example, between 2 and 8, and in IV_{1-6} between 2 and 5. As we have already noted, this is also the case at the song level between Lam II and IV.

It cannot be over-emphasised that what we have here is nothing more than a very compact and incomplete rendering of what is explained in a more thorough and documented way elsewhere. For this reason we refer the reader once again to the studies mentioned at the beginning of this section on method. Further reference can also be made to the literature proposed by De Moor.[20]

An analysis of Lamentations as a whole can be found in 1988, 294–396. One of the most important discoveries therein was the fact that many responses are also evident at the song level.[21] The literary arguments

[20] JCdMoor, 'The Integrity of Isaiah 40', in: MDietrich & OLoretz (eds), *Mesopotamica – Ugaritica – Biblica: Festschrift für Kurt Bergerhof zur Vollendung seines 70. Lebensjahres am 7. Mai 1992.* Neukirchen-Vluyn: Neukirchener Verlag 1993, 181–216.

[21] Cf the revised and enlarged survey of the song-responses on pp 636–641.

for the demarcation of units larger than the canticle can be found in the articles dating from 1988. Since closer exegetical research has provided the opportunity for submitting supplementary information on several points, the canticle analysis is offered once again in the present volume.

What is important for our explanation so far is that one begins to acquire a clearer insight into the mutual cohesion of the texts together with the thematic and substantial homogeneity of the various literary units. Thus the fact that the strophes appear to constitute thematic units particularly in their cohesion as canticles, provided the motivation for us to proceed with the exegesis at the canticle level. It goes without saying that the smallest units of the text provide the methodical point of departure for the exegesis as such. Clarification by way of the immediate and wider (parallel) context, however, can be enlightening and informative. As was the case with several texts in the book of Lamentations, the exegete can be greatly assisted by external parallelisms where uncertainty exists. By making more intensive use of the context of external parallelisms in the exegesis of Lamentations we have followed something of a new path, one which has occasionally led to a radical departure from long-standing interpretations. In every case, however, we have endeavoured to maintain the necessary prudence and have carefully tested the various arguments involved.

The Masoretic Text as contained in the Codex Leningradensis B 19^{A} (to be found in BHK and BHS) served as the basis for the exegesis against the background of the other text traditions. Grateful use was also made of the extremely thorough text-critical studies of, among others, Albrektson[22] and Gottlieb.[23]

Accepted exegetical methods and tools have been employed where appropriate. Concordances and grammars, for example, remain indispensable should one wish to do justice to the wider Old Testament context and to the Hebrew terminology. More recent theological dictionaries have also proved their worth as sources of information and dialogue partners although critical use of this and other secondary material was demanded.

---

22 BAlbrektson, *Studies in the Text and Theology of the Book of Lamentations, with a Critical Edition of the Peshitta Text*, STL 21, 1963.

23 HGottlieb, *A Study of the Text of Lamentations*, Acta Jutlandica XLVIII, Theology Series 12 Århus 1978.

Lamentations I

Canto I (1_{1-11})

1 א *Ah, how lonely she sits,*
that city, that Lady among her people.
She has become like a widow,
that Lady among the nations.
The princess among the provinces
has now been reduced to forced labour.

2 ב *She weeps aloud in the night,*
tears run down her cheeks.
No one comforts her,
not one among all her lovers.
All her friends have abandoned her;
they have become her enemies.

3 ג *Exposed is Judah by captivity*
and hard servitude.
She sits down among the nations,
she finds no resting place.
All her pursuers hound her
and press her hard.

---

4 ד *The roads to Zion mourn,*
for no one comes to the festivals.
All her gates are desolate.
Her priests groan.
Her young girls are deeply grieved,
and as for her – her lot is bitter.

5 ה *Her oppressors have become the masters,*
her enemies are without care,
because YHWH *grieves her deeply*
for the multitude of her transgressions.
Her children have been forced to depart,
as captives before the oppressor.

6 ו *From daughter Zion has departed*
all her majesty.
Her princes have become like stags
that find no pasture.
Without strength they fled
before the pursuer.

---

7 ז *Jerusalem ponders*
the days of her affliction and homelessness,
all the precious things
that were hers in days of old,
until her people fell into the hand of the oppressor,
and there was no one to help her.
Oppressors looked on mocking
over her downfall.

8 ח *Jerusalem sinned grievously,*
therefore she has become impure.
All who honoured her despise her,
for they see her nakedness.
Yes, she herself groans
and turns her face away.

9 ט *Her uncleanness clings to her skirts.*
She was not prepared for such an outcome.
Appallingly deep was her downfall,
and no one comforts her.
"Look, YHWH, *at my affliction,*
yes, the enemy has triumphed!"

---

10 י *The oppressor stretches out his hand*
over all her precious things.
Yes, she sees infidels
invade her sanctuary;
those of whom you command:
they may not enter into your congregation.

11 כ *All her people groan*
as they search for bread.
They trade their treasures for food
to restore their vigour.
"Look, YHWH, *and observe,*
how worthless I have become!"

Canto II (1_{12-22})

12 ל *You there, all who pass by,*
observe and see:
is there any sorrow like my sorrow,
which is being brought upon me,
with which YHWH *deeply afflicts me*
on the day of his fierce anger?

13 מ *From on high he sent fire;*
he made it go down into my bones.
He spread a net for my feet,
he turned me back.
He is ruining my life,
(making me) so faint all day long.

---

14 נ *He fastened the yoke upon me with my transgressions,*
by his hand they were fastened together;
they weigh on my neck.
He makes my strength founder.
Adonai has handed me over,
and I cannot endure.

15 ס *Piled up (like sheaves) are all my mighty ones,*
by Adonai in my midst.
He proclaimed a time of harvest for me,
to thresh my young men.
Adonai treads as in a wine press
the virgin daughter Judah.

16 ע *For these things I weep,*
my eye, my eye flows with water.
Yes, a comforter is far from me,
one to revive my vigour.
My sons are bewildered.
Yes, how mighty is the enemy.

---

17 פ *Zion stretches out her hands,*
(but) no one comforts her.
YHWH *has commanded against Jacob*
that his neighbours should become his oppressors.
Jerusalem has become
a filthy thing in their eyes.

18 צ *Righteous is he,* YHWH,
for I resisted his word.
Hear indeed, all you peoples,
and behold my sorrow:
my young women and young men
have gone into captivity.

19 ק *I called to my lovers,*
they, they deceived me.
My priests and elders
perished in the city,
while seeking food for themselves,
to restore their vigour.

---

20 ר *See,* YHWH, *how faint at heart I am;*
my bowels are aflame,
my heart turns upside down within me,
yes, how heedless I have been.
Outside, the sword bereaves me of my children,
in the house, death.

21 ש *Hear how I groan,*
no one who comforts me.
All my enemies delight to hear of my misfortune,
and it is you who brings it (upon me).
You brought on the day you had announced.
Let them become like me.

22 ת *Be attentive to all their evil*
and deal with them
as you have dealt with me
because of all my transgressions.
For my groans are many
and my heart is deathly sick.

* * *

LITERARY STRUCTURE OF LAMENTATIONS I

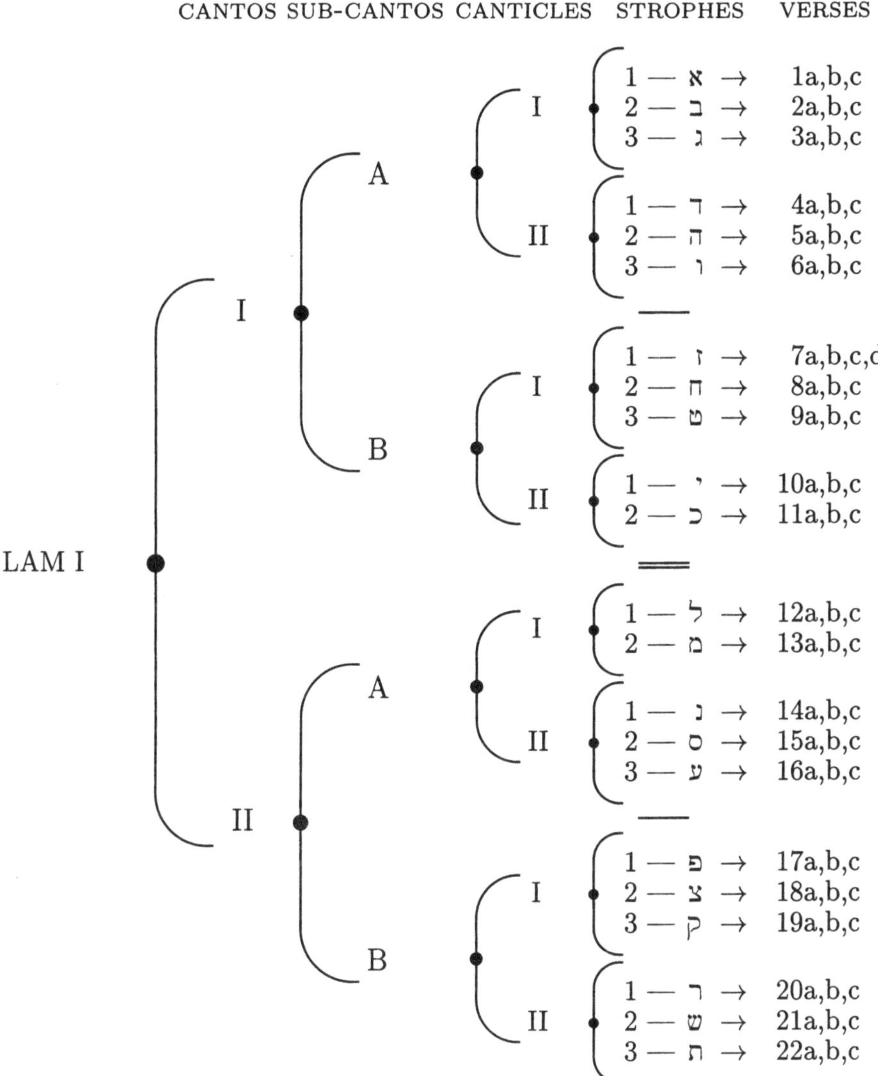

For the concentric structure of Lam I see 1988, 295ff.

figure 1

Essentials and Perspectives

If we look at the first song in terms of its size it may appear to be too large a 'pericope' to be representative of the main lines of exegesis. One decisive argument in favour of considering it in this way, however, is the clear and well-rounded literary unity formed by the alphabetic acrostic. The literary-structural design of this unity reflects the main themes of the song not only externally but also in terms of content. The song's concentric structure, for example, clearly indicates that the principle theme should be sought neither in the opening strophes nor in the conclusion, but rather in the central strophes $1_{11,12}$.[1] Personified as a woman, we hear Lady Jerusalem / daughter Zion lamenting over the indescribable distress that has befallen her: "look and see if there is any sorrow like my sorrow." She turns first in her distress to YHWH (1_{11c}) and then – having received no response – she turns to the people (1_{12a}), to whoever will witness her misery. Whatever happens, she is simply in need of help. At the same time, the central strophes indicate the ultimate roots of her misery. She complains before YHWH that she has become absolutely worthless (1_{11c}), a situation which is further articulated elsewhere in the strophe by the description of her dreadful and wasting hunger. Nourishment is the only thing that still matters. In addition to her physical and material distress she laments before the people over her spiritual privation: it is YHWH, her own God, who is oppressing her in this unparalleled fashion (1_{12c}).

While Jerusalem's worthlessness stands at the centre of the first song, it functions at the same time as a summary of the first main part of the book 1_{1-11}, within which we can distinguish four smaller units or canticles. By way of its own themata each smaller unit makes the distress and worthlessness of Lady Jerusalem and her country more explicit. The detailed description leads the reader/listener to sympathise with Lady Jerusalem as she cries out in anguish over her worthlessness, all the more so because the poets present her current situation in contrast with her former status which was once marked by extraordinary majesty, greatness and renown. The poets, however, do not restrict themselves to naming her exterior distress alone. The first canticle (1_{1-3}) begins with such a contrast figure: the city – personified as Lady Jerusalem – , who was once the highly honoured and admired princess, the very heart of her nation, now sits alone like a widow in mourning, abandoned by YHWH her husband,

[1] See 1988, 295–297.

isolated like a leper with no one to support or comfort her. If the nations trouble her (population) further it is only to put her to work as a slave, a lot all the more bitter to one who once commanded others in her employ. Her loneliness is colossal but there is no one to help and console her. Worse still: her former allies, the very ones from whom she might have expected some assistance, have now become her enemies as they take advantage of her helplessness. Although somewhat hidden within the central strophe (I_2) of this canticle, a theological interpretation is here implied for the disaster that has befallen Lady Jerusalem: she is passing through a period of judgement from YHWH; the night is upon her, the darkness of the dies irae, the day of YHWH.

What applies to the city applies equally to the land. Judah has also become like a defenceless widow; she too is suffering merciless oppression and abuse (I_3). This initial strophe is elaborated primarily in the final song.

The second canticle (I_{4-6}) focuses on the suffering brought about by the destruction of the Temple. At one time, Zion was visited by pilgrims from far and wide but now there is nothing except immense loneliness. No one comes to the festivals any more. Those who once inhabited the sanctuary, from the priest to the young girl who sang and danced in the liturgy, are intensely dejected. The destruction of the once magnificent sanctuary constitutes a further contrast, but the same can also be said of the people themselves whose present desolate situation is in stark contrast to the days when their rulers moved about the Temple in sumptuous apparel as they took part in the liturgy. Now the splendour and radiance of Zion's children and princes has vanished. Once again, however, and with even greater urgency, we hear a theological vision of the sanctuary's downfall resound in the central strophe (I_5): because of the great many sins that have been committed (there) YHWH has given the enemy free reign.

The third canticle (I_{7-9}) reveals the contrasts mentioned above in the life of Lady Jerusalem. Homeless and destitute, she endures the pain of her loss. The enormity of her deprivation actually extends beyond the limits of the human imagination. The unusual depth of her fall can only be the result of YHWH's censuring actions. If the first canticle (I_{1-3}) makes use of the objective image of a down at heel widow, lonely as a leper, this third canticle focuses more on a subjective description of her distress: she perceives herself as a naked, menstruating woman, exposed in her impurity for everyone to see, loathsome and vile. One further detail makes her situation all the more painful: none of this has befallen her by accident;

the cause of her distress is her sin. She has violated her common bond) with YHWH. Now He has handed her over to her fate. He no longer offers her his dedication and protection. His aloofness lays bare her nakedness and impurity. She had never imagined that her life would end up like this. Her distress and oppression is unbearable, however, and Lady Jerusalem knows only One who can help her in her need: YHWH. With a short but insistent prayer she turns to Him for help (1_{9c}).

The final canticle (1_{9-11}) of the first canto (1_{1-11}) provides a climactic description of the most tormenting privation: despoilment, desecration of YHWH's sanctuary, and finally dreadful starvation. In this situation of terrible need, Lady Jerusalem cries out for help once more and with even greater urgency to YHWH.

After her prayerful outcry at the end of the first canto, Lady Jerusalem continues to speak in the second canto (1_{12-22}) as daughter Zion. This becomes apparent from the central strophe of this canto: 1_{17}. The change of name makes her complaint even more intense precisely because the relationship 'YHWH – Zion' most profoundly expresses the relationship between Him and (the population of) his Temple city. Without response from YHWH, she turns in her need to the people. Her question to them, whether they know of any need comparable to her's, is essentially an urgent appeal for help. Since her need does not only consist of visible distress but also has a spiritual dimension, she gives words to this facet of her torment further on in the canticle: it is YHWH her God who has brought this great affliction upon her; He is the source of her malady. He who once loved her (cf. the explanatory remarks on 'like a widow' in 1_{1b}), has turned against her.

It is for this reason that daughter Zion experiences her misery so profoundly: it is not her enemies but YHWH himself who is doing this to her. Against this background she continues to describe her need in the following canticle (1_{14-16}), the theological interpretation of her lot constituting a new element: He, YHWH, is allowing her to bear the consequences of her sins; He has handed her over to the might of her enemies; He is the one who has rejected her warriors and crushed her young men. Such suffering brings her profound sorrow and tears and causes the very life within her to drain away. There is no one to comfort her or restore her to strength and vitality.

In the first strophe of the following canticle (1_{17-19}) daughter Zion falls silent for a moment. From a literary perspective this leaves the impression that her tears have overcome her and left her speechless. The poets fill the silence by describing her as they see her: with hands outstretched, in silent supplication for help in her need. Who else can she turn to? YHWH? Is it realistic to continue to hope for His help? When daughter Zion finds her tongue once more she confesses that in judging her in this way YHWH has acted justly. What more then can she expect from him? For this reason she turns once again to the people and asks them to behold her sorrow (1_{18}), but this also is to no avail. What can she expect from the people when even her lovers have deceived her (1_{19})? Her distress is still so vast: her priests and elders have died from starvation in the city; she is in desperate need of help. The extent of her privation causes her to turn back to YHWH, to the one from whom she can expect nothing, or perhaps (cf 3_{29}) there is still hope?

It is apparent from the final canticle of the first song (1_{20-22}) that in spite of her expectations, YHWH is still her only possible means of deliverance. From a thematic perspective, therefore, daughter Zion's prayer to Him is her last word. Once again – for the third time – she urgently appeals to YHWH for help because her need is unbearable. This concluding prayer offers a significant theological addition to her other petitions. Where she spoke of the power of her enemies in 1_{9c} – she now speaks of the inhuman evil they have brought upon her and in so doing she appeals to YHWH's justice. In her downfall He has already punished her sins; why then should her enemies continue to be free to commit such humiliating atrocities against her? The fact that she prays for their judgement and punishment is not a prayer of vengeance – as is sometimes said – but rather a means for daughter Zion to put an end to her distress. If YHWH were to judge and punish her enemies for their wickedness, as he punished daughter Zion for her sins, then their downfall would bring her the relief for which she longs.

Lamentations I

Scholarly Exposition

Content/Structure

The first canto (1_{1-11}) describes the distress in which Jerusalem and Judah find themselves and is to be considered as an overture to the rest of Lamentations. Each element of need – which will be developed further on in the book – is expressed therein: loneliness, treachery, destruction and desecration of the sanctuary, loss of former glory, oppression, hunger, guilt, and abandonment by God. At the same time, however, and in spite of this long litany of disaster, prayer to YHWH for help is also given expression. Jerusalem's need stands in the foreground. The city's sinful fate (cf $1_{5b,8a}$) is elaborated in successive canticles and by way of a personification: the city is presented as a woman, thereby permitting the description of her suffering in personal terms. The image of Lady Jerusalem dominates canto I, the first canticle (1_{1-3}) setting the tone with an image of her widowhood side by side with that of Judah. The situation of need is amplified further on the basis of this metaphor. The second canticle thus refers to the lost splendour of daughter Zion and her present oppression; the first canticle (1_{7-9}) of the second sub-canto presents a certain Lady Jerusalem, looking back nostalgically in her immense distress to the good days of yesteryear; in contrast, the second and last canticle (1_{10-11}) of the second sub-canto specifies her most terrible need: defilement and hunger. These depictions of privation are twice interrupted by a short prayer of petition: $1_{9c,11c}$.

The same misfortune is elucidated in the second canto (1_{12-22}) but this time by Jerusalem in the person of daughter Zion whose voice only serves to intensify the complaints. She first directs her lament to outsiders, pointing to the incomparable sorrow which has brought on her deep infirmity (1_{12-13}) and to the gravity of the burden of sin which YHWH has laid upon her (1_{14-16}). In 1_{17} the poets fill out the pause in her speech, describing her as a desperate woman begging for assistance. In 1_{18-20} the same woman takes the floor once again only to confirm that there is no one to help her ($1_{18,19}$); her only recourse is to pray to YHWH, to the one who has abandoned her (1_{20-22}).

Genre (see also Introduction III.2)

Gunkel designated the genre of Lam I, II and IV as *'politischen Leichenlieder'*.[2] It is said [3] that in so doing, Gunkel imitated Jahnow [4] but she did not in fact use such terminology. She understood Lamentations to be a derived form of *the dirge*, a derivative which no longer matched the original form on a number of essential points. She believed, for example, that the element of 'the incomprehensible' in the dirge form had been replaced in Lamentations by confessions of guilt, but such a position remains open to discussion.[5] A further important point is the fact that the dirge possessed a profane quality because Israel did not associate YHWH with the unclean sphere of the dead and their domain. In Lamentations, on the other hand, it is YHWH himself who is invoked. For this reason Jahnow sees the transformation from dirges to Lamentations as a transformation from the profane to the religious genre. "Auch literargeschichtlich läßt sie diese Entwicklung feststellen, nämlich als eine Beeinflussing durch die sonst streng vom Leichenlieder zu unterscheidende Gattung des Volksklagepsalms." [6] As a matter of fact, Jahnow's genre determination is not so far from that of Westermann [7] who adjudges Lam I, II and IV to be complaints of the people [8] with elements of the dirge incorporated therein. Westermann is right to consider that the particular character of Lamentations is to be found in this combination of elements. The difference with complaints of the people from before 587 lies in the seriousness of the calamity they are facing. The difference between then and now lies in the demise of temple and kingship, both essential, institutional elements in the existence of the people, the disappearance of which was experienced as (almost) deadly and was given expression in combination with elements from the dirge.

[2] In: RGG[2] III 1049ff; cf also Schunk, BHH 1069.
[3] Westermann, *Klagelieder*, 35.
[4] HJahnow, *Das hebräische Leichenlied im Rahmen der Völkerdichtung*, BZAW 36, Giessen 1923.
[5] Cf 1983, 294 note 302 together with the explanatory remarks on 3_{40}.
[6] Jahnow, 170.
[7] Westermann, *Klagelieder*, 88, 105.
[8] Literally: *'Klage des Volkes'*.

The character of the complaint of the people, the motifs of which can also be found in Lam I, is dominant as far as Westermann is concerned. Cf direct address to YHWH ($1_{9c,11c,20a}$), complaint addressed to YHWH ($1_{9c,11c,20a}$), the lodging of complaint (for example 1_{16}), complaints concerning the enemy ($1_{5a,9c,21b}$), confession of guilt ($1_{5b,8a,18a}$), prayer for attention ($1_{9c,11c,20a}$) and prayer against the enemy (1_{22}). Westermann considers it worthy of note that the expression of trust is missing, the reason for which, he suggests, is to be found in the unknown extent of the catastrophe. The present calamity is too great for the people to be able to fall back on God's former saving deeds.[9]

Bearing all this in mind, however, we still do not have an answer to the question of the genre of Lam I. No matter how many elements of the complaint of the people are present, it still does not make Lam I a classical example of such a complaint. In Westermann's explanation there is a constant tendency to try to identify the same sequence of motifs in Lamentations as one would expect to find in the complaint of the people and this is not without its difficulties. It leads him to a rearrangement of elements which he feels have been displaced under pressure from the alphabetic acrostic.[10] The structure of the song, however, is not that of a complaint of the people[11] nor is the alphabetic acrostic to be found in association with such complaints. Besides this, the question of the relationship between the individual songs and Lamentations as a whole remains. The fact that the songs cannot be considered in isolation implies that the quest for the genre of each individual song is, at the same time, a quest for the genre of Lamentations as a whole. Since the composition of Lamentations is unique in the OT, however, continued talk of genre as such has to be eliminated. This, of course, has repercussions for the way we look at each of the five songs. Making due allowance for the motifs familiar from other genres, therefore, we will have to examine each song as an essential component of the unique composition which is Lamentations.[12]

Exegesis

Prior to the exegesis as such, a word outlining the reasoning behind the coherence of the various strophes which form one canticle is provided. Verse divisions are indicated as follows: the Masoretic verse divisions are

[9] Cf, however, 3_{55f}.
[10] See Westermann, *Klagelieder*, 112f, 115.
[11] Cf NHRidderbos, *De Psalmen*, Kampen 1962, 23.
[12] Cf the general introduction III.3 on 'Sitz im Leben'.

maintained; successive bicola are indicated with lower case letters a,b,c,d; the first part of a bicolon with upper case A the second with upper case B. For synonymous and complementary parallelism a double German comma is used: //. Antithetical parallelism is represented by a double backslash: \\.

The canticles are enumerated according to the number per sub-canto, the sub-cantos according to the number per canto and the cantos according to the number per song.

Sub-canto I (1_{1-6})

Cohesion between the two sub-cantos of this canto is apparent from the extensive portrayal of need based on the common elements of loneliness, lost magnificence and enemy oppression. In the first canticle (1_{1-3}) this takes place with respect to Jerusalem ($1_{1,2}$) and Judah (1_3) while in the second canticle (1_{4-6}) it focuses on Zion.

Canticle I (1_{1-3})

Content/theme: *Jerusalem and Judah are like lonely, inconsolable and oppressed widows*

Literary argumentation:

inclusions:
אֵיכָה (1aA) // הַמְּצָרִים (3cB)
בַגּוֹיִם (1bB) // בַגּוֹיִם (3bA)
מַס (1cB) // עֲבֹדָה (3aB)
אַלְמָנָה (1bA) // לֹא מָצְאָה מָנוֹחַ (3bB) [13]

responses:
הָעִיר (1aB) // יְהוּדָה (3aA)
רַבָּתִי (1aB) // רֹב (3aB)
אַלְמָנָה (1bA) // אֵין־לָהּ מְנַחֵם (2bA) //
לֹא מָצְאָה מָנוֹחַ (3bB) [14]
מְּדִינוֹת (1cA) // רֵעֶיהָ (2cA)
אֹיְבִים (2cB) // רֹדְפֶיהָ (3cA)
רֵעֶיהָ (2cA) // רֹדְפֶיהָ (3cA)

ext. par.:
יָשְׁבָה (1aA) // יָשְׁבָה (3bA)

---

[13] Cf Ruth 1_9.

[14] Note the alliteration between מָנוֹחַ en מְנַחֵם.

Although the fate of both Judah and Jerusalem is raised in this canticle, it is striking that the poets pay twice as much attention to Jerusalem, the first two strophes being devoted to her lot while we must wait until the third strophe before our attention is drawn to Judah. It is evident from the frequency with which the various names are used that this division of attention is characteristic of Lamentations as a whole. Judah appears five times; Israel and Jacob three times each; Jerusalem seven times and Zion fifteen times. Jerusalem and Zion are thus mentioned twice as often as the other three combined.[15]

1aA *Ah, how lonely she sits,* אֵיכָה יָשְׁבָה בָדָד

In terms of structure, the first two bicola of this strophe are parallel while the third follows the second in a chiastic relationship. The poets begin the first song with a triple contrast, each bicolon consisting of an antithetical description of the desperate situation. Contrast itself is a characteristic of the Eastern dirge in which the enormity of the distress is made manifest by calling to mind former magnificence and glory in the midst of present misfortune.[16]

There is no question here of a sort of amorphous grief. On the contrary, the poets render the distress of Jerusalem with the utmost precision. This becomes apparent from their description of the city's appearance. Whoever draws near to Jerusalem can see how deeply she is immersed in a torment of death and destruction.[17] Their first utterance sets the tone for the entire song: אֵיכָה (see also 2_1 and 4_1). BHK and BHS are incorrect in presenting this word as a distinct introduction since it properly belongs with the first bicolon.[18] Normally the word אֵיכָה means 'how' but in the dirge genre איכ(ה) serves as a fixed term of introduction,[19] where אֵיכָה as an exclamation is stronger than אֵיךְ.[20] In this way the poets have elected to give this song the timbre of a dirge. The preferred translation of אֵיכָה ought, therefore, to be 'Ah'. To break into a dirge implies that one is affected by grief brought on by death.[21] The poets themselves then are not

---

15 Cf 1983, 86–89.

16 Cf Jahnow, 1923, 99. See also GAAnderson, *A Time to Mourn, a Time to Dance. The Expression of Grief and Joy in Israelite Religion*, Pennsylvania, 1991, 51.

17 Cf 2_{15}.

18 Cf Kraus and Westermann.

19 Cf Isa 1_{21}, Jer 48_{17}, II Sam 1_{19}.

20 Cf Waltke – O'Connor, *An Introduction to Biblical Hebrew Syntax*, Winona Lake, Indiana 1990, 329. See further Jahnow, 1923, 136.

indifferent bystanders, they are personally involved. The suffering they describe is the very cause of their own grief.

Timbre and contrast do not mean that the dirge form has been employed in its entirety. In disagreeing with this, Kraus is left with the paradox that the dead city is presented simultaneously as a living woman who mourns her own loss. Such a scene would be impossible to imagine. The image presented is not that of Jerusalem's death but that of the city as a woman in mourning who weeps over her great loss. "Daß sich die "Klagelieder" nicht mit der Leiche sondern mit der Hintergebliebenen beschäftigen, hat allerdings in der wirklichen Totenklage ein Vorbild. Auch hier gibt es Lieder, in denen weniger von dem Todesfall selbst als vom Schmerz der Hintergebliebenen und der bedrängten Lage, in die sie durch den Todesfall geraten sind, die Rede ist."[22] One might be able to speak of 'the dirge of one left behind'. אֵיכָה, however, is not placed on Jerusalem's lips but comes from the lips of others who are witnesses to her distress. For this reason the opening of this song should be typified as a 'lament over a woman in mourning' but given the lack of material – only here – it would hardly be correct to speak of a genre.

Her enormous grief has been brought on by a great loss which the poets have yet to identify. First they turn their attention to her appearance. She is sitting down (√ישׁב *qal* pf 3f sg). In combination with אֵיכָה her sitting indicates a mourning custom according to which the bereaved sat down or lay down in the dust of the earth as a sign of their grief at the death of a loved one.[23] It is possible that the custom's original purpose was to give the bereaved a sense of connection with the realm of the dead, the new domain of the one being mourned.[24] The word combination יָשְׁבָה בָדָד, however, evokes a different set of associations, as can be seen from the context in Lev 13_{46} where the same phrase is used. In the context of Leviticus 'sitting alone' is the lot of the leper who has been expelled from the community.[25] What is striking is the fact that a leper was obliged to follow certain customs which functioned at the same time as mourn-

[21] See, for example, David's dirge over Saul and Jonathan, II Sam 1_{19-27} and over Abner, II Sam 3_{33-34}.

[22] Jahnow, 172.

[23] Cf Gen 23_{2f}; II Sam 12_{16}, 13_{31}, Ez 26_{16}; Est 4_3; see also the explanatory remarks on Lam 2_{10} and 3_{16}.

[24] Cf Jahnow, 24ff and Anderson, 82: "the state of mourning itself is closely associated with the dead".

[25] Cf Num 12_{14f}, II Kgs 15_5 and the metaphorical usage in Jer 15_{17}.

ing rituals, customs such as letting one's hair hang loose or tearing one's clothing.[26] When Lamentations was composed, these customs had certainly been around for a long time. The confluence of two realms, one surrounding the mourner and one surrounding the leper, is the ultimate effect of these opening words.

The first bicolon, therefore, appears to be using imagery: the city is presented as a woman in mourning, down at heel, worthy of pity, lonely as a leper. The poets use these images to introduce one of their primary themes: Lady Jerusalem is alone. The use of a present tense translation for the perfect יָשְׁבָה flows from the fact that, having once sat down she remains seated.[27] 'She' is that city. The absence of a name gives the definite article a certain demonstrative significance. With the naming of the city in $1_{7,8}$ and the even earlier mention of '(daughter) Zion' in $1_{4,6}$, the poetic referent soon becomes apparent.

Westermann has alluded to the relationship between dirge and complaint of the people as characteristic of Lamentations. This does not only imply a sort of mixing of literary motifs, it also gives a whole new dimension to the complaint of the people. By presenting the people, in this case the population of Jerusalem, in the person of a woman, the poets locate the experience of the community in the context of personal experience: "Die Geschichte eines Volkes erhält in diesem Vergleich den Charakter des Personalen, des persönlich-menschlichen Schicksals, zu dem ins besondere die Möglichkeit des Leidens gehört." [28] The portrayal of Lady Jerusalem's suffering, therefore, is not simply a literary impression, rather it describes the actual calamity experienced by her population. The fact that the poets have chosen to do this in the figure of a woman is not without reason. Kaiser has rightly pointed out that the figure and experience of womanhood is the most appropriate way to express the depth and all-embracing character of humanity's acquaintance with suffering: "the Israelite poets "become women" when expressing the full intensity of the community's suffering." [29]

1aB *that city, that Lady among her people.* הָעִיר רַבָּתִי עָם

The apposition רַבָּתִי עָם has been translated in various ways. The word

[26] Cf Lev 10_6, 13_{45}, $21_{10f,15}$.

[27] Cf GES-K § 106*g* and Rudolph.

[28] Westermann, *Klagelieder*, 110.

[29] BBKaiser, 'Poet as "Female Impersonator": The Image of Daughter Zion as Speaker in Biblical Poems of Suffering', JR 67 (1987), 166.

רַבָּתִי, for the most part, is taken as a fem st cs (with י-*compaginis*) of the adjective רַב (many), and translated in the context as: 'the city, that once was full of people'.[30] The necessary addition of the temporal modifier 'once', however, makes for a less than precise translation. It is also possible to consider רַבָּתִי as a feminine form of the noun רַב, 'superior', a proposal supported by the presence of the same רַבָּתִי in the second colon where an adjectival interpretation does not fit. The concatenation of רַבָּתִי // רַבָּתִי // שָׂרָתִי in three consecutive bicola points in a similar direction.[31] In addition, the same expression is to be found in Ugaritic as an epithet for goddesses.[32] We consider רַבָּתִי, therefore, to be a noun. It might be possible to translate the word as 'mistress' but the idea of authority implied therein does not reflect the original intention. In any case, if one were to opt for a uniform translation, the word 'mistress' would not fit the phrase רַבָּתִי בַגּוֹיִם which does not call for a relationship of authority giving Jerusalem the status of ruler over the surrounding nations. It is better to focus on her status as capital, as Temple city, and on the esteem this status affords her in the land. Such a status is granted Jerusalem elsewhere in Lamentations (2_{15} and 5_{15}) and is consonant with Zion theology.[33] In order to express this we have chosen the translation 'Lady', a term which offers the advantage of being able to link up with the other images used with respect to Jerusalem in the first canto of Lam I such as 'widow', 'lovers' (1_2), 'immodesty' (1_8) and 'unclean clothing' (1_9). The poets thus present us a with a picture of how Jerusalem's former status has disappeared, thereby maintaining the contrast of the dirge form: the city, who was a Lady among her people, now sits alone, in mourning, isolated as a leper. Jerusalem no longer functions as capital and Temple City of Judah.

1bA *She has become like a widow,* הָיְתָה כְּאַלְמָנָה

We are now presented with a new image – although one derived from the basic metaphor of 'the city as woman'[34] – 'Lady Jerusalem has become

[30] See KJV, RVS, NEB etcetera; cf I Sam 2_5 and HAL 1093.

[31] See Waltke – O'Connor, 1990, 128 and BL 526 *k*.

[32] Cf Gordon, UT §19.2297, which renders *rbt aṯrt ym* as 'Lady Atirat of the Sea'; see likewise ThFMcDaniel, 'Philological Studies in Lamentations', Biblica 49 (1968), 29ff; JCdMoor, *The Seasonal Pattern in the Myth of Ba'lu*, AOAT 16, Neukirchen 1971, 143, and HGottlieb, *A Study of the Text of Lamentations*, Acta Jutlandica XLVIII, Theology Series 12 Århus 1978, 11.

[33] Cf Ps 48_{2-3} and further 1983, 281ff.

[34] Cf MCAKorpel, *A Rift in the Clouds*, Münster 1990, 26, and ChCohen, 'The 'widowed' city', JANES 5 (1973), 75–81.

like a widow'. The preposition כְּ emphasises the metaphorical character of the comparison. The metaphorical use of widow to describe a city is to be found elsewhere in the OT: Isa 47_8 (Babel), 54_4 (Jerusalem); cf Jer 51_5 (Israel and Judah). "Im bibl. Hebr. hat das wort eine völlig negative Nuance."[35] Although not directly apparent to us, one of the consequences of widowhood is childlessness (see more on this topic below). Brandscheidt and others see widow Jerusalem's childlessness as the point of comparison. It is true that loneliness as a consequence of childlessness is indicated in the first bicolon by יָשְׁבָה בָדָד but this is surely not the only purpose of the widow imagery. In Isa 47_{8f} the elements of widowhood and childlessness are both clearly distinguished. The essence of widowhood lies, in the first place, in the fact that a woman loses her husband and as a consequence of this loss she finds herself in an extremely vulnerable position. Without the protection of her spouse and in the absence of the male members of her family a woman could end up in the most dreadful state of affairs[36] and if there was a question of debt she might even lose her children who would be taken from her and sold into slavery.[37] It is for this reason that widowhood is associated with childlessness. Hence the commandments insist that one should not abuse the helplessness of widows.[38] Although the removal of her children is mentioned later ($1_{5c,18c}$) it is difficult to imagine that the most essential point of comparison, namely the loss of her spouse, would not have some role to play and that the metaphor's only purpose is to portray Lady Jerusalem's childlessness and vulnerability. The loss of her husband and her oppression both seem to be intended, but we are then faced with Rudolph's question: "wer sollte das sein?" (see likewise Van Selms). On the basis of the response between the first and the last song,[39] namely between 1_1 and 5_3, we might think of the city leaders, the king and the princes. It is stated in 1_6 (the centre of the first canto 1_{1-11}) that her princes were carried off. Together with the king they live in exile.[40]

It is probable, nevertheless, that the imagery used here betrays an even deeper sorrow. The prophets Hosea and Jeremiah were able to portray the relationship between YHWH and his people as a marriage relationship, one which broke down due to the woman Israel's infidelity.[41] The woman Is-

[35] TWAT I 309 (Hoffner).
[36] Cf TWAT I 311 (Hoffner).
[37] Cf II Kgs 4_1.
[38] Ex 22_{22}, Deut $24_{17,19ff}$; see also the explanatory remarks on 5_3.
[39] Cf our structural analysis of the entire book, 1988, 361–391.
[40] Cf the explanatory remarks on 2_{9bA} and 4_{20}.

rael's adulterous behaviour led to her ultimate widowhood because YHWH abandoned his people (Hos 1_9, Jer 3_8). Deutero-Isaiah's message of comfort ties in with this very situation when the prophet proclaims that YHWH is going to undo Zion's widowhood and become her husband once again.[42]

All this implies, therefore, that 'widow' Jerusalem is not simply in mourning over the loss of her king and leaders but primarily over the loss of her 'spouse': YHWH. This partly explains the metaphorical usage 'like a widow' (כְּאַלְמָנָה), since one can hardly say that YHWH is dead. In the conclusion of the final song we hear the complaint that YHWH has forgotten and forsaken his people. Since we can assume that there is an inclusion between the first canticle of Lam I and the last canticle of Lam V, we might also be justified in proposing a relationship between the two at the literary level and with respect to content. See also the prayer for restoration of former splendour in 5_{21} which corresponds with Lady Jerusalem's lost magnificence portrayed in this first canticle.

Bereft of king and princes, deprived of her children and, most importantly, abandoned by YHWH, Lady Jerusalem's widowhood seems to take on the features of an extremely profound loneliness.[43]

1bB *that Lady among the nations.* רַבָּתִי בַגּוֹיִם

It becomes evident that Lady Jerusalem's loneliness appears to extend even further when contrasted with another former relationship she enjoyed when she was still a Lady among the nations. Outright domination of the nations by Judah is not implied here, rather that Jerusalem enjoyed a certain status in the midst of the (neighbouring) nations who received 'the Lady' with deference. In a response in the following strophe they are even referred to as her lovers (רַבָּתִי בַגּוֹיִם [1_{1bB}] // אֹהֲבֶיהָ [1_{2bB}]).

Her status is not simply a figment of the poets' imagination, it was a political reality. Jer 27 comes to mind, by way of illustration, where king Zedekiah's Jerusalem appears to have been the centre of political negoti-

[41] Cf Hos 1–2, Jer 2–3; cf also Korpel, 219–232.

[42] Isa 54_{4ff}; cf Jer 51_5; see for Deutero-Isaiah's familiarity with the complaints of Lamentations: NKGottwald, *Studies in the Book of Lamentations*, London 1954, 44f, 115f, and 1983, 325–331.

[43] Cf JLHelberg, 'The Incomparable Sorrow of Zion in the Book of Lamentations', in: *Studies in Wisdom Literature*, WCvWijk (ed), OTWSA 15 & 16: Old Testament Studies, Papers read at the 15th and 16th Meeting of the OT werkgemeenskap Suid-Afrika 1972 and 1973. Edited 1976. See 33–35.

ations concerning resistance against the super power of Babylon.[44] This relationship has also come to an end (see explanatory remarks on 1_{2b}).

1c *The princess among the provinces* שָׂרָתִי בַּמְּדִינוֹת
has now been reduced to forced labour. הָיְתָה לָמַס

Having observed Jerusalem's intense loneliness we are now confronted with another consequence of her widowhood: oppression through misuse of her weak position. To this end, the poets employ a further contrast in the final bicolon of the canticle, this time portraying Jerusalem as a שָׂרָתִי, 'princess'. In contrast to what was implied in 1_{1bB}, the poets here do intend a relationship of authority, namely that of a 'mistress' over the מְּדִינוֹת. A מְדִינָה should be understood as a more or less autonomous region within a country: a province.[45] The provinces were governed from Jerusalem which meant that they bore joint responsibility for national revenues collected in the form of taxes and forced labour.[46] According to North: "מַס ist 'Frondienst', eine Art Arbeit, zu der man 'gezwungen' wird, ohne daß es sich um förmliche "Sklaverei" handelt." [47] On the basis of this we translate מַס as 'forced labour'. It is true perhaps that the texts mentioned deal with the period of David and Solomon but the Deuteronomistic redaction knew all too well what the kingship meant at this point in time (cf I Sam 8_{10-18}).

There are indications, in addition, that shortly before the fall of Judah, Josiah endeavoured to extend the boundaries of his kingdom to match those of David and Solomon's time. He did so, for one, by annexing the territories of the former tribal amphictyony as provinces. It goes without saying that such actions had a number of positive consequences for Josiah's treasury.[48] In any event, the contrast in the final bicolon reveals that the poets were also aware of forced labour which had to be done by the provinces. Given the response מְּדִינוֹת (1cA) // רֵעֶיהָ (2cA) one might think of territories outside of Judah over which Jerusalem no longer had any say (cf Josiah). Whatever the case, the situation is reversed: she who once forced her neighbours into service is now obliged to serve them in turn.[49]

---

44 Cf further 1983, 131 and the explanatory remarks on 2_{16}.
45 Cf Eccl 2_8, 5_7, Est 8_{11}, Neh 1_3.
46 Cf I Kgs 5_{13-18}, 11_{28}, 12_4.
47 TWAT IV 1007.
48 WEClaburn, 'The Fiscal Basis of Josiah's Reform', JBL 92 (1973), 11–22.
49 Cf II Sam 12_{31}, Isa 31_8; see further the explanatory remarks on Lam 5_5.

2a *She weeps aloud in the night,* בָּכוֹ תִבְכֶּה בַּלַּיְלָה
tears run down her cheeks. וְדִמְעָתָהּ עַל לֶחֱיָהּ

If the first strophe described Lady Jerusalem's appearance from a certain distance, as it were, we are now treated to a close up view of the wretched figure in the context of which the imagery is pursued further. It is evident from the paronomastic infinitive בָּכוֹ alongside the verbal form תִבְכֶּה[50] that her tears are quite intense. Singular forms are used for 'tears' and 'cheeks' which may be understood as collectives or as duals.[51] We have not translated the sf 3f sg of the term דִמְעָתָהּ because the same suffix of the term לֶחֱיָהּ functions anaphorically in its place. The plural 'tears' in the versions is a correction. The night time does not afford her the luxury of a refreshing rest. On the contrary, her grief leaves her restless and the darkness brings enormous heaviness of heart.[52] As a visible sign of her pain, her tears continue to flow on account of the calamity that has befallen her.[53]

There is reason to believe that more is intended by the use of the term 'night' than simply a temporal extension of Lady Jerusalem's sorrow. If we examine the opening canticles of the first four songs, we find responses therein which in one way or another have to do with darkness and gloom: יָעִיב (2_1), חֹשֶׁךְ וְלֹא־אוֹר (3_2) and יֻשְׁנָא (4_1). It is equally clear that in 2_1 and 3_1 the darkness in question has its source in YHWH's wrath (see the exegesis) while the faded gold in 4_1 is a consequence of his judgement. Given the frequency of responses there can be no question here of pure coincidence.[54] It seems reasonable to assume, therefore, that 'night' is not used literally here but that it has something to do with YHWH's judgement. Indeed, 'night' in the OT is also seen as the hour of YHWH's judgement. Cf Isa 15_1, Job 27_{19f} and $34_{20,25}$. For the cited texts see TWAT IV 560 (Stiglmair), where Mi 3_6, a text one might consider important in this respect, is not mentioned; for the exegesis of this text see Van der Woude[55] who is otherwise wrong in claiming that the metaphorical use of 'night' is only to be found in Mi 3_6. Cf further Keel: "Wie es räumlich bestimmte Bereich gibt, die an die Totenwelt grenzen, so auch zeitliche. Das Un-

---

50 Cf GES-K § 113*p*.
51 Cf GES-K § 123*b* and § 124*l*.
52 Cf TWAT IV 556 (Stiglmair).
53 Cf Job 30_{17}; Ps 6_7; Jahnow, 46ff, 99 and TWAT I 640 (Hamp).
54 See the survey on pp 636–641 and JRenkema, 'The Meaning of the Parallel Acrostics in Lamentations', VT XLV/3 (1995), 379–382.
55 ASvdWoude, *Micha*, Nijkerk 1976, 112–117.

heil und der Tod können einen Menschen zwar auch tags treffen, aber ihr eigentlicher Bereich ist doch die Nacht und das Dunkel. In der Nacht erscheinen Krankheit und jegliches Übel viel schlimmer als tags, und die Dichter der Klagelieder erzählen, wie sie die ganze Nacht unter Tränen und Seufzen wachgelegen haben (6,7 30,6 77,3)." [56], a quotation which can also be read as an explanation of 3_2. חֲשֵׁכָה 'darkness' in Mi 3_6 is synonymous with 'night', thereby providing some justification for our proposed link between לַיְלָה here and חֹשֶׁךְ וְלֹא־אוֹר in 3_2. The word 'night', therefore, has a theological meaning in our text: Lady Jerusalem weeps bitterly because she is passing through the hour of YHWH's judgement. Cf Jer 9_{17ff}.

Excursus: The 'Day of YHWH'

In the portrayal of night as the time of YHWH's judgement, we find an initial indication in Lamentations that the poets have accepted the pre-exilic prophetic announcement of judgement in the form of the 'day of YHWH' (יוֹם יְהוָה), which was also directed against Israel. Night, gloom, and darkness etcetera accompany this moment of divine judgement.[57] In the exegetical remarks which follow it will become apparent that other elements of the 'day of YHWH' are to be found elsewhere in Lamentations. An almost literal reference, for example, can be found in 1_{21cA}, in the phrase יוֹם־קָרָאתָ, 'the day you have announced'. Since the adoption of such prophetic 'day of YHWH'-preaching is partly determinative of the poets' theological presuppositions, a closer look at what is meant by the notion יוֹם יְהוָה would serve our purpose at this point.

Am 5_{18} represents the oldest text in which mention is made of the 'day of YHWH'. Amos is not introducing a new concept at this stage in his preaching. His approach is rooted, rather, in a notion which was current among his people with respect to the actions of YHWH over and against the enemies of Israel. For Israel, the 'day of YHWH' was a period of time in the near future in which YHWH would exercise judgement over the enemies of his people. Amos does not deny this aspect of the notion of יוֹם יְהוָה but he does add a new and hitherto unheard of element to it: Israel herself can also be counted among those enemies of YHWH who will be judged in his day. In doing so Amos attacks the sense of absolute certainty in which his

[56] In: OKeel, *Die Welt der altorientalischen Bildsymbolik und das Alte Testament*, Zürich-Einsiedeln-Köln-Neukirchen-Vluyn 1977², 67.

[57] Cf the extensive elaboration of this theme in Zeph 1_{14ff}.

audience had come to luxuriate. Grounded in a faith-conviction based on their experience of YHWH in the past, they firmly believed that he would protect them and destroy their enemies. After all, there had been 'days of YHWH' before, such as the 'Day of Midian', the time of YHWH's victory over the Midianite enemy of his people.[58] Amos' preaching undermined this sense of security which prevailed among his listeners and which they held in expectation of a new 'day of YHWH' (cf Ps 37_{13}). Even although Israel, thanks to YHWH, had repeatedly evaded her enemies, the people were not to assume thereby that the 'day of YHWH' could not and would not turn against Israel herself. According to Amos precisely such a course of events was immanent. That day of gloom and darkness would also turn against YHWH's own people on account of its sin.

Other pre-exilic prophets besides Amos preached in terms similarly related to the theme in question and elaborated it in their own fashion. In such contexts, however, use was made of the standard terminology associated with the יוֹם יְהוָה. For the most part such terminology was borrowed from descriptions of theophany in which the numinous was given expression by way of phenomena such as earthquake, volcanic activity and storm and their accompanying fire, smoke cloud and darkness which were seen as manifestations of the divine. The terminology of conflict and war was also employed, together with descriptions of human reactions thereto such as angst, bitterness, distress etcetera.[59] Similar terminology can be found in the Book of Lamentations and this will be indicated in the course of the exegesis.[60]

The adoption of that aspect of the יוֹם יְהוָה of the pre-exilic prophetic announcement of judgement in which YHWH turned against his own people is a clear indication that the poets of Lamentations experienced this day of YHWH in the downfall of Jerusalem and Judah. They recognised in their own lives that Amos and those prophets who preached a similar message were right. The fact that they applied this preaching to themselves without reserve is due to the evidently parallel situation created by the reversal of their expectations of salvation. Just as the יוֹם יְהוָה had been transformed by the prophets from a day of salvation for Israel into a day of judgement, so the salvific expectations of Zion theology were turned on their

58 Cf Isa 9_3; cf also Judg 7_{19ff} and Isa 10_{26}.

59 JJeremias, *Theophanie*, WMANT 10, Neukirchen 1977²

60 For a short summary of the material in question cf 1983, 277f and the literature referred to therein.

head by the hostile events brought about by YHWH. For this reason the poets recognised this day of judgement from YHWH to be their lot. Given the terminological echoes in the surrounding material, however, it remains surprising that the poets did not take over the expression יוֹם יְהוָה in its entirety. Spieckermann wonders if this is intentional: "Manifestiert sich darin vielleicht eine Scheu, den Jahwetag geschichtlich zu identifizieren, ihn zum Ereignis der Vergangenheit werden zu lassen?"[61] The answer is: Yes! It will become apparent that the poets yearned with great intensity for future days of YHWH, in particular towards a time when YHWH's wrath would turn decisively against their enemies. Cf the explanation of 1_{21c-22} and 4_{21f}.

2b *No one comforts her,* אֵין־לָהּ מְנַחֵם
not one among all her lovers. מִכָּל־אֹהֲבֶיהָ

In the second bicolon of this strophe we have our first encounter with the refrain which bemoans the fact that there is no comforter for Lady Jerusalem. The five repetitions of this refrain in Lam I ($1_{2,9,16,17,21}$ – according to the number of the songs?) makes it clear that we are dealing with a substantial and radical complaint. In addition to this, the phrase is given the central position in the first canticle thereby affording it unique emphasis. The *pi'el* of the root נחם broadly means 'to comfort'. People comfort one another in time of mourning (Gen 37_{35}, II Sam 10_{23}) and more generally in moments of sorrow (Gen 50_{21}, Ruth 2_{13}, Eccl 4_1 etcetera.). In the context of mourning, the comfort in question went hand in hand with certain rites of solace such as the eating of the bread of consolation and drinking from the cup of consolation (cf Jer 16_7).[62] Such acts of comfort implied more than simple expressions of sympathy and encouragement. At its deepest level, the *pi'el* of √נחם suggests the comforter's complete availability for the other in his or her time of sorrow. As a consequence the word can also imply practical assistance in a given situation, as is the case in Eccl 4_1. In Lam 1_{7cB}, however, the poets complain that Lady Jerusalem has no one to help her using the analogy of the absent comforter. It is worth mentioning that from the perspective of the Talmud (Sanhedrin 98b) the Messiah is the comforter who was born, according to Midrash

[61] HSpieckermann, 'Dies Irae: der alttestamentliche Befund und seine Vorgeschichte', VT 39 (1989), 205.

[62] Further material on this dimension can be found in HJahnow, *Das hebräische Leichenlied im Rahmen der Völkerdichtung*, BZAW 36, Giessen 1923, 7, 31f, 183 and in the explanation of 4_{10}.

Eicha Rabba, on the day of the destruction of the temple (Tisj'ah be-Av).[63] Such essential and sorrow alleviating comfort is now lacking. The situation becomes all the more wretched when one realises that from a human perspective there could have been comforters in the form of Lady Jerusalem's lovers. One would expect outsiders to be distant in moments of sorrow but Lady Jerusalem had lovers! From the very first strophe the status granted her by the neighbouring nations is drawn to our attention. Most exegetes suggest that the neighbours in question were Judah's allies in the resistance against the Babylonians.[64] Our dating of the material, the first song included, leads us to think of the nations mentioned in Jer 27_3: Edom, Moab, Ammon, Tyre and Sidon. It is certainly apparent that 'political love' is implied here given the use of the *qal* participle of the root אהב which tends to carry such a nuance in similar contexts,[65] although love of this type also possessed a religious implication in the form of the acceptance of the gods of one's allies.[66] Lady Jerusalem's lovers, however, have been unfaithful. In her moment of terrible suffering not one of them reaches out a hand to help and comfort her. Such behaviour might be expected from outsiders or strangers but from lovers it is unthinkable. Once again we are confronted with the depths of her loneliness.[67]

2c *All her friends have abandoned her;* כָּל־רֵעֶיהָ בָּגְדוּ בָהּ
they have become her enemies. הָיוּ לָהּ לְאֹיְבִים

Lady Jerusalem's suffering, however, is even more profound. Not only do her lovers maintain their cowardly distance, they have also betrayed her and even become her enemies. At this point the complaint reaches its climax. Circumstances have now far exceeded the prophetic prediction which saw Jerusalem's lovers going into captivity (Jer 20_{22}) or being forgetful of their beloved (Jer 30_{14}). The expression בָּגַד בְּ appears to be carefully chosen. In Ex 21_8 such terminology functions in the context of the legally effective arrangements surrounding marriage and implies a violation of one's legal duties or loyalties. The expression is more suggestive of a measurable social transgression and less of a deficient disposition.[68] Transposed from the metaphorical context of the relationship between Lady Jerusalem and

---

[63] For further information on the notion of comforting see THAT II 61f (Stoebe), TWAT V 380f (Simian-Yofre) and Anderson, 84f, 94.
[64] See, for example, Aalders, Rudolph, Kraus, Van Selms and cf 1983, 279.
[65] Cf JAThompson, 'Israel's "lovers" ', VT 27 (1977), 475–481.
[66] Cf, for example, II Kgs 16_{18}.
[67] Cf Ps 38_{12}, 88_{19}.
[68] Cf THAT I 262 (Klopfenstein).

her lovers to the context of the political relationship between Judah and her neighbours, the expression implies that former agreements, such as promises of mutual assistance in the event of a Babylonian aggression, had been broken. Cf Jer 27_{3ff}, in which mention is made once again of collective resistance against the Babylonians, although an earlier stage is being referred to here.[69] It is evident that new agreements were made at a later date, but when Nebuchadnezzar turned his might against Judah and the time had come for the allies to fulfil their part of the bargain, it would appear from their betrayal that their promises were worthless. Instead of rushing to assist they rejoiced in the downfall of their neighbour (1_{21}, $2_{7,16}$). Mention is made of this elsewhere in the Old Testament: cf Ezek 21_{28}, 25_{3}, Jer 40_{14}, 41_{15} with regard to the Ammonites, Ezek 25_{8} with regard to Moab and Ezek 26_{2} with regard to Tyre.

Lady Jerusalem did not only have to face passive hatred and betrayal from her lovers, however. It is evident from 1_{2cB} that their love was transformed into active hostility, a more pressing evil than the prophecy had foretold. Edom took pride of place in this hostile behaviour, having taken advantage of the upheaval which followed on Judah's downfall to invade and partially occupy her southern territory. The Edomites pillaged the land and either murdered or enslaved the refugees. They contributed, at the same time, to the destruction of Jerusalem. It is clear from the memories of Edom's deeds, which are to be found in various parts of the OT, that they were the cause of great bitterness in Judah. We hear about them for the first time in Lamentations itself: 4_{21f} and 5_{2ff} (see the explanation) and then later in Ezek $25_{12-14,35}$, Ob $_{10-14}$ and Ps 137_{7}. Bartlett minimises the historical content of Edom's antagonism toward Judah and suggests that the descriptions thereof in the OT are stereotypical and inspecific. According to him, Edom's characterisation as an evil doer is based on an historical prejudice in which that nation functioned as the archetypal enemy.[70] Bartlett is mistaken, however, in not considering the data of Lam V where the complaint of 5_{2-12}, for example, is quite concrete and far from stereotypical (see the explanation).

3a *Exposed is Judah by captivity* — גָּלְתָה יְהוּדָה מֵעֹנִי
and hard servitude. — וּמֵרֹב עֲבֹדָה

In the final strophe of this canticle attention is focused on Judah. Kraus wrongly proposes that there is no connection whatsoever between the

[69] Cf 1983, 131.

[70] JRBartlett, *Edom and the Edomites*, JSOT suppl series 77, Sheffield 1989, 156f.

second and third strophes prior to this verse. The conclusion of the second strophe points to the hostility of the neighbouring nations, the animosity of whom was not only directed towards Jerusalem. The fact that most exegetes tend to miss this connection is due to the difficulty presented by the interpretation of גָּלְתָה (= √גלה *qal* pf 3f sg). Most commentators opt for the translation: 'to go into exile'.[71] Problems then arise with respect to the interpretation of the preposition מִן for עֹנִי and רֹב which follow. If we interpret מִן in the locative sense as '(away) from', then we would have to translate the verse: 'Judah has gone into exile (away) from distress and hard servitude', as most commentaries including Provan's recent opus tend to do. Such an interpretation seems inappropriate, however, since it is unlikely that living in exile in Babylon was any easier than it was in Judah. If we hope to maintain the translation 'to go into exile' then the reference must be to the voluntary exile of those Judeans who had chosen to go to Egypt rather than stay in occupied Judah. The weakness of this interpretation, as Rudolph correctly points out, lies in the fact that forms of the root גלה are never used for voluntary exile. Rudolph's own exegesis suggests that עֲבֹדָה and עֹנִי refer to previous misfortune endured first at the hands of the Assyrians followed by the Egyptians and then by the Babylonians. This suggestion remains unconvincing given the fact that the poets are describing Judah's current misfortune. Gordis' suggestion that we interpret מִן as a rabbinical "Mem of condition", suggesting that the condition of Judah in exile was one of misfortune and oppression, is equally flawed.

It is remarkable that whenever the exile is mentioned in Lam I the expression 'captivity' (שְׁבִי) is used (see 1_{5cB} and 1_{18cB}). It would seem, therefore, that only part of the population, the young people, is involved (cf the explanation of 1_{5c}). Since the songs focus primarily on the dreadful condition of those who remained behind, including those in Judah (see Lam V), it is clearly not the poets' intention that we interpret this group of captives as *pars pro toto*. The fact that 1_3 is related to this is apparent from the literary structure of the first canticle. As usual a feminine is used for Judah (GES-K § 122*h,i*), given that the term refers metonymically to her inhabitants.[72] The inclusion כְּאַלְמָנָה (1bA) // לֹא מָצְאָה מָנוֹחַ (3bB) gives some indication of the poets' deeper intentions. The expression לֹא מָצְאָה מָנוֹחַ – as a characteristic of widowhood – can also be found in the Ruth 1_{19} (see the

[71] Cf KBL 182 and HAL 184.

[72] Cf BKWaltke – MO'Conner, *An Introduction to Biblical Hebrew Syntax*, Winona Lake, Indiana 1990, 104.

explanation of 1_{3b}). The implication is that the use of the widow metaphor in 1_3 is also being maintained for Judah, thus making it plausible that the term גלתה should not be read as 'to go into exile' but rather according to the original meaning of the root גלה 'to strip'.[73] As Van Selms has rightly pointed out, the idea of 'to go into exile' is derived from the original meaning in light of the fact that a land becomes open and bare when its inhabitants disappear. We opt, therefore, for the *pu'al* pf vocalisation גֻּלְּתָה, in common with Nah 2_8, and translate in the passive: 'the widow Judah is stripped'. The 'husband' who once clothed her and covered her nakedness (cf Ezek 16_8) has abandoned her (see 5_{20}). Nakedness is both a disgrace and a punishment.[74] In former times Nineveh was punished with nakedness as can be seen in Nah 2_8 and 3_{5-7}.[75] The same nakedness will be the future lot of Babylon (cf Isa 47_3). The reason for such a punishment is not evident in the text, although one can detect indirect influence from those prophetic announcements which portrayed Judah's apostasy and worship of other gods as playing the whore with foreign lovers, an offence which YHWH punished with shameful nakedness (cf the texts mentioned above).

Image and reality mirror each other. The notion of being stripped might best be rendered by the term 'exposed' (cf also 4_{22a}). Living and functioning, normal existence in fact, has become impossible in Judah because of the עֳנִי and the רֹב עֲבֹדָה, the preposition preceding which has a causal meaning.[76] עֳנִי is normally translated as 'suffering' or 'misfortune' but the term can also mean 'captivity'.[77] In any event, the notion of 'captivity' has an important role to play here as is evident from the concentric structure of the third strophe in which the first bicolon (3a) is parallel, to a certain extent, with the last bicolon (3c). In addition, the extremely concrete רֹב עֲבֹדָה, which means little less than slavery, provides further witness to the significance of the idea of 'captivity' in this context.[78] Slavery and captivity are joined inseparably together, thereby giving rise to the image of hostile troops roaming unconfined throughout Judah, hunting down refugees and taking them prisoner in order to put them to work

[73] Cf KBL 182, HAL 183.

[74] Cf Jer 13_{26}, Ezek 16_{37ff}, $23_{10,29}$, Hos $2_{5,12}$.

[75] For the correspondences between Nahum and Lamentations on this point see 1983, 180–183.

[76] Cf HAL 566 sv מִן (4,6).

[77] Cf HAL 810.

[78] Cf also Lam 5_5, Ex 1_{14}, 2_{23}, $5_{9,11}$, Lev 25_{39}, Deut 26_6 and TWAT V 1010f (Ringgren).

as slaves.[79] The people are no longer able to do their daily tasks; the fields are left untilled and the land is desolate. Given the fact that all of this horror is actually taking place we have translated in the present.

3b *She sits down among the nations,* הִיא יָשְׁבָה בַגּוֹיִם
she finds no resting place. לֹא מָצְאָה מָנוֹחַ

Whatever way one does it, when one ties in the first bicolon with the exile there are obvious consequences for the way one will interpret the following bicola. The phrase הִיא יָשְׁבָה בַגּוֹיִם, in such cases, is usually seen as a designation of the sojourn in Babylon; uprooted and homeless, Judah now lives in exile, in the midst of the גּוֹיִם. The customary explanation of the second colon 1_{3bB} would appear to follow smoothly upon the first. The 'rest' mentioned here is understood in terms of a concept borrowed from (pre-exilic) Deuteronomic theology referring to 'the redemptive rest of the land'. The notion in question signifies a safe and peaceful lifestyle in the land of the promise, a lifestyle from which everyone can benefit under his or her own vine and fig tree.[80] With the loss of their land the exiles have also lost the redemptive rest that went with it and they can find nothing to replace it in the land of their exile (cf Kraus, Kaiser and Boecker, among others).

A number of objections can be raised against the idea of a direct relationship with Deuteronomic theology. In the first place, the redemptive rest of the land is assigned a different form, namely מְנוּחָה, a form which one would also expect to see in 1_{3bB} if it were a question of a fixed theologoumenon. Deut 28_{65}, which in any event is considered Deuteronomistic,[81] constitutes an exception. It is precisely here, however, that we meet the second objection. In present day research it is accepted that the concept of 'redemptive rest' was only used in (later) Deuteronomistic theology[82] and stemmed, therefore, from a later date. Given our dating of the Book of Lamentations it would have been impossible for the poets to have borrowed such later usage. Thirdly, the concept מָנוֹחַ elsewhere has a more local meaning, namely 'place of rest'.[83] Finally, the use of the concept in

---

[79] Cf also 5_5 and the explanation thereof.

[80] Cf Deut 3_{20}, 12_{9f}, 25_{19}, 28_{65}, and GvRad, *Theologie des Alten Testaments, Band I, Die Theologie der geschichtlichen Überlieferungen Israels*, München 1966[5], 237.

[81] Cf GvRad, *Das fünfte Buch Mose. Deuteronomium*, ATD 8, Göttingen 1968[2], 124ff and HDPreuß, *Deuteronomium*, EdF 164, Darmstadt 1982, 158.

[82] Cf Preuß, *Deuteronomium*, 194.

[83] Cf Gen 8_9, Isa 34_{14} and TWAT V 305f (Preuß).

the Book of Ruth points in a direction which fits much more appropriately in the context of our canticle. Naomi is in search of 'rest' for Ruth. As events turn out it would appear that she finds it by urging her daughter-in-law to enter into a new marriage, through which she will be relieved of her widowhood. Naomi had already expressed such a wish in Ruth 1_9. A woman finds 'rest', therefore, in the house of her husband who obliges himself to care for her needs and protection. When a woman becomes a widow, however, she forfiets her 'rest'. It is evident from Ruth 1_9 and 3_1 that such 'restlessness' is a fact of widowhood. This in turn implies that the metaphor of the widow is still determinative of the language used in 1_{3bB}, albeit now applied to Judah. Widow Judah sits restless: she has lost both house and husband (cf also the explanation of song-response 5_3). Having said this, it is not our intention to imply that the Deuteronomist's later theological formulations with respect to 'redemptive rest' are not already present here in embryonic form (and with even older roots).[84] Indeed, as part of the metaphor, the restlessness of widow Judah corresponds at its deepest level with the rupture in the relationship between YHWH and Judah's inhabitants, which turned out for them to mean loss of house and home, peace and security. If we respect the concentric structure of the first song as a whole then the corresponding colon in 1_{20bA} provides further explanation: Judah's heart writhes within her because of her enemies' rage (cf the explanation of 1_{20} and the complaints in the final song).

Where is Judah to be located? What is the meaning of the term בַּגּוֹיִם? If we assume the first bicolon to refer to the exile then the גּוֹיִם in question must refer to the other (deported) peoples in Babylon, in the midst of whom the Judean exiles now find themselves. What then would we understand by Judah's restlessness? Are Judah's exiles without rest because of the hostile attitude of the other (deported) peoples? Given that all the exiles are more or less in the same boat such an interpretation of Judah's lack of rest would be highly improbable. For this reason, we take the גּוֹיִם to be Judah's neighbouring peoples, a proposal which is supported by the chiastic responses within the first canticle:

אֵין־לָהּ מְנַחֵם (2bA) // לֹא מָצְאָה מָנוֹחַ (3bB)
and כָּל־אֹהֲבֶיהָ (2bB) // בַּגּוֹיִם (3bA)

It is not only Lady Jerusalem who is like a 'widow' in the midst of the neighbouring nations, widow Judah is also lonely and unprotected. The

[84] Cf TWAT V 300 (Preuß).

hostile attitude she is presently enduring comes from the very people who were once her lovers (1_{2c}). The situation of the exile is not, in fact, mentioned in the songs. A final and compelling argument is provided by the song-response between the first and the last song:

לֹא מָצְאָה מָנוֹחַ (1_{3bB}) // לֹא הוּנַח־לָנוּ (5_{5bB})

In Lam v it is clear that the misfortune and suffering being described is that which prevailed in Judah after the downfall, a time when the neighbouring nations took advantage of widow Judah's defencelessness and, as enemies, robbed her of everything, including her rest.[85]

3c *All her pursuers hound her* — כָּל־רֹדְפֶיהָ הִשִּׂיגוּהָ
and press her hard. — בֵּין הַמְּצָרִים

This bicolon provides similar occasion not to interpret the situation in terms of the exile. As a matter of fact, one can then naturally conclude that the pursuers in question were the Babylonians who, after capturing Jerusalem, imprisoned the eligible inhabitants of both Jerusalem and Judah in preparation for deportation.[86] Kraus, Kaiser, Boecker and Stoll, among others, follow this line of thought. If, however, we give due respect to the response כָּל־רֵעֶיהָ (2cA) // כָּל־רֹדְפֶיהָ (3cA) then we are forced to interpret the pursuers as Judah's neighbours whose hostile attitude after Judah's downfall has already been mentioned in 1_{2cB}. After the departure of the Babylonians, the neighbouring nations took advantage of Judah's vulnerability and lack of defences to appropriate territory and cities and to force the population into labour. It is quite significant that such an interpretation is also supported by a response between the first and last songs, namely between 1_{3c} and 5_{5A} (... כָּל־רֹדְפֶיהָ הִשִּׂיגוּהָ // עַל צַוָּארֵנוּ נִרְדָּפְנוּ). This explanation proves that we are not dealing with the one-off disaster of the deportation to Babylon but rather with an ongoing time of distress which prevailed in Judah after the downfall (cf the exegesis of 5_5). The poets do not simply state the fact of this hostile invasion, they also indicate its effects on the population via the phrase בֵּין הַמְּצָרִים (3cB). The plural of מֵצַר is also to be found in Ps 118_5, where it has the collective meaning of prevailing fear and anxiety, and in Ps 116_3 where it refers to the specific fear of Sheol. מְצָרִים in 1_{3cB} is provided with no further specification. In the concentric structure of Lam I, however, 1_3 corresponds with

[85] Cf the exegesis of 1_{2cB} and the explanation of $5_{2,4-8}$.
[86] Cf II Kgs 25_{4ff}, Jer 40_1, $52_{15,28}$, Lam 4_{19f}.

1_{20} where Zion says: כִּי־צַר־לִי, which is made more explicit by the sword which bereaves in the streets and by death which reigns in the house. The correspondence leads us to assume that the anxieties brought about by death, lack of defences, chaos and lack of food after the downfall – themes which return in every song – are also intended in 1_3 (cf the inclusion with the opening word אֵיכָה).

Canticle II (1_{4-6})

Content/theme: *Zion without festival-goers or splendour*

Literary argumentation:

inclusions:	בָּאֵי (4aB) \\ וַיֵּלְכוּ (6cA)
	כֹּהֲנֶיהָ (4bB) // שָׂרֶיהָ (6bA)
	הִיא (4cB) // בַּת־צִיּוֹן (6aA)
	צָרֶיהָ (5aA) // צָר (5cB)
responses:	צִיּוֹן (4aA) // צִיּוֹן (6aA)
	מוֹעֵד (4aB) // כָּל־הֲדָרָהּ (6aB)[87]
	בְּתוּלֹתֶיהָ (4cA) // עוֹלָלֶיהָ (5cA)
	הָלְכוּ (5cA) // וַיֵּלְכוּ (6cA)
	לִפְנֵי־צָר (5cB) // לִפְנֵי רוֹדֵף (6cB)
ext. par.:	הָיוּ צָרֶיהָ לְרֹאשׁ (5aA) \\ הָיוּ שָׂרֶיהָ כְּאַיָּלִים (6bA)

The theme of abandonment and loneliness comes to the fore once again in the second canticle. One new element at the level of content, however, can be found in the special attention given to the consequences of the downfall with respect to Zion.

4a *The roads to Zion mourn,*	דַּרְכֵי צִיּוֹן אֲבֵלוֹת
for no one comes to the festivals.	מִבְּלִי בָּאֵי מוֹעֵד

The name of Zion is mentioned here for the first time. The name itself is not simply a synonym for Jerusalem. It is the unique term, rather, for Jerusalem as location of the cult, as the temple city, the dwelling place of YHWH.[88] As they begin to describe the details of the horror facing them, the poets turn their attention first to desolate Zion, revealing thereby that Zion beyond all other places is closest to their heart, and then to

87 Cf Ps 68_{25-30}.

88 Cf TWNT VII 298 (Fohrer), THAT II 545ff (Stolz) and TWAT VI 1008ff (Otto); on Zion theology see also 1983, 280–294.

the situation of distress within the city. Just as the poets of the Psalms spoke in personified terms of rejoicing mountains and rivers clapping their hands[89] so the poets of Lamentations use the image of roads in mourning. Indeed it is a characteristic of the dirge that even inanimate things are seen as animated and alive.[90] The feminine plural of the adjective אָבֵל is used which literally means 'to observe mourning customs', customs which make a person's mourning visible to others.[91] The poets are most interested in this visual dimension. The mourning of the roads to Zion is made clear by way of a powerful contrast. It goes without saying that the temple was the location of the daily liturgy with its sacrifices and prayers, priests and singers. At the same time, the maintenance and care of the buildings and the surrounding area demanded the constant presence of numerous people. Zion's roads were familiar with their coming and going. It was particularly during the major feasts, however, that the masses flocked towards the city and the temple from near and far.[92] In Isa 33_{20}, for example, Zion is referred to as the city of festive gatherings; we read in the Psalms of the processions which took place during such festivities.[93] Although the term מוֹעֵד is frequently related only to the (three) major feasts, it would perhaps be more accurate to afford it a broader interpretation.[94] Koch, for example, includes the feasts of Sabbath and New Moon.[95] The overcrowdedness of the city during such times is hinted at in Ezek 36_{38}.

Things have changed. Zion's roads, which were once so used to masses of festival-goers, are now dismally empty. Since normal activities were left undone during periods of mourning (cf Jona 3_7) the scene was set for an association between the once busy roads of Zion and the customs of mourning.

4bA *All her gates are desolate.* כָּל־שְׁעָרֶיהָ שׁוֹמֵמִין

The second bicolon is a logical continuation of the first: after the roads come the gates towards which they lead. The verb שׁמם[96] has several aspects; objective meanings include: 'to be ruined', 'to be abandoned';

[89] Cf, for example, Ps 89_{13}, 96_{12}.

[90] Cf Jahnow, 102f.

[91] Cf Gen 35_{34f}, 50_{10}, Ps 35_{14f} and TWAT I 47f (Baumann).

[92] RdVaux, *Les Institutions de l'Ancien Testament II*, Paris 1958, 383ff.

[93] Cf Ps 47, 68_{21-30}, 132.

[94] Cf TWAT IV 746f (Koch).

[95] Cf likewise RdVaux, 371ff and HJKraus, *Gottesdienst in Israel*, München 1954, 242ff.

[96] שׁוֹמֵמִין = *qal* pt pl masc. For the special form cf BL § 63*t* and § 9*a'*.

subjective meanings describe human reaction to the objective meanings: 'paralysis', 'rigidity', 'bewilderment' etcetera, brought about by death and destruction.[97] Although they coincide at this point, the relevant meanings are difficult to render in translation at one and the same time: the gates are abandoned because they are also ruined. The term 'to be desolate' reflects our best efforts to combine both meanings (cf also 2_{9aA}). A ruined and abandoned gate is the very model of profound contrast. The city gate was not only the place of meeting par excellence where people could always be found (cf 5_{14}), it was also the strongest part of the city wall.[98]

So far we have only dealt with the objective aspect of the term and most exegetes, with the exception of Lohfink, are content to go no further. Lohfink also points to the subjective aspect.[99] Besides the objective aspect of ruination, the poets also had the subjective, experiential dimension (of the animated gates) in mind. Just as human beings in mourning stand shocked and bewildered so Jerusalem's ruined gates are left rigid and lifeless, an echo of Isaiah's prophecy (Isa 3_{26}). The parallel with Zion's mourning roads from verse 4a is clear. At the same time, the internal parallelism with the 'groaning priests' of 1_{4bB} is made audible by way of the subjective aspect (cf 2_{9a} // 2_{10a} = response).

The context of festival-goers and priests inclines us to think here primarily of the gates which gave access to the temple complex. The destruction of the temple is mentioned independently in II Kgs 25_{8ff} and is described in detail in Lam 2_{4-9}.[100] In their description of the destruction endured by Zion, the poets begin and end with the temple (cf 1_4 and 5_{18}), revealing thereby that the fate of the temple was for them the most disturbing of all. Janssen has noted that the destruction of the temple by the Babylonians was not in the least a matter-of-course.[101] It was more likely, in fact, that the invaders would have been inclined to leave the sanctuary intact, given that tactless behaviour with respect to religious feelings had the power to generate enormous resistance among subjected peoples. For this reason, they tended to leave temples and their liturgical life undisturbed, although as victors they did require that their own Babylonian gods be worshipped alongside those of the conquered nations. The fact that the

97 Cf Ezek 26_{15f}, NLohfink, 'Enthielten die im Alten Testament bezeugten Klageriten eine Phase des Schweigens?', VT 12 (1962), 267f and THAT II 971f (Stolz).

98 Cf RdVaux, *Institutions II*, 31ff.

99 Lohfink, 276f.

100 Cf also, the explanation of $4_{1,11,22}$.

101 EJanssen, *Juda in der Exilszeit*, FRLANT NF 51, Göttingen 1956, 46f.

Babylonians did decide to destroy the temple has to do with the political significance it had attained over the years. The belief had emerged within Zion theology that Jerusalem was inviolable, protected as it was by YHWH who dwelt as King in the temple of his holy city.[102] This faith was thoroughly reinforced and absolutised by the fact that Jerusalem had shown herself to be invincible to the enemy on more than one occasion.[103] It was precisely this faith in the fundamental inviolability of Jerusalem which was partly responsible for the revolt against Nebuchadnezzar. By having his troops destroy the temple, Nebuchadnezzar shattered the faith of its inhabitants and thereby put paid to any thoughts of a renewed uprising.[104] The destruction of the sanctuary, however, left Lady Jerusalem grievously wounded at the religious level which was so essential to her. The Babylonians had shattered her faith both figuratively and literally. The ruined gates which gave entry to the forecourts of her temple now give witness to this terrible reality.

4bB *Her priests groan.* כֹּהֲנֶיהָ נֶאֱנָחִים

Having passed through the desolate gates, the poets come across the priests in the temple complex, groaning in their anguish (*niph'al* pt pl of √אנח). The participle form renders the idea of ongoing and continuous groaning. the verb אנח, which occurs several times in the first song[105] does not lend itself to everyday use; it is primarily found, rather, in the context of existential distress brought on by oppression (Ex 2_{23}), godless tyranny (Prov 29_{2}), serious illness (Ps 6_{7}, 102_{6}) or labour pain (Jer 22_{23}). Wherever it is found, it gives expression to the strenuous and wearisome as well as the visible and audible nature of such groans. With this in mind we translate with the verb 'to groan'.

It is not difficult to guess why the priests are in this constant state. Not only their faith but their very existence as priests has come under attack. They can no longer carry out their duties. Not only the temple but the altar itself has been destroyed (cf 2_{7a}). There are no festival-goers. They can no longer play their part in the daily sacrifices for which there is no longer any demand. Since the priests' very lives revolved around the liturgy (Lev $2_{3,10}$), its disappearance with the destruction of the temple has robbed them of their existence and of their daily bread.

---

102 Cf Ps 46, Jer $7_{4,10}$.
103 See also the explanation of Lam 4_{12}.
104 For a more thorough examination of this topic cf 1983, 136–138.
105 Lam $1_{4,8,11,21}$, cf also אֲנָחֹתֶי in 1_{22cA}.

4cA *Her young girls are deeply grieved,* בְּתוּלֹתֶיהָ נוּגוֹת

The priests are not alone in their misery; the poets also refer to the grief of the בְּתוּלוֹת of Zion, literally 'her girls'. The proximate reference to 'her priests' in verse 4bB suggests that the poets are not thinking of Jerusalem's young girls in general who perhaps ventured into the temple from time to time. It would seem more likely that the girls they had in mind were those who had some kind of special involvement in the liturgical life of the temple. Did the pre-exilic temple in Jerusalem have female cultic personnel? After discussing texts such as Ex 38_8 and I Sam 2_{22} De Vaux concludes that this was probably not the case except during syncretistic periods when there was even talk of sacred prostitution.[106] Orthodox Yahwism did not tolerate such practice; indeed, a different word[107] was used to refer to the young women in question. The term בְּתוּלָה, however, was usually reserved for a young, still unmarried girl.[108] For this reason it is probable that we are dealing here with young girls who sang and danced at festival gatherings in the temple.[109] It goes without saying that they were elated and full of joy at such events; their grief is all the more understandable, therefore, now that the temple has been reduced to rubble and the festivals have become nothing more than a painful memory. The *niph'al* of the root יגה is used to express the young girls' state of mind and, as with the priests in verse 4bB, the participle form is used to render the ongoing, continuous character of their grief. Dahood's suggestion that the term derives from the root נוג, 'to depart'/'to withdraw',[110] is incorrect since the context clearly calls for a derivative of √יגה.[111] Given the total number of occurrences of this verb in the OT, it would appear that its incidence in Lamentations is relatively frequent: 5x: $1_{4,5,12}$ and $3_{32,33}$. Since all the other occurrences in Lamentations have a strictly theological meaning, with YHWH as subject, it would make sense to assume that this is also the case here in verse 4cA. It is not the enemy who has robbed these young girls of their festivals but YHWH himself.[112] Absence of festival gatherings is not the only problem here. The whole atmosphere of the

[106] Cf II Kgs 23_7 and perhaps also Ezek 8_{14}. RdVaux, *Institutions II*, 248f.

[107] קְדֵשָׁה, see HAL 1005.

[108] Cf HAL 159f and TWAT I 872–877 (Tsevat).

[109] Cf Ex 15_{20} Judg 21_{21}, Ps 68_{26} and Jer 31_{13}.

[110] MDahood, 'Ugaritic Lexicography', Mélanges Eugène Tisserant I (Studi e Testi 231) Vatican City 1964, 95f; cf also Robinson (BHS).

[111] Cf, among others, Rudolph, Albrektson, Hillers, Wagner (TWAT III 410).

[112] Cf the reverse in Ps 30_{12}, Jer $31_{4,13}$.

sanctuary has undergone a change. When employed within the CI genre, the root יגה is used to render the theological context of God's aloofness and absence, a situation which brought about great distress and much sorrow.[113] As Scharbert points out: "יגה gibt ein tiefes seelisches Getroffenheit schlechthin wieder und deutet ein rein passives Verhalten der Betroffenen an... '.[114] In an attempt to do justice to the various accents suggested by the term יגה we translate it here as 'deeply grieved'.

4cB *and as for her – her lot is bitter.* וְהִיא מַר־לָהּ

In the final colon of this strophe the poets do not turn their attention towards one or other new group; without expressly stating the fact, rather, they focus once again on the whole picture, personified as 'daughter Zion'. It is evident from the personal pronoun הִיא and the inclusion: הִיא (4cB) // בַּת־צִיּוֹן (6aA), however, that 'daughter Zion' is the referent here. The designation בַּת־צִיּוֹן is also to be found in the parallel ד-strophe of the second song (2_{4cA}, song-response). Since 'she' is in fact 'daughter Zion', we will anticipate our explanation of 1_{6a} at this point and focus our attention for a moment on the phrase בַּת־צִיּוֹן. בַּת here does not convey its primary and most natural significance 'daughter' but can also refer in the broadest sense to a '(young) woman'.[115] This more general meaning explains the use of the term in personifications such as the presentation of a city as a woman[116] or as a temple city.[117] Examples of other cities referred to in this way include Tarshish (Isa 23_{10}), Sidon (Isa 23_{12}), Babylon (Jer 50_{42}, 51_{33}). The personification of a country or land as a woman is thereby related.[118]

Korpel sees a root metaphor in the image of the city as a woman because other metaphors can be derived therefrom (such as the widow metaphor in 1_{1bA}). As a woman, a city can also bear children in the same way as a land brings forth its harvest after sowing: "A city, like a woman, also brings forth 'children' namely its inhabitants."[119] This leaves us with a further metaphor derived from the root metaphor of the city as a woman, namely the city as mother (cf the explanation of 5_3). The context of the canticle,

---

[113] See Ps $13_{2,3}$, $31_{11,12}$, cf TWAT III 410 (Wagner).

[114] JScharbert, *Der Schmerz im Alten Testament*, Bonn 1955, 27.

[115] Cf Gen $6_{2,4}$, 30_{13}, Isa 32_{19} etcetera.

[116] For example, 'daughter Jerusalem'; cf II Kgs 19_{21}, Lam 2_{13aB}.

[117] Also referred to as 'daughter Zion'; cf II Kgs 19_{21}, Isa 16_1, Lam 1_6, 2_1 etcetera.

[118] Cf daughter Judah in Ps 48_{12}, 97_8, Lam 1_{15}, $2_{2,5}$; daughter Edom in Lam 4_{21} (cf GES-K § 122*h*).

[119] MCAKorpel, *A Rift in the Clouds*, Münster 1990, 261; cf also TWAT I 868ff (Haag).

however, compels us to envisage the personification בַּת־צִיּוֹן in 1_4 primarily as the sanctuary.[120] In this event בַּת־צִיּוֹן has to be distinguished from 'daughter Jerusalem'. The temple and its adjacent complexes occupied an extraordinary position in the overall plan of the city and therefore deserved a distinct personification.

The relationship between Zion and her inhabitants which is made present in the personification makes the following understandable: if it is said that daughter Zion is bitter at heart then the sentiments of the people of Zion are thereby expressed. In this respect the word מַר appears to have been very carefully chosen since it establishes a clear connection with the widow metaphor (1_{1bA}). The initial stages of widowhood went hand in hand with mourning and bitterness (cf Ruth $1_{13,20}$). A combination of mourning, woe cries and bitterness can also be found in the lament over Tyre in Ezek 27_{30ff}. At the same time, however, מַר has a theological dimension. We noted above (see excursus after 1_{2a}) that the poets had borrowed from the prophetic concept of the 'day of YHWH' as a day of judgement also intended for Israel. In several instances where the realisation of that judgement is described, there is talk of the bitterness brought about by it.[121] What is implied here in verse 4cB, therefore, is that daughter Zion's bitterness is a consequence of YHWH's judgement. In this way the correspondence with 2_4, where YHWH is portrayed as the hostile executor of judgement against Zion, becomes apparent once again. Although the poets make repeated use of the metaphor of Jerusalem (Zion) as a woman both here and in the following song, the personification of daughter Zion should prevent us from losing sight of the fact that we are always dealing with human beings. Such a possibility is not merely hypothetical, given the classification of the first two songs as political 'dirges'[122] which creates an unnecessary gulf between Lam I and II on the one hand and the far more personal Lam III on the other.[123] Such opposition is set up without good reason. The image of the city as a Lady does not only imply the houses, the walls, the palace and the temple, it also very much implies her inhabitants. It is not only the downfall of city and state that the poets lament; the consequences for the people also have their full attention (cf the central position of Lam III within the songs as a whole). Lady Jerusalem's state of mind, expressed in terms of lamentation, mourning

---

120 Cf also the song-response in 2_4: בְּאֹהֶל בַּת־צִיּוֹן.

121 Cf Amos 8_9, Zeph 1_{14}, Jer 6_{26} and TWAT V 19 (Ringgren).

122 HGunkel, RRG², 1049.

123 Cf Jahnow, 169.

and bitterness, is the state of mind of her inhabitants, a fact which is also made apparent in this canticle in light of the attention given to those individuals who were involved in some special way in the services surrounding the temple complex.

5a *Her oppressors have become the masters,* הָיוּ צָרֶיהָ לְרֹאשׁ
her enemies are without care, אֹיְבֶיהָ שָׁלוּ

Daughter Zion's anxiety and bitterness stand in glaring contrast to the position and frame of mind of her enemies. Their careless supremacy makes her suffering even more unbearable (cf Ps 13_5, 38_{19f}). The expression alludes to the military and/or the state being in control of things.[124] Daughter Zion's enemies have the power[125] and it is evident that they have no difficulty in maintaining their authority. They rule at their ease and without care.[126] Which enemies are we dealing with here? Brunet has hazarded the thesis that the צָרִים represent the Babylonians while the א(ו)יְבִים represent the pro-Babylonian party in Judah of which the prophet Jeremiah was also supposed to be a member. In this case Lamentations contains complaints concerning the betrayal of Judah and Jerusalem by fellow countrymen who made up this party. Against this background Brunet detects a protest against Jeremiah in Lamentations.[127] His position, however, is untenable and has found little support. He fails to appreciate the Hebrew parallelismus membrorum: א(ו)יְבִים and צָרִים are identical at the level of content.[128] The terms צָרִים and א(ו)יְבִים essentially refer to the Babylonians, a fact made apparent from the concentric structure of this strophe (cf the inclusion צָרֶיהָ [1_{5aA}] // לִפְנֵי־צָר [1_{5cB}]). Even the expression הָלְכוּ שְׁבִי in 1_{5c} points to the deportation into Babylonian exile (see II Kgs 25_{11} and Jer 40_1; cf Jer 20_6, Ezek 12_{11}.

5bA *because* YHWH *grieves her deeply...* כִּי־יְהוָה הוֹגָהּ

For a discussion of the root יגה 'to grieve' see 1_{4cA}. The poets themselves

124 Cf Judg 11_{8f} and I Chron 11_6.

125 Cf Deut $28_{13,44}$; for the relationship between Deut 28 and Lamentations cf 1983, 21–32.

126 Cf the meaning of the root שלה in Jer 12_1.

127 GBrunet, *Les Lamentationes contre Jérémie*, Bibliothèque de l' Ecole des hautes études. Sciences Religieuses 75, Paris 1968, 9.

128 For a thorough refutation of Brunet cf HGottlieb, *A Study of the Text of Lamentations*, Acta Jutlandica XLVIII, Theology Series 12 Århus 1978, 12f, RBrandscheidt, *Gotteszorn und Menschenleid. Die Gerichtsklage des leidenden Gerechten in Klgl 3*, TTS 41, Trier 1983, 217f and 1983, 140f.

do not provide any more specific clue as to the identity of the enemies and adversaries mentioned in 1_{5a}. The reason why becomes apparent in this bicolon. Daughter Zion's actual enemy is not Babylon and its henchmen but YHWH himself (see the song-response הָיָה אֲדֹנָי כְּאוֹיֵב in 2_{5aA}). He, in fact, is the one who has handed over daughter Zion into the hands of her enemies. An important theological insight is given expression here and supported by the central position of this bicolon in the canticle. Thus the poets were able to repudiate the notion prevalent among their fellow countrymen, namely that YHWH was not strong enough to stand up to the enemies of his people.[129] The downfall of Judah and Jerusalem, however, was not due to YHWH's powerlessness, but rather – as is evident from what follows – to his punishing actions on account of their sin. The acceptance of the prophetic preaching of Jeremiah and Ezekiel, for example, is evident at this point.[130] Such a confession of YHWH's might – even in its negative consequences – still leaves open the possibility of a change in the horrific situation of his people. YHWH alone is capable of bringing about this change and it makes sense, therefore, to turn to him in prayer and lament.

5bB ... *for the multitude of her transgressions.* עַל רֹב־פְּשָׁעֶיהָ

Johnson characterises the first canto (1_{1-11}) as the 'factual half' of Lam I and canto II (1_{12-22}) as the 'interpretative half'.[131] Such a distinction does not work with respect to this colon as it contains both fact and interpretation at once. The present calamity was brought about by daughter Zion's many transgressions (רֹב־פְּשָׁעֶיהָ). Although the word פֶּשַׁע usually refers to transgressions of the legal order, it is placed here in a theological context: Zion has repeatedly violated the legal order given by YHWH. It is not a question, therefore, of an inclination to do evil but of actual transgressions, committed, in fact, against YHWH. Where the notion of sin is concerned the term פֶּשַׁע carries the most weight. Micah, for example, saw it as his duty to denounce such transgressions among his people.[132] Compared with the poets' explicit portrayal of the people's suffering it is strange that they do not provide a more detailed description of the sins they have committed. At the same time, there are no evident external parallelisms as a source of clarification.[133] Only the sins of the prophets and the priests

[129] Cf 1983, 213–216.
[130] See 1983, 187–201.
[131] BJohnson, 'Form and Message in Lamentations', ZAW 97 (1985), 62f.
[132] Mic 3_8; cf Jer 5_{5f} and THAT II 492f (Knierim).
[133] For more on this topic see 2_{14b} and the hermeneutical epilogue of Lam III.

are explained in more detail (cf 4_{13}). Such vagueness with respect to the nature of the people's sins is bound up with, among other things, a particular understanding of what is implied by sin, namely that transgression is inclusive of its consequence and that the accent can shift from one to the other. In our case the seriousness of the sin is not measured according to the number of commandments transgressed; it is related, rather, to the extent of the misfortune it brings upon the transgressor. The metaphor of the 'yoke of transgressions' in 1_4 expresses the same notion of synthesis between sin and its consequences.[134] The greater the misfortune the greater the sin which brought it about must have been. According to the Old Testament way of looking at things it was also possible to commit sins without knowing it; only the reality of the corresponding misfortune made the sinner aware of his or her wrongdoing. Given the evident immensity of the disaster which has overcome the people, daughter Zion's sin must have been very great indeed. The fact that a certain amount of ambiguity exists with respect to the nature of the transgressions in question is apparent from the song-response between 2_{14} and 3_{40}: the sins are left undisclosed as a stimulus to further self-examination.[135] In contrast to those exegetes who consider this colon to be somewhat tangential within the fifth strophe (Rudolph, Weiser and Kraus), I adjudge such an understanding of sin to provide coherence and unity to the strophe at the level of content.

5c *Her children have been forced to depart,* עוֹלָלֶיהָ הָלְכוּ
as captives before the oppressor. שְׁבִי לִפְנֵי־צָר

This bicolon continues the description of Zion's destitution. It is almost as if the image of the empty temple square has taken hold of the poets and will not let them go. They only see priests and young girls. Where are all the others? The truth is that the children of daughter Zion have been led off into captivity. With these words the poets continue to exploit the widow metaphor; because of her faults, the defenceless widow has been robbed of her children.[136] The term עוֹלֵל is frequently used in parallel with יוֹנֵק to express the twin concept 'children and infants'[137] but here it stands on its own. For this reason we should not think of the smallest children being taken captive (cf 2_{11f}) nor of the population as a whole (cf

[134] Cf also Ps 31_{11}, 38_{4-6}, 39_9, 40_{13}.
[135] For more on this topic see 1983, 269–280.
[136] Cf II Kgs 4_1, Isa 47_{8f}; see also the explanation of 1_{1b} and 5_3 in the present commentary.
[137] Cf TWAT V 1131ff (Sæbø) for the variations in meaning.

Wiesmann, Hillers). The inclusion between 5c and 18c (בְּתוּלֹתַי וּבַחוּרַי) in the concentric structure of the first song offers an interpretative clue. With the disappearance of the young people, who were to be found in the temple forecourts with somewhat natural frequency, Lady Jerusalem's future has also disappeared. The expression שְׁבִי לִפְנֵי־צָר (שְׁבִי being understood adverbially) leads one to think of a band of people being driven along under guard. Zion's youth were led off in such a fashion.

6a *From daughter Zion has departed* וַיֵּצֵא מִן־בַת־צִיּוֹן
all her majesty. כָּל־הֲדָרָהּ

For the personification of the sanctuary as daughter Zion see 1_{4c}. On the basis of the LXX, Robinson (BHS) suggests we vocalise ויצא as a *pu'al* 'has been led off'. The LXX-tradition, however, is divided (see Albrektson). The passive translation seems to be a correction based on the idea that immobile things do not disappear of their own accord. The Masoretic vocalisation deserves preference, however, both because it is the more difficult reading and because of the fact that the princes mentioned in 1_{6bA} should be considered a facet of daughter Zion's majesty. This initial bicolon has a summarising character. The loss of her young children leads us to wonder what else daughter Zion has lost. The poets provide a summary response: 'all her majesty'. Rudolph and Weiser are too narrow in their interpretation, concentrating as they do on the children and the princes mentioned in the surrounding context. What the poets are referring to, rather, is everything (כָּל) that once bestowed majesty on daughter Zion. The term הָדָר can be used for the splendour of YHWH's kingship (cf Ps 104_1, 111_3, $145_{5,12}$); the radiance of YHWH's majesty in creation (cf Ps 29_4, Isa 35_2); YHWH is also the one who has bestowed such הָדָר on Jerusalem (cf Ezek $16_{6-13,14}$).[138] The canticle as a whole provides occasion for thinking primarily of the majesty of the temple. It is only natural, of course, that the beauty and majesty of an ancient city would find its point of convergence in temple and palace; indeed Jerusalem's temple radiated with the glory of YHWH.[139] The parallel strophe in the second song (2_6), which details the destruction and defilement of altar and temple, points in the same direction and gives (partial) substance to the lost majesty of daughter Zion. There is also a song-response in Lam III in which the loss of כָּל־הֲדָרָהּ

[138] Cf THAT I 469–472 (Wehmeier – Vetter) and TWAT II 357–363 (Warmuth).
[139] Cf Ps 48; 96_6; cf also the exegesis of תִּפְאֶרֶת יִשְׂרָאֵל in 2_{1bB} and the explanation of 2_{15c}.

is reflected in the lost magnificence of the גֶּבֶר (cf אָבַד נִצְחִי in 3_{18A}). The splendour of the first temple remained in memory long after the exile.[140]

II Kgs $25_{9,13-17}$ offers a description of how the temple was burned and torn down after its precious gold and copper had been hauled away (cf also 29_{aB}). Nothing remained but a scorched and ransacked ruin (see 4_1). This exterior dimension, however, was only one aspect of Zion's lost majesty, and not the most important one at that. The most profound source of grief was the departure of YHWH himself from Zion, YHWH whose very presence conferred splendour on the sanctuary and the people who filled and surrounded it (3_{18}, 4_7). The metaphor of widowhood is thus maintained, in the context of which we should note how adornment and splendour are inappropriate in times of mourning and sadness (cf Ex $33_{4,6}$). Since a widow did not wear jewellery (cf 2_1 and Jdt $10_{2,4}$) we can see evidence of an inclusion within the first sub-canto (1_{1-6}) – at the strophic level – between this colon and Lady Jerusalem in 1_1 who sits alone as a widow without any sign of her former majesty.

6b *Her princes have become like stags* הָיוּ שָׂרֶיהָ כְּאַיָּלִים
that find no pasture. לֹא־מָצְאוּ מִרְעֶה

It already became clear in 1_4 how the poets cannot envisage objects and places such as roads and gates without the pilgrims, priests and young girls normally associated with them. The majesty of daughter Zion, therefore, was also the majesty of those present in her midst in their festal attire, among whom her princes must have been especially outstanding (Ps 68_{28}). Should Zion's שָׂרִים share a degree of identity with the elders (זְקֵנִים), as De Vaux has suggested with reference to Judg $8_{6,14}$ and Isa 3_{14},[141] then we might be forgiven for envisaging the involvement of such princes/elders in the cult with respect to this bicolon. The Deuteronomistic history has, indeed, preserved such images.[142] Priests and elders are mentioned in the same breath in Lam 1_{19bA} and 4_{16bAB} and the same is true for elders and princes in 5_{14}.

It is well known that the city gate was the place where the elders were supposed to administer justice.[143] If our suspicion that a certain level of identity exists between the elders and the princes is well founded then we

140 Cf Hag 2_4 (MT 2_3).
141 RdVaux, *Institutions I*, 180ff.
142 Cf Judg 4_3, I Kgs 8_{3a}. Cf also Ezek 8_{11} and WZimmerli, *Ezechiel 1–24*, BKAT XIII/1, Neukirchen 1979², 216–218.
143 Cf Deut 21_{19}, 22_{15}, Job 29_{7-17}, Prov 31_{23}, Lam 5_{14} and TWAT II 646f (Conrad).

have evidence of yet another inclusion in this canticle, namely between שְׁעָרֶיהָ (her gates) in 1_{4bA} and שָׂרֶיהָ (her princes) in 1_{6bA}. Princes were the heads of important families, prominent individuals who often exercised high military and civil functions under the king who richly rewarded them for their services.[144] Such functions, however, often provided the princes with the chance to enrich themselves dishonestly.[145] In any event, the princes were no strangers to health and wealth.[146] Mention is made of their abundance in the fourth song ($4_{4,5}$) in terms of the former luxury enjoyed by the children (עוֹלָלִים) of Zion (cf עוֹלָלֶיהָ in 1_{5cA}). Lam 4_7 also describes their former majesty. The wealth of the princes would certainly have manifested itself in their rich festival attire, but now their noble splendour has disappeared together with the feasts. They themselves have fled the city. Without doubt, the poets chose the metaphor of the princes as stags in association with the notion of הָדָר (majesty). Stags and hinds symbolised the very essence of elegance, effortless grace and swiftness,[147] but such associations are not intended here. The poets lean more towards the element of contrast at this point in their description. The stags, once swift and elegant, can no longer find pasture and are left breathless and weak.

What is intended here is that the great famine which resulted from the long siege of Jerusalem[148] and continued to lay hold of the city for some time thereafter[149] had even affected the princes. Further discussion of the famine can be found with reference to 1_{11b}.

6c *Without strength they fled* וַיֵּלְכוּ בְלֹא־כֹחַ
before the pursuer. לִפְנֵי רוֹדֵף

Since no one is spared by such famine, even Zion's princes are without strength and are left powerless in their efforts to escape the pursuer – the Babylonians.[150] Given that the Babylonians considered the pro-Egyptian princes[151] to be partly responsible for inciting revolt in Judah, such individuals already had good reason to flee. After being taken prisoner, however, the pro-Egyptian princes were executed[152] while the others were

144 Cf I Sam 8_{14}, 22_7 and TWAT II 644ff (Conrad).
145 Cf Isa 3_{14}, Ezek 22_{25}.
146 See RdVaux, *Institutions I*, 108f, 114.
147 Song $2_{9,17}$, 8_{14}, Ps 18_{34}, Prov 5_{19}, Isa 35_6.
148 Cf Jer 37_{21}, 52_6, II Kgs 25_3.
149 Cf Lam $1_{11,19}$, $2_{11ff,19f}$, 3_4, 4_{3-5}.
150 Cf II Kgs 25_{4ff}, Jer 52_{7ff} and the explanation of Lam 4_{18-20}.
151 Cf Jer 37_{15}, $38_{4f,24ff}$.

deported. It was Babylonian policy to send the leaders of the people into exile in order to hamper any further attempts at insurrection. Lam 2_{9b} also mentions that the princes together with the king languish in exile.[153]

Sub-canto II (Lam 1_{7-11})

The elaboration of the various themes in the second sub-canto is characterised by the familiar contrast between former glory and present misery taken from the dirge. Her desperation having realised itself to the full, Lady Jerusalem recalls past times when her jewels (palaces) were many and her neighbours held her in high esteem.

Now things have changed. Now she is homeless and despised. Her incredible fall from grace is her own fault (1_{7-9}). What precious things were left to her are now desecrated and taken away by the enemy, while famine robs her of whatever remains (1_{10-11}). In the depths of her distress she cries out for help to YHWH and laments her worthlessness ($1_{9c,11c}$).

Canticle I (1_{7-9})

Content/theme: *Lady Jerusalem loses her former majesty on account of her sin*

Literary argumentation:

inclusions:	(9cA) אֶת־עָנְיִי // (7aB) עֲנִיָּהּ
	(9aB) אַחֲרִיתָהּ // (7dB) מִשְׁבַּתֶּהָ
responses:	(9aB) זָכְרָה // (7aA) זָכְרָה
	(8cB) וַתָּשָׁב אָחוֹר \\ (7dA) שָׂחֲקוּ
	(9aA) טֻמְאָתָהּ בְּשׁוּלֶיהָ // (8aA) חֵטְא חָטְאָה יְרוּשָׁלַםִ
	(9aA) טֻמְאָתָהּ בְּשׁוּלֶיהָ // (8aB) לְנִידָה
	(9cB) כִּי הִגְדִּיל אוֹיֵב // (7dA) צָרִים שָׂחֲקוּ
partial response:	(9cA) רְאֵה יְהוָה // (7dA) רָאוּהָ צָרִים
ext par:	(9bB) אֵין מְנַחֵם לָהּ // (7cB) אֵין עוֹזֵר לָהּ
	(9aB) אַחֲרִיתָהּ \\ (7bB) מִימֵי קֶדֶם

In this canticle the poets depart from the sanctuary, as it were, and focus their attention on the city as a whole. It is apparent from the suffixes (3f

---

152 See II Kgs 25_{18-21}, Jer 39_{6}, $52_{10,24-27}$.

153 For further discussion of the political factions and their objectives see 1983, 132–139.

sg) and the imagery employed in 1_8 that Jerusalem is still being presented as a Lady. In her deep distress she thinks back on her former majesty and realises just how deep her downfall has been.

7aA *Jerusalem ponders...* זָכְרָה יְרוּשָׁלַםִ

Lady Jerusalem ponders. What is the object of her pondering? Several exegetes (Aalders, Kraus, Kaiser, Stoll) opt in response for 1_{7aB}: 'the days of her affliction...', in which case the verb זכר is understood as meaning 'to recall': Lady Jerusalem recalls the days of her affliction and homelessness. Such an explanation, however, places Lady Jerusalem's distress in the past. Kraus also suggests that זָכְרָה might refer to a community commemoration in the context of the liturgy. The objection remains, nevertheless, that the rest of the song places Jerusalem's affliction firmly in the present. For this reason, commentators such as Rudolph, Gordis and Boecker see 1_{7aB} as an adverbial, temporal modifier (although יְמֵי lacks a preposition) and assume כֹּל מַחֲמֻדֶיהָ to be the object of זָכְרָה: 'in the midst of her affliction Lady Jerusalem recalls the treasures that were hers from of old'. While such an approach to the problem creates a strong connection with 1_{7b}, we are left once again with the verb זכר being understood as 'to recall'. Given the meaning of this verb in the remaining songs, however, the question remains whether such an interpretation is correct. Once again an evident external parallelism calls for our attention.

It is certainly not by accident that √זכר can also be found in the ז-strophe of the third song (3_{19-21}). A song-response is alluded to at the same level. In the first place we have the imperative זְכָר (3_{19}) which is directed to YHWH in the form of a prayer.[154] In addition, the self-same objects are mentioned: וּמְרוּדִי and עָנְיִי, thus soundly confirming the song-response. The prayer of 3_{21} does not ask YHWH to remember the affliction of the pious warrior, the גֶּבֶר (cf 3_{1A}) as something from the past, but to realise the affliction the גֶּבֶר is now facing, to look at his affliction. The imperative זְכָר can be found in one other place in Lamentations, namely in 5_{1A}, where the parallel with 5_{1B} further specifies its content: "look and see our disgrace!" (cf the explanation of 5_1). In both instances a translation of the imperative זְכָר as 'recall' would be inadequate since the intended meaning is much closer to 'to realise', 'to place before one's eyes'. In this sense זָכְרָה has "gegenwärtige Gegebenheiten welche die Existenz prägend bestimmen"[155] as its object. Nevertheless, one can still ask oneself whether

[154] Cf the explanation of 3_{19}.

זָכַר has to carry this meaning where Lady Jerusalem is concerned. Is it really necessary for her to realise her affliction, to place it before her eyes, when she is right there in the midst of it (cf 1_{1aA})? The exegesis of 3_{20}, where the גֶּבֶר is the subject of זָכוֹר תִּזְכּוֹר, provides further assistance at this point. What preoccupies the גֶּבֶר here is quite evident: the affliction, homelessness, wormwood and gall mentioned in 3_{19}. The objection that Lady Jerusalem and the גֶּבֶר are experiencing their affliction now and have no need, therefore, to call it to mind, no longer holds water. Their recollection implies much more than 'looking their affliction in the face', it also implies that they realise just how deep their misery really is! This becomes apparent if we look at $3_{17,18}$ where visible, outward affliction [156] is described side by side with inner, spiritual struggle.[157] Both aspects are constituents of the one same affliction being endured by Lady Jerusalem and the גֶּבֶר. For this reason we can paraphrase √זכר as 'pondering' and take 1_{7aB} as the object of זָכְרָה: Lady Jerusalem ponders on and realises the full extent of what she is now undergoing, both at the material and the spiritual level.

7aB *... the days of her affliction and homelessness,* יְמֵי עָנְיָהּ וּמְרוּדֶיהָ

The content of Lady Jerusalem's experience is initially indicated by the term עֳנִי which means 'affliction'. The implications lying behind such 'affliction', however, can only be deduced from the context in which the word itself is used. Elsewhere in the OT, the concept is interpreted in ways which fit particularly well with its use here and in the rest of Lamentations, such as the affliction endured by orphans and widows in Isa 10_2, (cf Lam 1_1, 5_3). Such an interpretation underlines the coherence between 1_7 and 1_6, via the loss of Jerusalem's princes described therein.[158] Other correspondences include: the affliction of the hungry in Isa 58_7;[159] the affliction of the naked in Isa 58_7 (cf Lam 1_8); the affliction of those bowed down in spirit in Isa 66_2 (cf Lam 3_{20}). Affliction, however, can also have a significant influence on a person's spiritual condition. In times of distress, a person who is forced to endure affliction is led to realise his or her dependence on YHWH to whom he or she cries out in prayer for assistance or deliverance.[160] This seems to be the case in the canticle under discussion,

155 See THAT I 511 (Schottroff).
156 Such as that mentioned in 1_{16}; cf the explanation thereof.
157 See, in addition, the explanation of 3_{20}.
158 Cf, in addition, the explanation of 1_1 and 5_3.
159 Cf Lam 1_{11}, 2_{11}, 4_{10}, 5_{10} etcetera.

at the end of which Lady Jerusalem calls out to YHWH in the depths of her distress (cf, in this regard, the evident inclusion זָכְרָה יְרוּשָׁלַםִ ... עָנְיָהּ [7aA] // רְאֵה יְהוָה אֶת־עָנְיִי [9cA]; see in addition $1_{11c,20a}$, $3_{20,55ff}$).

Next to affliction we have the term מְרוּדֶיהָ (from מָרוּד, pl + sf 3f sg), a word derived from the root רוד.[161] The meaning of this verb is uncertain although the lexica usually translate it as 'to wander' (Rudolph: 'Heimatslosigkeit'). 'To wander', however, appears to be a derivative meaning, since 'wandering' is what one does when one no longer has a roof over one's head. Nevertheless, the one does not necessarily imply the other. Although Lady Jerusalem does not have a roof over her head she does not wander around, she sits down (cf 1_{1a}). For this reason we opt for the translation 'homelessness' together with Van Selms and understand the plural to be an intensive form.[162] The concrete interpretation [163] of the homelessness of Lady Jerusalem and the גֶּבֶר is provided by parallel strophes and canticles in the other songs: the destruction of temple, palace, city, walls and gates portrayed in 2_{6-8}, the recollection of the punishment of Sodom in 4_6. Lady Jerusalem is homeless. The house she once thought could never be taken from her (Lam 4_{12}) is a ruin (cf also 4_{11b} and Zeph 3_7). The people of Judah are likewise without hearth and home; in their case the result is 'wandering' (see the explanation of 5_6).

7b *all the precious things* כֹּל מַחֲמֻדֶיהָ
that were hers in days of old, אֲשֶׁר הָיוּ מִימֵי קֶדֶם

The treasures which Lady Jerusalem once owned prior to her downfall are also the subject of her pondering. In shrill contrast to her present homelessness and affliction mentioned in the foregoing bicolon, she realises just how prosperous and magnificent her life once was. In this way both bicola combine to exemplify the familiar style feature of the dirge: contrast between former majesty and present distress.[164] Without having lived through better times it is not easy to put one's experience of affliction into words. In this sense, the extent to which Jerusalem has fallen into ruin is only clear to those who have seen and known her glory intact and undiminished. Löhr, Aalders, Wiesmann, Kraus and Kaiser (cf BHK and BHS) are mistaken, therefore, in dropping this bicolon.

160 See, for example, Ps 34_7 etcetera; cf THAT II 344f (Jenni)
161 Cf HAL 598.
162 Cf GES-K § 124*e*.
163 Cf GES-K § 83*c*.
164 Cf Jahnow, 99.

What treasures does Lady Jerusalem have in mind as she ponders on their loss? The term מַחֲמָד is found several times in Lamentations: $1_{7,10,11}$ [165] and 2_4. In 1_{11}, however, the term refers to the personal treasures of the city's population. The reference in 1_{10} points once again to Lady Jerusalem's treasures but without more detailed description of what is intended this text does not provide much assistance in our search for the content of מַחְמָד. The remaining reference, 2_4, points unquestionably to material treasures. An inclusion is evident within this canticle of the second song (2_{4-5}) between כֹּל מַחֲמַדֵּי־עָיִן (2_{4bB}) // כָּל־אַרְמְנוֹתֶיהָ (2_{5bA}) from which it becomes apparent that Zion's treasures and her palaces are more or less identical. Bearing Ps 78_{47} in mind – in which the root הרג has things rather than people as its object (cf also Ezek 24_{21}) – it seems reasonable to assume that the treasures implied here in verse 7b are the temple complex and the adjacent royal palace. Such an interpretation is confirmed by the parallel canticle 2_{6-7} in which the destruction of temple, altar and palace is specified. It should be noted, in addition, that Ps $48_{3,13-15}$ intones the splendour of Zion's towers, walls and palaces.[166] It would have been quite justifiable, therefore, to speak of the centuries old temple of Solomon – which still existed at that point – as well as the royal palace as treasures belonging to Lady Jerusalem 'from of old'.

7c *until her people fell into the hand of the oppressor,* בִּנְפֹל עַמָּהּ בְּיַד־צָר
and there was no one to help her. וְאֵין עוֹזֵר לָהּ

Before an infinitive, the preposition בְּ denotes an adjunct of time: 'at that time', 'then', 'in those days', 'when'.[167] For this reason we understand 1_{7cA} to be a temporal adjunct with respect to the preceding bicolon 1_{7b}: the treasures Lady Jerusalem possessed up to the moment when her people fell into the hands of the enemy. 1_{7cB} is appositional, providing the detail that it was precisely at that moment that Lady Jerusalem was unable to find protection, either for her people or her treasures.

From the point of view of content we are dealing here with a complaint: when it came to the crunch, Lady Jerusalem stood alone; there was no one to help her (אֵין עוֹזֵר). From the perspective of Lam 4_{17} – see the term עֶזְרָתֵנוּ – we might be tempted to interpret this lack of assistance as purely political: at the critical moment Judah's ally Egypt did not come to her assistance (see the explanation of 4_{17}), but there is more to it than that. As

165 For the different vocalisations see BL 493*y,z*.

166 Cf also Ps 50_2 and the explanation of Lam $2_{5,15}$.

167 Cf, for example, Gen 9_{14}, Ex 3_{12}, Num 35_{19}, Isa 1_5; see HAL 101 sv בְּ (21).

a matter of fact, the root עזר not infrequently implies 'protection in time of war' and is used to refer to YHWH's help against the enemy (cf Ps 22_{12}), the realisation of which is the responsibility of the king (cf Ps 72_{12}). It comes as no surprise, therefore, that YHWH's 'protective help' holds a significant place in Zion theology.[168] The profound sense of disappointment that, in spite of the faith and expectation of its inhabitants YHWH did not help or protect his city, is hereby made audible. Not only YHWH was absent; Lady Jerusalem had no one to help her.

7d *Oppressors looked on mocking*
over her downfall.

רָאוּהָ צָרִים שָׂחֲקוּ
עַל מִשְׁבַּתֶּהָ

We understand this conclusion to be a continuation of the apposition set up in 1_{7cB}, introducing the additional element of painful mockery. Lady Jerusalem was not alone in her conviction that YHWH would protect her, her enemies were similarly persuaded. No one believed, in fact, that any adversary or hostile force could ever breach the gates of the city.[169] The fall of Jerusalem, however, put an end to such 'belief' and turned what once was respect into mockery and abuse. The fact that Lady Jerusalem's anguish achieved even greater depths thereby is made apparent by frequent reference to the mockery in question: 1_{21}, 2_{16}, $3_{46,61-63}$, 5_{1}. Here in 1_{7d} we hear mention of the mocking tones of the enemy for the first time. They see Jerusalem's helplessness and laugh (tauntingly) over her מִשְׁבָּת. In line with Rudolph, Kraus, Hillers, KBL 572, HAL 607 and Stolz (THAT II 863), among others, we understand this noun to be a derivative of the root שׁבת[170] meaning 'to (come to an) end' (cf 5_{14}). In the negative sense, the term is used for the cessation of Israel's power and pride, brought on by divine judgement.[171] Such an understanding is well suited to the term מִשְׁבַּתֶּהָ which we translate here as 'her downfall'. Lady Jerusalem cannot let go of that bitter moment nor the tauntingly hostile spectators who witnessed it. That moment is not far from her thoughts as she ponders her situation and it forces her to wonder in her anguish why YHWH did not intervene to protect her. The following strophe takes up the question.

A few remarks with respect to the irregularity of 1_7 are necessary, however, before we move on. In contrast to the remaining strophes, the ז-strophe

[168] Cf Ps 46_6 and TWAT VI 15 (Lipiński).

[169] Cf the exegesis of 4_{12}.

[170] Cf BL 490z, 558c.

[171] Cf Isa 17_3 with כָּבוֹד; cf מַכְבַּדֶּיהָ in 1_{8bA} and Ezek 33_{28} (destruction of Israel's 'proud might').

consists of four instead of three bicola. For this reason, almost every exegete (with the exception of Gordis and Stoll) treats one of the bicola as a gloss and eliminates it. Surprisingly enough, there is little unanimity as to which of the bicola deserves to be thus eliminated. 1_{7b} is scrapped by Aalders, Wiesmann, Plöger, Van Selms, Kaiser and Brandscheidt, while 1_{7c} is dropped by Rudolph, Weiser, Albrektson, Gottlieb and Boecker. Rudolph is of the opinion that 1_{7c} is a marginal, explanatory note on 1_{7a} which crept into the main text when the manuscript was copied. Hillers assumes the presence of two different text traditions, one with 1_{7b} and another with 1_{7c}. Neither explanation is satisfactory. It is hardly imaginable that a glossator or copyist would not have noticed the interpolation of a marginal note that disturbed the evidently regular structure of three bicola per strophe. Indeed, the opposite would have been more likely given that copyists suffered from the precise temptation to iron out difficulties wherever they encountered them. If this had been the case here there would certainly have been evidence thereof in the various text traditions but not so. The versions are also unanimous in rendering 1_7 with four bicola. We hold the more difficult reading (four bicola) to be the original and can provide further arguments in defence of such a position. From the perspective of Hebrew poetry, for example, one is more likely to encounter 'expansion'.[172] Structural analysis also tends to uphold the more difficult reading. The arguments presented above in support of the unity of canticle 1_{7-9} revealed how literary building blocks found in both 1_{7b} and 1_{7c} exercised a function within the canticle as a whole. Similar literary arguments can be brought forward in support of the unity and cohesion of the sub-canto Lam 1_{7-11}, arguments in which literary elements from both 1_{7b} and 1_{7c} also function. cf:

inclusions: הָיוּ *(7bB)* // הָיְתִי (11cB)
עַמָּהּ *(7cA)* // עַמָּהּ (11aA)
כֹּל *(7bA)* // כָּל (11aA)
מַחֲמֻדֶיהָ *(7bA)* // מַחֲמוֹדֵיהֶם (11bA)

responses: בְּיַד־צָר *(7cA)* // יָדוֹ פָּרַשׂ צָר (10aA)

This kind of evidence suggests that both 1_{7b} and 1_{7c} function on a higher

[172] This is an elaboration on the part of the poet or reciter; cf WGEWatson, *Classical Hebrew Poetry. A Guide to its Techniques*, JSOT suppl series 26, Sheffield 1984, 349ff; MCAKorpel – JCdMoor, 'Fundamentals of Ugaritic and Hebrew Poetry', in: The Structural Analysis of Biblical and Canaanite Poetry, (eds WvdMeer and JCdMoor) JSOT suppl series 74, Sheffield 1988, 23ff.

literary level within the song. Generally speaking, however, glosses would be more likely to have already disrupted less remote literary connections. The responses between this verse and the remaining songs also provided a source of argumentation in favour of the more difficult reading. The exegesis pointed to a connection between the 'treasures' of 1_{7b} and the temple and palaces mentioned in 2_7. A similar agreement exists between 1_{7cA} and 2_{7bA}: בְּיַד־צָר // בְּיַד־אוֹיֵב, with which לֹא־חָלוּ בָהּ יָדָיִם of 4_{6bB} is parallel at the canticle level (cf פֹּרֵק אֵין מִיָּדָם of 5_8). The final bicolon of this verse, 1_{7d}, is parallel with 2_{7c}. Evidently, therefore, every bicolon of 1_7 has a song-response in one or other of the remaining songs. We noted above how 1_{7a} and 1_{7b} together exhibit the dirge pattern. At the same time, we also saw that it was incorrect to assume that 1_{7c} introduces nothing new to the strophe as a whole (Weiser) since אֵין עוֹזֵר לָהּ, from the theological perspective, does in fact provide a new element (see the exegesis). 3_{18B} responds hereto: 'gone is ... my hope in YHWH'. Such a lament – formulated at the very core of the book of Lamentations – is profound indeed: there is no help to be found in YHWH. It is possible, perhaps, that the poets consciously employed literary irregularity in order to express the precise extent to which YHWH's aloofness had knocked Lady Jerusalem off balance. Something similar appears also to be the case in 2_{19}, where the subject of the great distress of the starving children is raised.

8aA *Jerusalem sinned grievously,* חֵטְא חָטְאָה יְרוּשָׁלַםִ

In like fashion to the central verse of the second canticle (1_{5bB}) we find mention of Lady Jerusalem's sin as the origin of her downfall here in the middle of the third canticle. A literal translation would render the colon: 'a sin Lady Jerusalem has sinned'. It is frequently suggested that we read חטא as a paranomastic infinitive (cf GES-K § 113*n*) and vocalise it as such. This is unnecessary, however, given that the construction with the noun is also to be found bearing the same meaning (cf GES-K § 117*p*).

The term employed for 'to sin' is not the root פשע but rather the verb חטא. As such, therefore, the transgression of commandments or injunctions should not be our primary thought. The actual content of the root חטא points more towards a breach of community relationships, thus placing the accent on the fact of the transgression rather than on the inclination to transgress.[173] Where norms and rules exist in a community then the root חטא also implies their transgression.[174] Such transgressions can also

[173] Cf THAT I 543 (Knierim).

take place without the perpetrator being aware of it (cf I Sam 14_{24ff}). The transgression implied here in 1_{8aA} points towards an actual breach in Jerusalem's relationship with YHWH. At its very core, the sin is directed towards YHWH because the rules for community relationships were established by him. Jerusalem's downfall, therefore, is not rooted in the enemy's superior force but in the sanction of YHWH. Indeed, the song-response in 2_8 describes the city's destruction at YHWH's hands. He has evaluated Jerusalem's sin and avenged it with destruction of wall and gate. The poets do not offer any detail as to the content of Lady Jerusalem's wrong-doing although 2_{14}, 4_{13} and 5_7 provide a good case for thinking that the sins in question are those of her leaders (see the exegesis of the respective verses).

8aB *therefore she has become impure.* עַל־כֵּן לְנִידָה הָיָתָה

Once again the poets return to the metaphor of Jerusalem as a Lady. The fact that the relationship in which she was once involved has come to an end is apparent from the fate she is now being forced to endure: she has become נִידָה. There are two distinct positions with respect to the meaning of the term נִידָה. Several exegetes[175] suggest that the term is a derivative of the verb נוד meaning 'to shake'/'move' and see Jerusalem as an object of scorn before which onlookers would shake their head in a gesture of mocking (cf Ps 44_{10}, Jer 48_{27}). The same interpretation is implied in Jer 16_{18}, although the word ראשׁ has been added here (for the sake of clarity?). If this is correct then there is a unmistakable concatenation between this and the previous strophe which ends with the enemy's mocking laughter. The fact that similar concatenations are frequent in Lamentations between successive literary units might provide an argument in favour of such an interpretation. Other commentators, such as Aalders and Albrektson, consider נִידָה to be a variant spelling of נִדָּה, which is also to be found in 1_{17c} signifying the impure condition of a menstruating woman. While this image of impurity clearly reaches out in advance to the images of nakedness and impure separation in the following verses, it also fits well with the חֵטְא of the preceding colon: because of her sin, communion with YHWH, the Holy One, has become impossible. The poets employ the image of impurity to express this situation (cf also the clear connection between חַטָּאת and נִדָּה in Num 19_9, 31_{23}, Zech 13_1). Although opting for one or other of the two suggestions is no easy task, our preference goes to the latter

[174] Knierim, 545; TWAT II 860 (Koch).
[175] Rudolph, Kraus, Hillers, Boecker; cf HAL 657 and TWAT V 252 (Milgrom – Wright).

since in 2_{16} the enemy's mockery is rendered in different terminology. Lady Jerusalem's nakedness, introduced in the following bicolon, also relates better to the idea of impurity.

8b *All who honoured her despise her,* כָּל־מְכַבְּדֶיהָ הִזִּילוּהָ
for they see her nakedness. כִּי־רָאוּ עֶרְוָתָהּ

Those referred to as having once honoured Lady Jerusalem are her former lovers (cf 1_2). The peoples who formerly treated Lady Jerusalem with the respect due to her political position[176] – cf Jer 27_{1ff} – and perhaps also her name and fame (cf 2_{15} and Ezek 16_{14}), now despise her. The root זלל here means 'to despise'/'disparage'[177] and firmly establishes the contrast between Lady Jerusalem's former position of respect and her current situation. Those who now despise her are the very ones who used to honour and respect her. The immediate cause of all of this is her present state, her nakedness. Nakedness is a polyvalent concept, although broadly speaking it stands for shame and disgrace. Such nakedness, and particularly the exposure of the genitals, constituted an almost insuperable disgrace.[178] The concept appears in prophetic announcements of judgement as a punishment from YHWH. Disgrace of this kind was also used in the portrayal of the fate of certain (personified) cities who had undergone YHWH's judgement, for example, Nineveh (Nah 3_{5f}) and Jerusalem (Jer 13_{26}). Deutero-Isaiah employs the image in the announcement of judgement against Lady Babylon in Isa 47_3. The notion of nakedness presented here also underlines the fact that the gulf between YHWH and Lady Jerusalem had become a reality: He no longer intends to cloth her.[179] In the *Sfire* inscription 1A 40–41, nakedness is also presented as a punitive sanction against covenant violations. See also ANET^3 660 where nakedness is rendered by 'slavery'.[180] In Ezek 16_8 we find the original situation: as he passes by Lady Jerusalem, YHWH tenderly covers her nakedness and takes her in marriage.[181] With respect to the judgement, nakedness is given concrete form in terms of despoilment and destruction[182] which is equivalent to the removal of majesty

[176] The meaning of the root כבד in the *pi'el*, cf THAT I 797 (Westermann), TWAT IV 19 (Stenmans).

[177] Cf KBL 258, HAL 261.

[178] Cf Gen 3_7, 9_{20-27}, Isa 3_{17}, 20_4, Ezek $16_{7,8}$.

[179] Cf Ex 21_{10}, Isa 4_1, Hos 2_{8f} (MT 2_{11f}); see also HWWolff, *Dodekapropheton 1, Hosea*, BKAT XIV/1, Neukirchen 1965^2, 45.

[180] Cf, however, ASvdWoude, *Jona Nahum*, Nijkerk 1978, 117.

[181] Cf also MCAKorpel, *A Rift in the Clouds*, Münster 1990, 228–231 and TWAT IV 372 (Niehr).

and splendour (תִּפְאֶרֶת, cf Lam 2_{1bB}). Where a city is concerned, nakedness implies openness and vulnerability or lack of protection.[183] The stripping of Judah is evident, therefore, from the destruction of the fortified cities alluded to in Lam $2_{2,5}$. The same applies to Jerusalem. The walls and gates of the city have been torn down (cf the song-response 2_{8f}). The city once considered impregnable (4_{12}) now lies wide open and exposed, accessible to one and all. As a matter of fact, all the dimensions mentioned so far are tied up in one image, the nakedness of Lady Jerusalem: she has been made a disgrace (3_{45}), abandoned by YHWH (5_{20}), ruined and left without protection; the enemy have free access and can do whatever they please (cf 1_5 and 5_{1-13}).

8c *Yes, she herself groans* גַּם־הִיא נֶאֶנְחָה
and turns her face away. וַתָּשָׁב אָחוֹר

It is evident from her reaction – she herself groans – that the very disdainful glances of her former admirers bring Lady Jerusalem to the full realisation of her shame. Since there is no one else who groans in the immediate context, גַּם in its usual meaning 'also', makes no sense here. McDaniels offers an attractive solution. He suggests that we should understand גַּם at this point as it is understood in Ugaritic, namely 'loud',[184] We have already referred to the audible character of the root אנח (cf 1_{4b}). If we were to adopt this interpretation our translation would run as follows: 'loudly she groans'. Nevertheless, some doubts remain. Gottlieb has argued that the root אנח in Hebrew is never intensified with an adverb. For this reason we are more inclined to understand גַּם as an accentuation of the subject.[185] Lady Jerusalem groans under the mocking and disdainful gaze of her enemies and tries to avoid it but turning her face. Literally: 'she draws back'.

9aA *Her uncleanness clings to her skirts.* טֻמְאָתָהּ בְּשׁוּלֶיהָ

It is known that small bells were attached to the seams of the high priest's clothing, which served to keep impure demonic powers at bay.[186] In this

---

182 Cf Ezek 16_{39f}, 23_{29}, Nah 3_7, Hab 3_{13}, Zeph 2_{14} and Ps 137_7 (in this text עָרוּ עָרוּ can be translated as 'strip, strip').

183 Cf Mic 1_{11} and ASvdWoude, *Micha*, Nijkerk 1976, 48ff as well as Gen $42_{9,12}$ and TWAT IV 373 (Niehr).

184 ThFMcDaniel, 'Philological Studies in Lamentations', Biblica 49 (1968), 31f. Compare Hillers translation.

185 Cf HAL 188 sv גַּם 5.

186 Ex 28_{33ff}, 39_{24-26}; cf, for example, FCFensham, *Exodus*, Nijkerk 1970, 200.

context Keel notes: “Die Säume signalisieren die Schwäche und gefährdete Randzone einer Persönlichkeit”.[187] Lady Jerusalem has paid no attention to the purity of her clothing. On the contrary, her defiling menstrual blood flowed with such ‘sickly persistence’ (Van Selms) that it soaked through even to the very seams of her clothing. One might ask how it is possible to speak here of Lady Jerusalem's clothing when the previous strophe referred to her nakedness. The same sequence is also found, however, in Ezek 16_{37-39}: YHWH first uncovers the shame of adulterous Jerusalem after which former lovers will strip her of her clothing and make her nakedness complete (cf also 4_{22a}). In other words: YHWH uncovers Jerusalem's sin and the enemy carry out his sentence. The responses mentioned above:

חֵטְא חָטְאָה יְרוּשָׁלַםִ (8aA) // טֻמְאָתָהּ בְּשׁוּלֶיהָ (9aA)
לְנִידָה (8aB) // טֻמְאָתָהּ בְּשׁוּלֶיהָ (9aA)

clearly show that Jerusalem's impurity has to do with her sin, with respect to which no further detail is provided in the immediate context. Elsewhere, however, we find the idea that the spilling of innocent blood makes a city ritually impure (cf Ps 106_{38-39}). Prophets see such impurity as the result of adulterous liaisons with idols and foreign nations but bloodshed is also part of their purview.[188] In the wider context of the entire book of Lamentations, the sin of bloodshed is indeed mentioned among the sins of Jerusalem's prophets and priests who were thereby considered impure (cf $4_{13,14}$ and the explanation thereof). Lam 1_9 focuses on another aspect of impurity, namely social isolation (cf יָשְׁבָה בָדָד in 1_{1aA} and the explanation thereof). Impurity implies unavoidable separation (cf Lev 18_{19}) and makes it impossible to enter into the arena of the holy.[189] Everyone steers clear of Lady Jerusalem because of her visible impurity. It should be noted that this approach to sin employs terms which differ from the (prophetic) terminology of social injustice. This also provides a clue as to the provenance of the authors of Lamentations. To speak of sin in terms of ritual impurity was the custom primarily in priestly circles.[190]

9aB *She was not prepared for such an outcome.* לֹא זָכְרָה אַחֲרִיתָהּ

The poets hark back at this point to former times when Jerusalem lived without a care, without paying attention to the warning voices (cf 1_{18a}

[187] OKeel, YHWH-*visionen und Siegelkunst*, SBS 84/85, Stuttgart 1977, 69.
[188] Hos 5_3, 6_{10}, Jer 2_{23}, Ezek 16_{37f}, $23_{7,13}$, 24_{6-14}.
[189] RdVaux, *Institutions II*, 353–358.
[190] STerrien, ‘The Omphalos Myth and Hebrew Religion’, VT 20 (1970), 334ff.

and the explanation thereof). She did not think for one moment that her life would turn out like this, nor did she realise that such distress and abandonment would be her lot.[191] Literally speaking אַחֲרִיתָהּ means 'her end', although the term doubtlessly has a theological significance in this colon. Jerusalem's end is not guided simply by fate, it is YHWH's judgement upon the city. In Amos 8_{10} and Jer 5_{31} the term carries a similar significance. The Amos text is particularly meaningful with respect to the Jerusalem's 'end'. It appears in the context of the 'day of YHWH' (see excursus following the exegesis of 1_{2a}) where it is characterised as a day of intense mourning and as a bitter (מָר) end (אַחֲרִית).[192] Lady Jerusalem had not expected YHWH to intervene in such a way. Now – in her final moments – her heart is full of bitterness.[193]

9b *Appallingly deep was her downfall,* וַתֵּרֶד פְּלָאִים
and no one comforts her. אֵין מְנַחֵם לָהּ

In the text critical apparatus of BHS, Robinson suggests we read a *hoph'al* imperfect instead of a *qal* imperfect which would then render the translation: 'she was brought down'. Since there is a lack of textual witnesses in support of such an emendation, however, and since Lady Jerusalem's active role in her own downfall – emphasised in the preceding verses – would be weakened thereby, Robinson's suggestion remains unconvincing. The phrase וַתֵּרֶד פְּלָאִים constitutes a further reflection on Lady Jerusalem's end, focusing on the way it came about. The adverb פְּלָאִים contains echoes of an inversion. The verb פלא, 'to be extraordinary, wonderful, miraculous', together with the נִפְלָאוֹת, 'wonders, miracles', derived therefrom, point in particular to the saving deeds of YHWH which elicit wonder and amazement in those who witness them.[194] "Die Tatsache, daß פלא vor allem auf das Rettungshandeln Gottes bezogen ist, zeigt, daß Wunder im AT nicht das Durchbrechen einer objektiv feststehenden Ordnung (z.B. des Naturgesetzes) meint, sondern das Überschreiten des von einem Menschen in seiner Situation konkret Erwarteten und für möglich Gehaltenen."[195] 'The miraculous' is what people do not expect or even imagine possible in their particular situation. YHWH's 'wonderful' deeds can also have neg-

---

191 With respect to the future meaning of the root זכר cf TWAT II 574f (Eising), Isa 47_7 and Eccl 11_8.

192 Cf, in addition, the explanation of 1_{4cB}.

193 See also the explanation of 2_{17} and 4_{18b}.

194 Cf Jer 21_2, Mic 7_{15}, Ps 77_{12}.

195 See THAT II 417 (Albertz).

ative implications, however, especially when he pronounces judgement.[196] It goes without saying that we can assume a similarly negative implication for the colon under discussion. The negative 'wonder' of Jerusalem's downfall is presented in the form of a breakdown in a pattern of expectation: Lady Jerusalem – and according to 4_{12} she was not the only one – relied on YHWH's protection, but when the enemy advanced against her he withdrew his hand (2_{3b}). More serious still: YHWH's hand was the agent of her destruction (cf the song-responses in $2_{8,9}$). Surrounded by the destruction brought about by YHWH, Lady Jerusalem sits in despair, naked and destitute, wretched and despised.

The phrase אֵין מְנַחֵם לָהּ in 1_{9bB} is not simply a repetition of the cognate complaint in 1_{2bA}. In the latter case the primary focus was on the absence of lovers as a source of comfort. In 1_{9bB}, however, the lament moves to a deeper level: YHWH, whose 'wondrous' deeds brought about her downfall, now leaves Lady Jerusalem to her remaining fate. He is not moved to mercy nor does he stretch out his hand to help her. The fact that the poets concretely envisage the absence of priestly Torah and prophetic word of guidance in this regard is made apparent in the song-response of 2_9 (אֵין תּוֹרָה and לֹא ... חָזוֹן). Such material implications of 'comforting' are discussed in 1_{2bA}.

9cA *"Look,* YHWH, *at my affliction,* רְאֵה יְהוָה אֶת־עָנְיִי

Lady Jerusalem's situation has become unbearable. Her affliction is truly unimaginable and there is no one to help or comfort her. Nevertheless, if she is to survive she must find help and her cry of distress is evidence that she is aware of this. To whom can she turn? There is only One who can help her: YHWH. Paradoxically, in spite of the fact that YHWH has abandoned her, it is to him that she turns in prayer. She declares her conviction that he alone has the power to help her. It was already apparent in 1_{5b} and 1_{8a} that YHWH was behind Lady Jerusalem's misfortune and not her enemies. He had handed her over to them, only he had the power to save her from them. The same idea emerged in our exegesis of the previous bicolon (1_{9b}). If it is true that Jerusalem's present affliction is entirely due to YHWH then he alone has the power to bring it to an end. Lady Jerusalem has no other option than to place her trust in the very God who has punished her so severely. Structural analysis reveals how the placing of this prayer together with that of 1_{11c} was well considered.

[196] Cf Deut 28_{59}, Isa 29_{14} and Job 10_{16}.

Within Lam I there are song-responses between 1_{9} and 1_{20} (רְאֵה יְהוָה // רְאֵה יְהוָה) and between 1_{11} and 1_{22} (רְאֵה יְהוָה // תָּבֹא ... לְפָנֶיךָ). The prayer of confidence in $1_{9,11}$ is likewise to be found in the second sub-canto of the third song, namely in 3_{22-23}, in the form of song-responses in which the גֶּבֶר places his trust in YHWH. Given that Lam III holds a central position within the book of Lamentations as a whole, one can say that these short exclamatory prayers in Lam I mirror, in summary form, the trust of the devout one of the third song. Together with Rudolph we can characterise each prayer as a "winziger Klagepsalm". The relationship we have been discussing makes it clear once again that the metaphor of Jerusalem as a Lady does not only refer to the city as such but also to the inhabitants thereof whom she represents. Her appeal to YHWH is their cry of distress, revealing their unabated expectation in YHWH's assistance. What will be said later concerning the faith struggle of the גֶּבֶר is presented here in reduced and summary fashion (cf also the remarks relating to 1_{4cB}).

Lady Jerusalem begs YHWH to 'look' at her affliction, a core expression within the songs as a whole (see the explanation of $3_{36B,50}$). YHWH's 'looking' as not a neutral kind of looking. From the very beginning, Israel had experienced YHWH, in contrast to the idols who do not 'look', as a God who had an eye for and paid heed to the affliction of people in distress. It was considered part of his nature, therefore, that he would be ready to help.[197] Lady Jerusalem now appeals with great urgency to that readiness. The *qal* imperative of the root ראה is used, a form which is characteristic of the lament genre.[198] At the same time, however, a glance in the concordances reveals that the formulation רְאֵה יְהוָה – with the imperative followed directly by the tetragrammaton – is only to be found in Lamentations and more specifically in $1_{9,11,20}$ and 2_{20}. It would appear that the more widespread use of such a direct imperative was considered too categorical and was felt, therefore, to be inappropriate. The fact that the formulation רְאֵה יְהוָה was used here and considered justified nevertheless, simply emphasises the extremity of Jerusalem's distress. At the same time, the prayer reflects Lady Jerusalem's feeling that YHWH is no longer looking at her and thus does not observe her affliction (cf 3_{50}); YHWH is keeping himself hidden (3_{44}). The oppression to which he is subjecting Jerusalem (1_{5b}) is a consequence of his distant aloofness. He has intentionally turned away his gaze because he does not want to see what she is enduring (see also

[197] Cf Ex 3_{8} and THAT II 696f (Vetter).
[198] HGunkel – JBegrich, *Einleitung in die Psalmen*, Göttingen 1975[3], 128.

3_{36}). For this reason her enemies have a free hand. If only YHWH would look down and see the dreadful situation they have brought about in his city; such is the profound intention of this exceptionally urgent prayer (cf also $1_{11,20}$, 3_{50} and 5_1 and the explanation thereof).

The combination עָנְיִי and רְאֵה can be found in Ps 9_{14}, 25_{18}, 31_8 and 119_{153}. The function of the strophes of the present canticle is evident in this prayer in which the content of Jerusalem's sin is not the primary point of interest but rather the description of the dreadful fate she is facing on account of her sin. It is apparent from the inclusion עָנְיָהּ (1_{7aB}) // עָנְיִי (1_{9cA}) that such is the true substance of Lady Jerusalem's affliction, an affliction YHWH must see with his own eyes. The substantive is in frequent use in the OT and is, according to Gerstenberger, "stark konzentriert in den liturgisch-weisheitlichen Schriften und in kultischen Zusammenhängen. Es hat ein kompaktes Bedeutungsfeld: "Elend", das zum Himmel schreit". Gerstenberger also notes that the term is primarily connected to affliction brought about by God, thus making his intervention necessary.[199] All we have said so far is appropriate to the imperative of רְאֵה. For the actual content of Jerusalem's עָנְיִי see the explanation of $1_{7,8b,9b}$ together with the elaboration thereof in the following canticle. In the apparatus of BHS, Robinson suggests we read 'her affliction' (עָנְיָהּ) in which case it would not be Lady Jerusalem who turns in prayer to God but the poets in her stead. From the text critical perspective this emendation is weak and gives the impression, moreover, that it is trying to smooth out a more difficult reading by avoiding a sudden change of speaker between 9b and 9c.

9cB *yes, the enemy has triumphed!"* כִּי הִגְדִּיל אוֹיֵב

The affliction Jerusalem is facing is brought about by a triumphant enemy. The meaning of the transitive use of the *hiph'il* of the verb גדל I can be summarised as follows: 'to behave arrogantly and audaciously superior at the expense of others'.[200] With reference to 2_{21ab} one might imagine a reign of terror on the part of Jerusalem's enemy (cf, in addition, $2_{16,17}$, $3_{46,52}$). The כִּי here has both an explanatory and an emphatic significance.

Having expected mourning and confession of guilt, both Rudolph and Kraus are surprised that Jerusalem's affliction and the superiority of the enemy are named in the prayer as the ground of appeal. Aside from the fact that there will be a confession of guilt later on in the song (1_{18a}),

[199] In TWAT VI 256f.
[200] Cf TWAT I 942f (Mosis) and TWAT III 226 (Kutsch); cf also Zeph $2_{8,10}$.

both commentators fail to recognise an essential element of Israel's understanding of God at this point: YHWH is a God who takes heed of the human person in need. It is continuously apparent from Israel's history that God allows himself to be moved to help his people when they call out to him in distress. Such an awareness is present in almost all the traditions of the Old Testament[201] and can even be found affirmed by YHWH himself.[202] In prophetic announcements of judgement the very seriousness of the situation is underlined if there is a threat that YHWH will no longer listen.[203] Nevertheless, it is evident from Judg 10_{10ff}, for example, that such a situation need not be seen as YHWH's final word.[204] Judg 2_{18} expresses a particularly significant theological insight: when placed in the balance, an authentic cry of distress carries more weight than sins which have already been committed. The poets of Lamentations were evidently aware of this in that they first bring Lady Jerusalem's cry of distress into relationship with the enemy whose dominanation is bringing her such great affliction.[205]

Canticle II (1_{10-11})

Content/theme: *Loss of treasures brought about by violent hostility and hunger*

Literary argumentation:

inclusion:	יָדוֹ פָּרַשׂ צָר ... (10aA) // כִּי הָיִיתִי זוֹלֵלָה (11bB)
responses:	כָּל (10aB) // כָּל (11aA)
	גוֹיִם בָּאוּ מִקְדָּשָׁהּ (10bAB) // כִּי הָיִיתִי זוֹלֵלָה (11cB)
	אֲשֶׁר צִוִּיתָה (10cA) // רְאֵה יְהוָה (11cA)
ext par:	כִּי־רָאֲתָה גוֹיִם (10bA) // כִּי הָיִיתִי זוֹלֵלָה (11cB)
key words:	מַחֲמַדֶּיהָ (10aB) // מַחֲמוֹדֵיהֶם (11bA)
	רָאֲתָה (10bA) // רְאֵה (11cA)

These verses constitute the second and last canticle of sub-canto B, Lam 1_{7-11}. 1_{9c} clearly provides a link with the preceding canticle, setting up

201 Cf Ex 2_{23f}, 3_{7f}, Judg 2_8, $3_{9,15}$, 10_{10ff}, 15_{18f}, 16_{28}, Ps 22_{5f}, 81_8, 107.

202 Ps 50_{15}, 91_{15}.

203 Ezek 8_{18}; cf Lam $3_{8,44}$.

204 Cf also 1983, 321–323.

205 For additional information on the essential relationship between distress and prayer cf HGunkel – JBegrich, *Einleitung in die Psalmen*, Göttingen 1975^3, 125ff and part VII of the introduction of the present volume on the theology of the poets.

concatenation via אוֹיֵב and צָר. The enemy's supremacy is elaborated in chiastic fashion: 1_{10} describes enemy behaviour, which consists of despoilation and desecration, while 1_{11} exposes the extremity of Jerusalem's hunger. Both 'enemy' and 'hunger' alike rob her of her treasures (מַחְמָד joins both strophes together). The canticle concludes with an even more urgent prayer than that in 1_{9c}.

10a *The oppressor stretches out his hand* יָדוֹ פָּרַשׂ צָר
over all her precious things. עַל כָּל־מַחֲמַדֶּיהָ

Whose words are these? It is apparent from the 3f sg suffix of מַחֲמַדֶּיהָ that they are not Lady Jerusalem's words. Once again it is the poets who come to the fore at this point, describing the distressful state of their city. From a stylistic perspective this bicolon makes 1_{9c} into a short (pleading) exclamatory prayer (cf the response with 1_{8c} גַּם־הִיא נֶאֶנְחָה) which is fully in line with the portrayal of Lady Jerusalem in the previous canticle.

The enemy's hostile activity is once again the subject of the poets' craft although they do not simply repeat themselves. Time and again they fill out some new aspect of their depiction of events or elaborate upon a dimension of the situation mentioned in a previous verse. Expansions on themes from the first song are particularly evident in the second. After destruction (1_4), deportation (1_5) and persecution (1_6), reference is now made to the plunder of Lady Jerusalem's priceless things. The oppressor stretches out his hand, יָדוֹ פָּרַשׂ. The same expression is to be found in 1_{17} where it is used to express a desperate gesture in prayer.[206] The enemy sets out with a passion to appropriate all Lady Jerusalem's treasures. Rudolph's interpretation of the implied treasures as restricted to those of the temple is too narrow. The treasures in question were intended for the victorious king Nebuchadnezzar and, as such, also included the riches taken from the royal palace. According to II Kgs 25_{13-17}, such treasures were carried off in an orderly fashion. Temple artefacts later resurfaced in Babylonian temples and royal treasuries.[207] The phrase כָּל־מַחֲמַדֶּיהָ, however, certainly includes treasures beyond those of temple and palace: gold, silver, jewellery etcetera which belonged to the ordinary people, particularly the women. It is worthy of note that in Lam I, II, IV and V the distress of such women is always spoken of in the central strophes.[208] The

[206] Cf the response 1_{17aA} // 1_{20aA} in sub-canto B of the second canto (1_{17-22}) at the canticle level together with Ps 143_6, although in this case the hands are stretched out in a gesture of taking.

[207] Cf Dan 1_2, $5_{2,23}$, Ezra $1_{7,8}$, $5_{14,15}$; cf also the decree of king Darius in Ezra 6_{3-5}.

theft of their jewels constituted a part of their affliction. The women of Jerusalem were famous for their jewellery. The judgement predicted in Isa 3_{16-24} in this respect has now become a reality: enemy soldiers have robbed them of their treasures. After a one and a half year siege the purse was empty and thus the soldiers turned to enthusiastic plundering. As a matter of fact, the soldiers were obliged to provide their own equipment and upkeep and whatever 'salary' they were able to put together consisted of booty collected in battle (cf Ezek 29_{19}). It is also possible that the jewels in question referred to the women of Jerusalem themselves[209] which would mean that the soldiers assaulted the women. Such an event is in fact stated, in so many words, in the central verse of the fifth song (5_{11}). This bicolon leaves us with an image of soldiers bursting into houses and homes, threatening their occupants, raping the women, turning everything upside down and carrying off whatever suited them.

10b *Yes, she sees infidels*	כִּי־רָאֲתָה גוֹיִם
invade her sanctuary;	בָּאוּ מִקְדָּשָׁהּ

By way of an emphatic כִּי, 'Yes',[210] the sanctuary is expressly brought to the fore. The term מִקְדָּשׁ can refer to the temple complex as a whole but can also designate individual parts thereof.[211] In this context the likely reference is to the walled part of the temple, the forecourts and the actual temple building itself. It goes without saying that the richly endowed temple complex would not be left out when a city was being plundered by enemy invaders (cf also 2_{7b}). Stylistically and at the level of content, however, the poets set about their task with great subtlety at this point. It would have been completely in line with the preceding bicolon if they had continued to focus attention on the removal of the temple treasures and this is indeed implied in their words. The גוֹיִם who enter the sanctuary are soldiers charged with the task of demolishing it and carrying off whatever is of value.[212] Nevertheless, the poets are not inclined to present events in such a way. No matter how appalling the destruction and plunder of the temple might be to them (cf 4_1), there is another matter which they find even more shocking and which they insightfully know must be an affront

208 Cf also the explanation of 3_{51}.
209 See the expression 'the delight of your eyes' as a reference to Ezekiel's wife in Ezek 24_{16}.
210 For the emphatic use of the particle כִּי cf HAL 448 sv כִּי II.1.
211 Cf HAL 591f.
212 Cf II Kgs $25_{8ff,13ff}$.

to YHWH: each time soldiers enter the sanctuary, YHWH's ban (cf 1_{10c}) on infidel access to the temple is transgressed. In contrast to former times, there are no longer gatekeepers to hold back these גּוֹיִם. No one stands in their way. An echo of this complaint can be found in Jer 51_{51}.

10c *those of whom you command:* אֲשֶׁר צִוִּיתָה
they may not enter into your congregation. לֹא־יָבֹאוּ בַקָּהָל לָךְ

For the division of the cola see the Masoretic *zāqēf qāṭōn* with צִוִּיתָה. A difference of opinion exists on the significance of the suffix of לָךְ. The LXX and the Peshitta read it as a 2m sg suffix and understand it to refer to YHWH: they are forbidden to enter into 'your congregation'. Wisemann, Gottwald and Meek, among others, follow this line of thought. Keil, Albrektson and Gottlieb, on the other hand, read a 2f sg suffix which they understand to refer to Lady Jerusalem: גּוֹיִם are forbidden to enter into her congregation. The latter interpretation fits better with the direct speech of צִוִּיתָה and with the content of the ban. Israel itself had to safeguard the purity and integrity of the assembly.

Together with the situation of famine mentioned at the beginning of the following strophe, the transgression of the ban on גּוֹיִם in the assembly stands at the centre of this canticle and is thereby given extra moment as a complaint. An analogous ban can be found in Deut $23_{3,4}$, where the Moabites and the Ammonites in particular are denied access to Israel's liturgy to the furthest generation because of their hostile behaviour towards Israel on its way to Canaan. On account of the common use of the word-pair אֲשֶׁר צִוָּה and the term קָהָל, it might be suggested that a reference is being made in Lam 1_{10} to Deut $23_{3,4}$. One might even propose an historical argument in favour of such a suggestion. It is well known that Nebuchadnezzar, in reacting to king Jehoiakim's rebellion, made use of the services of Moabite and Ammonite troops.[213] It is certainly not outwith the bounds of possibility that Moabite and Ammonite troops also joined forces with the Babylonian army in 587. Should such troops have been deployed in carrying off the temple's precious artefacts then their presence in the sanctuary would have constituted a direct violation of the ban in Deut $23_{3,4}$.

The link proposed above is well established in the Jewish tradition.[214] As such, it is presupposed that the text from Deuteronomy is the older

[213] Cf II Kgs 24_2 and Hab 3_{16}; cf also 1983, 123, 184.
[214] Cf Midrash Eichah Rabba and Lechem Dim'ah of Rav Shmuel de Uzeda (1557).

of the two. Such a suggestion might support Albrektson's hypothesis that Lamentations was dependant on Deuteronomy,[215] a position which Kaiser and Brandscheidt follow uncritically. In doing so, however, both commentators fail to recognise the distinction between Deuteronomic (pre-exilic) and Deuteronomistic (post-exilic), a failure which leads in Kaiser's case to a much later dating of Lamentations (cf the introduction III.1).

Von Rad follows a different line of approach.[216] The later Deuteronomistic redaction of Deuteronomy notwithstanding, he detects the preservation of "ein prächtiges Stück altjahwistischen Sakralrechtes" in Deut 23_{2ff}, although not in its oldest form. He considers the exclusion of the Moabites and the Ammonites from the sanctuary on the basis of data from salvation history to be of a later date. It is reasonable indeed to suggest that the specific provision which banned the Moabites and the Ammonites from Israel's liturgy was a later accentuation of an older, more general rule which denied access to the Yahwistic liturgy to all foreigners.[217] Whether this is true or not, the specific exclusion under discussion already suggests as such that we are dealing with a more specific interpretation of an already existing general rule. The more generous specification with respect to the grandchildren of the Edomites and the Egyptians gaining access to the Yahwistic community in Deut 23_{7-8} provides a similar example. This means that the formulation of Lam 1_{10c} is dependant upon the general rule relating to foreigner access to the liturgy and not the specification of Deut $23_{3,4}$. A further argument can be presented in support of this claim: it is clear that the term גוים in 1_{10bA} must refer to 'infidels' in general and not any particular nation or people (cf Ps 79_1). As is already apparent from 1_{10b}, the poets use גוים in the broadest sense of the word to signify the alien soldiers who found their way into the temple. There is reason to accept, moreover, that Babylonian troops, and not those of Moab or Ammon, had charge of the dismantlement of the sanctuary. The tradition has in fact preserved the name of the chief of Nebuchadnezzar's body-guards, Nebuzaradan, who was charged with the removal of valuables from the temple.[218] As captain of the elite guard (literally: chief [among] the trusted ones) Nebuzaradan held a position of immense trust. After his victory, Nebuchadnezzar needed such a trusted figure to oversee the settlement of his affairs in Judah and Jerusalem. Given the enormous

---

[215] Cf 1983, 21–32.

[216] GvRad, *Das fünfte Buch Mose. Deuteronomium*, ATD 8, Göttingen 1968[2], 104.

[217] Cf Ex 12_{43}, Lev 22_{25}, Ezek $44_{7,9}$.

[218] Cf II Kgs 24_{13-15}.

value of his newly acquired treasures it was only natural that he would be disinclined to hand over their collection and removal to ordinary soldiers who were more concerned with their own purse than with that of the king. Foreign mercenaries such as the Moabites and the Ammonites would have been even less likely candidates for such a job. Nebuzaradan, for his part, will have chosen trustworthy soldiers to carry out his orders, most likely from among his own Babylonian ranks. On the other hand, it is quite imaginable that he fobbed off much of the 'dirty' and (also theologically) more dangerous work of tearing down the temple complex on his foreign (Edomite?) troops.[219]

The violation of the ban on alien troops entering the sanctuary remains the essential focus of this bicolon. The violation itself is more serious than it might appear at first sight. The general ban on access to the sanctuary for גוֹיִם was formulated in order to keep strangers out, even despite their positive intention to worship YHWH, the God of Israel, in his temple. The specifications evident in Deut 23_{3-4} and 23_{7-8} were made precisely in order to remove this more painful side of the ban for foreigners who had long been resident in Israel and had become worshippers of YHWH. The soldiers who invaded the temple precincts, however, were far from well intentioned. On the contrary, their purpose was to plunder and desecrate (cf 2_7). For that reason there was little point in informing these men of the fact that they were violating YHWH's ancient ban and trying to stop them was equally pointless. In such circumstances the poets were aware of only one meaningful addressee for their complaint: the one who had promulgated the ban in the first place, YHWH himself (cf the direct speech and the use of the second person singular). We have translated the perfect צִוִּיתָה in the present. While it is true that the ban was promulgated by YHWH in the past, as far as Israel was concerned it was still an effective in the present. As such, the expression of the tension between the ban and its violation became more acute, thereby allowing the complaint to take on the character of an indictment or accusation. Now that the community was unable to hold off the invasion of the sanctuary by alien troops, the task of upholding the ban had to be turned over to YHWH himself (cf II Sam 6_7). The community, however, were left without response! The focal point of their complaint remains: why have you let them enter your sanctuary?

This passage – together with other passages in Lamentations – is strongly reminiscent of Ezek 7 (cf 7_{21-26} and 24_{21}). This is partly due to their

[219] Cf the explanation of 4_{22aB}.

common use of יוֹם יְהוָה terminology and partly to the secondary sections of Ezek 7 which provide a supplement to the original form of the text from the perspective of events surrounding 587.[220]

11a *All her people groan* כָּל־עַמָּהּ נֶאֱנָחִים
as they search for bread. מְבַקְשִׁים לֶחֶם

For the first time the poets explicitly turn their attention to the relentless theme of famine and hunger. Structural analysis reveals that in their conception of the five songs the famine took a literally central position. Here too – in the very heart of the first song – reference is made to the immense hunger which is afflicting the population. At the same level, in the centre of the secondsong, the desperate hunger of the little children is described in urgent detail (2_{11}). In the third song the same complaint for lack of food resounds in the heart of the first canto.[221] At the same level as Lam I and II the hunger theme is echoed responsively in the fourth song (4_{10}) where the appalling event is related in which the women of Zion resorted in their hunger to eating the corpses of their children, an event already mentioned at the end of Lam II (2_{20}). In this context Kaiser rightly speaks of "eine Umwertung aller Werte" which has brought about this hunger. The sorrow of the poets brought on by the tragic situation of these women is placed on the lips of the devout one of the third song (3_{51}) in the centre of the second canto of song three (see the explanation). In the final song, the poets also devote their attention to the hunger raging in the land (cf $5_{9,10}$). In addition to these central locations the famine theme is also described in 1_{19}, 2_{19}, $4_{3-5,7-9}$ and 5_{6}.

The structural setting of the theme of hunger is an indication of the profound emphasis placed upon it by the poets. Such emphasis cannot be explained away by poetic imagination. It is the result rather of a horrifying reality which had its origins in the long siege of Jerusalem and which continued to worsen before the poets' eyes.[222] It goes without saying that when the decision was made to rebel against Nebuchadnezzar (cf II Kgs 24_{20}) emergency supplies were stockpiled within the city. It is equally clear, however, that the same supplies proved to be hopelessly inadequate, not only because of the extended duration of the siege but also because there were many more mouths to feed in Jerusalem given the fact that hoards of refugees from the countryside had fled to the city in

220 WZimmerli, *Ezechiel 1–24*, BKAT XIII/1, Neukirchen 1979², 172ff.
221 Lam 3_{1-33}; see 3_{16} and the explanation thereof.
222 Cf II Kgs 25_{3}, Jer 32_{24}, 37_{21}, 38_{9}, 52_{6}.

an effort to escape Babylonian hostilities. Such mouths were also in need of nourishment. The same thing happened during Nebuchadnezzar's first siege of Jerusalem under king Jehoiakim, cf Jer 32_7.[223] Jer 35 tells us that at that time even the Rechabites sought refuge in the city.

After one and a half years of the second siege, famine had claimed a multitude of victims. For the survivors the hunger is unbearable. Daily life turns around one single obsession: food. The population are engaged in a continuous[224] search for nourishment and given the form of the verb אנח (*niph'al* participle) the groans brought on by such a burden are equally unrelenting (cf 1_{4bB}). One might wonder whether the worst of the situation was not over once Jerusalem had surrendered. After that point communications were re-opened with the countryside and it was possible once again to import food into the city. The use of participial forms reveal, however, that such was not the case. After the surrender, the famine continued unabated and not without reason. During the period of the Babylonian invasion, the economic life of the countryside was also brought to a standstill. A significant portion of the rural population fled into the city while others took their chances in foreign lands.[225] Since Nebuchadnezzar, according to II Kgs 25_1, advanced against Judah during the winter – Tebeth or the tenth month coinciding with December/January – there would have been no customary farming activity in the following spring and summer. Such activity would have been even less likely in the following year, during the months prior to the fall of Jerusalem (= the 9th of Tammuz [in June/July]). Lam 1_{3a} attests that Judah was forced into labour on behalf of the enemy, to the extent that her own fields lay uncultivated (see the explanation of 1_{3a} together with 4_{9bB}); in other words, Judah's fields produced nothing.[226] The first grain harvests would only have been possible in the following year. Moreover, any food grown during the siege would have been used up by the Babylonian troops who would certainly have ransacked the entire countryside in search of hidden stores of food.[227] As sources of nourishment the fruit and olive trees as well as the vines tended to ripen somewhat later and were less dependant on human labour for their survival. In the autumn of the same year it would have been possible to harvest such fruits, perhaps even in abundance (cf Jer $40_{10,12}$). Up

[223] See AvSelms, *Jeremia deel II*, Nijkerk 1974, 92.
[224] Cf the *qal* participle מְבַקְשִׁים.
[225] Cf Jer 40_{11} and the explanation of Lam 5_6.
[226] See also the exegesis of $5_{5,6}$.
[227] Cf Jer 41_8 and the explanation of Lam 5_9.

to that point in time the famine must have remained extremely severe.

It would be too limiting to view the famine as an expression of exclusively material need. Famine also had a theological significance, given that YHWH and not the land was the true provider of Judah's daily bread.[228] At its core, therefore, lack of bread could be considered his punishment.[229] Famine was thus a sign of rejection by YHWH.

11b *They trade their treasures for food* נָתְנוּ מַחֲמַדֵּיהֶם בְּאֹכֶל
to restore their vigour. לְהָשִׁיב נָפֶשׁ

As is always and everywhere the case there are also people who still have something to trade and as is always and everywhere the case such a situation will give rise to a black market. Jerusalem is no exception. Prices are driven upwards by the enormous scarcity, leading the inhabitants to bring their personal treasures out of hiding, valuables they had managed to conceal from the plundering invaders. Gold and silver change hands for food which is barely edible. At any rate this is how I interpret the term מַחֲמַדֵּיהֶם.[230] On the basis of Hos 9_{16} where the term מַחְמַד signifies 'children' (NRSV: 'the cherished offspring of their womb'), Hillers, followed by Gordis, considers מַחֲמַדֵּיהֶם to refer to the children of Jerusalem who were exchanged as a form of payment for food. Ezekiel's wife is referred to in the same manner in Ezek 24_{16}. Nevertheless, Hillers interpretation cannot be supported here, a fact which also becomes apparent from our structural analysis of the text in question. In the first place there is external parallelism in this canticle with מַחֲמַדֶּיהָ in 1_{10aB} where children are certainly not the point of reference (cf the explanation of this colon). What actually happened to the children emerges from the song-response with the second song, 2_{11}, where it is stated that they wasted away on their mothers' laps. The song-response in 4_{11} exposes their final and dreadful fate. Hillers' interpretation does not hold water from the practical perspective either. Indeed, the Babylonians did not need to buy children. As conquerors they could enslave whoever they wished, even the children (cf $1_{5c,18c}$). For fellow Israelites the use of children as currency can hardly have been an attractive proposition. Children had no real value as such and as extra mouths to feed they would have placed further strain on the food reserves of those who received them in payment. The use of silver and gold would have provided greater purchasing power.

228 Cf Deut 11_{14}, Ps 132_{15}, 147_9.
229 Cf Am 4_6, Jer 5_{17}, Ezek 4_{16f}.
230 Read the *qᵉrē*, cf text critical apparatus of BHS.

That the hungry were very much the worse for their experience is evident from the fact that food and nourishment alone were necessary to restore their vigour. The NBG translates 'to prolong their lives' which implies a certain dimension of vitality. The root שׁוב (*hiph'il*) here means 'to cause to turn back', while the term נֶפֶשׁ is best translated as 'vigour'.[231] The phrase portrays the starving people of Jerusalem as barely conscious individuals who are interested in only one thing: food.

11cA *"Look,* YWHW, *and observe,* רְאֵה יְהוָה וְהַבִּיטָה

For the compellingly urgent prayer of appeal רְאֵה יְהוָה expressed in this colon see also 1_{9c}. The first canto now concludes with an even more urgent prayer on the lips of Lady Jerusalem. This becomes evident from the addition of the imperative וְהַבִּיטָה and the location of the colon in the centre of the first song. Lady Jerusalem implores YHWH not only to 'look' but also to 'observe'. The root נבט might perhaps be considered a synonym of the root ראה; nevertheless, in several texts the visual observation implied by √נבט appears to refer to something more attentive. For this reason, according to Ringgren[232] the root is frequently found in "sinngeladenen Kontexten". Hab 1_{13} provides us with a key to the explanation of the deeply penetrating and profoundly theological character of this prayer. According to Van der Woude[233] this text is of special significance because Habakkuk "was wholly initiated in the cultic traditions of Israel ... and perhaps even belonged to one of the most prominent families in Jerusalem." Other commentators refer to Habakkuk as a cultic prophet pure and simple.[234] This implies that the poets who composed Lamentations belonged to the same spiritual milieu as the prophet in question. Habakkuk knows that YHWH's vision is too pure to 'look' upon evil (ראה) and that he is unable to stand back and 'observe' (נבט) injustice at work. Such an understanding of YHWH is an essential element in the theological thinking of the poets. They call upon him to consider the injustice being done to them by their enemies in the hope that he will bring it to an end.[235] The radical nature of this awareness is made evident in its relationship with the primary theme of the entire book expressed in $3_{17,50}$: if YHWH looks down upon his people then the affliction will come to an

[231] Cf 2_{12} and THAT II 79, 88 (Westermann); TWAT V 544 (Seebass).
[232] In TWAT V 137ff; cf Hab 1_5.
[233] ASvdWoude, *Habakuk-Sefanja*, Nijkerk 1978, 9.
[234] Cf 1983, 184.
[235] Cf 1_{9c}, 1_{11c}, 1_{20-22}, 2_{20-22}, 5_1.

end (see the explanation). Broadly speaking, three distinct arguments can be distinguished in the poets' efforts to move YHWH to bring their affliction to an end: a. description of the dreadful affliction; b. confession of guilt; c. the derision, pride and injustice of the enemy. See part VII of the introduction for more detail on the poets' theology.

11cB *how worthless I have become!"* כִּי הָיִיתִי זוֹלֵלָה

The first canto concludes with Lady Jerusalem's complaint: she has become זוֹלֵלָה. This term is mostly translated with the word 'scorned' or 'disdained', in which case the accent is placed on the value judgement of others. First and foremost, however, we are dealing with the reality of the situation Lady Jerusalem has brought upon herself by her frivolous behaviour. The *qal* form of the root זלל means 'to waste', 'to dissipate'.[236] Lady Jerusalem's complaint is that she has found herself in a condition of worthlessness (part fem), an interpretation which fits well with her loss of honour (desecration of the temple), vitality (hunger) and treasures. Her new situation is one of stark contrast with her former glory and beauty, when she was a source of joy for all the land (Ps 48_2, Lam 2_{15}) and YHWH's splendour radiated auspiciously over the people of Zion (cf 3_{18}, 4_2). The prayer also reveals a theological contrast: can YHWH, who once loved Zion and chose this place as his dwelling (cf the song-response in 4_{11}), now bear to look down and see that his city and his people have been plundered?[237] Nowhere else in the canonical prophetic tradition can one find a complaint such as this.

Canto II (Lam 1_{12-22})

In terms of style, the change of voice throughout this canto is striking, although there is concatenation present between 1_{11c} and 1_{12a} via the imperatives of √נבט and √ראה and the subject. Where the poets themselves had priority in describing Lady Jerusalem's suffering and pain in the first canto, now she herself takes the floor. The female voice implies an intensification of the complaint.[238] The only place in the canto where she

[236] Cf Deut 21_{20}, Prov 23_{21}, 28_7.

[237] Cf the complaint in Ps 80_{13f} and 89_{42}.

[238] BBKaiser, 'Poet as "Female Impersonator": The Image of Daughter Zion as Speaker in Biblical Poems of Suffering', JR 67 (1987), 166.

does not speak is 1_{17}, where – at the very centre of the second canto – the poets themselves cut in with a word to express the canto's thematic content: 'Zion has no one to comfort her'. A balance between this canto and the first is created by this simple shift of speaker. Lady Jerusalem's short exclamatory prayers in the first canto ($1_{9c,11c}$) are thereby brought into relationship with the poets' words in 1_{17}: Zion is afflicted by YHWH and lacking any solace. One should also note the change of name which takes place in this central strophe, a change, in fact, which applies to the entire canto. Lady Jerusalem of canto I fades into the background to be replaced by 'daughter Zion' (cf $1_{4,6}$). With respect to the first canto, this points once again to an intensification of the complaint since the name 'daughter Zion' constitutes the most intimate expression of Jerusalem's relationship with YHWH, with the one who so afflicts her.

Sub-canto I (Lam 1_{12-16})

This sub-canto is a complaint of daughter Zion in its entirety, a complaint which is not addressed to YHWH this time but to 'those who pass by'. In this way she turns to anyone who will give her time, anyone who is willing to pay the slightest heed to her distress. In the opening canticle she emphasises the profundity of her affliction by referring to the incomparable suffering YHWH has brought upon her. He is the one who has made her faint with the fire of his judgement (1_{12-13}). The concluding canticle (1_{14-16}) presents this in a more concrete way. It is a complaint about the enemy, the invader into whose hands YHWH has handed her over, the adversary who is breaking and destroying her children. Lonely daughter Zion is plunged into desperate sadness.

Canticle I (1_{12-13})

Content/theme: *An appeal for pity and compassion*

Literary argumentation:

inclusions:
(13cB) כָּל // (12aA) כָּל
(12b) כְּמַכְאֹבִי אֲשֶׁר עוֹלַל לִי
// (13aA) פָּרַשׂ רֶשֶׁת לְרַגְלַי
(13aA) שָׁלַח־אֵשׁ // (12cB) חֲרוֹן אַפּוֹ

incl/resp:
(12b) כְּמַכְאֹבִי אֲשֶׁר עוֹלַל לִי
// (13bB) הֱשִׁיבַנִי אָחוֹר

responses:
(13cA) נְתָנַנִי שֹׁמֵמָה // (12cA) הוֹגָה יְהוָה
(13cB) כָּל־הַיּוֹם דָּוָה // (12cB) בְּיוֹם חֲרוֹן אַפּוֹ

12aA *You there, all who pass by,* לוֹא אֲלֵיכֶם כָּל־עֹבְרֵי דֶרֶךְ

1_{11c} was characterised as a short exclamatory prayer. This appears to be open to negotiation given that Lady Jerusalem is still speaking, albeit as daughter Zion. Commentators suggest, nevertheless, that there is clearly a new beginning here in that daughter Zion turns to the passers by and no longer to YHWH.

The meaning of the opening phrase לוֹא אֲלֵיכֶם is unclear. The fact that the ל of לוֹא is written in smaller script in some older manuscripts shows that even the Masoretes did not consider the text to be in perfect order. The versions, however, still seem to follow the present Hebrew text, as is also evident from the variants in the LXX tradition.[239] Three main types of solution have been proposed in the history of the exegesis of this phrase: a. textual emendation; b. לוֹא understood as the negative לֹא; c. לוֹא understood as a variant of the exclamatory לוּ, 'O'.

a. The most frequently followed emendation is that of Praetorius[240] who changes both opening words into the imperative לְכוּ, 'come'. Such a solution seems unacceptable. It remains unclear how לוֹא אֲלֵיכֶם could be reduced to a simple לְכוּ. In terms of content, moreover, such an imperative seems to say little. By virtue of what they are, the passers by are 'passing by'. In addition, the imperative לְכוּ usually means 'go' rather than 'come'.[241]

b. The suggestion that לוֹא be understood as a negative leads Albrektson to assign the meaning 'the man in the street' to כָּל־עֹבְרֵי דֶרֶךְ and to paraphrase the whole colon as follows: "(This is) not for (=nothing which concerns) ordinary people, this does not happen to everybody." Brandscheidt follows a similar line. In light of 2_{15aB}, however, such an indirect interpretation of the phrase כָּל־עֹבְרֵי דֶרֶךְ is unacceptable.

A different exegetical approach, exemplified by the Talmud (Sanhedrin 104b), Midrash Echa Rabba, Soncino Bible and Zlotowitz, discerns a wish in this colon that the passers by will not themselves be touched by such horrendous suffering. If this were the case, however, the first colon would be brought to stand in complete isolation and this would be the only place in the entire book where daughter Zion/Lady Jerusalem showed any concern for others. In terms of her personal concerns there is only one thing that matters to Lady Jerusalem, one thing she cares about the

239 Cf textcritical apparatus BHS.

240 FPraetorius, 'Threni I,12,14; II,6,13', ZAW 15 (1895), 143.

241 Cf Gen 41_{55}, 42_{19}, Ex $5_{4,11}$ etcetera.

most: the sorrow that afflicts her children (cf, however, the explanation of 4_{11}). Such specific orientation towards Jerusalem's sorrow appears more warranted in Gottwald's exegesis. While maintaining the idea of negation he presents 1_{12a} as an anticipative question: "Is it nothing to you, all you who pass by?" (cf also NRSV which points out in a footnote that the Hebrew is uncertain).

c. Although the aforementioned explanation provides, for the most part, a reasonable rendering the intention of the text, our preference remains with a third option in which לוא is understood as a variant of לו.[242] Since לא in an imperative context usually carries a nuance of urgency (cf Gen 23_{13}) and given that אֲלֵיכֶם clearly suggests address, both words together serve to attract attention and to introduce the imperatives of the following colon.

12aB *observe and see:* הַבִּיטוּ וּרְאוּ

A clear concatenation exists between this and the previous canto, via both the repetition of the imperatives and the fact that the same speaker has the floor; only the addressee has changed. Where daughter Zion first turned to YHWH now she turns to whoever is passing by. She continues to speak for the remainder of the first sub-canto of canto II (1_{12-16}). This fact is not without significance. The first canto closed without Lady Jerusalem receiving an answer from YHWH to her prayers of 1_{9c} and 1_{11c}. Lam II further elucidates this in the form of a song-response: her prophets no longer receive visions of YHWH ($1_{9c,[11c]}$ // 2_{9c}; see the explanation of this bicolon as well as that of $3_{8,44}$). She is still alone![243] As we can see from the repeated complaint that there is no one to comfort her, however, it is evident that without help she cannot endure the enormity of her affliction and sorrow. Since YHWH has not answered her urgent plea she turns in despair to whoever will listen to her, to the passers-by on the street. The fact that the same verbs are used in the imperatives here signifies that for daughter Zion it is not simply a question of taking a neutral glance at her distress. As she had hoped that YHWH would look upon her as a helper[244] so her hope continues that when the passers-by see her affliction they will be moved to assist her. Attracting attention in such a way is reminiscent of Ps 31, the complaints and expressions of trust in verses 10–19 of which strongly remind one of those found in Lamentations as a whole.[245] The

[242] Cf HAL 495f.
[243] Cf the canto-response with יָשְׁבָה בָדָד 1_{1aA}!
[244] Cf $1_{9c,11c,20a}$, $3_{36,50}$, 5_1.

complaint in Ps 31_{11}: "those who see me in the street flee from me" offers some explanation of daughter Zion's invitation in Lam 1_{12aB}. Her suffering is so horrible that those who pass by prefer to hurry on their way and not to look. Given that people on the road are more likely to stop and stare at the sensational, this in itself is already an indication of how ghastly her condition must be (1_{1aA}). The phrase עֹבְרֵי דֶרֶךְ means random passers-by, people who have to pass Jerusalem on their journey elsewhere,[246] which implies a certain lack of inhibition in the response they might give to daughter Zion's appeal.

12bA *is there any sorrow like my sorrow,* אִם־יֵשׁ מַכְאוֹב כְּמַכְאֹבִי

Daughter Zion urgently demands that those who pass by not only look at her sorrow but compare it with the sorrow of others. Of course, she is not asking for an objective comparison with a neutral judgement of her situation, her question, rather, is a rhetorical one. She wants to convince the passer-by that they have never seen anything so terrible. She endeavours to involve them emotionally in her cruel fate. She describes her suffering with the noun מַכְאוֹב from the root כאב 'to have sorrow' (cf HAL 433). The use of this verb raises the question whether only the subjective experience of grief is intended or whether we are dealing more with grief that can be observed by others, objective grief.[247] In Lam 1_{12}, however, this turns out to be a false dilemma.[248] Human beings tend to turn away from sorrow but daughter Zion makes no distinctions and demands with some emphasis (cf the imperatives) that her grief be observed. She does, however, allude to and illustrate her grief verbally, speaking of the fire of YHWH which is poured out upon her (cf 2_{4c}) and her imprisonment and faint condition (1_{13}). For outsiders these things can be observed in the fact that fire has destroyed the city, the condition of the inhabitants is feeble, and the enemy is victorious. Much of this is made more concrete in the form of song-responses. $2_{11,12}$, for example, with its mention of children dying of starvation – daughter Zion's greatest sorrow – is most insistent. The other song-responses are as follows: oppression by the enemy (3_{34-36}), the destruction of Jerusalem ($4_{11,12}$), the rape of the women of Zion, the hanging of her princes and the humiliation of her elders ($5_{11,12}$). The effect of all this actual affliction, however, is mirrored in the face of the comfort-

245 Cf 1983, 241f.

246 Cf Ps 80_{13}, 89_{42}, Prov 9_{15}.

247 JScharbert, *Der Schmerz im Alten Testament*, Bonn 1955, 41–47, 55–58.

248 Cf TWAT IV 8f (Mosis).

less, mourning Lady who sits alone and calls out helplessly to those who pass by (cf 1_{1a}). Her efforts are in vein. There is no mention either here or elsewhere in the book that anyone came to her assistance. The passers-by reach the conclusion, nevertheless, that daughter Zion has been afflicted with incomparably great suffering.[249]

12bB *which is being brought upon me,* אֲשֶׁר עוֹלַל לִי

In this colon and in the remainder of this and the following canticle, daughter Zion turns her attention to a comprehensive description of one aspect of her distress, one which those who pass by would never be able to observe objectively: her spiritual affliction. Her suffering is not accidental. The sorrow that she feels has been deliberately forced upon her. The question arises as to the source of her grief. עוֹלַל is the *po'al* pf of the root עלל I and has a passive meaning here.[250] Once again we understand the perfect to have a present nuance: the distress daughter Zion is experiencing had its origins in the past but it continues undiminished in the present. Together with the suffixed preposition, the phrase can be rendered 'is being brought upon me'. Other dimensions of the root עלל I, however, are not given expression by this translation. In the *qal*, the root means 'to act'/'to do'.[251] The contexts in which the root is used (e.g. for the gleaning of corn fields and vineyards) make it clear that a quite deliberate and attentive action is involved here. In the figurative sense it is also used for the 'gleaning' of an enemy in retreat.[252]

A further dimension implied by the root has to do with bringing evil upon another.[253] The associations with harvest and gleaning are also represented in the present use of the verb. This is clear from the fact that the latter part of the sub-canto speaks of YHWH's judgement using the image of the harvest (cf 1_{15}) and that of a retreating enemy.[254] Daughter Zion's affliction is not accidental, rather it is quite calculated and precise. With great reserve she avoids any direct identification of the one who is treating her this way.

---

249 Cf the response at the canticle level with the second song in 2_{13} and its existing response with 2_{15} within sub-canto 2_{11-17}.

250 Cf GES-K § 67*l*.

251 Cf HAL 789.

252 Cf Lev 19_{10}, Deut 24_{21}, Judg 20_{45} and especially Jer 6_9! Cf also TWAT VI 153 (Roth).

253 Cf, for example, Lam 3_{51}, Ex 10_2, Num 22_{29}, Isa 3_{12}.

254 Cf $3_{47,52}$, 4_{18f}.

12c *with which* YHWH *deeply afflicts me* אֲשֶׁר הוֹגָה יְהוָה
on the day of his fierce anger? בְּיוֹם חֲרוֹן אַפּוֹ

The truth comes out, however, in a clause introduced once again by the relative pronoun: it is YHWH himself who is so deeply afflicting daughter Zion.[255] The *hiph'il* of the verb יגה means 'to be grieved at a profoundly psychological level', a fact which is reflected in the resigned demeanour of those involved (cf 1_{4cA}). In songs of the CI genre people tend to be plunged into sorrow and distress by YHWH's aloofness (Ps 13_3, 31_{11}).

Here the situation is even worse: the source of daughter Zion's pain is not YHWH's absence but his fierce anger. What daughter Zion is being forced to undergo is experienced as a time of YHWH's burning anger, חֲרוֹן אַפּוֹ. אַף literally means 'nose' but in a derived sense it can also mean 'anger' since one's breathing becomes more intense when one is angry or 'snorting with rage'.[256] Such an understanding of 'anger' accentuates its physical and visible aspects.[257]

The adjective חָרוֹן is derived from the verb חרה I 'to be hot', 'burning' and is only used in the figurative sense to designate the destructive power of God's anger. It is understandable that destruction by fire (see אֵשׁ in the following colon) would be easily combined with the notion of God's fierce and burning anger.[258]

Excursus ' YHWH's anger'

According to Stoll, "Die Aussagen über den Zorn Gottes und sein Gericht fallen uns heute nicht leicht. Wir habben uns daran gewöhnt, von der Liebe Gottes auszugehen."[259] A good assessment from a hermeneutical perspective. Efforts have been made to get rid of the less palatable aspects of the metaphor of God's anger.[260] Among Old Testament scholars, Vriezen, for example, stresses the correlation between God's love and his anger and points out that the prophets who focus most on God's love tend also to be most pointed in their description of his rage. Their preaching of such divine anger has its roots in an awareness of the wounded love of YHWH. His deepest concern is the life of the sinner and his actions are characterised by the will to save.

---

[255] The 1 sg suffix read by the LXX is an elucidation of the present Hebrew text.
[256] Cf THAT I 223 (Sauer).
[257] Cf THAT I 582 (Sauer).
[258] Cf TWAT III 185f (Sauer).
[259] CDStoll, *Die Klagelieder*, Wuppertal 1986, 80.
[260] Cf, for example, KBarth, KD II/I 308.

The unintended ambivalence in Vriezen's interpretation is evident in his explanation of the flood narrative: "...in the bible, the will to save holds sway; prior to executing His judgement, Yahweh decides to save Noah and thereby preserve humanity. In all of this, God's actions are not only driven by anger, they are filled with remorse for the fact that He made human kind (Gen 6_6). Even at this dreadful moment in world history, God's love and desire to save are apparent." [261] Nevertheless, anger loses out to love and one is forced to forget the image of people drowned in the flood.

When we stay close to the texts, however, our songs of Lamentation give no occasion whatsoever for theological 'Umwertung'. Where God's anger is mentioned the reference is without exception to the destructive, devastating and deadly effects of that anger.[262] The reality of divine anger is made visible in precisely this devastation and the victims who accompany it. The poets are not interested in the other side of God's anger, their deepest concern is whether his anger has not gone too far and whether they can survive it (cf 5_{22}).

The metaphor of God's anger must be understood, therefore, as analogous to human anger. Given that the divine anger is ultimately deadly, however, there are limits to the extent to which the analogy can be drawn. This is also the reason why the restraint and short duration of God's anger is often spoken of. Nevertheless, whatever the duration or restraint involved, it is always a grievous experience for humanity. God's anger is almost always brought about by human misconduct with respect to his essence or his commandments, although one cannot reduce his anger to this, since God as creator does not have to justify himself before his creation.[263] Here in Lamentations there is also clear admission that Israel has given YHWH occasion to be angry.[264]

The location par excellence for talk of God's anger is in the description of the 'day of YHWH' (cf excursus after 1_{2a}; cf also the occurrences of the expression in Isa $13_{9,13}$, Nah 1_6, Jer $4_{8,26}$, 25_{37f} together with Zeph 2_2). Zephaniah provides us with the most comprehensive description of the 'day of YHWH' (cf the *'dies irae, dies illa'*), which is of some importance given that the fulfilment of his prophecy – as we are frequently reminded in Lamentations – is taking place in Judah in these very days.

[261] Cf ThCVriezen, *Hoofdlijnen der theologie van het Oude Testament*, Wageningen 1966[3], 331ff.

[262] Cf, for example, $2_{1,3a,6c,21c,22}$, $3_{43,66}$, 4_{11}.

[263] Cf Sauer, THAT I 223f.

[264] Cf the explanation of $1_{5,8,18}$, 2_{14}, 3_{42}, 4_{13}, 5_{16}.

In spite of hermeneutic endeavours to soften the blow, we have to take God's anger and its affects seriously at this point in Lamentations and not try to contradict the texts by giving them a different complexion. Although anger, for God, is an alien reality, it does not have anything capricious or mercurial about it in the OT; it is a very well defined expression of God's heart. Only when it pleases him, does it make way for the expression of his love (cf Isa 54_{6-8}).

13aA *From on high he sent fire* מִמָּרוֹם שָׁלַח־אֵשׁ

Here and in the following bicola daughter Zion herself puts her suffering into words. Using a variety of images she describes the grief she has been forced to endure at YHWH's hands, grief he continues to inflict. With exceptional expertise, the poets choose her words in such a way that they not only refer to the actual events which surrounded the fall of Jerusalem but are also appropriate to the personification which they employ as a means to describe the intimate suffering of daughter Zion. The connection with the previous strophe is made clear via the concatenation between חֲרוֹן 'burning'/'fierce' (1_{12cB}) and אֵשׁ 'fire' (1_{13aA}).

'From on high he sent fire'. מָרוֹם literally means 'high place' and is synonymous here with 'heaven' as the place of God's dwelling.[265] Several exegetes (e.g. Kraus and Stoll) find this phrase reminiscent of the destruction of Sodom and Gomorra (cf Gen 19_{24f}). Van Selms also sees the connection but considers it unintentional in light of the personification. He is apparently unaware of the fact, however, that the literal and figurative meanings merge into one another at this point. Another allusion to Sodom can be found in 4_6, where Zion's lot is portrayed as even worse than the downfall of the city of the plain, a fact which fits strikingly well with the incomparable grief mentioned in 1_{12b}. The occurrence of the standard term for the punishment of Sodom, namely the terminus technicus √הפך (cf $4_{1bA,6bA}$), also points towards a comparison with this city, the term in question being used in Lamentations in the context of the destruction of Jerusalem (cf 1_{20b}). Slightly more deep-lying evidence can be found in the song-responses. The punishment of Sodom is the classical example of the punishment meted out for unforgivable sins. In 2_{14} and 4_{13} (cf 3_{39}), the extraordinary downfall of Jerusalem (see 2_{13}) is blamed on the sin of false prophets[266] whom Jeremiah characterised precisely as

[265] Cf HAL 598f and CHoutman, *De hemel in het Oude Testament*, Franeker 1974, 235–238.

[266] Cf 1983, 156–177.

inhabitants of Sodom and Gomorra.[267] Gen 19_{24} speaks of God's judgement falling on Sodom like a rain of fire from heaven, a reference often made in prophetic announcements of judgement. It is clear from the word combinations שָׁלַח־אֵשׁ (Lam 1_{13a}) and וַיַּצֶּת־אֵשׁ (Lam 4_{11bA}), employed with precise reference to the downfall of ungodly cities/Jerusalem, that the fire of YHWH's judgement certainly had a role to play in the poets' train of thought.[268] The strictly theological character of the descriptions is always striking, however. Daughter Zion does not ascribe her ruined state to the enemy but to YHWH himself. The Babylonians did not gain victory under their own steam. They did nothing more than slay a lion that had already been beaten (Midrash Eicha Rabba). YHWH is thus the real 'Executioner'. From the theological perspective, the advantage of such an interpretation is that there can be no talk of YHWH himself being humiliated (via the destruction of his sanctuary by the Babylonians). At the same time, all the prayers in Lamentations are rooted in this awareness: if YHWH is the only source of daughter Zion's affliction, then YHWH must be the only source of salvation therefrom.

13aB *he made it go down into my bones.* בְּעַצְמֹתַי וַיּוֹרִדֶנָּה

In terms of translation, the phrase בְּעַצְמֹתַי וַיִּרְדֶּנָּה at the end of this bicolon is somewhat problematic. The Masoretes read בְּעַצְמֹתַי with the first colon: 'from on high he sent fire into my bones'. This reading would seem to favour the ו-consecutive with יִרְדֶּנָּה, thus making וַיִּרְדֶּנָּה function as the (somewhat imbalanced) second half of the bicolon. The Masoretes derive the term from the root רדה I, *qal* impf 3m sg with sf 3f sg, the suffix referring to עַצְמֹתַי understood as a collective. Given the meaning of the root רדה I, 'to trample' or 'to rule over', אֵשׁ is taken to be the subject: 'it (fire) rules over her' (= invades my bones). Gordis, for example, attempts a translation using 'to trample' but this does not work well with אֵשׁ. We are left with problems with respect to the imbalance in the bicolon and the gender of אֵשׁ (fem). In line with LXX, the Peshitta and several modern exegetes we prefer to derive וַיִּרְדֶּנָּה from the verb ירד (*hiph'il* impf 3m sg energicus), assuming an interchange between the ו and the י.[269] We consider וַיּוֹרִדֶנָּה to be the original form.[270] Arguments in favour of such a

[267] Cf Jer 23_{14} together with Isa 1_{10} and TWAT V 760f (Mulder).

[268] Cf Am $1_{4,7,10,12,14}$, $2_{2,5}$, Hos 8_{14}, Jer 17_{27}, 49_{27}; TWAT I 245f (Stolz) and TWAT I 459ff (Hamp).

[269] Cf EWürthwein, *Der Text des Alten Testaments*, Stuttgart 1973[4], 104 and ETov, *Textual Criticism of the Hebrew Bible*, Assen/Maastricht, 1992, 245.

proposal include: a. the occurrence of the same verb in 1_{16aB} (response at the canticle level); b. a more balanced bicolon; c. the combination of אֵשׁ and ירד in II Kgs $1_{10,12,14}$. In terms of meaning, however, little difference is involved between both derivations (√ירד or √רדה I), unless one is determined to render רדה with 'to trample' on the basis of Joel 4_{13}.

We are clearly not dealing with the destruction of the bones but with a sort of feverish condition brought on by the fiery rain from on high. The poetic personification is dominant at this point: the burning fire of YHWH's judgement has weakened daughter Zion through and through.[271] There is clearly an inclusion in this strophe between 1_{13a} and 1_{13c} (cf the parallelism in the inclusion between מֵעַי חֳמַרְמָרוּ [20aB: 'my stomach churns'] and וְלִבִּי דַוָּי [22cB: 'my heart is deathly sick'] in the final canticle). The term 'bones' is a reference to the hardest and most interior part of the human body,[272] but even this is affected by the fever. 4_{11b}, in which the literal destruction of Zion is in the foreground, is clearly parallel to this bicolon.

13b *He spread a net for my feet,* פָּרַשׂ רֶשֶׁת לְרַגְלַי
he turned me back. הֱשִׁיבַנִי אָחוֹר

Danger for daughter Zion did not only come from on high but also from below, as the poets make clear with their use of hunting imagery. It is not a question here of the pursuit of fish or birds but of much larger animals for which the hunting nets were used in a variety of ways. One option was to throw the net over one's prey which would then get entangled and trapped.[273] Another option was to stretch the net under camouflage over a pit, in which case one's prey would either get trapped in the net or fall into the pit.[274] The hunting scene provided a rich source of metaphors for people in relation to one another and in relation to their own falls and entanglements.[275]

The image in 1_{13bA} suggests a net buried in the sand along a well trodden path. Suddenly one finds oneself trapped in its mesh, one falls to the

[270] Cf Rudolph, Weiser, Hillers and Brandscheidt.

[271] See דְּוָה in 13cB and cf Job 30_{30}, Ps 102_4 and Jer 20_9.

[272] ThStruys, *Ziekte en genezing in het Oude Testament*, Kampen 1968, 167f.

[273] Cf Ezek 12_{13}, 17_{20} and 19_{18}.

[274] Cf Ps 35_7, 57_7, $140_{9,10}$, Prov 29_5.

[275] Cf Ps 7_{16}, 9_{16}, 19_9, 35_{7f}, 57_7, 140_6; cf also AvDeursen, *De achtergrond van de Psalmen*, undated, 128–135, OKeel, *Die Welt der altorientalischen Bildsymbolik und das Alte Testament*, Zürich-Einsiedeln-Köln-Neukirchen-Vluyn 1977², 78–85 and MCAKorpel, *A Rift in the Clouds*, Münster 1990, 453–458.

ground and the edges of the net are pulled tighter. Thus YHWH has taken daughter Zion by surprise and imprisoned her. She never thought for one moment that such a thing could happen, that He, the one who protected her, could turn out to be the hunter. Once again we are confronted with a contrast. There was once a time when the people of Jerusalem praised YHWH and confessed him as a God who set free from the net (Ps 25_{15}, 31_5).

The phrase הֱשִׁיבַנִי אָחוֹר, literally: 'he makes me turn around, turn back', clearly points to a connection with the first bicolon of this strophe. In order to escape the fire from on high daughter Zion takes flight, but she then finds herself trapped in a net hidden on her path with which YHWH drags her back. Thus she must face the inevitability of her fate. In terms of imagery and theme, the beginning of the second canto of Lam I is strongly reminiscent of the beginning of the first canto of the third song (cf 3_{1-6}).

13cA *He is ruining my life,* נְתָנַנִי שֹׁמֵמָה

נְתָנַנִי שֹׁמֵמָה literally means: 'he is giving me ruin'. The basic meaning of the verb שׁמם can be defined as 'to be ruined'/'to be cut off from life'. Depending on the context, either the objective or the subjective aspect can predominate.[276] Of course, the objective element is present to some extent. שֹׁמֵמָה has its 'Sitz im Leben' in the curses related to the violation of covenant regulations[277] and in the description of prophetic announcements of doom.[278] In light of the poetic personification and the internal parallelism in this bicolon (cf the parallel with sickness), however, the emphasis in the present bicolon should be placed on daughter Zion's subjective experience of her ruin: she feels herself crushed, abandoned, cut off from life, deeply sick (as she says herself in the final colon).

13cB *(making me) so faint all day long.* כָּל־הַיּוֹם דָּוָה

נְתָנַנִי also governs the second colon. YHWH 'gives' her sickness and she feels faint (cf the prophetic prediction in Mic 6_{13} in which sickness is also mentioned in parallel with ruin) The noun דוה is carefully chosen. דוה differs from the usual noun referring to sickness (cf √חלה in Mic 6_{13}) in that it is related to the sickness and nausea associated with menstruation and goes together with affliction and dejection.[279] In this sense the term links

---

276 Cf TWAT II 971ff (Stolz).

277 Cf Lev 26_{33} (positive in Ex 23_{29}).

278 Cf Isa 1_7, 6_{11}, 17_9, Mic 6_{13}.

279 Cf ThStruys, 391f; HAL 207 sv דוה/דוי and TWAT II 963 (Seybold).

up closely with $1_{8,9}$: the נִידָה and טֻמְאָתָהּ of daughter Zion. The aforementioned notions of affliction and dejection also fit well in the context of the songs. The somewhat intensive translation 'so faint' is supported by both שֹׁמֵמָה in the first colon and the parallel with 'my bones' in 1_{13aB} (cf the explanation of 1_{22cB}).

Canticle II (1_{14-16})

Content/theme: *Adonai has handed her over into the power of her enemies*

Literary argumentation:

inclusions:	פְּשָׁעַי (14aA) // בָנַי שׁוֹמֵמִים (16cA)
	הִכְשִׁיל כֹּחִי (14bB) \\ מֵשִׁיב נַפְשִׁי (16bB)
	נְתָנַנִי אֲדֹנָי בִּידֵי (14cA) // עַל־אֵלֶּה אֲנִי בוֹכִיָּה (16aA)
	אֲדֹנָי (15aB) // אֲדֹנָי (15cA)
responses:	אֲדֹנָי (14cA) // אֲדֹנָי (15cA)
	עַל־צַוָּארִי (14bA) // עָלַי (15bA)
	לֹא־אוּכַל קוּם (14cB) // כִּי גָבַר אוֹיֵב (16cB)
concatenation:	via 1 sg suffixes

14aA *He fastened the yoke upon me with my transgressions,* נִשְׂקַד עֹל פְּשָׁעַי

The meaning of נִשְׂקַד is unknown and the verb שׂקד is only to be found here in the OT. Ancient translators and modern exegetes have emended the text in order to arrive at a more or less acceptable proposed meaning. שׂ is frequently changed to שׁ.[280] The *qal* of the root שׁקד means 'to keep watch over', which leads some commentators (e.g. Löhr and Wisemann) to interpret the עֹל as a preposition: 'He (YHWH) keeps watch over my sin'. Others take פְּשָׁעַי as the subject: 'my sin keeps watch over me'.[281] Both interpretations tend to leave the second colon (1_{14aB}) unclear. A third approach suggests we read נִשְׂקָה instead of נִשְׂקַד based on the root קשה I (*niph'al* participle, 'to be oppressed'; cf Isa 8_{21}) with the translation: "heavy was the yoke of my transgression".[282] Apart from the grammatical objections to this translation (cf HAL 1512) it appears to be too much of an anticipation of the content of the following bicolon.

280 Cf LXX and the Peshitta as well as KBL 929 and HAL 1258.
281 Cf text critical apparatus BHS.
282 Cf Rudolph, Brandscheidt, Boecker, Gross among others.

There are exegetes who believe – and not without reason – that it is not always justifiable to simply emend a *hapax legomenon.* Although the meaning may be unclear, the word in question need not necessarily have been poorly or faultily transmitted. Ewald, Aalders (unintentionally) and Albrektson, for example, assume that the verb שׂקד is a terminus technicus for the fastening on of a yoke, in which case we would be dealing here with a *niph'al* perfect: 'He fastened the yoke upon me with my transgressions', the translation we have chosen to follow. In this instance we are dealing with an action executed by YHWH, the consequences of which continue into the present. Although the sins in question were committed in the past, their consequences remain fully visible in the present. For the meaning of פֶּשַׁע see the explanation of $1_{5b,8a}$). The image of the yoke of transgressions which daughter Zion is being forced to bear reveals that the authors not only intend to include sins committed long in the past but also the future consequences of such sins. In this sense פֶּשַׁע is not detached from its possible effect. It also becomes clear that YHWH is the one who actualises the effects of sin; indeed, he is the one who binds the yoke of transgression upon daughter Zion (cf בְּיָדוֹ in 1_{14aB}).

The metaphor shows that the poets did not see sin and its effects as two unrelated entities. In fact, they assume a close relationship between the two: sin carries its effects within it and the former brings about the latter. Koch proposes a rather mechanical relationship between the two and speaks of a 'Schicksalwirkende Tatsphäre' or a 'Tun-Ergehen Zusammenhang'.[283] Nevertheless – and although this is not always directly stated – it remains a profound reality for Israel that YHWH is always the one who either executes or (in forgiveness) does not execute punishment. The duality of sin and its effect makes it possible to react inversely: where devastation is understood as the punishment for sin, then those who are confronted with devastation must have sinned, a line of thought against which the book of Job constitutes a strong protest (cf also Joh 9_{22ff}). Sin in Lamentations is indeed seen as the cause of the terrible lot being endured by Judah. Apart from the transgressions of the leaders (2_{14}; 4_{13}), it is not completely clear to the poets which sins of the people have brought about this calamity.[284] Where they do know the sins in question they are unwilling, for hermeneutical reasons, to explain them in any detail.[285]

[283] Cf KKoch, 'Gibt es ein Vergeltungsdogma im AT', ZThK 52 (1955), 1–42 and KKoch (ed), *Um das Prinzip der Vergeltung in Religion und Recht des Alten Testaments*, WDF CXXV, Darmstadt 1972, 130–181.

[284] Cf the explanation of 3_{40} as well as 1983, 268–80.

14aB *by his hand they were fastened together;* בְּיָדוֹ יִשְׂתָּרְגוּ

This colon clearly does not imply that the yoke itself was made out of daughter Zion's sins, which is the impression one gets from the translation provided by the NBG: 'woven together by his hand'. A yoke was usually carved from wood and placed on a farm animal as means for pulling a plough, for example (cf Deut 22_{10}, I Kgs 19_{19f}, Am 6_2), or a threshing sledge.[286] In this way daughter Zion is presented like a beast of burden, forced by the yoke to bear the burden of her transgressions. The fact that daughter Zion's sins are numerous (cf 1_{5bB}: רֹב־פְּשָׁעֶיהָ) makes the meaning of the phrase בְּיָדוֹ יִשְׂתָּרְגוּ somewhat clearer. A multitude of detached and different sins is not suited to being dragged along by means of a yoke. For this reason, YHWH has bound together all the sins which have remained unpunished into one compact whole (cf HAL 1261).The verb שׂרג is to be found in only one other place in the OT, namely Job 40_{12} (MT 40_{17}), where it implies the knotting of muscles. The consequences of many sins now press down on daughter Zion's neck/shoulders all at once.

14bA *they weigh on my neck.* עָלוּ עַל־צַוָּארִי

Those exegetes who change the word 'yoke' in the first bicolon into the preposition עַל are forced to introduce the same 'yoke' in the first part of the second bicolon.[287] Emendation, however, is unnecessary. The verb עלה I can be used for placing a yoke on an animal's neck (cf Num 19_2). In our context, however, the 'yoke' is not the subject, rather the plural עָלוּ (*qal* pf 3m pl) suggests that the subject consists of the multiple sins of daughter Zion. She feels the full weight of her transgressions via the yoke upon her neck, a pain she cannot endure. The metaphor of the yoke already points in this direction given that עֹל is always used for a yoke intended for beasts of burden. The metaphor itself, therefore, points to a burden too great for human beings to bear.[288]

14bB *He makes my strength founder.* הִכְשִׁיל כֹּחִי

The burden of daughter Zion's sins is beyond her strength. Several exegetes take the 'yoke' from the first colon as the subject of הִכְשִׁיל and

[285] Cf on this topic the hermeneutical epilogue of Lam III.

[286] Cf Deut 25_4; cf also Dalman, *Arbeit und Sitte*, 1932 II, 99–105, together with the images in BHH 869 and BRL[2] 255.

[287] Cf Robinson in the text critical apparatus BHS.

[288] Cf I Kgs $12_{4,9-11,14}$, Isa 9_3, 47_6, Jer 27, 28, 30_8.

translate: 'it makes my strength founder'[289] but this does not fit the poetic image. It is not the yoke which makes the pulling so burdensome nor is any animal with a yoke likely to haul a heavy plough or threshing sledge on its own initiative. The latter only happens after some encouragement from the drover and such encouragement is not always equally good-natured (Judg 3_{31}, Acts 26_{14}). The subject, therefore, is YHWH who has fastened the yoke with her sins attached on daughter Zion's shoulders and now lets her haul her burden (cf 3_3). Such effort exhausts her and she becomes tired and listless (cf Isa 40_{29ff}). She loses the power of her muscles and founders.[290] As in Ps 31_{11} the poets of Lamentations use their words sparingly. The phraseology here is reminiscent of the CI genre in the Psalms.[291]

14c *Adonai has handed me over,* נְתָנַנִי אֲדֹנָי בִּידֵי
and I cannot endure. וְלֹא־אוּכַל קוּם

The same thought process continues in this bicolon. Broadly speaking, the expression נתן ביד ('to give into the hand') means 'hand over' (cf II Chron 25_{20}) which would leave us with the translation: 'The Lord has handed me over, I cannot endure'. The construct form בִּידֵי, however, suggests a closer relationship between the two cola, usually rendered in translation as 'into the hands of them, before whom I cannot endure' (cf NBG, where ידי is the *nomen regens* and the rest of the clause functions as *nomen rectum*). The grammatical possibility of such a translation is referred to in GES-K § 130*d*. In terms of content, however, this interpretation appears to give greater emphasis to the power of the enemy which is somewhat out of place given that the canticle as a whole focuses exclusively on Adonai as the origin of daughter Zion's downfall. For this reason we follow the Syriac ביד[292] without the final י which we read as a ו. Confusion and interchange between the two letters in not uncommon.[293] We read the ו as part of the second colon and translate נתן ביד with 'to hand over' as in the aforementioned II Chron 25_{20}. Adonai has not forgiven daughter Zion's sins (cf the song-response 3_{42}). He has withdrawn his protective right hand (cf 2_{3b}) and handed his people over so that the enemy has free reign. Furthermore, the supplementary parallelism between 'floundering'

[289] Cf Keil, Meek and Rudolph.
[290] Cf TWAT IV 370 (Barth).
[291] Cf Barth, ibid, 371f.
[292] Robinson wrongly gives only ידי in BHK; cf Albrektson.
[293] Cf EWürthwein, *Der Text des Alten Testaments*, Stuttgart 1973[4], 104.

in 1_{14bB} // 'and I cannot endure' in 1_{14c} is thereby respected. Daughter Zion has become so exhausted from dragging the burden of her sins that she no longer has energy enough to resist her enemies. Her floundering becomes her fall (cf also the explanation of 5_{14} [song-response]).

With respect to the divine name it is rather striking that the term אֲדֹנָי is used here for the first time in place of יְהוָה. The replacement in numerous manuscripts of Adonai with YHWH is doubtlessly due to textual adaptation. The more difficult אֲדֹנָי, however, ought to be maintained. The use of the term is certainly not a merely stylistic variation as Aalders and Hillers, for example, would have it. Formal justification for my own position came to light in the structural analysis of the songs in which it became clear that the poets use one divine name per canticle or at least allow one divine name to dominate.[294] In examining the canticles of the first song we noted that the divine name אֲדֹנָי only appears in the sixth canticle. In terms of content there is a certain distinction between this and the parts which employ the name יְהוָה. The poets use the tetragrammaton preponderantly in prayers and expressions of trust.[295] In a survey of the other places where the term יְהוָה is to be found we are left either with the context of his oppression in $1_{5,9}$ (with its roots in his aloofness; cf 1_{4c} together with $2_{3b,9c}$) or it is said in general terms that he executes judgement.[296] If we compare this with the verbal context in which the name אֲדֹנָי occurs then we tend to find somewhat 'harsher' terminology: 'He hands over...', 1_{14c}; 'He piles up the mighty (like sheaves)...', 1_{15a}; 'He treads as in a wine-press...', 1_{15}; 'He engulfs with clouds of anger...', 2_1; 'He destroys...', 2_2; 'He is like an enemy...', 2_5; 'He casts out...', 2_7, 3_{31}. In expressions of trust the name אֲדֹנָי is considerably less frequent than יְהוָה, although that is to be understood (cf 3_{58}). It would appear, therefore, that in contexts where the term אֲדֹנָי is used, God's authority and (superior) power are allowed to dominate. Such an interpretation is in full agreement with the basic meaning of the term which in profane terms means 'Lord'/'Commander of inferiors', a meaning which is also maintained in theological usage.[297] The use of אֲדֹנָי in the present context seems quite fitting, given the metaphor of applying the 'yoke' together with the harsh images which follow. Daughter Zion is confronted with Adonai's distance, harshness and superiority and nothing of the closeness, solidarity and pro-

[294] Cf 1988, 318–320.

[295] Cf $1_{9,11,20}$, 2_{20}, $3_{22,24-26,50,55,59,61,64,66}$, $5_{19,21}$.

[296] Cf 1_{17}, $2_{6,17,22}$, $4_{11,16}$.

[297] Cf THAT I 32ff (Jenni) and TWAT I 62–78 (Eißfeldt).

tection she associates with YHWH her husband (cf the exegesis of 1_{1b} and 5_{20f}).

15a *Piled up (like sheaves) are all my mighty ones* סִלָּה כָל־אַבִּירַי
by Adonai in my midst. אֲדֹנָי בְּקִרְבִּי

The phrase 'all my might ones' refers to daughter Zion's powerful leaders, the dignitaries of the city. In the parallel strophes of the other songs they, together with the fate that has befallen them, are further specified. The dignitaries in question are the priests and prophets, elders and princes.[298] In order to describe what has happened to them the poets use the verb סלה I with אֲדֹנָי as subject and אַבִּירַי as object. The verb סלה I is only to be found in one other place in the OT, namely in Ps 119_{118} (*qal*) where it means 'to despise' or 'to scorn' (cf KBL 658 and HAL 714). The *pi'el* form used in our text is most often tentatively rendered with the verb 'to reject' or 'to dismiss'. In the context of the present canticle, however, such an abstract translation is inadequate. The actual meaning of the verb is not fixed and is usually derived from the context in which it occurs. The translations are merely conjectural (cf Albrektson). Hillers proposal that √סלה is a scribal error for √סלל is of interest. He understands the latter verb to mean 'to pile up', the object consisting of the sheaves about to be threshed on the threshing floor. Daughter Zion's mighty ones are thus piled up like sheaves in her midst. A similar image can also be found in Jer 50_{26}. The Peshitta seems to preserve a similar line of thought, given the translation: 'to tread underfoot' with 'ears (of corn)' as its object. A clear parallel is thereby established with the גַּת דָּרַךְ, the treading of the grapes in the wine-presses in 1_{15c}. The Targum also offers a similar understanding of the text with the translation: 'gather'/'collect' (cf the discussion in Gordis).

The most convincing aspect of this proposed interpretation lies in the fact that harvest imagery is frequently employed in the OT to describe YHWH's judgement. Hillers list [299] can be supplemented with several other texts in some of which one also finds reference to the wine harvest.[300] What follows the description of YHWH's judgement in Zephaniah, moreover, has striking parallels with Lam 1_{15}. In Zeph 1_{7f} there is mention of a זֶבַח, a sacrificial meal at which YHWH sanctifies his soldiers in preparation for the execution of his judgement which will be visited upon the princes etcetera.[301] Such

298 Cf 3_{34} together with 2_{20cB}, 4_{14-16}, $5_{12,14}$.
299 Isa 41_{15f}, Jer 9_{21} (MT 9_{22}), 51_{33}, Mic 4_{12-13}.
300 Cf Joel 3_{13} (MT 4_{13}), Am 2_{13}, Hab 3_{12} and Zeph 1_{2f}.

a sacrificial meal reminds one of the מוֹעֵד which is mentioned in 1_{15bA}. In addition, the common 'day of YHWH' framework with respect to YHWH's judgement in both Lamentations and Zephaniah together with the continuation of the harvest imagery in the following bicolon (15b) and the association with the 'yoke' used for pulling the threshing sledge (cf Deut 25_4, Hos 10_{11}) in the previous strophe, all seem to favour the existence of a parallel relationship.

15bA *He proclaimed a time of harvest for me,* קָרָא עָלַי מוֹעֵד

The term מוֹעֵד signifies a fixed time, such as the harvest time in the natural cycle,[302] or the solar, lunar or stellar orbits.[303] In terms of the cult it refers to a time of festival, a feast day (cf 1_{4aB}). In our context the reference is to the harvest in the figurative sense of the word: Adonai has fixed the time of his judgement. The use of the verb קרא would suggest, in the first instance, a festal (cultic) gathering (cf Zeph 1_{7f} once again) to which the people were solemnly summoned (cf Lev 23_{2ff}, Num 16_2). Adonai has now taken the initiative, establishing the time of the harvest and summoning reapers. A similar מוֹעֵד is entoned in Ps 75 as a time at which YHWH executes judgement upon the godless and raises up the righteous.[304] Where Jerusalem is concerned, the aforementioned ideas run quite unexpectedly together in the mention of the מוֹעֵד. The festal gathering proclaimed by Adonai is not for daughter Zion but for her enemies. They are summoned to celebrate her fate as their own harvest feast. They are permitted to realise her punishment for their own profit. The (harvest) joy of the enemy is comprehensively developed in the parallel canticles of the second and third songs (cf especially 2_{16} and 3_{46}).

15bB *to thresh my young men.* לִשְׁבֹּר בַּחוּרָי

With the phrase לִשְׁבֹּר בַּחוּרָי, the second part of this colon provides a further description of the purpose of the מוֹעֵד proclaimed in 15aB. בָּחוּר is a young adult, an as yet unmarried man (cf HAL 114). The colon is frequently rendered: 'to destroy my young men' (cf NEB) but, given the imagery employed in these verses and continued in the present colon, such a translation is too abstract. We noted above that מוֹעֵד can also be used to mark the time of the harvest.[305] Israel's major feasts are also related to

301 Cf also Zeph 3_3, together with ASvdWoude, *Habakuk-Sefanja*, Nijkerk 1978, 94f.
302 Cf Hos 2_8 (MT 2_{11}).
303 Gen 1_{14}, Ps 104_{19}; cf also TWAT IV 746ff (Koch).
304 Cf Ps 75_{3ff} together with Ex 9_5 and Jer 47_7.

different harvests.[306] Moreover, there seems to be a relationship between שׁבר I 'to break'/'to crush' and corn (שׁבר II; cf HAL 1305) since the process of threshing breaks and crushes the grains of corn. The Akkadian verb *šebēru* may mean to thresh or crush grain (cf GES-B 805 and HAL 1303). In this way the imagery is allowed to continue with the call to the harvest feast as the time of Adonai's judgement placed at the centre of the strophe. Daughter Zion's mighty ones lie piled up like sheaves on the edge of the threshing floor and her young men are crushed like grains of corn (cf Mic 4_{12f}, Hab 3_{12}). The image points to the actual condition of defeat before the foe; some of the young men were killed in the attack.[307] The survivors among daughter Zion's young men are left to face humiliation and exploitation (cf 5_{13}).

The mention of אַבִּיר and בָּחוּר constitutes a merism. From daughter Zion's mighty men down to her young warriors not one remains untouched by the harvest of Adonai's judgement. All of this is but a variation of the central complaint: daughter Zion is alone, without a helper, with no one to comfort her, defenceless.

15c *Adonai treads as in a wine press* — גַּת דָּרַךְ אֲדֹנָי
the virgin daughter Judah. — לִבְתוּלַת בַּת־יְהוּדָה

The structure of this strophe corresponds with that of the first canticle (1_{1-3}) in which the first two strophes refer to the suffering of Jerusalem while the third deals with the suffering of Lady Judah. In the present strophe, the first two bicola refer to the suffering of daughter Zion while the third refers to the suffering of daughter Judah. It is quite clear that the harvest imagery continues to dominate the text, this time in the form of the grape harvest upon which Isa 63_{1-6} provides the best commentary (cf also Jer 25_{30}). The same sequence of grain harvest followed by wine harvest (probably based on the actual sequence of events for both harvests) can also be found in Joel 3_{13} (MT 4_{13}) which supports our exegesis of this text. The land outside Jerusalem also had to suffer the consequences of the war and it is certain that blood will have flowed during the downfall of the surrounding strongholds (cf $2_{2,5}$). After the capture of Jerusalem, however, the destruction was not at an end (cf 1_3, 5_{11}). Daughter Judah is forced to endure the same judgement as daughter Zion. In light of the

305 Cf Hos 2_8 (MT 2_{11}).
306 Cf RdVaux, *Institutions II*, 383–403, and TWAT IV 742f (Koch).
307 Cf √שׁבר in Isa 14_{25}, Jer 17_{18}, 19_{11}, 48_{38}.

continuation of the terror we translate the perfect as a present. 'Daughter Judah' should also be understood as a poetic personification.[308] The construct relationship בַּת־יְהוּדָה should be read as a genitive of apposition.[309] Rashi[310] is of the opinion that בְּתוּלַה refers to Jerusalem itself as the daughter of daughter Judah (cf likewise Aalders, Smit, Stoll). Such an interpretation is unjustified. However, since it does not square with 1_{1c} where Lady Jerusalem and not Judah is 'princess among the provinces'. בְּתוּלַת (construct state) should also be seen as a genitive of apposition.[311] The term בְּתוּלָה means a still young, healthy and marriageable or already married woman[312] and as such places extra emphasis on the bitter fact that such a young woman should be struck by Adonai's judgement in this way. The preposition לְ before בְּתוּלָה serves to designate the object of the action (גַּת דָּרַךְ).[313] The Hebrew perfect is understood once again as a present because the action of treading the wine press is ongoing. See also the continuous crying (participium) in the following bicolon.

16a *For these things I weep,* עַל־אֵלֶּה אֲנִי בוֹכִיָּה
my eye, my eye flows with water. עֵינִי עֵינִי יֹרְדָה מַּיִם

The ע-strophe constitutes the conclusion of this canticle together with that of sub-canto 1_{12-16}. For this reason עַל־אֵלֶּה should be seen as causal. It refers back to the content of the complaints daughter Zion has expressed in this sub-canto and to which the present strophe alludes in an abridge fashion. Daughter Zion is brought to tears by the dreadful events which have overcome her (cf also 1_2). Tears are a universal human reaction to sorrow and distress,[314] but daughter Zion's tears have no end. The use of the participle בוֹכִיָּה[315] together with the personal pronoun אֲנִי makes the ongoing character of her weeping very clear,[316] a fact which is reconfirmed in the second colon.

By far the majority of exegetes scrap one עֵינִי assuming it to be a question of dittography.[317] Text critical commentators usually point out that the

[308] Cf TWAT I 868f (Haag).
[309] Cf GES-K § 128*k* and Brockelmann § 70*d*.
[310] Cf MZlotowitz, מגילת איכה, New York 1979[6], 67.
[311] Cf GES-K § 130e together with Isa 23_{12}, 37_{22}, Jer 14_{17}.
[312] Cf Jer $31_{4,21}$ and TWAT I 875 (Tsevat).
[313] Cf GES-K § 117*n*.
[314] Cf TWAT I 639f (Hamp).
[315] Cf BL 590*h* and Joüon–Muraoka § 79*p*.
[316] Cf Joüon–Muraoka § 121*d*, GES-K § 116a.
[317] See Löhr, Rudolph, Haller, Wiesmann, Weiser, Kraus, Boecker, Kaiser but not

double עֵינִי עֵינִי has been problematic since the earliest days. The LXX, Peshitta and Vulgate together with several Hebrew manuscripts render the colon with only one עֵינִי. The Targum, in contrast, seems to assume the presence of a double עֵינִי עֵינִי. We prefer to uphold the MT since such doubling is not an unknown phenomenon in Hebrew.[318] Similar repetition can also be found in direct addresses.[319] Repetition of this sort serves an emphatic function and the poets employ it to show how desperately daughter Zion's eyes run down with tears. The argument which suggests that the double עֵינִי disturbs the metric line is not convincing. Such metrical irregularities may also have been consciously used in order to draw attention to the content of the text (cf 1_7).

16b *Yes, a comforter is far from me,* כִּי־רָחַק מִמֶּנִּי מְנַחֵם
one to revive my vigour. מֵשִׁיב נַפְשִׁי

In light of the retrospective עַל־אֵלֶּה which opened the previous bicolon we prefer to understand כִּי here as emphatic (cf HAL 448 כִּי II [1]) rather than causal. It is not the absence of a comforter which brings daughter Zion such horrendous sorrow. Her complaint now focuses on the fact that she must carry all this alone because there is no one to lighten her burden. It is evident that the first colon seems to constitute an alternative to the formula אֵין מְנַחֵם ($1_{2,9,17,21}$) although given the presence of the verb רחק, something more than a stylistic variation is clearly intended. On the basis of Ps 38_{12} and $88_{9,19}$ one might assume a similar meaning as in 1_{2b}, but the verb is also used in other places in the Psalms in specifically theological contexts. Psalms 10_1 and 22_2 (cf Isa $59_{9,11}$) speak of the 'distance of YHWH and his salvation'. When he hides himself such moments of distress give rise to prayers that he will not stay afar off.[320] It seems reasonable to assume, therefore, that this complaint is not rooted in the absence of any comforter but in the absence of a particular comforter, YHWH himself. This seems likewise to be the case in the background of 1_{9b} (cf the explanation thereof). Nevertheless, there is a significant distinction between 'unavailable' (אַיִן) and 'afar off' (רָחַק) which should not go unnoticed. A person who is 'afar off' is not gone altogether and no matter how far YHWH distances himself from his people, he is still there. It is still worth

Gordis and Brandscheidt; cf also BHK and BHS.

318 Cf Deut 16_{20}, Isa 21_9 (quoted in Rev 14_8, 18_2 [cf Debrunner 493.1]); Ps 68_{13}, Lam 4_{15}.

319 Ps 22_2, II Kgs 2_{12}, 4_{19}, 13_{14}; cf Mt 25_{11}, Lk 8_{24}.

320 Cf Ps $22_{12,20}$, 35_{22}, 38_{22}, 71_{12}; cf also THAT II 770 (Kühlewein).

the effort to try to reach him. Others may observe that there is no one to comfort and help daughter Zion (1$_{2b,7c,9b}$) but she herself keeps open the possibility that YHWH will look upon her in this moment of distress. We outlined the meaning of the term מְנַחֵם in the exegesis of 1$_{2b}$ but this text differs with the present text in that it provides no further concretisation of the absent comforter. In the present bicolon daughter Zion makes quite clear what she desires from her comforter: that he will restore her 'vigour' or spirit for life.[321] Once again these words highlight the seriousness of her condition. Her pain and sorrow are so great that her very life is in danger. She is close to death.

16c *My sons are bewildered.* הָיוּ בָנַי שׁוֹמֵמִים
Yes, how mighty is the enemy. כִּי גָבַר אוֹיֵב

In light of the strong connection with what precedes, we should not consider this concluding bicolon as a separate complaint. Daughter Zion can expect no comfort from YHWH because he has hidden himself from her. Even her sons can offer her no assistance since they themselves lie broken. Given the juxtaposition of 'sons' in the first colon and 'might of the enemy' in the second, it is not as obvious that the referents of בָנַי are the inhabitants of Jerusalem as Aalders and Kraus, for example, would have us believe. It seems more reasonable to assume that the mighty ones and strong young men from the previous strophe are intended here. Their strength and power has been broken because they were forced to undergo the threshing judgement of Adonai; they can do nothing more to protect daughter Zion from her mighty enemy. The plural participle שׁוֹמֵמִים[322] renders the subjective elaboration of objective ruin. Daughter Zion's sons are bewildered and stunned. It is possible that the text is referring at this point to part of a mourning ritual in which the mourners sat silently on the ground.[323] In this event כִּי should not be understood as causal but rather as an emphatic introductory כִּי, analogous to that of the previous bicolon. Our translation 'Yes, how mighty is the enemy' honours both the emphatic element as well as the comparative aspect inherent in the verb גבר.[324] The coherent character of the present canticle provides a further reason to understand כִּי as non-causal. It is not the enemy who lies at the

[321] נֶפֶשׁ + *hiph'il* of √שׁוב, the same expression as in 1$_{11b}$.
[322] Cf the explanation of 1$_{4b}$ and 1$_{13c}$.
[323] Cf Ezek 26$_{16}$; NLohfink, 'Enthielten die im Alten Testament bezeugten Klageriten eine Phase des Schweigens?', VT XII (1962), 269–275, and the explanation of 2$_{10a}$.
[324] Cf TWAT I 902f (Kosmala).

roots of the downfall of daughter Zion's mighty ones and strong young men, but Adonai himself who has summoned a solemn מוֹעֵד to that end.

Sub-Canto II (Lam 1_{17-22})

The first canticle of the present sub-canto commences with the portrayal of the desperate daughter Zion. She stretches out her hands for help but must face the fact that there is no one to comfort her. Other people are also powerless to help because YHWH is the one who has ordered this hostility against her. Daughter Zion begins to realise both realities: YHWH's punishment is justified and her former lovers are not there to help her children in their distress. To whom can she turn? There is only one: YHWH. The final canticle (1_{20-22}) constitutes her prayer to him. He alone has the power to end her suffering.

Canticle I (Lam 1_{17-19}).

Content/theme: *Zion finds no comfort because of* YHWH*'s justified punishment*

Literary argumentation:

inclusions:	לְיַעֲקֹב (17bA) // בָּעִיר (19bA)
	לְנִדָּה בֵּינֵיהֶם (17cB) // הֵמָּה רִמּוּנִי (19aB)
responses:	פֵּרְשָׂה צִיּוֹן בְּיָדֶיהָ (17aA) // קָרָאתִי לַמְאַהֲבַי (19aA)
	אֵין מְנַחֵם לָהּ (17aB) // הֵמָּה רִמּוּנִי (19aB)
ext par:	צִוָּה יְהוָה (17bA) // צַדִּיק הוּא יְהוָה (18aA)
	בְּתוּלֹתַי וּבַחוּרַי (18cA) // כֹּהֲנַי וּזְקֵנַי (19bA)
assonance:	בַשֶּׁבִי (18cB) // וְיָשִׁיבוּ (19cB)

A change of voice occurs within this canticle. In our introduction to the second canto of Lam I, we pointed to the fact that the poets themselves only take the floor in the פ-strophe (1_{17}). This takes place with great stylistic subtlety and in a well chosen place, namely the exact centre of the present canto following precisely on daughter Zion's final complaint in 1_{12-16}. The literary effect of this stylistic feature is that after her complaint, daughter Zion seems to be overcome with tears and, as it were, falls silent for a moment. The poets fill in the tearful silence with a description of her appearance: desperate, hands outstretched for help in this incomparable distress.

After verse 17 daughter Zion returns as speaker, but there appears to have been an significant change in the interim. Although complaints and reflections on her situation continue anew in a section of equal length, the tone clearly differs from that presented in the first sub-canto. It is no longer enough for daughter Zion to express her great suffering in the presence of a human audience. Her intentions in doing so were left unresolved since none of those around her or those passing by paid any attention to her lot; nobody stopped to offer comfort and a helping hand. The first sub-canto of Lam 1_{11-22} concludes with a complaint concerning these mortal onlookers. In the present canticle she confesses the justified nature of her punishment (1_{18a}), a confession which can function in prayer as a basis or ground for appeal. In 1_{18bc} we hear the dying echo of a cry for help directed towards the nations and concerning her lost children, the disappointment of being abandoned by her lovers and the unsparing hunger. In the final canticle (1_{20-22}), therefore, she turns definitively to YHWH, the only one who can really help her.

It is clear that a transposition of the פ-strophe and the ע-strophe[325] based on the sequence found in Lam II–IV but without the support of important textual witnesses would constitute a serious disruption of the acrostic structure. The introduction (III.4) offers a possible explanation for the various alphabetical sequences in Lam I, on the one hand, and Lam II–IV on the other.

Exegesis

A few remarks with respect to the structure of this strophe seem in order here. In light of the change of subject, 1_{17} possesses a greater independence within this seventh canticle. This fact is also underlined by the strophe's distinctly concentric structure:

inclusions: צִיּוֹן (17aA) // יְרוּשָׁלַם (17cA)
אֵין מְנַחֵם לָהּ (17aB) // לְנִדָּה בֵּינֵיהֶם (17cB)

Both inclusions surround the centre of the strophe, namely 1_{17b}, an extremely compact summary of the poets' theological vision of the downfall: it has come about at the command of YHWH. One should also take note of the use of names in this strophe: צִיּוֹן // יַעֲקֹב // יְרוּשָׁלַם. Here too we find the customary ratio: 2x the capital to 1x the land. Via the central positioning of יַעֲקֹב, however, the land is given extra emphasis and the entire strophe is brought into balance.

[325] Cf Wiesmann.

17a *Zion stretches out her hands,* פֵּרְשָׂה צִיּוֹן בְּיָדֶיהָ
(but) no one comforts her. אֵין מְנַחֵם לָהּ

Here in the second canto daughter Zion is directly named as subject. The transition from the first (1_{1-3}) to the second canticle (1_{4-6}) in the first canto (1_{1-11}) is encountered once again in the transition from the first (1_{12-16}) to the second sub-canto (1_{17-22}). Why is 'daughter Zion' now the focus of attention? Realistically speaking there need not be much of a difference between both 'women'. See the equivalence between Lady Jerusalem and daughter Zion presented by the inclusion in 1_{17}: צִיּוֹן (17a) // יְרוּשָׁלִַם (17c); see also the inclusion between בַּת־צִיּוֹן (2_{8aB}) // בְּתוּלַת יְרוּשָׁלִָם (2_{10cB}). Zion, however, is a 'chiffre' for Jerusalem as the temple city of YHWH.[326] The relationship between YHWH and daughter Zion, therefore, is the most intimate of the portrayals of the relationship between Him and his people (cf the explanation of 4_{11}). The intentional intimacy serves to underline the contrast: daughter Zion, once sheltered and protected by YHWH, must now stretch out her hands in search of help. This very contrast makes her prayer in the present sub-canto all the more urgent.

What is the significance behind daughter Zion's outstretched hands? The same combination of words (פָּרַשׂ יָד) is used in 1_{10aA} where it refers to the enemy stretching out their hands towards daughter Zion's treasures. Such an explanation would hardly fit the present circumstances. In addition, the more intensive *pi'el* form is used here in place of the *qal* while the use of the preposition בְּ emphasises the fact that it is precisely with her hands that daughter Zion makes this gesture of reaching out.[327] A survey of texts which employ the *pi'el* of √פרשׂ in combination with יָד (or כַּף) gives rise to a number of possible interpretations. In Isa 25_{11} the combination is used for swimming while in Isa 65_2 it constitutes an inviting gesture from God directed towards his people. In the context of Ps 143_6, Isa 1_{15} and Jer 4_{31} it refers to a gesture accompanying prayer but given the usage in Isa 25_{11} and 65_2 such an interpretation need not exclude others. In light of this it seems right to search for the meaning from the relevant context. Lam 1_{17} appears to use the combination פֵּרַשׂ בְּיָד in an absolute fashion. The immediate context of the strophe does not seem to offer any definitive explanation but this changes when one looks at the wider context. A broader view of the text suggests two possibilities, neither of which are mutually exclusive: a. a gesture of pleading towards the passers-by based

326 Cf the explanation of $1_{4a,c}$.
327 Cf Joüon–Muraoka § 125*m*.

on the response between the beginning of both sub-cantos in the second canto (1_{12a} // 1_{17a}); b. a gesture accompanying the urgent prayer to YHWH from the last sub-canto based on the response between the beginning of both canticles in the last sub-canto (1_{17a} // 1_{20a}). Given the presence of responses it would seem that both interpretations were intended. Daughter Zion stretches out her hands for help to whoever is willing to listen (cf also the core of Lam I, $1_{11c,12a}$). The text reminds one of Zadkine's statue of the mourning figure in Rotterdam in the Netherlands.

The summarising character of the present strophe is quite evident from all we have said thus far. The second colon reveals a similar character with its refrain like repetition of the lack of a comforter (for the meaning of אֵין מְנַחֵם לָהּ cf $1_{2aA,9bB,16bB}$). The absence of a comforter here, however, is a much more heavily laden notion: no one comforts daughter Zion, not even YHWH. The use of names is also well considered. We have already mentioned the inclusion set up within the strophe between צִיּוֹן (17aA) and יְרוּשָׁלַםִ (17cA). צִיּוֹן, however, also has a function within the macro-concentric structure of Lam I, namely: צִיּוֹן (6aA) // צִיּוֹן (17aA).[328] For the meaning of the term צִיּוֹן see the explanation of $1_{4a,c}$.

17b YHWH *has commanded against Jacob* צִוָּה יְהוָה לְיַעֲקֹב
that his neighbours should become his oppressors. סְבִיבָיו צָרָיו

In contrast to the previous canticle the use of the tetragrammaton is restored here and not without significance. The combination with יַעֲקֹב implies that this affliction which has overcome the people was not caused by foreign gods, but by YHWH, the God of Jacob; a quite far reaching thought given the theological context of the time. The traditional notion held that when a nation fell in battle to another, the god(s) of the victor was (were) stronger than that (those) of the vanquished. According to this line of thought YHWH must have been weaker than the gods of Babylon.[329]

The Moabite Stone provides a different theological explanation for a situation not unlike the present one. The stone regards Israel's temporary victory and dominion as the consequence of Kamos' anger against his people which takes the form of his distance: Moab's national god hands his people over to their fate. This was the only way the Moabites could explain the fact that the Israelite king could gain the upper hand.[330] In

328 Cf 1988, 296.
329 Cf 1983, 214f for a more detailed discussion of this topic.
330 Further information on the Moabite Stone can be found in ELipiński, 'Etymological

the present context, however, the victory over Jacob cannot be explained by YHWH's anger, as a consequence of his distant absence. The theological vision of the poets is much more radical. It is not YHWH's powerlessness or absence which has led to the downfall of Jacob but his very supremacy over the other nations. It was not the gods of the nations but YHWH himself who commanded the neighbouring nations, as Jacob's enemies, to be the ruination of his people.[331]

In a certain sense this theological explanation is an overture to the theology of Deutero-Isaiah in which the gods are explicitly portrayed as powerless and insignificant (Isa 44_{6-20}) or YHWH is portrayed as the Unrivalled One who determines the fate of the powerful on earth (Isa 40_{23}) or the one who gives them the power to be victorious (Isa 41_{2}, 45_{1ff}). The authority of YHWH's word of command is also evident from the fact that the *pi'el* of the root צוה is also used in the context of creation. Thus the heavenly bodies follow their pre-ordained course. The obedience of Cyrus on the historical level is paralleled with the same stellar obedience. Cf Isa 45_{12f}.[332]

The absolute character of YHWH's command corresponds with the choice of the name Jacob, whereby two specific accents are determined: totality and radicality. The name Jacob suggests that all of Judah was affected by this great affliction and not only Jerusalem. After the fall of the northern kingdom Judah was the sole representative for all of Israel and could therefore be referred to as Jacob after the patriarch of the same name. In addition to this, the name Jacob is used both in the prophets and the Psalms to designate the close relationship which existed between YHWH and his people, a relationship which had already become visible between YHWH and Jacob their forefather via the election, blessing, promise and liberation which he received from his God.[333] Thus with great brevity the poets reformulate their portrayal of the unbelievable disaster which has befallen them: YHWH himself has commanded their downfall, He is behind the ruin of his own faithful people (cf 1_{5b}).

---

and Exegetical Notes on the Mesa Inscription', Orientalia 40 (1971), 325–340; cf JCdMoor, 'Narrative Poetry in Canaan', in: A. Dearman (Ed.), *Studies in the Mesha Inscription and Moab*, Atlanta 1989, 149–171 for literary structure and translation.

331 For the interpretation of סְבִיב as 'neighbouring' cf Jer $48_{17,39}$, Ps 76_{12}, 89_{8} together with the explanation of 1_{2c}.

332 See in addition THAT II 533f (Liedke).

333 Cf TWAT III 771–773 (Zobel).

17c *Jerusalem has become* הָיְתָה יְרוּשָׁלַם
a filthy thing in their eyes. לְנִדָּה בֵּינֵיהֶם

If נִידָה in 1_{8a} appeared somewhat ambiguous in its meaning, the reference in the present context unequivocally places the emphasis on the aspect of impurity. נִ(י)דָה refers to the separation of the menstruating woman who was considered to be impure.[334] Ezra 9_{11} indicates that the image can also be used for a land: an impure and defiled land. Indeed a similar notion is evident in the present use of the metaphor. Menstruating and thus impure, Lady Jerusalem (as representative of her land) is set apart. Her neighbours keep their distance.[335] Assistance and rapprochement are out of the question, a fact underlined by the connection with 'the absence of comforters' in 1_{17a}. In this way the poets bring Lady Jerusalem's intense loneliness into focus at the very heart of the second canto (1_{12-22}). Cf also יָשְׁבָה בָדָד at the introduction to the first canto (1_{1aA}).

18aA *Righteous is he,* YHWH, צַדִּיק הוּא יְהוָה

Once again daughter Zion takes the floor, as we can see from the response between 1_{17a} and 1_{19a} within the present sub-canto: daughter Zion's appeal to her lovers for help remains unanswered; they have deceived her. She is now thrown back upon YHWH, the one with whom she enjoyed so close a relationship for so long. With YHWH on her mind she confesses that he is צַדִּיק. By placing this term in the first position of a nominal clause the poets firmly underline this characteristic of their God.[336]

Recent literature has tended to emphasise the notion that the root צדק and its derivative forms are part of the context of the mutual relationship which exists between God and humanity and that they therefore carry a positive significance. Koch is among the main proponents of such an interpretation. In THAT II 507–530 he renders צדק as 'gemeinschaftstreu/heilvoll sein'.[337]

While it might be correct to point out that the context of mutual relationship is being accented in the present colon, it would be rather onesided to suggest that YHWH's righteousness is exclusively salvific. It is true that the scriptures very often speak of the salvation which YHWH realises for his people in need by his righteous deeds.[338] That the vast majority of

[334] Cf Lev $12_{2,5}$, 15_{19-33}.
[335] Cf TWAT V 251f (Milgrom – Wright) and II Chron 29_5.
[336] Cf Brockelmann § 30a.
[337] Cf also TWAT VI 905f (Johnson).
[338] Cf, for example, Ps 31_2, 116_5, 145_{17}.

the relevant Old Testament texts should speak of YHWH in such a fashion, however, is due to the manifold situations of distress which are brought to his attention in which he is called upon to bring about justice. As such, the prevalent understanding of צדק is not absent from the book of Lamentations, given the song-responses which represent similar appeals to YHWH in great distress.[339] This positive dimension, however, should not close our eyes to the relational dimension which is present in every act of righteousness, a dimension which is quite evident, for example, in Ps 72: if the king, in YHWH's name, does justice to the wretched and saves the poor, this implies simultaneous doom and punishment for their oppressors (Ps $72_{4,14}$, cf 129_4 and Ex 9_{27}). When Israel itself is guilty of oppression and injustice, however, and thereby damages its mutual relationship with YHWH, then we can only expect that YHWH will respond with a corresponding act of justice. The fact that such an act can take the form of severe punishment is apparent from II Chron 12_6, Isa 10_{22},[340] Ezra 9_{15}, Dan 9_{14} as well as here in Lam 1_{18}. This element is also paralleled at the canticle level in the other songs where it is understood as fulfilled prophecy of doom (2_{17}): the coming of the end (4_{18b}) and the destruction of Zion (5_{18}). Cf the explanation of the texts in question.

Nevertheless, the punishing and liberating dimensions of YHWH's deeds implied in his צְדָקָה do not carry equal weight. The notion's centre of gravity is without question YHWH's salvific צְדָקָה. The fact that the punishing dimension literally fades into the background is evident from the component of duration: YHWH's salvific justice is eternal (cf Ps 111_3, 119_{142}) while his anger is passing in nature (cf Isa 54_{7f}). Passing or not, however, YHWH's punishing צְדָקָה is far from unreal. Von Rad is of the opinion that צַדִּיק הוּא יְהוָה in Lam 1_{18a} has nothing to do with punishment.[341] The text, according to Von Rad, contests an incorrect accusation against YHWH, who has been indicted for bringing misfortune upon his people, and proclaims that YHWH only brings about salvific צְדָקָה. The fact that such an indictment against YHWH is nowhere to be found in the text undermines Von Rad's position. Moreover, the righteousness of YHWH's behaviour is not a matter of dispute in the present context: the previous strophe portrays the downfall of Judah as the consequence of YHWH's command while the following strophe establishes a causal relationship between his צְדָקָה

339 Cf 2_{18}, 3_{54ff} together with the explanation of 5_{19}.

340 Cf TWAT VI 904 (Johnson).

341 GvRad, *Theologie des Alten Testaments, Band I, Die Theologie der geschichtlichen Überlieferungen Israels*, München 1966[5], 389.

and daughter Zion's sin. If she confesses that YHWH is צַדִּיק, she does not imply thereby that he is being accused of injustice but that he is justified in allowing this fate to overcome her. Her reasons for speaking thus become apparent in the following colon.

18aB *for I resisted his word.* כִּי פִיהוּ מָרִיתִי

Daughter Zion points to her past behaviour and she confesses her guilt: כִּי פִיהוּ מָרִיתִי, she resisted YHWH's word (mouth). What is meant by such an expression? A number of commentators believe that daughter Zion is pointing not only to her previous violations of YHWH's commandments but also to the fact that she ignored the exhortatory preaching of the prophets.[342] It is most unlikely, however, that she is focusing her confession on violations of YHWH's תּוֹרָה. Firstly, we hear the complaint voiced in 2_9 that the Torah is no longer being taught.[343] Such a complaint reveals that the teaching of the Torah was missed with sadness, a fact which is hard to reconcile with (conscious) violations of the same תּוֹרָה. A second and more compelling reason is based on the fact that in the Old Testament, the expression מָרָה פֶּה is always used for resistance to a particular command given in a particular situation,[344] but never for disobedience with respect to commandments which have eternal validity.[345] For this reason the text here must refer exclusively to daughter Zion's resistance to the preaching of the prophets who had warned her about the consequences of her behaviour and had announced YHWH's judgement upon it.

The meaning of מָרָה פֶּה certainly points in this direction, given that the expression is appropriate to the direct preaching of the pre-exilic prophets of doom who called for a change of heart in concrete situations on pain of sanctions from YHWH. At the time, however, daughter Zion paid no attention to such warning voices. She was only willing to listen to those prophets who promised her YHWH's salvation and protection, promises which appeared to be quite in line with her (theological) traditions.[346]

The literary structure of the songs confirms this interpretation. A glance at 2_{17a} reveals that we are dealing here also with the word of these warning prophets, namely that concerning YHWH's word of destruction which is now coming to fulfilment which finds its echo in the call to arms announced

---

342 Cf Aalders, Kraus and Kaiser.

343 אֵין תּוֹרָה; cf Lev 10_{11}, Deut 31_{9ff}.

344 Cf Num 20_{24}, 27_{14}, Deut $1_{26,43}$, 9_{23}, Josh 1_{18}; I Kgs $13_{21,26}$ and 1983, 273.

345 Contra Schwienhorst, TWAT V 9f.

346 Cf 1983,156–177 on prophecies of salvation and doom.

by YHWH against Jacob in the preceding strophe (1_{17b}). The poets endorse the fact that daughter Zion's disobedience gave rise to this situation. At the same time, there is an inclusion between 1_{18a} and 1_{21c} within the sub-canto (1_{17-22}) which suggests that the 'day of YHWH' has dawned. The reference implies that the prophetic announcements of doom are being realised in the form of YHWH's reaction on his day to the sins of Lady Jerusalem.

All in all, daughter Zion admits that she threw all the prophetic warnings to the wind and that her present fate is her own fault and should not be blamed on YHWH. Her confession could have functioned as the basis for a prayer of appeal to YHWH for help, but she does not turn as yet to prayer. The very recognition and confession of her guilt makes the gulf between them seem too great. For this reason she appeals once again for human compassion.

18b *Hear indeed, all you peoples,* שִׁמְעוּ־נָא כָל־עַמִּים
and behold my sorrow: וּרְאוּ מַכְאֹבִי

It is not necessary to follow Robinson's suggestion in the text critical apparatus of BHS and emend this text; instead one can read the *kᵉṯîḇ*.[347] The present bicolon is reminiscent of 1_{12ab} but a comparison of the two makes the difference between them more apparent. Where passers-by are appealed to in 1_{12}, here the nations are the addressees and the impression is given that the range of address has become much wider. Those near at hand offered no assistance. The reinforced imperative שִׁמְעוּ־נָא, 'hear indeed', confirms this impression. The passers-by in the ל-strophe (1_{12}) were able to observe Lady Jerusalem's affliction from the roadside. In the present circumstances the nations must hear of her situation first before they have the chance to see it for themselves.[348] Lady Jerusalem sums up for her wider audience the events which have brought on this unparalleled distress.

18c *my young women and young men* בְּתוּלֹתַי וּבַחוּרַי
have gone into captivity. הָלְכוּ בַשֶּׁבִי

The focus of daughter Zion's list of grievances is more than evident. First of all we hear her lament over the loss of her children (cf Isa 49_{15}). The present bicolon is reminiscent of 1_{5c}. As with 1_{18b}, however, a comparison of the two bicola brings the difference to the surface together with

[347] Cf GES-K § 127c.

[348] For the meaning of מַכְאוֹב cf the explanation of 1_{12b}.

the variation the poets intended by their repetition. Where 1_{5c} spoke of Jerusalem's younger inhabitants, here the reference is to her more mature young men and women.[349] 1_{15b} spoke of the young men who perished in the day of judgement. The mention of בַּחוּרַי in the present colon must therefore refer to the remaining young men who survived the struggle or who were too young at the time to have been involved in it. These also, however, have been lost together with her young daughters. A further variation with respect to 1_{5c} is the use of the preposition בְּ before שֶׁבִי. For this reason we understand שֶׁבִי here to be a noun and translate: 'have gone into captivity'.[350]

Once again the poetic repetition appears to imply a new dimension. Where daughter Zion's younger children were carried off as prisoners in 1_{5c}, here her older youth are afflicted with the condition of captivity itself. Without a doubt the allusion being made is to the exile. As far as daughter Zion is concerned it does not matter. All she knows is that she has been robbed of her children.

19a *I called to my lovers,* קָרָאתִי לַמְאַהֲבַי
they, they deceived me. הֵמָּה רִמּוּנִי

The present bicolon, in which daughter Zion speaks of what led up to her current situation, is reminiscent of 1_{2bc} in which the poets are the speakers. After the loss of her children she singles out her sense of disappointment over the behaviour of her former allies. Once again there is variation in terminology between the two texts. Instead of the *qal* participle we now have a *pi'el* participle of the verb אהב. With respect to a political alliance the *qal* need not carry any negative implications (cf I Kgs 5_1) but the *pi'el*, in contrast, is clearly negative. It is used exclusively to designate the adulterous character of the relationship in question. In the context of Hosea it is used directly to indicate improper love for the Baalim.[351] Elsewhere it refers to the inappropriate placing of one's trust in one's allies and their gods.[352] With daughter Zion as the religious subject (cf $1_{4a,c}$) in the present context, it seems plausible that the religious duties which go hand in hand with such political alliances are the focus of the text.[353] In the wake of her confession of guilt in 1_{18a}, daughter Zion lets it be known

349 For בְּתוּלָה in the sense of a young, marriageable woman cf 1_{15c} and for בָּחוּר cf 1_{15b}.
350 Cf HAL 1294.
351 Hos $2_{7,9,12,14,15}$; cf also Zech 13_6.
352 Cf 1_{2bc} together with Jer $22_{20,22}$, 30_{14}, Ezek $16_{33,36,37}$, $23_{5,9,22}$.
353 Cf II Kgs 16_{10ff}.

that having been deceived she is now aware of the improper nature of her alliances. By trusting her old political friends (and their gods in the process) she had simultaneously displayed a certain lack of confidence in YHWH (cf Isa 30_{15}). Her disappointment, however, remains undiminished. The fact that she sinned does not yet justify the deceptive behaviour of her allies. Where the poets speak in similar contexts of infidelity, daughter Zion speaks of malicious and wilful deception.[354] The 3m pl pronoun of the second colon is worthy of note. It is certainly used to stretch the colon to a more acceptable length, but at the level of content it also provides some extra emphasis. Daughter Zion called out in vain and by the way of their behaviour her former lovers have become partly to blame for the loss her children and the dreadful famine (cf 1_{2b} on the identity of these allies).

19b *My priests and elders* כֹּהֲנַי וּזְקֵנַי
perish in the city, בָּעִיר גָּוָעוּ

Having singled out the loss of her children and the faithless deception of her allies daughter Zion now turns her attention to the unmitigated hunger. The poets already spoke of the famine in general terms in the כ-strophe (1_{11}). The change of voice between the poets and daughter Zion, however, prevents simple repetition. At the same time her description of the situation is much sharper and more focused. She points out how hunger has affected her priests and elders. Their high civil position offered them no special protection against the all pervasive famine.

The combination of priests and elders is worthy of some attention. It suggests that in one way or another the elders were also responsible for the cult, a notion quite appropriate to the present speaker, daughter Zion. Our explanation of 1_{6b} revealed a certain level of identity between the princes and the elders. Such an explanation is understandable if one realises that these very elders were the wealthy and distinguished heads of the most prominent families, individuals who exercised considerable influence in matters of state during the period of the monarchy.[355] Immediately prior to the fall of Judah, the princes also exercised significant influence on foreign policy and were partly responsible for the direction it would take in that they insisted on forming an alliance with Egypt.[356] Their foreign

354 This the meaning of √רמה II in the *pi'el*; cf Gen 29_{25}, Josh 9_{22}, I Sam 19_{17}, 28_{12}, II Sam 19_{27}, Prov 26_{19}; in I Chron 29_{25} the meaning is even more direct: 'to betray'.
355 Cf I Sam 30_{26}, II Sam 5_3 19_{11f}, II Kgs $10_{1,5}$; cf also TWAT II 644–650 (Conrad).
356 Cf Jer 37_{15}, $38_{4f,24ff}$.

policy, however, was a disaster. Egypt turned out to be powerless before the might of the Babylonians (cf Lam 4_{17}) and the other allies slipped one by one into betrayal (cf 1_{2c}). The famine was a consequence of all of this, revealing at the same time that the elders were the victims of their own political manoeuvring.

The mention of priests here is partly due to the literary structure of the text. The inclusion at the level of the entire song between כֹּהֲנֶיהָ (1_{4bB}) and כֹּהֲנַי (1_{19bA}) makes this evident. This inclusive repetition, however, reveals another situation. The various events and situations described by the poets may very well be simultaneous. In 1_{4b} there are still priests in the temple. Here in 1_{19bA} they wander round the streets of the city, weakened to the point of death (גָּוָעוּ). The root designates the moment of perishing and death.[357] It is not insignificant that we find the priests and elders away from the temple and gate where they respectively belong. See the inclusion in the second canticle between שְׁעָרֶיהָ (1_{4bA}) and שָׂרֶיהָ (1_{6bA}) which shows that it was not uncommon for princes to also be elders.

19c *while seeking food for themselves,* כִּי־בִקְשׁוּ אֹכֶל לָמוֹ
to restore their vigour. וְיָשִׁיבוּ אֶת־נַפְשָׁם

Here we see the reason why the priests and elders have wandered from their posts. Even such dignitaries as these are driven out into the street by the famine. The unparalleled severity of the situation is thereby exposed. The priests were permitted to take a share for themselves of the offerings brought to the temple while the elders were usually taken care of by their families. In the present situation, however, it is no longer possible to care for the elders as before and the people no longer bring offerings. It is a question of 'every man for himself'. The priests and elders are thereby humiliated and debased, hunger has reduced them to the same level as the rest of the population. The poets' choice of words makes this abundantly evident. Almost the same terminology is used here as in 1_{11ab}. Just like everyone else these prominent individuals are forced onto the streets in search of something to eat. The term אֹכֶל is also used for animal 'feed'.[358] Exhausted, feeble and starving they stumble through the streets of Jerusalem. They no longer have time to think of others (cf לָמוֹ, 'for themselves'); self-preservation is all that matters.[359] We have translated the imperfect וְיָשִׁיבוּ as a infinitive based on the fact that ו +

[357] Cf Gen 6_{17}, $25_{8,17}$ etcetera; HAL 176.
[358] Cf Job 9_{26}, 38_{41}, 39_{29}, Ps 104_{21}.
[359] For the meaning of וְיָשִׁיבוּ אֶת־נַפְשָׁם cf 1_{11b}.

impf can indicate the intention of an action.[360] The plus found in LXX (cf text critical apparatus BHS) and the Peshitta: 'and they found nothing', appears to be a later explanatory addition.

A few remarks with respect to the use of perfects are appropriate here. Perfects are employed because they either describe actions which have their beginning in the past while their effects are still felt in the present, for example the deportation of the children or the infidelity of the allies or actions which themselves are ongoing (cf the perfect יָשְׁבָה in 1_{1aA}). Aalders is of the opinion that the affliction described here is past tense and that the use of the perfect indicates a retrospective position. Kraus follows along similar lines. He proposes that the priests and elders are already dead, although such an idea is not otherwise implied by the verb גוע. The death of the priests and elders is not in itself improbable. The famine has endured for a long time (cf the exegesis of 1_{11ab}) and over the weeks and months it is certain that, depending on their physical condition, many priests and elders would have succumbed while others would have survived.[361] The affliction is not over, however, and there can be no question of retrospection as daughter Zion's repeated appeals for help make clear.[362]

Nevertheless, as the text of Lamentations reveals time and again, there is no response. Not one of the nations steps in to help and comfort daughter Zion. Thus her desperate need throws her back once again on the Only One who perhaps might intervene: YHWH. The following canticle begins, therefore, with a renewed appeal to YHWH.

Canticle II (1_{20-22})

Content/theme: *A prayer for revenge against the evil deeds of her enemies*

Literary argumentation:

inclusions:
(22cA) כִּי־רַבּוֹת אַנְחֹתַי // (20aA) כִּי־צַר־לִי
(22cB) וְלִבִּי דַוָּי // (20aB) מֵעַי חֳמַרְמָרוּ
(22bB) עַל כָּל־פְּשָׁעָי // (20bB) כִּי מָרוֹ מָרִיתִי

responses:
(22aA) תָּבֹא // (20aA) רְאֵה
(22bA) כַּאֲשֶׁר עוֹלַלְתָּ לִי // (21bB) כִּי אַתָּה עָשִׂיתָ

---

360 Cf GES-K § 107*q*, 142*d*, 165*a*, Joüon–Muraoka § 116*e* and HAL 248 sv ו (10).

361 Cf 2_{20c}, 4_{16b} and 5_{12b}.

362 Cf 1_{18b} and 1_{20-22}.

כִּי־צַר־לִי (20aA) // כִּי נֶאֱנָחָה אָנִי (21aB)

ext par: אֲנָחֹתַי (22cA) // כִּי נֶאֱנָחָה אָנִי (21aB)

וְלִבִּי דַוָּי (22cB) // נֶהְפַּךְ לִבִּי בְּקִרְבִּי (20bA)

In the present final canticle daughter Zion turns for the third time and definitively to YHWH. None of this is obvious, however. The poets let it emerge little by little via the context. In the first canto we find only two short – albeit insistent – exclamatory prayers ($1_{9c,11c}$ [canto-responses with $1_{20,22}$]), interim laments as it were, as if she is not yet ready to turn completely to YHWH. Now that she fully realises that none of her former lovers is going to comfort her and that she can expect nothing from the passers-by and the neighbouring nations (the appeal in the previous canticle went unanswered), she submits herself fully to YHWH (1_{20-22}). In the last analysis he is the Only One left to whom she can turn. For this reason, the prayers of $1_{9c,11c}$ are now expanded.

20a *See,* YHWH *how faint at heart I am;* רְאֵה יְהוָה כִּי־צַר־לִי
my bowels are aflame, מֵעַי חֳמַרְמָרוּ

The extraordinarily intense character of the imperative appeal which introduces this bicolon was already apparent in $1_{9c,11c}$. We translate כִּי as emphatic.[363] It would be incorrect to interpret these words as if YHWH was being informed of daughter Zion's present state of need. She herself has already stated that He is behind her affliction (1_{12c-15}). The precise intention of this bicolon is to focus on the distress which she is now being forced to endure at YHWH's hand. At the song level the phrase כִּי־צַר־לִי corresponds in the form of an inclusion with הַמְּצָרִים in 1_{3cB} in which the connotation of mortal terror was evident. Indeed, the intransitive *qal* of √צרר I does not only designate the objective situation of need in which one finds oneself (at the hands of one's enemies), it also indicates the subjective feelings brought on by the terror of that situation.[364] Here, at the end of the song, it makes little sense to inquire into the origins of daughter Zion's fears. In this respect the previous canticle already summarised matters. No new themes are introduced at this point only points of emphasis. Implicit reference is made to the affliction already described as the actual content of daughter Zion's distress. The subjective component, however, is given much greater weight. It is not the chaos in the land or the ruined

363 Cf HAL 448 sv כִּי II (1).

364 Cf the similar context in Ps 31_{10}, 69_{18ff}, 102_3.

city or the disordered society that YHWH is called to look upon, rather it is a fearful woman. Zion's distress represents the heavy-heartedness, anxiety and fear of the remaining inhabitants of the temple city.

The subjective experience of distress is underlined by the internal parallelism in the present bicolon: her bowels burn. This expression is only found in Lamentations (1_{20} and 2_{11}). Even the verbal conjugation is rare.[365] The intended disposition is not easy to describe. It is clear that מֵעַי[366] functions as the seat of interior feelings or emotions (cf the saying 'butterflies in the tummy'). In Hebrew the מֵעִים can be carriers of a variety of emotions such as love (Song 5_4), pity (Isa 63_{15}) dismay (Jer 4_{19}), poignancy (Jer 31_{20}).[367] The combination with √חמר III (a *poalal* form) 'to be aflame'/'to burn' or with √חמר II[368] meaning 'to seethe' or 'ferment' is unique to this verse in the OT.[369] Unpleasant heat and/or movement in the abdominal region – fever? (cf 1_{13a}) – constitutes the physical counterpart to the feeling of angst mentioned in the first colon. In the broader context of the entire canticle it would appear that this expression is just one element of the poets portrayal of physical discomfort. The inclusion with 1_{22c} via the parallel with 'my heart is faint' (cf the explanation of 1_{13c}) and the concatenation with the 'heart turned upside down' in the next colon (1_{20bA}) makes this fact clear. The expression reappears in 2_{11} where the feeling of dismay is primary. In the present context the feelings of fear and mortal anxiety are primary.

This unique expression within the OT refers to an unknown but powerful emotion which justifies the extremely intense and likewise unique imperative appeal רְאֵה יְהוָה (see the explanation of 1_{9c}).

20bA *my heart turns upside down within me,* נֶהְפַּךְ לִבִּי בְּקִרְבִּי

In the portrayal of human kind in the OT the heart also constitutes the seat of a person's vigour, emotion, knowledge and will/disposition.[370] The combination הָפַךְ לֵב, therefore, can designate a change of disposition or a 'change of heart'[371] but that is not the authors' intention here. The context shows that the phrase is referring primarily to aspects of the life

365 Cf Joüon–Muraoka § 59*d*.
366 A pl st cs with sf 1 sg; cf BL 588*l*.
367 Cf TWAT IV 1037f (Ringgren).
368 Likewise *poalal* – cf BL 285g' and HAL 316f.
369 Cf both options in TWAT III 1f (Ringgren).
370 Cf THAT I 861ff (Stolz) and TWAT IV 425–447 (Fabry).
371 Cf Ex 14_5, I Sam 10_9, Ps 105_{25}, Hos 11_8.

force and the emotions. The heart is more sensitive than any other organ to physical and emotional stress. One's heart(beat) registers every change in one's emotional environment. Daughter Zion feels her heart turn upside down within her because her very life itself is completely on its head.

It is possible, however, that the expression carries further implications. The context speaks of the city in metaphorical terms. With the use of the root הפך, associations are brought into play with the Sodom and Gomorra tradition in which 'turning upside down' is the *terminus technicus* for the downfall of these cities.[372] In other words: Jerusalem feels herself turned upside down, just like Sodom and Gomorra and perhaps even worse. The broader context of Lamentations underscores this interpretation as we can see from 1_{13a}[373] and one of the central strophes of the fourth song (4_6) in which the fate of Jerusalem is compared with the fate of Sodom while a connection is simultaneously established with sin as the cause of that fate. The selfsame connection also exists between the first and second colon of 1_{20b} thus making the interrelated character of this canticle all the more visible. The actual subject of this 'turn around' is not the heart of daughter Zion but YHWH himself who lies at the origin of everything Judah has been forced to endure. The connection with the prophetic announcement of judgement, in which Israel's wickedness and downfall (and that of other lands) is compared with that of Sodom and Gomorra, is thereby confirmed.[374] Isa 13_{9-22} is particularly interesting in this regard since the judgement terminology used therein can also be found in Lamentations. The same terminology, moreover, is used in the context of the 'day of YHWH' (Isa 13_9) which is likewise part of the content of the present canticle (1_{21c}).

20bB *yes, how heedless I have been.* כִּי מָרוֹ מָרִיתִי

Had the phrase נֶהְפַּךְ לִבִּי בְּקִרְבִּי from the previous colon been used only to express a sense of unease and nothing more then the connection with Israel's recalcitrance would have remained somewhat vague. On the other hand, should there be something contained in the first colon to suggest the city's bitter and sinful fate then the mention of former unruliness would not be out of place at this point. For this reason the כִּי should not be translated as causal which would be unnecessary in the context of

372 Cf Gen $19_{21,25,29}$, Deut 29_{22f}, Isa $1_{7,9}$, 13_{19}, Jer 20_{16}, 49_{18}, 50_{40}, Am 4_{11} together with TWAT II 458 (Seybold).

373 Cf the exegesis thereof.

374 Cf Am 4_{11}, Isa 13_{19}, Jer 50_{40}, cf also Isa 1_{10}, Jer 23_{14} and TWAT V 766f (Mulder).

addressing YHWH in this way. Once again an emphatic rendering[375] offers more clarity: 'yes, I have offered strong resistance (against you)'. Thus the colon functions as a confession of guilt, although here in the context of prayer. That Israel's heedlessness is directed towards YHWH is confirmed by the fact that the verb מרה in its OT usage always has YHWH as direct or indirect object.[376]

It goes without saying, of course, that one should interpret the aforementioned recalcitrance in the context of the sub-canto, following along the lines of 1_{18aB} in which resistance to the prophetic announcements of judgement seemed to be the primary intention. Pre-exilic Israel was unwilling to listen to such words of doom. In the present context the paranomastic כִּי מָרוֹ מָרִיתִי has precisely the same meaning. Jerusalem's fate is the consequence of her unwillingness to obey the many pre-exilic, prophetic exhortations and appeals for conversion.[377] Israel's 'deafness' was such that the prophet Ezekiel characterised the people as a 'rebellious house' (cf Ezek 2_{5ff}).

20cA *Outside the sword bereaves me of my children,* מִחוּץ שִׁכְּלָה־חֶרֶב

Since the first two bicola of this strophe lay the accent on subjective experience and not on the actuality of daughter Zion's situation it would be wrong to interpret the final bicolon as an exclusively objective representation of her affliction. The murderous sword is the source of daughter Zion's mortal anxiety. YHWH is called to look upon terrified human beings who are still being confronted with dreadful misfortune. The first colon reveals a certain correspondence with 1_{18c}. In summing up her suffering before the surrounding nations, daughter Zion singled out the loss of her children as her primary source of anguish. In the present context she does the same thing, only this time before YHWH: מִחוּץ שִׁכְּלָה־חֶרֶב, which literally means: '(coming) from outside, the sword makes childless'. Once again, therefore, she mourns the continuing loss of her children.

Within the canto there is a relationship between this colon and 1_{15} in which daughter Zion's warriors and young men are slain in her very midst. The situation is that of after the fall of Judah when daughter Zion was helplessly delivered into the hands of her enemies who exploited her helplessness by invading her territories, routing her population, plundering,

---

375 Cf HAL 448 sv כִּי II (1).
376 Cf TWAT V 7 (Schwienhorst).
377 Cf Schwienhorst, 8f.

enslaving and murdering. Structural analysis supplies the grounds for further interpretation. Within the concentric structure (at the song level) there exists an inclusion with the third strophe (1_3) which describes the misery of widow Judah. It became apparent in the exegesis of this strophe that the reference being made was to the hostile behaviour of Edom (cf Ob $_{10-14}$). In a song-response between 1_{21} and 4_{21}, the name Edom recurs. The second song refers in the form of a song-response to the violent death of priests and prophets – in the sanctuary no less (2_{20c}) – while 2_{21ab} mentions further victims of the murderous sword.

The words of this colon, however, are even more telling. The allusions to concrete aspects of daughter Zion's misfortune raise clear thematic associations with prophetic announcements of judgement. The similarities involved should not surprise us since the prophet's portrayals of judgement and doom are borrowed in their turn from actual situations of war and famine which had plagued the countries of the ancient Near East throughout their history. The present complaint also has something thematic about it. The same expression can be found in Deut 32_{25}: 'In the street the sword shall bereave' (מִחוּץ תְּשַׁכֶּל־חֶרֶב) while similar expressions can also be found in Lev $26_{22,25}$, Jer $15_{7,9}$, Ezek 5_{17}, $14_{15,17}$ (cf also Hos 9_{12}).

All these texts are located in announcements of judgement which portray the dreadful consequences of Israel's disobedience to YHWH. By formulating her complaint as a sort of repeated confession of her guilt, daughter Zion affirms that it is not some accidental or undefined misfortune that has come upon her but YHWH's judgement. Once again the link with pre-exilic announcements of doom, which we observed with respect to the preceding bicolon and elsewhere (1_{18a}) becomes apparent.[378]

20cB *in the house, death.* בַּבַּיִת כַּמָּוֶת

The second colon is somewhat problematic, particularly with respect to the meaning of the כ before מָוֶת. Textual corruption is unlikely since LXX, Targum and the Vulgate assume the Masoretic text. Alternative interpretations are by no means obvious. Perles, for example, followed by Rudolph and Wiesmann, reads the Akkadian *kamûtu* 'captivity' for כמות, without realising, however, that the internal parallelism is thereby disrupted.[379]

---

[378] Cf 1983, 262–267. For further discussion of the presumed dependence of Lam 1_{20} on Deut 32_{25} cf 1983, 28f.

[379] FPerles, 'Was bedeutet כמות in Threni 1,20?', OLZ 23, 1920, 157f.

Likewise, Hillers' emendation of כַּמָּוֶת to כָּפָן 'hunger' (cf Job 5_{22}, 30_3) demands too much textual surgery. Two more recent attempts to explain the text with new argumentation come from Albrektson and Gordis. The former points out the possibility that the preposition בְּ may have fallen out after the comparative particle כְּ [380] and interprets מָוֶת, on the basis of Ps 6_6, as the equivalent of שְׁאוֹל, the kingdom of the dead. He thus translates the text as: "inside (the house) it is as if in שְׁאוֹל." We consider this suggestion improbable since the passive dimension of שְׁאוֹל is not implied here but rather the act of dying itself which robs daughter Zion of her children (cf Jer 9_{21}). The predicate שִׁכְּלָה has a double subject: חֶרֶב and מָוֶת. Our preference falls, therefore, to the interpretation of Gordis [381] who suggests that the כ should be taken as an 'asseverative Kaph'.[382] The emphatic dimension is difficult to render in translation. One might imagine something like: 'yes, death indeed!' It is not difficult, however, to guess why death appears to have free reign 'in the house'. The parallel strophe in the second song (2_{20}) relates the story of the dreadful famine which claims young and old alike as its victims (cf 4_9) Weakness brought on by lack of nourishment will have ensured that sickness preceded death.

Here too we hear echoes of the prophetic announcements of doom in the frequently used trio of terms: sword, famine and plague.[383] Ezek 7_{15} is particularly reminiscent of Lam 1_{20c}. One might be left wondering why the mention of plague (דֶּבֶר) is absent from the present text. This might be explained, however, by the fact that מָוֶת constitutes a synonym thereof; so much so that the term 'plague' in LXX is translated almost everywhere with the term θάνατος.[384] Jer 15_2 with its catalogue of death, sword, famine and captivity, reveals something of the way the poets of Lamentations have taken over this quartet of themes from the prophecy of doom in the present, final, sub-canto, albeit in reverse sequence: captivity (1_{18c}), hunger (1_{19bc}), sword and death (1_{20c}; cf also Jer 43_{11}).

21a *Hear how I groan,*	שִׁמְעוּ כִּי נֶאֱנָחָה אָנִי
no one who comforts me.	אֵין מְנַחֵם לִי

[380] Cf Joüon–Muraoka § 133*h*.

[381] RGordis, 'The Asseverative Kaph in Ugaritic and Hebrew', JAOS 63 (1963), 176–178.

[382] Cf also GES-K § 118*x* and HAL 448 sv כְּ (5) where it is referred to as a '*Kaph veritatis*'.

[383] 15x in Jer; cf TWAT II 134 (Mayer); cf also the summary in Jer 28_8 and Ezek 6_{11f}.

[384] Cf also Jer 15_2 where the text refers to death instead of plague.

By far the majority of exegetes and translators emend the Masoretic text at this point, changing the *qal* 3m pl pf שָׁמְעוּ to a *qal* imperative sg שְׁמַע, directed to YHWH. Albrektson (followed by Gottlieb) has been a recent defender of the MT. He dismisses Rudolph's argument that 1_{21b} in the MT is a redundant repetition of 1_{21a} as unconvincing. On the contrary, Albrektson notes, the repetition, far from being redundant, may even be intentional. In support of his claim he points to the style figure in which a theme is further explained in what follows via the repetition of the verb (cf 2_{5ab} and $3_{59,60}$). In spite of these arguments, emendation remains the most appropriate approach to the text. Textual corruption might be blamed on *aberratio oculi* by way of which the שָׁמְעוּ of 1_{21bA} was read instead of שְׁמַע.

If we accept an imperative reading of the text then it would appear that the canticle exhibits a triple response: רְאֵה (1_{20aA}) // שְׁמַע (1_{21aA}) // תָּבֵא (1_{22aA}). In addition, the parallel with the last sub-canto of Lam III, in which an appeal to YHWH exhibits precisely the same verbal sequence, further substantiates our claim: רָאִיתָה יְהוָה ($3_{59A,60A}$) // שָׁמַעְתָּ (3_{61A}) // תָּשִׁיב (3_{64A}). It is stated with confidence in the parallel ש-strophe of the third song (3_{61}) that YHWH will hear, thus constituting a song-response with an imperative שְׁמַע here in 1_{21a}. Even from the perspective of content an imperative seems more appropriate here than a 3m pl, and as such the second colon becomes more meaningful. In an appeal to YHWH to hear the intense weeping of daughter Zion,[385] the second colon takes on a causal function: 'because there is no one else to comfort her'[386] YHWH is implicitly called upon to be her comforter, an appeal which is completely in line with what follows.

21b *All my enemies delight to hear of my misfortune,*	כָּל־אֹיְבַי שָׁמְעוּ רָעָתִי שָׂשׂוּ
and it is you who brings it (upon me).	כִּי אַתָּה עָשִׂיתָ

Once again the theme of enemy joy returns. In 1_{7d} this was related to the downfall of Jerusalem. There are two possible reasons for the present jubilation in the enemy camp: either daughter Zion's misfortune or the fact that YHWH has brought misfortune on his own people. The *zāqēf qāṭōn* in the Masoretic text indicates that the division should be placed after שָׂשׂוּ thereby relating the enemy's delight with רָעָתִי, that is to say daughter Zion's misfortune and not YHWH's modus operandi. It is somewhat surprising that almost every commentator seems to ignore this division,

385 כִּי is once again emphatic; for the implications of the root אנח cf 1_{4b}.

386 Cf the meaning of מְנַחֵם in $1_{2b,9b,16b,17a}$.

given that the resulting translation: *'they rejoice that you have done it'* is not without problems at the theological level. If we ignore the division we are left with a situation in which the enemy also recognises YHWH as the *auctor intellectualis* of the downfall of his people. Nowhere else in Lamentations, however, can we find such an affirmation, not even in 2_{17} where the enemy's delight is once again related to the fate of Jerusalem and not to the fulfilment of YHWH's word.[387] A further argument against the customary interpretation is the fact that the god of a vanquished people was also considered to be vanquished.[388] Mocking the loser or the underdog in a battle always had negative repercussions with respect to their god. Israel certainly experienced enemy derision in this way.[389] The downfall of his people places YHWH's own honour in jeopardy.

The suggestion that the traditional division of the text creates an imbalance in the bicolon by adding an extra beat to the first half thereof is not convincing. It is possible that 1_{21bA} has not been correctly transmitted. Compare, for example, Aalders and Wiesmann who both drop שָׁמְעוּ.

From the perspective of content, 'to hear' is indeed peculiar, giving the impression that the enemy is only now hearing of the fate of Jerusalem while the previous verses had made it quite apparent that they themselves were major contributors to that fate.[390] The notion of the enemy 'hearing', therefore, only has meaning if it has to do with the continuation of daughter Zion's distress. The enemy hear that her problems have not been solved and that further campaigns against Judah would not only be possible but would probably require little effort (cf 2_{17cB}). In this case daughter Zion's misfortune would have to include more than just the one-off downfall of Jerusalem. The famine, sword and death which followed upon that downfall are also part of the image. The notion that her ongoing misfortune is the cause of her sorrow (cf 1_{18bB}) is supported by the incl/resp מַכְאֹבִי (1_{18bB}) // רָעָתִי (1_{21bA}) at the sub-canto level.

A further objection to the elimination of שָׁמְעוּ is the fact that the verb שׂושׂ would thereby find itself in an unusual position with respect to syntax.

387 Cf also 3_{61ff}, 4_{21}.
388 Cf 1983, 213–216.
389 Cf Prov 14_{31}, 17_5, I Sam $17_{26,36}$, II Kgs $19_{10-19,22f}$. Similar texts from exilic times have also been preserved. Cf Ps $74_{10,18,22}$, $79_{10,12}$, Isa 46_{1f}, together with TWAT III 225f, 228 (Kutsch).
390 Cf, for example, the second strophe of the first song (1_2) which declares the enemy's infidelity.

Moreover, one would then expect a construction with the preposition עַל or בְּ.[391] The transmitted text of 1_{21b} seems to have solid credentials.

The verb שׂושׂ is used to express spontaneous joy, mostly in relation to a specific event.[392] Joy at the misfortune of another is considered especially hurtful.[393] and understood as something reprehensible.[394] Our understanding of the text is that the enemy delights in daughter Zion's misfortune which she knows has its origin in YHWH (cf $1_{5b,12c,17b}$). This does not undermine the fact that the idea expressed in יְהוָה עָשָׂה רָעָה is both theologically contentious and rarely used. Such activity is not what YHWH's people expect from him[395] and when it does happen it is quite exceptional. Nevertheless, daughter Zion has found herself in one of those exceptions: YHWH has brought this great affliction upon her. See for a similar line of thought and theological tension the conclusion of the first canto of the third song (3_{33}) together with its explanation.

21cA *You brought on the day you had announced.* הֵבֵאתָ יוֹם־קָרָאתָ

The present colon is closely connected to the preceding colon via concatenation at the level of content. Daughter Zion now sees her misfortune in the theological context of the 'day of YHWH' (cf the excursus after 1_{2a}). YHWH has brought on the day he had announced and that 'day' continues unhindered. In recognising this context daughter Zion also admits that she had been warned and that YHWH has kept to his word by bringing the former preaching of the prophets of doom to fulfilment (cf 2_{17}).

Our proposal here runs counter to that most honoured by exegetes and commentators, namely that the 'day' intended here is not the present 'day' of Jerusalem's misfortune but rather a future 'day' in which the prophecies of doom against the nations will be fulfilled. In her prayer, daughter Zion asks whether YHWH still intends to send out his judgement over the nations, which would imply the simultaneous punishment of her enemies. Such a proposal, however, requires some textual emendation which, based on an appeal to the Peshitta, provides the following Hebrew text: הָבֵא אֶת יוֹם־קָרָאתָ (imp *hiph'il*), 'bring on the heralded day!'[396]

---

391 For much more radical emendations cf text critical apparatus of BHK.

392 Cf THAT II 830 (Ruprecht); cf also the meaning of the root שׂמח in 2_{17cA}.

393 Cf Ps $35_{15,19,24}$, Isa 14_{29}.

394 Cf Prov 17_5, 24_{17} and Job 31_{29}.

395 Cf THAT II 799f (Stoebe).

396 Cf Robinson (BHK), Haller, Meek, Gottwald, Rudolph, Weiser, Kraus, Gottlieb, Brandscheidt, Groß, Stoll.

In spite of the apparent exegetical unity surrounding this colon we are unable to share the proposal. In the first place we object to the fact that the text requires emendation, especially since the LXX is at odds with the Peshitta and in agreement with the MT. Secondly, the references noted much earlier indicate that it is the prophetic prediction of YHWH's 'day' against Jerusalem which has come to fulfilment.[397] On the basis of $1_{12,15}$, Albrektson suggests that we are dealing here with the 'day' of the commencement of YHWH's judgement against Israel. This is confirmed from the perspective of structural analysis via the responses in the present canticle between מִחוּץ שִׁכְּלָה־חֶרֶב (1_{20cA}) // הֵבֵאתָ יוֹם־קָרָאתָ (1_{21cA}) // כִּי־רַבּוֹת אַנְחֹתַי (1_{22cA}). Gottlieb disagrees with Albrektson, pointing out that without any connection with what precedes it, the second colon (וְיִהְיוּ כָמוֹנִי) is left too isolated. All this provides Budde (followed by Wiesmann) with the incentive to make fundamental changes in the final two strophes of the present song: reading 1_{22bB} in the place of 1_{21cB}, placing 1_{21cB} after 1_{22aA} and switching 1_{22b} and 1_{22c}. The history of the transmission of the text, however, offers no support for such a radical set of emendations. At the same time, the argument that a present tense interpretation of the text places the second colon (1_{21cB}) in isolation, pays insufficient attention to the character of the 'day of YHWH'.[398] Albrektson's interpretation reinforces this by proposing that the 'day of YHWH' had something to do with the judgement against Israel (cf likewise Boecker). This, however, is incorrect. YHWH's day was primarily a time of judgement against Israel's enemies. Nevertheless, since Amos, it can be noted in the pre-exilic prophetic announcements of judgement that this day could also turn against Israel itself if she were to behave as an enemy of YHWH. The original content of the day, however, should not be lost sight of. Because of their crimes, YHWH's judgement was also announced against the foreign nations. The relevant prophecies from among the canonical prophets[399] directly confirm this although it can also be indirectly derived from a variety of other texts (cf excursus). Given the historical context, the situation prior to the downfall of Judah is significant at this point. One might think, for example, of the controversy between Jeremiah and Hananiah in which the words of the prophets are characterised as prophecies of war, famine and pestilence against mighty nations and great kingdoms (Jer 28_8). We can also determine from Jer 23_{33-40} that such prophets of doom (the מַשְׂאוֹת)

[397] Cf $1_{2a,4c,9c,12c,13a,15a}$.
[398] Cf the excursus after 1_{2a}.
[399] Cf Amos 1–2, Isa 13–21 etcetera.

were even common just before 587.[400] This fact is of vital importance for a correct understanding of the conclusion of this and the following strophe. It is unbelievably painful for daughter Zion to see the announcements of doom prophesied against her, expressed in the יוֹם יְהוָה-preaching of bygone prophets, coming to fulfilment. At the same time, the preaching in question is given a new and exciting topicality. Up to this point only a part of their prophetic announcement has been fulfilled: that directed against daughter Zion. The remainder, that directed against the nations, is still to be awaited.

21cB *Let them become like me.* וְיִהְיוּ כָמוֹנִי

If YHWH keeps to his word with respect to his own people, then why not also with respect to the other nations? Even prophets of doom such as Jeremiah foretold that the nations would have to drink the cup of YHWH's wrath.[401] Jer 25_{29} in particular expresses the prophetic conviction that the nations will not get off scot-free. Nevertheless, now that judgement has fallen upon the very house of God (I Peter 4_{17}), where is YHWH's judgement against the nations? For daughter Zion such a question is an extremely pressing one since many of these nations have become her enemies and have behaved towards her in a more than scandalous manner. When YHWH applies equality of treatment and likewise punishes the trespasses of her enemies, daughter Zion will be granted a substantial clarification of her present distress to say the very least. For this reason we can paraphrase the final bicolon of this strophe as follows: 'You have brought your day upon me, bring it also upon my enemies!' We have therefore translated the imperfect as a jussive: 'let them become'. It is an urgent call for consistency in YHWH's behaviour. It is apparent in 3_{64-66} and 4_{21} that faith in such behaviour is not absent. In the present context such faith is the basis of daughter Zion's prayer.

Several exegetes (Rudolph, Van Selms, Kaiser) detect a prayer for revenge in this final part of Lam I. On the basis of such prayers, including the so-called 'psalms of vengeance',[402] people have considered the OT to be religiously inferior to the NT because of the latter's command to love one's neighbour. Characterising the present prayer as a prayer for revenge, however, is completely mistaken. Desire for revenge has its origin in the

400 Cf 1983, 174f and the explanation of 2_{14}.

401 Cf 25_{15-38} together with the explanation of Lam 4_{21}.

402 Cf AHJGunneweg, *Vom verstehen des Alten Testaments*, Göttingen 1977, 139.

sensitivity of human beings who consider themselves to have been injured by another. It is a desire for atonement, detached from any possible reparation for the damage endured (cf the classic 'eye for an eye, tooth for a tooth'). Such a description does not apply to Lady Jerusalem's prayer for two important reasons. Firstly, her prayer does not arise from hurt feelings, rather it is an appeal to YHWH's just and righteous behaviour.[403] Secondly, she does not call for punishment for the enemy detached from the context of her own situation. The true intention of her prayer is not revenge against the enemy but her own liberation. She longs to be set free from the unbearable distress in which her enemies have submerged her. The following strophe offers further explanation.

22a *Be attentive to all their evil* תָּבֹא כָל־רָעָתָם לְפָנֶיךָ
and deal with them וְעוֹלֵל לָמוֹ

We understand the impf *hiph'il* 2m sg תָּבֹא (√בוא) as jussive. YHWH has not ignored the sins of his people, let him now not ignore the wickedness of the enemy. The meaning of רָעָה varies according to whether one does evil or is forced to endures it. In the former case one speaks of 'wickedness', 'evil' or 'crime', in the latter of 'disaster' or 'misfortune'.[404] In the immediate context there is a clear relationship between רָעָתִי, the ruinous misfortune daughter Zion is being forced to endure (1_{21bA}) and כָל־רָעָתָם, all the evil deeds brought about by her enemies; the latter being the cause of the former. Given the wider context of the song, however, a difficulty arises with respect to context. Daughter Zion has already come to the realisation that it is YHWH himself who is the source of her oppression and not her enemies (cf $1_{5b,12c}$). YHWH himself has commanded the enemy to press hard against his people ($1_{14c,17b}$) which means in essence that they cannot be blamed for their actions since they are simply carrying out His orders! A prayer for revenge against the enemy in this instance is without meaning. Clearly the poets, in speaking of all the evil of the enemy, intend more than their contribution to the fall of Jerusalem alone. We pointed out above (1_{21b}) that a theological uneasiness is set up when YHWH is brought into connection with the doing of רָעָה. The OT is extremely reserved in this regard. It is also frequently stated that YHWH has remorse for the destruction he had planned to do.[405] YHWH only allows

403 Cf also the inclusion in the present sub-canto between צַדִּיק הוּא יְהוָה (1_{18aA}) // הֵבֵאתָ יוֹם־קָרָאתָ וְיִהְיוּ כָמוֹנִי (1_{21c}).
404 Cf THAT II 796ff (Stoebe).
405 Cf THAT II 799 (Stoebe).

such רָעָה to become reality when every other avenue has been exhausted (cf Ezek 22_{30f}). YHWH's minimal force intervention, however, has become a maximum force intervention at the hands of daughter Zion's enemies. A precedent exists which illustrates our point: in Isa 10_{5-19} daughter Zion experiences the malicious behaviour of her enemies as no longer in proportion to the just punishment due from YHWH and far surpassing the prophetic predictions of doom (cf 1_{2c}). Moreover, victory and supremacy do not discharge an enemy from his duty to treat the vanquished in a humane manner.[406] The inclusion at the canticle level with the first canticle (1_{1-3}) makes it clear that the wickedness in question here has to do with the enemies continuing exploitation of daughter Zion.[407] Therefore she prays that YHWH will intervene against her enemies and their ongoing wickedness towards her people.[408]

22b *as you have dealt with me* כַּאֲשֶׁר עוֹלַלְתָּ לִי
because of all my transgressions. עַל כָּל־פְּשָׁעָי

Taken together this and the preceding bicolon constitute a clear chiasm. Besides וְעוֹלֵל לָמוֹ and עוֹלַלְתָּ לִי, כָּל־רָעָתָם and כָּל־פְּשָׁעָי are also parallel. The latter pair is of interest with respect to the aforementioned characterisation of these words as a prayer for revenge (cf 1_{21cB}). Once again it appears that daughter Zion is not moved to pray for YHWH's intervention out of wounded feelings. As a matter of fact, daughter Zion appeals to the 'Selbigkeit' of YHWH: if he punishes one evil he must also punish the other. In doing so she is not attempting to exonerate herself. On the contrary, she places her own former transgressions on the same level as the wickedness of her enemies. She does not shy away from using the weightiest and most concrete expression for 'sin' at her disposal in order to represent her transgressions (for the meaning of פֶּשַׁע cf 1_{5b}), an expression which, as such, corresponds appropriately with מָרוֹ מָרִיתִי (1_{20bB}) thereby forming an inclusion within the canticle. In addition, there is an evident relationship with pre-exilic prophecy of doom, given that the prophets in question denounced the transgressions (פְּשָׁעִים) of their people.[409] If YHWH attends to her prayer, then the salvific dimension of his justice will become visible once again (cf 1_{18a} and 5_{19}). Punishment by YHWH and the ensuing powerlessness of the enemy will alleviate her distress.

---

406 Cf Isa 47_5 and Zech 1_{15}; cf also ASvdWoude, *Zacharia*, Nijkerk 1984, 39.
407 Cf הָיְתָה לָמַס, the enslaving of the population, in 1_{1cB}; cf also 1_{3a} and 5_5.
408 For the specific meaning of the *polel* of √עלל I see 1_{12bB}.
409 Cf Mic 3_8, Jer 5_5 together with THAT II 492f (Knierim).

22cA *For my groans are many* כִּי־רַבּוֹת אַנְחֹתַי

A break in enemy hostilities is essential since daughter Zion's distress is so immense. In interpreting this colon it is important to note the canticle-inclusion between כִּי־צַר־לִי (1_{20aA}) and כִּי־רַבּוֹת אַנְחֹתַי (1_{22cA}). In the exegesis of 1_{20a} we noted that emphasis was on the subjective experience of distress (צַר) and this is confirmed by the inclusion since אֲנָחָה, 'loud groan', has a similar nuance. For more on the meaning of אֲנָחָה cf Ps 6_{7f}, 31_{11} and 38_{10}; cf also the exegesis of $1_{4bB,8cA,11aA}$, texts which employ the verbal form. The latter cola provide some indication as to what lies behind daughter Zion's groans. The inclusion at the song level between רַבָּתִי (1_{1aB}) and רַבּוֹת (1_{22cA}) provides a further indication of the immensity of her affliction via the enormous contrast which it encloses: the once mighty and powerful city is now only mighty in the heaviness of her many and loud groans.

22cB *and my heart is deathly sick.* וְלִבִּי דַוָּי

A second inclusion exists between the final colon of this song and 1_{20aB}: מֵעַי חֳמַרְמָרוּ and וְלִבִּי דַוָּי (22cB). At the same time there is an inclusion at the song level between the present colon and יָשְׁבָה בָדָד in 1_{1aA} rooted in the connotations surrounding leprosy. In the present context דַוָּי stands as an adjective in relation to לִבִּי. In 1_{13cB} the same term appeared to be related to menstruation, making it probable that the same is implied in this (sub-)canto via נִדָּה in the central colon 1_{17cB}. The focus is on the state or condition of the heart of daughter Zion which is profoundly sick.[410] It would appear that heart in the present context has to do with vitality. Intense sickness threatens her very life. The same expression can be found in two other places in the OT: Isa 1_5 and Jer 8_{18}, both of which are not without significance for the explanation of this colon. In Isa 1_5 the image of an ailing body is used to describe the destruction of Judah where the Assyrians had ruined the land (cf the explicative Isa 1_7). The metaphor, therefore, has an objective dimension, that of destruction (cf שֹׁמֵמָה in 1_{13cA}). The use of the expression in Jer 8_{18} is also preceded by a description of enemy destruction, an objective fact which nevertheless resonates on a subjective level with the prophet, making his heart sick and thus expressing the emotional side of the experience of destruction. Both elements deserve to be honoured in our explanation of this final colon of Lam I: because of the horrific devastation of her land and her very self daughter Zion feels herself deathly sick.[411] One specific dimension of the

[410] דַוָּי is an intensive form of דוה, cf GES-B 158; cf also 1_{20bA} on לֵב.

ruin she is facing wounds her most directly and most intensely: the death (from starvation) of her (little) children. This aspect of her desolation is indicated by the response with 1_{20c} (the sword that carries off her children) within the canticle together with the parallel with the final colon of the second song (2_{22c}).

[411] Cf the ongoing connection within the songs with elements from the dirge.

Lamentations II

Canto I (2_{1-10})

1 א *Ah, how he has engulfed in his anger,*
Adonai, daughter Zion.
He has cast down from heaven to earth
the splendour of Israel.
He has not thought of his footstool
on the day of his anger.

2 ב *Adonai has destroyed without mercy*
all the pastures of Jacob.
He has torn down in burning wrath
the fortified cities of daughter Judah.
He has torn to the ground and defiled
the kingdom and its princes.

3 ג *Seething with anger he has hewn off*
all the horns of Israel.
His right hand has pulled back
in the sight of the enemy.
He has burned against Jacob as a flaming fire
which has consumed all around.

---

4 ד *He has bent his bow like an enemy,*
his right hand in the assault
like an adversary; He has killed
every delight for the eye.
In the tent of daughter Zion
he has poured out like fire his fury.

5 ה *Adonai has become like an enemy.*
He has destroyed Israel.
He has destroyed all her palaces,
He has ravaged his fortified cities.
Everywhere in daughter Judah he has brought
great sadness and mourning.

---

6 ו *With violence he has demolished his hut as in a garden,*
he has destroyed his festival site.
He has abolished, YHWH, *in Zion,*
festival and sabbath.
He has rejected in accursed anger
king and priest.

7 ז *Adonai has scorned his altar,*
annulled his sanctuary.
He has delivered into the hand of the enemy
the walls of her palaces.
They have celebrated this tumultuously in YHWH*'s house*
as on the day of a festival.

---

8 ח *It was* YHWH*'s determination to destroy*
the wall of daughter Zion.
He stretched out the measuring line and has not withheld
his hand from destroying.
He lets wall and rampart languish,
together they waste away.

9 ט *Her gates lie collapsed on the ground,*
her bars he has shattered and broken.
Her king and princes dwell among the nations.
(Priestly) guidance is no more.
Even her prophets no longer find
revelation from YHWH.

10 י *They sit on the ground and are dumbfounded,*
the elders of daughter Zion.
They have thrown dust upon their heads,
put on mourning attire.
They press their faces to the ground,
the young girls of Jerusalem.

Canto II (2_{11-22})

11 כ *Blinded with tears are my eyes,*
my insides burn.

My spirit is torn asunder
at the wound of my daughter, my people,
at the pining of children and infants
in the squares of the city.

12 ל *To their mothers they cry:*
"Where is corn and wine?",
while they, parched and gaunt,
in the squares of the city
pour out their lives
on their mothers' lap.

13 מ *What example shall I hold up to you,*
with what compare you, O daughter Jerusalem?
To what shall I liken you,
how comfort you, maiden, daughter Zion?
For vast as the sea is your wound!
Who shall heal you?

---

14 נ *Your prophets have witnessed for you*
what was baseless and vain.
They have not exposed your iniquity
to restore your fortunes.
They witnessed oracles for you,
baseless but alluring.

15 ס *They clap their hands at you*
all who pass along the way.
They hiss and shake the head
at daughter Jerusalem:
"Is this the city that was called:
'perfect in beauty,
the joy of all the land'?"

---

16 ע *They open wide their mouths at you,*
all your enemies.
They hiss and gnash their teeth.
They say: "We have devoured!
Yes, this is the day we so hoped for.
We have uncovered it and see it!"

17 פ YHWH *has done what he planned:*
he has consummated his word
which he ordained long ago.
He has destroyed without mercy.
The enemy rejoices over you.
He has raised the horn of your adversaries.

---

18 צ *Their heart cried out to Adonai:*
"Rampart of daughter Zion!"
Let tears stream down like a flood,
day and night!
Do not rest,
give the apple of your eye no respite!

19 ק *Rise up, cry out in the night,*
from the first watch of the night!
Pour out your heart like water
before the presence of Adonai!
Lift up your hands to him,
for the lives of your children
who perish from hunger
on the corner of every street!

---

20 ר *Look,* YHWH, *and observe*
against whom you are doing this!
Must women eat their own fruit,
the children they carried upon their hands?
Must (they) be murdered in Adonai's sanctuary
priest and prophet?

21 ש *They are lying on the ground in the streets*
from the youngest to the oldest!
My young women and men
fall by the sword!
You kill on the day of your anger,
you slaughter without mercy!

22 ת *You have assembled – as on a festival day –*
my assailants from all around!

On the day of YHWH*'s anger*
no one escapes or survives!
Those whom I caried upon my hands and reared
my enemy murders!

* * *

LITERARY STRUCTURE OF LAMENTATIONS II

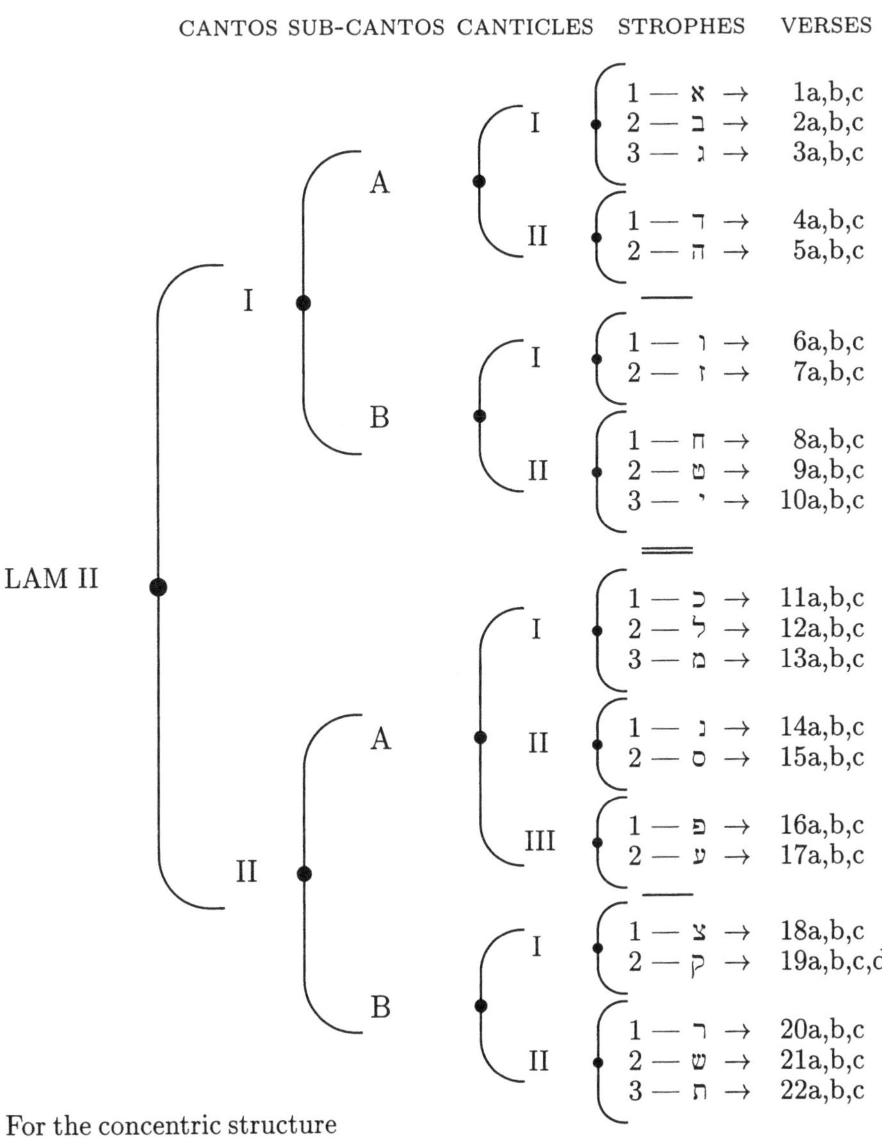

For the concentric structure
of Lam II see 1988, 307ff.

figure 2

Essentials and Perspectives

In a manner similar to that of the first song, the composition of Lamentations II draws us to its central core in which we find agreements on the level of content with the central strophes of Lam I, namely with respect to the common theme of famine. The differences are to be found in the details. While the first song speaks of the dreadful hunger of Jerusalem's population in general terms, here we find the death by starvation of the smallest of the children given central place. The detailed description of the distress of the population and the theological explanation thereof is characteristic of Lam II. The agony of the youngest children is certainly the most serious of Jerusalem's misfortunes but it is not the only one. Every kind of human affliction is to be understood as a consequence of the fall of Zion. The poets begin the song with a detailed description of such affliction.

Canto I (2_{1-10})

In the first canto (2_{1-10}) the poets abandon the style figure of the lamenting daughter Zion from Lam 1_{12-22} and now speak for themselves. With respect to Lam I there is barely any repetition. Time and again new facets and unmentioned details are brought to the fore. One clear distinction with respect to the first song, for example, can be seen in the broader attention given to the land which is expressed in the use of the designations Israel, Jacob and Judah. Such attention provides the primary focus of the first sub-canto (2_{1-5}). It should be noted that from the perspective of structural analysis the desolation of Zion encloses that of the land and constitutes the primary theme of the second sub-canto (2_{6-10}). This is evident from the fact that the song opens with a description of daughter Zion who has encountered the full force of YHWH's wrath while the final canticle of the canto concludes with the destruction of Jerusalem's walls and gates ($2_{8,9}$). In addition, the central verses of the canticle place the destruction of the temple (2_{6a}) alongside the suffering of Judah (2_{5c}).

The first canticle (2_{1-3}) depicts the fall of Zion and Judah. The glory and might of Jerusalem and the land have completely vanished. The profoundly theological character of the description is evident in the fact that YHWH himself is presented as the subject of each and every humiliation and act of destruction while the terrestrial enemy is nowhere mentioned. It was YHWH who brought down the glory of daughter Zion and ruined the fortified cities of Judah (2_{2b}). He alone sapped Israel of its strength and humiliated the kingdom ($2_{2,3}$). YHWH's destructive deeds are packed with theological tension as they connect him to such devastation. The extent of the tension can be seen in the fact that he did not restrain from destroying what was his own property: Zion and the temple (2_{1bc}). In consistently describing Zion's ruin as the first and the last (1_4, $4_{1,12}$, 5_{18}), the poets relate how unbelievable this event has been for them.

The following canticle (2_{4-5}) takes a step further in using the rather daring metaphor of YHWH as enemy. Such an ambivalent comparison makes it possible to consider two lines of thought in conjunction. On the one hand, the metaphor offers the possibility of ascribing hostilities to YHWH. On the other hand, however, it reveals a certain theological reserve in that YHWH is never spoken of in absolute terms as the 'Enemy'. At the same time, the metaphor permits us to interpret YHWH's actions in a different fashion while betraying the hope that he will perhaps change his current course. Such is the hope to be found in all of the songs. See, for example, the conclusion of the final song.

Once again the destruction of Zion (2_{4bc}) is mentioned as the first hostile act, followed only then by that of the land. The conclusion of the canticle makes it clear, moreover, that next to famine and death, the devastation of city and land constitute a substantial aspect of Judah's distress.

The first canticle (2_{6-7}) of the second sub-canto begins with the description of a paradoxical event: YHWH's destruction of his own temple. The importance of this theme is evident from its central position within the first canto (2_{1-10}). Here we find an answer given to those who wish to know the identity of the one responsible for the ruin of the house of God. The context should be understood as that of the critical issue of YHWH's power (cf 3_{34-36}). The response provided, however, is also full of theological tension if one considers the fact that YHWH is evidently rejecting and destroying the place he once chose for himself. This goes for Zion as well as the people who served there in YHWH's name: the king and the priest (2_{6c}). An important element of the poets' theological evaluation is thus brought to the fore: YHWH's wrathful deeds are inconsistent with his true nature and are ultimately damaging to himself also (cf the explanation of 3_{31-33}).

The final canticle (2_{8-10}) of the second sub-canto appears to offer a repetition of Zion's downfall and the fate of the population. Nevertheless, a new and very important theological element is also introduced at this point.

Where earlier canticles gave the impression that YHWH was engaged in an uncontrolled act of wanton destruction, the present verses describe his deeds as considered and carefully assessed. Although it is not mentioned directly, the parallel context makes it clear that the sin of Jerusalem is the occasion of YHWH's actions.

After the fall of Zion is recalled once again via the destruction of her gates and the shattering of her bars, the ongoing consequences for the population become the focus of discussion. The people are summed up as those for whom the loss of YHWH's nearness and protection constitutes a serious problem. Ultimately the entire population is affected from the least infant to the king himself. It would appear that the sequence is determined by social importance although this is only partly true given that the poets opt for a fresh approach via a new canto (2_{11-22}) when dealing with the lot of the children and employ the style figure of daughter Jerusalem who is deeply moved at the fate of her little ones. The reaction of the remaining elders and young women of Jerusalem to this event should be understood as a silent prayer to YHWH resulting from profound distress.

An endeavour is thus made in this first canto to provide a theological perspective on the destruction as a part of human distress. Attention should be paid in this context to the alternation between perfects and presents. It is clear that only the perfect lends itself to the description of a one-off and prior act of material destruction at the hands of the Babylonians while the ongoing distress of the people is most fittingly rendered with a present. See also the alternation of tenses in the transition from 2_9 to 2_{10}.

Canto II (2_{11-22})

In the second canto the element of destruction fades into the background as the poets focus their description on the experiences and ultimate fate of the people. The canto begins with the central strophes of the entire song (2_{11-12}) which concentrate our attention on the starvation and death of the children of Jerusalem. The city is once again personified as a woman whose heart is rent asunder by what has happened to her children. The unavoidable question as to the reason for this dreadful occurrence is posed. The first sub-canto (2_{11-17}) concludes with a description of her dreadful lot – from which her prophets did nothing to protect her – which elicits horror among those who pass her by and joy in the camp of the enemy. The second sub-canto consists of a summons to prayer together with the prayer itself which raises up daughter Jerusalem's most distressing affliction before YHWH, namely the terrible fate of her children.

The first canticle (2_{11-13}) focuses immediately on the fate of the children and infants. From a human perspective their death from starvation must have been the most painful of daughter Jerusalem's afflictions (cf the return of this theme at the end of the song [2_{18-22}]). She concretises the pain and anguish mentioned in 1_{13}. Her immense sorrow can be heard in her broken voice. Following this the poets take the floor once again, seeking in vain for words of comfort (2_{13}). Their inability to do so simply serves to underline the unsurpassed nature of daughter Jerusalem's anguish (1_{12}).

The following canticle (2_{14-15}) establishes a logical connection with the first by raising the unavoidable question of guilt. Who or what has brought all this about? Once again the poets go into further detail. In contrast to Lam I, however, they turn their attention away from the sins of the people and point the finger first at the prophets of Jerusalem. Without denying the guilt of the people, the prophets are burdened, nevertheless, with particular responsibility for the city's downfall since they failed in their task of pointing out abuses and alienation from YHWH. In a politically deteriorating situation, they continued to preach YHWH's unremitting protection and thereby set the people's fears at rest. Their words, it is clear, were without justification. Their failure is held against them vigorously. Had they raised the question of violations of the covenant relationship with YHWH they would have offered the people the chance to turn back from their sin and protected them thereby from ultimate downfall. Unfortunately, they failed to do so and as deceptive spiritual leaders they bear particular responsibility for the affliction now facing the city without removing the share of guilt to be borne by the people. The canticle concludes with the dreadful loss Jerusalem's beauty, the result of YHWH's nearness to her, indicating thereby that the prophets in question are not only to blame for the death of the children.

The third canticle (2_{16-17}) of this sub-canto describes a further consequence of the prophets' neglect: the cutting exultation of the enemy. While this element has been mentioned before,[1] 2_{16} adds a new dimension in the enemy's pretence that they themselves had brought about the fall of the city. The poets counter this claim by pointing to the words once spoken by YHWH through his prophets, words with which the fall of unrepentant

[1] Cf 1_{21}, 2_7.

Israel had already been announced. Since Israel did not change its ways, YHWH carried out his promise and it is for this reason alone that the enemy can rejoice. They received their victory from YHWH. Such a theological interpretation, however, leaves room for a new possibility: if it was YHWH who gave power to the enemy then he can take it away and reverse the fortunes of his people. Such an eventuality is all the more significant given the fact that the poets constantly observe how YHWH's present deeds of destruction are so out of harmony with his former salvific acts and how much against his will all this must be. With this in mind they attempt to move him to save once more by referring in prayer to the intensity of the people's anguish.

The prayer itself is to be found in the final sub-canto (2_{18-22}) following upon a summons to prayer. In the first canticle of this sub-canto daughter Jerusalem is called upon to prayer in spite of everything for the life of her children. The summons is related to 2_{11-12} where Jerusalem's voice is choked with sorrow and her eyes clouded with many tears. Nevertheless she is forced to lift up her hands and cry out in a prayer of self-surrender, raising the affliction of her children before YHWH. Their situation is all the more poignant since they themselves cannot be held responsible for Jerusalem's downfall. They are the innocent victims of intense suffering. The concluding canticle (2_{20-22}) reveals how daughter Jerusalem obeys the summons to prayer. She lays the suffering of all her children both small and great before YHWH. She begs him to look upon those who are being forced to suffer his wrath and perish. In this way she endeavours to draw YHWH's attention to the consequences of this raging anger which is so uncharacteristic of him. The unmistakable question is present in the background: how long does he intend to maintain this disturbing behaviour? See the explanation of 5_{22}.

Lamentations II

Scholarly Exposition

Introduction

The second song continues the description of sorrow and affliction begun in the first. The difference with respect to Lam I, however, is to be found primarily in the details. From the theological perspective, Judah's fate is presented entirely as the result of YHWH's destructive actions. The devastation mentioned in passing in the first song is now the focus of the poets' attention with the destruction of Zion occupying a central position. The depiction of human suffering is dominated by the anguish brought about by the horrendous famine facing the people. The poets pause for a moment to convey the fate of the children, the most vulnerable victims, as well as the powerlessness and distress of their mothers. Where the first song spoke in general terms of sin and guilt, the second song treats the topic more systematically and even points the finger at the guilty parties. Having expressed her grief, in prayer daughter Jerusalem explicitly names those who are so urgently in need of YHWH's assistance.

Content/structure

In canto I (2_{1-10}) the ruin of Zion and the land is presented together with the consequences thereof for the population. The first sub-canto (2_{1-5}) commences with the destruction of Zion and then moves on to describe the devastation of the land. The second sub-canto (2_{6-10}) focuses on the destruction of the temple and of Jerusalem. Both sub-cantos conclude (2_{5c} and 2_{9-10}) with reference to the consequences of the disaster for the people of Judah and Jerusalem.

The second canto (2_{11-22}) takes up the first and is characterised by its emphasis on the distress of the population. The canto begins and ends with reference to the horrendous and indescribable fate of the children of

Jerusalem. Death by starvation of the children and infants stands at the beginning of the canto (2_{11-13}) while the concluding verses (2_{20-22}) return to the theme anew. With respect to the first song, Lam II goes into more detail regarding the question of guilty parties, those who are responsible for the starvation and death of Jerusalem's children, while focusing more closely on the horror of those who pass by and the exaltation of the enemy. Everything seems to point the finger at the shortcomings of Jerusalem's prophets. In contrast to their empty proclamations of salvation YHWH has fulfilled his true prophetic word (2_{14} versus 2_{17}). Such accusations do not mitigate the distress of the innocent children, reason why Lady Jerusalem must turn to YHWH for help (2_{18-22}).

Genre and 'Sitz im Leben'

What was said with respect to the genre of Lam I remains valid and appropriate for the second song. Here too we find a manifest association between lament and dirge. Compare the explanation of $2_{4b,5c,10}$ etcetera. See also the section dealing with genre in the general introduction (III.2 and III.3).

Sub-canto I (Lam 2_{1-5})

The description of the fall of Zion and the devastation of the land reveals a profoundly theological tone. YHWH is repeatedly mentioned as the subject of hostile activities depicted in a variety of images: he hurls down, does not remember, destroys, raises to the ground. In the present sub-canto, such metaphorical language for the destructive activity of YHWH is strongly influenced by military enterprise.[2] Material devastation is heavily emphasised, with attention focusing primarily on Judah and to a lesser extent on Jerusalem. The quantitative difference is compensated for via the first positioning of the downfall of Zion in 2_1.

Canticle I (2_{1-3})

Content/theme: *Zion and Israel encounter the wrath of Adonai*

Literary argumentation:

inclusions: יָעִיב בְּאַפּוֹ (1aA) // וַיִּבְעַר (3cA)
בְּיוֹם אַפּוֹ (1cB) // בָּחֳרִי־אַף (3aA)
בַּת־צִיּוֹן (1aB) // יַעֲקֹב (3cA)

[2] See MCAKorpel, *A Rift in the Clouds*, Münster 1990, 511–513.

responses: קֶרֶן יִשְׂרָאֵל (3aB) // בַּת־צִיּוֹן (1aB)
הָרַס (2bA)[3] // הִשְׁלִיךְ מִשָּׁמַיִם אֶרֶץ (1bA)
כֹּל קֶרֶן יִשְׂרָאֵל (3aB) // כָּל־נְאוֹת יַעֲקֹב (2aB)
מִבְצְרֵי בַת־יְהוּדָה (2bB) // תִּפְאֶרֶת יִשְׂרָאֵל (1aB)

ext par: קֶרֶן יִשְׂרָאֵל (3aB) // מִבְצְרֵי בַת־יְהוּדָה (2bB)
לָאָרֶץ (2cA) // אֶרֶץ (1bA)
יַעֲקֹב (2aB) // יִשְׂרָאֵל (1bB) //
יַעֲקֹב (3cA)[4] // יִשְׂרָאֵל (3aB)

1a *Ah, how he has engulfed in his anger,* אֵיכָה יָעִיב בְּאַפּוֹ
Adonai, daughter Zion. אֲדֹנָי אֶת־בַּת־צִיּוֹן

The introductory אֵיכָה (cf 1_{1a}) sets the tone for the second song as that of the dirge as it did for the first. The openings of both songs, however, reveal striking differences. Kaiser is of the opinion that the second song is older than the first on the basis of the fact that, among other things, the first song is more theological in character than the second. The latter only refers to sin as the root cause of Zion's lot in 2_{14} in contrast to references in $1_{5,8,18,22}$ of the first song. The opposite, however, appears to be more defensible: while the first song only mentions the fall as the work of YHWH as late as 1_{5b}, song two is theological from the very beginning, 2_1 commencing with the description of YHWH's judgement – which functions in fact as a 'title' for the entire song – 'Adonai engulfs daughter Zion in his anger'. It is immediately striking that daughter Zion is the first to be mentioned in the second song,[5] meaning that the poets are focusing their attention on Jerusalem/Zion. The present canticle does offer a certain counter-balance with respect to the first canticle of Lam I (1_{1-3}) in that the final strophes (2_{2-3}) relate the fate of Judah in reverse order. A clear balance is thus present between the description of the distress of the city and of the land. Secondly, the imperfect is used in the present canticle while the following verbs with Adonai as subject are perfects. The imperfects signify that Adonai's anger is ongoing while the perfects portray events which have already taken place. In this sense the imperfects 'include' the perfects.

Once again – in the context of the OT at least – we come face to face with a new expression. The verb עוב (here *hiph'il* impf) is a *hapax*. Several com-

[3] Cf Ezek 13_{14}.
[4] Note the frequent alternation.
[5] Cf also 1_6, the central strophe of the first canticle of Lam I.

mentators[6] associate it with the noun עָב 'cloud' (Aramean עִיבָא) which occurs with greater frequency. This interpretation is supported by the LXX and the Peshitta. Ehrlich, Meek, Kopf[7] and Rudolph are inclined to relate the term to the Arabic verb *'yb* 'to disgrace', an explanation which finds support in the Targum.[8] In contrast, McDaniel,[9] followed by Hillers and Brandscheidt, defends the notion that the verb is a form of the root יעב. This verb is only found in a derived form in the OT, namely as תּוֹעֵבָה 'horrible', and is used with reference to idolatry, cultic impurity etcetera (cf HAL 1568f). Such an interpretation, however, implies a theological contradictio in terminis: the Holy one makes somebody or something תּוֹעֵבָה. Such an idea is never expressed so directly. We opt, therefore, for the traditional interpretation 'to engulf with cloud', noting that structural analysis provides a further argument in its favour. In our explanation of 1_{1a} we already pointed to the fact that the first four songs each contain images of darkness in their opening canticle (לַיְלָה [1_{2a}] // חֹשֶׁךְ וְלֹא־אוֹר [3_{2B}] // יִשְׁנֶא [4_{1a}]), all of which stand for the consequences of YHWH's judgement. In the opening of the final song this corresponds with its consequence: 'disgrace' (5_1, cf Ezek 5_{15}).

The interpretation of יָעִיב as 'to engulf' fits comfortably into the series as an image of darkness. In a certain sense this may also be true for the alternative suggestion: 'disgrace', 'indignity'.[10] Hillers chooses this alternative because he is of the opinion that 'to engulf in cloud' can be found nowhere else in the OT as an image for divine judgement. The material collected by Holmberg,[11] however, provides for a different conclusion. Dark cloud is one of the accompanying phenomena associated with the appearance of YHWH (theophany). YHWH envelops himself in dark cloud.[12] The texts from II Sam 22_{12} and Ps 18_{12} constitute important parallel texts in that the terminology varies between them, thus implying that a certain descriptive freedom is evident. They are also important because the purpose of theophany described therein has to do with liberation from the hand of

[6] Among others Keil, Budde, Löhr, Haller, Wiesmann, Weiser, Kraus, Boecker and Stoll.

[7] See LKopf, 'Arabische Etymologien und Parallelen zum Bibelwörterbuch', VT VIII (1958), 188f.

[8] Cf also SBergler, 'Threni V – nur ein alphabetisierendes Lied? Versuch einer Deutung', VT XVII (1977), 316.

[9] ThFMcDaniel, 'Philological Studies in Lamentations', Biblica 49 (1968), 34f.

[10] Cf GES-B 568 and see also חֶרְפָּתֵנוּ in 5_1.

[11] See TWAT V 980f.

[12] Cf Ex $19_{9,16}$, II Sam 22_{12}, Ps 18_{12}; cf also Job 22_{14}.

the enemy (cf II Sam 22_{15ff} and Ps 18_{12ff}). It is obvious that darkness is understood as a threatening element among the theophanic phenomena, indeed human beings certainly experience it as such (cf Ps 23_4, Isa 8_{22f}). The dark cloud in which YHWH wraps himself can also surround human beings if he draws near to punish their evil ways. The classical descriptions of the day of YHWH provide excellent examples of such a notion.[13] The darkness of the pillar of cloud can be interpreted as threatening for Egypt even in a difficult text such as Ex 14_{20}. In a related complaint of the people such as Ps 44 the situation of YHWH's judgement is typified as darkness (Ps 44_{10}; cf also Jer 13_{16}!). Given the relationship with the day of YHWH terminology – which can also be found in parallel strophes in the other songs – it seems appropriate to opt for the interpretation 'to engulf with cloud'. In contrast to Ps 18 and II Sam 22, it is 'daughter Zion' who is here confronted with the darkness of YHWH's wrath and not the enemy.[14] Once again in contrast to the conclusion of the final song the tetragrammaton is not used at this point but the divine name אֲדֹנָי. BHS is incorrect to propose that we read יְהוָה here.[15] For the meaning of the divine name and its usage see the explanation of 1_{14c}.

1b *He has cast down from heaven to earth* הִשְׁלִיךְ מִשָּׁמַיִם אֶרֶץ
the splendour of Israel. תִּפְאֶרֶת יִשְׂרָאֵל

With the exception of Mic 7_{19}, the *hiph'il* of the root שׁלך with YHWH as subject almost always carries negative connotations.[16] The preposition מִן before שָׁמַיִם has a locative function, pointing to the heavens as the place from which YHWH has cast down. The fact that YHWH has cast down from heaven 'to earth' reveals the vast extent of the fall.[17] The combination √שׁלך + אֶרֶץ is not uncommon. See Ezek 19_{12} where it refers to destruction together with Deut 29_{27} and Jer 22_{28} (*hoph'al*) where exile is implied by the notion of being cast down into another land. In combination with שָׁמַיִם the idea of exile from heaven is included in the image.[18] Such a mighty fall is what usually overcomes earthly kings who in their pride consider themselves to be like gods.[19] In the present text, however, we are not dealing with the casting down or exile of persons but of the

[13] Cf Zeph 1_{14f}, Joel 2_2, Ezek 30_3 cf Isa 19_1.
[14] For the meaning of בַּת־צִיּוֹן cf the explanation of 1_{4cB}.
[15] Cf 1988, 318f.
[16] Cf THAT II 919 (Stolz).
[17] Cf Prov 25_3; cf also Lam 1_{9b}.
[18] Cf CHoutman, *De hemel in het Oude Testament*, Franeker 1974, 245.
[19] Cf Isa $14_{15,19}$ and Ezek 28_{17} together with the commentary of KSpronk, *Beatific*

תִּפְאֶרֶת יִשְׂרָאֵל, the 'glory of Israel'. The term תִּפְאֶרֶת is found in a variety of contexts in the OT and can be used in general to refer to what is considered beautiful or to the things that make people proud: adornment, splendour, beauty, as well as non-material things such as victory etcetera.[20] Rudolph follows such a line in his commentary. The problem remains, however, as to how such things can be cast down from heaven to earth. The phrase תִּפְאֶרֶת יִשְׂרָאֵל must imply something which belongs (belonged) in heaven. For this reason the suggestion of Kraus, Kaiser, Boecker and Brandscheidt, among others, who propose that the phrase refers to the glory of the city of Jerusalem, remains unconvincing. Van Selms follows a similar line of thought in considering the casting down of the תִּפְאֶרֶת to refer to the destruction of Jerusalem's tall ramparts.

Weiser correctly points out that the notion of the divine mountain is present here in the background. Reference can be made in this regard to Ps 48_{2f}, a Zion psalm which also exhibits several connections with Lamentations at both the literary level and the level of content.[21] Psalm 48 speaks of the ancient idea of the divine mountain, the top of which reached up to heaven and served as the dwelling place of the gods. In light of YHWH's unicity, Israel transferred the notion to mount Zion and to the temple in Jerusalem where YHWH made his home.[22]

The idea of YHWH's enthronement in the temple, however, need not run counter those texts which say that his throne is in the heavens,[23] since both heaven and earth encountered one another in the sacred space of the temple. The Psalmist is free, therefore, to employ synonymous parallelism in singing:

> "YHWH *is in his holy temple,* YHWH*'s throne is in heaven.*"[24]

The glory of YHWH which abides in the heavens radiates over his earthly sanctuary in Zion, the temple.[25] The Israelites survey YHWH's splendour

Afterlife in Ancient Israel and in the Ancient Near East, AOAT 219, Neukirchen-Vluyn 1986, 213–226.

[20] Cf THAT II 387 (Vetter).

[21] Cf 1983, passim.

[22] Cf Ps 80_2, 99_1, Isa 37_{16}, II Kgs 19_{15}.

[23] Cf, for example, Ps 14_2, 20_7.

[24] Ps 11_4; cf Jer 25_{30}, cf also MMetzger, 'Himmlische und irdische Wohnstatt Jahwes', UF 2 (1970), 139–158, TNDMettinger, *The Dethronement of Sabaoth. Studies in the Shem and Kabod Theologies*, Coniectanea Biblica, Old Testament Series 18, Lund 1982, 29ff and TWAT III 1025–1032 (Görg).

[25] Cf Ps 89_{18}, 96_6.

and are moved to praise (cf Ps 71_8). Where it is said in the present colon that YHWH has thrown down this splendour of Israel from the heavens then the implication must be that he has severed the connection between his heavenly throne and his earthly sanctuary and that Zion as a consequence has to do without YHWH's presence. The destruction of the temple is the visible consequence thereof.[26]

Here also we find that structural analysis supports the suggestion that תִּפְאֶרֶת יִשְׂרָאֵל refers to the temple, namely via the response relationship with the following canticle: תִּפְאֶרֶת יִשְׂרָאֵל (1bB) // כֹּל מַחֲמַדֵּי־עָיִן (4bB) (cf also the parallel with 1_4). Moreover, within the first canto of Lam II, 2_4 constitutes an inclusion with 2_7 where the destruction of the temple is likewise the focus of description. The combination temple/Israel is quite understandable. Jerusalem and her sanctuary were the joy and possession of the whole land (cf 2_{15c}). The name Israel resounds here by design for the first time and refers to the people.[27] The naming of Israel at this point reveals an enormous contrast: Israel – the people of YHWH – is forced to face the fact that YHWH has cut them off. The image of the widow in the parallel colon of the first song is significant here: Lady Jerusalem has lost her husband YHWH (1_{1b}). A further connection with the א-strophe of the first song is evident: a widow wore no adornment and in mourning wore no make-up.[28] YHWH himself has made Israel into a widow and removed her adornment from her.[29]

1c *He has not thought of his footstool* וְלֹא־זָכַר הֲדֹם־רַגְלָיו
on the day of his anger. בְּיוֹם אַפּוֹ

Our interpretation of 2_{1b} is well suited to what follows in 2_{1c}, regardless of whether the 'footstool of his feet' refers to the temple (mountain) itself or to the ark. Albrektson, Weiser and Kraus are of the opinion that the reference here is to the ark while most other exegetes opt for the temple. It is not easy to choose between the two. In the early monarchy, the ark was understood as the footstool in front of YHWH's throne.[30] The image

26 Cf Ezek $24_{21,25}$. For further details and literature on this topic see 1983, 281–287.
27 Cf THAT I 784 (Gerleman) together with the remarks on יַעֲקֹב in 1_{17bB}.
28 Cf II Sam 13_{19}, Isa 61_3.
29 Cf Isa 3_{16}–4_1, Ezek 16_{39}, Judith 8_5, 9_1, 10_{2ff}. together with the explanation of Lam 4_{22aB}.
30 Cf Ps 99: response between יֹשֵׁב כְּרוּבִים (99_{1B}) // לַהֲדֹם רַגְלָיו (99_{5B}). See also Mettinger, 23, Ps 132_7 and I Chron 28_2, together with the drawings in OKeel, *Die Welt der altorientalischen Bildsymbolik und das Alte Testament*, Zürich-Einsiedeln-Köln-Neukirchen-Vluyn 1977^2, 146, 232ff.

of the footstool set in front of YHWH enthroned accurately reflects the relationship between the earthly and heavenly domains (cf Isa 6, where the hem of YHWH's royal cloak fills the temple – the hem, according to Keel being the weakest and least significant part of a person's clothing).[31]

The response in Ps 99: וְהִשְׁתַּחֲווּ לַהֲדֹם רַגְלָיו (5B) // וְהִשְׁתַּחֲווּ לְהַר קָדְשׁוֹ (9B), in which it is apparent that mount Zion can be understood as YHWH's footstool, makes it clear that the expression 'footstool of his feet' need not exclusively refer to the ark. Fabry is of the opinion that this extension from ark to Zion was the result of an increasing awareness of YHWH's magnitude.[32] In light of the response it is more probable that proskynesis on the part of the entire people had become impossible and as a result the temple (mountain) took the place of the ark. This was possible because the holiness of the ark extended to both temple and mountain and even to the city.[33] The transfer of the sacred character of the ark to the adjacent territory gained its own independence and no longer needed to be related to the ark per se. All this explains why the ark is rarely mentioned by the prophets during the period of the monarchy, although this need not imply that it had been removed altogether. The idea of complete removal would require some explanation. Spieckermanns' suggestion that the ark was quickly removed from the temple domain in Jerusalem after the division of the kingdom "weil sie sich als religiöses Einheitssymbol nicht bewährt hatte" is not convincing.[34] Indeed, Jerusalem's political pretension to being the only capital of all Israel would have been given significant support precisely by the ark's presence. As a matter of fact, Judah never gave up its claims over the entire kingdom (cf Josiah) while the North not only created its own national sanctuary in order to undermine the political status of Jerusalem (cf I Kgs 12) but also made imitations of the ark.[35] Since it is fairly reasonable to assume that the ark was still present, it was possible, therefore, that the mention of the one (the ark) may have implied the other (the temple [mountain]) and vice versa. On the level of content, the choice between Zion and ark is equally difficult. Were we to opt for Zion/temple, then a clear inclusion becomes evident in the strophe: בַּת־צִיּוֹן (1aB) // הֲדֹם־רַגְלָיו (1cA) (cf also בְּאַפּוֹ [1aA] // בְּיוֹם אַפּוֹ [1cB]), with the central bicolon appearing likewise to refer to the temple. Such

[31] OKeel, YHWH-*visionen und Siegelkunst*, SBS 84/85, Stuttgart 1977, 69.
[32] In TWAT II 356.
[33] Cf Ps 46_5, Isa 52_1; see also THAT II 603f (Müller).
[34] HSpieckermann, *Heilsgegenwart. Eine Theologie der Psalmen*, Göttingen 1989, 93.
[35] Cf Jer 3_{16} and AvSelms, *Jeremia deel I*, Nijkerk 1972, 73.

evidence suggests strong internal consistency within the present strophe, but little difference is made if we were to opt for the ark instead. While the ark can also stand for mount Zion, at the same time it is the ancient symbol (cf Num 10_{33-36}) of YHWH's presence, a sign of his relationship with his people. In this event also the present colon would follow on well from what precedes. In fact both options are not mutually exclusive, both are implied by this colon.

Perhaps the disappearance of the ark is being referred to here. Some further historical reflections would be relevant in this context. In our explanation of 1_{4b},[36] we already noted the exceptional nature of the destruction of the temple by the Babylonians as a means to prevent further insurrection. Jerusalem's sanctuary had achieved such political importance because, as YHWH's dwelling, the people believed it to be inviolable. By destroying the temple, the Babylonians effectively undermined the people's faith. It is difficult to see how such faith in the inviolability of Zion could be maintained and strengthened if the ark – symbol of YHWH's presence par excellence – had been taken as booty by an invading enemy at some prior stage of Israel's history.[37] At the same time it is hard to imagine that such a thing could transpire without there being an entire narrative to accompany it.[38] The most reasonable suggestion continues to be that the ark remained in Jerusalem until its downfall in 587. It is hardly imaginable that the poets, as former adherents of Zion theology, would have made no allusion to the loss of such an ancient symbol of faith had such a loss already occurred.[39]

It is evident from their choice of words that they were trying to give theological expression to the evident division between YHWH and Zion. Ruined Zion was no longer identical with YHWH's dwelling which was now clearly situated in the heavens.[40] Within the ruins of Zion, however, the very distance between the poets and YHWH provided the grounds for maintaining their faith in him.

A final remark with reference to 2_{1cB}. The expression בְּיוֹם אַפּוֹ provides a further reminder of the day of YHWH which has now become a reality for Israel. See the excursus on the day of YHWH above together with the explanation of 1_{21c}; for the meaning of YHWH's anger see 1_{12c}.

---

36 See the relevant pages of the present commentary as well as 1983,143f.

37 Cf the possibilities mentioned in TWAT II 403f (Zobel).

38 Cf I Sam 5 and 6.

39 Cf, the explanation of 4_1.

40 Cf the use of מִשָּׁמַיִם together with the explanation of 5_{19}.

2a *Adonai has destroyed without mercy* בִּלַּע אֲדֹנָי לֹא חָמַל
all the pastures of Jacob. אֵת כָּל־נְאוֹת יַעֲקֹב

The root בלע I carries the basic meaning 'devour' with the accent on haste: one sees food and one devours it in an instant.[41] Figuratively speaking, human beings are frequently the object of devouring (Hos 8_8, Jer 51_{34}). The *pi'el* form employed in the present colon further underlines the destructive character of the act. The context in which the term is used frequently indicates that the pious, the just or the innocent are the ones who are under threat of such radical annihilation at the hands of the enemy.[42] The hostile character of Adonai's punishing deed is evident from the first word. Indeed, Adonai will be referred to as the enemy below in 2_{5a}.

The *qal* of √חמל can be confidently translated by the term 'mercy', especially in light of the element of temporal duration implied therein. Given his compassion and desire for a change of heart,[43] YHWH is moved to tolerate and spare for a while those who deserve punishment. The combination לֹא חָמַל points to YHWH's resolution in carrying out his judgement.[44] The fact that the expression does not appear in the Psalms allows us to assume the influence of the prophetic announcements of doom here also.[45] With YHWH as subject, the verb is to be found in Jer 13_{14} and 21_7; cf Jer 15_5 and Isa 30_{14}. The expression occurs most frequently in Ezekiel. While Ezekiel announces that YHWH will exercise no compassion in his judgement over Israel[46] we find a repeated response in Lamentations that YHWH has indeed shown no compassion ($2_{2,17,21}$, 3_{43}). Nevertheless, the expression is more than a simple response: it betrays dismay and alarm. There is no trace of hesitation or compassion left in YHWH's hostile actions towards his people. According to the *q^e^rē* וְלֹא, whereby the ו serves as reinforcement, the Masoretes have provided a further accent at this point.[47] The second colon introduces a further mark of contrast. The objects of Adonai's devastating deeds are not human beings but the נְאוֹת יַעֲקֹב. נְאוֹת is plural[48] of נָוֶה, 'pasture', referred to in Jer 25_{37} as the 'peaceful folds'.[49] In the context of a prophetic judgement the use of such pastoral images is

41 Cf TWAT I 659f (Schüpphaus) together with Isa 28_4 and Hos 8_8.
42 Cf Ps 124_3, Isa 49_{19}.
43 Cf Joel 2_{18} and II Chron 36_{15}.
44 Cf TWAT II 1043f (Tsevat).
45 Cf 1983, 262–267.
46 See Ezek 5_{11}, $7_{4,9}$, 8_{18}, 9_{10}.
47 Cf HAL 247 sv ו (3).
48 Cf BL 215g.
49 Cf Ps 16_6 in which an agreement is evident between the pious and the innocent

ambivalent. It is said, for example, that after destruction a land is useful for nothing other than pasture.[50] The opposite, however, is also true: the judgement announces that even the pasture itself will be destroyed.[51] The conclusion of Jer 25 reveals substantial agreements with the judgement terminology found in Lamentations.[52] Initial impressions would lead us to suppose that the destruction in question was that brought about in the countryside of Judah, at first by the Babylonians and then later by a variety of enemies.[53] The devastation of Judah's pastures, however, appears to have metaphorical significance, equating them with residential areas. Such is the case with respect to the announcements of salvation in Jer 23_3, 50_{19} and Ezek 34_{14} (cf Ps 23_2) and it is evident here in the parallelism with the 'fortified cities of Judah' in the following colon. The poets' use of this expression implies the destruction of both city and land (cf Ps 79_5).

2b *He has torn down in burning wrath* הָרַס בְּעֶבְרָתוֹ
the fortified cities of daughter Judah. מִבְצְרֵי בַת־יְהוּדָה

As is evident from the use of the root הרס, the present colon provides further detail on what precedes it. The term is often used to describe the destruction of cities as well as the pulling down of walls.[54]

The object of the verb also appears to offer further detail. It does not refer to the cities of Judah in general but rather singles out the fortified cities, the מִבְצְרֵי בַת־יְהוּדָה,[55] the destruction of which had already been predicted within the framework of Zephaniah's day of YHWH preaching (Zeph 1_{16}, cf Jer 5_{17}). מִבְצָר is derived from √בצר III. In Ugaritic the verb means 'high' and by extension 'inaccessible'.[56] It is known that Rehoboam built fortified defensive cities, strategically situated along his borders, to act as buffers should Jerusalem come under threat of attack.[57] The summary in II Chron 11 mentions the cities of Lachish and Azekah, two fortress towns which are also mentioned in Jer 34_7 as the only cities besides Jerusalem

---

who are confronted by a destructive action (√בלע I *pi'el*).

50 Cf Ezek 25_5, Isa 27_{10}, Zeph 2_6.

51 Cf Am 1_2, Jer 10_{25}, $25_{30,36f}$.

52 Note that the prophecy of the poisonous cup is exclusive to Jer 25 and Lam 4_{21}.

53 Cf 1983, 151–154 and the explanation of 3_{64-66}, 4_{21}, $5_{5,8}$.

54 Cf the texts mention by Münderlein in TWAT II 499, although Mic 5_2 deserves special mention, given its corresponding formulation as a prophecy of doom.

55 For the expression בַת־יְהוּדָה cf 1_{4c} and 1_{15c}.

56 Cf HAL 142 and TWAT IV 638 (Haag); cf also Deut 3_5.

57 II Chron 11_{5-10}; for further specifics see KRoubos, *II Kronieken*, Nijkerk 1972, 123–126; RdVaux, *Institutions II*, 31–40; BHH 475–479 and BRL² 80ff.

which had not yet fallen into the hands of the Babylonians. This reference has been confirmed by extra-biblical sources, namely the Lachish ostraca (nr IV).[58] The contrast found in the destruction of Jacob's charming pastures is paralleled here in the destruction of Judah's fortifications.

The subject of these acts of destruction is not the enemy but Adonai himself, thus lending the description a theological character once again. The verb הרס, for example, is specifically used to describe YHWH's exercise of judgement.[59] The destruction itself does not take place without emotion. Where the first bicolon in this strophe only suggests emotion by stating that YHWH has destroyed without mercy, the present bicolon makes it explicit, even specifying the burning wrath (בְּעֶבְרָתוֹ) with which YHWH went about his deeds. עֶבְרָה (cf also 3_{1B}) stands alongside אַף 'anger' (cf 1_{12}), חֵמָה 'glowing anger' (2_4, 4_{11}), חָרוֹן 'burning anger' (1_{12}, 4_{11}), זַעַם 'cursed anger' (2_6) and the root קצף 'to be wrathful' (5_{22}) as part of the terminology employed to describe YHWH's rage. As such, the notion also has a place in the description of the day of YHWH. The theological consequences of YHWH's anger are explained above with reference to 1_{12c}.

The term עֶבְרָה specifically implies an emotionally laden and forceful outburst of anger (cf Gen 49_7). The divine form of the term carries the idea of burning and devouring and constitutes a force which cannot be resisted, a force which was once directed against Israel's enemies.[60] Now God has turned his anger against Israel itself. The poets' use of the term is undoubtedly inspired by the speed and effectiveness with which the city and the land were burned to the ground and destroyed. One must be attentive, however, to the theological limits of the metaphor. The poets do not imply that YHWH is beside himself with anger or that he has lost control (cf the explanation of 2_8 and 5_{22}). While the reasons for YHWH's עֶבְרָה are mentioned elsewhere[61] they remain absent from the present verses and their surrounding context, thus placing the accent on the wrathful outburst itself.

By placing the *'aṯnāḥ* under לָאָרֶץ, the Masoretes intended to include the expression הִגִּיעַ לָאָרֶץ from the following colon in the present bicolon. Such a procedure remains improbable, however, given that the idea of 'pulling

[58] Cf ANET[3], 322 and TGI[2], 76f.
[59] Cf Jer 1_{10} and TWAT II 500f (Münderlein).
[60] Cf TWAT V 1038 (Schunck).
[61] Cf, for example, Isa 9_{18}, Ezek 22_{21}, Jer 7_{29}.

down to earth' is already included in the meaning of הרס. Moreover, the strophe would be severely imbalanced thereby.

2c *He has torn to the ground and defiled* הִגִּיעַ לָאָרֶץ חִלֵּל
the kingdom and its princes. מַמְלָכָה וְשָׂרֶיהָ

The final bicolon of verse 2 expresses the total character of what has happened: the entire kingdom has been affected by YHWH's judgement. The *hiph'il* of √נגע literally means 'to cause to touch' (cf HAL 631) while with לָאָרֶץ it might be translated 'to cause to touch the earth' or by extension 'to tear down to the ground'. The expression can be used of walls[62] or a high city (Isa 26_5) and in the figurative sense of a political entity such as the kingdom of Judah and its leaders. It is unnecessary to emend the MT and read: חִלְּלָם מַלְכָּהּ וְשָׂרֶיהָ 'He has defiled them, her king and her princes (namely those of daughter Judah)' as the LXX does (cf Albrektson). Attempts to interpret מַמְלָכָה personally as 'king' create more difficulties than they explain (cf Gottlieb). Given the unity of this strophe, the parallelism between נְאוֹת יַעֲקֹב (2aB) // מִבְצְרֵי בַת־יְהוּדָה (2bB) // מַמְלָכָה (2cB) strongly suggests the matter-of-fact interpretation of מַמְלָכָה as 'kingdom' (also supported by the meaning of הִגִּיעַ לָאָרֶץ). The poets' enormous respect for their land of Judah/Israel as a religious datum further sustains such an interpretation.[63] The personal touch is supplied, nevertheless, by the use of שָׂרֶיהָ, the destruction of the kingdom having a particularly devastating effect on its leaders.[64]

As in the preceding bicolon the present bicolon also reveals a theological dimension (cf the parallelism between בִּלַּע אֲדֹנָי [2aA] // עֶבְרָתוֹ [2bA] // חִלֵּל [2cA]). The *pi'el* form of √הלל I 'to defile' thereby provides the theological consequences of YHWH's destructive actions. The basic meaning of the verb carries the notion of 'unbinding'.[65] In the OT context of the sacred, the term takes on the meaning of 'defilement', implying that the relationship between the holy and the Holy One has been ruptured. As subjects of the verb, human persons can cause a rupture in the relationship by their impure/sinful behaviour. Since his Name is bound to that of Israel, YHWH can forego punishment (cf Ezek $20_{9,14}$) but not for an unlimited time. Israel's sin can reach such proportions that YHWH himself is forced to bring about a rupture in their relationship. In the fashion of a response,

---

62 Cf Isa 25_{12}, Ezek 13_{14}.

63 Cf the explanation of 5_2 and the prayer for restoration in 5_{21}.

64 For the significance and functions of the princes cf the explanation of 1_{6b}.

65 Cf THAT I 571 (Maass) and TWAT II 972 (Dommerhausen).

this is also rendered in a number of places with the *pi'el* of √חלל I, but now with YHWH as subject: he himself actively defiles Israel. The fall of Jerusalem in 587 is understood as such a defilement.[66] The same is true here. After such devastation daughter Zion is now outlawed. She can no longer rely on YHWH. He has cut his connections with her.

Note the agreements and differences between 1_2 and 2_2. While both strophes deal with a complete change of disposition, the first focuses on that of Israel's allies, the second that of YHWH.

3aA *Seething with anger he has hewn off...* גָּדַע בָּחֳרִי־אַף

In comparison to the previous strophe, Rudolph (along with Brandscheidt) sees YHWH's immediate actions coming to the foreground here. In the three bicola of verse 2, YHWH is always subject of the act of devastation, in the present strophe this is twice the case. The central bicolon reveals the enemy to be the executors of YHWH's divine judgement. The poets imply no further emphasis. Thus we do not find the construction חֲרוֹן אַפּוֹ but rather בָּחֳרִי־אַף in which the term חֳרִי is roughly the equivalent of חֲרוֹן (cf HAL 339). There is, however, a striking difference in the contextual use of both terms: חֲרוֹן (cf 1_{12c}) is only found as an adjective describing divine wrath whereas the adjective חֳרִי also and more frequently describes human anger.[67] YHWH's anger is presented with a more anthropomorphic colouring in the present colon and thereby becomes more humanly conceivable. For this reason the 3m sg suffix is unnecessary with אַף, a fact which is wrongly corrected in the versions.[68] From the grammatical perspective the suffix is likewise unnecessary given that the 3m sg is already anaphorically present in the 3m sg of the verb גדע.

3aB *...all the horns of Israel.* כֹּל קֶרֶן יִשְׂרָאֵל

YHWH goes to work against כֹּל קֶרֶן יִשְׂרָאֵל with the strength usually reserved for the hacking down of mighty trees (Isa 10_{33}), The horn (of a bull or wild ox; cf Ps 92_{11}, Deut 33_{17}) symbolises the strength/defences of human persons and land.[69] In light of the additional mention of the name Israel, the present expression thus transcends the other expressions of destruction of Judah's fortified cities. With a single blow, YHWH has

66 Cf Isa 43_{28}, 47_6, Ezek 22_{16}.
67 Cf THAT I 633 (Sauer).
68 Cf the text critical apparatus of BHS.
69 Cf Mic 4_{13}, Ps $89_{18,25}$.

reduced everything that was strong and mighty in Israel to weakness. It would not be illogical to follow Kraus here and envisage Israel's military forces as the object of YHWH's attack since the following bicolon tends to point in that direction.

3b *His right hand has pulled back* הֵשִׁיב אָחוֹר יְמִינוֹ
in the sight of the enemy. מִפְּנֵי אוֹיֵב

אָחוֹר + *hiph'il* √שׁוּב means 'to withdraw' or 'to pull back' (cf $1_{8c,13b}$). The subject of the verb is Adonai who has withdrawn his right hand. While Hillers' suggestion that the right hand belongs to Israel is grammatically possible it fails at the level of content since Adonai is subject of the first colon of each of the three bicola of this strophe. The anthropomorphic image of YHWH's right hand symbolises his strength in battle[70] as well has the creative power with which he established the earth and spread out the heavens. If we read this expression against the background of the Psalms, in which YHWH's right hand is spoken of in hymnic terms, it becomes evident what is meant by the withdrawal thereof. YHWH's right hand supports the king,[71] protects the pious,[72] is unlimited in its outreach[73] and generous in giving.[74] In addition to these, there are texts which profess that the land was given to Israel by YHWH's right hand[75] which also offers protection against the enemy.[76] The poets of Lamentations can no longer speak of YHWH's right hand in this fashion, the loss of its protective force being the particular focus of the present context. As the enemy approached, Israel's protector withdrew his powerful right hand. The disappointment of the people is partly explained in Ps 77, the author of which describes himself as wounded and ailing because the right hand of the Almighty had changed (Ps 77_{11}).

3c *He has burned against Jacob as a flaming fire* וַיִּבְעַר בְּיַעֲקֹב כְּאֵשׁ לֶהָבָה
which has consumed all around. אָכְלָה סָבִיב

The withdrawal of YHWH's right hand should not be seen as a sign of passivity on his part. While the enemy rage, it is in fact Adonai who is at

[70] See Ex $15_{6,12}$, Ps $89_{11,14}$.
[71] Ps 18_{36}.
[72] Ps 63_{9}, 118_{15f}, 138_{7}; cf Isa 41_{10}.
[73] Ps 139_{10}.
[74] Ps 16_{11}.
[75] Ps 44_{3f}, 78_{54}, 80_{16}.
[76] Ps 20_{7}, 21_{9}, 60_{7}, 98_{1}, 108_{7}.

work. The poets bring this fact to the fore at the conclusion of the present canticle by way of a daring and climactic image: the hostile fire which consumes all in its wake is YHWH himself. The subject of וַיִּבְעַר is not Adonai's anger[77] but rather Adonai himself. The verb here ought to be understood intransitively. The terminology is reminiscent of theophany[78] although its directness is uncommon nevertheless. In theophanic descriptions it is usually the indirect notion of God's anger[79] or wrath[80] which burns (cf his 'fire' in Num 11_1). The intention here is not to suggest that YHWH is in the fire[81] but rather that he himself has become like a flaming fire.[82] Devouring fire is also found as a theophanic element in the description of judgement of the day of YHWH.[83] In Ps 18_{7-20}, YHWH's theophanic wrath turns against the enemy of Israel's king. Here, however, it is turned against Israel itself. Adonai has turned against Jacob, his own people (cf 1_{17b}), as a devouring fire. The fire has taken hold and destroys all around it. It cannot be escaped.

Canticle II (2_{4-5})

Content/theme: *Adonai destroys Zion and Judah as an enemy*

Literary argumentation:

inclusions: דָּרַךְ קַשְׁתּוֹ כְּאוֹיֵב (4aA) // וַיֶּרֶב ... תַּאֲנִיָּה וַאֲנִיָּה (5c)
וַיַּהֲרֹג (4bA) // בִּלַּע (5bA)
כֹּל (4bB) // כֹּל (5bA)
בַּת־צִיּוֹן (4cA) // יִשְׂרָאֵל (5aB)
שָׁפַךְ כָּאֵשׁ חֲמָתוֹ (4cB) // הָיָה אֲדֹנָי כְּאוֹיֵב (5aA)
incl/resp: מַחֲמַדֵּי־עָיִן (4bB) // אַרְמְנוֹתֶיהָ (5bA) // מִבְצָרָיו (5bB)
responses: כְּאוֹיֵב (4aA) // כְּאוֹיֵב (5aA)
בַּת־צִיּוֹן (4cA) // בַּת־יְהוּדָה (5cA)

The present canticle differs from the previous one on two points. Firstly, the present text focuses almost equal attention on Zion (cf 2_{5b}) and Judah. Secondly, the image of Adonai is elaborated further in these verses. The

77 Thus KBL 140 and HAL 140 sv בער.
78 Cf TWAT I 28f (Ringgren).
79 Isa 30_{27}, Ps 2_{12}.
80 Jer 4_4, 7_{20}, Ps 89_{47}.
81 Cf Gen 15_{17}, Ex 3_2, Deut $4_{12,15}$.
82 Cf Deut 4_{24} and Ex 24_{17}.
83 Cf Isa 10_{17}, 30_{27ff}, Zeph 1_{18}.

poets look back at the devastation which has taken place as the enemy conquered Jerusalem and the land. Such retrospection, however, does not yet imply that the poets are looking back from a time of restoration.

4aA *He has bent his bow like an enemy,* דָּרַךְ קַשְׁתּוֹ כְּאוֹיֵב

The first colon confronts us with the direct image of Adonai as a hostile archer. The image itself is quite unique, appearing only once outside Lamentations (cf 3_{12f}) in Ps 7_{13} in the similar context of divine judgement. On the other hand, YHWH's arrows, which symbolise his judgements, are referred to with greater frequency (see 2_{4b} below). The comparison כְּאוֹיֵב is also unique, appearing only here in the OT. Gordis wrongly suggests that we read the כ of כְּאוֹיֵב as an *emphatic kaf* (asseverative Kaph): "the Lord has indeed become the enemy". Given the unusual character of the comparison, especially with respect to Adonai, the text is better understood as the result of a certain hesitance on the poets' part to actually call him 'the enemy', a hesitance which led them to uphold the metaphorical element introduced by the כ. If Adonai were the enemy in the absolute sense of the word then there would be no more point in turning to him for help. The text reveals an immense theological tension in which the poets continually find themselves. It is perhaps true that YHWH is not the 'direct cause' (cf 3_{37f}) of the present disaster, but in reacting to Israel's sin he behaves like an enemy since he is the ultimate 'commander' of the hostile force invading the land (cf 1_{17b}). This sketch of the situation also contains an unexpressed positive element. As 'commander', YHWH alone is in a position to bring the hostilities to an end and restore the good things of the past (cf 5_{21B}). Were YHWH the absolute enemy then a reversal of fortunes would be forever out of the question. The tension between accusation and expectation also resounds in the final canticle of Lam II where Lady Jerusalem prays to YHWH in a final prayer while referring to him at the same time as her only enemy (cf 2_{22cB}).

4aB *his right hand in the assault...* נִצָּב יְמִינוֹ

The *niph'al* participle נִצָּב in the second colon appears to present a difficulty. Rudolph emends the text and reads חִצּוֹ בִּימִינוֹ, 'his arrows in his right hand'. Weiser reads a singular 'arrow' (cf also HAL 674f sv √נצב). A scribal error leading to the replacement of ח with נ is improbable,[84]

[84] Cf EWürthwein, *Der Text des Alten Testaments*, Stuttgart 1973[4], 213 and ETov, *Textual Criticism of the Hebrew Bible*, Assen/Maastricht, 1992, 244–253.

however, and there is also a lack of logic in the idea that YHWH bent his bow while holding his arrows in his right hand. Kraus proposes that we maintain the MT and translate: 'his right hand is raised' in the sense of 'ready to fire'. Albrektson follows a similar line although he is closer to the meaning of the *niph'al* of √נצב in the suggested reading 'at the ready' which he proposes with reference to Isa 3_{13}. Adonai is then taken as subject and his right hand as an accusative. The metaphorical suggestion of Adonai as a hostile archer is thereby maintained. Albrektson's suggestion appears to be the most attractive, given the appropriate meaning it establishes while avoiding the need for emendation. The notion of 'readiness for action', moreover, is also present in Num $22_{23,31}$, Judg 18_{16}, Ps 82_1 and Prov 8_2.[85] It is interesting to note how the same imagery returns in the parallel strophes of the third song, with the use of √נצב[86] with precisely the same meaning as we have suggested here: the archer taking aim at his target. The entire action involved in shooting an arrow with a bow should be imagined here: the bow is bent; the archer's right hand sets the arrow on the string and raises it to eye level; he takes aim and fires.

In terms of content, there is evidence here of a quite remarkable theological proposition made apparent, among other things, via the use of YHWH's right hand. Where the previous strophe spoke of withdrawal, here YHWH's right hand turns against his people. Once again, therefore, we see the inversion of a theme from salvation history: YHWH, who so often struggled against the enemies of his people, now struggles as an enemy against Israel. The tradition inverted is taken from the theme of Holy War.[87] A similar turn about was evident in the day of YHWH preaching with respect to YHWH's orientation towards Israel (cf the excursus on the day of YHWH above). The element of YHWH's struggle against other adversaries, however, is not completely eclipsed by such inversions.[88]

The notion that YHWH could fight against his own people is quite rare in pre-exilic prophecy although it is present nevertheless.[89] The remarkable character of such a notion is evident from Isa 28_{21} where YHWH's struggle against his own people is called a strange and unusual work.[90] Israel now

---

85 For the literal use of √נצב cf 1 Sam 19_{20}, 1 Kgs 22_{48}, Ruth 2_{5f}.

86 See 3_{12} *hiph'il* impf + sf 1 sg.

87 Cf RdVaux, *Institutions II*, 73–83; HMLutz, *Jahwe, Jerusalem und die Völker*, WMANT 27, Neukirchen–Vluyn 1968, 177–189.

88 Cf Lutz, 130–146.

89 Cf Am 2_{13-16}, $9_{1,4}$, Isa 28_{20f}, Jer 6_{1-6}; cf also JASoggin, 'Der prophetische Gedanke über den heiligen Krieg als Gericht gegen Israel', VT X (1960), 79–83.

stands face to face with this uncommon and strange behaviour on the part of YHWH. His once saving right hand has now turned in hostility against his own people. The magnitude of the turn becomes apparent in the next colon.

4bA *...like an adversary; He has killed...* כְּצָר וַיַּהֲרֹג

At first sight, the consecutive imperfect in the first colon appears to be in a strange location. The Masoretes solved the problem by employing the disjunctive *zāqēf qāṭōn*, thereby attaching כְּצָר to the previous colon. Such a reading, however, creates a heavy imbalance between the first and the second bicola. The arrangement followed by BHK/BHS is much more balanced, although it is lacking in logic in terms of meaning: 'like an enemy and he kills'. In their efforts to solve the problem, commentators frequently resort to transposition, reading וַיַּהֲרֹג כְּצָר.[91] Gordis goes even further, reading as follows: דָּרַךְ קַשְׁתּוֹ כְּאוֹיֵב נִצָּב כְּצָר / וַיַּהֲרֹג יְמִינוֹ כֹּל מַחֲמַדֵּי־עָיִן. Gottlieb is of the opinion that such a transposition possesses the same level of probability as the more common option. The fact that the text tradition of Lamentations gives no occasion for such a radical re-arrangement makes Gordis' suggested emendation somewhat unlikely.

Hillers takes a different route in search of a solution for the problem, suggesting a logical and therefore attractive option. He proposes that a now missing verbal form once stood in the text prior to the consecutive imperfect. Such a suggestions not only explains the present location of the consecutive imperfect but also obviates the need for a drastic re-arrangement of the text. Based on the combination of the verbs הרג and נכה found in Isa 27_7 and Ps 136_{17f}, Hillers suggests that the missing verb form must have been a *hiph'il* perfect of the root נכה. נִצָּב from the previous bicolon is treated as a noun meaning the 'hilt (of a sword)' with which the striking took place (cf Judg 3_{22}). Since 'the sword' has been lifted up he attaches the preposition בְּ before יְמִינוֹ. His reading of the text then emerges as follows: נִצָּב בְּיְמִינוֹ כְּצָר הִכָּה וַיַּהֲרֹג.

The advantage of this suggestion lies in the fact that no (difficult to explain) transposition is required. The disadvantages, however, lie in the overly artificial interpretation of the somewhat laboured image of the sword, the necessary addition of the preposition בְּ and the strained assumption of a missing verb נכה.

---

[90] Cf HWildberger, *Jesaja 28–39*, BKAT X/3, Neukirchen 1982, 1079f.

[91] Cf, for example, Meek, Rudolph, Weiser, Kraus and Boecker.

A better suggestion emerges if one takes the parallel verses in the third song into account where YHWH the hostile archer is still the focus of the poets' attention. In Lam 3_{12f} there is also mention of the archer bending the bow after which he takes aim at his target (= וַיַּצִּיבֵנִי כַּמַּטָּרָא לַחֵץ). The act of firing the arrows is not mention, only the consequence thereof: penetration of the vitals (3_{13}). A verb describing the shooting of the arrows, therefore, would appear to be more logical than Hillers' artificial *hiph'il* form of נכה. The root ירה I (*qal*) carries such a meaning and can be found in combination with the accusative חֵץ in I Sam 20_{36} and Prov 26_{18}. One advantage of ירה over נכה is that the absence of ירה can be explained via *aberratio oculi* and *metathesis*. Indeed, the consonants thereof can be found in the preceding and following words. Moreover, the fact that the י at the beginning of ירה and the ר at the end of כְּצָר are written in a similar fashion in ancient Hebrew explains how they could have been confused.[92] The same holds true for the י and the ו. In addition, the ר and the ה follow each other in וַיַּהֲרֹג. The second song thus shows a plus (the shooting of the arrows) compared to the third song, as is the case the other way round with respect to the target and the mention of arrows. The text would then run as follows: כְּצָר יָרָה וַיַּהֲרֹג. The question remains, however, as to the actual need for emendation of the text. No emendation is necessary if we assume that the poetic line at this point runs into the following line (*enjambment* – a not uncommon phenomenon in Hebrew poetry).[93] Our translation is based, therefore, on the unemended text.

YHWH's arrows are sufficiently well known as an image for his judgements throughout the OT.[94] It is interesting to note that in Ezek 5_{16} YHWH's arrows stand for famine. Hunger is similarly implied in Deut 32_{23f} but with the additional notions of sickness and poison included.[95] It is difficult to make a choice here since the colon appears to be open to a double interpretation (cf the following colon).

4bB ... *every delight for the eye.* כֹּל מַחֲמַדֵּי־עָיִן

What are the poets referring to with the expression כֹּל מַחֲמַדֵּי־עָיִן? Given

[92] Cf Würthwein, 213 and Tov, 246.

[93] Cf WGEWatson, *Classical Hebrew Poetry. A Guide to its Techniques*, JSOT suppl series 26, Sheffield 1984, 333f.

[94] Cf Num 24_8, Deut 32_{42}, Ps 7_{14}, 18_{15}, 38_3, 64_8, Ezek 5_{16}.

[95] Cf likewise Deut 32_{42}; for the correct interpretation and translation of Deut 32_{24} see JCdMoor, '"O Death, Where Is Thy Sting?"' in: LEslinger & GTaylor (eds), *Ascribe to the Lord. Biblical and other Studies in Memory of PCCraigie*, Sheffield 1988, 105.

the fact that the verb הרג almost always has people as its object, most commentators have tended to understand the phrase as referring to human beings. In this event כֹּל מַחֲמַדֵּי־עָיִן might then be interpreted as Zion's beloved children whom YHWH has killed by starvation. In terms of structure, the song-response with the fourth song, which speaks of the hunger of Zion's precious (4_2) well-cared for and pampered children (4_{4f}), supports such an interpretation. It is possible, therefore, to employ מַחֲמַדֵּי־עָיִן as a reference to human persons as is the case in Hos 9_{16}: מַחֲמַדֵּי בִטְנָם 'the cherished offspring of their womb', and in Ezek 24_{16} in which the prophet refers to his wife with the expression מַחְמַד עֵינֶיךָ. It is also possible, however, that כֹּל מַחֲמַדֵּי־עָיִן refers to the magnificent temple buildings and precincts, a possibility which is also supported by the literary structure of the songs. Within the canticle we can point to the inclusion/response מַחֲמַדֵּי־עָיִן (4bB) // אַרְמְנוֹתֶיהָ (5bA); within the sub-canto there is a response between תִּפְאֶרֶת יִשְׂרָאֵל (1bB), where explanations likewise point to the temple, and מַחֲמַדֵּי־עָיִן (4bB). The magnificence of the palaces is spoken of in Ps 48_{14} (cf Ps 122_3). In Ezek 24_{21}, moreover, the temple is referred to as the 'delight of Israel's eyes' (מַחְמַד). In addition, the song response with 1_4 in which Zion's destruction is the point of focus in similar fashion to 2_4, also establishes a concatenation with the preceding colon. The objection that the verb הרג exclusively refers to persons is not completely correct (cf Ps 78_{47} with 'vine' as object) and is indeed mitigated by the fact that the personification 'daughter Zion' in the following colon is anticipated here. Within the strophe, the significance of the destruction of the temple – as a fait accompli – has preferential place. Indirect association with the ongoing theme of starvation, however, appears also to be present.[96]

4c *In the tent of daughter Zion* — בְּאֹהֶל בַּת־צִיּוֹן
he has poured out like fire his fury. — שָׁפַךְ כָּאֵשׁ חֲמָתוֹ

If we are correct in suggesting that the use of the image of YHWH as an enemy archer is continued in the second bicolon then it would not be unreasonable to propose that there are also echoes of the metaphor of YHWH's 'arrows of judgement' in the present bicolon. It is not unusual to find YHWH's arrows described in the context of theophany as 'arrows of fire' or 'bolts of lightning'.[97] These burning arrows have now fallen upon the 'tent of daughter Zion' and set it ablaze.

[96] Cf the connection between starvation and the destruction of Zion in the fifth canticle of the fourth song (Lam 4_{10-11}).

[97] Cf II Sam 22_{15}, Ps 18_{15}, 144_6, 77_{18f}, Hab 3_{11}, Zech 9_{14}.

What exactly is intended by the expression אֹהֶל בַּת־צִיּוֹן? In the present context אֹהֶל can have two meanings: Jerusalem as a dwelling place or the temple in Jerusalem. Aalders, Meek, Rudolph and Boecker[98] opt for the former while Van Selms, Kaiser, Brandscheidt, Groß[99] opt for the latter. References to the temple as אֹהֶל are not infrequent in the Psalms[100] and are also reminiscent of the desert sanctuary.[101] Reference to Jerusalem as a tent can be found in Isa 33_{20} and 54_{2}. Jeremiah uses the image of a Bedouin tent being torn down in his description of ruin (Jer 10_{20}). The image of the city as a tent would appear to fit particularly well with the image of YHWH's burning arrows. Canvas is much more likely to catch fire than stone. A response is thereby clearly established with the conclusion of 2_{3} where the all consuming fire of Adonai's judgement was already mentioned. Boecker is of the opinion that the text here refers to the city alone since the destruction of the temple is only raised later in 2_{6f}. Both ideas are not mutually exclusive, however: the reference is to Jerusalem in its entirety, the temple included. Nothing escapes the fire of YHWH's judgement. Temple and dwellings are even mentioned in the same breath in the description of the actual destruction.[102] The more detailed description of the destruction of the temple in the following canticle simply makes explicit what is already implicit in the present canticle.

In the final colon of this verse we are faced with the problem of harmonising the images of the 'pouring out' of YHWH's burning anger and the 'shooting' of Adonai's fiery arrows. The verb שפך appears to be primarily concerned with liquids such as water (Lam 2_{19}), blood (Lam 4_{13}) etcetera According to Koch the negative aspect of שפך is particularly evident in such texts: "das nirgends ein wachstumförderndes Begießen bedeutet, sondern stets ein abruptes gewaltsames Ausschütten." [103] Examples of the figurative use of the term with a variety of objects abound: with the liver (as the seat of the emotions, Lam 2_{11}), with life (Lam 2_{12}), with stones (Lam 4_{1}), with divine anger (Lam 4_{11}) and with blood (Lam 4_{13}). The combination שָׁפַךְ (כָּ)אֵשׁ, however, is unique to this verse. It appears to be a poetic supplement to the frequently occurring expression 'to pour out blazing

[98] Cf also Koch: "Die Wohnung der als Grundlegend betrachteten nomadischen Urzeit wird zum feierlichen Ausdruck für das "heimatlichen Herd".", TWAT I 130.

[99] Cf VFritz, *Tempel und Zelt*, WMANT 47, Neukirchen 1977, 94f.

[100] Cf Ps 15_{1}, 27_{5}, 61_{5}, 78_{60}.

[101] Cf TWAT I 134f (Koch).

[102] Cf II Kgs 25_{9} and Jer 52_{13}.

[103] KKoch, 'Die Rolle der hymnischen Abschnitte in der Komposition des Amos-Buches', ZAW 86 (1974), 518.

anger' (שָׁפַךְ חֵמָה) which is found especially in Ezekiel.[104] Other words for anger such as זַעַם (Ezek 21_{36}) and עֶבְרָה (Hos 5_{10}) as well as חֲרוֹן אַף (Lam 4_{11}) are also evident as objects of the root שׁפך. Zeph 3_8 is important here because it likens the pouring out of YHWH's wrath to burning anger and devouring fire (cf Lam 2_3, 4_{11}). In Hos 5_{10}, however, YHWH's anger pours out like (destructive) water. The images need not exclude one another. In the context of the Sodom tradition in Gen 19_{24} (cf the explanation of Lam $1_{13,20}$, 4_6), mention is made of a 'rain of fire'. Within the genre of theophany, the combination of storm, lighting, fire, rain etcetera. is not unusual.[105] Adonai's fiery arrows rain down on various parts of the city and set them ablaze. Reference is without doubt being made here to the Babylonians setting the temple, palace and houses of Jerusalem alight (cf II Kgs 25_9).

This devastating fire should also be seen in a theological context. The destructive fire of the Babylonians was in fact the burning wrath of YHWH, as is apparent from the use of the fixed prophetic expression שָׁפַךְ חֵמָה. The notion חֵמָה appears here in Lamentations for the first time and is evidently well chosen for the context. The noun חֵמָה is derived from the verb יחם, a form related to the root חמם meaning 'to be hot'.[106] The noun can be translated as 'burning anger'. Sauer notes a possible distinction between אַף and חֵמָה.[107] On the basis of Hos 7_5, where חֵמָה is used for warming of the body from within by wine drinking, אַף, he suggests, should be understood as outwardly visible anger (snorting) and חֵמָה as more of an interior emotional movement. Nevertheless, such interior burning wrath can be poured out and thus bring about exterior effects such as 'setting ablaze' (cf, for example, II Kgs $22_{13,17}$; Jer 4_4). In Jeremiah, חֵמָה signifies YHWH's poisonous wine, the drinking of which has the destruction of Jerusalem and Judah as its consequence.[108]

5a *Adonai has become like an enemy.* הָיָה אֲדֹנָי כְּאוֹיֵב
He has destroyed Israel. בִּלַּע יִשְׂרָאֵל

Primarily because of the final bicolon of the preceding strophe, it became apparent that the poets were focusing their attention on Zion. In the final

---

104 Ezek 7_8, 9_8, 14_{19}, $20_{8,13,21,33f}$, 22_{22}, 30_{15}, 36_{18}; cf also Ps 79_6, Jer 6_{11}, 10_{25} and Isa 42_{25}.

105 Cf Isa 30_{27ff}, especially 30_{30}, Mic 1_4, Ps 18_{8-16}, 77_{17ff}, 92_{2ff}, Nah $1_{3,6,8}$.

106 Cf THAT I 581 (Sauer) and TWAT II 1032 (Schunck).

107 Cf THAT I 582.

108 Cf Jer 25_{15ff}, the exegesis of Lam 4_{21} and the excursus on YHWH's anger after 1_{12c}.

strophe of the present canticle they turn to the fate of the entire land and its population. This is evident from the use of the name Israel (cf 2_{1b}) although Zion is, nevertheless, mentioned separately (cf the exegesis of 2_{1c}). The implication remains that the destruction of the people is not yet complete. The expression כְּאוֹיֵב is also used in Lam 2_{4a}. The difference in the present verse is that Adonai is directly named in the comparison, thereby giving it greater emphasis. For the meaning of √בלע I see the exegesis of 2_{2a}. For the usage and meaning of the divine name אֲדֹנָי see the exegesis of 1_{14c}.

5bA *He has destroyed all her palaces,* בִּלַּע כָּל־אַרְמְנוֹתֶיהָ

The repetition of the √בלע I establishes concatenation with the preceding bicolon. Acts of destruction which have already taken place are now mentioned. A problem exists with the 3f sg suffix of the object (אַרְמְנוֹתֶיהָ) of this verse which does not square with יִשְׂרָאֵל in verse 5a which is masculine. For this reason the object is frequently emended and read as אַרְמְנוֹתוֹ, thus placing the suffix in agreement with the following noun מִבְצָרָיו (cf text critical apparatus of BHS). Although it is only a small emendation it still remains unnecessary. The LXX supports the MT. Kraus is of the opinion that the 3f sg refers back to daughter Zion who is mentioned in the final bicolon of the preceding strophe. Albrektson follows a similar line of thought and correctly points out that the palaces were primarily related to Zion (cf Ps $48_{4,14}$) whereas the fortified cities were related to the entire land (cf Keil). Structural analysis within the strophe proves them correct (cf the incl/resp מַחֲמַדֵּי־עָיִן [4bB] // אַרְמְנוֹתֶיהָ [5bA]). It already became apparent in our explanation of מַחֲמַדֵּי־עָיִן (4bB) that the primary focus of thought ought to be the temple complex. In this regard, Albrektson refers to Ps 48_4: 'Within (Zion's) citadels God has shown himself a sure defence' and rightly notes that there is an evident contrast in the present complaint: Zion, the protective refuge, has been destroyed by Adonai himself. In descriptions of Israel's destruction, it is typical that that of Zion is mentioned first.

5bB *He has ravaged his fortified cities.* שִׁחֵת מִבְצָרָיו

Here in the second colon Judah becomes the focus of attention. From the perspective of content, the present colon is a contraction of 2_{2a} employing a different object and verb. According to Vetter, the root שחת (*pi'el* pf) has two aspects which are particularly important here, namely the sudden/unexpected character of the intended devastation: "bei *šḥt* pi. werd das völlig passive Objekt in das erreichte Ergebnis der Handlung versetzt: »plötzlich verdorben/vernichtet machen« (resultativ)" together with the notion of √שחת as a *terminus technicus* taken from military parlance (cf, for example, Jer 22_7).[109] It almost goes without saying that both aspects are well placed here. Adonai has swept away the fortified cities of Judah as an enemy soldier (for further explanation of the 'fortified cities' see 2_{2b}). The imagery of 'daughter Judah' found in 2_{2bB} and in the following bicola makes the 3m sg suffix 'his fortified cities' appear somewhat unusual, leading us to expect a 3f sg suffix. Such would have been the case had the poets simply been thinking of 'אֶרֶץ Judah' (= fem). It is probable, however, that the 3m sg suffix refers back to יִשְׂרָאֵל at the end of the preceding bicolon. יִשְׂרָאֵל is masculine when it refers to the people and thereby the cities of the people.[110] A similar sort of alternation can be found in Hos 8_{14}. It is not impossible that at a much deeper level of meaning the poets had even intended the suffix to refer to Adonai himself and that YHWH's relationship with the cities of Judah was primary in their minds. In 5_3 – as for Jerusalem in 1_1 – the widow metaphor is used once again for these cities (cf the exegesis) thus making the event all the more horrifying. YHWH has destroyed his own cities. With respect to the sudden, unexpected element of √שחת (cf Isa 29_5) we might imagine the bitter disappointment felt by those who had rooted their trust and expectations in Zion theology only to witness YHWH turn against them.[111]

5c *Everywhere in daughter Judah he has brought great sadness and mourning.* וַיֶּרֶב בְּבַת־יְהוּדָה תַּאֲנִיָּה וַאֲנִיָּה

Within the second canticle and the first sub-canto the present colon clearly exercises a concluding function by providing a thematic summary. It is remarkable how the poets strive for concentricity even in smaller units such as this. Daughter Judah stands in the centre (cf 1_{15c}) surrounded and included by תַּאֲנִיָּה וַאֲנִיָּה and וַיֶּרֶב. The *hiph'il* of √רבה I means 'to make numerous' or 'to make great' (cf HAL 1098). Both meanings are present in the text of 2_{5c}: everywhere in Judah there is sadness and mourning and they are great indeed. The use of assonance and alliteration draws our attention to the combination תַּאֲנִיָּה וַאֲנִיָּה. In Hebrew poetry, alliteration emphasises the cohesion between the words in question; assonance too

109 See THAT II 892.

110 Cf GES-K § 122*i* and also JLHelberg, 'Land in the Book of Lamentations', ZAW 102, 1990, 375f.

111 Cf 1983, 132–139.

exercises a strong associative character.[112] וַאֲנִיָּה and תַּאֲנִיָּה mutually fortify one another, further indicating the magnitude of the mourning and sadness already introduced by וַיֶּרֶב. The nouns תַּאֲנִיָּה וַאֲנִיָּה are both derived from the same verb אנה I which only appears in Isa 3_{36} and 19_8. Both texts consist of prophecies of doom and predict mourning, downfall, anguish and death. As such they vouch for the interpretations 'sadness'/'mourning' in the present context. The word-pair is also to be found in one other place, namely Isa 29_2 in the context of a prophecy of doom against Zion. This is striking because the following strophe speaks of the destruction of Zion, thus making it evident that concatenation exists between both bicola and that the present context has borrowed from the prophecy in Isa 29_2. The reality confronting Zion, however, is more horrific than Isaiah had predicted. In Isa 29_{1-8}, salvation for Zion comes along at the last minute.[113] In the present context salvation still seems far off.

The poets' exceptional composition techniques are once again evident in this portion of the second song. While 2_{5c} constitutes the concluding and summarising bicolon of the second canticle, it unites at the same time with the following bicolon to form the central core of the first canto (2_{1-10}), thereby indicating the thematic focal point: the destruction of Judah and Jerusalem. Moreover, the human consequences of the disaster are only referred to within this sub-canto (2_{1-5}), as is apparent from a response with the conclusion of the second sub-canto (2_{6-10}) where this is likewise the case (cf also the parallel between יְהוּדָה [2_{5c}] and יְרוּשָׁלִָם [2_{10c}]).

Sub-canto II (Lam 2_{6-10})

The second sub-canto is characterised by its concentration on the destruction of Zion (in $2_{6b,8a,10a}$). Note how the first canticle (2_{6-7}) focuses on the destruction of the temple buildings while the focus is transferred to the destruction of the surrounding walls and doors in the second canticle (2_{9-10}). It is striking that the final canticle immediately describes the consequences of Zion's fall for those who are involved in the temple cult. They are mentioned in sequence, according to their importance: first the king with his princes, then the priests (via Torah in 2_{9b}), followed by the prophets (2_{9c}), the elders (2_{10a}), and finally the young girls of Jerusalem (2_{10c}). In the first song the king and the prophets are not mentioned. The present sub-canto harbours two significant theological moments. The first

[112] Cf WGEWatson, *Classical Hebrew Poetry. A Guide to its Techniques*, JSOT suppl series 26, Sheffield 1984, 224–228.

[113] Cf HWildberger, *Jesaja 28–39*, BKAT X/3, Neukirchen 1982, 1102f.

consists of YHWH's destruction and rejection of his chosen place (Zion) and chosen people. It is evident, therefore, that YHWH's hostile actions not only pain his people but they also turn back against himself. It is reminiscent of YHWH's complaint which Jeremiah directed to Baruch: "I am going to break down what I have built, and pluck up what I have planted."[114] The second moment has a corrective function with respect to the first sub-canto (2_{1-5}) where the mistaken impression may have been given that YHWH's destructive actions were out of control. Such an impression is removed here by the reference to the fact that forethought and calculation lie at the heart of YHWH's wrathful behaviour (2_8).

Canticle I (2_{6-7})

Content/theme: YHWH *destroys his own temple and altar*

Literary argumentation:

inclusions:
שֻׂכּוֹ (6aA) // בֵּית־יְהוָה (7cA)
צִיּוֹן (6bA) // אַרְמְנוֹתֶיהָ (7bB)
מוֹעֲדוֹ (6aB) // מוֹעֵד (7cB)
וַיִּנְאַץ (6cA) // זָנַח (7aA)
כֹהֵן (6cB) // מִזְבְּחוֹ (7aA)

responses:
שֻׂכּוֹ (6aA) // מִזְבְּחוֹ (7aA)
שֻׂכּוֹ (6aA) // מִקְדָּשׁוֹ (7aB)
מוֹעֲדוֹ (6aB) // מִקְדָּשׁוֹ (7aB)
בְּצִיּוֹן (6bA) // חוֹמֹת אַרְמְנוֹתֶיהָ (7bB)

6a *With violence he has demolished his hut as in a garden* וַיַּחְמֹס כַּ(ב)גַּן שֻׂכּוֹ
he has destroyed his festival site. שִׁחֵת מוֹעֲדוֹ

At the end of our explanation of 2_5 we already noted the central place of 2_{6a} within the first canticle (by analogy with 1_6, 3_{17}, 4_6 and $5_{6,7}$), thus providing the present bicolon with extra import. From a text critical perspective, the first three words are often incorrectly understood. Commentators have considered it theologically impossible for YHWH to be the subject of the verb חמס since the verb in question and its derived noun have to do with the perpetration of unjustified violence[115] which one cannot apply to YHWH. Robinson (BHK) suggests, therefore, that we follow

[114] Jer 45_4; we thereby take leave of our former opinion in this regard expressed in 1983, 193, note 100.

[115] Cf Jer 22_3, Ezek 22_{26}, Zeph 3_4.

the Syriac which reads the *qal* imperfect of √הרס, ‘to tear down’. Kaiser follows a similar line. Nevertheless, we encounter the paradox of YHWH perpetrating violence in one other place in the OT: Job 19_7.[116] Emendation of וַיַּחְמֹס implies a reduction in terms of content and is at the same time unnecessary. The text is not referring to an objective appropriation of the content of YHWH’s deeds but rather to the subjective experience of those deeds by human persons.[117] The poets continue to employ very risky propositions in which YHWH figures as an enemy. In so doing they are attempting to render the experience of a group of people who have seen their world turned upside down by YHWH’s actions. We have already noted several times how the poets have turned the received theology on its head (cf the explanation of $2_{2c,3b,4a}$). The use of the verb חמס is part of this process, although given that the direct object is constituted by buildings and not people, the formulation is cautious. The fact that people are affected nevertheless is apparent from the song-response with 1_6. It was once possible to confess that YHWH hated violence (Ps 11_5) and rescued people from it (Ps 18_{49}, $140_{2,5}$) while the prophets proclaimed that he was aware of it and would exercise judgement over it.[118] Now YHWH himself is the perpetrator of violence and as a consequence there can be no helper. The paradox rests in the fact that in doing violence to his own temple, YHWH also does violence to himself.[119]

Although no theological motivation for YHWH’s behaviour is directly alluded to in the first canto, indirect allusions are present via the song-response with the central verse 4_6 where the magnitude of the people’s sin is referred to (cf, in addition, the song-response between 2_7 and 5_7).

As far as we are concerned, the term שֻׂכּוֹ refers to the temple.[120] Together with several Hebrew manuscripts we read סֻכּוֹ from the noun סֹךְ ‘hut’.[121] For reference to the temple as a ‘hut’ see Ps 76_3 and Ps 27_5, as well as text critical apparatus of BHS. Aalders, Brandscheidt and Stoll, among others, consider שֻׂכּוֹ to be a derivative of √שָׂכַךְ (cf GES-B 785) and a reference to the enclosure surrounding the temple complex. Such an interpretation,

116 Cf THAT I 587 (Stoebe) and TWAT II 1058 (Haag).

117 Albrektson and Haag (TWAT II, 1053) rightly point this out.

118 Cf Zeph 1_{9f}, 3_4, Jer 22_3, Ezek 7_{23}, 8_{17f}.

119 Cf the explanation of 4_{10-11} together with Jer 45_4.

120 Cf the same motif already present in the lament over Ur (ANET^3 617 [331]).

121 Cf also LXX (τὸ σκήνωμα) and the Vulgate (*tentorium suum*); idem GES-B 542, Zorell 799b together with Löhr, Meek, Albrektson, Kraus, Plöger, Van Selms, Gottlieb, HAL 711 and 1236.

however, disrupts the evident parallelism with מוֹעֲדוֹ in the following colon. Rudolph raises the question as to the meaning of the comparison between 'hut' and 'garden' (כַּגַּן). The translation 'he did violence to his hut like a garden' does indeed make little sense. For this reason LXX reads ὡς ἄμπελον (= כַּגֶּפֶן) 'like a vine' which Löhr then interprets as the people on the basis of Jer 2_{21}, Ps 80_{9} etcetera. A comparison between objects of such unequal magnitude is unlikely, however, as is the combination גֶּפֶן and √חמס.

We maintain the MT while accepting, along with Albrektson, that after the comparative particle כְּ, the preposition בְּ has fallen out, a not uncommon phenomenon.[122] In this way Rudolph's objection is answered while the MT achieves greater sense. The metaphor of the temple as a hut offers more than one comparative dimension. Ps 27_{5}, for example, provides a positive point of comparison, suggesting that the temple is a place to hide in time of need. In the same way as hut offers shelter from the sun, the temple offers sanctuary from the enemy – a primary element in Zion theology.

It is possible that the expression wishes to underline, at the same time, the humble character of the divine dwelling: in a temple built by human hands (cf I Kgs 8_{27}). Such an impression is carried by the notion of fragility associated with a garden hut which is built from the simplest materials (cf Job 27_{18}) and can be demolished without much effort (cf Isa 5_{5}). It is in this dimension that the *tertium comparationis* should be sought with respect to the present text: with the ease with which one demolishes a garden hut, Adonai has destroyed his temple. Influence from Isa 1_{8} should not be excluded here. In this text, unsteady daughter Zion nevertheless remains upright and does indeed appear – in light of Isa 22_{1b} – to be a hiding place, all of which refers to Sennacherib's failed attempt to conquer Jerusalem in 701 BCE.[123] The meaning of this event for Zion theology is evident: YHWH once protected his city,[124] but now the people are confronted with the opposite: YHWH himself has demolished his temple, his people's place of refuge. Such an unimaginable turn about also contributes to the explanation of the use of the verb חמס: it describes YHWH's inappropriate violence towards daughter Zion. The once unbelievable and horrifying prophecy concerning the destruction of the temple has become a visible reality.[125]

---

122 Cf Joüon–Muraoka § 133*h*.

123 Cf OKaiser, *Der Prophet Jesaja*, Kapitel 1339, ATD 18, Göttingen 1973, 114ff and HWildberger, *Jesaja 13–27*, BKAT X/2, Neukirchen 1978, 812–816.

124 Cf 1983, 97–105.

125 Cf Mic 3_{12}, Jer 7_{14}, $26_{6,18}$.

In the second colon מוֹעֲדוֹ is parallel to סֻכּוֹ. The term מוֹעֵד, therefore, should not be understood as 'fixed (festival) times' (cf $1_{4a,15b}$) but as '(festival) site' (cf HAL 528). Moreover, given that מוֹעֲדוֹ is object of שׁחת (pf *pi'el*) with Adonai as subject, the term requires a more material interpretation. We already pointed out the military and unexpected character of the destruction. The latter dimension should be understood here in terms of the disappointment of the devotees of Zion theology (cf the explanation of 2_{5b}).

6b *He has abolished,* YHWH, *in Zion,* שִׁכַּח יְהוָה בְּצִיּוֹן
festival and sabbath. מוֹעֵד וְשַׁבָּת

The consequences of the destruction of the temple for the liturgy are the focus of the this and the following bicola. Now that the place of assembly has been destroyed, feast and sabbath can no longer be celebrated: YHWH has 'abolished' them. It is clear that the *pi'el* of √שׁכח (only in Lam 1_{26}) does not imply that YHWH has caused the festivals of long ago to disappear from the memory of his people. On the contrary, they remain quite alive in the memory of the poets (cf 1_{4a}). Indeed, it is precisely the fact that feast and sabbath cannot be celebrated which constitutes the core of the present complaint. The 'abolition' in question must mean that YHWH's destruction of the temple has made the celebration of feast and sabbath simply impossible and that the community might as well forget the sabbath and festival liturgy in the sense of 'omitting' it altogether.[126] As we noted above with regard to the use of חמס, the poets continue to express the paradoxical aspect of YHWH's deeds. It is not for nothing that they return in the present canticle to the use of the divine name YHWH. They do so in order to call to mind that this temple is still his holy place (cf I Kgs 9_3). It was YHWH himself who established the rules for the temple liturgy and commanded that feast and sabbath be celebrated there.[127] His prophets took great exception to violations of this command.[128] Now YHWH has made the fulfilment of his own command impossible. It seems that the poets wish to say that YHWH's violence is turned against his own ordinances.[129]

Lam 2_{6b} is one of the texts which leads us to believe that the sabbath as a day of rest and festival was also celebrated in cultic fashion in pre-exilic

126 Cf THAT II 900 (Schottroff).
127 Cf Ex 20_8, $23_{12,14-17}$, 34_{21-23}, Lev $19_{3,30}$, Deut 16_{1-17}.
128 Cf, for example, Jer 17_{19ff}, Ezek 20_{12ff}, $22_{8,26}$, 23_{38}.
129 For the meaning of מוֹעֵד cf the explanation of 1_{4a} and 1_{15b}.

times. Other similar texts include Isa 1_{13}, Hos 2_{13}, prophetic critiques which allow us to deduce the festive character of the sabbath celebration together with that of the other feasts. Celebrations were accompanied by sacrifices, prayers, song and music.[130] Thus the present bicolon corresponds with $1_{4a,6a}$ where it is lamented that 'festival goers' have disappeared and that 'all majesty' has departed from Zion. Moreover, in the central text 3_{17}, the גֶּבֶר (the devout one of the third song) laments that he must forget the good things [טוֹבָה] of God's house (cf 5_{15}).

6c *He has rejected in accursed anger* וַיִּנְאַץ בְּזַעַם־אַפּוֹ
king and priest. מֶלֶךְ וְכֹהֵן

In contrast to 2_{6ab}, YHWH's judgement against the most important persons who had a place in the cult, namely the king and the priests, now becomes the focus of attention. There is clearly a connection with the preceding bicolon since the celebration of feast and sabbath not only involved the priests but included the king also. The temple in Jerusalem was a state sanctuary and the priests were in the king's service (cf I Kgs 4_2 where the prince [שַׂר] Azaraiah appears also to have been a priest [cf Lam 1_{6b}]). Priests could be appointed or removed by the king (cf I Kgs $2_{27,35}$), indeed the king bore responsibility for the sanctuary (cf II Kgs 12_{4ff} and 22_{3ff}).

There are also texts, however, which speak of the priestly activities of the king, albeit in special circumstances: the transfer of the ark (II Sam 6), the dedication of the temple (I Kings 8) and the conclusion of the covenant under Josiah (II Kgs 23_{1-3}). The sacral function of the king was long established among the Canaanites and as time went on Israel's kings also appear to have striven for priestly functions,[131] although a tension remained with respect to the scope of the king's authority in this regard.[132] From the theological perspective, the position of the king is closely defined in the OT. As God's adopted son[133] he represented the people before God. He also bore the duty to realise YHWH's justice in his governance.[134] Even after the exile, room was left for a 'princely' function within the design for

130 Cf Isa 1_{13ff}, Am 5_{21ff}, for theories concerning the origin of the sabbath cf RdVaux, *Institutions II*, 371–277 and THAT II 865–869 (Stolz).

131 Cf, for example, I Kgs 8_{14}, 12_{33}, II Kgs 16_{12-15}, 23_{1-3}; cf also JCdMoor, *New Year with Canaanites and Israelites*, Kampen 1972, 14–22 and JASoggin, 'Der Beitrag des Königtums zur Israelitischen Religion', in: *Studies in the Religion of Ancient Israel*, VTS 23, Leiden 1972, 9–26.

132 Cf I Sam 10_8, 11_{15}, 13_{8ff}, II Chron 26_{18}.

133 See II Sam 7_{14}, Ps 2_{6f}, 110_1.

134 See Ps 72; cf also the explanation of 4_{20}.

the new temple and its cult.[135] We can deduce from the present text that the king not only took part in the festivals but that his active presence in the sabbath liturgy was the norm. There is no question here, however, of a causal relationship between the destruction of the temple and the end of cultic function of the king and the priests. The opposite is in fact the case (cf 4_{12ff}). Since the king and the priests had been personally affected by Adonai's judgement, an end had come to the cult and their function therein. The destruction of the temple was the consequence of their transgressions. This is said directly of priests and prophets in 2_{14} and 4_{13}. In the present verse, the same is said indirectly of the king by way of the verb נאץ. In an indirectly theological context, the *qal* of √נאץ means 'to scorn' or 'insult'. With YHWH as subject, the theological consequence of his scorn can be drawn out, leaving us with the idea of 'rejection' – the actuality of which is made clear in YHWH's deeds: he rejects his people.[136] It is worth noting that YHWH can also be the object of √נאץ, although the *pi'el* form is used in every case. In contrast to the *qal*, however, the *pi'el* limits the act of scorn to the disposition of the subject. Thus it is possible to despise YHWH.[137]

In Isaiah we find an intensification in which the scornful disposition actually implies the breakdown of one's relationship with YHWH.[138] This idiomatic affinity shows that rejection *by* YHWH is in fact a result of rejection *of* YHWH.[139] Thus the reason behind the rejection of priest and king is implicitly stated here. No concrete reference is made to their sins (cf, however, 4_{13b} with respect to the priests). The direct result of rejection by YHWH is loss of one's place in the cult. At the material level, the performance of the liturgy has been made impossible by the destruction of the sanctuary, at the personal level by the exile of the king (2_{9b}, 4_{20a}), the murder of the priests (2_{20c}) or their expulsion. (4_{16b}). This event also goes hand in hand with a level of theological tension. YHWH himself is affected by his act of rejection as he was by the destruction of his temple: the people he once chose as king and priest he is now forced to reject.

---

135 Cf Ezek $45_{17,22-24}$, 46_2.

136 Cf Deut 32_{19}, Jer 14_{21}, 33_{24}.

137 Cf Deut 31_{20}, Ps $10_{3,13}$, $74_{10,18}$, cf also THAT II 4f (Wildberger) and TWAT V 132 (Ruppert).

138 Cf the use of parallel synonyms such as √עזב I 'to abandon' and √מאס I 'to reject' alongside √נאץ (*pi'el*) in Isa 1_4 and Isa 5_{24}. Both concepts can be found in the final prayer of Lam 5_{20ff}.

139 Cf TWAT V 134 (Ruppert).

The description of YHWH's wrathful behaviour employs a new term here, namely the noun זַעַם which serves as an adjective alongside אַפּוֹ. YHWH's anger (for אַף see the explanation of 1_{12c}) is further qualified by זַעַם. When used between persons √זעם means 'to curse',[140] which in a sense conceals the present implication of the term, namely the actual damage done to the one who is cursed.[141] With YHWH as subject and human persons as the most frequent object, the notion behind the term זַעַם should be understood as an element in the description of YHWH's righteous anger. This is clearly the case in the present context: YHWH's 'cursing' anger is expressed in reality in the rejection of priest and king.

7aA *Adonai has scorned his altar,* זָנַח אֲדֹנָי מִזְבְּחוֹ

With God as subject, the verb √זנח II 'to scorn' is a typical lament in the CI and CP genres,[142] the object of scorn always being an individual or the people. Lam 2_7, however, cannot simply be classified among such laments since it has a material and not a human object, namely YHWH's altar.

The language employed by the poets is quite remarkable, giving the impression that the destruction of the altar somehow has a personal dimension.[143] The impression is confirmed by the realisation that the combination of √זנח II and √נאר only appears in one other place, namely Ps $89_{39,40}$ where it refers to the derision of the king.[144] It is equally remarkable that the rejection of the king was the subject of the preceding colon. A literary-structural relationship exists between 2_{6c} and 2_{7a}. Within the third canticle (Lam 2_{6-7}) these bicola constitute the most central inclusion. We already pointed out the inclusions between וַיִּנְאַץ (6cA) // זָנַח (7aA) and כֹּהֵן (6cB) // מִזְבְּחוֹ (7aA). With respect to 6cB, where כֹּהֵן and מֶלֶךְ are side by side, we already discussed the cultic function of the king. If we accept that there is a chiasm between כֹּהֵן / מֶלֶךְ ⟺ מִקְדָּשׁוֹ / מִזְבְּחוֹ, then Adonai's scorn for his altar also carries an element of scorn for the priests (with the destruction of the sanctuary including the anullation of the covenant with the king).

If we are correct, then 2_{7aB} likewise includes a memory of the relationship between the king and the temple. The fact that the concrete destruction of the altar is implied here is made evident via the response within the

140 Cf Num 23_{7f}, Prov 22_{14}, 24_{24} (// √ארר).

141 Cf TWAT II 622 (Wiklander).

142 Cf Ps 43_2, $44_{10,24}$, $60_{3,12}$, 74_1, 77_8, 88_{15}, 89_{39}.

143 Cf also the explanation of $4_{1a,10-11}$.

144 For the affinity between this Psalm and Lamentations see 1983, 235, 238, 251f.

canticle between סָכּוֹ ... וַיַּחְמֹס (6aA) // זָנַח אֲדֹנָי מִזְבְּחוֹ (7aA). For the use of the divine name אֲדֹנָי cf the explanation of 1_{14c}.

Mention of the altar before the temple in the present colon is fully in line with the level of importance of both objects. At a later period the altar became the most essential element of the sanctuary and the sacrifice the most essential part of the liturgy. Altars can exist without a temple but there can be no temple without an altar (cf, however, Judg 17_{1-13}). The altar is mentioned on its own in Isa 17_8 and 19_{19} while the function of the priest is often simply designated as 'altar service'.[145] At the same time, the final end of the sanctuary at Bethel is predicted in terms of an announcement of the downfall of its altar.[146] The absence of a reference to the building of the altar of burnt sacrifice in the report of the building of the temple has led commentators to assume that the altar in question was already built prior to the construction of the temple.[147]

7aB *annulled his sanctuary.* נִאֵר מִקְדָּשׁוֹ

Since this second colon continues with reference to the sanctuary we can understand 2_{7aB} as an expansion of 2_{7aA}. מִקְדָּשׁ can refer to the entire temple complex as well as to some of its constituent parts (cf HAL 591f). In light of the parallel with מוֹעֲדוֹ in 2_{6aB} and the separate mention of the enclosing walls in 2_{7b}, it would seem reasonable to interpret the term as a reference to the forecourts and buildings within the walls (see like wise 1_{10b}). As we already noted, the verb נאר (*pi'el*) employed here is only found elsewhere in Ps 89_{40} (with YHWH as subject and the covenant with the Davidic king as object) where it is parallel with √חלל I *pi'el* 'to desecrate'. In the present bicolon √נאר *pi'el* is parallel with √זנח II, although the response שִׁחֵת מוֹעֲדוֹ (6aB) // נִאֵר מִקְדָּשׁוֹ (7aB) within the canticle is of importance with regard to its meaning. The aforementioned parallel appears to be the strongest, thus allowing us to see √נאר *pi'el* as a synonym of √שחת *pi'el* 'to destroy' (cf 2_{5b} and 2_{6a}). This is supported by the inclusion ... בְּאֹהֶל בַּת־צִיּוֹן שָׁפַךְ ... (4c) // נִאֵר מִקְדָּשׁ (7aB) within the canto, which is why we translate 'to annul' even though the notion of 'desecration' would fit just as well in the context. Once again the two notions are not mutually exclusive: the desecration of the sanctuary becomes visible in its physical destruction. This is the result of YHWH's scorn which itself implies

145 Cf, for example, Num 18_5, I Sam 2_{28}.
146 Cf I Kgs 13_{1ff}.
147 Cf TWAT IV 792ff (Dohmen).

the removal of his protection. The manner in which YHWH executed his destructive deeds is the topic of the following bicolon.

7bA *He has delivered into the hand of the enemy...* הִסְגִּיר בְּיַד־אוֹיֵב

Once again the poets focus on the relationship between YHWH's deeds and the advance of the enemy. This is no surprise. The critical question remained whether Zion's downfall should not be blamed on YHWH's powerlessness.[148] At the thematic level, an answer to this question already emerged in 1_{17}, the centre of the second canto of the first song: YHWH gave orders to the enemy to advance against Jacob. Downfall and its consequent oppression and distress were seen in 1_{17} as YHWH's judgement on the sins of his people (cf $1_{5b,8a,14a,18a}$). One would seek in vain in the first song, however, for a theological explanation of the downfall of the temple. The poets restricted themselves in Lam I to the mention of the devastation of Zion (1_4) and the forced infiltration and plunder of the sanctuary by unbelievers (1_{11}).

The fate of the temple and the people should not be placed on one and the same line. It would appear that just prior to the downfall, observers saw a clear distinction. In Jeremiah's preaching of doom, it is not his criticism of the misconduct of the people which is so shocking but rather the related announcement of the downfall of the temple (cf Jer $26_{6,9,11}$). Evidently, the predicted disaster was to be understood in terms of the people's sins.[149] In contrast to this, however, the announcement of the destruction of God's dwelling was taken as blasphemy. Without doubt this has to do with the understanding of the temple as YHWH's dwelling. He had chosen Zion and he protected his house against the enemy. Up to this point his protection had been a reality.[150] In line with this theological train of thought and no matter how bitter a pill to swallow, personal misfortune had to be accepted as the consequence of personal sin. The enemy destruction of the temple, however, was another matter altogether. Such a course of events implied the paradox of a God who did not protect his own sanctuary, a realisation which led to the understandable conclusion that YHWH was not as strong as the enemy gods. Such a conclusion was also drawn in reality.[151] The poets' theological vision on this precise point is contained in the first canticle (2_{6-7}) of the present sub-canto. They stress

[148] Cf 1983, 213–216.
[149] Cf 1983, 169ff.
[150] Cf 1983, 142ff.
[151] Cf 1983, 214ff.

that YHWH himself took the initiative to destroy his own dwelling. In the centre of the ז-strophe, and with sublime poetic sensitivity, they make reference to this fact by speaking of the destruction of that which made the protection of the temple complex a reality, namely the walls of Zion. The concentric structure (2_{7aB} // 2_{7cA}) of the present strophe ought to be respected and viewed, therefore, as the focal expression of the poets' thoughts. The destruction of the sanctuary and the joy of the enemy at gaining access to the temple are the consequence of the fall of the walls.

7bB ... *the walls of her palaces.* חוֹמֹת אַרְמְנוֹתֶיהָ

The fact that the colon חוֹמֹת אַרְמְנוֹתֶיהָ is often considered to be corrupt,[152] makes it apparent that a linear reading of the text will prevent us from seeing its cohesion. In spite of the agreement of the versions with MT, Rudolph considers the sudden mention of palaces here to be misplaced since the context refers exclusively to the temple. At the same time, the term אַרְמוֹן 'palace' is normally used exclusively for secular buildings, particularly the dwellings of prominent citizens and the king (cf HAL 86). Such objections, however, remain unconvincing. The 3f sg suffix of אַרְמְנוֹתֶיהָ refers back to Zion in 2_{6b}.[153] Furthermore, one can reliably view the אַרְמְנוֹתֶיהָ in relation to the temple complex. The temple complex and the royal palace did not only constitute an integrated whole from a religious perspective but also from an architectural perspective.[154] Albrektson points in the context to the song of Zion, Ps 48, in verses 4 and 14 of which the palaces of Zion are mentioned.[155] Moreover, sections of the temple enclosure also functioned as walls for the royal apartments.[156] Given the connection between palace and temple, it is evident that for the enemy force which knew how to break through the walls of the palace, the way to the temple itself lay open.

Löhr unjustifiably objects that the phrase הִסְגִּיר בְּיַד always has human beings as its object and that חוֹמֹת of the MT is therefore inappropriate. However, the phrase appears in the same meaning 'to hand over' with 'livestock' as object in Ps 78_{48} and 'a city' as object in Am 6_8.

152 Cf Löhr, Meek, Rudolph, Weiser, Kraus; cf also Robinson's proposed emendation in the text critical apparatus of BHS.

153 See 2_{5b} and 2_{4c} for a similar association between Zion and אַרְמוֹן.

154 Cf BRL² 160 (Galling).

155 Cf HSpieckermann, *Heilsgegenwart. Eine Theologie der Psalmen*, Göttingen 1989, 186–196.

156 Cf BHH 831f, 839 together with II Kgs 11_{19}, Jer 26_{10} and Ezek 43_{7f}.

Adonai has handed over the walls to the advancing enemy powers (cf Jer 52_7) and in so doing he has opened the way for the destruction of his sanctuary. It would be unacceptable to suggest that the poets came to this conclusion by themselves. For the adherents of Zion theology,[157] the devastation of the temple was a heart rending and inconceivable event, a fact clearly underlined by the song-response in the third song in which the גֶּבֶר states that his soul is bowed down within him when he thinks of his misfortune and homeless state which is the direct result of the destruction of the temple and the impossibility of celebrating the liturgy.[158] The poets' explanation of the downfall of the temple, therefore, must be rooted in the acceptance of the prophetic announcements of doom which had predicted the fall of Zion. The prophecy of Micah springs immediately to mind in this regard. On account of the corrupt nature of the cult, Micah saw the temple mountain transformed into a hill overgrown with thicket, a place for wild animals (Mic 3_{12}), a byword for misfortune, 'as if struck by a bomb'.[159] The echoes of this prophecy continued to resound in Jeremiah's time (cf Jer 26_{18}) who repeated Micah's prophetic warning in his own fashion.[160] Lam 5_{18} speaks of the fulfilment of these prophetic announcements.

7c *They have celebrated this tumultuously in* YHWH*'s house* קוֹל נָתְנוּ בְּבֵית־יְהוָה
as on the day of a festival. כְּיוֹם מוֹעֵד

What does the expression נָתַן קוֹל mean?[161] Generally speaking, it refers to loud (vocal) noise. With YHWH as subject it is used for thunder.[162] Elsewhere, however, the meaning is dependant on the context.[163] As we can see from the song-response 1_{7c}, צָרִים שָׂחֲקוּ 'the enemy laugh', these noisy invaders are expressing their joy. This is confirmed in the present context by the comparison made in the second colon: כְּיוֹם מוֹעֵד 'as on a day of festival'.

The comparison in question is quite unusual. In 1_{10b}, the poets referred to the transgression of YHWH's ban on admitting pagans to the temple.

157 Cf 1983, 255–260.

158 Cf the explanation of $1_{7b,13}$, 3_{17}, 5_{17f}.

159 Cf ASvdWoude, *Micha*, Nijkerk 1976, 123.

160 Cf Jer 7_{1-5}, 26_{1-6}; see also Ezek 24_{21}.

161 For an overview of texts containing this combination of words compare TWAT V 696 (Lipiński).

162 See, for example, Ex 9_{23}, I Sam 12_{17}, II Sam 22_{14}; Ps 18_{14}.

163 For example, birds singing or lions roaring (Ps 104_{12}, Jer 2_{15} and Am 3_4); human's shouting loudly (Jer 22_{20}, Prov 1_{20}); war cry (Jer 4_{16}) and loud weeping (Gen 45_2, Num 14_1) etcetera.

A similar line of thought may have been operative here also. Loud noise was not appropriate in the hallowed atmosphere of the sanctuary.[164] Thus the poets could have pointed to the enemy's unfitting behaviour, as we find in Ps $74_{4,23}$, but they refrained. The comparison here leads us to think that the poets were referring to the hubbub of a festival rather than the unfitting ribaldry of the enemy soldiers. In Ps $31_{8,9}$ the psalmist rejoices because YHWH did not hand him over into the hands of the enemy (וְלֹא הִסְגַּרְתַּנִי בְּיַד־אוֹיֵב, 31_{9a}). In the present text, the poets listen to the enemy rejoicing and celebrating a feast in the temple because YHWH has handed over his people into their hands (cf 1_{7c}). In stark contrast, YHWH's own people are forced to forget their feasts (2_{6b}). Once again, therefore, we are confronted with a turn about in the people's historical experience of YHWH's saving deeds (cf $2_{2c,3b,4a,6a}$).

Canticle II (2_{8-10})

Content/theme: *A city in tears, its inhabitants defeated*

Literary argumentation:

inclusions:	בַּת־צִיּוֹן (8aB) // בְּתוּלַת יְרוּשָׁלָם (10cB)
	אֻמְלָלוּ (8cB) // יֵשְׁבוּ לָאָרֶץ (10aA)
	חֵל וְחוֹמָה (8cA) // בַּת־צִיּוֹן (10aB) [165]
	טָבְעוּ בָאָרֶץ שְׁעָרֶיהָ (9aA) // נְבִיאֶיהָ (9cA) [166]
responses:	חוֹמַת בַּת־צִיּוֹן (8aB) // שְׁעָרֶיהָ (9aA)
	בַּת־צִיּוֹן (8aB) // בַּת־צִיּוֹן (10aB)
	יַחְדָּו אֻמְלָלוּ (8cB) // הוֹרִידוּ לָאָרֶץ (10cA)
	טָבְעוּ בָאָרֶץ (9aA) // יֵשְׁבוּ לָאָרֶץ (10aA)

This canticle constitutes the final verses of the first canto and the second sub-canto and as such it has the character of a conclusion. It begins by mentioning the systematic destruction of Zion's walls by YHWH. The second strophe constitutes a bridge between the destruction of the walls and the consequences for those who lived within them. At this point the poets clearly focus on those who were involved in the temple liturgy in on way or

164 Cf JCdMoor, 'The Sacrifice Which is an Abomination to the LORD', in: *Loven en Geloven*, Fs NicHRidderbos, Amsterdam 1975, 217–220.

165 See חוֹמַת בַּת־צִיּוֹן in 2_{8aB}; cf 2_{18aB}.

166 Cf the cohesion between 4_{12} and 4_{13}.

another. A clear succession of dignity is established in their overview: king, princes, priests, prophets, elders and finally the young girls of Jerusalem (cf Jer 32_{32}).

8aA *It was* YHWH*'s determination to destroy...* חָשַׁב יְהוָה לְהַשְׁחִית

Up to the present, the poets have spoken of the violent appearance of Adonai as an enemy. The devastating destruction and widespread death and decay might leave one with the impression that the divine wrath was and is out of control (see our remarks with regard to 1_{12c}). The verb שחת 'to destroy' reappears here (cf 2_{5b} and 2_{6a}), this time in the *hiph'il*, designating an act of YHWH. The meaning 'to destroy' continues to hold but where the *pi'el* focused primarily on the sudden, resultative character of the destruction in question (cf 2_{5b}) the present *hiph'il* "bezeichnet das aktuelle, absichtliche (...) Verderben".[167] The intended aspect of the destruction is a new element and is further elucidated via the √חשב (*qal*) which has YHWH as subject. There is no reason to follow the LXX at this point and read: Καὶ ἐπέστρεψεν κύριος τοῦ διαφθεῖραι = *hiph'il* שוב + √שחת, 'further destroying', which simply accentuates the impression of uncontrolled anger. The root חשב implies two constitutive moments of meaning: the moment of reckoning – including modifications such as blaming, charging, debiting and settling up, and the moment of planning, of thinking through.[168] YHWH's destructive behaviour is no unbridled attack; it has its roots in his measured and well-planned judgement. Mic 2_{1-3}, where there is talk of analogous retribution in the prophetic 'woe' oracle, provides a further illustration of what we have in the present text. Micah likewise employs the verb חשב; against those who devise evil, YHWH will devise evil in turn.[169] With respect to Lam 2_{8a}, this means that YHWH has assessed the evil of his people and they must pay for it in the form of the present destruction and downfall. No particular sin or guilt is mentioned in 2_{8a} as the basis of YHWH's planned intervention, however, leaving the use of the verb חשב with no apparent basis. The song-response with the first song provides the missing object, namely the behaviour of Jerusalem. Jerusalem has sinned grievously (1_{8a}) and thus her fate is well deserved. Jeremiah also refers to Jerusalem's sin (Jer 32_{31}) which she committed from the very moment she was built. It is interesting to note in the context of the third song, however, how the גֶּבֶר observes that Jerusalem's present lot is not (yet)

167 See THAT II 892 (Vetter).
168 Cf THAT I 643 (Schottroff) and TWAT III 245 (Seybold).
169 Cf ASvdWoude, *Micha*, Nijkerk 1976, 65–69.

equal to the evil she has done (cf 3_{22}: כִּי לֹא־תָמְנוּ). In spite of the prevailing misfortune and distress (cf 4_8 and 5_8), the prophetic prediction of the final end of Israel[170] has not yet become a reality. With the capture of Jerusalem the people feared that the end had come[171] but that end does not appear to have been final. There are still survivors in both the city and the land, a fact which can only be due to the goodness of YHWH.[172]

8aB ... *the wall of daughter Zion.* חוֹמַת בַּת־צִיּוֹן

YHWH's planned intervention has cost the people the walls of Jerusalem, the primary motif of the present strophe. It ought to be said, however, that the poets are extremely deliberate in their formulations. Given the fact that the present strophe is situated at the centre of the second sub-canto (2_{6-10}), it is evident that the aforementioned thematic prominence, which is further elaborated in the remainder of the sub-canto, is supported by the literary structure. A great deal is said with very few words. The same is true from a theological perspective. The fact that YHWH's destructive behaviour does not directly concern human beings but falls first upon stone and rock is evidence of the poets' subtlety. Nevertheless, the destruction of the wall affects more than the stones from which it was made. The protective function of the wall vanishes alongside those fallen rocks and stones. The image of the wall, in fact, is *pars pro toto.* If the wall collapses, the city too will fall and the enemy will gain access to the sanctuary within. As a consequence, the inhabitants from the king to the smallest infant are outlawed (2_{9-11}).

The wall of Jerusalem, however, did not only posses a profane, strategic value, it was simultaneously the visible symbol of faith in Jerusalem. The protective power of Zion's fortifications was not guaranteed by the quality of its stones nor the height or thickness of its walls but by YHWH's presence alone. For this reason YHWH himself is praised as Zion's Rock, fortress and defensive wall.[173] The demolition of the wall implied the simultaneous demolition of the people's unconditional faith[174] and at the same time the withdrawal of YHWH's presence from Zion (cf also 2_{3b}). The fact that the poets do not describe YHWH as the 'Guilty One', while continuing, nevertheless, to consider him responsible for the death and de-

[170] Cf Am 8_{2f}, Hos $1_{6,9}$, Isa 6_{19ff}, 22_{14}, Jer 7_{15}, 15_6.
[171] Cf the explanation of 4_{18}.
[172] Cf once again the song-response 3_{22}.
[173] Cf Ps 9_{10}, 18_3, 27_5, $46_{8,12}$, 48_4, $59_{10,17f}$, $62_{3,7}$, 94_{22}, 144_2; cf also Zech 2_5 (MT 2_9).
[174] Cf 1983, 169–172.

cay which surrounds them, is evidence of the extreme difficulty they must have encountered in distancing themselves from their faith convictions (cf also 2_{21c}).

8bA *He stretched out the measuring line and has not withheld* נָטָה קָו לֹא־הֵשִׁיב

The poets now provide us with further detail on YHWH's deliberate and calculated actions. He has stretched out the measuring line. The expression נָטָה קָו implies 'measurement' and can be used, for example, of a carpenter (Isa 44_{13}, cf Job 38_5). In Jer 31_{38f} and Zech 1_6 it is used with reference to the measurements which had to be made in the context of the rebuilding of Jerusalem. The opposite is the case, however, in II Kgs 21_{13} where the measurement functions in the context of the demolition of Jerusalem. Thus the context in which the act of measurement takes place is determinative of its meaning. In line with II Kgs 21_{13}, measuring in the present context clearly has negative connotations. YHWH has carefully calculated the portion of Zion's wall which is to be demolished. He has measured those (strategic) portions of the wall which must be raised to the ground. YHWH's deeds are far from uncontrolled.

8bB ... *his hand from destroying.* יָדוֹ מִבַּלֵּעַ

Within the bicolon 2_{8b} as a whole there is evidence of far-reaching use of associative language. In light of the לֹא־הֵשִׁיב, the root נטה also appears to have יָד as its object alongside קָו. In stretching out the measuring line YHWH has also stretched out his hand which he does not intend to withhold. נָטָה יָד is a fixed expression, meaning that a person is about to do something, getting ready to complete an action, and in most cases a hostile action.[175] Ringgren is of the opinion that, with YHWH as subject, the expression presents the image of YHWH as a warrior, a notion which is not out of place in the context of the entire first canto. Furthermore, there are echoes of Isa 14_{24ff}, especially in the use of similar terminology, although the Isaiah text has to do with YHWH's judgement against Assyria.[176] II Sam 24_{16} is an interesting text from the point of view of content in that it also refers to the threatened destruction of Jerusalem while partially employing the same terminology (יָד, שַׁחֵת). The influence of Zion theology in this text is unmistakable, however, since the angel of destruction is forced to withdraw his hand because of YHWH's remorse.[177]

[175] Cf TWAT V 409 (Ringgren).

[176] Against Israel: cf Isa 5_{29}, $9_{11,16,20}$, 10_4, Ezek 6_{14}, 14_9, 14_{13}, 16_{27}; cf also II Sam 24_{16}.

[177] Cf the echo in I Chron 21_{15}.

The contrast with the present circumstances is thereby made all the more clear: YHWH has not withheld his hand.[178]

8c *He lets wall and rampart languish,* וַיַּאֲבֶל־חֵל וְחוֹמָה
together they waste away. יַחְדָּו אֻמְלָלוּ

This bicolon presents the implementation of YHWH's plans. Wall and rampart languish. חוֹמָה and חֵל are object while YHWH is subject of וַיַּאֲבֶל (*hiph'il* impf of √אבל I; cf Ezek 31_{15}). The combination חוֹמָה and חֵל can also be found in Isa 26_{1}, Nah 3_{8} and II Sam 20_{15f}, the latter text giving the impression that the rampart was somewhat lower, standing in front of the actual city wall and serving as an initial fortification against enemy attack.[179] Rampart and wall languish. HAL 6f distinguishes two roots: אבל I, 'to languish' and אבל II 'to dry out'. According to Baumann there is only one verb at stake here which means 'to observe the customs of mourning', specifically during the entire mourning period.[180] The focus here is specifically on outwardly visible signs of mourning (cf 1_{4ab}). What would this imply? The enemy would have burrowed under the walls (cf II Sam, 20_{15f}) thus causing them to rupture. At strategic points they have been pulled to the ground altogether, leaving the city open and vulnerable.[181] Within the present canticle there is an inclusion with יֵשְׁבוּ לָאָרֶץ in 2_{10a}. Just as Zion's elders fall to the ground in mourning so the city walls also lie down in mourning.[182] Signs of rupture in the walls are also reminiscent of clothes torn in mourning.[183] Baumann is of the opinion that we are not dealing here with mourning over a death because there is actually no dead person to mourn.[184] Such a suggestion does not do justice to the context, nor to the constantly present relationship with elements of the dirge. The death and decay which have confronted both city and land are mentioned throughout the canto (cf 2_{4b} with וַיַּהֲרֹג). It remains true, however, that wall and rampart are used in the figurative sense as 'animated' objects (cf the roads and gates in 1_{4}). We already noted how Jahnow referred to the animation of things as part of the dirge (cf the explanation of 1_{4a}).[185]

---

[178] For the meaning of √בלע see the explanation of 2_{2a}.
[179] Cf, in addition, RdVaux, *Institutions II*, 35–38 and TWAT II 807ff (In der Smitten).
[180] In TWAT I 46f.
[181] Cf the references to Lady Jerusalem's nakedness in the song-response 1_{8b}.
[182] Cf the explanation of 2_{10c}; cf also the use of √טבע (to collapse) in the following colon and in II Sam 13_{31}; Isa 3_{26}, $47_{1,5}$, Ezek 26_{16}, Job 2_{13}.
[183] Cf, for example, Gen 37_{34}, II Sam 1_{11}; II Kgs 2_{12}.
[184] See TWAT II 48.
[185] See Jahnow, 102f.

Kutsch's proposal has made it reasonable to accept that the notion of observing the customs of mourning need not only be an expression of sadness but may also reflect the idea of humility towards YHWH in the hope of reprieve.[186] In addition, mourning customs were also observed when a person was humiliated by another (cf II Sam 13_{19}). These various dimensions of the observation of mourning customs can be found in the song-response between 1_8 and 2_8. In the latter text wall and rampart are humiliated by the violence done to them; in 1_8 Lady Jerusalem is humiliated by those who once honoured her.[187] The observation of mourning customs as an act of humility is also mentioned in Lam 3_{28ff}.[188]

Besides √אבל the root אמל I is also used (*pul'al*, BL 285*f*), a term which refers to the 'withering' of plants (Isa 16_8, Joel 1_{12}) or, metaphorically speaking, 'wasting away'.[189] Perhaps the poets envisaged the further collapse of the walls due to lack of repair and maintenance (cf also the collapse of the gates in the following bicolon) and being overgrown with weeds and thicket. It is striking that both verbs appear frequently in combination.[190] In Hos 4_3 the land languishes and wastes away in response to the sins of its inhabitants. The other texts constitute parts of prophetic announcements of judgement. Both ideas are resonant here: the walls languish and waste away because of YHWH's judgement over the sin of his people.

9aA *Her gates lie collapsed on the ground,* טָבְעוּ בָאָרֶץ שְׁעָרֶיהָ

The imagery employed in the previous bicolon is continued here in a climactic fashion: not only Zion's walls but even her much stronger gates have given up the ghost. Such a fate is likewise described in the context of human experience.[191] Just as human beings lie down on the ground in mourning so do Zion's (animated) gates.[192] Besides Isa 3_{26}, the imagery is strongly reminiscent of Jer 14_2, although there is a clear difference in the use of √קדר: 'uncared-for' which is equivalent to 'in mourning' (cf HAL 1002), in place of √טבע. A further difference can be seen in the use of לָאָרֶץ

186 EKutsch, «Trauerbrauche» und «Selbstminderungsriten» im Alten Testament, Theol Stud 78, 1965, 25–42; cf II Sam 12_{16ff} and I Kgs 21_{27f}.

187 For the relationship between (partial) nakedness and dirge cf Gen 37_{34}, Isa 32_{11}, Mic 1_8 and Jahnow, 18.

188 Cf also the explanation of 2_{10}.

189 Cf I Sam 2_5, Isa 19_8, KBL 60 and HAL 61.

190 Cf Isa 19_8, $24_{4,7}$, 33_9, Jer 14_2, Hos 4_3.

191 Cf Jahnow, 102f.

192 Cf II Sam 13_{31}, Isa 3_{26}, $47_{1,5}$, Ezek 26_{16}, Job 2_{13}; cf also the explanation of Lam 1_{4b}.

instead of the present בָּאָרֶץ. In Jer 14_2 the image is one of the mourning city walls leaning in dilapidation towards the ground. While they may have fallen into disrepair, the Jeremiah text does not speak of destruction. In Lam 2_{9a}, however, טָבְעוּ points to the actual act of 'collapsing' (cf Jer 38_6, Ps 9_{16}, $69_{3,15}$). In combination with בָּאָרֶץ one is left with the imagine of the collapsed gates surrounded by rubble (cf the explanation of 4_1) as if they had simply subsided.

9aB *her bars he has shattered and broken.* אִבַּד וְשִׁבַּר בְּרִיחֶיהָ

For metrical reasons, several commentators propose that we drop either אִבַּד or וְשִׁבַּר from the second colon (cf text critical apparatus of BHS). From a text critical perspective, however, there is no reason to make such an emendation. Both LXX and the Peshitta include both verbs. Gordis suggests that different versions of the text with אִבַּד and שִׁבַּר as variants circulated very early on. Later copyists who did not want to choose between the variants simply included both verbs and joined them with a ו. The weakness of such a proposition is that Lamentations does not appear to give evidence of any similar variants. Gordis, moreover, find the present reading illogical. This would indeed be the case if one interpreted √אבד (*pi'el*) as 'to lose' (Eccl 3_6), in the sense of 'let vanish', which does not fit logically with the idea of 'shattering' (שׁבר *pi'el*) bars which follows. Even with such a meaning, however, the present text can make logical sense if one were to construe the significance of the ו prior to שׁבר as an indicator of choice: 'or'.[193] YHWH has caused the bars to vanish, i.e. as valuable metal removed by the Babylonians (cf I Kgs 4_{13} and II Kgs 25_{13ff}), or he has let them be smashed to pieces during the siege. A more realistic interpretation, however, would be to understand √אבד *pi'el* and √שׁבר *pi'el* as more or less synonymous with the meaning 'to shatter'/'to smash to pieces',[194] where אבד renders the more general notion of 'shattering' an object and שׁבר the more focused idea of 'smashing to pieces' (of the larger chunks; cf II Kgs 25_{13} [with שׁבר *pi'el*]). It is striking that when אבד has to do with material objects in our example texts, the objects in question are always idol shrines or other objects related to idol worship (cf also Isa 37_{19}). The bars of Zion are now being confronted with the same fate. The formulation thus betrays the poets' intention: the destruction of the temple has to do with doctrinal and liturgical purity (cf 3_{40}).

193 Cf HAL 248 sv ו (6).

194 Cf, for example, Num 33_{52}, Deut 12_2, II Kgs 19_{18}, 21_3, Ezek 6_3, Zeph 2_{13} (// נָטָה יָד, cf 2_{8b}).

From the point of view of content, therefore, there is no question of a meaningless repetition but rather of a logical sequence of actions. In addition, both verbs also function elsewhere in the songs. An echo can be heard in 3_{18}, for example, – the central strophe of the first canto of this song! – the splendour of the גֶּבֶר is lost through the shattering of the bars. The same is true for √שׁבר I: alongside the breaking of the bars of the gates, Lady Jerusalem's young men could also be broken (1_{15b}), the גֶּבֶר considered himself broken (3_4), and there is talk of a 'rupture of the people' ($2_{11,13}$). As was the case in 1_7, the metrical irregularity of the present text appears to be quite deliberately employed to indicate emphasis. In a certain sense, the present bicolon is both a conclusion and a new beginning at the same time, a feature of Hebrew poetry which is frequently marked by longer units.[195] From this point on in the canto there is no further mention of the destruction of material things. The destruction of Jerusalem's gates and bars constitutes, as it were, the lowest point. Only the fate of the people remains to be settled although this is presented as a direct result of the breaking open of the gates. The new theme thus explains the opening of a new strophe (contra Kraus and Westermann, for example, who prefer to associate 2_{9a} with the previous strophe).

We are confronted here with more than just an, albeit significant, part of the destruction as a whole. While the poets position the destruction of the temple at the centre of the present canto ($2_{5,6}$), they frame it with the devastation of daughter Zion (2_1) and her gates (2_9). The gates form a vital part of the fortifications of the city and are a sign of strength.[196] As such they function as protection and thereby have their place in Zion theology.

What was said above with respect to the city walls (2_{8a}) is equally valid with respect to the gates and their bars. They can only offer the city any protection if YHWH vouches for them. The association between walls and gates is also evident within the songs, as is clear from the special positioning of this verse in the literary structure of Lamentations as a whole. At the level of the entire book, there is an inclusion with 4_{12}, the beginning of the last sub-canto of the fourth song, while 2_9 stands at the end of the first canto of the second song (cf שְׁעָרֶיהָ [2_{9aA}] // שַׁעֲרֵי יְרוּשָׁלָם [4_{12bB}]). 4_{12} reflects on the people's faith in Jerusalem's invincibility: no one believed

[195] Cf PvdLugt, *Strofische structuren in de bijbels-hebreeuwse poëzie*, Kampen 1980, 510–517.

[196] Cf Deut 3_5, Judg 16_3.

that an enemy would ever be able to get through her gates. If we are to understand the gates as a chiffre for Jerusalem's impregnability then their destruction must have been a deeply shocking event for the poets. A further song-response is evident with 1_9, וַתֵּרֶד פְּלָאִים 'Appallingly deep was her downfall', which corresponds with the aforementioned collapse of her gates (תֵּרֶד // טָבְעוּ) as well as with the fate of Jerusalem's nobility: once they paraded in magnificent splendour (cf 3_{18}), now they roam through the streets of the city, grey from hunger (cf Lam 4_{7-8}).

9bA *Her king and princes dwell among the nations.* מַלְכָּהּ וְשָׂרֶיהָ בַגּוֹיִם

It is equally consistent with Zion theology that the fate of the king should follow on the description of the destruction of the city's walls and gates. Such theology stands on two pillars: YHWH's election and protection of Zion and his election and legitimation of the Davidic king.[197] Strikingly enough, the fate of the Davidic king (and his kingdom) is raised at the same points within the present canto as the fate of Zion: in the centre and in the framing canticles (cf מַמְלָכָה [2cB] // מֶלֶךְ [6cB] // מַלְכָּהּ [9cA]), thus implying that the rejection of Zion is likewise the rejection of the king. The poets render this rejection in expressive language. With the loss of protection for the city, the person of the king was also left unprotected. Thus the Davidic king was taken prisoner and carried into exile in fulfilment of Ezekiel's prediction.[198]

Imprisonment and exile was not the fate of the king alone but also of the princes. As early as 2_{cB} it became apparent that their existence was inextricably bound to that of the kingdom itself and their splendour to Zion's splendour (cf the explanation of 1_6). The fall of Zion, therefore, signified the fall of her princes. It is clear that they too were carried into exile since בַגּוֹיִם – in contrast to 1_{3bA} – can only mean exile in the present context. There is evident progression with respect to 1_6 where the princes were in full flight. Here they are prisoners, exiles in a foreign land. Next to simultaneous events the poets also portray sequential events (cf the progression of הָלְכוּ בַשֶּׁבִי [1_{18c}] with respect to הָלְכוּ שְׁבִי [1_{5c}]). This argues against the suggestion that Lam II is an older song or the oldest of the songs (cf, for example, Kaiser). The absence of king and princes means that there is no leadership left in Zion. Indeed the people have been handed over to the caprice of the enemy (cf the explanation of $5_{3,8}$).

---

197 Cf 1983, 91f, 281–294.

198 Cf Ezek 12_{11-13}, 17_{16}; cf also Lam 4_{20}, II Kgs 25_7, Jer 52_{11}.

9bB *(Priestly) guidance is no more.* אֵין תּוֹרָה

There is some dispute as to how one should connect the אֵין תּוֹרָה of this second colon with the first. If one were to follow the Masoretic punctuation, then 2_{9b} would constitute one sentence and one would be obliged to read that the king and the princes dwell in exile among a people who have no Torah, i.e. among pagans. Given the fact that we are dealing here with a sort of summary description of events, the fate of the prophets being next in line, it is clear that this cannot be the original meaning. The vast majority of exegetes accept, therefore, that the lack of torah-teaching points to the 'absence' or 'non-functioning' of the priests.

Kaiser has defended a different approach, proposing the idea of a royal torah. In order to connect king and torah here he points to the analogous association in the following colon: prophets no longer receive visions from YHWH.[199] Van Selms, who is convinced of the correctness of Kaiser's proposal, offers further details, suggesting that the royal torah consisted of the teachings of court functionaries. Ultimately, neither Van Selms nor Kaiser are convincing. While it is certain that wisdom was practised in the court, the fact that there is no further explicit mention of such an institutional, royal torah, is a strong counter argument to their proposition. Even the profane torah, in the sense of education as such, had its primary 'Sitz im Leben' in the family home rather than in the court.[200] Although Kaiser distances himself from this position in his later commentary (1981), it remains necessary, nevertheless, that we establish some kind of relationship between the first and the second cola. It does indeed appear to be referring to the priestly torah, but this does not mean that there is no relationship between the king and such torah. In our explanation of 1_{6b} we noted the evident association between the princes and the cult, while it was clear from 2_{6c}, where king and priest are mentioned in the same breath, that reference was being made to the royal guarantee to maintain the said cult. With the loss of the king as protector, an important pillar of the liturgy also disappeared, a fact which also had serious consequences for the priestly teaching associated therewith.

Hag 2_{10-13} relates an episode of priestly torah,[201] in which a distinction is made between pure and impure, sacred and profane. Ezekiel rebuked

---

199 OKaiser, *Der Königliche Knecht*, FRLANT NF 75, 1959, 31.

200 Cf THAT II 1033ff (Liedke – Petersen).

201 Cf JBegrich, *Die priesterliche Tora*, BZAW 66, 1936, 63–88; also in: JBegrich, *Gesammelte Studien zum Alten Testament*, ThB 21, München 1964, 232–260.

the priests because they overlooked such distinctions (Ezek 22_{26}; cf also Lev 10_{11}). It was the task of the priests to teach the people what was appropriate and what was not in their relationship with YHWH.[202] The Haggai text makes it clear that it was not simply a question of teaching the 'great' and widely known commandments but primarily about more practical regulations such as how one ought to behave in particular circumstances. Casuistry was a matter for the priests. At the same time, they had to judge whether a particular sacrificial animal would be acceptable or not.[203] Although the priests were able to draw upon written tradition, their teaching was for the most part orally presented (Hag 2_{10-13}, Mal 2_6). Now their teaching is gone. This need not imply that there were no longer any priests. Indeed, in Lam 1_{4b} there is even mention of the presence of priests in the ruined temple (cf 2_{20c}). It remained possible, therefore, to ask the priests for teaching but they are no longer able to offer it. Their fate makes their silence evident: YHWH has rejected them also in his burning anger (cf the explanation of 2_{6c}), a fact made clear by his destruction of the sanctuary and the altar ($2_{6,7a}$). It appears from $4_{13,16}$ that the priests had lost their spiritual authority, so necessary for their role as teachers. This was a disastrous situation for the remaining YHWH-believers. In their unsettled, even chaotic society, faced as it was with so many new, terrible and frightening circumstances, they could no longer turn to the priests for leadership. The danger was thereby created that the people might act against YHWH's will without knowing it and incur even further guilt. The distress referred to here had already been portrayed in Ezekiel's announcement of doom in Ezek 7_{25f}: "When anguish comes, they will seek peace, but there shall be none [...] they shall keep seeking a vision from the prophet; instruction shall perish from the priest, and counsel from the elders."

9c *Even her prophets no longer find revelation from* YHWH.

גַּם־נְבִיאֶ֕יהָ לֹא־מָצְא֥וּ
חָז֖וֹן מֵיְהוָֽה

If the 'institutional' revelation of YHWH's will embodied in the priestly torah has vanished then so has any ad hoc revelation, the revelation provided by the prophets. The prophets no longer received visions from YHWH. Given the prophecies uttered by Jeremiah and Ezekiel after the downfall, the present text must be referring to other prophets. The 3f sg

202 Cf Deut 33_{10} and GvRad, *Das fünfte Buch Mose. Deuteronomium*, ATD 8, Göttingen 1968², 258f.

203 Lev 22_{17-25}; RdVaux, *Institutions II*, 206–209; THAT II 1035f (Liedke–Petersen).

suffix of נְבִיאֶיהָ suggests that the prophets in question are those of daughter Zion and in light of the combination with the priests from the preceding colon, it is probable that the said prophets were involved in the cult. Much has been said in this regard over the question of 'false prophets' but this qualification is not found in lamentations. Moreover, the notion might lead to the erroneous conclusion that the prophetic deception of such individuals was evident.[204] Although cultic prophets spoke about the situation of the entire people (cf 2_{14}) they also prophesied in a pastoral context for individuals. They were qualified to speak a word from YHWH on behalf of an Israelite in need who genuinely sought YHWH's help.[205] Given the parallel with priestly teaching in the previous colon it is probable that the present lack of prophetic advice was at a more personal level. Such prophetic revelation was now at an end.

Although the noun חָזוֹן 'vision' originally had to do with prophetic visions, referring to the way divine revelation was received in earlier prophecy, the notion of an added auditory dimension would not have been unusual.[206] Later, the non-visual element even gained predominance (compare Isa 1_1 [חָזוֹן] with Isa 2_1 [הַדָּבָר]).[207] In the present text, however, no particular means of receiving divine revelation is implied, simply prophetic revelation in general. Jepsen presupposes the following coherence between 2_9 and 2_{14}: the text of 2_9 states that the prophets no longer receive revelation from YHWH. If they continue to prophesy, however, as they do in 2_{14}, then their prophecies must indeed be false.[208] Aalders follows a similar line of thought but both he and Jepsen are incorrect. It is not a matter here of the faulty nature of the prophecies in question. The text simply states that the prophets no longer receive revelation from YHWH. They simply do not prophesy at all, neither true prophecy nor false prophecy. This is also evident from the context. Cultic life and everything associated with it has become impossible, including prophetic activity. The perfect לֹא־מָצְאוּ clearly indicates that this situation has taken hold, but the fact that it is still ongoing warrants a translation in the present.[209] After the downfall, 'false prophecy' was not a matter of course. The prophets of Jerusalem

---

[204] Cf 1983, 156–177.

[205] Cf JCdMoor, *De tijd van het heil*, Kampen 1970, 14–23.

[206] Cf, for example, Num $24_{3ff,15ff}$, II Sam $7_{4,17}$, Ps 89_{20}.

[207] More detail can be found on this topic in TWAT II 823–835 (Jepsen); compare also LKöhler, *Theologie des Alten Testaments*, Tübingen 1966[4], 87–89.

[208] Jepsen, TWAT II, 831.

[209] Cf Löhr, Meek, Rudolph, Weiser, Kraus, Gordis, Van Selms, Hillers, Brandscheidt, Stoll.

– among whom we can envisage figures such as Hananiah (cf Jer 28) – must have undergone a serious crisis of faith after the collapse of their city. Indeed, their words of salvation for Jerusalem were never disclosed. On the contrary, this certainly must have led to much reflection as to why their words had not come true, a fact which must also have given rise to strong reservations with respect to new prophetic activities. On the other hand, it remains possible that, in such a state of distress, the people still longed for the liberating 'visions' of the prophets no matter what. The use of the root מצא (active finding = seeking) allows us to deduce that the prophets in question continued to try to receive 'words' from YHWH.[210] Nevertheless, a widespread mistrust of their prophetic activity had taken root (cf the explanation of 2_{14}) and with far-reaching consequences. In 4_{13}, it appears that they have lost their credibility on account of their sins. Ps 74_9 – although a somewhat later text – allows us to further deduce that cultic prophecy as a whole had completely vanished. In contrast – as we can see throughout Lamentations[211] – those prophets who had predicted YHWH's judgement of Jerusalem and the ultimate fall of the city increased their authority. Among such prophets we might once again refer to Micah (cf the explanation of 2_{7b}) whose prophecy of doom over the temple agrees both verbally and at the level of content with the present text. As one of the reasons for the coming destruction of Zion he mentions misplaced prophetic proclamations of salvation. In addition, he describes their future fate: it will become night for them, 'without vision' (מֵחָזוֹן); they will beseech but God will not answer them.[212] In Ezek 7_{26}, the absence of a prophetic word (of salvation) is mentioned alongside the absence of priestly torah as an element in YHWH's judgement.[213] It is only human to want to cling to the least glimmer of hope in such situations of great distress but even that has been rendered impossible. The civil and religious order has been turned upside down. The song-response between the present text and 1_9 is thus made clear. 2_9 concretises 1_9: king and princes are gone and there is no more revelation from YHWH. The tortured prayer extended directly to God in the song-response 1_{9c} is thus likewise understandable: "See, YHWH, my distress...". The faith lying behind this prayer is represented in the corresponding טוֹב יְהוָה-strophe of the third song (3_{25-27}).

210 Cf TWAT IV 1066 (Wagner).
211 Cf 1983, 262–267.
212 Cf Mic 3_{6f} together with the explanation of 1_{2a}.
213 Cf Isa 2_3 and Mic 4_3 for the reverse situation.

10a *They sit on the ground and are dumbfounded,* יֵשְׁבוּ לָאָרֶץ יִדְּמוּ
the elders of daughter Zion. זִקְנֵי בַת־צִיּוֹן

The Masoretic punctuation of the verbal forms יֵשְׁבוּ and יִדְּמוּ (impf) ought to be upheld. The perfect employed by the versions[214] is an accommodation to the perfects from the previous strophe. If one were to read perfects here then the elders would be given a place in the sequence king, princes, priests and prophets. The difference with the king and the princes, however, is that the elders are still present in the city and in contrast to the priests and prophets they still seem to be functioning; they are the only ones left who can still offer some kind of leadership to the people. It is not a question of 'sitting' in the past but of sitting now. Together with the young maidens they are, as it were, the only ones to remain in the city and as such they must witness the entire downfall without the slightest possibility of help. Their reaction is that of mourners lamenting the death of a loved one; they sit dejected on the ground.

The positioning of their 'sitting' within the structure of the songs is noteworthy. We already noted the criss-cross correspondences (present at the canticle level) between the beginning and end of the cantos in Lam I and II (cf also Lam III below).[215] The beginning of the first canto of Lam I returns at the conclusion of the first canto of Lam II and vice versa. The same is true for second cantos (with respect to the first cantos: יָשְׁבָה [1_{1aA}] // יֵשְׁבוּ [2_{10aA}]; מִקְדָּשָׁהּ [1_{10bB}] // תִּפְאֶרֶת יִשְׂרָאֵל and הֲדֹם־רַגְלָיו [$2_{1bB,cA}$]; with respect to the second cantos: עוֹלַל [1_{12bB}] // עוֹלַלְתָּ [2_{20aB}] etcetera. See also יוֹם [חֲרוֹן] אַפּוֹ in 1_{12cB} and 2_{22bA} together with מֵעַי חֳמַרְמָרוּ [1_{20aB}] // חֳמַרְמְרוּ מֵעַי [2_{11aB}]).

In exegetical terms, this means that there is a correspondence between Lady Jerusalem who sits in mourning and the elders of daughter Zion who do likewise. If one bears the use of personification in mind it would appear that both texts refer to one and the same act of mourning. The mourning of the city is the mourning of its inhabitants, represented here by their elders. They must now bear the responsibility but they too are crushed and disheartened. The exegesis of 1_{1aA} made it clear that sitting on the ground in this fashion was an element in the ritual of mourning. In the present bicolon, however, a new element is added, 'silence'. On the basis of Ugaritic parallels, commentators have proposed that we interpret the verb דמם as 'to lament' or 'to weep'.[216] The parallel with $3_{26,28}$, however,

[214] Cf the text critical apparatus of BHS.
[215] Cf 1988, 390.

contradicts such an interpretation. We derive our translation, therefore, from √דמם I which means 'to be silent' (cf LXX with ἐσιώπησαν), rendering יִדְּמוּ with 'they are dumbfounded', their silence being the result of a sort of paralysis brought on by terrible fear or overpowering sorrow.[217] On the basis of Job 2_{11f}, Ezra 9_{3ff} and Ezek 26_{16ff}, Lohfink has suggested with good reason that stylised expressions may have been applied to such moments of insensibility.[218] Whether the 'silence' of the elders should be explained in exclusively psychological terms, however, remains a question. We already suggested in our exegesis of 1_{1a} that the original intention behind the ritual act of sitting on the ground might (conceivably) be partly explained by a desire to participate in the realm of the dead. Given the unclear distinctions between the roots דמה, דום, דמם[219] it is possible to interpret the verb as √דמה meaning 'to be alike', thus 'alike' with the dead. The intention behind the action, therefore, would appear to be a desire to share in the silence of the dead, made real by their own silence and paralysis. Of course, this does not imply that such ritual acts were not genuine expressions of sorrow, far from it.

10b *They have thrown dust upon their heads,* — הֶעֱלוּ עָפָר עַל־רֹאשָׁם
put on mourning attire. — חָגְרוּ שַׂקִּים

Here we have two more frequently mentioned mourning customs. The sprinkling of dust upon the head in mourning can be found, for example, in Jos 7_6, I Sam 4_{12}, II Sam 1_2, 15_{32}. Jahnow considers the act of placing fine dust upon one's head to be a rite of communication with the dead, at least in origin.[220] Dust constitutes an element of the dead.[221] Indeed, the dead dwell in the dust (cf Isa 26_{19}). We can deduce from Jer 6_{26}, Ezek 27_{30} and Mic 1_{10} that, at times of mourning, people even rolled around in the dust and thus spent their entire day 'in the dust'. Perhaps the sprinkling of dust upon the head should be seen as a stylised version of a former more unrestrained ritual. In either case, the mourner sat covered in dust from top to toe.

---

[216] Cf HAL 217 sv דמם II and ThFMcDaniel, 'Philological Studies in Lamentations', Biblica 49 (1968), 38ff.

[217] Cf JScharbert, *Der Schmerz im Alten Testament*, Bonn 1955, 117.

[218] In: NLohfink, 'Enthielten die im Alten Testament bezeugten Klageriten eine Phase des Schweigens?', VT XII (1962), 260–277; cf also Hillers, Boecker and TWAT II 281 (Baumann).

[219] See TWAT II 280 (Baumann) and TWAT II 266 (Preuß).

[220] Jahnow, 23f.

[221] Cf Gen 3_{19}, Job 17_{16}, 20_{11}, 34_{15}, Eccl 3_{20}, Ps 22_{30}, 104_{29} etcetera.

Tearing one's clothing and putting on mourning attire can be found, for example, in Gen 37_{34}, II Sam 1_{11}, 3_{31}, 13_{31}. The שַׂק was made from cheap, unbleached goat or camel hair[222] and took the form of a tunic, with holes for the head and the arms, worn over the naked body.[223] Both practices appear to be stylised versions of original total nakedness during mourning (cf Isa 32_{11}, Mic 1_{18}). Commentators differ as to the actual meaning of such practices.[224] It is possible that the association between nakedness and death had a role to play (cf Job 1_{21}, Eccl 5_{14}) which would be in line with our explanation of the other customs outlined above. The question remains, however, as to whether people were still aware of the original meaning.[225] Frequently such practices begin to take on their own meaning and ceased to be understood as well-know and familiar expressions of mourning. Only when the context offers reasonable clues to suggest such a state of affairs should one seek further into the matter.

10c *They press their faces to the ground,* הוֹרִידוּ לָאָרֶץ רֹאשָׁן
the young girls of Jerusalem. בְּתוּלֹת יְרוּשָׁלָם

Most commentators envisage the present bicolon to mean that the young girls of Jerusalem 'hang their heads'. Such an explanation, however, tends to leave לָאָרֶץ together with the strophe-inclusion לָאָרֶץ (10aA) // לָאָרֶץ (10cA) more or less unexplained. Since the expression יָרַד רֹאשׁ cannot be found elsewhere in the OT, we are somewhat bound to the context for its meaning. In light of the evident association with 1_{4c} it would seem natural to interpret the posture of Jerusalem's young girls as an expression of profound grief and despondency. Is the present text simply restating 1_{4c} in different words, however? From the point of view of content, it is striking that the text explicitly refers to the elders as people in mourning while it only provides an impression of the young girls standing nearby with heads bowed. The question remains, therefore, whether the expression יָרַד רֹאשׁ לָאָרֶץ means more than simply 'to hang one's head'. Although the expression is not used elsewhere in the OT as an expression of mourning it seems reasonable to propose such a possible interpretation. In so doing we respect the homogeneity of the strophe to a greater degree together with the designation לָאָרֶץ which, in any event, meant 'to the ground' in the first bicolon (2_{10a}; cf also 2_{2cA}). The corresponding conclusion to the first canto

---

222 Cf II Sam 21_{10}, Isa 3_{24}, 50_3.
223 See II Kgs 6_{30}, II Mac 3_{19}.
224 Cf Jahnow, 18–21.
225 Cf Oßwald, BHH 2021ff.

of the second song (3_{28-33}) offers some clarification. It should be noted that in 3_{32} the verb יגע which was employed in 1_{4c} (*niph'al*) reappears with reference to Jerusalem's young girls. This supports our assumption that the gesture of 'bowing one's head' is a response to being afflicted by YHWH. Within the final canticle, however, there is an inclusion יִתֵּן בֶּעָפָר פִּיהוּ (3_{29A}) // הוֹגָה (3_{32A}) which gives the impression that oppression leads to being pressed down into the dust (cf Isa 51_{22}). For this reason we should take the fact that the girls let their heads fall to the ground much more literally. Having one's head on the ground is roughly equivalent of having one's mouth in the dust, the latter functioning as a response to the former, i.e. to affliction. If we are correct, then the expression in question also means that the girls are bowed down with their faces to the ground, a posture which can be seen as parallel to that of the elders who have sprinkled themselves with dust. Thus we have another variation of the mourning ritual of rolling oneself in the dust.[226] The girls, in their own fashion, have surrounded themselves with dust and thereby join the elders in a gesture of mourning. Such an interpretation confirms the unity of the strophe at the level of content.

One might ask why the poets conclude the present canto with the mention of the mourning girls of Jerusalem. There can be no doubt, however, that this has to do with their cultic role. In this canticle, the poets have listed, in order of importance, all those who had a part to play in the cult.[227] We are faced once again with the question whether this show of mourning was an exclusively personal expression. In our explanation of 2_{8c}, we mentioned Kutsch's proposition which made it reasonable to accept that such expressions of mourning also bore witness to the humility of those involved who thereby hoped for mercy before YHWH. The location of the present strophe within the structure of the songs as a whole leads us to believe that the mourning gestures of the young girls and the elders had a similar intention.

Perhaps these words are even more profound. Indeed, the total loss of the entire cult, from temple to prophet, is the subject of poetic portrayal from 2_6 onwards in the present sub-canto. Sacrifice and song are no more; prayer and intercession no longer resound within the temple walls. The liturgical path to YHWH's forgiveness and reconciliation has thus been

226 Cf Jer 6_{26}, Ezek 27_{30} and Mic 1_{10}.

227 Cf 1_{19b} for the relationship of the elders with the cult and 1_{4c} for that of the young girls who assisted in liturgical dance and song.

lost. Only the despoiled, the destitute, the naked and afflicted remain lying in the dust, constituting, without liturgy, a silent prayer to YHWH. Thus we have a response with the conclusion of the second canto in which the final canticle (2_{20-22}) functions as a prayer. The first canto of Lam I (1_{11c}) likewise concludes with a prayer of supplication. In addition, there is a firm association with the end of the first canto of Lam III based on the common use of terminology (√ישב, √דמם I and עפר) in the י-strophe (3_{28-30}). Nevertheless, a further expression of hope, however reserved, can also be detected in 3_{29B}.

Canto II (Lam 2_{11-22})

The first canto focused primarily on the various levels of destruction endured by the city, mentioning only the fate of those who had a function within the cult. The second canto focuses, in contrast, on the remaining members of the population and their terrible distress, especially that of the children of Jerusalem. Furthermore, direct reference is made to those who in the first instance must be held responsible for the current situation. The description employs the same alternation of speaker as in the first song. Daughter Jerusalem/Zion speaks in $2_{11,12,20-22}$ while the poets take the floor in the remaining verses speaking directly about her further anguish ($2_{13,15f}$) and its cause ($2_{14,17}$). The first sub-canto (2_{11-17}) is thereby concluded. The second sub-canto (2_{18-22}) sees the poets urging daughter Jerusalem to pray on behalf of her dying children ($2_{18,19}$). Finally she acquiesces to their pleas (2_{20-22}).

Sub-canto I (Lam 2_{11-17}).

Jerusalem's prophets stand at the heart (2_{14}) of this first sub-canto. They and their misleading visions are the primary cause of the present famine confronting the children of the city. Seeing her children die in their mothers' lap brings unmeasurable sorrow to daughter Jerusalem. The prophets must also accept responsibility for the city's lost splendour and her enemy's joy on account of that loss (2_{15-17}). The latter's presumption that they alone have brought Jerusalem to her knees is misplaced. All of this is the work of YHWH. In spite of the failure of Jerusalem's prophets, YHWH has brought the true prophetic word to fulfilment (2_{17} contra 2_{14}).

Canticle I (2_{11-13})

Content/theme: *Daughter Jerusalem weeps for her children dying from hunger*

Literary argumentation:

inclusions:	חֳמַרְמְרוּ מֵעַי (11aB) // מִי יִרְפָּא־לָךְ (13cB)[228]
	בַּת־עַמִּי (11bB) // בְּתוּלַת בַּת־צִיּוֹן (13bB)
	קִרְיָה (11cB) // יְרוּשָׁלַם (13aB)
	אִמֹּתָם (12aA) // אִמֹּתָם (12cB)
responses:	בֵּעָטֵף עוֹלֵל וְיוֹנֵק (11cA) // בְּהִשְׁתַּפֵּךְ נַפְשָׁם (12cA)
	עִיר (12bB) // צִיּוֹן (13cA)
ext par:	שֶׁבֶר (11bB) // שִׁבְרֵךְ (13cA)

11a *Blinded with tears are my eyes,* כָּלוּ בַדְּמָעוֹת עֵינַי
my insides burn. חֳמַרְמְרוּ מֵעַי

What is the identity of the first person speaker who begins this second canto? The direct address of the poets themselves would appear to have something to say for it, given that within the canticle, 2_{13} speaks of 'daughter Jerusalem' in the third person.[229] Closer inspection, however, shows that this interpretation is incorrect. Wiesmann offers better arguments in favour of daughter Jerusalem as the speaker. In terms of structure, this is supported by the song-response with her exclamatory prayer in 1_{11c}, 2_{11} being an expansion thereof. With regard to the content level of Lam I, we can also point to daughter Zion's complaint in 1_{16a} where she herself explicitly mentions her incessant weeping. After an appeal to YHWH, the mention of indignity, tears and physical suffering constitute a well-known sequence within the OT lament form.[230] Moreover, within the second canto (2_{11-20}), the inclusion on the canticle level with the final canticle (2_{20-22}) – likewise a prayer of daughter Zion – shows that she must also be the speaker in the first canticle (2_{11-13}). Finally, we can also point out the literal correspondence with 1_{20aB}: מֵעַי חֳמַרְמָרוּ (= lament of daughter Zion) // חֳמַרְמְרוּ מֵעַי (2_{11aB}). We can thus formulate the theme of the present canticle as follows: 'daughter Jerusalem weeps for her children dying of hunger' (for the same style figure cf Jer 31_{15}). By the time we come to the מ-strophe (2_{13}), however, the poets take to the foreground once again as the speakers as they (hopelessly) grasp for words to comfort daughter Jerusalem. Such an alternation of speakers within a canticle is not altogether uncommon (cf $1_{9,11}$) and it likewise appears to have been employed

[228] See דְּוָי in 1_{22cB} // with מֵעַי חֳמַרְמָרוּ in 1_{20aB}.

[229] Cf Calvin, Aalders, Haller, Rudolph, Weiser, Kraus, Hillers, Kaiser, Brandscheidt, Boecker, Groß, Stoll.

[230] Cf Job 16_{20}, Ps 31_{10f}, 69_4, 102_{3f}, 116_8, 143_7.

at the literary level with significant purpose (cf the explanation of 2_{13}). With respect to 1_{16}, one can speak anew (cf the explanation of 2_{9b}) of a certain progression from intense weeping to the consequences thereof. Once again we translate the perfect in the present tense.[231] The root כלה I refers to an action which brings something to an end or an event in which something reaches its end.[232] The meaning here suggests that daughter Jerusalem's eyes no longer function because of her many tears. She can no longer see what is going on around her.[233] Luther translates as follows: "Ich hab schier meine Augen ausgeweinet". Significantly, the verb כלה reappears at the end of the present canto: her eyes have reached their 'end' because YHWH has made an 'end' of the life of her children. See the explanation of 2_{22c}.

What might the function of such weeping be? It does indeed express the subjective experience of daughter Jerusalem's sorrow but at the same time it is also a conscious weeping in the presence of YHWH; daughter Jerusalem makes her sorrow visible to him through her tears which thus take on the character of a silent prayer.[234] For the significance of חֳמַרְמְרוּ מֵעַי see the explanation of 1_{20a}.

11bA *My spirit is torn asunder...* נִשְׁפַּךְ לָאָרֶץ כְּבֵדִי

Translated literally, this first colon provides an image which is unknown in our language usage: 'poured out on the ground my liver'. Close expressions in more modern phraseology would be those which include the term 'gall' (cf Job 16_{13}). As a 'heavy' (כָּבֵד) and important organ, the liver played an important role in occult divination in Israel's Umwelt (cf Ezek 21_{21} [MT 21_{26}]). Stenmans presumes that the infrequent mention of the liver in the OT hints at a rejection of the practice of liver inspection.[235] By analogy with the heart, the liver should be understood as the seat of the emotions. This was already the case in Ugarit. Cf CTA 3:B.25f: *tgdd. kbdh. bṣḥq // ymlu. lbh. bšmḫt // kbd. 'nt. tšyt*: "her liver swelled up with gladness // her heart was replete with joy // the liver of Anat with triumph".[236] Similar usage can be found in the OT.[237] Daughter Jerusalem is turned

[231] Cf the explanation of 1_{1a}.
[232] Cf TWAT IV 167 (Helfmeyer).
[233] Cf Jer 14_6, Ps 6_{7f}, 69_4.
[234] Cf, for example, Ps 38_{10f}; cf also the explanation of 2_{19}.
[235] See TWAT IV 22.
[236] Cf JCdMoor, *The Seasonal Pattern in the Myth of Ba'lu*, AOAT 16, Neukirchen 1971, 88, 94.
[237] Cf THAT II 794 (Westermann).

inside out and thus reveals her feelings for all to see. Related images can be found in the lament of the individual genre in the context of deathly affliction and abandonment by God.[238] Together with the references in the previous bicolon we now have a sequence of three allusions to daughter Jerusalem's emotional state. The cumulative effect of such a sequence serves to profoundly accentuate the cause of her deep sorrow which she will soon put into words.

11bB *... at the wound of my daughter, my people,* עַל־שֶׁבֶר בַּת־עַמִּי

As we can deduce from the prophetic idiom, the word שֶׁבֶר – mostly translated as 'rupture'/'break' – in the present context signifies a 'wound' brought about by a blow or stab. The root שׁבר, in combination with √נכה and √רפא, is used in similar contexts.[239] It is true that the present canticle does not employ the √נכה, but a song-response – this time with the third song – does reveal that it is present in the context (cf לְמַכֵּהוּ in 3_{30A}). The aforementioned prophetic phraseology has to do with disasters and catastrophes which are to confront the people as the outcome of YHWH's judgement. It is clear that the present affliction is to be understood as the direct fulfilment of such an announcement of doom. The fact that the authors of Lamentations interpret the situation in this fashion is evident from their use of this specific idiom. Where the older written prophets may have spoken in more general terms of a 'break' (cf Am 6_6, Isa $30_{14f,26}$), the idiomatic usage of Jeremiah, in contrast, is firmly consonant with that of the poets of Lamentations. The phrase שֶׁבֶר בַּת־עַמִּי, for example, can be found in several places in Jeremiah (6_{14}, $8_{11,21}$) as can the word combination שֶׁבֶר + גָּדוֹל,[240] although the latter combination is not unique to Jeremiah since the expression שֶׁבֶר גָּדוֹל can already be found in Zephaniah in the precise context of the יוֹם יְהוָה theme (Zeph 1_{10}). Nah 3_{19} also portrays the fall of Nineveh with similar terminology. Nevertheless, it remains reasonable to assume that the poets here are harking back to the prophetic vision of Jeremiah. We can deduce this not only from the significant agreements at the level of diction but also from a connection at the level of content. In the first sub-canto of the following canticle, the poets interpret the misleading visions of Jerusalem's prophets as the cause of her 'wound' (שֶׁבֶר); Jeremiah makes the same connection.[241] This is significant,

---

[238] Cf Ps 6_{7-8}, 31_{10ff}, 38_{6ff}, 42_4, 69_4, 88_{10}.

[239] Cf Isa 30_{26}, Jer 14_{19}, 15_{18}, $30_{12ff,17}$; cf also THAT II 807 (Stoebe).

[240] Jer 4_6, 6_1, 48_3, 50_{22}, 51_{54}.

[241] Jer 6_{14}, 8_{11}, 14_{13-22}.

of course, for the tone of the canticle as a whole. The poets interpret what they experiences as the fulfilment of a prophetic announcement of doom over their people. בַּת־עַמִּי, '... daughter, my people', is a personification in which the people are presented as a woman.[242] Daughter Jerusalem thus laments over the terrible fate of her people.

11c *at the pining of children and infants* בֵּעָטֵף עוֹלֵל וְיוֹנֵק
in the squares of the city. בִּרְחֹבוֹת קִרְיָה

It is evident from the central positioning of $2_{11,12}$ that what afflicts daughter Jerusalem the most in her present distress is the fate of her young children and infants. These strophes contain an accumulation of similar terminology: √שפך (11bA, 12cA), √עטף (11cA, 12bA), בִּרְחֹבוֹת (11cB, 12bB), אִמֹּתָם (12aA, 12cB), even more than was the case with the central strophes of the first song (√נבט and √ראה [$1_{11c,12a}$]). Moreover, within the second song as a whole, the poets have created a clear progression via the succession from king (2_{9bA}) to child (2_{11c}). Thus the literary structure of Lam II shows that by placing them in the centre – which also functions as the opening of the second canto – the small(est) children may be the last but they are certainly not the least to be mentioned. Their dreadful fate and suffering are significantly underlined.

We are left with the impression that a veiled question is at work here as to the justification and purpose of the suffering of the children and infants. Although the poets proclaim that YHWH is rightly punishing daughter Jerusalem because of her sins ($1_{5,18,22}$) based on the insight that the unjust behaviour of parents also has an effect on their children,[243] such knowledge does not reconcile with the terrible lot these children have to face, given that they are not (yet) able to accept personal responsibility. While the present text does not deal explicitly with the problem, 3_{27} clearly calls the relationship between YHWH and the suffering of the younger generation into question. Later, in the ק-strophe (2_{19}), the monstrous fate of her children becomes the focal ground of appeal for daughter Jerusalem's prayer. In this and the following strophes, the starvation and death of the children is rendered in some detail, while the poets relate what happens to their mortal remains in a progression at the conclusion of the canticle (2_{20b}).

The word יוֹנֵק refers to a babe in arms, an infant at the breast.[244] In the present context, however, this implies older children than we would recog-

---

[242] Cf Isa 22_4, Jer 4_{11} and TWAT I 869 (Haag).

[243] Cf Ex 20_5, Jer 44_7, Jos 7.

[244] Cf 4_{4aA} and TWAT III 666 (Ringgren).

nise as infants in our contemporary western culture. Children were weaned in Israel for a long time.[245] The term עוֹלֵל does not refer to the tiniest infants but rather to the younger children who were still dependant on their parents.[246] The combination עוֹלֵל וְיוֹנֵק represents a (limited) merism (cf I Sam 22_{19}) which implies that all the children between the וְיוֹנֵק and the עוֹלֵל were confronted with the same fate.

Sæbø wrongly suggests with respect to Lam 2_{11}: "Es gibt wohl ... kaum ein besonderes Interesse an den 'Kleinkindern' als solchen; doch ist ihre Erwähnung, insbesondere die Erwähnung ihres Todes, ein Ausdruck der völligen Ausrottung einer Bevölkerung oder des Volkes...". The fate of these children, however, is soundly described in the present text with the root עטף (inf cs *niph'al* + prep בְּ with elision of the ה, understood nominally)[247] which carries overtones of 'languishing/pining' and 'growing weak'.[248] The following strophe provides the reason why.

In the present strophe the poets limit themselves to giving a first impression, that of the place where this horror has taken place: the squares of the city. This locative phrase is striking, all the more so for the fact that it is repeated in the following strophe. It is clear that the poets are once again setting up a situation of contrast. Jerusalem's city squares were better suited to the daily round of public life than her narrow streets.[249] The large open spaces around the city gates come immediately to mind.[250] People had a chance to meet one another and enjoy themselves in such places and it would certainly come as no surprise that they were the playgrounds par excellence for the children.[251] Where the city squares once offered a lively prospect of children at play (cf Job 29_8), however, the poets see nothing more than breathless, starving children with no more lust for life.

The fact that the unweaned infants are mentioned implies that the mothers were also present in the city squares to care for their young ones. In situations of grave distress people seek one another out. Thus, as in the

---

245 Cf I Sam 1_{22f}, II Macc 7_{28} (3 years).

246 Cf 4_{4bA} and TWAT V 1133f (Sæbø).

247 Cf GES-K § 114a; for the form see BL 228*z* and GES-K § 51*l*.

248 Cf HAL 770 sv עטף II.

249 Cf Isa 59_{14}, Zech 8_4, Job 29_7, Ps 144_{14}.

250 Cf the parallel with שַׁעַר in Job 29_7 and see HAL 1131 sv רחב I.

251 Cf Zech 8_5; cf also the use of the term קִרְיָה which, while basically meaning 'city', also suggests the idea of 'gathering' (KBL 855 and HAL 1065); the term is likewise appropriate for its poetic tone. See Isa $1_{21,26}$, Mic 4_{10}, Ps 48_3.

first song, the poets give central place to their depiction of the famine and its dreadful consequences.[252] In this second song, however, they focus in more detail on the horrific consequences of the people's hunger.

12. Before continuing with the exegesis, a short remark concerning the structure of the following strophe might be appropriate here.[253] What would appear in the translation to be a rather colourless repetition constitutes, in the Hebrew text, a quite intentional and meaningful inclusion: אִמֹּתָם (12aA) // אִמֹּתָם (12cB). The mothers are mentioned at the beginning and the end and thus they embrace (in literary terms) their weakening children and dying infants; another example of the way the poets have placed the structural composition of the songs at the service of their content.

12a *To their mothers they cry:*	לְאִמֹּתָם יֹאמְרוּ
"Where is corn and wine?",	אַיֵּה דָּגָן וָיָיִן

Hunger leads the children to beg their mothers for food and drink. Of course, it is the עוֹלָל who ask for corn and wine, the weaned children, not the infants. The formulation of their request is quite striking, however, and testifies to the poets' acute powers of observation. At first listening, one would have expected the more common phrase 'bread and wine'.[254] Indeed, elsewhere in Lamentations לֶחֶם 'bread' is mentioned with some frequency.[255] In Lam 4_4, in fact, the children ask the same question in indirect speech and the poets employ the term לֶחֶם. The present context, however, is one of direct speech: לְאִמֹּתָם יֹאמְרוּ. The children's words are thus presented literally in a combination which appear here and nowhere else in the OT: 'corn and wine'. Albrektson rightly points out the unusual assonance created by the quadruple *qāmeṣ*, although he wrongly suggests that the poets chose this combination for euphonic reasons. Given the direct speech it seems more reasonable to imagine that the poets were in fact imitating child talk, the repeated a-sound being primary in infancy, no matter what the language.[256] The children cry out for corn (דָּגָן) and not bread (לֶחֶם). The poets reveal thereby that they do not have the final

[252] Cf the description of the famine in 1_{11}.

[253] Cf also the methodology on pages 64ff.

[254] Cf Gen 14_{18}, Judg 19_{19} etcetera.

[255] Cf 1_{11} (where we also find the more general term אֹכֶל 'food'), 4_4, $5_{6,9}$.

[256] Cf HWinitz & OCIrwin, 'Infant Speech: Consistency with Age', in Journal of Speech and Hearing Research, 1958(b) I, 245–249, and AMSchaerlaekens, De taalontwikkeling van het kind, Groningen 1985², 81f.

stage of baking bread in mind – i.e. the bread itself – but the initial stage, the baking of the bread. It would be natural to find young children at home when the bread was being prepared for baking. The mother would grind the corn into meal, prepare the dough and bake the bread in front of them. The children had something to watch in the process and could look forward to something to eat at the end of it. Now, however, there is no more baking because the materials are no longer available. There is no more corn and the children are aware of this; hence their question. The horror of what happens between the children and their mothers is mentioned on a further two occasions. Within the present canto this is the case via an inclusion at the canticle level: 2_{12} // 2_{20b} (2_{12} is part of the opening canticle of canto II [2_{11-22}]). In addition, 2_{12} is parallel with 4_{10} (4_{10} is part of the final canticle of the first part of the fourth song thus forming an inclusion with the present canticle within the book of Lamentations as a whole). In the aforementioned texts there is allusion to the women cooking and eating, but what...? If one focuses on the song-responses, then there appears to be a clearly intended association with 1_{12} where tormented Lady Jerusalem asks if there is any sorrow greater than her sorrow. At the response level it would appear that her primary thoughts were with the dying children and their powerless mothers in 2_{12}.

Reasoning that young children do not drink wine, a number of exegetes are inclined to scrap יַיִן [257] or emend it to וְאַיִן which renders 'and there is none' [258] instead of 'and wine'. It is well known, however, that in wine producing countries, children are introduced to wine at an early age, albeit mixed with water.[259] Moreover, given that the preparation of wine is not a daily household activity it would not, therefore, have been a familiar sight to Jerusalem's children.[260] Thus the children ask directly for wine.

12b *while they, parched and gaunt,* — בְּהִתְעַטְּפָם כֶּחָלָל
in the squares of the city... — בִּרְחֹבוֹת עִיר

First of all we are presented with the reason behind the children's appeal for food and drink. It is not the objective fact of famine which motivates their petition, however, but rather their subjective experience thereof. In contrast to 2_{11cA}, the *hiph'il* is used in the present text instead of the *niph'al*. The meaning is reflexive: the children feel themselves parched and

257 Budde, Löhr, Kraus, cf BHK.
258 Cf Erhlich and Gottwald.
259 Cf Song 7_2, Isa 65_{11}.
260 Cf BHH 2194f (Fohrer).

weak.[261] Their appeal is to no avail. There is no more food in the city and it is among the children in particular that the famine is taking its toll. Their growing bodies and lack of reserves make them more vulnerable than the adults.

Whereas the following bicolon describes the consequences of famine for the infants at the breast, the present bicolon focuses on the consequences of the starvation suffered by the עֹולָלִם, the younger children. Once again the poets depict the situation in the form of a contrast. Where these children once raced around and played in the squares of the city – see the explanation of 2_{11cB} – now they can only drag themselves along, gaunt and emaciated, weak and exhausted, dying from lack of food and nourishment. The adjective חָלָל together with the comparative particle כְּ suggests that we are dealing with a metaphor at this point: 'like impaled or gored ones'. The comparison points literally to the wounds brought about by the sword.[262] Metaphorically speaking, however, it remains a somewhat unusual image. Indeed, as a metaphor for hunger, the idea of a sword injury seems an unfortunate choice. A sword hits its target with speed, accuracy and visibility; hunger, in contrast, is a slow process without immediately observable results. Such an objection, nevertheless, need not be conclusive with regard to the image in question.[263]

It is possible that the use of the adjective חָלָל raises even further associations in Hebrew. The term is derived from the root חלל II which, besides meaning 'to pierce/impale', can also mean 'to hollow out'. Both meanings are mutually connected.[264] Piercing with a sword, therefore, appears to be a derived meaning, especially when one notes that where it is intended, the adjective חָלָל is often accompanied by the word חֶרֶב 'sword' itself. Thus, in Lam 4_{9a} the expression חַלְלֵי־חֶרֶב means 'pierced with a sword' and implies a deadly wound. In the present context, however, the poets do not employ the accompanying term חֶרֶב which perhaps implies that the notion of 'hollowing out' is the stronger. Such an interpretation fits well with the consequences of long-term hunger.[265] The poets thus present the dreadful tableau of Jerusalem's impassive children languishing in the city squares, gaunt and haggard and doomed to death.

---

261 Cf HAL 770.

262 Cf, for example, Lam 4_{9a}, Isa 22_2, Jer 14_{18}; see also HAL 307 sv חלל II.

263 Cf the references to the 'arrows of famine' in Ezek 5_{16} and Deut 32_{23}; cf also the explanation of 2_{4b}.

264 Cf TWAT II 981f (Dommershausen).

265 Cf also the explanation of 4_{9a}.

12c *...pour out their lives* בְּהִשְׁתַּפֵּךְ נַפְשָׁם
on their mothers' lap. אֶל־חֵיק אִמֹּתָם

The fact that the mothers still have these children on their lap implies that the reference is to the youngest children, babies at the breast and infants. They too have no food or drink to satisfy them since their starving mothers will no longer have been able to produce milk. In despair, in the struggle between life and death, many will have withheld their final efforts for themselves (cf 4_{3f}). What kind of struggle could the smallest ones have put up?! Where adults are forced to fight for their lives (cf $1_{11a,19bc}$), the smallest ones are left with little say and helplessly they 'pour out their lives on their mothers' lap'. Literally translated, the text states 'as (their) life flows away' ([בְּ]הִשְׁתַּפֵּךְ = *hithpa'el* inf). Live is thus envisaged as something which 'flows' probably because the נֶפֶשׁ, as the 'principle of life', was associated with blood.

13. The poets now bring out the fact that there are no words to describe such a dreadful and poignant situation by once again introducing a change of speaker. Daughter Jerusalem falls silent, without words; paralysed and tearless from unthinkable sorrow, her voice fails her. She has become a silent picture of profound affliction. The contraction in 3_{51} and the specific location of this text within the book of Lamentations as a whole bears witness to the central significance of the consuming affliction of Jerusalem's women. The poets (hesitatingly) address daughter Jerusalem,[266] but they are at a loss to find appropriate words and images to place her suffering in the context of human experience. It is quite human to compare one's suffering with the much greater suffering of another and thereby endeavour to lighten it a little. The poets, however, can find no mitigating comparisons. In line with 1_{12} ([sub-]canto response at the song level), where daughter Zion herself points implicitly to the incomparable nature of her sorrow in the form of a question which remains unanswered, the poets search in vain for a comforting response. The triple repetition of מָה, twice in the following bicolon and once in the bicolon thereafter, serves to underline their plight.

13a *What example shall I hold up to you,* מָה־אֲעִידֵךְ
with what compare you, o daughter Jerusalem? מָה אֲדַמֶּה־לָּךְ הַבַּת יְרוּשָׁלַםִ

Many exegetes are tempted to emend מָה־אֲעִידֵךְ.[267] Gottlieb follows the suggestion of Gordis who presumes a chiasm between מָה־אֲעִידֵךְ and וַאֲנַחֲמֵךְ

[266] Cf the 2f sg suffix and the direct address in 2_{13aB}.

('how comfort you' in 2_{13bA}) and, on the basis of the then synonymous meaning, derives אֲעִידֵךְ from √עוד I which in the *po'el* means 'to help someone to get back on his/her feet', 'to set up/establish'.[268] The present *hiph'il* form is said to have the same meaning. A reasonable case for the suggestion that the verbal forms אֲעִידֵךְ, אֲדַמֶּה (2_{13aA}), אַשְׁוֶה and וַאֲנַחֲמֵךְ (2_{13bA}) form a chiastic structure, however, is not made.

For our own interpretation we will allow 1_{12} to direct us. The question raised there as to the comparability of daughter Zion's sorrow is taken up in the present bicolon via the realisation that there is nothing to which it can compare. The triple repetition of what amounts to the same question serves to underline such an implication.[269] For this reason our preference goes to the solution proposed by Rudolph. In his exegesis of these words, he chooses to interpret אֲעִידֵךְ as the *hiph'il* of √עוד II 'to call to witness': "Was soll ich dir als Zeugnis [d.h. als Beleg, als Beispiel] anführen?", understanding the suffix ךְ as a dative.[270] Rudolph also offers an alternative possibility: instead of the *hiph'il* of √עוד II one can read the *qal* of √ערך[271] meaning "to set (sth.) against' and by extension 'to compare' (cf HAL 837). The latter suggestion requires a fairly small emendation to the consonantal text: reading ר instead of ד – based on a not uncommon scribal error.[272] In terms of meaning there is no difference between Rudolph's alternative and our preferred solution. The *pi'el* form of the verb דמה I is likewise to be found in Isa 46_5 (cf also Isa 40_{25}).

13bA *To what shall I liken you,* מָה אַשְׁוֶה־לָּךְ

For the meaning of √שוה *hiph'il* see, once again, Isa 46_5. The LXX differs from the MT here and reads: 'who shall save and comfort you?' (cf text critical apparatus of BHS. Scholars have assumed that LXX's 'to save' is based on the root in the present Hebrew text. It is more likely, however, that the verbs ἰσόω 'to make/be equal' and σῴζω 'to save' were mixed up in the Greek tradition/transmission, in which case the MT deserves preference.[273] Moreover, the triple repetition of the question of comparability

---

267 Cf text critical apparatus of BHS and the text critical discussions of Albrektson and Göttlieb.

268 Cf Ps 146_9, 147_6 and Ps 20_9 (*hithpol'al*); cf also SDaiches, 'Lamentations II 13', ET 28, 1917, 189 and HAL 751.

269 Cf the clear parallel with Isa 46_5.

270 Cf likewise Plöger, Van Selms and HAL 751.

271 Cf also Robinson in the text critical apparatus of BHS.

272 Cf EWürthwein, *Der Text des Alten Testaments*, Stuttgart 1973[4], 104, and ETov, *Textual Criticism of the Hebrew Bible*, Assen/Maastricht, 1992, 244.

intentionally accents the very incomparability of daughter Jerusalem's suffering.

13bB *how comfort you, maiden, daughter Zion?* וַאֲנַחֲמֵךְ בְּתוּלַת בַּת־צִיּוֹן

Hillers disagrees with a number of exegetes who suggest that comparative reference to the suffering of others somehow softens one's own pain: "one explanation (Jahnow, Rudolph) is that a person will feel better if he is shown that his case is not unique, but this is rather unconvincing." I am inclined to believe, however, that this is a misinterpretation of human nature on Hillers part.

The refrain 'there is no comforter' ($1_{2,9,16,17,21}$) establishes a clear connection between the present colon and the first song. Unable to provide any comparable suffering, even the poets themselves do not know how to comfort daughter Jerusalem. Further contrast is established by the use of the appellation בְּתוּלַת בַּת־צִיּוֹן. The term בְּתוּלָה implies a young woman in the prime of her life (cf the explanation of 1_{15c}). Such a woman is now being forced to endure this incomparable suffering without any form of comfort. The second appellation 'daughter Zion' simply serves to further underline the contrast: the temple city is bereft of comfort from her God.[274] The reference to 'daughter Zion' remains in force until 2_{15} where 'daughter Jerusalem' takes over once again.

13cA *For vast as the sea is your wound!* כִּי־גָדוֹל כַּיָּם שִׁבְרֵךְ

The poets manage at this point to offer a parallel image, but a comparison with the prophetic idiom, in which the phrase 'great wound' frequently occurs, demonstrates that it is far from a comforting one.[275] What is new in the present context is the comparison with the sea. Van Selms considers this a rather moderate comparison and is of the opinion that something more must be implied such as 'enormously great'. Indeed, he had not expected such a worn out comparison as this. Did the LXX translator, who wrongly renders the text as ποτήριον (= כּוֹס, 'cup'), have the same feeling?[276] Such interpretations do not seem to get to the true meaning of the text, however. Having searched in vain for an appealing comparison, the poets ultimately opted for a unique image which, from a literary

---

[273] Cf Albrektson's discussion of the matter.

[274] Cf the explanation of 1_{4a}; for the meaning of 'comfort' in the present context cf the explanation of 1_{2a}.

[275] For שֶׁבֶר and גָּדוֹל see the explanation of 2_{11b}.

[276] Cf TWAT IV 108 (Mayer).

perspective, is expressed in the fact that 'sea' is employed only here in Lamentations. For a people of the land such as Israel, the expanse of the sea was beyond their imagination and they were constantly overawed by its immensity and depth (cf Mic 7_{19}). Indeed, the sea's dimensions set the very limits of their imaginative powers.[277] The immensity of the sea was proverbial (cf Ps 104_{25}), exceeded as it was by God alone (Job 11_{7-9}). Thus the poetic use of this comparison continues the notion of incomparability. In addition, 'sea' in the OT was seen as a source of hostility, danger and chaos (cf Ps 46_3, Jonah 2_{16}) with the old Canaanite sea god, the murderous and destructive Yammu, always present in the background.[278] Thus the fall of Jerusalem was incomparably immense and chaotic.

13cB *Who shall heal you?* מִי יִרְפָּא־לָךְ

Who is there who can heal daughter Zion's terrible wound? The theological point of such a question is unmistakable. In fact there is only One who has this power: YHWH himself, who is greater and more powerful than the sea, YHWH the one and unique Healer.[279] Ps 89, which is closely related to Lamentations,[280] speaks thus of YHWH: "You rule the raging of the sea; when its waves rise, you still them".[281] As a matter of fact, the question as to who has the power to heal is a question concerning YHWH. Once again, however, the circle of hopelessness is thereby complete. It is precisely the same YHWH, the only possible healer, who acts like an enemy, bringing destruction and sickness day in day out. The intense responsive cohesion between the songs is once more underscored here: נְתָנַנִי ... כָּל־הַיּוֹם דָּוָה (1_{13c}) // מִי יִרְפָּא־לָךְ (2_{13c}). Once again the people are confronted with the fulfilment of a prophetic word: YHWH will not bring healing but rather terror and plague.[282]

Canticle II (2_{14-15})

Content/theme: *the fate of Jerusalem on account of the failures of her prophets arouses utter dismay*

---

[277] Cf Job 28_{14}, Ps 139_9, Isa 11_{7-9} etcetera, together with a variety of other OT idioms.

[278] Cf OKaiser, *Die mythische Bedeutung des Meeres in Ägypten, Ugarit und Israel*, Berlin 1962² and THAT II 1029 (Westermann); TWAT III 650f (Ringgren).

[279] Cf JCdMoor, 'Rapi'uma Rephaim', ZAW 88 (1976), 323–345, and JCdMoor, *The Rise of YAHWISM*, Leuven 1997², 313.

[280] Cf 1983, 251f.

[281] Ps 89_{10}; cf also Ps 65_8 and the aforementioned Job 11_{7-9}.

[282] Cf Jer 8_{18}, $14_{12,19}$.

Literary argumentation:

inclusions: (14aA) נְבִיאַיִךְ חָזוּ לָךְ ... // (15c) הֲזֹאת הָעִיר ...[283]
(15b) שָׁרְקוּ ... עַל ... יְרוּשָׁלָםִ // (14bB) שְׁבִיתֵךְ

incl/resp: (15bB) עַל // (14bA) עַל

responses: (15aA) סָפְקוּ עָלַיִךְ כַּפַּיִם // (14aB) שָׁוְא וְתָפֵל
(15aA) עָלַיִךְ // (14aA) לָךְ
(14cA) וַיֶּחֱזוּ לָךְ ... // (15c) הֲזֹאת הָעִיר[284]

ext par: (15c) הֲזֹאת הָעִיר ... // (14bB) שְׁבִיתֵךְ

At first sight, it would appear that the literary cohesion between these two strophes is not so strong, indeed, one would be inclined to suggest that the cohesion between 2_{15} and 2_{16} is more solid. See the following responses:

(16aA) פָּצוּ עָלַיִךְ פִּיהֶם // (15aA) סָפְקוּ עָלַיִךְ כַּפַּיִם
(16aB) כָּל // (15aB) כָּל
(16bA) שָׁרְקוּ // (15bA) שָׁרְקוּ
(16cA) זֶה // (15cA) הֲזֹאת[285]

Upon closer inspection, however, it would seem incorrect for a variety of reasons to consider 2_{15} and 2_{16} together as one canticle. Firstly, there is a thematic difference between the two strophes: the ס-strophe speaks of the dismay of the passers-by while the פ-strophe refers to the joy of the enemy. Secondly, if one were to link 2_{15} and 2_{16}, 2_{14} (and 2_{17} for that matter) would be left somewhat detached within the song. In addition, the unity of 2_{16} and 2_{17} as one canticle can be defended with reason at both the literary level and the level of content.[286] Nevertheless, the literary cohesion between 2_{14-15} on the one hand and 2_{16-17} on the other is quite striking. One explanation for this might be that within the first sub-canto (2_{11-17}) of canto II, the poets have endeavoured to form a chiastic structure between the second (2_{14-15}) and the third (2_{16-17}) canticle, internal parallelism being constituted by the dismay of the passers-by and the joy of the enemy (2_{15} // 2_{16}). The external parallel would then be antithetical in character and theologically quite unusual: the unauthorised and empty words of Jerusalem's prophets set in contrast to the true prophetic words

283 As cause and effect.
284 Again as cause and effect.
285 Both bicola are a quotation.
286 Cf the introduction and the exegesis of the canticle in question (2_{16-17}).

of YHWH which take their effect in spite of the prophets (2_{14} \\ 2_{17}). Such an antithetical thematic relationship explains the broader cohesion. This also appears to be the case in the second sub-canto (2_{18-22}) where the thematic unity of the component canticles is evident from their content: the first canticle (2_{18-19}) is a summons to a prayer of supplication; the prayer itself follows in the final canticle (2_{20-22}).

The first canticle (2_{11-13}) of the first sub-canto (2_{11-17}) speaks of the fate of the children of Jerusalem, the cause of which, in the first instance, is presented as the misleading prophecies of Jerusalem's prophets. The same relationship can be found in the fourth song between sub-canto responses 4_2 and 4_{13}. Jerusalem's downfall, which is only possible because YHWH himself brought it about (2_{17}), is a source of joy for the enemy, nevertheless (2_{16}).[287] If coherence at the level of content within the first sub-canto is thus made visible, it is equally evident that the נ-strophe takes centre stage therein (also constituting the beginning of the central canticle!). Such literary accentuation provides 2_{14} and its statement concerning the prophets of Jerusalem with extraordinary weight. Indeed, this is likewise evident from the fact that the content of their prophecies are discussed here for the first (and the last) time.

Kaiser is of the opinion that we can draw a conclusion from this section with regard to the date of Lam II. According to him, the apparent dependence on Ezekiel (cf the explanation of 2_{14}) shows that the second song could not have been written any earlier than ± 470. Kaiser appeals to Zimmerli for the date of the relevant verses in Ezek 13[288] but it is not clear how he ultimately arrives at his conclusion with respect to the date of Lam II.[289]

14a *Your prophets have witnessed for you* נְבִיאַ֫יִךְ חָזוּ לָךְ
what was baseless and vain. שָׁוְא וְתָפֵל

The description of the dreadful fate of Jerusalem's children brings us to the low point of this second song. The poets draw their exposé of the affliction which has brought on the city's downfall to a close. Now they unavoidably turn their attention to the cause of this immense catastrophe. Who or what is to blame? It is striking that poets do not focus immediately on the sins of the people in this regard, as was the case in Lam I

[287] Cf the thematic connection with 1_{21b}.
[288] WZimmerli, *Ezechiel 1–24*, BKAT XIII/1, Neukirchen 1979².
[289] Cf Zimmerli's dating, 15* and 298f.

(cf $1_{5,8,18,22}$). The focus of attention is rather the role of the prophets as the decisive element in the matter. They turn first to the content of the prophetic visions,[290] characterising their oracles as שָׁוְא. Broadly speaking שָׁוְא means 'deceit', 'malice' or 'falsehood', but in a more mitigated form it can also mean 'vain' or 'baseless'.[291] With respect to Lam 2_{14}, Sawyer opts for the stricter interpretation 'deceit' but it remains uncertain whether he is correct or not in doing so. If one opts for the stricter interpretation 'deceit' then, at the same time, one also typifies the prophets as malicious liars. The OT makes it clear that such brutal usurpers of God's word did exist.[292] Given the wider context, however, it is improbable that such criminal elements masquerading as prophets are intended here in Lamentations. Indeed, the concentric structure of the second song leads us to suspect a different understanding of the prophets in question. At the song level, 2_9 and 2_{14} form an inclusion and in both strophes it is clear that the same prophets are the object of interest. In contrast to a significant number of translations and commentaries which employ the qualification 'false prophets', however, neither strophe actually characterises them as personally untrustworthy individuals.[293] One is left with the impression that the untruthfulness of their prophecies was simply evident, yet prior to the fall of Jerusalem, the difference between false and true prophets was far from being as clear as it was to the generations which followed it. Later generations had the opportunity to test the words of the prophets against history itself and it would appear that Deut 18_{21f} was formulated with this in mind. It was the downfall of Jerusalem and its far reaching consequences which proved her prophets to be wrong and led to their condemnation in the present strophe. The fact that the text continues to speak of these individuals as 'prophets' is proof that their personal integrity was not so much at issue but rather the way they fulfilled their task as prophets together with the content of their prophecies. Both these points are the subject of criticism. At the same time, it is unnecessary to suggest that the poets themselves did not belong to those circles which adhered to Zion theology (cf Weiser contra Kraus). Why, after the downfall, should critique of one's own assumptions be considered impossible? On the contrary, such critique would appear to be natural and would

290 For the meaning of √חזה in this context cf the explanation of 2_{9c}.

291 Cf the texts mentioned in THAT II 882f (Sawyer).

292 Cf Zeph 3_4, Mic 2_{11}, 3_5, Isa 28_{7ff}, Jer 23_{14}.

293 Cf, for example, LHvdMeiden, *De Klaagliederen van Jeremia*, Baarn 1952, 104 and RKHarrison, *Jeremiah and Lamentations*, London 1973, 219.

certainly not be out of place within the general sense of disappointment which predominates in Lamentations as a whole (cf $4_{12,20}$). Weiser does not account for the possibility of closer reflection which is already apparent here in 2_{14} via the echo of criticism of the prophets who announced the city's downfall against the city's prophets (cf the confrontation between Jeremiah and Hananiah).

Content (see the following bicolon) and terminology (תָּפֵל [only in Ezek and Lam] and שָׁוְא) are indications that the poets turned for inspiration at this point to Ezekiel rather than to Jeremiah. Several commentators point out that it is impossible to understand Lam 2_{14} without prior knowledge of Ezek 13_{11-14}. Such a suggestion is not so strange if we account for the fact that the poets would have been more likely to consider themselves related to the Jerusalemite priest/prophet Ezekiel (cf Zimmerli, 24*) than with Jeremiah who was much more critical with respect to Zion traditions and, indeed, did not come from Jerusalem. What is striking here is that the poets have borrowed the concept שָׁוְא from Ezekiel's prophecy concerning false prophets but not the much harder term כָּזָב 'lie' (cf Ezek 13_{6-9}) while the frequently employed qualification for 'false prophecy' in Jeremiah, שֶׁקֶר (cf Jer $23_{26,32}$) is likewise absent from Lamentations.[294] Indeed, the fact that the poets mention the prophets in the same breath as the priests as individuals under particular threat from the enemy is evidence of a certain ongoing respect in their regard. The poets, nevertheless, have come to the awareness that precisely Jerusalem's prophets are responsible in significant measure for the downfall of the city.[295] The prevailing ambivalence can be explained if one realises that the prophets in question were not dealing in gross deceit. Their prophecies – which they continued to utter right up to the fall of the city – were in line with current Zion theology and had a veneer of truth about them. In addition, despite the evident wrongness of their preaching, the very enthusiasm with which they upheld their convictions must have been grounds for respect. The prophets, however, were not condemned for their enthusiasm but rather for the negative outcome of their endeavours.[296]

Such prophets based their pronouncements on established dogmas such as those concerning YHWH's protection of Jerusalem and his fidelity to the

294 √שקר means 'to deceive'/'to mislead'; cf TWOverholt, *The Threat of Falsehood*, London 1970, 49ff, Renkema 1983, 157 and THAT II 1015f (Klopfenstein).

295 Besides 2_{14} cf also 4_{13} and 5_7.

296 Cf the explanation of 4_{13}; for a more detailed treatment of this material cf 1983, 156–177.

Davidic dynasty.[297] At the same time, that they continued to preach salvation even when it was more and more flagrantly in conflict with political reality, is evidence of the fact that they were far from being opportunistic charlatans. Unabated, they continued to preach YHWH's protection of Jerusalem and his fidelity to his people.[298] Only the bitter counter-reality brought them to silence (cf Jer 37_{19}). The fact of the downfall of the city forced the poets to realise after the event that the prophecies which they too had lovingly praised were nothing more than vain and empty talk. Zimmerli refers to the ambiguous use of the term תָּפֵל in Ezek 13_{10f} via its phonetic association with the root טפל 'to plaster'.[299] The latter verb can be used in a figurative sense to refer to the 'whitewashing' of sins and acts of injustice.[300] Thus the term תָּפֵל here does not only mean 'vain' or 'baseless', it also has clear associations with the 'cover up' effect maintained by the absolute nature of the salvific expectation contained in the prophecy, an expectation which remained unrelated to the people's actual disposition towards YHWH (cf Jer 23_{17}). This shortcoming is the subject of the following bicolon.

14b *They have not exposed your iniquity* וְלֹא־גִלּוּ עַל־עֲוֹנֵךְ
to restore your fortunes. לְהָשִׁיב שְׁבִיתֵךְ

The literary composition of the נ-strophe reveals that the poets considered this utterance to be of particular significance. Such can be deduced from the fact that the inclusion formed by the strong similarity between the surrounding bicola: חָזוּ לָךְ שָׁוְא (14a) // וַיֶּחֱזוּ לָךְ ... שָׁוְא (14c) makes the strophe highly concentric, thus placing (the content of) 2_{14b} in the centre (cf also 2_{12}).

This central statement concerns the key task of prophecy: not predicting the future but rather fulfilling the divine task of testing the actual relationship between the people and YHWH against the precepts of the covenant (cf Mic 3_8). Future expectations of salvation or doom were based on the outcome of such tests, but not absolutely; outcome remained dependant on (further) disobedience or conversion (cf Jer 18). To be intent on the purity of the people's relationship with YHWH and to be prepared to step into the breach when that relationship was endangered were the primary prophetic tasks. A description of that task along similar lines can be found

297 Cf, for example, Ps 46; 48; 76 and Ps 2. See also 1983, 32–39, 281–294.

298 Cf Jer 14_{13}, 23_{17}, 27_{16}, 28_{2ff} together with 1983, 162–173.

299 Zimmerli, 283, 294.

300 Cf Job 13_4, 17_{14} and HAL 362.

in Ezekiel ($13_{4,5}$; cf 22_{30}). The prophets of Jerusalem, however, have not kept watch over Israel's purity and fidelity. Without listening to YHWH's counsel (cf Am 3_7, Jer 23_{22}) they spoke from their own hearts and followed their own thoughts (Ezek 13_{1-3}, Jer 14_{14}). Reference is without doubt being made here to the prophets' unauthorised preaching of the future validity of dogmas relating to YHWH's protection and plan of salvation with which they proceeded without reference to the estrangement which had grown up between the people and YHWH and the degeneration of their own relationship with the people (Ezek 22_{1-30}). Under such circumstances, their 'blind spot' made any prediction of salvation and protection meaningless. The focal point of their activities should have been the public evaluation of Judah's life and faith. Here lay their only chance for preservation in such crucial times. It is evident from the present bicolon that the poets completely share this opinion and that they make Ezekiel's reproach their own.

The phrase גִּלָּה עַל *pi'el* is found only here in Lamentations and in 4_{22}. √גלה *pi'el* means 'to unveil' while the preposition עַל is related to the object. One can interpret the expression גִּלָּה עַל, therefore, as 'to draw away the veil from...'. The object of unveiling is the עָוֹן of daughter Zion. Translations of עָוֹן vary from 'sin' or 'wrongdoing' to 'guilt', 'punishment' or 'injustice'.[301] Such notions are not unrelated: injustice engenders guilt and punishment follows. Koch[302] speaks in this regard of 'Schicksalwirkende Tatsphäre' or of a 'Tun-Ergehen-Zusammenhang', whereby the consequences of wrongdoing return sooner or later on the heads of those who perpetrate it without any mention of direct divine intervention.[303] Perhaps such a perspective is too one-sided, given the fact that every wrongdoing, whether directed against oneself or against another, is ultimately against God's will. God's interest in human עָוֹן, therefore, cannot only be indirect. Koch, nevertheless, does not deny divine involvement completely, nor does he believe in a purely mechanical (dynamic) relationship between wrongdoing and its ultimate reward: "Obwohl עָוֹן also eine dingähnlich wirkende Wesenheit auf Erde is, wird sie zugleich von Gott wahrgenommen und verfolgt, indem Er die Wirkung der Untat-Unheils-Sphäre am Täter aktiviert und deren verderbliches Wirken beschleunigt."[304] God's intervention, however, can turn aside the effects of עָוֹן.[305]

301 Cf HAL 756.
302 Cf TWAT V 1164–1177.
303 Cf also THAT II 244 (Knierim).
304 Cf Koch, 1167f.

According to Knierim, the fact that עָוֺן is a "Formalbegriff der sich auf alle Arten von Vergehen beziehen kann"[306] is of additional significance in the exegesis of the present bicolon. It is likewise important that the poets are aware that the punishment associated with such עָוֺן is not irreversible. Given the choice of the formal term עָוֺן, which can be related to all sorts of wrongdoing, it would seem likely that the poets either could not or did not want to be more explicit about the specific wrongdoing which resulted in the fall of the city. It is possible that different actions (e.g. the strictly liturgical as opposed to the customs of popular piety) were evaluated differently in terms of their licitness.[307] Whatever the case, it is clear that in the syncretistic atmosphere surrounding the fall of Jerusalem not everybody was equally clear on what was appropriate and what was not.[308] The very choice of imagery such as 'to unveil' or 'to remove the veil from' is an indication that the poets understood the sins in question – committed, as they were, before the present decline – to have been concealed sins, sins which were not clearly visible, mostly unconscious sins. Even now, immediately after the fall of the city, not everyone was completely clear as to the sins and acts of wrongdoing which had motivated YHWH to intervene in this manner. We can draw such a conclusion from the song-response with the נ-strophe from the third song (3_{40}) where we find the addressees encouraged to examine themselves more closely on this point.[309] Having said this, we do not wish to suggest that the poets had absolutely no clue as to what had gone wrong. Indeed Lam 4_{13} gives witness to the contrary. Given their overall purpose in writing the songs, however, it is clear that they saw no great value in providing detailed descriptions of the sins of their people (cf the hermeneutical epilogue of Lam III).

The fact that daughter Zion is now forced to carry this terrible burden of sin (cf the song-response with the נ-strophe in the first song, 1_{14}) was not an entirely unavoidable scenario. Had Jerusalem's prophets done their job and 'unveiled' her עָוֺן (see above), then they would have opened up the possibility conversion. Had daughter Zion changed her ways, then it is clear to the poets that YHWH would have forgiven her sins and turned aside this dreadful disaster (cf Ezek 18_{23} and 22_{30}). In the present context, the

305 Cf Ps 32_5, 85_3, $103_{3,10}$, 106_{43-46}, 130_8 etcetera.

306 Cf THAT II 247.

307 Cf MRose, *Der Ausschließlichkeitsanspruch Jahwes*, BWANT 106, Stuttgart-Berlin-Köln-Mainz 1975, 196–212.

308 See 1983, 213f.

309 Cf also the explanation of $1_{5b,8a,14a}$ together with 1983, 268–274.

expression שׁוּב שְׁבוּת (*hiph'il*) employed for this 'turn about' means 'to turn around (impending) fate (for the better)'. 'Fate' here stands for more than just the exile, it includes everything associated with the present affliction. Where the expression is used it is mostly with YHWH as subject.[310] Had Jerusalem's prophets truly spoken the word of God, then this positive 'restoration of fortunes' would have actually taken place.[311] Their words, however, were words of ruin and death (cf Jer 14_{15f}).

One is left wondering whether this complaint against the prophets is justified? Were there no prophetic voices to be heard before the diaster struck which took their divine task seriously and exposed the people's wrongdoing? Multiple references to the 'canonical' prophets in 1_{18} and elsewhere clearly show that the poets would not have denied the presence of such voices. Nevertheless, there are indications which partly explain the poets' complaint. It is probable, for example, that much of the criticism of Israel's sin, uttered before the downfall by prophets who would only later come to be seen as 'canonical', was articulated on a redactional level, based on (post)-exilic reflection after which it achieved greater prominence. Only then were practices roundly condemned which had still been considered acceptable in the syncretistic atmosphere prior to the downfall (e.g. child sacrifice). Indeed, Jeremiah was forced to state quite explicitly that YHWH had never requested such offerings and did not desire them.[312] At the time of the downfall, however, a prophet such as Jeremiah did not have the same status as the prophets of Jerusalem. For many, these prophets and these alone belonged to the true prophetic profession which formed part of the temple clergy in Jerusalem. This image was underlined by the fact that their prophecies of salvation had their place in a long, ancient and honourable prophetic tradition[313] which employed classical terminology. Moreover, their prophecies were underpinned by the fact that Judah's history constantly confirmed those dogmas related to YHWH's protection of Jerusalem and his fidelity to the royal house of David.[314] Prophets who preached otherwise were considered to be heretics and were often threatened and even killed for their alleged blasphemy.[315] In hindsight, the poets are now forced to admit that they and the people were wrong in blindly

[310] Cf, for example, Jer 32_{44}, Ezek 16_{53}, 39_{25}; cf also THAT II 887 (Soggin).
[311] Cf HAL 1289f sv שְׁבוּת.
[312] Cf Jer 19_{5} and 32_{35}.
[313] JCdMoor, *De tijd van het heil*, Kampen 1970.
[314] For further details cf 1983, 90–145 and 156–177.
[315] Cf Jer $11_{19,21}$, 20_{10}, $26_{9ff,20-23}$; cf also the explanation of 4_{13}.

following the words of Jerusalem's prophets. In light of its natural authority, the official clergy bore the greatest responsibility and they should have tested such prophecies for their truth content.[316] The ordinary faithful, however, should not simply have accepted official standpoints without thinking. It is evident that their religious attitudes also contributed to the fall of Jerusalem and that they too were thus partly responsible (cf 3_{40}).

14c *They witnessed oracles for you,* וַיֶּחֱזוּ לָךְ מַשְׂאוֹת
baseless but alluring. שָׁוְא וּמַדּוּחִים

For שָׁוְא and √חזה see the explanation of 2_{14a} which, even in terms of content, is very similar to the present bicolon. The new element in 2_{14c} consists of the qualification of the oracles as מַדּוּחִים, a (plural) term derived from the verb נדח (cf BL 494*g*) which in the *hiph'il* can mean 'to tempt'/'to allure'.[317] The term can also be interpreted as 'to dispel', a fact which has led some translations and commentaries to interpret מַדּוּחִים as 'outcasting', i.e. prophecies which drive into exile.[318] Together with the Peshitta, Targum, KBL, Gottwald, Albrektson and Kraus, among others, we interpret the *hapax* מַדּוּחִים as 'alluring'.[319] In contrast to a rather unexpected mention of the exile, our option fits well into the context. We also translate the ו preceding מַדּוּחִים as adversative.

The bicolon appears, to a certain extent, to offer an apology for the degree of attachment the population of Jerusalem had to the oracles of the city's prophets: their words were both plausible and attractive. From the human perspective such belief was quite understandable. Not only did the oracles of the temple prophets appear to have a sound pedigree, their content was also pleasing and alluring. In the midst of Judah's unstable and, at the last, seriously distressing political situation, the natural temptation to place one's faith in words which offered a sense of future must have been extreme. Where there is hope there is life,[320] and Jerusalem's prophets preached oracles of hope. The use of the *terminus technicus* מַשָּׂא is evidence of this optimism. The term is mostly an indicator of a prophecy of doom against the alien nations.[321] De Boer sees a connection with the

---

316 Cf JRenkema, 'A note on Jeremiah xxviii 5', VT XLVII (1997), 253f.
317 Cf Deut 13_{14}, Prov 7_{21}.
318 Cf, for example, LXX, Luther, Calvin, Löhr, Rudolph.
319 Cf also HAL 520 and ELevine, *The Aramaic Version of Lamentations*, New York 1976, 117.
320 Cf Jer 38_{1-4}.
321 Cf Isa 15_1, 17_1, 19_1, Nah 1_1 etcetera.

verb נשׂא, 'to carry', and treats מַשָּׂא figuratively, in the sense of God's judgement being a 'burden': "מַשָּׂא as used in prophecy suggests often the idea of judgement and catastrophe", and "In the headings of prophetic oracles מַשָּׂא means 'burden imposed on...'".[322] Others consider the term to be a derivative of the expression נָשָׂא קוֹל, 'to raise one's voice' = 'to make a pronouncement'. Müller, for example, argues primarily that מַשָּׂא can have the very general meaning of 'pronouncement' as such,[323] although he realises, nevertheless, that in the context of a prophetic oracle it is mostly related to the proclamation of judgement against the alien nations.[324] With reference to Jer 23_{33-38},[325] however, he points out that this need not exclude a possible association with משׂא II ('pronouncement') and משׂא I ('burden'). The aforementioned Jeremiah pericope does indeed contain a word-play based on the concepts of 'burden' and 'pronouncement'. It seems natural to assume that Lam 2_{14} is also to be understood as a prophecy of doom for the nations announced by the prophets of Jerusalem. YHWH's judgement of the enemy clearly implied accommodation, security and ultimate salvation for Judah. The Jeremiah pericope (23_{33-38}) shows that the people liked to hear such prophecies and that they even asked Jeremiah himself to prophesy YHWH's judgement upon the enemy. The prophet was forced to take the opportunity to polemicise against prevailing proclamations of salvation for Judah. With the use of word-play, he announces that Judah herself has become a 'burden' to YHWH and that he intends to throw off that 'burden'.[326]

15a *They clap their hands at you* — סָפְקוּ עָלַיִךְ כַּפַּיִם
all who pass along the way. — כָּל־עֹבְרֵי דֶרֶךְ

Since her prophets failed in their duty and did not offer daughter Zion the chance to change her ways, appalling disaster has fallen upon Jerusalem. The city's fate elicits a reaction of shock among those unbiased passers-by who happen to witness the ongoing aftermath of recent events.[327] Given the fact that Jerusalem's affliction has not yet passed and that the sight of the city continues to evoke horror and alarm, we translate the perfects

322 PAHdBoer, *An Inquiry into the Meaning of the Term* משׂא, OTS V (1948), 197–214; cf THAT II 116 (Stolz).

323 Cf also Prov 30_1, 31_1 and HAL 604 sv משׂא II.

324 Müller, TWAT V 22.

325 Cf TWAT V 24.

326 For concrete examples of מַשָּׂאוֹת as words of judgement for the nations which simultaneously implied salvation for Judah cf Jer 27_{16}, 28_{2ff}, 28_8.

327 For the explanation of כָּל־עֹבְרֵי דֶרֶךְ cf 1_{12a}.

here as presents. It is quite surprising to note how the vast majority of commentators unjustly interpret the attitude of the passers-by as one of mockery and derision. It is true, perhaps, that such words and gestures might also appear to be at home in a context of mockery – see the following bicolon – but this is not exclusively the case. While the connection is usually made between the enemy in 2_{16} and the passers-by in the present bicolon,[328] it has to be insisted, nevertheless, that a passer-by need not necessarily be an enemy.[329] Why would those who happen by accident to be passing by turn to mockery and derision? Since Jerusalem was on their route and given their expectations of the city (cf 2_{15c}) it seems more reasonable to assume that the sight of the ruins shocked them to the core. Such horror and alarm is frequently expressed in somewhat stereotypical terms in the OT. See I Kgs 9_8 (with כָּל־עֹבֵר and שָׁרַק), Mic 6_{16}, Jer 18_{16} (with כֹּל עוֹבֵר and the noun שְׁרוּקַת 'mockery' from √שרק = 'to whistle' / 'to hiss').[330] The terminology employed in Lam 2_{15}, therefore, does not exclude the notion of horror and alarm. The expression סָפַק כַּפַּיִם, '(once off) to clap one's hands', is not frequent in the OT – only elsewhere in Num 24_{10} and Job 27_{23}. In the Numbers text there is no question of mockery and derision, far more anger and shock (contra Jagersma;[331] correct Noth[332] who considers it an expression of indignation: "Gemütsbewegung des Unwilens"). The meaning of the Job text is unclear although in Job 34_{37}, the use of the root ספק without כַּף certainly does not imply mockery of God but rather alarm and anger. Nah 3_{19} also speaks of clapping of hands but it is clear here that it is an expression of joy as is likewise the case in Ps 47_2. Both texts, however, do employ an alternative expression, תָּקַע כַּף, which implies a different, more repeated clapping (contra Kraus).

15b *They hiss and shake the head* שָׁרְקוּ וַיָּנִעוּ רֹאשָׁם
at daughter Jerusalem: עַל־בַּת יְרוּשָׁלָםִ

Once again we return to the specific mention of 'daughter Jerusalem', revealing that we are not dealing with Zion alone but with the fate of the entire city. Texts which employ forms of the root שרק 'to whistle'/'to hiss' more clearly allude to a sense of horror at a shocking event like the de-

---

[328] For example, Löhr, Aalders, Meek, Rudolph, Albrektson, Weiser, Kraus, Plöger, Van Selms, Hillers, Brandscheidt, Boecker, Provan and Ringgren (TWAT V 909).

[329] Cf Calvin and Thenius.

[330] Cf HAL 1527; cf Jer 19_8, 49_{17} with respect to Edom and 50_3 with respect to Babylon.

[331] HJagersma, *Numeri deel II*, Nijkerk 1988, 158.

[332] MNoth, *Das vierte Buch Mose, Numeri*, ATD 7, Göttingen 1973², 167.

struction of a city than the hand clapping of the preceding bicolon. Ezek 27_{36} can be added to the list of texts mentioned above in this regard. The hissing of the merchants concerning Tyre is far from an expression of mockery at the downfall of a competitor,[333] it is rather a sign of dismay at the disappearance of what was thought to be an unassailable trading partner from whom they were set to earn a great deal.[334] Besides hissing, the present bicolon also mentions the gesture of head shaking in the form of the expression הֵנִיעָה רֹאשׁ (*hiph'il*), a word combination which is more frequently found in the context of mockery.[335] The context, however, rather than the expression itself, is what makes the derisory character of the gesture evident. Nevertheless, this is not true of every text. It would be difficult to explain Job 16_4, for example, as a mocking text. In Job 16, as with the present text, the nuance appears to one of compassion.

Rudolph, Van Selms, Kaiser and Brandscheidt (cf KBL 1011 and HAL 1527 sv שׁרק), among others, suggest the presence of an additional aspect in the actions of shaking the head, hissing and clapping the hands. In their opinion these gestures also had a so-called apotrophaic dimension as gestures of exorcism. The ruins of cities were said to house ghosts and demons which people could keep at bay by clapping their hands, whistling and shaking their heads.[336] In this regard Rudolph refers to Jahnow who has pointed out this possible interpretation on the basis of a number of biblical texts, an interpretation many scholars have accepted without much hesitation. In so doing, however, many exegetes forget that Jerusalem – in spite of the destruction and death she had undergone – was still substantially inhabited and was hardly the place one would expect to find ghosts. Rudolph himself, however, expresses a degree of reserve here, suggesting that the 'ghostly' interpretation may relate to the original purpose of the gestures in question but that, given the context, later interpretations would appear to prevail. Indeed, if one consults Jahnow, it turns out that she too is much more reserved in her statements on the matter than the many others who have taken over her conjectured position,[337] to the extent that she also points out a contrary option: "Sonst freilich scheint Pfeifen und Zischen nicht dem Verscheuchen, sondern gerade dem

---

333 Cf WZimmerli, *Ezechiel 25–48*, BKAT XIII/2, Neukirchen 1969, 658.

334 Cf also Ezek $27_{33,35}$.

335 Cf II Kgs 19_{21}, Isa 37_{22}, Ps 22_8, 109_{25}.

336 Cf LKöhler, *Der hebräische Mensch*, Tübingen 1953, 122f.

337 Cf Jahnow, *Das hebräische Leichenlied im Rahmen der Völkerdichtung*, BZAW 36, Giessen 1923, 44, 187.

Anlocken der Geister zu dienen, vgl. Lasch, Archiv f. Religionswiss. 18 (1915), S. 589ff." The question remains as to how conscious people were of the original meaning of customs and gestures such as these and whether their animistic background could be reconciled with Yahwism.[338] Both the present context and the wider context of the songs as a whole provide no reason to interpret the actions of 2_{15f} as related to some form of incantation. Parallel strophes at the song level (1_{15c}, 3_{45}, 5_{15}) likewise refer to the city's horrific fate, without any suggestion of magical gestures of whatever kind; their primary meaning being scorn, dismay and hostile mockery (cf 3_{45f}, 4_{15}).

15cAB *"Is this the city that was called:* הֲזֹאת הָעִיר שֶׁיֹּאמְרוּ
'perfect in beauty, כְּלִילַת יֹפִי

Our conviction that the preceding bicolon constitutes an expression of dismay rather than mockery is the reason why we interpret the concluding tricolon of the present canticle as a rhetorical question implicitly expressing the expectant image the passers-by would have had with respect to Jerusalem based on the city's eminence and fame. Jerusalem was well known for her beauty, characterised here as כְּלִילַת יֹפִי. כְּלִילַת[339] means 'complete'/'total'. The noun יֹפִי, 'beauty', has to do with exterior, observable beauty such as that of human beings, trees or, as in this case, cities. Although the term is never used to refer to God, as it is in Egypt,[340] it can refer to his earthly dwelling place, namely Zion.[341] Ps 48 praises Zion's beauty in some detail but not as a fact in itself, rather as the reflection of God's magnificence and strength.[342] Zion's beauty which radiates over Jerusalem must be seen, therefore, in a theological context. The city's splendour is not grounded in the aesthetically pleasing nature of its secular architecture; it is rather divine in origin. The identical description of Tyre in Ezekiel employing the same expression כְּלִילַת יֹפִי (cf Ezek $27_{3,4,11}$) ought thus to be related to Ezek 28_2 where Tyre is praise by her king as a divine dwelling (מוֹשַׁב אֱלֹהִים), an action which is negatively condemned as *hubris*.[343] The fact that the terminology of Ps 48_3 and 50_2 is placed

[338] Cf also the concluding remarks on 2_{10b}.
[339] Adj fem st cs of כָּלִיל, in agreement with the gender of עִיר; cf GES-K § 128x.
[340] Cf TWAT III 787ff (Ringgren).
[341] Cf Ps 48_3, 50_2; cf also Ps 122_3.
[342] Cf the obvious cohesion in Ps 48_{13-15} and see also NHRidderbos, *De Psalmen II*, KV, Kampen 1973, 120f.
[343] Cf also TWAT III 789 (Ringgren).

on the lips of the passers-by does not intend to suggest that they considered Jerusalem to be pretty but ordinary. On the contrary, they knew Jerusalem as a sacred place where the glory of the divinity who dwelled there once radiated for all to see. Thus their horror at the dreadful ruin of Jerusalem is also of a theological nature. Their reaction implies a hidden question: 'Why did the divinity allow his holy city to be devastated in this way?' This question is to be found explicitly expressed elsewhere in the 'Wirkungsgeschichte' of the OT, namely in the deuteronomistic history: "Why has YHWH done such a thing to this land and to this house?" (I Kgs 9_8). See also the divine subject in the song-response 3_{45}: 'You have made us filth and rubbish...' (...סְחִי וּמָאוֹס תְּשִׂימֵנוּ).

15cC *the joy of all the land'?"* מָשׂוֹשׂ לְכָל־הָאָרֶץ

In relation to the context outlined above with respect to Jerusalem's beauty, the expression מָשׂוֹשׂ לְכָל־הָאָרֶץ should likewise not be understood in secular terms as a referring to the people's pride in their magnificent capital (which Wielinga describes in wonderful detail).[344] What is a stake here is religious joy, the kind experienced by the population during festival gatherings.[345] Hosea 2_{10} (MT 2_{13}) also refers to the joy surrounding cult and liturgy with the term מָשׂוֹשׂ. Frequent parallelism between √שׂושׂ and √גיל also calls for a similar interpretation, the latter verb indicating an expression which had its 'Sitz im Leben' in the cult. Westermann remarks in this regard: "Es ergibt sich: *gil* gehört in das Wortfeld, das mit unserem Wort »Freude« bezeichnet werden kann. Dieses Wortfeld is im Hebr. sehr viel reicher entwickelt als in den modernen Sprachen, weil mit Freude hier nicht primär ein Gefühl, eine Empfindung oder Stimmung gemeint ist, sondern die sich äußernde Freude, also ein Vorgang in der Gemeinschaft."[346] which is equally true of מָשׂוֹשׂ in a cultic context. All this has consequences for the translation of כָל־הָאָרֶץ which many exegetes render as 'for all the earth' (cf NEB). The universalistic interpretation implied in such an interpretation does not appear to be justified. If it is a matter of joy experienced, celebrated and expressed in a cultic setting, then, as far as the poets are concerned, Jerusalem is certainly the centre of the entire land but not of the entire world, unless they are referring

---

344 BWielenga, *De Bijbel als boek van schoonheid*, Kampen 1960^6, 54–56.

345 Cf 1_4, 2_{6c} and parallel 5_{15}, the latter text likewise with מָשׂוֹשׂ; similarly Ezek 24_{25} (cf 24_{21}). See also GAAnderson, *A Time to Mourn, A Time to Dance*, Pennsylvania, 1991, 37ff.

346 In THAT I 415.

to eschatological expectations that the nations will one day worship in Jerusalem (cf Isa 2_{1-4}) and thus setting up a contrast via the words of the passers-by: how can such joy be celebrated in this ruin? Such exegesis reads too much into the text, indeed the song-response with (the context of) 5_{15} runs counter to any interpretation along these lines. In 5_{15} the same מָשׂוֹשׂ is employed to refer to the (vanished) joy of the community as it laments over the destruction of Zion. Moreover, when the term אֶרֶץ in Lamentations has the broader meaning of 'the world' then this is always made clear by the context.[347] The passers-by see Jerusalem as the cultic centre of the land par excellence. The fact that Jerusalem fulfilled such a function in Israel was also important for Zion theology, on which point deuteronomistic theology was in complete agreement.[348]

A final text critical remark by way of conclusion. Many exegetes consider 2_{15c} to be too long[349] and, for metrical reasons, drop a word (combination). Albrektson (cf his summary of those who would emend the text) agrees with Kraus that the MT should be maintained because of the fact that we are dealing with a quotation. He is of the opinion that the unusual length of the tricolon is rooted in the mention of Jerusalem's titles of honour. Structural analysis supports this line of argument, noting that a tricolon, which commonly functions as an indicator of separation, is not unusual at the end of a literary unit.[350] 2_{15c}, therefore, constitutes the tailpiece of the present canticle (2_{14-15}). In terms of content, there appears to be no question of duplication. Given that the versions also presuppose the MT, the latter's reading should be maintained without further ado.

Canticle III (2_{16-17})

Content/theme: *The enemy rejoices, but only at* YHWH*'s behest*

Literary argumentation:

inclusions: פָּצוּ עָלַיִךְ פִּיהֶם (16aA) // וַיְשַׂמַּח עָלַיִךְ אוֹיֵב (17cA)
כָּל־אוֹיְבַיִךְ (16aB) // אוֹיֵב (17cA)

---

[347] Cf 4_{12}: מַלְכֵי־אֶרֶץ; cf also אֶרֶץ עוּץ in 4_{21}. In addition, the term אֶרֶץ in Lam II always has the meaning 'ground', cf $2_{1,2,9,10,11,21}$; in 3_{34} it means 'land' as in the present context.

[348] Cf 1983, 204–207.

[349] Cf also text critical apparatus BHK and BHS.

[350] Compare MCAKorpel – JCdMoor, 'Fundamentals of Ugaritic and Hebrew Poetry', in: *The Structural Analysis of Biblical and Canaanite Poetry*, (eds WvdMeer and JCdMoor) JSOT suppl series 74, Sheffield 1988, 33.

כָּל־אוֹיְבַיִךְ (16aB) // צָרָיִךְ (17cB)
אָמְרוּ בִּלָּעְנוּ (16bB) // הָרַס וְלֹא חָמָל (17bB)
הַיּוֹם שֶׁקִּוִּינֻהוּ (16cA) // בִּצַּע אֶמְרָתוֹ (17aB)
מָצָאנוּ רָאִינוּ (16cB) // עָשָׂה יְהוָה (17aA)

incl/resp: בִּלָּעְנוּ (16bB) // הָרַס (17bB)

ext par: בִּלָּעְנוּ (16bB) // הֵרִים קֶרֶן צָרָיִךְ (17cB)
הַיּוֹם שֶׁקִּוִּינֻהוּ (16cA) // צִוָּה מִימֵי־קֶדֶם (17bA)
אָמְרוּ (16bB) // אֶמְרָתוֹ (17aB)

Based on a surface reading it would appear that the פ-strophe and the ע-strophe deal with two distinct and unrelated themes, namely the joy of the enemy (2_{16}) and the fulfilment of YHWH's word (2_{17}). The structural analysis outlined above, however, shows that the poets have in fact linked both strophes very closely together. It is not only justifiable, therefore, to consider both strophes as constituting one canticle but also to assume a more profound cohesion at the level of content: certainly the enemy rejoice, but they only do so at YHWH's behest. In light of this relationship between the strophes, the initially rather abrupt looking transition from 2_{17ab} and 2_{17c} within the ע-strophe turns out not to be so surprising. Indeed, the same connection can be found in 1_{21} where, besides agreement at the level of content, there is also a structural indication of association. If we consider 1_{21} to form the centre of the final canticle of the first song, then on a larger scale, the present (seventh) canticle forms the centre of the second canto. This canto does indeed possess a thematic character: only because YHWH has brought his word of judgement to fulfilment can the enemy rejoice over Jerusalem's lot. The role of the enemy in Jerusalem's downfall, however, remains subordinate. Within the broad picture of the city's misfortune they are only mentioned twice in the second song: here and in 2_7. The relationship between these two strophes is not accidental. They correspond with one another in a concentric structure at the song level; not only on a literary level but also in terms of content: the enemy's joy over Jerusalem's ruin is YHWH's doing (cf הִסְגִּיר בְּיַד־אוֹיֵב in 2_{7bA}).

16a *They open wide their mouths at you,* פָּצוּ עָלַיִךְ פִּיהֶם
all your enemies. כָּל־אוֹיְבַיִךְ

The expression פָּצָה פֶּה is used in a metaphorical sense when it implies the devouring of blood or human persons.[351] In Ps 22_{14}, the gaping mouth of

351 Cf Gen 4_{11}, Num 16_{30}, Deut 11_6.

the enemy is likened to the mauling jaws of wild animals.[352] Clearly the expression has a more negative significance than is implied in the simple act of opening one's mouth. In non-hostile contexts the phrase suggests 'boasting'/'bragging' (cf Judg 11_{35f} and Job 35_{16}). The various elements implied in the expression thus appear to have a joint role in the present context.[353] Given what follows, it is clear that the accent should be placed in the first instance on the enemy's malicious taunting at the downfall of daughter Jerusalem, an event which certainly brought them great joy (cf the inclusion with 2_{17c}). The perfects are translated once again as presents since the joy and bragging of the enemy is ongoing. The theme of enemy rejoicing is quite common in the CI and CP genres. In the present context, however, we are not dealing with a topos from the lament genre without any direct roots in historical reality. This can be deduced from the words of judgement uttered by the canonical prophets over the alien nations whose malicious taunting at the fall of Judah is the subject of their confrontation (cf the explanation of 1_{2cB}). The element of taunting and mockery coming from the Ammonites, Moabites, Philistines and Tyre is explicitly mentioned in Ezek $25_{3,6,15}$, 35_{15}, and of the Edomites in Ob $_{12,13}$. Such enemies should be our first suspects in the present context (cf Lam 1_{2c}, 3_{63}, 4_{21} and 5_5).

16bA *They hiss...* שָׁרְקוּ

It is quite understandable that hissing has been understood as an expression of mockery on the basis of this bicolon. This is indeed what the term means in the present context but such an interpretation need not have consequences for our explanation of 'hissing' in the previous strophe (2_{15cb}). It appeared that hissing had its 'Sitz im Leben' in the dirge, a notion we consider reasonable given the texts mentioned above together with the material from Jahnow. It appears thus that the present text is also evidence of a relationship between lament and dirge.

Hissing as an expression of mourning, however, need not always have the same intention behind it. Tears of mourning can also be crocodile tears, depending on the individuals doing the mourning. In the present text, the difference in subject is explicitly stated: happenstance passers-by and patent enemies. One would be wrong to lump both groups together in the same category and interpret the 'intention' of their hissing as the same.

---

[352] Cf Ps 35_{21} (with √רחב instead of √פצה) and Job 16_{10} (with √פער).

[353] Cf $1_{7d,9c,16c,21b}$; see also the exegesis of 2_{7c} and the response between 3_{46} and 3_{52}.

Mourning a deceased enemy is parody and statements such as 'Alas! He is dead!' (or 'hissing') are intended to be ironic. The figurative application of mourning rituals can be found elsewhere in the OT.[354] In any event, the poetic parody in no way diminishes the dreadful reality of daughter Jerusalem's affliction.

16bA ... *and gnash their teeth.* וַיַּחַרְקוּ־שֵׁן

The context makes it clear that something different is intended here than we would commonly understand by 'gnashing of teeth' as an expression of anger. In the wider context of the OT as a whole, the phrase חָרַק שֵׁן is employed to express a variety of emotions. In Ps 35_{16} it accompanies mockery; in Ps 37_{12} it implies menace or threat; in Ps 112_{10} irritation. In the present context, mockery would seem to be the best interpretation. At the same time, however, the immediate context of Ps 35_{16} and Job 16_9 would lead us to assume that here the expression implies something more than just mockery from the enemy camp. In Job 16_9, for example, the expression is used in parallel with the verb טרף which means 'to tear apart' (as by wild animals[355]), while the 'gnashing of teeth' in Ps 35_{16} is placed on the same level as being threatened by lions. We noted with regard to the preceding bicolon that the expression פָּצָה פֶּה also could imply the gaping jaws of a wild animal, a possible metaphor for the attitude of the enemy (Ps 22_{14}). We are left thus with the image of a wild animal with open jaws revealing its ominous teeth. The image continues in the present text: the animal grinds its lower jaw against its upper jaw such that the grinding of its teeth is audible and its intention to 'tear apart' evident (cf the same image in Ps 124_6). This interpretation finds confirmation in Ps 35_{25} where the poet fears that the enemy, like lions (17) with open jaws (21), will devour him. Strikingly enough, the verb בלע I ('to destroy'/'to devour') is used in both Ps 35_{25} and Lam 2_{16c}. The following enemy reference to what they have already devoured makes it clear that the 'gnashing of teeth' is no empty gesture.

16bB *They say: "We have devoured!* אָמְרוּ בִּלָּעְנוּ

The usual translation of this colon is not entirely satisfactory, since the use of the form בִּלָּעְנוּ clearly echoes the already used √ בלע I (cf $2_{2,5[2x],8}$). Given

[354] Cf the singing of a song of mourning over a person who is still alive: Amos 5_{1-3}; cf also Jahnow's explanation of the parodical use of the dirge in relation to Isa 1_{21-23}, 14_{4-21} and Ezek 32_{19-32}; Jahnow, 231.

[355] Cf HAL 363 sv טרף I.

the military context of earlier uses of the term, we translated the verb as 'to destroy' even although the basic meaning has to do with 'devouring' (cf 2_{2a}). In light of the wild animal imagery in the present context, however, we have chosen to translate the term here with 'to devour' (cf Ps 35_{25}, Jer 51_{34}). In so doing, the nuance of speed is thereby maintained. With respect to the subject of √בלע I there is some tension with the previous canto where YHWH was always the subject of destruction while here it is the enemy who claim to have devoured daughter Jerusalem. Such enemy pretension is unjustified, however, and the poets refute it in the following strophe.

16cA *Yes, this is the day we so hoped for.* אַךְ זֶה הַיּוֹם שֶׁקִּוִּינֻהוּ

The enemy's joy was already a part of the poets' portrayal of events in $1_{7,21}$. In the present colon the same enemy speak of their long cherished hope that they would one day see the downfall of Judah. Such hope is best ascribed to the neighbouring nations referred to in 1_{2c} whose aspirations confirm that the expression רַבָּתִי בַגּוֹיִם (1_{1b}) is not simply an honorific title with little or no meaning. On the contrary, one can deduce from such an expression that Jerusalem played a dominant role in the region of Syria/Palestine/Trans-Jordan and in such a manner that her neighbours preferred to be rid of her. The still recent period under the kingship of Josiah springs to mind here. Noth points out that Josiah not only expanded his own territory by incorporating the former lands of the northern kingdom but also by annexing Philistine land and parts of Trans-Jordan.[356] Where the latter region was concerned, Josiah's annexation involved territory which had formerly belonged to Israel but which had constituded the Assyrian province of Gilead since 722. After the Assyrian empire had begun to diminish, the province was taken over by the Ammonites and Moabites (cf Zeph 2_8), but they had later been forced to relinquish their dominant position to Josiah. Josiah's moves also had financial implications for the peoples involved (cf 1_{1c}) and ongoing territorial claims were not easy to brush aside.

Judah's prominent position can also be deduced from the Babylonian Chronicles. After the fall of Ashkelon in 605, the Chronicles focus exclusively on the city of Judah (Jerusalem) as the target of the Babylonian offensive (cf TGI[3], 74). Jer 27_{1ff} also refers to Jerusalem's former political leadership. The 'love' shown to Judah by her allies was in fact dictated by

[356] MNoth, *Geschichte Israels*, Göttingen 1969[7], 247.

her position of power in the region. Daughter Jerusalem's lovers, however, were mere opportunists and their true intentions were otherwise: to escape Judah's might at the first opportunity. Ezekiel's prophecies reveal that he was well aware of the jealousy, derision and vindictiveness of nations such as the Ammonites, the Moabites and the Philistines (cf Ezek $25_{3,6,8,15}$). This also implicitly refers to their once cherished but futile hope for a turn around in their relationship with Judah.

The futile nature of the enemy's hopes is made evident in the chosen terminology. The root קוה I (meaning in the *pi'el*: 'to [tensely] wait for something') has a negative tone in profane usage and is frequently employed in situations where the exact opposite happens to what one had expected.[357] With this in mind, Westermann remarks: "das Hoffen muß also besonders dort bewußt geworden sein, wo das Erhoffte nicht eintrat. Es macht sich dort bemerkbar, wo es lange hinzieht, ohne Erfühlung zu finden."[358] A further context in which √קוה I is used in the *pi'el* is that of an enemy lying in wait to take a life.[359] Ps 56 seems to present the image of the enemy as a wild animal lying in wait for its prey. Thus the enemies of Lady Jerusalem are aware that they had long lain in wait for (the moment of) her downfall but that they had felt like wild animals chasing a prey they were actually unable to catch. If such a metaphor is at work here, then we not only have substantial consistency in imagery within the present strophe (a fact which is not easy to express in translation) but also with the parallel canticle in the third song where the imagery of bird hunting is employed (3_{52}; cf 4_{19}). At the same time, YHWH's actions are described in 3_{10} as those of a wild animal lying in wait. In addition, there is a clear link with 4_{12} where the futile character of the enemy's hope is further explained: how could Judah ever fall? Jerusalem, for that matter, was an invincible city!

It thus becomes clear that the enemy's hope was not a question of patiently awaiting their chance but rather a tense, impatient lying in wait for something which was considered in fact impossible: the end of Judah and Jerusalem's domination. The fact that the chance of such an event becoming reality was so small makes their joy all the more significant.

16cB *We have discovered it and see it!"* מָצָאנוּ רָאִינוּ

[357] Cf Job 6_{19f}, 30_{26}, Ps 69_{21}, Isa $5_{2,4,7}$, Jer 13_{16}, 14_{19} etcetera.

[358] In THAT II 622.

[359] Cf Ps 56_7 and 119_{95}.

Wagner notes: "Nicht nur Suchen, sondern auch Hoffen und Erwarten zielen auf Finden ab (Ps 69,21 *qwh pi*)".[360] It would appear, therefore, that what we might consider unusual phraseology was quite common in Hebrew: to find is the same as to discover what one had hoped for. Strikingly enough, the same expression is used in the context of hunting: the hunter discovers his game (Gen $27_{3,7,20}$), once again pointing to the consistent imagery of the present strophe. Thus the enemy have found (and continue to find) what they were looking for. 'Seeing' what they have found simply underlines the fact. We have translated רָאִינוּ as a present – in contrast to the foregoing perfect מָצָאנוּ – not in order to establish opposition between the two but to show that an act in the past (perf מָצָאנוּ) continues in the present. The enemy's 'seeing' has to do with visually observable reality, the root ראה being used in this sense throughout Lamentations. The enemy have observed and continue to observe the downfall of Lady Jerusalem with their own eyes (Ps 35_{21}); there is no better proof! We already noted elsewhere the contrast concealed in these words and the link between Ps 48 and Lam $2_{15,16}$ to which it points.[361] YHWH's protection of Jerusalem was not only a theological construction but also a reality actually experienced by Judah. It is clearly stated in Ps 48_9 that the people have 'seen' that YHWH has repulsed the enemy.[362] Although Judah once witnessed YHWH's defeat of her enemies, now she must witness their triumph over Jerusalem. The formulation of the present colon points, therefore, to the contrast which daughter Jerusalem finds so painful to endure.

17aA YHWH *has done what he planned:* עָשָׂה יְהוָה אֲשֶׁר זָמָם

For the cohesion between this and the previous strophe see the introduction to the present canticle above. While the enemy do indeed witness the downfall of Jerusalem, they do not observe true reality as the poets do from their theological perspective. Judah's devastation at the hands of her enemies is merely the visible effect of YHWH's own plans. Thus, in this thematic strophe the poets repeat what they portrayed in more detail in the first canto. For them the enemy are merely a tool in YHWH's hands, carrying out his plans (√חשׁב in 2_8) and orders (1_{17b}). Once again we have evidence that there is no question of a sudden outburst of anger and wrath on the part of YHWH (although such seemed to be the case, cf עֶבְרָה in

360 In TWAT IV 1062.
361 Cf 1983, 226.
362 Cf 1983, 34 note 80 and 105 note 34. For more detail on the verification of the dogma of Jerusalem's invincibility cf 1983, 90–145.

2_{2b}) but rather of a well thought out plan. √זמם refers to a pre-meditated and well thought through action.[363] The same word combination can be found in Jer 51_{12} in the context of a prophecy of doom directed against Babylon.

17aB *he has consummated his word...* בִּצַּע אֶמְרָתוֹ

What might the origin be of the theological insight of the previous colon? It certainly cannot simply be derived from an inspection of the ruins of the city. The poets borrow the insight of previous prophecies which interpreted God's word with respect to the downfall of the city. The terminology they employ to render this insight is striking, however, the word combination אִמְרָה and √בצע *pi'el* being unique to the present colon. As a divine utterance, the term אִמְרָה in the Psalms has the connotation of 'clarity', 'purity', 'trustworthiness'.[364]

In terms of content, the author of Ps 119 employs the term to designate YHWH's statutes and ordinances.[365] In Isa 28_{23}, the term is used to refer to the word of the prophet while in Isa 32_{9} it specifically refers to the prophetic announcement of judgement. The various semantic elements surrounding the term each have a contribution to make to its usage here in 2_{17} where it refers to a trustworthy and clear prophetic announcement of judgement uttered in YHWH's name. Thus the present text constitutes an explicit recognition of a distinct prophetic voice. The words of former prophets, who were once despised and oppressed, have been proven right in contrast to the words of Lady Jerusalem's prophets. The failure of the latter serves to canonise the prophetic words of the former which foresaw this disaster now confronting Judah. This is underlined by the fact that the poets of Lamentations have borrowed a range of ideas from the canonical prophets.[366]

Given the terminology employed by the poets here it would be something of an overstatement to suggest that the aforementioned recognition of the words of the canonical prophets was a source of joy. The common translation: 'He has fulfilled his word' (NEB) is too flat, especially if one realises that other verbs are normally used to express the idea of 'fulfilment' in the OT: √מלא, √שׁלם or √קום.[367] The root בצע, in contrast, is a *terminus techni-*

[363] Cf Prov 30_{32}, 31_{16}. See also TWAT III 600 (Steingrimsson).
[364] Cf Ps 12_{7}, 18_{31}, II Sam 22_{31}, Prov 30_{5}.
[365] See TWAT I 372 (Wagner).
[366] Cf 1983, 262–267 and passim in the present commentary.
[367] Cf TWAT IV 880f (Snijders).

cus taken from 'weaving' terminology and meaning 'to cut off (a finished piece [of fabric])'.[368] In the same sense one can understand the figurative use of בצע as 'to make a profit', to 'cut off' one's portion. The term is used in a similarly figurative manner in the expression: 'to cut short someone's life' as an image for premature death.[369] With YHWH as subject, the term can also be found in Isa 10_{12} where is means 'to complete' (cf Zech 4_9) which is in line with the aforementioned weaving terminology. In light of the biblical usage and the association with the previous colon we have chosen to translate the term as 'to consummate'. In so doing, however, we intend a negative undertone which we find evident in the second colon of each of the bicola in this strophe (הֵרִים קֶרֶן צָרָיִךְ // הָרַס וְלֹא חָמָל // בִּצַּע אֶמְרָתוֹ). 'He has consummated his word' means here that YHWH has brought his word of judgement in its entirety into effect. This has echoes in 4_{11}, for example, in the satisfaction of YHWH's wrath. YHWH's judgement is complete; there is nothing more to add (cf 4_{22B}). The precise nature of that word of judgement is elaborated in the following colon.

17bA ... *which he ordained long ago.* אֲשֶׁר צִוָּה מִימֵי־קֶדֶם

Kaiser asks whether YHWH's word here is exclusively related to pre-exilic prophecies of doom or whether it also implies the curse stipulations formulated with respect to violations of the covenant laws in Lev 26_{14ff} and Deut 28_{15ff}, i.e. from the older, pre-exilic portions (the aforementioned chapters are frequently supplemented and re-formulated from the perspective of the fall of Judah and the exile). In the Jewish tradition, for example, Rashi was of the opinion that the fall of Jerusalem could be inferred from the warnings given in the Torah, especially in Lev 26_{27ff}.[370] Nevertheless, there is no real contradiction involved here. It is quite significant that later redactions formulated the covenant stipulations of blessing and curse as words of Moses. Moses, however, was also seen as a prophet.[371] Thus later prophetic announcements of judgement which took account of the contemporary situation ought to be seen as extensions of the (more ancient) curse stipulations. Jer 34_{8-22} is a striking example of this.

Rather than relating the present text to a former and (from a literary perspective) unique proclamation of the covenant with its associated blessings

[368] Cf HAL 141 and TWAT I 734 (Kellerman).

[369] Cf Isa 38_{12}, Job 6_9.

[370] Cf his commentary on Lev 26_{27ff} in ויקרא, Amsterdam 1977², 378ff.

[371] Cf HSchmid, *Die Gestalt des Mose. Probleme alttestamentlicher Forschung unter Berücksichtigung der Pentateuchkrise*, EdF 237, Darmstadt 1986, 69f.

and curses, however, it would be better to view it in light of the ongoing prophetic announcement of judgement, given that the notion of 'completion' and the phrase מִימֵי־קֶדֶם 'from long ago' point towards the continuity of this announcement. Such an interpretation is in line, moreover, with 1_{18a} where resistance against the preaching in question and the consequent enemy attack are called to mind.[372] At the same time, with their use of the phrase מִימֵי־קֶדֶם the poets give a further indication of something which was already evident, namely that they did not limit themselves to the prophetic preaching immediately prior to the downfall of Judah but that they were also attentive to earlier, consonant prophetic voices.[373] One might think, for example, of the prophecies of Micah: Mic 1_{8ff}, 2_4, 3_{12}, 6_{13f}.[374] Given the multiplicity of texts which refer to the threat of sword, fire and devastation, it would appear that the menace of enemy hostility was in fact a permanent, structural element of prophetic announcements of judgement.[375]

It is clear that the poets of Lamentations have a particular understanding of prophecy. They do not subscribe to the static view which would insist that once a divine command is uttered it must one day come to fulfilment. Although the individual prophetic judgements of former times, the דְּבָרִים, together constitute the one single אִמְרָה of YHWH, the realisation of the judgements in question has not yet been fixed or established. Jonah's prediction of doom and destruction did not have to reach fulfilment if he succeeded in bringing the people of Nineveh to conversion before the divine ultimatum had expired. On this very point the poets are explicit in their disappointment. The formulae they employ lead us to assume that the prophetic word of judgement against Judah and Jerusalem need not have ended as it did. All this death and destruction had been unnecessary and even avoidable. They were well aware that prophetic announcements of doom were not absolute, static and unchangeable; their primary purpose was to express YHWH's categorical desire for conversion. The realisation of his word was dependent on such conversion or the lack of it because YHWH was willing to exchange justice for mercy (cf Jer 18 and Lam 2_{14}). Here the poets witness the sudden (cf 2_{5b}) halt (√ בצע *pi'el*) of the dynamic progression of such conversion oriented divine judgements. YHWH

[372] Cf 1_{17b} where the same root צוה *pi'el* is employed: YHWH himself commanded this hostile invasion.

[373] Cf 1983, 262–267.

[374] Cf also Am 2_4, Isa 5_{25-30}, Zeph 2, Hab 1_{6ff}.

[375] Cf also the standard use of the threat of war by the false prophets, Mic 3_5.

has brought his judgement to completion in this present act of devastation.

The poets not only show their disappointment, however, they also reveal their insight into the fact that the true prophetic word – no matter how it might appear at first sight to the contrary and no matter how it might appear to have been preached by outsiders – must ultimately serve the purpose for which it was uttered, i.e. conversion or, in its absence, the ultimate destruction which it predicts. We were already able to deduce this at the structural level from the chiastic cohesion between the sixth and the seventh canticle wherein the empty words of Jerusalem's prophets are unable to prevent the actual realisation of YHWH's word. What Jeremiah predicted with respect to the wayward prophecy of Jerusalem's prophets is hereby confirmed: in spite of their empty words YHWH will not rest until he has carried out the plans of his heart (מְזִמּוֹת לִבּוֹ, from √זמם!).[376]

The realisation of the devastation leads the poets to conclude that the people have not responded to this prophetic word by converting and changing their ways (3_{40}); thus YHWH has acted justly (cf 1_{18a}).

17bB *He has destroyed without mercy.* הָרַס וְלֹא חָמָל

Contrast and disappointment are clearly evident in this colon. The ו in וְלֹא should be understood adversatively. No sense of reserve could be detected in the way YHWH went about the fulfilment of his word. For the significance of √הרס and the combination לֹא חָמָל see the exegesis of 2_{2ab}. The importance of the latter expression is evident in the concentric structure of the entire song: לֹא חָמָלְתָּ in 2_{21c} forming an inclusion with לֹא חָמַל in 2_{2a}. There is still further agreement with 2_2: if 2_2 constitutes the centre of the first canticle then 2_{16-17} (as a canticle) constitute the centre of the second canto: in both places we find the combination לא חמל and the √הרס, thus pointing to the thematic nature of the expression. From a theological perspective it is indeed justified to speak of the disaster in terms such as those employed in this colon.

17c *The enemy rejoices over you.* וַיְשַׂמַּח עָלַיִךְ אוֹיֵב
He has raised the horn of your adversaries. הֵרִים קֶרֶן צָרָיִךְ

The transition back to the theme of enemy rejoicing appears rather abrupt, at least at first sight. Internal cohesion within the canticle makes it clear, however, that the present bicolon is not an isolated expression. The very

[376] Cf Jer 23_{16-20}, 30_{23f}.

possibility of enemy rejoicing, rather, is rooted in the fact that YHWH has been left with no other option than to uphold his judgement against his people. The relationship between enemy rejoicing and YHWH's actions, which we have explained in some detail in the exegesis of the previous strophes, makes it impossible to accept Brunet's suggestion that אוֹיֵב implies a domestic enemy and צַר the Babylonians (cf 1_{5a}). Parallelism, together with a causal relationship between the two cola is, however, more than evident.

As the final bicolon of canticle III and of sub-canto I, the present bicolon has a clearly summarising character. The downfall of Judah brought about by YHWH turns out to be a feast for the enemy and a source of spontaneous joy for them: "שׂמח meint in der Regel... die sich spontan und elementär äußernde Freude... Diese Freude ist ihrem Wesen nach überschwänglich bis dahin, daß man außer sich gerät vor Freude."[377] According to Ruprecht, hand clapping and shouts of exultation are among the expressions of such joy. The concluding colon emphasises once again that this rejoicing on the part of the enemy is not based on any victory they themselves have achieved; their victory was brought about by YHWH and He alone empowered them in their actions: 'He has raised up their horn'. This metaphor (for קֶרֶן cf 2_{3a}) is used fairly frequently in the OT. Stähli[378] provides a number of examples and cites Gunkel with respect to its meaning: "das Bild ist vom Wildochsen (Ps 92,11) hergenommen, der mit hochaufgerichtetem Horn in der Fülle seines Kraftgefühls, den Gegner herausfordernd, dasteht, ein Bild, das auch den Babyloniern bekannt ist."[379] The contrast with 2_{3a} is clear: YHWH has hacked off all the horns of Israel.

No matter how sad and disappointing the conclusion to this present sub-canto appears, a fundamentally important option remains open at the theological level. If it was not YHWH who handed victory to the enemy, then the enemy themselves, or rather their gods, have been left with the final word. Former faith and trust turns out to be nothing more than an illusion and the existence of Israel as the people of YHWH a mere fiction. If YHWH is indeed the true power behind the enemy victory, however, then he can also bring about a change in their fortunes. The coherence of the following sub-canto is based on such an awareness.

---

377 See THAT II 829f (Ruprecht).

378 See THAT II 756.

379 Cf HGunkel, *Die Psalmen*, HKAT II/2, Göttingen 1926⁴, 327.

Sub-canto II (Lam 2_{18-22})

In the preceding sub-canto, both canticles revealed a clearly interrelated and coherent character. The beginning of the sub-canto was difficult to understand as a direct continuation of the preceding strophe, thus making the inauguration of a new sub-canto all the more evident. At the level of content, however, the link between the first sub-canto and what preceded it was quite discernible: the superior might of the enemy also had its effect on the children of Lady Jerusalem. The first sub-canto opened with the starvation of the children (2_{11-17}). The poets take up this theme once again in a response at the sub-canto level in the first canticle of the present sub-canto. Although she no longer has any tears left (2_{11a}), the poets urge daughter Jerusalem to weep before YHWH for the life of her starving children (2_{18-19}). In the final canticle (2_{20-22}) she obeys their appeal and turns in prayer to YHWH.

Canticle I (Lam 2_{18-19})

Content/theme: *Daughter Zion is forced to pray for the life of her children*

Initial remarks: As with Lam 1_7, Lam 2_{19} appears at first sight to be a rather 'irregular' strophe. Most exegetes are tempted to make emendations to the text in order to make it fit the 'model' (cf, for example, Robinson in the text critical apparatus of BHS). The 'irregularity' of the strophe appears to disappear, however, if one recognises the expansion at the end of the strophe. 2_{19c} and 2_{19d} do not constitute two separate bicola but rather one single quatrain. The content of the strophe makes this clear: 2_{19d} functions as a further explicitation of the final colon 2_{19c}. It seems justifiable, therefore, to consider 2_{19c} and 2_{19d} as a unit within the literary analysis of the various external parallelisms to be found in the text.[380]

It is interesting to note how the present sub-canto is, in fact, an expansion of 2_{5c}, 'the great sadness and mourning in Judah'. At the song level, 2_5 and 2_{18} constitute an inclusion although the latter text reveals a plus: Judah's distress is drifting ultimately towards prayer. Such prayer is an indication of the enormous tension in which YHWH's faithful find themselves: they pray to the one who was once Zion's wall of defence, but who now even destroys her palaces (בִּלַּע כָּל־אַרְמְנוֹתֶיהָ [2_{5b}] \\ חוֹמַת בַּת־צִיּוֹן [2_{18a}]).

[380] Cf MCAKorpel – JCdMoor, 'Fundamentals of Ugaritic and Hebrew Poetry', in: *The Structural Analysis of Biblical and Canaanite Poetry*, (eds WvdMeer and JCdMoor) JSOT suppl series 74, Sheffield 1988, 29.

Literary argumentation:

inclusions:
צָעַק (18aA) // הָעֲטוּפִים בְּרָעָב (19dA)[381]
לִבָּם (18aA) // נֶפֶשׁ עוֹלָלַיִךְ (19cB)
חוֹמַת (18aB) // חוּצוֹת (19dB)
כַנַּחַל (18bA) // כַמַּיִם (19bA)
אַל־תִּדֹּם בַּת־עֵינֵךְ (18cB) // קוּמִי רֹנִּי בַלַּיִל (19aA)

response:
הוֹרִידִי כַנַּחַל דִּמְעָה (18bA) // שִׁפְכִי כַמַּיִם לִבֵּךְ (19bA)

ext par:
לִבָּם (18aA) // לִבֵּךְ (19bA)
אֲדֹנָי (18aA) // אֲדֹנָי (19bB)
לַיְלָה (18bB) // בַלַּיִל (19aA)

The literary cohesion between both strophes of the present canticle is also apparent in the common use of 2nd pers fem sg impf. The conclusion of the canticle is marked by the (long) quatrain (cf the remarks with regard to 2_{15c}).

18aA *Their heart cried out to Adonai:* צָעַק לִבָּם אֶל־אֲדֹנָי

Gordis begins his exegesis of this strophe with the following: "The opening stich צָעַק לִבָּם is extremely difficult. The suffix of לִבָּם has no antecedent." In so doing he provides a succinct description of the problems raised by classical exegesis with respect to this text. Most commentators solve the problem by resorting to emendation, frequently reading צעק as a 2nd pers fem sing imperative צַעֲקִי (which, given the content, is highly unlikely; see below). Such a procedure, however, is simply an attempt to fit the present text in with the imperatives which follow. Other exegetes emend the suffix ם (3rd pers masc pl) to read ךְ (2nd pers fem sing) and understand the entire text as an imperative directed at daughter Jerusalem, urging her to cry out to YHWH.[382] A solution along these lines, however, is not supported by any variants in the transmission of the text nor can it be explained on the basis of a possible scribal error. Indeed, the LXX, for example, provides a literal translation of the MT: Ἐβόησεν καρδία αὐτῶν πρὸς κύριον. Even attempts to interpret לִבָּם as a word with a different meaning (Albrektson, for example, reads לַבָּה 'revenge') are nothing more than speculation.

It would indeed appear to be a problem, at least initially, to envisage an antecedent for the suffix of לִבָּם, but this is due to the fact that a

[381] See explanation.

[382] Cf text critical apparatus BHS, HAL 976 sv צעק, together with many others. For an overview of the entire text critical discussion see Albrektson and Gottlieb.

linear reading thereof offers very little to assist us in the process of interpretation. We are left with the question as to the identity of an already mentioned group to whom 'their heart' can refer. At the level of content, it would be impossible to identify such a group as the enemy from the preceding strophe (cf the meaning of √צעק). If one respects the poets' concentric thought processes, however, then an alternative possibility immediately emerges. Indeed, the multiple inclusions evident in the canticle strongly underline its concentric structure. The most obvious inclusion in our present context is that between לִבָּם (2_{18aA}) and נֶפֶשׁ עוֹלָלַיִךְ (2_{19cB}), especially since לֵב and נֶפֶשׁ are often employed as synonyms.[383] If we are correct then the poets are referring here to the heart of Lady Jerusalem's languishing children! They indeed are the ones who long for help in their present affliction.

Further arguments can be cited in support of the latter interpretation. For example, since we are dealing here with a new canticle and thus with a new beginning, it would seem reasonable to expect an indicative at this point as a basis for the five (!) imperatives and two prohibitives which follow. In any event, an indicative is clearly present in the concluding quatrain 2_{19cB}: עַל־נֶפֶשׁ עוֹלָלַיִךְ, daughter Zion is urged to pray 'for the life of her children'. The imperatives are intended for Jerusalem. If she is the addressee then she too must know – or at least come to know – who is being referred to in 2_{18a}. The conclusion of the canticle makes it crystal clear that she is being urged to pray for her children, indeed the very abundance of imperatives underlines this entreaty with some intensity. The introduction of a further, less important reason for the necessity of Jerusalem's prayer would simply lead to fragmentation, a textual condition which would be out of place with respect to the usual thematic homogeneity of the canticles. The concentric structure of the present canticle makes it logical to assume that 2_{18a} contains a parallel to the indicative in 2_{19cB}. It seems obvious, therefore, that לִבָּם (collective) refers to the hearts of Jerusalem's languishing children. In such an event, 2_{18a} and 2_{19cBd} form an inclusion. At the same time, we can assume a response between the beginning of both sub-cantos in the present canto: 2_{11c} // 2_{18a}.

Ultimately, the text's concentric 'tendencies' are not only indicative of thinking and speaking but also of listening. In other words, the Israelite audience did not only listen in a linear fashion on the basis of what was

[383] Cf THAT I 864 (Stolz) and TWAT IV 426 (Fabry).

previously said, they were also already attentive to what could be said on the basis of a previous utterance. For those who are sensitive to such concentric thinking/speaking, the initial objection raised by Gordis can be rejected: לָכֶם does have an antecedent and closer exegesis confirms this assumption.

The √צעק is only found here in Lamentations. It refers primarily to the scream of a human person in acute distress and, as such, an imperative interpretation (cf the emendations) remains highly improbable. No similar cry of distress can be found as the subject of an order in the OT. In Jer 22_{20} two imperatives can be found but these are used in the specific situation of prophetic announcements of doom in which they have indicative significance.[384] Albertz offers a reasonable definition of √צעק as follows: "So meint die Wurzel *ṣʿq* den Vorgang des menschlichen Notschreis, der zugleich Schmerzensschrei (...) und Hilferuf (...) ist...".[385] Albertz also notes the primordial aspect of the cry of distress: "Beide Aspekte (distress and help, JR) haben ihren Grund in dem urtümlichen Bewußtsein kreatürlicher Zusammengehörigkeit der Menschen, welches bewirkt daß jeder, der den Schmerzensschrei eines anderen Menschen hört, diesem ganz selbverständlich zu Hilfe eilt." Initially, therefore, the cry of distress was an inarticulate yet extremely recognisable exclamation which somehow obliged the help of another.

Given the fact that God let himself be compelled to assist his people in need, such cries of distress also applied to him.[386] When the cause of the distress was not visible, it could be indicated in some way (cf II Kgs 4_{40}). The person of faith directed his or her cry of distress to YHWH, knowing that he was attentive to the cries of those in need and was in a position to help.[387] Israel also frequently cried out to YHWH in distress from Egypt.[388] An important text for our exegesis at this point is Ex 22_{23} where it is stated that YHWH pays attention to the cries of help of the oppressed widow and orphan (mentioned also in Lam 1_1 and 5_3). Gen 41_{55} and II Kgs 6_1 are similarly important in that the distress they describe consists of severe hunger which gives rise to a cry for help. The starvation of the children is clearly portrayed in the central canticle of the present song

384 Cf Isa 14_{31} and Ezek 21_{17}.
385 See THAT II 569f; cf also TWAT II 631 (Hasel).
386 Cf THAT II 569f (Albertz).
387 Cf Ps 9_{13}, 34_{18}, 77_2, 88_2 etcetera.
388 Cf Ex 2_{23}, 3_7 etcetera; cf also Ps $107_{6,28}$, TWAT II 625 (Hasel) and the explanation of Lam 3_{56}.

(2_{11-12}). Although the cry for help has parallels in similar situations of hunger, the present cry is nevertheless a unique utterance. Albertz[389] rightly points out that what makes the cry for help unique is its loud, impassioned character. The present context, however, speaks of nothing of the sort. The children do not scream or cry. Nevertheless, the poets are not misusing the language here. They have clearly shown in the preceding verses that the children have become feeble. One cannot expect to hear loud and powerful cries of help from such children. It is striking, therefore, that the poets do not hear the feeble voice of Jerusalem's starving children, they hear the cry of their hearts. "There is a silent language of tears which no one, not even the angels, can hear or understand except God."[390] The fact that לֵב can constitute the subject of a variety of human acts is evident throughout the OT.[391] Thus the heart can 'speak' (Ps 27_{8}), 'fail' (Ps 73_{26}), 'rejoice' (Ps 84_{3}) etcetera.

The image of daughter Jerusalem left over in our minds from the previous sub-canto portrayed her in terms of her dumfounded sorrow over the downfall of her people, particularly the death of her languishing, starving children (2_{11-12}). One would be justified in asking: what now? What is there left for her to do or say? Everything has already been said: the extent of her downfall, the fall of her leaders, the loss of her splendour, the hunger of her children, the admission of her iniquity, the shock of those who pass by and the abuse of her enemies. Is there anything else she can do other than shoulder her fate to the bitter end, whatever that end might be? The remainder of the song, however, strongly opposes such fatalism. The poets see a new lead, a new way forward: her children in the throws of death. Is YHWH able to endure such a scene? In our exegesis of 2_{11c} we already noted the emergence of the question concerning the justifiability and even the sense associated with the starvation of children who are too young to (be able to) bear responsibility for wrong doing. The impression emerging in 2_{11} is firmly underlined in the present verses. The poets, however, still do not know how such suffering can be justified. The only remaining option is for still silent daughter Jerusalem to turn to YHWH and address him, to pray for her starving children.

The question as to the precise interpretation of the term לֵב here remains open. Are we dealing with the actual prayer of the children themselves

389 See THAT II 569.
390 KHMiskotte, *Als de goden zwijgen. Over de zin van het Oude Testament*, Haarlem 1966, 196.
391 Cf TWAT IV 422f (Fabry).

welling up from the depths of their hearts or is their ever weakening condition already a prayer in itself?[392] It is indeed true that לֵב can represent the entire person,[393] in which case the very sight of these starving children would be more than enough to move Lady Jerusalem to prayer. In light of the content of the following colon, however, we prefer to follow the first option.

18aB *"Rampart of daughter Zion!"* חוֹמַת בַּת־צִיּוֹן

Several commentators also suggest emendations to the present text but none are convincing enough to uphold and the MT ought to be preserved. Our translation follows Gottwald who, with reference to Zech 2_5 (MT 2_9), understands the term 'rampart' to be a metaphor for YHWH. In his commentary *Lechem Dim'ah* (1557) cited by Zlotowitz,[394] Rabbi Shemuel Uzeda already affirms a similar line of thought.[395] In addition, we consider the entire colon to be the direct speech of Jerusalem's children, not only because the cry of distress from the first colon has to be given some sort of content but also because it is difficult to imagine such a prayer on the lips of a collection of disillusioned adults whose faith in YHWH's protection via the walls of Jerusalem has been profoundly contradicted by the reality confronting them. The adults are too frustrated in life and faith (cf 3_{30}) for such a uninhibited prayer to find its way onto their lips (cf also the explanation of 3_{14}), but such a thing cannot be said of the children. Their appeal, their cry to God is not from the intellect but from the heart which functions as the seat of their emotions. They are unaware of any theological contradiction; their reactions are primal: if mother cannot help them (2_{12a}) then they must turn to God. Just like all children, they borrow the language they hear around them, including the language of the liturgy,[396] in order to express this elementary awareness. Associated notions of protection and care are certainly in the background here (cf the exegesis of 2_{8a}).

The (sub-canto) response 3_{55}, in which one of Lady Jerusalem's older children cries out in the depths of distress to YHWH, provides an extension to the present situation. The use of לֵב does not only appear to function via its subtle connection with the cry of distress (צעק), it also plays an

[392] Cf Gen 21_{15-17}!
[393] Cf THAT I 863 (Stolz).
[394] MZlotowitz, מגילת איכה, New York 1979[6], 86.
[395] Cf also the references mentioned in the exegesis of 2_{8a} in the present commentary.
[396] Cf RdVaux, *Institutions I*, 83f.

essential role in light of the ancient confession that YHWH knows the hearts of human persons. He knows what is going on in the hearts of his people[397] and listens to the cries for help which arise from the afflicted heart. Hosea's prophetic accusation (Hos 7_{14}) is instructive here: "They do not cry to me from the heart...". Evidently YHWH is only moved by a true appeal from the heart and no other. While elsewhere the children lead the way in praise of God (Ps 8_3),[398] here they lead the way in genuine lament.

The poets' interest in the children of Jerusalem is also significant from another perspective. In the mind of Israel, YHWH, as a God who dwells in the highest yet stoops to the lowest, has always shown special concern for the poor and the lowly![399] The poets confirm this fact in daughter Jerusalem's appeal to this specific feature of YHWH's pity.

18b *Let tears stream down like a flood,* הוֹרִידִי כַנַּחַל דִּמְעָה
day and night! יוֹמָם וָלַיְלָה

The feeble cry of the children of Jerusalem must also touch the hearts of the people around them (cf quotation from Albertz above). The children surely need help but who is there who can really intervene? Are the people in any condition to assist?[400] Their thoughts return to the one who is their final and only refuge: Adonai.

With an urgency unequalled in the entire OT, the poets now wield the imperative: not once, but seven times (including the two prohibitives)! In so doing they endeavour to move daughter Jerusalem, so weakened by sadness and tears, to prayer.[401] As a person in distress weeps before God as an expression of his or her sorrow,[402] the poets urge Lady Jerusalem to pray ceaselessly with her tears. Such tears usually accompany the sort of prayer which appeals to God's pity.[403] In this light, the manifold imperatives are quite understandable. In Lam $1_{2,16}$, Lady Jerusalem's weeping is described as intense, so intense that there are no tears left in her eyes. She has cried herself out (cf Luther's 'ausgeweinet' [2_{11a}]). In spite of this,

397 Cf Ps 7_{10}, 26_2, 139.
398 Cf NHRidderbos, *De Psalmen I*, KV, Kampen 1962, 119f.
399 Cf Ps 113_{5-7} and Lam 3_{50}.
400 Cf Lam 4_4.
401 For the significance of 'seven' as being the precise and necessary number with respect to an action, cf Gen 4_{24}, Jos 6_4, II Kgs 5_{10}, Job 2_{13}.
402 See Deut 1_{45}, Isa 38_3, II Kgs 22_{19}.
403 Isa 30_{19}, Ps 6_{7-9}, 39_{13}, 56_9; cf TWAT I 641 (Hamp).

however, she is still called upon to weep bitterly before YHWH on behalf of her afflicted children.

Compared with other complaints of the people in which 'weeping before YHWH' is mentioned, the extent of Jerusalem's present tears is heavily accentuated here by way of the unique image of a ravine which, after heavy rainfall, guides the water downwards with enormous intensity.[404] It is possible that a lament ritual, familiar at the time of writing, lies hidden behind the present text (cf the explanation of 2_{19b}). The poets, however, not only urge Lady Jerusalem to weep with great intensity they also indicate the duration of her weeping. The expression 'night and day' follows the more ancient sequence, dating from before the exile, when the day was counted from evening to evening.[405] The expression itself is a merism, implying the full 24 hours of a normal day.[406]

18c *Do not rest,* אַל־תִּתְּנִי פוּגַת לָךְ
give the apple of your eye no respite! אַל־תִּדֹּם בַּת־עֵינֵךְ

Intensity and duration are underlined here by way of prohibitives. The *hapax* פוּגַת is derived from the root פוג meaning 'to rest'.[407] Daughter Jerusalem cannot allow herself a moment's rest. The second colon underlines this with a further prohibitive. References to the apple of one's eye with the same combination בַּת־עָיִן in Ps 17_8 and Zech 2_{12} (2_8 MT) and with אִישׁוֹן עָיִן ("Männlein [in Auge]"),[408] in Deut 32_{10} and Prov 7_2, point to a figurative usage which still functions to the present day, namely the apple of one's eye as a metaphor for a person's most precious possession. In association with weeping, however, the physical significance – the pupil of one's eye – takes precedence. The eye is a valuable but also vulnerable organ of sense; one is advised to be careful with it in order to avoid damaging it. While overabundance of tears can impair the functioning of the eye (cf 2_{11aA}), Lady Jerusalem is not in any position to take notice of such a fact. Something much more important is at stake and as such she must not spare 'the apple of her eye' by resting or pausing in her tears. The connection with the central strophe in the third song (3_{49}) is noteworthy here, both 3_{49} and the present bicolon employing a *hapax* (פוּגָה // פְּגוֹת [derived from the same √פוג] and √דמם I ['to rest', cf HAL 217] // √דמה II

---

[404] Cf JNegenman, *Een geografie van Palestina*, Kampen 1982, 90.
[405] Cf TWAT IV 554 (Stiglmair).
[406] Cf RdVaux, *Institutions I*, 275f; TWAT IV 555 (Stiglmair).
[407] Cf Ps 77_3; HAL 866.
[408] Cf HAL 43 sv אִישׁוֹן.

['to come to rest']). Daughter Jerusalem's weeping is identical to that of the devout one of Lamentations III.

19aA *Rise up, cry out in the night,* קוּמִי רֹנִּי בַלַּיְל

Here the poets provide us with a further explanation of the duration of Jerusalem's tears. The aforementioned יוֹמָם וָלַיְלָה (24 hours) is to be taken seriously. Daughter Jerusalem is told she must get up in the night, that the hours usually given over to sleep must be given over to tears. There is even further contrast in the fact that while the night is normally a time of silence, Lady Jerusalem is being called to cry out and scream. No doubt the poets are aware of the fact that everything sounds loud(er) in the silence of the night. The contrast serves to underline the exceptional nature of what Lady Jerusalem is being urged to do. Night offers an extra dimension to lament and as such it is a more appropriate time for prayer and weeping.[409] Where the tears of 1_{2a} were an expression of deep sorrow, here they are an expression of grieving prayer. The root רנן means 'to scream', but the type of scream intended by its use depends on the context. It is frequently employed to refer to cries of joy and rejoicing but the verb is also found in the context of lament and prayer.[410]

19aB *from the first watch of the night!* לְרֹאשׁ אַשְׁמֻרוֹת

We can determine from this and other OT texts that the hours of darkness were divided into three night watches. Thus the term לְרֹאשׁ אַשְׁמֻרָה refers to one of the divisions of the night during which a watchman kept vigil when it was considered necessary.[411] Ex 14_{24} and I Sam 11_{11} speak of the last watch or morning watch (2.00–6.00), Judg 7_{19} of the middle watch (22.00–2.00) and here in Lam 2_{19} we have mention of the first watch (18.00-22.00).[412] It is evident that the poets do not intend daughter Jerusalem to restrict her lament to the first watch, they simply urge her to persevere in her tearful prayer even when the usual time has arrived for rest and sleep.

19b *Pour out your heart like water* שִׁפְכִי כַמַּיִם לִבֵּךְ
before the presence of Adonai! נֹכַח פְּנֵי אֲדֹנָי

409 Cf Num 14_1, I Sam 15_{11}.
410 Cf Ps 17_1, 61_2, 88_3, Jer 7_{16}, 11_{14}. See also THAT II 783 (Ficker) and HAL 1163f.
411 Cf √שׁמר I = *qal*: 'to keep watch over'/'to guard'.
412 Cf RdVaux, *Institutions I*, 278; THAT II 984 (Sauer) and TWAT IV 554f (Stiglmair).

Hosea's prophetic reproach (Hos 7_{14}; cf Lam 2_{18a}) seems to have inspired the poets here also. Daughter Jerusalem's lament should not only be an exterior matter, it must come from the heart. She must pour out her heart with her tears (cf the response between 2_{18b} and 2_{19b}). The image of pouring out water is reminiscent of I Sam 7_6 – likewise in the context of a complaint of the people – in which water is drawn from the well and poured out before the presence of YHWH.

Found only here in the OT, exegetes have been forced to speculate as to the meaning of the ritual. Goslinga, for example, suggests it is a symbolic action "whereby one turns to YHWH and empties oneself before him", the water being a symbol for the heart.[413] Van Zijl proposes that we understand it as "an act of abandonment of one's unhappy life (cf Deut $12_{16,24}$, Ps 22_{15}) leading to complete surrender to YHWH (Lam 2_{19})."[414] The response הוֹרִידִי כַנַּחַל דִּמְעָה (18bA) // שִׁפְכִי כַמַּיִם לִבֵּךְ (19bA), however, suggests something different. The image of a briskly flowing stream is out of proportion with that of human weeping no matter how intense the tears might be. It may, nevertheless, have its roots in a lament ritual known to the poets which consisted of pouring out water before YHWH as a symbol for the tears of the people (cf the explanation of 2_{18b}). In metaphorical terms, the fluid and formless shape of water signify boundless excess.[415] Thus the heart must be poured out without reserve in an act of complete surrender. לֵב stands here for the very core of the person in which the human will and human existence have their origin. In a certain sense, the heart is the person in miniature.[416] The preposition נֹכַח underlines the fact that this 'emptying of the heart' has to take place in the presence of YHWH. As the following colon confirms, Jerusalem's prayer of tears must be oriented to him alone.

19cA *Lift up your hands to him,* שְׂאִי אֵלָיו כַּפַּיִךְ

According to Ps 63_5 and 141_2 which employ the same word combination (נָשָׂא כַּף, found only in these places), it would seem that a gesture of raising one's hands accompanied prayer of this kind. כַּף primarily means the palm of the hand, the raising of which implied that one desired to receive something and was thus an appropriate gesture in the context of prayer. Both Ps 63 and Ps 141 express the notion of expecting help from

413 CJGoslinga, *Het eerste boek Samuël*, Kampen 1968, 182.
414 AHvZijl, *I Samuël, deel I*, Nijkerk 1988, 100.
415 Cf TWAT IV 858 (Fabry).
416 Cf TWAT IV 426 (Fabry).

YHWH (cf also Ps 119_{48}). The poets' final imperative in urging Jerusalem to pray would appear, therefore, to have an extra confirmatory significance (cf Neh 8_7 [MT 8_6]).

19cB *for the lives of your children...* עַל־נֶפֶשׁ עוֹלָלַיִךְ

Evidently, Jerusalem's prayer is intended as a prayer of intercession on behalf of her children. The use of the noun עוֹלֵל and the adjective עָטוּף (19d, also reminiscent of the forms of √עטף in $2_{11c,12b}$) lead us, in the first instance, to think of the children mentioned in 2_{11c} which likewise deals with the dreadful situation of famine, although it does not employ the term רָעָב 'hunger'/'famine' (cf 2_{19d}).

Lam 1_{19} also refers to the deadly famine in the city. The song-response between 1_{19} and 2_{19} is unmistakable: גָּוְעוּ כִּי־בִקְשׁוּ אֹכֶל (1_{19bcA}) // הָעֲטוּפִים בְּרָעָב (2_{19dA}). In 1_{19}, however, it is not children who are in search of food but the priests and elders. This leads us to suspect that the children spoken of here in 2_{19cd} are probably the same younger children as those mentioned in 2_{11f}. Nevertheless, the poets do not restrict themselves to this younger group but also include daughter Jerusalem's other children, even her adult 'children' such as her priests and elders. This is underlined by the fact that both texts speak of the preservation of the נֶפֶשׁ: וְיָשִׁיבוּ אֶת־נַפְשָׁם (1_{19cB}) // עַל־נֶפֶשׁ עוֹלָלַיִךְ (2_{19cB}).

The poets' ongoing use of metaphor is in no way impeded by the aforementioned assumption (cf the exegesis of יְתוֹמִים in 5_3 and the meaning of עוֹלֵל in 1_{5c}). Since her entire population is being threatened by famine, daughter Jerusalem is called upon to pray for all of her children, young and old. The following colon and the final canticle confirm this supposition.

19d *...who perish from hunger* הָעֲטוּפִים בְּרָעָב
on the corner of every street! בְּרֹאשׁ כָּל־חוּצוֹת

When compared with $2_{11,12}$, the localisation here in 2_{19d} is somewhat unusual. In the former text it is stated twice and with a certain emphasis that the children are to be found languishing in the city squares ($2_{11c,12b}$) while the present text locates them on the corner of every street. We are left with the impression that Lady Jerusalem's languishing children are to be found throughout the city, searching for food on every street corner.

The natural reliance of the youngest children on their mothers suggests that they were not included in the search. Indeed, it is expressly stated that they '...pour out their lives on their mothers' lap' (2_{12c}). The song-response between בָּעִיר (1_{19b}) and בְּרֹאשׁ כָּל־חוּצוֹת (2_{19dB}) further confirms this likelihood, the alternative location suggesting that the feeble and starving priests and elders of 1_{19} are to be considered here also among daughter Jerusalem's perishing children.

It is significant that the expression בְּרֹאשׁ כָּל־חוּצוֹת is not original. The poets have borrowed it, among other idioms, from Nahum's prophecy of doom against Nineveh.[417] The adoption of such terminology once again suggests the notion of a change of fortunes: YHWH's judgement, formerly uttered against the godless city of Nineveh, has now become a terrible reality for Jerusalem, his very own city.

Canticle II (2_{20-22})

Content/theme: *The prayer of daughter Zion*

Literary argumentation:

inclusions:	לְמִי עוֹלַלְתָּ כֹּה (20aB) // אֹיְבִי כִלָּם (22cB)
	בְּמִקְדַּשׁ אֲדֹנָי (20cA) // כְיוֹם מוֹעֵד (22aA)
	כֹּהֵן וְנָבִיא (20cB) // מוֹעֵד (21aB)
responses:	לְמִי עוֹלַלְתָּ כֹּה (20aB) // נַעַר וְזָקֵן (21aB)
	יֵהָרֵג (20cA) // הָרַגְתָּ (21cA)
	נָפְלוּ בֶחָרֶב (21bB) // וְלֹא ... פָּלִיט וְשָׂרִיד (22b)
ext par:	בְּיוֹם אַפֶּךָ (21cA) // בְּיוֹם אַף־יְהוָה (22bA)
	יְהוָה (20aA) // יְהוָה (22bA)
	טִפֻּחִים (20bB) // טִפַּחְתִּי (22cA)

The present canticle constitutes the conclusion of the second canto, the conclusion of the second song and, in a certain sense, the conclusion of the first two songs combined. Daughter Zion acquiesces to the entreaty of the previous canticle and brings her affliction before YHWH in prayer. From the thematic perspective, there is a striking difference between this canticle and the concluding canticle of the first song where enemy oppression was central. The same enemy oppression is present here but only in the margins (2_{22cB}). Jerusalem's lament focuses now on the dreadful fate of her children and is clearly linked to the preceding appeal to pray for their lives. The material devastation of the city, described in detail in the

417 Nah 3_{10}; cf 1983, 182.

first canto (cf also 2_{15}), is not simply repeated here. The poets focus their attention and ours on the central theme of this song, namely the terrible affliction confronting the people with its climax in the appalling fate of daughter Zion's children. In so doing they summarise the sufferings of the city as they are described in the first two songs.

This point in the composition of Lamentations constitutes an important division. We noted elsewhere that in terms of size, Lam I and II represent almost half of the book and that from a thematic perspective both songs are closely related in their description of the affliction of daughter Jerusalem/Zion.[418] The third song introduces a fundamental change (cf the introduction to the first canticle of Lam III). Instead of the voice of the personified city or of those who address her, we now see one of the city's inhabitants take centre stage. Exegetically speaking this means that Lady Jerusalem/daughter Zion has the floor for the last time within the context of Lam I and II. Thus she turns her attention to the most essential and urgent dimension of her affliction: the dreadful fate of her children/inhabitants.

20aA *Look,* YHWH, *and observe...* רְאֵה יְהוָה וְהַבִּיטָה

For the extraordinarily insistent character of the present combination of imperatives see the explanation of 1_{9cA} and 1_{11cA}. At the song level there is an evident response between 1_{20a} and 2_{20a} (רְאֵה יְהוָה). In addition, this final canticle returns to the central theme elaborated in the first song (רְאֵה יְהוָה וְהַבִּיטָה [1_{11cA}] // רְאֵה יְהוָה וְהַבִּיטָה [2_{20aA}]). As the logical follow up to such a combination of imperatives, the poets concentrate in a summary fashion on the fate of their people (as is also evident in 5_{1B}). Furthermore, by way of the structural association with 1_{20a} (song-response with 2_{20a}), the poets hint at daughter Jerusalem's interior torment (cf the parallel כִּי־צַר־לִי [1_{20aA}]). Since her prayer does not refer to some disaster from the past we have rendered the perfects here as presents. The day of YHWH has arrived and the hour of his judgement continues unabated. Victims have fallen and continue to fall. In all its stark reality, however, the very immensity of Jerusalem's affliction cannot but elicit YHWH's sympathy and move him to intervene on her behalf.

20aB *...against whom you are doing this!* לְמִי עוֹלַלְתָּ כֹּה

[418] Cf 1988, 388.

Daughter Jerusalem is not asking YHWH to take a look at his own deeds. Her prayer only has meaning if one is led to think of the deeds of the enemy, empowered as they are by YHWH. The question, therefore, is whether YHWH will look down and see what has happened and is happening to her children under his mandate. It is evident from the specific formulation of her complaint [419] that she senses that boundaries have been transgressed in the punishment due for her sins. The intention of the poets is clear: to give daughter Jerusalem the chance to express the extremity of her affliction before YHWH and – given her claims – to consider him in a certain sense responsible. In so doing they employ Jerusalem's prayer to instil a sense of unease in YHWH as he looks down on these dreadful deeds committed in his name, deeds which are far from his heart (cf the explanation of 3_{33}). It would be wrong, therefore, to render Jerusalem's affliction as a past event thus making her prayer somewhat redundant. The fact that her distress is far from over gives meaning and purpose to her prayer: she uses it to try to move YHWH to bring an end to the dreadful affliction under which her children are dying daily in the streets and squares of the city.

Although it is not stated directly, the death of Jerusalem's children would appear to be the primary focus of this colon. The connection between the final sections of Lam I and II confirms this. The burning innards (מֵעַי חֳמַרְמָרוּ, 1_{20aB}) – also mentioned at the beginning of the present canto (2_{11aB}) – appear to be caused by the fate of the younger children and the infants (cf 2_{11ac}). This returns in an inclusion on the canticle level within the second canto (2_{11-22}; cf בֵּעָטֵף עוֹלֵל וְיוֹנֵק [2_{11cA}] // לְמִי עוֹלַלְתָּ כֹּה [2_{20aB}]). The word play between the verb עלל (+ לְ = 'to take action against') and the noun עוֹלֵל (child) is quite striking in the Hebrew. The verb was used for the first time in 1_{12bB} (cf the latter colon for the meaning 'to bring evil upon'/'to glean'). It is daughter Zion's intention to make the identity of the victims of his judgement clear to YHWH: innocent children who cannot be held responsible for the present disaster.

Rudolph reads more into the text than is actually present by interpreting the לְמִי as an allusion to Israel's election: YHWH is doing this to his chosen people. There are no associations with the notion of Israel's election in the present canticle, however. At the same time, the poets are not suggesting that the present distress is some theologically absurd attack on

---

[419] Cf the similarities with 1_{9cA} (אֶת־עָנְיִי), 1_{11cB} (כִּי הָיִיתִי זוֹלֵלָה), 1_{20aA} (כִּי־צַר־לִי), 5_{1B} (אֶת־חֶרְפָּתֵנוּ).

YHWH's chosen ones. Their primary purpose is to bring this profound and incomprehensible human suffering to the fore and thereby touch YHWH and move him to intervene. Such is the fundamental ground of appeal in Jerusalem's prayer. The imperatives explicitly call for YHWH's saving intervention on behalf of his afflicted people. The following bicola fill in the meaning of the לְמִי in summary form. With great urgency, daughter Jerusalem draws YHWH's attention to the actual victims of the present distress.

20bA *Must women eat their own fruit,* אִם־תֹּאכַלְנָה נָשִׁים פִּרְיָם

אִם functions here as an introduction to an interrogative sentence.[420] The 3rd person fem pl impf תֹּאכַלְנָה is jussive. The women of Jerusalem have been forced into this horrifying act by the extremes of famine. Kraus is incorrect to speak of cannibalism in this regard. Human cannibalism is never related to exceptional situations of hunger nor are the children of those involved its object (cf II Kgs 6_{24-29}). The present lament over this dreadful and inhuman deed recurs in more detail in 4_{10a}.

The present canticle does not only focus on the distress of the women of the city but goes on to offer a summary description of all those who have been afflicted by death and destruction. It is striking, however, that the poets turn first to the fate of the women and their children. The inclusion within the canto (at the canticle level) between the mothers of 2_{12ac} and the women mentioned here underlines this poetic emphasis. There is also an evident progression between the mention of Jerusalem's dying children at the beginning of the canto (2_{11-12}) and the eating of their corpses in the present colon. The scenario is unimaginably horrifying.

Commentators such as Wiesmann have noted that this picture (and the rest of the suffering described in Lamentations) does not originate from eye witness accounts.[421] Such a vision of things does not only tend to justify a later dating of the songs, it also gives witness to the horror with which these passages were met: these dreadful events cannot possibly have been real.

Nevertheless, a number of points suggest that this approach is incorrect. If the portrayal of the actions of the women of Jerusalem is merely a literary fiction then the work of the poets involved in its composition is

[420] Cf HAL 59 sv אִם (5), and I Kgs 1_{27}.

[421] HWiesmann, 'Der Verfasser des Büchleins der Klagelieder – ein Augenzeuge der behandelten Ereignisse?', Biblica 17 (1936), 71–84.

far from fortunate. From a theological perspective, moreover, it would seem inappropriate to trouble YHWH with a form of prayer which had no roots in reality. Indeed, it was known that YHWH could not be misled and that baseless complaints in fact provoked his wrath (cf Num. 11_{1ff}).

The fact that we are dealing with an event which actually took place is made evident by the central strophe of the second canto of the third song (3_{51}) where the devout one states that his eyes are pained by the sight of (the suffering of) the women of his city. In so doing, he highlights his own heart-rending situation as an eye witness.[422]

Similar situations of terrible famine are also to be found elsewhere in the OT: Lev 26_{29}, Deut 28_{53}, II Kgs 6_{28}, Jer 19_9 and Ezek 5_{10}. The evidential value of Deut 28_{53} is somewhat limited, however, given that the verse in question may have been formulated after the exile and under the very influence of Lam 2_{20} and 4_{10}.[423] The same objection might also raised with respect to Lev 26_{29} and Jer 19_9, the latter text possibly originating from the pen of the deuteronomistic redaction of the Book of Jeremiah.[424] The objection does not apply to the text from II Kgs 6_{28}, however, which appears to date back to older Elisha traditions.[425] Further Ancient Near Eastern sources reveal that extreme famine could indeed lead to such desperation that people were forced to appease their hunger in ways similar to that described here in Lamentations.[426]

While the modern reader will certainly find such a description of events horrific and unbelievable we can be assured that the same must have been true for the poets of Lamentations. Indeed they had to endure the said events at first hand and it was a truly painful sight (3_{51}). The very unbelievable dimension of Jerusalem's suffering, however, is what constitutes the core of her prayer, a heart rending lament which must surely stir YHWH's sympathy. In addition to this, the drama of Jerusalem's affliction does not restrict itself to inhuman suffering. The children constitute the future of a nation; thus the poets insinuate the absence of a future for

---

422 Cf the parallel lament of Lady Jerusalem: נֶהְפַּךְ לִבִּי בְּקִרְבִּי ('my heart turns within me', 1_{20bA}).

423 Cf 1983, 25f.

424 WThiel, *Die deuteronomistische Redaktion von Jeremia 1–25*, WMANT 41, Neukirchen 1973, 221.

425 For Ezek 5_{10} cf WZimmerli, *Ezechiel 1–24*, BKAT XIII/1, Neukirchen 1979², 134.

426 Cf, for example, DJWiseman, *The Vassal-Treaties of Esarhaddon*, London 1958, 62. See also ANET³ 533 and 1983, 26.

Israel in their horrendous portrayal of events. The 'fruit' eaten by the women of Jerusalem must have been terribly bitter to the taste.

20bB *the children they carried upon their hands?* עֹלֲלֵי טִפֻּחִים

The contrast contained in the preceding colon is further elaborated and underlined here. The adjective טִפֻּחִים is derived from the √טפח II, a verb which is only found elsewhere in Lam 2_{22c}. The meaning of both √טפח I and √טפח II has been established on the basis of related verbs in other Semitic languages as well as the Hebrew context: √טפח I 'to spread out (one's hands)' and √טפח II 'to bear healthy children'/'to raise (children)'. The latter meaning is ascribed to the verb on the basis of its parallel relationship with √רבה in 2_{22cA}.[427] The suggestion proposed by HAL is unacceptable, however, given that a translation employing 'healthy children' would hardly fit the context. In light of their starving situation, the children of Jerusalem would have appeared anything but healthy (cf also $2_{11,12}$). Our translation is supported by the structural association with the first canticle of the fourth song (4_{1-2}). Both these canticles constitute an inclusion at the level of the entire book. In 4_2 the poets speak of the children of Zion who were considered more valuable than fine gold. In 4_5 (in response with 4_{2a}), the luxurious treatment enjoyed by the children of Zion before the present disaster is portrayed. Both these notions together with the possible meanings of √טפח II are well represented in the expression 'to carry upon one's hands' (cf Van Selms). The fact that Zion's children were spoiled and pampered only underlines the dreadful contrast expressed in Jerusalem's painful lament: the mothers are forced to do such things to the children they once loved so much.

20c *Must (they) be murdered in Adonai's sanctuary, priest and prophet?* אִם־יֵהָרֵג בְּמִקְדַּשׁ אֲדֹנָי כֹּהֵן וְנָבִיא

Lady Jerusalem refers YHWH to the distress of her other 'children' brought on by the continued presence of the enemy who are murdering her population on the streets of the city.[428] The murder of her priests and prophets is a heart-rending experience for her. One might be at liberty to speak here of a psycho-theological insight on behalf of the poets if one considers that they focus YHWH's attention on the fate of his priests and prophets – a fate which must concern him deeply – immediately after that of the

[427] Cf HAL 362.

[428] Cf the song-response with 1_{20c} (מִחוּץ שִׁכְּלָה־חֶרֶב).

women and children. At the canto level there is an evident response with the conclusion of the first canto (cf 2_{9bB}). Priest (implicitly) and prophet are mentioned in the same sequence. 2_{20c} reveals something of a progression: in the present canto we are dealing with the death of the priests and prophets where in the first canto there was only talk of the cessation of their ministerial (liturgical) functions. The addition of a stipulation of place – in Adonai's own sanctuary – is also striking. The fact that the prophets are included here is evidence of the cultic context in which they performed their ministry.[429]

The murder of the priests in the sanctuary is indicative of a bitter turn of events. The very ones who normally took care of the slaughtering of animals for sacrifice are now themselves slaughtered in the very same place. In 1_{19bc} there is mention of priests who wander through the city in search of food. Evidently other priests and prophets remained in their place among the ruins of the temple (cf $2_{6,7}$ and 1_{4b}). In our explanation of 1_{4b} we already referred to the unusual methods of the Babylonians in their destruction of the temple in Jerusalem. In conquering a city it was the Babylonian custom to leave the temples untouched although they insisted that Babylonian gods be venerated alongside those of the indigenous population. Indeed, it was wise to be careful where matters of divinity were concerned. With the present conquest, however, they wanted to bring the image of Jerusalem as an inviolable city to an absolute end (cf, in addition, the explanation of 1_{4b}).

It is reasonable to assume that the priests and prophets who remained in the temple were put to death as part of this destructive policy. The Babylonians were well aware of the political inclinations of many of Jerusalem's citizens.[430] Indeed, they were aware of the extent to which the salvific announcements of Jerusalem's cultic prophets stimulated long term resistance to their siege. By murdering these very prophets (and priests) the Babylonians exposed the falsity of their claims with respect to the inviolability of the city and made the further repetition of their salvific announcements impossible. Daughter Jerusalem herself, however, views this as an absurd affliction: YHWH's servants and spiritual leaders are murdered on his own sacred ground (cf 5_3). Can he truly let such a thing happen?

---

429 Cf JJeremias, *Kultprophetie und Gerichtsverkündigung in der späten Königszeit Israels*, Neukirchen 1970, 2–10; 1983, 164–166; TWAT IV 77f (Dommerhausen) and THAT II 10 (Jeremias).

430 Cf HJagersma, *Geschiedenis van Israël*, Kampen 1979, 251 and 1983, 150.

21a *They are lying on the ground in the streets* שָׁכְבוּ לָאָרֶץ חוּצוֹת
from the youngest to the oldest! נַעַר וְזָקֵן

It is clear that 'murder by the sword' mentioned in 1_{20cA} corresponds at the song-response level with the dead of Jerusalem, the young and the old alike, who now lie slain on the ground. Next to conscious assassinations, undisciplined murder squads appear to have control of the streets. We noted in the exegesis of 1_{10a} that the Babylonian soldiers and mercenaries from among the surrounding nations set about plundering the city with great fervour after the long siege. Their coffers had been empty for a long time and their (gambling) debts were serious. It seems obvious, therefore, that they would intimidate the people of the city until they brought out their hidden treasures. The arbitrary killing of passers-by in order to threaten the remaining population was and is a tried and tested means of intimidation. The merism נַעַר וְזָקֵן should be understood in this light and can be freely translated as 'from the youngest to the oldest'.[431]

The absence of the 1st person sg suffix (as with בְּתוּלֹתַי וּבַחוּרַי in 2_{21b}) is a further indication that the poets were speaking in more general terms here. Without respect for person, the enemy has had free reign of the city to terrorise and murder. Corpses lie where they fell throughout the streets of the city (cf also 4_{14}).

Note that the terminology found in this strophe is also to be found in Isa 51_{17-23} where there is mention of YHWH having given the cup of his judgement to Jerusalem to drink.[432] It is possible that the שָׁכְבוּ בְּרֹאשׁ כָּל־חוּצֹת in the Isaiah text should be considered an interpolation based on the very presence of the expression in Lam 2_{19} and 4_1 (note, however, Nah 3_{10} with the same context), but this may also have been the work of Deutero-Isaiah himself.[433] The use of the root שׁכב is simply necessary. It is more significant, however, that Isa 51_{17-23} locates terminology from the conclusion of Lamentations II in the context of the 'cup of judgement' image. The cup in question is mentioned in Lam 4_{21} where it is stated that daughter Zion has drunk YHWH's 'cup of judgement'. Other terms which Lamentations has in common with Isa 51_{19}, such as שֶׁבֶר (Lam $2_{11,13}$, $3_{47,48}$, 4_{10}), רָעָב (2_{19}, 4_9, 5_{10}) and חֶרֶב (1_{20}, 2_{21}, 4_9, 5_9), are also part of this judgement context. Jer 13_{12-14} speaks of the drunkenness associated with YHWH's judgement which leads to an unreserved act of destruction on YHWH's part (לֹא־אֶחְמוֹל

[431] Cf TWAT V 512f (Fuhs).
[432] Cf שָׁכְבוּ לָאָרֶץ חוּצוֹת (Lam 2_{21a}) and שָׁכְבוּ בְּרֹאשׁ כָּל־חוּצוֹת (Isa 51_{20}).
[433] Cf JLKoole, *Jesaja II, deel II Jesaja 49 tot en met 55*, Kampen 1990, 165.

[Jer 13_{14}]; cf לֹא חָמָלְתָּ in 21c). In other words, the affliction expressed here by daughter Jerusalem is the direct consequence of drinking the cup of YHWH's judgement.[434] What follows also points in this direction.

21b *My young women and men* בְּתוּלֹתַי וּבַחוּרַי
fall by the sword! נָפְלוּ בֶחָרֶב

Lady Jerusalem continues to lament her affliction unabated. From the stylistic perspective, the present colon constitutes an augmentation of the merism נַעַר וְזָקֵן in 21a. Although the groups 'in between' are to be assumed in the context of the merism, they are now mentioned, nevertheless, by name: the young women and young men of the city. The formulation בְּתוּלֹתַי וּבַחוּרַי has already been used by the poets in 1_{18c} where it is said that the upper age group of Jerusalem's youth lived in exile. Given the present verse, exile was clearly not the fate of all the young people of the city. Deportation to Babylon was selective. Young men and women who did not 'qualify' for deportation remained in Jerusalem but, given the terror at large in the city, their fate was worse than that of the deportees. The vigorous and attractive youth are often the very ones to draw the most attention and become the enemy's particular target: they were put to death by the sword. To this end the poets employ the expression נָפַל בֶּחָרֶב which we already noted in Jeremiah's prophecy concerning the cup of judgement (cf Jer 25_{27} and the song-response 4_{21}).

This lament also reveals a certain element of progression with respect to 1_{18}: exile is not as final as death. For daughter Jerusalem, the difference is insignificant; she has been robbed of your vigorous young men and women, indeed she has been robbed of her very future.

21cA *You kill on the day of your anger,* הָרַגְתָּ בְּיוֹם אַפֶּךָ

For the 'day of anger' as the hour of YHWH's judgement, see the excursus on the day of YHWH following the exegesis of 1_{2a} and the excursus following the exegesis of 1_{12c}. Once again the poets cut through any possible misunderstanding: these events are not at the initiative of the enemy, YHWH himself is behind them. The mention of 'death by the sword' may have given the impression that the enemy had taken charge but Lady Jerusalem clearly ascribes the misfortune confronting her and her children to YHWH. Given the literal statement in the song-response 1_{21bB}

434 Cf also the explanation of the song-response in 4_{21bB}.

(כִּי אַתָּה עָשִׂיתָ), it is clear in Jerusalem's mind that he alone is responsible for what has happened and for what continues to happen.

21cB *you slaughter...* טָבַחְתָּ

The fact that YHWH is responsible for Jerusalem's affliction is further elaborated in 'cutting' terminology. Besides the more general term 'to kill' (√הרג), daughter Jerusalem speaks of 'slaughter'. The root טבח is only found in Lamentations. Alliteration is evident between this term and the root טפח II 'to pamper', 'to spoil' from 2_{20bB}, although both terms are widely contrasting in terms of meaning. The verb is at home among the terminology surrounding the day of YHWH[435] and the prophecy of the cup of judgement in Jer 25_{34f}.[436] The term would appear to evoke a number of associations. In Ezekiel, for example, the enemy sword is the instrument of slaughter among the population (Ezek 21_{15}), a fact which corresponds with the mention of the sword (חֶרֶב) in the preceding bicolon. At the same time, there appears to be a connection with the dreadful image of the women who are forced to eat their offspring. Thus in 4_{10} there is mention of the women boiling/cooking their children. In ancient culture, slaughter and cooking were more closely related than they are in our contemporary world in which they are seen as more or less unrelated activities. The noun טַבָּח derived from √טבח, however, means 'cook' in Hebrew.[437]

The Septuagint translation is quite revealing here in that it renders the notion of slaughter with 'You have cooked' (ἐμαγείρευσας). The preparatory work necessary for the women to eat the meat of their dead children – i.e. their slaughter – is at its core the work of YHWH himself. A further association can be derived from the fact that the slaughter of lambs and sheep was often employed as a metaphor for the killing of harmless and innocent individuals.[438] The applicability of such a metaphor to the young children of Jerusalem requires no further defence. The judgement of which the prophets spoke in terms of famine, sword and slaughter has now become a reality for daughter Jerusalem down to the last detail and beyond!

21cB *... without mercy!* לֹא חָמָלְתָּ

---

[435] Cf Isa 30_{25}, 34_6, Jer 12_3.

[436] See the exegesis of Lam 4_{21}! Cf Zeph 1_7 and TWAT III 305f (Hamp).

[437] Cf I Sam 8_{13}, 9_{23f}; cf also TWAT III 302f (Hamp).

[438] Cf Jer 11_{19}, Ps 44_{23}, Isa 53_7; cf also TWAT III 304f (Hamp).

YHWH's lack of mercy was already mentioned in 2_{2aA} and 2_{17bB}.[439] Nevertheless, the present text differs in detail from the aforementioned verses. The combination of YHWH's lack of mercy and the root הרס in $2_{2,17}$ reveals that the said lack of compromise manifested itself in relation to the destruction of the cities of Judah. Cities, walls and houses, however, are not people, far less innocent children. The destruction of material possessions is clearly easier to endure than the suffering and death of infants and young children, let alone the fact that their corpses were afterwards eaten. Even now, while the people are confronted with such intense suffering, YHWH continues to execute his judgement unabated. Thus daughter Jerusalem presses on with her painful lament.

22a *You have assembled – as on a festival day –* תִּקְרָא כְיוֹם מוֹעֵד
my assailants from all around! מְגוּרַי מִסָּבִיב

Ewald[440] has offered a unique interpretation of this text based on the LXX reading (παροικίας) in which מְגוּרִים appears to be derived from √גור I 'to dwell (as a stranger)'. The מְגוּרִים are thus understood as the inhabitants of the unprotected villages and towns of Judah. Such people left their homes on feast days to travel up to Jerusalem. In the present crisis they turn once again to Jerusalem, not for a feast but for protection against the enemy (cf Jer 35_{11}). Keil, however, had already rejected such an interpretation as laboured and inappropriate. The vast majority of exegetes understand מְגוּרַי as a suffixed form of the noun מָגוֹר meaning 'terror'/'fear'. The combination with סָבִיב can also be found in Ps 31_{14}, Jer 6_{25}, $20_{3,10}$, 46_{5}, 49_{29}. Jerusalem is subject to terror from every side. Keil leaves the content of מָגוֹר open, seeing it as an expression of the multiplicity of Jerusalem's terrors, i.e. not only her hostile enemies but also famine and disease (cf 1_{20}).

In explaining this summarising strophe we need to take the entire context of the first two songs into account. The expression כְּיוֹם מוֹעֵד was already mentioned in 2_{7c} where it refers to a victory feast celebrated by Jerusalem's enemies in the temple, a fact which the poets deplore since it was only made possible by YHWH himself who had abandoned her walls and palaces into their hands. The present text states that it was YHWH who assembled them for this feast.[441] In the central strophe of the sec-

[439] See the exegesis of these texts for the meaning and structural placing of the notion in the second song.

[440] Cf also Löhr and KBL sv *מְגוּרִים.

ond canto of Lam I (1_{17}) we find סָבִיב in combination with the enemies of Judah who were commanded by YHWH to attack Jacob. The concluding strophes, moreover, speak repeatedly of the enemy and their deeds (1_{22}, 3_{64-66}, 4_{22}). The final bicolon of the present strophe is no exception (cf אֹיְבִי כִלָּם [2_{22cB}]). In addition, the final cola of the three concluding bicola constitute external parallelisms: אֹיְבִי כִלָּם // וְלֹא . . . פָּלִיט וְשָׂרִיד // מְגוּרַי מִסָּבִיב. The bulk of the evidence has led commentators to assume, therefore, that the term מְגוּרַי should be understood as enemy invaders in person (cf the Vulgate: *qui terrerent me*), even although this requires the emendation of מְגוּרַי to read מְגוֹרְרַי (*polel* of √גור III) meaning 'those who terrorised me'.[442] McDaniel remains closer to the consonantal text in reading a participial *hiph'il*: מְגִירַי, which can also be understood as a derivative of √גור II 'to attack' (cf Ps 59_4; Isa 54_{15}).[443]

22b *On the day of* YHWH*'s anger* וְלֹא הָיָה בְּיוֹם אַף־יְהוָה
no one escapes or survives! פָּלִיט וְשָׂרִיד

The enemy day of feasting is YHWH's day against Israel (cf the excursus following the exegesis of 1_{2a}). By placing this *theologoumenon* in the song's summarising conclusion the poets underline its importance in a fashion similar to the first song.[444] At the same time, identical content and responsive speech concerning the cup of judgement can be found at the end of the fourth song (cf $4_{21b,22a}$). For the notion of YHWH's wrath see the exegesis of 1_{12c}.

In the present bicolon, the poets continue the line of thought of the preceding colon: the enemy surrounds Lady Jerusalem shutting her in so tightly that there can be no thought of escape, a fact which the poets emphasise by placing לֹא in first position. The use of the fairly common word-pair פָּלִיט וְשָׂרִיד (Josh 8_{22}, Jer 42_{17}, 44_{14}) also provides an element of accentuation. We already noted a similar combination in 2_{5cB} (תַּאֲנִיָּה וַאֲנִיָּה) where commentators point out the assonance and alliteration which bind the words together and create emphasis.[445] The nouns in the present text,

---

441 For the present meaning of √קרא see Am 5_8, 9_6.

442 Cf, for example, Rudolph and Robinson in the text critical apparatus of BHS; cf also HAL 177.

443 See ThFMcDaniel, 'Philological Studies in Lamentations', Biblica 49 (1968), 42–44. For the graphic confusion between ׳ and ו see EWürthwein, *Der Text des Alten Testaments*, Stuttgart 1973^4, 104 and ETov, *Textual Criticism of the Hebrew Bible*, Assen/Maastricht, 1992, 246f.

444 Cf יוֹם־קָרָאתָ in 1_{21cA} and עוֹלַלְתָּ לִי in 1_{22bA}.

however, are derived from different verbal roots. √פלט in the *qal* means 'to escape' while √שׂרד, also in the *qal*, refers to the notion of 'survival' in the specific context of a defeat at the hands of the enemy (cf Num. 21_{35}, Josh 8_{22} etcetera). Both meanings fit well in the context.

What the poets intended by this situation of no escape remains something of a question. It would be difficult to maintain a literal interpretation since, given the mention of refugees in Jer 40_{11}, there were evidently people who did manage to escape. The same text also speaks of a remnant which remained in Judah, probably implying the country dwellers rather than the inhabitants of Jerusalem. Lam 3_{22A} – which speaks of surviving the disaster – proves, nevertheless, that the poets did not have the complete annihilation of Jerusalem's population in mind. Their use of terms here is strictly theological in character and is determined by the day of YHWH theme. In his announcement of YHWH's judgement over Israel 'on that day', the prophet Zephaniah leaves open the possibility of survival where there is conversion and the fostering of justice and humility (Zeph 1_7).

In the present bicolon the poets make it clear that the people have missed their chance. No one can hide from the wrath of YHWH. Once again the first and the second songs complement one another in the form of responses. In 1_{22b}, Lady Jerusalem confesses that YHWH has brought this affliction upon her on account of all her sins (עַל כָּל־פְּשָׁעָי). A certain tension remains, nevertheless. There is also no escape for Jerusalem's dying children. Does Jerusalem's confession of sin also apply to them (cf 2_{18a})?

The difficult issue of the relationship between collective and individual responsibility raises its head at this point, as does the problem of innocent suffering in time of judgement (cf Ezek 18; Jer 45; 49_{12}). The poets provide no easy answers. For them the tension must remain. In light of the (implicit) confession of guilt, they appear, on the one hand, to accept a collective responsibility: children may suffer because of their parents' guilt (cf Ex 20_5). On the other hand, however, they appear to employ the hunger and death of the children and infants as the basic argument of their prayer in the very presence of YHWH, complaining as they do that a consistently maintained collective approach to the guilt of Jerusalem is unreasonable and inhuman. Is YHWH able to endure such horrors? Must more children die in this way?

[445] Cf WGEWatson, *Classical Hebrew Poetry. A Guide to its Techniques*, JSOT suppl series 26, Sheffield 1984, 224–228.

22c *Those whom I carried upon my hands and reared my enemy murders!* אֲשֶׁר־טִפַּחְתִּי וְרִבִּיתִי אֹיְבִי כִלָּם

The present bicolon justifies our inclusion of the destiny of the infant children of Jerusalem in our explanation of 2_{22b}. The fact that they too cannot escape this dreadful situation is provided here with separate confirmation. The terminology used especially for the children in 2_{20bB} also returns at this point (√טפח II). In our explanation of 2_{20bB} we argued for the translation 'to carry upon one's hands' which points to an active element in the relationship between the mothers and their children. This in turn corresponds with daughter Jerusalem's psychological condition as it is described in the final bicolon of the first song: her heart is sick. Jerusalem's incomparable anguish (1_{12b}, 2_{13}) has its primary roots in the distress of her dying children. The content-based inclusion in the present canto with the first canticle (2_{11-13}) is crystal clear in its implications. It is also striking, from a literary perspective, that the present canto begins and ends with the same verb: √כלה I. The relationship is unmistakable: tears have dimmed the light in Lady Jerusalem's eyes because the enemy are killing her children. Thus the poets provide the significant and profoundly moving character of the theme of Jerusalem's dying children with an element of structural visibility.

New here is the use of the term 'to raise' (√רבה I *pi'el*), a reference to the fact that Jerusalem is not only referring to her youngest children but also to those she raised to adulthood. The singular is somewhat unexpected. In 1_{21bA} Jerusalem employs the plural but here, at the end of the second song, she is no longer focused on her many enemies. The plural employed by the LXX (ἐχθρούς μου) misinterprets the intention of the text. Daughter Jerusalem's summarising prayer is not about her enemies in the plural, it is about the one and only real enemy of her people whose very name she is afraid to mention (cf $2_{4a,5a}$). She thus appeals to God against God.

Lamentations III

Canto I (3_{1-33})

1 א *I am the devout man who looks upon affliction*
under the scourge of his anger.
2 א *He drives me forth and makes me go*
into darkness and no light.
3 א *Yes, against me again and again turns*
his hand all day long.

4 ב *He makes my flesh and skin waste away,*
he breaks my bones.
5 ב *He builds a rampart about me and surrounds me*
with poison and hardship.
6 ב *He makes me dwell in dark places,*
like the dead of long ago.

---

7 ג *He builds a wall around me, I cannot escape;*
he makes heavy my metal chains.
8 ג *Even when I cry out and call for help*
he rejects my prayer.
9 ג *He walls off my ways with hewn stones,*
my paths he makes twisted.

10 ד *He is a bear lying in wait for me,*
a lion in ambush.
11 ד *I want to escape, but he rips me open;*
he destroys me.
12 ד *He bends his bow towards me in attack,*
as target for his arrow.

---

13 ה *They penetrate my innards,*
the arrows from his quiver.
14 ה *I am the laughing stock of all my people,*
their mocking-song all the day.
15 ה *He fills me with bitter herbs,*
gives me bitterness to drink.

16 ו *He makes me grind my teeth on gravel,*
he presses me down in ash.
17 ו *Cast out from peace is my soul,*
I am forced to forget good things.
18 ו *And I said, "Ravaged is my splendour,*
my expectation from YHWH."

19 ז *Realise my affliction and wandering,*
bitterness and poison.
20 ז *My soul is abundantly aware of it*
and it pities me.
21 ז *(But) this I shall once again take to heart,*
therefore still hope:

---

22 ח *It is (due to) the favours of* YHWH *that we do not perish,*
for his mercy never ceases.
23 ח *New (signs of favour) every morning;*
manifold is your faithfulness.
24 ח *"My portion is* YHWH*", says my soul,*
therefore I will hope in him.

25 ט YHWH *is good to those who wait intently for him,*
to the soul that seeks him.
26 ט *Good is he. May one quietly wait*
for YHWH*'s help.*
27 ט *He is good to a devout one when he must bear*
a yoke in his youth.

---

28 י *May he sit down alone and be silent,*
for He has imposed it on him.
29 י *May he press his mouth to the dust,*
perhaps there is still hope.
30 י *May he turn his cheek to the one who strikes him,*
may he be filled with insults.

31 כ *For He does not reject forever,*
Adonai.
32 כ *Whenever he has grieved, he has compassion*
according to his many favours.

33 כ *For it does not conform to his heart: oppression*
and grieving of human persons.

Canto II (3_{34-66})

34 ל *To be trampled under (the enemy's) foot*
serve all the prisoners of the land;
35 ל *to be subverted (serves) the right of a devout one*
before the presence of the Most High;
36 ל *human persons (serve) to be agrieved in their rights,*
and Adonai does not want to see it!

37 מ *Who spoke, that such a thing should happen?*
Adonai did not command it!
38 מ *From the mouth of the Most High come not*
evil words, but the good!
39 מ *Why then should a survivor grumble,*
a devout one concerning his sin-fate?!

---

40 נ *Let us search and scrutinise our ways,*
and return to YHWH*!*
41 נ *Let us lift up our heart along with our hands*
to God in the heavens.
42 נ *We, we sinned and were rebellious!*
You, you have not forgiven!

43 ס *You cover yourself with anger and pursue us!*
You kill and have no mercy!
44 ס *You wrap yourself in a cloud,*
inaccessible to prayer!
45 ס *You make us into filth and rubbish*
in the midst of the peoples!

---

46 פ *They open wide their mouths about us,*
all our enemies!
47 פ *Panic and pitfall come upon us,*
the devastation and the disintegration!

48 ע *My eye flows with torrents of water*
because of the disintegration of my daughter, my people.

49 פ *My eye gushes with water, restless,*
without sleeping,
50 פ *until he looks down and sees,*
YHWH *from the heavens.*
51 פ *My eye causes me deep pain*
because of all the daughters of my city.

52 צ *They hunted me like a bird,*
my enemies, without reason.
53 צ *They let my life waste away in a pit*
and have thrown stones upon me.
54 צ *Water flows over my head;*
I thought, 'I am lost.'

---

55 ק *I call upon your name, O* YHWH,
from the depths of the pit.
56 ק *You hear my voice, do not close your ear*
to my gasping and crying for help.
57 ק *You are near on the day I call to you;*
you say: "Fear not!"

58 ר *You, Adonai, battle always for my soul,*
you free my life.
59 ר *You see, O* YHWH, *my oppression,*
do me justice.
60 ר *You see all their malice,*
all their plots against me.

---

61 ש *You hear their taunts, O* YHWH,
all their plots against me,
62 ש *the whispers of my adversaries and their jeers*
over me, all day long.
63 ש *Their sitting and rising you observe;*
I am their mocking-song.

64 ת *You shall pay them back, O* YHWH,
according to the work of their hands.
65 ת *You shall give them an anguished heart,*
your curse upon them.
66 ת *You shall pursue them in anger and destroy them,*
from under the heaven of YHWH.

* * *

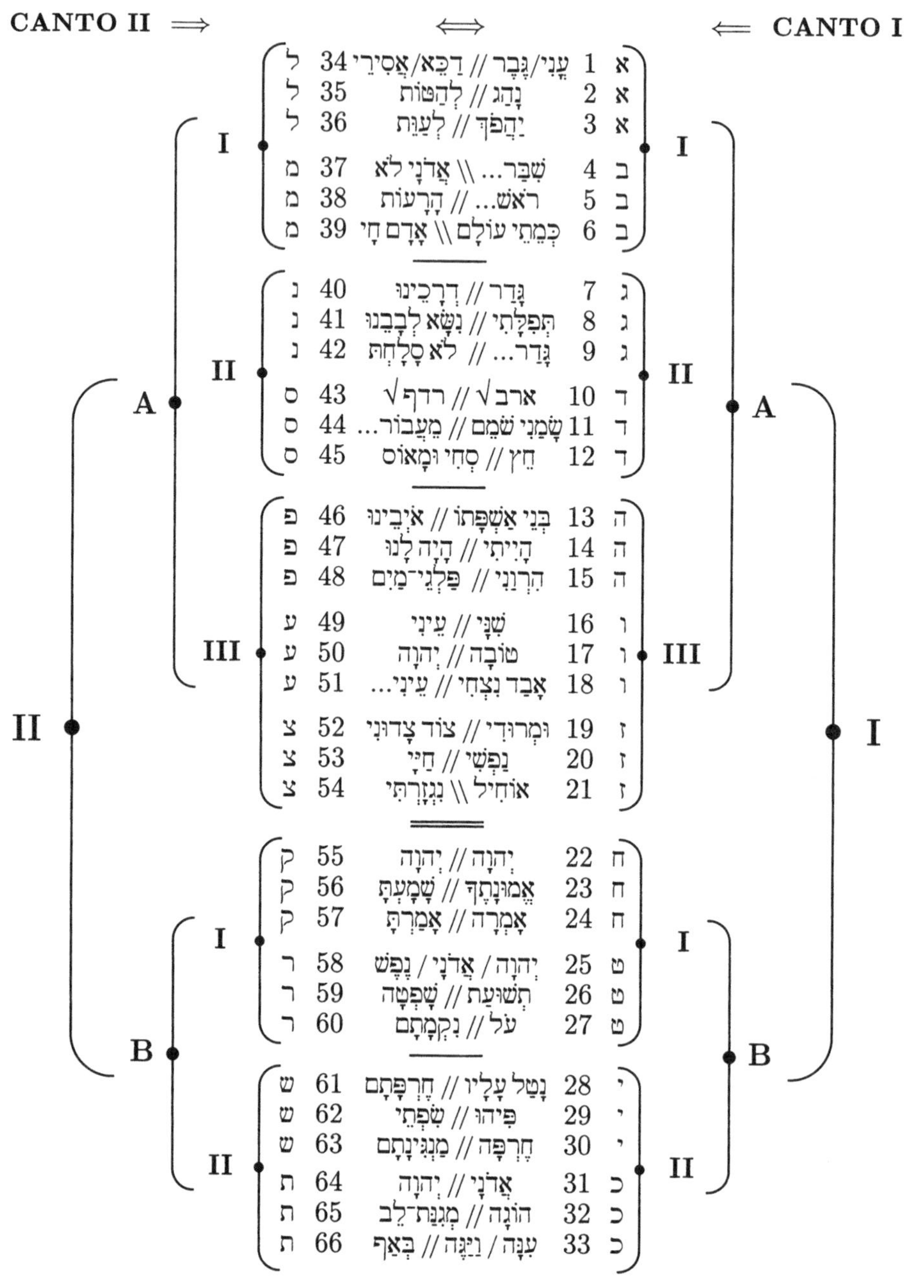

figure 3

Essentials and Perspectives

The third song differs from Lam I and II in a variety of respects, the two most important of which we will be our initial focus as we introduce the exegesis. Firstly, the collective voice of Lady Jerusalem, so poignantly present in the first two songs, makes way in the third for that of one of her inhabitants, a devout man who introduces himself at the beginning of the song (3_{1A}). Secondly, there is a significant difference in literary structure between the present song and songs I and II. Concentricity at the song level – so evident in the first two songs – is absent in the third which is structured on the basis of well-rounded panels, independent units, each constituting a canto. The cantos in question cannot and should not be separated from one another since they not only mirror one another at the level of content they also detail or clarify one another via responsive connections. Thus both panels constitute the third song as a whole, each following the same sequence of lament and prayer. This form and structure is further distinguished by its triple alphabetic acrostic (cf III.6). In our introduction to the main exegetical features of the song, therefore, we will focus on the two panel structure. From a literary perspective, both are strongly concentric, with 3_{17} in the first panel and 3_{50} in the second constituting the central core of each. Read side by side, both panels supply the thematic content of the song and, indeed, of the entire book:

Cast out from peace is my soul,
I am forced to forget the good (3_{17})
until he looks down and sees,
YHWH *from the heavens.* (3_{50})

The first panel, canto I (3_{1-33}), consists of two parts: sub-canto I (3_{1-21}) and sub-canto II (3_{22-33}). Both sub-cantos are remarkable in their totally contrasting antithetical tone: the first characterised by a bitter sense of abandonment, the second by continued faith and trust. The second panel displays exactly the same structure and shift of tone: sub-canto I (3_{34-54}) and sub-canto II (3_{55-66}). The antithetical transition between the central strophes of the song (3_{31-33} and 3_{34-36}) reveals one of the poets' focal theological insights: the refusal to look on affliction and distress in the land is not after YHWH's heart, it is not his way. Such inner conflict in God himself is the ground of their hope. Their complaints become increasingly focused on trying to point out to YHWH how his deeds run counter to his very self in judging his people thus and how diametrically opposed all this is to his many past deeds of salvation on behalf of his people Israel.

In the first sub-canto (3_{1-21}) of the first canto we hear the story of a devout inhabitant of Jerusalem. He recounts the various afflictions he has been forced to endure at the hands of YHWH using impressionistic, metaphorical language. Although concrete facts and details are missing, we are still left with the sense that this devout man is experiencing the most profound affliction. In making such a stylistic choice, the poets almost certainly intended to make their present distress emotionally recognisable for future generations. Nevertheless, closer exegetical inspection reveals that the pain of the devout man is a direct result of the fall of Zion. He suffers side by side with his city and his people. This alone makes his experience recognisable to his fellow Israelites. At the same time, his distress is portrayed as incomparable; there is no one who can claim to be suffering more than he.

At its core, however, the devout man's deepest agonies are not a result of his outwardly observable affliction, the latter being a mere product of his much deeper and theologically proportioned sorrow: in the midst of a unique relationship of trust in YHWH, the devout man is being forced to suffer terribly at the hands of his own God. It is YHWH himself who is afflicting him thus. The bitterness arising from such a situation sets the tone of the first three canticles of the third song. It is not a question here of lament or prayer; the devout man utters defiant accusations and in the presence of third parties he laments over YHWH, the very one who is behind the affliction of his faithful one, the God whose present deeds completely contradict everything Israel once appreciated and confessed of him.

Thus, after the devout man introduces himself, the first canticle (3_{1-6}) focuses on his experience of the night of YHWH's judgement. Hunger-stricken, physically broken and exhausted, he is hunted down by YHWH and shrouded in hopeless darkness. In such a desperate situation he ultimately considers himself left for dead.

In the second canticle (3_{7-12}), the devout one characterises his existence as that of a prisoner hermetically shut-off in his cell. He feels himself guarded by a God who behaves like a merciless jailer, who pays no attention to his cries for clemency. On the contrary, his Guard afflicts him in a multitude of ways.

The third canticle (3_{13-21}) concretises the devout man's afflictions. The arrows of YHWH's judgement reach into the very marrow of his being. As a devout disciple who desires to sustain his special relationship of faith and trust in YHWH, his pain is all the more acute. By maintaining such a stance in the midst of the present affliction he becomes a focus of derision for he own people. The majority of his fellow Israelites are far from prepared to accept the fact that YHWH could be responsible for their present state and they choose to bid their God farewell. It is unacceptable that YHWH should treat human beings in such a manner! Whoever would endeavour to remain faithful to such a God simply makes himself laughable in their eyes. The devout man is clearly and painfully confronted with this reality (3_{14}). In a somewhat veiled manner the devout man goes on to speak of the hunger and thirst brought on by YHWH's judgement. He sums up his affliction by stating that his existence no longer brings him the slightest pleasure (cf 3_{17}); the core of his lament: all peace has been driven out of his soul. YHWH's rejection of altar and temple ($2_{6,7}$) is echoed in these verses. Zion, the visible sign of the Source of everything that is good, is ruined. His relationship of trust and faith has turned out to be a one-way affair: as a devout disciple he calls out to YHWH but YHWH turns a deaf ear (3_8) and offers him no hope, no future expectation (3_{18}).

The devout man has not spoken his final word, however. In the depths of his affliction he knows of only One who has the power to rescue him from this deathly darkess: the God who is the very perpetrator of his punishment. While such knowledge appears to be paradoxical, it is consistent, nevertheless, in terms of power and might. In the first song, Lady Jerusalem comes to the same conclusion: since no human person has the strength to help her she turns to the very One who rejected her and prays to YHWH for help. The devout man's self-pity offers him no perspective on the future. He too sees only one way out: holding fast to his hope in YHWH, the God who caused his loss of hope.

In the second sub-canto (3_{22-33}), therefore, it is evident that the devout man has chosen a different perspective together with a completely different language, that of fidelity and trust. His sense of trust emerges from an alternative evaluation of the reality confronting him, one rooted in a reflection on the very essence of YHWH himself.

Having commenced with a portrayal of all the negative dimensions of his experience (3_{1-20}), the devout man now discovers that in spite of everything there remain positive aspects to his existence and to that of his fellow Israelites, aspects which now command his attention in the first canticle (3_{22-27}) of the second sub-canto. No matter how great his affliction is he cannot place everything in his life under this same heading.

He has experienced things which are not in line with YHWH's judgement. Thus he realises that there is still a chance of survival, in spite of the fact that YHWH has commanded his prophets to foretell the end of Israel. His judgement is not yet total and the devout man must consider such a fact as a favour from YHWH. He realises also that in the midst of his distress each new day offers new opportunities for survival. Little by little his faith in YHWH is restored; now he can even say that in spite of his affliction YHWH is still 'his portion' (3_{24}). His confession of continued communion with YHWH allows him also to share once again in that characteristic feature of his God: the goodness (3_{25-27}) which he has manifested throughout the history of his people, the same goodness which can be found expressed in the confessions of Israel's faith.

The second and final canticle (3_{28-33}) of the first sub-canto puts into words the devout man's insight with respect to his relationship with YHWH. Accusation and rebelliousness are inappropriate and undeserved. Such is not the way to move YHWH to restore his former favours. A different attitude is required, one of humility and silent endurance of affliction, in the fragile hope of ultimate liberation by YHWH. In the final strophe (3_{31-33}) of the present (sub-)canto, at the centre of the book as a whole, the poets give foundation to this awareness with the most fundamental theology.

Thus the devout one states that God does not reject forever. If one were to inquire as to the source of such an insight then one would have to turn to the implicitly assumed relationship between God's wrath and his rejection. Israel was well aware that YHWH's anger might be intense but, in principle, it was short in duration. An additional dimension of Israel's faith emerged from the experience that human persons in their deepest need were always able to move YHWH to acts of mercy which he performed, without obligation, as deeds of his essential fidelity and goodness. Israel knew that in the long run YHWH's mercy would win out over his wrath. The final and perhaps most fundamental insight to which the devout one holds fast is his absolute certainty that the affliction with which human persons are confronted does not conform to the heart of YHWH. God's heart, by its very nature, is a place of goodness and friendship. As such, when he is forced to grieve and distress, he not only does violence to human beings, he also does violence to himself. Such discord in God is a source of hope, hope that he will ultimately reverse the present sorrow and affliction. The devout man has had his say. He has expressed his bitter suffering and has reasoned that there is hope in spite of it all. He has nothing more to do than to pray in humble fidelity and to wait upon the salvific intervention of YHWH his God.

The second canto (3_{34-66}) reveals the same structure as the first both at the literary level and the level of content and even mirrors the same antithesis between the two constituent sub-cantos. Distress and affliction constitute the focal point of the longer first section of the canto (= sub-canto I [3_{34-54}]). Here too the transition is made from murmuring accusation to silent humility ($3_{39,40}$). The question of the cause of the present affliction, the answer to which reveals Jerusalem's personal failure, brings about a change in the accusations and prayerful laments. The second sub-canto (3_{55-66}) breaths once again with a spirit of trust and fidelity as the devout man speaks of his hope that YHWH will save him and his people.

The sentiment of the first strophe of canto II is in sharp contrast to the renewed faith and trust expressed in the verses preceding it. As with the beginning of the first canto, we are confronted with an atmosphere in which the devout man laments over the disaster he has been forced to endure (3_1). Here too we encounter great bitterness at the injustice, affliction and oppression confronting the land towards which YHWH appears to remain so passive. It would be incorrect, however, to isolate this return to the negative from the positive renewal of faith with which canto I concluded. In their very antithetical character, the central strophes of the third song (3_{31-33} and 3_{34-36}) provide us with an insight into an essential aspect of the poets' intention: not only is the contrast between YHWH's nature and his concrete aloofness made visible in their words, the poets also make it clear that the faith and trust of the devout man did not come into existence after the present affliction; it was born in the midst of it, in a context of profound violation of justice and severe oppression in the land.

It goes without saying that, in such circumstances, a pious and accepting fidelity to God together with its supporting theology would be the subject of a certain amount of protest. Indeed, faith and experience clash quite violently in these passages! The devout man may well be inspired to speak of God's mercy and goodness but the fact remains that the actual experience of his fellow Israelites is of a different character: YHWH has closed his eyes to the immense agony being endured by his people, "Adonai does not see!" (3_{36B}). The bitter realisation with which his people confront him reminds the devout one of his own former attitude and evaluation of the situation (3_{1-20}). In contrast to this, however, he raises the question of guilt: who lies behind this great anguish, who is responsible? The terminology employed by the poets reveals that not YHWH – who is responsible only for good – but another is to blame for the affliction. The primary guilty parties are the prophets of Jerusalem who unjustly pretended to be speaking the word of YHWH but, in fact, led the people astray with dishonest and crooked words. They did not disclose the sin of Jerusalem and Judah which had covered them both with guilt and ultimately must have brought on YHWH's judgement (cf 2_{14} and 4_{13}). The people, therefore, ought not to blame YHWH for their lot; Jerusalem's prophets are the guilty ones although those who accuse them ought also to examine their own consciences.

In line with the consequences of the given response, the tone of the second canticle (3_{40-45}) changes from one of bitter complaint to one of self-examination and confession of guilt. Conversion is called for because the people have sinned to such an extent that YHWH is not only unable to forgive, his very wrath is awakened by it. By insisting at this point on self-examination and conversion, the devout man in fact repeats his already stated conviction: in the presence of YHWH there can only be humility and silent expectation. He calls his people to respond in this way. As their representative he puts their collective guilt into words (3_{42}). The following strophe makes it evident once again that this attitude of faith did not emerge after but during the still scourging affliction which was brought on by God's wrath (cf 5_{22}). In great humility he addresses his words to YHWH, pointing out again and again how such divine behaviour is self-destructive (cf 3_{33}).

The third canticle (3_{46-54}) of the present sub-canto is central to canto II (3_{34-66}). It constitutes an implicit appeal to YHWH rooted in the insight that human beings in whatever form of distress can move him to clemency. For this reason, the devout man restates the affliction of his people in the presence of YHWH: the mockery of the enemy, the fall of the city, the horrendous sorrow of Jerusalem's women. At the same time, he does not omit his own personal experience of being hunted down and taken prisoner, locked up in a cistern. In the midst of all this he emphasises the intended duration of his lament: he will not cease to place his suffering and that of his people before YHWH until He abandons His indifference. The primary intention behind each and every lament in the book of Lamentations is thereby expressed.

The second sub-canto (3_{55-66}) of canto II reveals a different tone, the primary lament mode – which dominated the preceding sub-canto – giving way once again to the sense of faith, trust and hope which coloured 3_{22-33}. The only difference between the present sub-canto and 3_{22-33} lies in its more detailed and more explicit portrayal of the devout man's trust in YHWH. If it is impossible for YHWH to passively endure the affliction of a human person, then this is even more the case when such individuals continue to humble themselves before him, confess their guilt and publicly and in all helplessness confirm their trust in him. As far as the devout man is concerned, YHWH cannot and will not shame such a person. It is in this sense that we must understand the final sub-canto: as an anticipation of the professed salvation which – the devout man is certain – YHWH will realise.

The constituent canticles of the second sub-canto further elaborate the devout man's professed trust and expectation. In 3_{55-60}, he confesses YHWH's closeness: YHWH hears him and clearly sees the affliction which he has been forced to undergo. The final canticle (3_{61-66}) focuses this closeness on the enemy: YHWH also hears their mockery and is aware of their plans. For this reason, the devout man is sure that YHWH – who is just (1_{18}) – will repay their crimes against him and his people. More detailed exegesis reveals that the devout man is not set upon revenge pure and simple; he desires only a return to the former state of well-being and the recovery of the land annexed by the enemy. Thus the third song concludes with a prayer of trust and expectation, and, perhaps more significantly, with the very name of YHWH.

Lamentations III
Scholarly Exposition

Introduction

As we already noted in the introduction to 2_{20-22}, the third song departs significantly from the first two in terms of style, the literary figure of the lamenting and weeping Lady Jerusalem making way for a new motif. By continuous use of the first person singular 'I', however, the poets have allowed for a smooth transition from 2_{20-22} to 3_1. While this may suggest a certain identity between both figures, we are, nevertheless, no longer confronted with the lamenting Lady Jerusalem or with those who observe her affliction and put it into words; we are now faced with an inhabitant of the city ($3_{1,51}$), one who has first hand experience of the disaster which has befallen her. In a certain sense one can talk of a turn away from 'the outside' towards 'the inside'. A collective interpretation – which would simply be a repetition of Lady Jerusalem's claims from the first two songs – of the 'I' in the third song, therefore, would not receive much support. Together with the vast majority of exegetes[1] we opt for an individual (literary) interpretation, accepting at the same time that the individual experience of the devout man has meaning, nonetheless, for the entire people (cf the explanation of 3_{1A}). The personal element is primary in binding the second song block (Lam III-V) together (cf אֲנִי [3_{1A}] // לָנוּ [5_{1A}]). Since 3_{1A} introduces the second half of the book as a whole, we can permit ourselves to speak of a perfect balance in terms of the division of the material.

From a structural perspective, the present literary twist constitutes the centre of the book of Lamentations. Although it will become apparent that Lam III deals with the same affliction as the first two songs, the focus turns from the fall and destruction of the city and the land to the human

[1] See, for example, Keil, Budde, Löhr, Haller, Weismann, Meek, Rudolph, Weiser, Kraus, Hillers, Brandscheidt, Westermann.

person who – in his relationship with YHWH – is being forced to endure and assimilate these events. Relating the affliction to YHWH results in two contrary assertions: bitterness versus renewed faith and trust in God. The content of the sub-cantos mirrors this antithesis. The personal experience of the devout man is not exclusive to him alone. In taking the floor in Lam III he includes others in his thoughts and considerations (cf the use of 'us' throughout the song). The poetic account of his personal affliction comes accross as short and somewhat vague, a stylistically impressionistic portrayal of events consciously chosen to make the suffering of the main character of the third song all the more recognisable. At the same time, however, the aforementioned vagueness remains relative. Given the fact that from the perspective of structure and content Lam III constitutes the well considered literary core of Lamentations, a core which has to be read and explained in responsive relationship with the other songs, it becomes evident that the affliction of this devout inhabitant of the city is the same as that described elsewhere in the book. Structurally speaking this can be seen in the many literary and topical/thematic agreements on equivalent levels with the other songs.[2]

Genre

Any attempt to determine the genre of Lam III cannot be made in isolation from the book of Lamentations as a whole (cf introduction III.2). No matter how much Lam III differs at first sight from the other songs, there is evidence here too of markedly characteristic connections between lament and elements of the dirge form (cf $3_{6,16,53,54}$). Westermann does not support such a relationship.[3] According to Westermann, the composite Lam III is dominated in terms of genre by "der Klagepsalm eines Einzelnen", which, in his opinion, constitutes a gauge for distinguishing authentic from secondary material.[4] Neither his determination of genre nor his distinction between individual and collective lament are correct, however. The very repetition of the term 'us' clearly reveals that we are

2 For more detailed argumentation see 1988, 361–391 and the exegesis per verse.

3 CWestermann, *Die Klagelieder, Forschungsgeschichte und Auslegung*, Neukirchen-Vluyn 1990, 70, 181; cf, however, 21f: "In 3,42–51 liegt das Fragment einer Volksklage vor, vom Schuldbekenntnis (42) bis zur angedeuten Bitte um Gottes Zuwendung... Motiv der Totenklage ist die Schilderung des Schmerzes in 48,49,51 sowie die Ausagge aus 47: »Grauen und Grube ward uns zuteil«; eine feste Wendung, wie etwa Jes 24,17; Jer 48,43 zeigen." Nevertheless, $3_{47-49,51}$ need not refer to a dirge.

4 Westermann, 142.

dealing here with more than personal affliction and bitterness to which others are not a party (cf the already noted impressionistic portrayal of events intended to stimulate recognition). The strong relationship with elements from the dirge form need not detract from this. Note, for example, Keel's remark: "Es ist meistens müßig zu fragen, ob der Beter eines bestimmten Klagepsalms als unreiner Kranker außerhalb des Ortes in einer Grabhöhle hauste, ob er sich als Gefangener in einem Zisternenkerker befand oder alles symbolisch gemeint sei. In all den vielen ähnlichen Gestalten trat dem Israeliten mitten in seiner alltäglichen Welt das Totenreich entgegen. Es manifestierte sich tatsächlich in diesen Wirklichkeiten, die es aber andererseits doch auf häufig transzendiert, so daß diese Wirklichkeiten auch wieder nicht als Chiffren sein können für die Enge und Verlorenheit, die den Israeliten jederzeit und überall bedrängten und zu Jahwe hindrängten, der angesichts solcher Bedrohungen allein festen Halt gewähren konnte." [5]

While the suffering of the devout man in the third song is typical of the suffering of many others surrounding him, it is also recognisable to suffering people of later generations who have experienced similar affliction. For this reason, his struggle with renewed faith and trust in God can also be seen as having an exemplary function. Individual experience in Lam III is at the service of the faith community. We will return to this point in an epilogue at the end of the exegesis of the present song.

It would be incorrect, nevertheless, to characterise Lam III as a didactic song on the basis of its paradigmatic significance. Imitation need not imply any notion of learning. Indeed the very concept of 'learning' would be far too detached for the present context and would constitute a gross misunderstanding of the profundity of the affliction. Suffering cannot be alleviated by rules and regulations nor by the transfer of experiential wisdom. Kaiser's qualification of Lam III as 'literature influenced by wisdom' is therefore misplaced.[6] Wisdom, in fact, is incapable of explaining such affliction (cf Job).[7]

Structure/Content

With respect to the analysis of the cantos and sub-cantos we refer to

[5] OKeel, *Die Welt der altorientalischen Bildsymbolik und das Alte Testament*, Zürich-Einsiedeln-Köln-Neukirchen-Vluyn 1977², 63.

[6] Cf OKaiser, *Klagelieder*, ATD 16/2, Göttingen 1992, 160; cf also Kraus, 1968, 55f.

[7] For further detail on the (minimal) influence of wisdom see 1983, 261f together with the exegesis of 3_{27}.

1988, 321–334, the results of which point to a responsive diptych structure. Lam III consists of two equally large cantos. While each canto retains its own independence, in thematic and linguistic terms they clearly mirror and/or supplement one another in their parallel strophes (canto-responses).

Canto I (3_{1-33}) consists of two sub-cantos. In the first (3_{1-21}), the devout man introduces himself and provides a report of the suffering he is being forced to endure. In the second (3_{22-33}), the same devout man relates how he continues to place his hope in YHWH in spite of everything he has suffered.

Canto II (3_{34-66}) is, in a certain sense, a duplicate of canto I in that it too begins with a bitter tale of suffering, this time with regard to the devout man's fellow citizens (3_{34-54} = sub-canto I). Reflection on the origin of the people's suffering takes the second canto a step further than the first. In response, the people are called upon to turn their bitter accusations into prayerful lament (3_{40-54}). The devout man takes the lead in a renewal of hope and trust resulting from this called for change of heart. The second sub-canto (3_{55-66}) repeats and elaborates on his hopes and expectations.

Sub-canto I (Lam 3_{1-21})

At the core of the book as a whole, the present sub-canto embraces much of the theological tension with which those who remained faithful to YHWH were confronted after the downfall of Jerusalem. The said tension is represented by the experiences and thoughts of the devout man, the גֶּבֶר. The first sub-canto portrays his confrontation with immense affliction in some detail. The devout man speaks for himself, frequently employing bitter expressions and powerful images in order to depict YHWH's attitude and actions. Time and again we are reminded of the threats contained in the prophetic announcements of judgement concerning Israel while, in terms of gravity, the content of his lament goes far beyond that of the CI found in the Psalms. In this sense it is also incorrect to speak of laments or complaints since the lament dimension of the CI/CP is essentially an appeal for compassion which – when directed to God – becomes a prayer for his slavific intervention. Such is the opinion of Westermann who proposes that this first part of Lam III should be understood as a complaint of the individual.[8] It would seem more appropriate, however, that we characterise the words of the גֶּבֶר as a sort of indictment. Defiantly bitter, he

[8] Westermann, *Klagelieder*, 142.

laments over the affliction YHWH has brought upon him although he does not mention YHWH by name. In this respect it is striking that the גֶּבֶר does not address his complaint directly to God but rather to those around him. It is to them that he speaks of the terrible affliction to which YHWH has given his consent. Thus the first sub-canto is in fact a further elaboration of the lament of Lady Jerusalem to those who passed by: "look and see if there is any sorrow equal to mine" (1_{12}), focused in the present verses on the personal suffering of the גֶּבֶר.

Canticle I (3_{1-6})

Content/theme: *In his anger* YHWH *strikes the devout man and shuts him in as if he were dead.*

Literary argumentation:

inclusions:	(6A) בְּמַחֲשַׁכִּים הוֹשִׁיבַנִי // (1B) בְּשֵׁבֶט עֶבְרָתוֹ
	(6B) כְּמֵתֵי עוֹלָם // (1A) אֲנִי
	(5B) רֹאשׁ וּתְלָאָה // (2B) חֹשֶׁךְ וְלֹא־אוֹר
responses:	(4A) בִּלָּה בְשָׂרִי וְעוֹרִי // (1A) רָאָה עֳנִי
	(4B) שִׁבַּר עַצְמוֹתָי // (1B) בְּשֵׁבֶט עֶבְרָתוֹ
	(5B) רֹאשׁ וּתְלָאָה // (2B) חֹשֶׁךְ וְלֹא־אוֹר
	(6B) עוֹלָם // (3B) כָּל־הַיּוֹם
ext par:	(6A) בְּמַחֲשַׁכִּים // (2B) חֹשֶׁךְ
consonance:	(6A) הוֹשִׁיבַנִי // (3A) יָשֻׁב

1A *I am the devout man...* ...אֲנִי הַגֶּבֶר

The גֶּבֶר opens the third song by introducing himself, a unique event in the OT. The entire first strophe focuses with some emphasis on the personal fate of this individual: אֲנִי // אוֹתִי // בִּי. Our Western tendency would be to immediately inquire into the identity of the גֶּבֶר. The suggestion that the poet himself is speaking at this point (Weiser) is far from satisfactory. As a matter of fact, the text itself provides little direct information on the speaker and, as such, speculation abounds. In line with many of his predecessors, Wiesmann, for example, follows the tradition that Lamentations was written by Jeremiah and proposes, therefore, that we should understand the speaker in Lam III as the prophet in question. Rudolph considers such a suggestion impossible since one cannot say that Jeremiah was personally affected by God's wrath. Rudolph does not distance himself to any great extent from the tradition, however. He proposes that a follower of Jeremiah is availing himself of the prophet's voice here, pointing out how Jeremiah overcame the affliction his prophetic ministry had brought him and holding him up as an example to be followed in overcoming the present distress. Rudolph's own objection to the traditional perspective on this text, however, remains valid: he ultimately ignores the difference between the גֶּבֶר and the prophet.

Van Selms offers a quite distinct interpretation. The introductory אֲנִי leads him to think of the style employed by royal inscriptions which leads him further to hypothesise that the present speaker is a humiliated king. In his opinion, the description of the suffering endured by the גֶּבֶר fits well in the context of the Babylonian captivity of king Jehoiakin. Van Selm's proposal is not entirely new, given that Jehoiakin had already been connected with (the authorship of) Lamentations.[9] His arguments in this regard, however, remain unconvincing. What he suggests as applicable to the king might just as easily apply to any other individual. Indeed the presentation formula upon which he builds much of his hypothesis is not exclusive to kings since it is also employed in the opening words of the decalogue for YHWH. In addition, one might object that it is not clear that allusion is being made to the king in Lam III while in the other songs his very exile is in fact presupposed (cf 2_9, 4_{20}). In contrast, the present text portrays the גֶּבֶר as fully participating in the affliction confronting the city and the land. Van Selms is also incorrect to suggest that the גֶּבֶר was not an eye witness (cf 3_{49-50} and the accompanying commentary).

Our approach to the problem is based on the close relationship between the five songs and their firm responsive interconnectedness at both the literary level and the level of content. If we honour this cohesion which the poets so carefully created then we become free to borrow information from the other songs as a means to increase our knowledge of the גֶּבֶר. Thus it appears that he is being afflicted by the same judgement with which YHWH is confronting Lady Jerusalem. Her 'night' is his 'darkness' (cf בַּלַּיְלָה [1_{2aA}] // חֹשֶׁךְ וְלֹא־אוֹר [3_2]). One can further deduce from the responsive connection with the second song that the גֶּבֶר, as an inhabitant of Jerusalem, is closely related to Zion, since being engulfed in YHWH's anger is also part and parcel of his own darkness (cf יָעִיב בְּאַפּוֹ ... בַּת־צִיּוֹן [2_{1a}] // חֹשֶׁךְ וְלֹא־אוֹר [3_{2B}]).

[9] "Erst der gelehrte Sonderling Herm. von der Hardt hat in einem 1712 zu Helmstädt edirten Programme die Abfassung derselben von Jeremia in Anrede gestellt und die fünf Lieder dem Daniel, Sadrach, Mesach, Abednego und dem Könige Jojachin zu geschrieben." Cited by CFKeil, *Biblischer Commentar über den Propheten Jeremia und die Klagelieder*, Leipzig 1872, 548.

It is not beyond the bounds of possibility that the גֶּבֶר actually lived in the temple complex which has now become a dark and deathly place (compare יָעִיב בְּאַפּוֹ ... בַּת־צִיּוֹן [2_{1a}] with the external parallelism in this canticle between חֹשֶׁךְ וְלֹא־אוֹר [3_{2B}] // בְּמַחֲשַׁכִּים [3_{6A}]).[10] The song-response with the fourth song points in a similar direction: 4_1 speaks of the darkness of Zion as a result of the dulling of the temple gold; 4_2 laments over the 'breaking' of the בְּנֵי צִיּוֹן, the inhabitants of Zion, while the גֶּבֶר complains in the following strophe of the present song that YHWH has broken his bones (3_{4A} // 4_2). In addition, one should take note of the song-response between the ה-strophes of the third and the fourth songs (3_{13-15} and 4_5) from which one can deduce that the גֶּבֶר may be included among the 'spoiled' children of Zion. Furthermore, in the description of the aristocracy found in $4_{7,8}$, there are indications that the גֶּבֶר (in the literary sense) was among their number also. For a variety of reasons, therefore, we are inclined to envisage the גֶּבֶר as a prominent inhabitant of Jerusalem residing in Zion. Indeed, the גֶּבֶר also speaks of the city of Jerusalem as 'his city' (3_{51B}). In spite of the various possible indications of his identity, however, the poets are never explicit. In any event, a direct identification would not fit their general purpose since the suffering of the גֶּבֶר in Lam III is not associated with a specific individual: his suffering and affliction is in fact the same as that of his fellow citizens. This common bond between the גֶּבֶר and his compatriots also constitutes the primary ground upon which they ought to follow his lead in renewing their faith and trust in God. To provide the גֶּבֶר with too distinct a profile or even identify him as someone known to them would hinder such a transformation. Unique and extraordinary individuals – such as the king, for example, – provide difficult role models for ordinary people to follow. It almost goes without saying, therefore, that the poets' references to the גֶּבֶר allow his fellow citizens to see him as no more and no less than one of their own, one of ruined Zion's afflicted inhabitants. Given the use of the expression בְּנֵי צִיּוֹן, we can be sure that such individuals were not few and far between.

We are confronted with an unavoidable question at this point: is the גֶּבֶר – in spite of that fact that he cannot be identified – an historical figure or simply the literary product of the poets' imagination? The answer: he is both! It is clear that we are not dealing with a fictional character here, in the sense that the poets invented him without any reference to real persons and real circumstances. The very opposite is in fact the case:

---

[10] For Zion as necropolis see the explanation of $2_{20c,21}$ and 5_{18}.

it would be impossible even to conceive of the גֶּבֶר without the disaster which confronted the people of Jerusalem and Judah in 587 BCE. These are authentic, historical events experienced by real people. The figure of the גֶּבֶר is both literary and historical at the same time: literary, because he does not constitute a single historical individual and historical because he embodies those devout individuals who are tormented by their experiences, questions and doubts and who turn to God in the midst of their confusion. In this sense one can speak of a collective personality: the גֶּבֶר, as he is described in Lam III, represents the people who have been forced to endure all of this affliction.

It remains striking, however, that the poets choose to render this 'everyman' with the term גֶּבֶר instead of the more general term אִישׁ with which גֶּבֶר is frequently paralleled.[11] Why הַגֶּבֶר? The definite article clearly has a demonstrative function: 'this strong man'.[12] In what respect does the notion of 'everyman' relate to the גֶּבֶר? The noun itself consists of two important aspects: 'physicality' – a גֶּבֶר was a strong individual of about thirty years of age (cf I Chron 23_3; the term בָּחוּר is used for younger men), virile, healthy and fecund – and 'fidelity' – a גֶּבֶר enjoyed a special relationship of faith and trust in God. The term would appear to suggest a sort of spiritualisation of the physical: a man only becomes truly strong when he enjoys a close relationship with God and does what God asks of him with faith and reverence. The גֶּבֶר is frequently presented thus in the Psalms.[13] Where the emphasis is placed on the spiritual dimension of being a גֶּבֶר then the question of age becomes less important (cf 3_{27B}). While it is clearly almost impossible to render both dimensions in a single translational equivalent, they remain of vital importance for our understanding of the text because they function in revealing the extent of the גֶּבֶר's suffering. Indeed, it is in precisely these two fundamental aspects of his existence that this man has been so profoundly affected: the spiritual trial brought on by his loss of hope in YHWH (3_{18B}) together with the terrible hunger he has been forced to endure have brought him physically to his knees. His devastated state is described in greater detail later in the canticle. Thus the poets continue to make use of the contrast element of the dirge by placing the גֶּבֶר's former 'magnificence' side by side with

[11] Cf Jer 22_{30}, Mic 2_2 and the inclusion in the present canto between גֶּבֶר (3_{1A}) // בְּנֵי־אִישׁ (3_{33B}).

[12] Cf GES-K § 126*a*,*b*.

[13] Cf Ps 37_{23}, 34_9, 40_5 etcetera; for further argumentation see TWAT I 913–917 (Kosmala).

this present affliction which has left him almost dead (3_{6B}). With a minimum of words – אֲנִי הַגֶּבֶר – they achieve the maximum of eloquence. On the one hand, the preservation of the גֶּבֶר's anonymity makes it possible for other devout individuals to identify themselves with him while, on the other hand, the intensity of suffering suggested by the contrast between the magnificent past and the dreadful present is so great that no one dare say 'my suffering is worse', a possible excuse not to follow the גֶּבֶר on his path towards renewed faith and trust in YHWH.

While the introductory formula is אֲנִי הַגֶּבֶר is unique in the OT, the terminology employed in the present canticle is reminiscent of the sentiment portrayed in perhaps the darkest of all the Psalms, Ps 88. Kraus characterises this third song as a Psalm in which the scent of death infiltrates every line.[14]

1A ...*who looks upon affliction...* רָאָה עֳנִי

Several authors prefer to deny that the affliction described in Lamentations has its source in the first hand experience of one or more eyewitnesses. I am more inclined to believe, however, that the poets are presenting their audience with their own observations and experiences in these songs (cf also the explanation of 2_{22bA}). Such is the purpose of the indirect statement offered here: the גֶּבֶר looks upon affliction.[15] Elsewhere in Lamentations the verb 'to look upon'/'to see' means to 'visually observe'. In the present context, however, the additional implication is that the גֶּבֶר is personally enduring the affliction of which he speaks. עֳנִי is without a definite article, undetermined. We are not yet informed of the content of the affliction referred to here, although we know from the use of עָנִי in Lam $1_{3aA,7aB,9cA}$ that elsewhere the term points to the affliction suffered by Judah and Jerusalem and this may provide a clue to our understanding. In the remainder of the song, however, the גֶּבֶר is left to express his affliction in his own words and further exegesis will have to determine the extent to which his עֳנִי is identical with that of the city and the land.[16]

1B ...*under the scourge of his anger.* בְּשֵׁבֶט עֶבְרָתוֹ

While the content of the גֶּבֶר's affliction remains unspecified, the same cannot be said for its cause: בְּשֵׁבֶט עֶבְרָתוֹ. שֵׁבֶט can sometimes refer to the

[14] For the many parallels with Ps 88 see 1983, 235, 238 and 250.

[15] Present tense: cf 1_{1aA} and GES-K § 106*g*.

[16] For the present colon as a relative subordinate clause with a change of actant see GES-K § 155*f*.

sceptre of a ruler or king (cf Ps 45_7 and 125_3) but it can also signify a scourge or rod with which one beats those who have transgressed in some way (cf Ex 20_{21}) and this latter interpretation is clearly intended here.

Scourging was considered a form of punishment or discipline.[17] In the present context the scourge is used in a figurative sense, providing an image of the repercussions of the anger with which the גֶּבֶר is confronted. The present strophe does not identify the one wielding the scourge but it seems reasonable to assume that the suffix of עֶבְרָתוֹ refers back to the end of the second song. Since, as we already noted above, the first person singular also extends from 2_{22} into 3_1, then 2_{22aB} בְּיוֹם אַף־יְהוָה provides the clue to the identity of the scourger. עֶבְרָה is similar in meaning to אַף.[18] Thus it would appear that the devouring anger confronting the גֶּבֶר is none other than that of YHWH himself.[19] The fact that the גֶּבֶר must endure this same wrath is further proof that the catastrophe confronting the land is also a source of personal affliction for him.

The image of YHWH's anger as a scourge or rod is not new. Its earlier use in Isa 10_5 is somewhat illuminating because the author of this verse employs it to embody YHWH's anger in the form of a foreign power (Assyria), a notion which also firmly coincides with the theological train of thought found in Lamentations. Time and again the poets express their conviction that YHWH is at work behind the rage of the enemy.[20]

2A *He drives me forth and makes me go...* אוֹתִי נָהַג וַיֹּלַךְ

'To drive (forth)' is the *qal* of √נהג I, the original meaning of which had to do with the actions of a shepherd leading his flock towards their destination.[21] The shepherds actions could be gentle (Isa 11_6) or hard (Gen 31_{13}). In combination with different objects, the verb took on a variety of meanings such as to ride a chariot (II Kgs 9_{20}), to deport prisoners of war (Isa 20_4), to drag off human beings as booty (I Sam 30_2) or to take one's family members with one (I Sam 30_{22}).

The present context shows that √נהג I – with YHWH as subject and גֶּבֶר as object – certainly does not imply peaceful intentions. YHWH has driven the גֶּבֶר forth as a victorious army its prisoners.[22] Given the *hiph'il* imperfect of

[17] Cf Prov 10_{13}, 22_{15} etcetera.
[18] Cf TWAT V 1037 (Schunck).
[19] For further detail on the significance of עֶבְרָה see the explanation of 2_{2aA}.
[20] Cf $1_{17,21}$, $2_{17,20,22}$ etcetera.
[21] Cf HAL 637f.
[22] Cf TWAT V 276f (Groß).

√הלך, it would appear that YHWH's actions have a determined destination in mind.

2B ... *into darkness and no light.* חֹשֶׁךְ וְלֹא־אוֹר

At first hearing this tautological phrase comes across as somewhat impressionistic. The repetition clearly indicates a place of absolute darkness but what sort of actual experience does it intend to imply? Both the immediate and the broader context suggest that we should understand the image as the consequence of YHWH's judgement. Thus the final cola of each bicolon within the first strophe are parallel: שֵׁבֶט עֶבְרָתוֹ (1B) // חֹשֶׁךְ וְלֹא־אוֹר (2B) // יָדוֹ כָּל־הַיּוֹם (3B). We already noted the responsive relationship between the individual songs on this point: בַּלַּיְלָה (1_2) // יָעִיב (2_1) // חֹשֶׁךְ וְלֹא־אוֹר (3_2) // יְשֵׁנָא (4_1). If we respect this relationship at the level of content then the גֶּבֶר must be referring to the 'night' of Lady Jerusalem and the fall and destruction of Zion. Within the א-strophe (3_{1-3}), the parallelism between the final cola of each bicolon shows that these are the effects of YHWH's wrath. Thus the expression 'darkness and no light' suggests an implicit recognition of the fulfilment of a former announcement of judgement on the part of YHWH since חֹשֶׁךְ וְלֹא־אוֹר is borrowed from earlier prophetic announcements of judgement. It can be found literally stated in Amos' proclamation of the day of YHWH as the hour of God's judgement over Israel (Am 5_{18}).

3 *Yes, against me again and again turns* אַךְ בִּי יָשֻׁב יַהֲפֹךְ
his hand all day long. יָדוֹ כָּל־הַיּוֹם

Whenever the root שׁוב is accompanied by another verb one must interpret the action implied by the verb in question as repeated action,[23] in the present case the action implied by the expression (בְּ) הָפַךְ יָד. This expression is used elsewhere for the action of driving or steering a chariot, and is suggestive of the charioteer pulling on the reins to steer his horse in a different direction (cf I Kgs 22_{34}; II Kgs 9_{23} and HAL 243). KBL 240 considers the combination of √הפך and √שׁוב to be a gesture of rejection and Seybold follows this line of thought.[24] There are, however, no alternative texts which might confirm such a claim. It seems preferable, therefore, to stick with the translation 'pull on the reins', especially since the image it suggests is quite fitting in the context. Given that the בְּשֵׁבֶט עֶבְרָתוֹ in 3_{1B}

[23] Cf KBL 952 and HAL 1331.
[24] See TWAT II 455.

has already portrayed the image of YHWH's anger as a hostile power and given that the גֶּבֶר in the previous bicolon was portrayed as a prisoner of war being driven forth by his captor (√נהג I), the impression given in the present bicolon of YHWH as a charioteer careering from side to side in hot pursuit of a prisoner who is attempting to escape is far from being an inapprpriate metaphor. The גֶּבֶר employs these images to reveal how profound his feeling of being hounded by YHWH really is and to show that there is no possibility of escape from the disasters confronting him (חֹשֶׁךְ וְלֹא־אוֹר). As with the first two songs, the present situation is also marked by ongoing affliction which has its roots in past disaster. Indeed, the temporal indicator כָּל־הַיּוֹם, 'all day long', appears to confirm this fact and further supports a present translation of the perfects (cf 1_1).

A theological contrast is also evident in the present text. On two earlier occasions in the songs there was mention of YHWH's hand: 1_{14} in which YHWH binds the yoke of Lady Jerusalem's sins to her back and 2_{18} in which YHWH does not withold his hand from destruction. The present usage is equally negative. The contrast with salvation history is clear: in former times YHWH's hand was turned against the enemy and was a source of protection for Israel.[25]

4A *He makes my flesh and skin waste away,* בִּלָּה בְשָׂרִי וְעוֹרִי

The *qal* of √בלה means 'to be consumed'/'to be worn out'. The *pi'el* form employed here has an intensive function and suggests 'to make disappear'.[26] What the poets are implying here are the physical and visible consequences of the affliction being endured by the גֶּבֶר. The fact that his skin is 'wasting away' is a powerful reference to the emaciation brought on by the famine. At the same time, however, it also points to the unbearable tension and restlessness confronting the גֶּבֶר.[27] A person's skin can reflect his or her psychological condition. Hunger makes one's skin dry out, thereby causing it to fade and lose its lustre. It is worth noting that $4_{7,8}$ portrays a similar physical consequence of famine, setting up a contrast with the once radiant good health of the aristocracy. It is possible that the poets are suggesting here that the גֶּבֶר might be (on the literary level) one of the aristocracy mentioned in 4_{7aA}. The enormous contrast described in the latter verses is also present here.

[25] See TWAT III 448f (Ackroyd).
[26] Cf HAL 127.
[27] See also the exegesis of 3_{20}.

4B *he breaks my bones.* שִׁבַּר עַצְמוֹתָי

If one compares this colon with the laments found in the Psalms then one cannot fail to note that precisely the same combination of words is employed in Ps 32_3: עֶצֶם + √בלה: 'my bones waste away'. The lament in question is certainly superceded in seriousness by the present complaint. There would appear to be an almost conscious opposition being set up between this colon and the content of Ps 34_{21} where YHWH in contrast protects the bones of the righteous so that not one of them is broken. Where it was still possible to offer a fairly literal explanation of the previous colon, the expression employed here calls for a figurative interpretation, 'bones' standing for something other than the actual bones of the גֶּבֶר. There is much to support the assumption that the bones represented the entire person.[28] Our modern day expression 'flesh and blood' had is Hebrew equivalent in the expression 'flesh and bones'.[29] Indeed, in both Ps 6_3 and 22_{15}, 'bones' are paralleled with the human person as such.[30] In Ps 51_{10}, the author prays that his shattered bones might rejoice once again. In Isa 38_{13} the dying Hezekiah laments that YHWH has broken his bones like a lion (combination of עֶצֶם + √שׁבר), thus revealing the presence of a response at the canticle level within the present canto: שִׁבַּר עַצְמוֹתָי (3_{4B}) // אַרְיֵה בְּמִסְתָּרִים (3_{10B}).

If one interprets the 'bones' of the גֶּבֶר as representative of his entire person then the significance of the expression becomes clear: he is a broken man. The human skeleton carries and supports the body and without it no one could remain standing. The expression can be similarly understood in the spiritual sense: the withdrawal of YHWH's support in life is exactly the same as the breaking of person's bones (cf Isa 38_{13}). The cola 3_{4A} and 3_{4B} both point to a totality: flesh and skin constitute, in a certain sense, the visible exterior of the human person while bones signify the load bearing interior. Attack both and you attack the entire person. Finally, note should be taken of the song responses between the present colon and Lam II and IV. In Lam 2_2, YHWH breaks apart both city and land, here in 3_{4B} he makes a broken man of the גֶּבֶר while in Lam 4_2 the children of Zion are compared with broken pieces of pottery. What happens to a person externally resonates to his very core.

---

[28] OKeel, *Die Welt der altorientalischen Bildsymbolik und das Alte Testament*, Zürich-Einsiedeln-Köln-Neukirchen-Vluyn 1977[2], 57 and TWAT VI 328f (Beyse).

[29] Cf Gen 2_{23}, 29_{14}, Judg 9_2, II Sam 5_1.

[30] Cf also Prov 16_{24B} with נֶפֶשׁ // עֶצֶם and Ps 53_6.

5A *He builds a rampart about me and surrounds me...* בָּנָה עָלַי וַיַּקַּף

The combination of √בנה + the preposition עַל is a *terminus technicus* for the building of a siege wall against a city.[31] The following consecutive imperfect וַיַּקַּף (from √נקף II) meaning 'to surround' is employed in similar military circumstances (cf II Kgs 6_{14}, 11_{8}) and as such can also be found in laments in which the petitioner is surrounded by his or her enemies (cf Ps 17_{9}, 88_{18}). Once again a responsive connection with the ב-strophe of the second song (2_{2}) is clearly present, especially via the cogent agreement between the central bicola. The ב-strophe also speaks of the tearing down of the (walls of) fortified cities which were first surrounded then hemmed in with siege walls. The imagery employed here is perfectly appropriate. The antithetical word-pair הרס \\ בנה also occurs with relative frequency.[32]

5B *... with poison and hardship.* רֹאשׁ וּתְלָאָה

Van Selms considers the imagery employed in the first colon to be continued here and, although without proper argumentation, is convinced that the terms רֹאשׁ and תְּלָאָה refer to some sort of building material because the customary interpretation of 'poison' and 'hardship' seem out of place in the second colon. LXX understands רֹאשׁ simply as κεφαλήν μου, 'my head'[33] and does not appear to concern itself further with the meaning of the expression. Gordis and Hillers both emend רֹאשׁ to read רִישׁ, 'poverty' (cf Prov 6_{11}) and Gordis proposes the translation: "He has built and surround me with poverty and trouble." In the last analysis, neither Van Selms nor Gordis are convincing.

Objections to the MT are, in my opinion, unfounded. Both nouns appear – in similar contexts – with some frequency in the OT.[34] רֹאשׁ refers to a vegetable based poison derived from plants and is compared or used instead of snake venom in Deut 32_{33}. The actual identity of the plant(s) in question is not clear.[35] תְּלָאָה is employed to refer to the hardship Israel endured in Egypt under Pharao's regime and thereafter (cf Num 20_{14ff}). Neh 9_{32} characterises the entire period from the Assyrian oppression to the exile and beyond as a time filled with תְּלָאָה.

---

31 Cf Deut 20_{20}, Ezek 4_{2} and Eccl 9_{14}.

32 Cf Jer 24_{6}, 42_{10}, 45_{4}, Ezek 36_{36}, Mal 1_{4}, Ps 28_{5}, Prov 14_{1}, Job 12_{14} etcetera.

33 Cf text critical apparatus of BHS.

34 Cf HAL 1089 sv רֹאשׁ and 1600 sv תְּלָאָה.

35 See the detailed discussion in WMcKane, 'Poison, Trial by Ordeal and the Cup of Wrath', VT XXX (1980), 478ff.

It remains a question whether 'poison' and 'hardship' indicate the consquences of enemy hostility and nothing more. McKane is of the opinion that there is a relationship with YHWH's judgement: the drinking of the cup of judgement in which the wine becomes poisonous because of the people's guilt (cf Num 5_{11-31}). To support his line of thought he points, for example, to Jer 8_{14} where there is mention of an immanent hostile invasion of Judah. The text in question displays a certain internal contradiction. On the one hand, the people flee to the fortified cities in order to escape the enemy while, on the other hand, their flight turns out to be pointless because the fortified cities cannot hold back YHWH's judgement: he soaks them with רֹאשׁ and, in spite of their fortified cities, they die because they have sinned. In light of this Jeremian text the song-response between 3_{5B} and 2_{2b} is all the more striking, since in the latter text there is mention of YHWH's destruction of the fortified cities. Poison and hardship, therefore, are not simply the consequence of enemy hostility, they are the result of YHWH's judgement which has enemy hostility as its consequence. The גֶּבֶר is in fact suffering the results of YHWH's judgement[36] but that does not yet imply that personal sin was its cause. As a matter of fact, the גֶּבֶר's bitter tone denies such a possibility. The songs themselves are aware of other individuals who are primarily to blame for the present disaster and who must bear the lion's share of the responsibility. Nevertheless, the consequences of their transgressions do not leave the גֶּבֶר unaffected. The external facts of conquest and destruction resonate in the interior of the גֶּבֶר and he experiences at a personal level the affliction which results therefrom. His bitterness in this regard also determines the tone of the present sub-canto, as we can see from the comparison of the canto-response with the מ-strophe (3_{37-39}) in canto II, in particular with 3_{39} where there is mention of murmuring among the גְּבָרִים. The connection between the *hithpolel* of √אנן in 3_{39} and תְּלָאָה here is determined by the so-called wilderness tradition (Num 20_{14ff}). In our context it is in fact the גֶּבֶר who is murmuring and it is clear that his fate has, in a sense, forced him into it.

6 *He makes me dwell in dark places,* בְּמַחֲשַׁכִּים הוֹשִׁיבַנִי
like the dead of long ago. כְּמֵתֵי עוֹלָם

Ps 143_3 is identical to and probably dependant upon this verse.[37] The noun מַחְשָׁךְ 'dark place' can be found a further six times in the OT. While

[36] Cf the inclusion חֹשֶׁךְ וְלֹא־אוֹר (3_{2B}) // רֹאשׁ וּתְלָאָה (3_{5B}).
[37] See 1983, 254f.

its use in Isa 29_{15} suggests 'hidden places' where things happen which do not deserve to see the light of day – a similar interpretation being possible for the difficult text of Ps 74_{20} [38] – such a translation is not quite so obvious in the present context. The remaining texts where the term can be found are Isa 42_{16} and Ps $88_{7,19}$, texts in which the meaning of מַחְשָׁךְ leans in the direction of deadly affliction and calamity.[39] Given the many other points of correspondence with Ps 88,[40] however, the use of the term in this psalm is certainly the most interesting. In Ps 88_{18} we encounter the combination נקף עַל ('to surround'), terminology also found in the present immediate context, namely in Lam 3_5. We are thereby justified in seeking an interpretation of the Lamentations use of the term מַחְשָׁךְ in the light of Ps 88. At the same time Ps $88_{6,7}$ are strongly reminiscent of Lam 3_6. Thus the use of מַחְשָׁךְ in the present colon implies the realm of the dead. The following colon confirms this, calling up ideas of the grave.[41] The גֶּבֶר is already a part of this dark realm, a fact confirmed in 3_{16B} and in 5_{18} where Zion, the dwelling place of the גֶּבֶר is described as a necropolis. There is a clear relationship present here, therefore, between the lament as such and the mourning lament or dirge (contra Westermann who does not consider this to be the case in Lam III). Threatened by ultimate death at the hands of the enemy – a consequence of YHWH's poison and hardship –, the גֶּבֶר stands with one foot already in the grave (cf 2_{20c}). One of the characteristic afflictions of the underworld is the experience of abandonment by God. Although YHWH retains his power in this realm,[42] he does not pay heed to it.[43] For his/her part the human person is also no longer able to praise YHWH.[44] The metaphor of Lady Jerusalem the 'widow', abandoned by her husband YHWH, appears to be made more concrete here in the deathly abandonment experienced by the גֶּבֶר.

The image of the underworld also implies separation from the (beloved) living. Ps 88_{19} speaks of אֹהֵב (pt) and רֵעַ, the dearest and nearest who have deserted the sorely afflicted lamenter. The sense of abandonment is

---

38 Cf JRidderbos, *De Psalmen II*, Kampen 1958, 263, KBL 515 and HAL 542.

39 For Isa 42_{16} see JLKoole, *Jesaja II, deel I Jesaja 40 tot en met 48*, Kampen 1985, 180.

40 See 1983, 235, 238 and 250.

41 For our translation of עוֹלָם as 'long ago' cf THAT II 230 (Jenni).

42 Cf Ps 139_8, Am 9_2.

43 Ps 6_6, 88_6; cf GvRad, *Theologie des Alten Testaments, Band I, Die Theologie der geschichtlichen Überlieferungen Israels*, München 1966[5], 401.

44 Cf Ps 6_6, 30_{10}, 88_{11f}, 115_{17}; see also KSpronk, *Beatific Afterlife in Ancient Israel and in the Ancient Near East*, AOAT 219, Neukirchen-Vluyn 1986, 283f.

expressed once more with the term מַחְשָׁךְ: the lamenter sits in darkness and can no longer see another soul (cf Ps 88_9). It appeared from the previous bicolon that the poets had made an intentional connection with Lam 2_2. In the present context, the connection is clearly with Lam 1_2 where there is likewise mention of אֹהֲבֶיהָ (1_{2bB}) and רֵעֶיהָ (1_{2cA}), the lovers and intimates of Lady Jerusalem who betrayed her and left her in the lurch. Lady Jerusalem's 'night' is identical with the darkness into which YHWH has driven the גֶּבֶר.

Canticle II (3_{7-12})

Content/theme: *the sentry leers at his prisoners like a beast of prey*

Literary argumentation:

inclusions:	גָּדַר (7A) // דָּרַךְ (12A)[45]
ext par:	נְתִיבֹתַי עִוָּה (9B) // דְּרָכַי סוֹרֵר (11A)
	דְּרָכַי (9A) // דְּרָכַי (11A)
alliteration:	גָּדַר (7A) // גָּדַר (9A)
	דְּרָכַי (9A) // דְּרָכַי (11A) // דָּרַךְ (12A)[46]

The delimitation of the present canticle is not a simple matter. One might defend the idea that, at the level of content, 3_7 is a continuation of 3_6: YHWH stands guard over the prisoners in his underworld prison. The continuation of a line of thought, however, does not oblige us to apply the same boundaries to the literary units as we do to 'thought-units'. This is already evident at the strophe level where the literary units are clearly marked by the alphabetic acrostic. At the level of content, there is no doubt that bicola 3_{12} and 3_{13} belong together but at the literary level they constitute consecutive strophes. For this reason we can speak of concatination (at the content level) between strophes and canticles, literary units being linked to one another by way of smooth transitions.

7A *He builds a wall around me, I cannot escape;* גָּדַר בַּעֲדִי וְלֹא אֵצֵא

The *qal* of √גדר means 'to erect a wall'.[47] Such a wall could also serve as a sort of barricade, blocking a road or path.[48] Hos 2_8 and Job 19_8 are

[45] Metathesis. Cf also the inclusion between 3_{46} and 3_{54}: פָּצוּ // צָפוּ. See note 397.

[46] Cf WGEWatson, *Classical Hebrew Poetry. A Guide to its Techniques*, JSOT suppl series 26, Sheffield 1984, 227.

[47] Ezek 13_5, 22_{30}; cf HAL 173.

[48] Cf Hos 2_5 (MT 2_8) Job 19_8.

not infrequently chosen as the guiding principle for the translation of this verse: 'He blocks my path' (cf NBG). Our preference remains, however, with the first interpretation. The preposition (here with suffix 1 sg) can mean 'behind' but it can also mean 'around' (cf HAL 135). We opt, therefore, for the latter interpretation 'around'.[49] The dark places into which YHWH has forced the גֶּבֶר have now become a hermetically sealed prison from which there is no possibility of escape. Once more there is evidence of a turn about in the גֶּבֶר's salvific expectations: God, who provided and, indeed, was a protective rampart, has now set up a prison wall. גדר can signify a city wall (Ps 89_{41}, Mic 7_{11}). Ezra 9_9 reports that YHWH provided a wall (גָּדֵר) around his people, or was himself that wall.[50] There is little doubt that the image of YHWH as a protective wall is in line with pre-exilic Zion theology.[51] YHWH is guarantor of his people's safety. The parallel verse in Lam 2_3 reports the opposite: YHWH removes his people's protection by cutting off the horns of Israel. Here in 3_7, the same notion is further explicated in reverse, as it were: YHWH does not only destroy the protective wall surrounding his people (cf Ps 89_{41}), he builds a new wall, a prison wall to incarcerate his people.

7B *he makes heavy my metal chains.* הִכְבִּיד נְחָשְׁתִּי

Chained up in his prison, the גֶּבֶר is barely able to move (cf 3_{9B}). He is held fast with brass/bronze chains, perhaps the strongest chains possible (cf Deut 33_{25}). As fetters, brass chains are known elsewhere in the OT.[52] The גֶּבֶר's brass chains, however, are not the work of human hands but that of YHWH who makes them heavy and strong. They constitute, thus, maximum security chains from which there is absolutely no escape. To break such chains is an impossible task for human beings. There is only One who can destroy them: the One who made them and used them to bind the גֶּבֶר fast. Given the fact that the term for 'chains' is found elsewhere in the dual form,[53] the singular נְחָשְׁתִּי of the present verse is unusual. Rudolph and BHS are thereby inclined to propose that we vocalise נְחָשְׁתַּי as a dual with a 1 sg suffix. The singular of the LXX (χαλκόν μου), however, argues otherwise. Where foot and hand restraints are concerned

---

49 Cf NEB: "He has walled me in...".

50 Cf HHGrosheide, *Ezra – Nehemia*, Kampen 1963, 260 and TWAT II 811 (In der Smitten).

51 See the explanation of 2_{9a}.

52 Cf Judg 16_{21}, II Kgs 25:7 etcetera; cf also HAL 653.

53 Cf II Sam 3_{34}, Jer 39_7 etcetera.

the dual form would seem the most natural but a single chain also appears to be a possibility. One can determine from Ps 105_{18}, for example, that a sort of neck-chain was also employed as a kind of fetter, although the interpretation of this text has been the subject of dispute.[54] Figure 134 in Keel[55] supports the notion of a neck-chain. On the basis of the final bicolon of the present strophe we interpret the singular as a collective (cf Ps 107_{10}). The reference is to 'chains' in general without specification of sort.

8A *Even when I cry out and call for help...* גַּם כִּי אֶזְעַק וַאֲשַׁוֵּעַ

Imprisoned and fettered with no chance of escape, the גֶּבֶר has only one option left to make contact with the outside world: his voice. He cries out and appeals to his jailer for help. HAL (266) ascribes the same meaning to √זעק as it does to √צעק in 2_{18a} 'the cry of a human being in acute distress'. The present context, however, evidently does not employ the same notation as in 2_{18a} (ז instead of צ). Albertz[56] explains the difference in notation as a question of dialect. Hasel,[57] however, correctly points out that this has not been proven. It is interesting that both 'spellings' should occur side by side in the same textual corpora (also in Aramaic, Arabic and other Semitic languages) as is clearly the case here in Lamentations. On the basis of this observation Hasel assumes that in reality both spellings were employed in an arbitrary fashion. Such an explanation remains unsatisfactory. One possible explanation for the use of √זעק instead of √צעק may be the combination in the present colon with √שוע I, a fairly frequent combination[58] which suggests a more or less fixed expression. Where both verbs are combined the 'spelling' זעק is always used. The root צעק stands for the utterance of a primitive cry of distress by a person suffering acute affliction. The root זעק, on the other hand, – when combined with √שוע implies greater flexibility of meaning. When addressed to YHWH, forms of √זעק function as prayers of entreaty.[59]

---

54 Cf HJKraus, *Psalmen, 60–150*, BKAT XV/2, Neukirchen 1978[5], 890.

55 OKeel, *Die Welt der altorientalischen Bildsymbolik und das Alte Testament*, Zürich-Einsiedeln-Köln-Neukirchen-Vluyn 1977[2], 92. His explanatory remarks concerning "Gefängnis, Zisterne und Fallgrube" on pages 60–63 are also enlightening in relation to the general atmosphere of the third song.

56 In THAT II 568, in line with BL 28*v*.

57 See TWAT II 630.

58 See Hab 1_2, Job 19_7, 35_9; cf Exod 2_{23}.

59 Cf Ps 18_{42}, 22_{25}, 88_{14}, Jona 2_3 etcetera.

8B *...he rejects my prayer.* שָׂתַם תְּפִלָּתִי

The fact that the root שׂתם is found only here perhaps explains why a number of manuscripts employ the better attested √סתם.[60] The basic meaning of the root is 'to hide, conceal'. In the light of 3_{44}, however, the idea that YHWH 'hides' the prayer of the גֶּבֶר is far from evident. At the same time, a reflexive interpretation of the *qal* here (YHWH hides himself) would appear to be inadmissible. Followed by Gottwald and Albrektson, Driver opts for a derivative of an Arabic verb meaning 'to reject'/'to frustrate' (a desire or prayer).[61] Something similar seems to be implied in the present context. The sense of bitter contrast is certainly more than apparent: YHWH, the very one who hears his people's prayer (Ps 65_3), now refuses to listen. The term תְּפִלָּה, 'prayer' primarily suggests the notion of supplication,[62] the sort of prayer one directs to YHWH in time of distress. It is quite understandable that the גֶּבֶר resorts to this kind of prayer. YHWH has fettered him, only YHWH can undo his fetters (cf Ps 107_{16}). The song response between 3_8 and 2_{3b} appears to resonate in this fashion, with the mention of the withdrawal of YHWH's right hand and the consequenct distress and restlessness (cf 1_{3b} and 5_3) which are its result. In lamenting YHWH's unwillingness to listen to his prayer, the גֶּבֶר himself makes a distinction between his bitter complaint and prayer as such. The fact that YHWH refused to hear him must, at the very least, have given the גֶּבֶר much food for thought (cf Isa 1_{15}).

9A *He walls off my ways with hewn stones,* גָּדַר דְּרָכַי בְּגָזִית

The root גדר obviously bears the same meaning here as it does in 3_{7A}, namely 'to build a wall around...'. The term suggests a square shaped, hewn stone intended for wall building.[63] The 'hewn stone' element is new in respect to 3_{7A}. Isa 9_9, among others, suggests that the term refers to sound and sturdy building material. The authors are telling us here that YHWH has not only walled the גֶּבֶר in but he has used the sturdiest materials for the purpose. Hewn stone building blocks fit together prefectly, are too heavy to move and therefore cannot be levered apart. The גֶּבֶר thus underlines the inescapable nature of his prison. No matter where he turns he is confronted by walls.

[60] Cf KBL 933 and 688, HAL 1271 and 728.

[61] GRDriver, 'Hebrew Notes on "Song of Songs" and "Lamentations" ', Fs ABertholet, Tübingen 1950, 139.

[62] Cf Ps 102_1 and THAT II 430 (Stähli).

[63] Cf I Kgs $7_{9,11}$, Ezra 6_4 etcetera.

9B *my paths he makes twisted.* נְתִיבֹתַי

The term נְתִיבָה 'path' can be used literally as well as figuratively and is a synonym of the term דֶּרֶךְ 'way'. The basic meaning of the verb עוה is 'to bend'/'to twist' as can be found in Ps 38_7 (*niph'al*: 'I am bent'). Both Knierim (THAT II 244) and Koch (TWAT V 1161f) offer an interpretation of the present usage of the verb, Knierim: "den (Lebens-)Pfad krümmen"; Koch: 'to make one's path through life impassible'. In light of the other images employed in the context, however, a more concrete interpretation would appear to be more fitting. If one imagines the wall which YHWH has built around his prisoners then one might picture a round prison within which the גֶּבֶר with his heavy chains can only walk around in circles. We noted elsewhere[64] via a similar word combination (√ גדר and נְתִיבָה) in Hos 2_5 (MT 2_8) that the present text had affinities with an announcement of doom. In the Hosea text YHWH builds his wall with thorns and stones in order to cut off the path of his adulterous wife, Lady Israel, towards her lovers.[65] While YHWH's salvific intention to win back his people is implicit in Hosea, the wall he builds in the present context is clearly intended to separate him from his people. With the reversal of this implicit announcement of salvation, the גֶּבֶר reveals how radical his separation from YHWH has become.

10 *He is a bear lying in wait for me,* דֹּב אֹרֵב הוּא לִי
a lion in ambush. אֲרִיֵה בְּמִסְתָּרִים

At first sight it would appear that the image of the גֶּבֶר as prisoner is being superseded in the present bicolon by the metaphor of YHWH as a beast of prey which has set its sights on the גֶּבֶר as its next meal. On closer inspection, however, such an interpretation seems improbable since it interrupts the evident consistency of the poets' chosen imagery which portrays YHWH as the enemy and the גֶּבֶר as his prisoner. At the end of the strophe, the poets continue to employ the image of YHWH as a hostile soldier standing guard over the גֶּבֶר. While the same is ultimately true for the present bicolon, therefore, we can understand the metaphors of the bear and the lion lying in ambush as a sort of descriptive elaboration on the image of YHWH as a prison warder introduced in the preceding verses.

The beast of prey metaphors employed here by the poets are far from abstract images. Both lion and bear were well known in the Old Tes-

[64] See 1983, 264.
[65] That is to her idols; cf CvLeeuwen, *Hosea*, Nijkerk 1968, 60.

tament period.[66] Jer 49_{19} and 50_{44} speaks of the lion concealed in the thickets beside the river Jordan (cf Jer 4_7). The bear was well known for its aggressive nature (cf Prov 28_{15}), especially the female bear when it was robbed of its young.[67] Keel points out that the dangerous Syrian bear was also known in Egypt. Both bear and lion are mentioned together on several occasions in the OT,[68] thus making it all the more striking that the bear is absent from the animal imagery employed in the Psalms. Keel explains this as follows: "Die Pss bewegen sich stärker als andere atl Bücher in einer gemein-altorientalischen Vorstellungs- und Formenwelt. Da der Bär in den flachen Flußtälern Mesopotamiens und Ägyptens fehlt, fehlt er auch in ihren Dämonenschilderungen und Königsvergleichen."[69] The image of the bear and the lion lying in ambush, in contrast, is well represented among the prophecies of doom and it is from this source that the poets of Lamentations have borrowed the comparison. In prophecies of doom, being devoured by lion and bear was employed as an image of YHWH's judgement.[70] Once again there are strong connections evident with Hosea's prophecy of doom. Hosea employs the powerful image of YHWH as a lion(ess) tearing its prey to pieces and as a young female bear which has been robbed of its young (cf Hos 5_{14}, 13_{7-8}). Via the context of calamity to be expected on the day of YHWH, the connection between Am 5_{19} and Lam 3_{10} is even closer.

The link with such prophecies of doom, however, is far from complete. The absence of the image of 'being devoured' constitues an important difference with respect to Hos 13_{7f} where it is employed to portray the very end of Israel's existence. The absence of the image in the present context is significant: no matter how dreadful the גֶּבֶר's situation, he is still alive. This realisation, nevertheless, must remain marginal, given the aforementioned canticle response between YHWH as a lion and the broken bones of the גֶּבֶר in 3_{4B} (cf Isa 38_{13}). The גֶּבֶר is face to face with the threat of complete anihilation at the hands of YHWH.

The use of the expression בְּמִסְתָּרִים places the emphasis on the image of

[66] Cf the drawings of lions in AOB 399 and ANEP 228.

[67] See II Sam 17_8, Prov 17_{12}; cf II Kgs 2_{24}.

[68] Cf I Sam 17_{34ff}, Prov 28_{15}, Isa 11_7, Hos 13_8, Am 5_{19}.

[69] In OKeel, *Die Welt der altorientalischen Bildsymbolik und das Alte Testament*, Zürich-Einsiedeln-Köln-Neukirchen-Vluyn 1977[2], 78.

[70] For the use of theriomorphic metaphors in the context of YHWH's judgement see Botterweck (TWAT I 413) and MCAKorpel, *A Rift in the Clouds*, Münster 1990, 538–541.

beasts of prey lying in ambush, ready to attack. The term מִסְתָּר suggests a 'hiding place',[71] although the present context leans more towards the notion of a concealed spot from which a beast of prey might suddenly attack its quarry (cf Ps 10_9). For this reason we translate 'in ambush'. The גֶּבֶר is thus confronted with his divine jailer: a prison warder without emotion or reason, a beast of prey awaiting the first opportunity to kill and devour him. The image of wild animals lying in ambush has its actual equivalent in the lurking enemy observing the Judeans' desperate flight.[72] Such contradictory behaviour on the part of YHWH is extraordinary indeed (cf Job 10_{16}).

11A *I want to escape, but he rips me open;* דְּרָכַי סוֹרֵר וַיְפַשְּׁחֵנִי

Up to the present day, the *hapax* √פשׁח and the unique *polel* form סוֹרֵר have been the cause of much brain racking among exegetes. Rudolph interprets סוֹרֵר as a verb derived from the noun סִי(רָה) (= 'thorn') and translates: "er sperrte meine Wege mit Dornen."[73] His objection to the more usual derivation from √סור (= 'bend'/'yield') claims that we would then be left with a simple repetition of 3_{9B}. Such an objection, however, remains unnecessary. The present bicolon ought to be understood as a continuation of the metaphor of the jailer as a beast of prey lying in ambush. Anyone confronted with a wild animal which is ready to attack would certainly try to escape (cf Job 10_{16}). Such is the intention of דְּרָכַי סוֹרֵר וַיְפַשְּׁחֵנִי, literally: 'He makes my ways evasive'. The presence of √סור with the same meaning in 4_{15} supports our translation 'to escape'.[74] The prisoner evades his guard but not completely. While it is true that the גֶּבֶר is not dead, the claws of the beast of prey tear at his flesh nevertheless. Thus we ought to understand the expression וַיְפַשְּׁחֵנִי as a derivative of the *hapax* √פשׁח, 'to rip open'.[75]

11B *he destroys me.* שָׂמַנִי שֹׁמֵם

The text literally states: 'he sets me (up) for destruction', which in more modern terminology might be expressed as: 'he has turned me into a

---

71 Cf Hab 3_{14}, Jer 23_{24}.

72 Cf 4_{18f}, likewise with √ארב I and 1_{3c}.

73 Cf the imagery employed in Hos 2_5 (MT 2_8).

74 Cf TWAT V 806: "Auch das einmalige *polel* hat kausative Bedeutung: '(der Löwe) hat mich vom Weg getrieben und zerrissen.'" (Snijders).

75 Cf HAL 921 as well as Rudolph who, nevertheless, maintains the idea of 'thorns' as the subject.

complete mess'. Lady Jerusalem says as much of herself in 1_{13cA} and of her sons in 1_{16cA}. In light of the use of the same verb, there is an apparent causal connection between material ruin and the 'ruination' of human persons: the destruction of Jerusalem destroys the inhabitants. It is hardly surprising, therefore, that the song-response with 1_{4bA} speaks of Zions's ruined gates (כָּל־שְׁעָרֶיהָ שׁוֹמֵמִין, cf 2_4) while 4_5 also echoes responsively in mentioning the ruination of Zion's children from hunger (נָשַׁמּוּ בַּחוּצוֹת).

Once again there appears to be a link between the גֶּבֶר and the sons of Jerusalem via the use of √שׁמם in 1_{16cA}. The primary purpose of the imagery employed here is to show how the imprisoned גֶּבֶר is suffering and being broken down by the spiritual and physical torments of his jailer. If we inquire into the reality behind such imagery then we can point to the parallel texts which speak of the destruction of his city and the debilitating famine.

12 *He bends his bow towards me in attack,* דָּרַךְ קַשְׁתּוֹ וַיַּצִּיבֵנִי
as target for his arrow. כַּמַּטָּרָא לַחֵץ

We already encountered the metaphor of YHWH as archer in the song-response in 2_4 where YHWH's arrows were employed as an image for his judgement which the inhabitants of Judah and Jerusalem were having to face in the form of famine, death and fire. Agreement with the present verse is apparent at the literary level in the common use of the expression דָּרַךְ קַשְׁתּוֹ and the √נצב (here in the *hiph'il*, meaning 'to establish'/'to position'; cf HAL 674f). YHWH himself is the subject, or more specifically 'his right hand' as mentioned in 2_{4aB} (using the same verb). When taking aim with a bow and arrow, the right hand is brought up to eye level and the target is fixed upon. The image is consistent with the remainder of the canticle. The גֶּבֶר is locked up in prison. Not only is he unable to escape but he is constantly tormented and threatened with death from the bow and arrow of his jailer. Thus the גֶּבֶר experiences his life as constantly overshadowed by YHWH's judgement.

Canticle III (3_{13-21})

Content/theme: YHWH *pounds his prisoner with derision, acrimony, hunger and thirst and deprives him of every hope*

Literary argumentation:

inclusions: בְּכִלְיוֹתָי (13A) // לִבִּי (21A)
הָיִיתִי שְׂחֹק (14A) // וְתָשִׁיחַ עָלַי נַפְשִׁי (20B)

(19B) לַעֲנָה // (15B) לַעֲנָה
(19A) וּמְרוּדִי // (15A) בַמְּרוֹרִים
(18B) אָבַד . . . וְתוֹחַלְתִּי מֵיְהוָה // (16B) הִכְפִּישַׁנִי בָּאֵפֶר
responses: (21B) אוֹחִיל // (18B) וְתוֹחַלְתִּי
(20B) נַפְשִׁי // (17A) נַפְשִׁי
asson/allit: (16B) הִכְפִּישַׁנִי בָּאֵפֶר // (15A) הִשְׂבִּיעַנִי

In terms of structure, the present canticle is positioned at the centre of the first canto (3_{1-33}) and, at the same time, at the end of the first sub-canto (3_{1-21}), both literary indications that these verses constitute a focal point in the composition. Within the canticle, two inclusions can be noted on the basis of similar sounding phraseology. As a matter of fact, the very number of inclusions evident in the canticle makes it is possible to speak of a strongly concentric structure, with the core formulation in 3_{17} – the centre of the present canticle – focusing on the distress and affliction of the גֶּבֶר (cf the introduction to the main exegetical features). 3_{17} is one of the two pivotal verses in the entire book, 3_{50} being the other.[76] Taken side by side they express the primary theme of the songs as a whole:

(3_{17}) וַתִּזְנַח מִשָּׁלוֹם נַפְשִׁי נָשִׁיתִי טוֹבָה
(3_{50}) עַד־יַשְׁקִיף וְיֵרֶא יְהוָה מִשָּׁמָיִם

13 *They penetrate my innards,* הֵבִיא בְּכִלְיוֹתָי
the arrows from his quiver. בְּנֵי אַשְׁפָּתוֹ

In spite of the fact that we begin a new canticle at this point, the imagery of YHWH as an archer continues on from the previous verse.[77] The partial repetition of 2_{4ab} provides the metaphor in question with a degree of emphasis. With regard to the conclusion of the previous canticle there is also a distinct progression in the present verse. Where the preceding canticle placed the accent on YHWH as a jailer lying in wait for the opportunity to injure his prisoner, the present verses portray the גֶּבֶר as one already wounded to the depths of his being.[78]

The arrows fired from YHWH's bow reach their target and deeply wound the גֶּבֶר, penetrating into his kidneys. Kellerman is perhaps correct in pointing out that such an image calls to mind the sharp pains associated with kidney stones, an ancient and well-known phenomenon.[79] Texts

[76] For more detailed argumenation see 1988, 321–334.

[77] For further detail on this phenomenon see the introduction to the second canticle (3_{7-12}).

[78] For 'arrows' as an image of YHWH's judgement see the explanation of 2_4 and 3_{12}.

dating back as early as those from Ugarit were already familiar with the image of arrows in the kidneys.[80] This does not, of course, exclude the further possibility of metaphorical usage. If the heart is to be understood today as the seat of every kind of human emotion, the kidneys functioned in a similar fashion in the world of the Old Testament (cf Prov 23_{15f}). The heart and the kidneys, therefore, are often found parallel to one another, as is the case here in the context of the inclusion בְּכִלְיוֹתָי (13A) // לִבִּי (21A).[81] The fact that the kidneys were understood as an essential part of the human person is apparent from Ps 139_{13} where God's formation of the human person in the womb of his or her mother is paralleled with the creation of his or her kidneys or inward parts. If the גֶּבֶר's kidneys have been breached by YHWH's arrows then it is clear that he feels himself pierced to the very essence of his being. It cannot get any worse than this! His very existence as a person is in the balance.[82]

The imagery employed here for the depths of human suffering is rather impressionistic in nature. Similar terms are used in the book of Job to indicate the depths of existential conflict (cf Job 16_{13}). Nevertheless, if one takes account of the parallel verses in the second song, the source of the גֶּבֶר's suffering is given a rather surprising concretisation. In the second song there was also talk of YHWH as a hostile archer whose arrows spelled death to 'all that pleased the eye' (2_{4bB}). The expression כֹּל מַחֲמַדֵּי־עָיִן appeared to refer to Zion's beloved children as well as her magnificent buildings. Some human beings are able to observe such matters in a detached way and then simply get on with the rest of their lives but with the גֶּבֶר the opposite is the case. Every fibre of his life is woven together with that of Zion and her children. Their destruction is his destruction, wounding him at the very core of his being.

14 *I am the laughing stock of all my people,*	הָיִיתִי שְּׂחֹק לְכָל־עַמִּי
their mocking-song all the day.	נְגִינָתָם כָּל־הַיּוֹם

The present bicolon contains a long standing exegetical crux which has had its repercussions in both the textual traditions and in the translations, namely the complication introduced by the singular 'my people'. The ridicule engaged in by the גֶּבֶר's countrymen and women would appear to be somewhat misplaced. Given that they are sharing the same

79 See TWAT IV 189.
80 Cf KTU 1.82.3.
81 The same parallel can be found in Ps 7_{10}, 26_2, 73_{21}, Jer 11_{20}, 17_{10}, 20_{12}.
82 Cf also TWAT IV 189 (Kellerman).

fate, their laughter and mockery must ultimately be seen as self-ridicule. For this reason the text is often emended to read 'my peoples'.[83] It has to be said, however, that the singular 'my people' is much more firmly anchored in the text tradition than the plural 'peoples'. Gordis also notes that the nature of the *sebirin*, which warn against obvious but nevertheless inaccurate readings, is often misunderstood.[84] One argument for a plural reading at the level of content might be borrowed from the suggestion that Lam III is a collective song, the 'I' in 3_{1A} being understood as a collective for Israel as a whole and not a single person. In such a view, the mocking laughter of the (surrounding) peoples is no longer out of place. The canto-response with 3_{46-48} (cf 2_{16}), where the mockery of the enemy is heard without ambiguity, further confirms this line of argument. We would appear, therefore, to have sufficient reason to reject our translational option for the singular 'my people' (see the introduction to Lam III). In 3_{46f}, however, there is clear evidence of a plural suffix (cf עָלֵינוּ).

The strongest objection to the singular עַמִּי is the apparent mocking laughter of the גֶּבֶר's countrymen and women who are nevertheless being confronted with the same affliction as he. The question remains, however, as to whether such an objection is valid. If the גֶּבֶר's own suffering were the butt of ridicule then the objection would be quite understandable, given that his people share a similar lot. The mocking laughter of the גֶּבֶר's people, however, appears to focus an another object altogether: not his affliction but rather his continued faith and trust in God. The bitter irony surrounding Job's wife, who at least partly endured the same suffering as her husband, serves as an analogy.[85] The concentric structure of the present canticle serves to confirm our analysis. There is an inclusion evident between הָיִיתִי שְּׂחֹק (3_{14A}) // וְתָשִׁיחַ עָלַי נַפְשִׁי (3_{20AB}) which establishes a quite striking link with Ps 42_{10-12} in which the same terminology and theme are present, the jeering question 'Where is your God?' being hurled at the oppressed yet faithful individual who is bent low under the weight of such mockery. One might argue, in my opinion incorrectly, that such faith and trust in God on the part of the גֶּבֶר is not the question here. As a matter of fact, the גֶּבֶר's faith and trust has always been implicitly present since his very 'גֶּבֶר-ness' implies a special relationship of trust in

[83] Cf, for example, Robinson, text critical apparatus of BHS, among other things on the basis of the *sebir*; cf also the detailed text-critical remarks in Albrektson and Gottlieb.

[84] See also ETov, *Textual Criticism of the Hebrew Bible*, Assen/Maastricht, 1992, 64.

[85] Job 2_9; cf Jer 20_{7f}, Job 12_4, Ps 69_{11ff}, Mk 15_{32} par.

YHWH (cf the explanation of 3_{1A}). It is also noteworthy that the גֶּבֶר never ascribes his personal suffering to an earthly enemy. Although he never names names, YHWH is the single cause of the גֶּבֶר's greatest and deepest affliction (cf 3_{1B}). This devout man is being visibly confronted with the enormous tension involved in continuing to have faith in a God who simultaneously frustrates and hurts him in every manner possible.

Those who ridicule him have clearly given up the struggle and have lost their faith in YHWH. In the very mention of כָל־עַמִּי (cf I Kgs $19_{10,14}$) we hear the frustration of the vast majority of his countrymen and women loudly echoed. Disillusioned by Zion's downfall, profoundly disappointed in their faith expectations, demoralised by hunger and left at death's door, the גֶּבֶר's people are without hope or dream. In such circumstances, who would dare to continue to call himself 'devout'? The גֶּבֶר's own words have turned him into a laughing stock (שְׂחֹק = laughter) and he knows it. It hurts too! Derision and insult can cut to the quick, especially when they come in the form of a mocking-song with which everyone can sing along.[86] Clearly the content of the present bicolon functions in the strophe as follows: the גֶּבֶר has stated that God has striken him in the worst possible way (3_{13}) and now his own people are adding insult to injury.

15A *He fills me with bitter herbs,* הִשְׂבִּיעַנִי בַמְּרוֹרִים

Commentators frequently opt for a figurative explanation of the present colon, the bitter herbs being seen as a symbol of the גֶּבֶר's bitter disposition as a result of the mocking laughter confronting him.[87] On the basis of the evident cohesion with the remaining songs, however, we opt for an alternative, more realistic interpretation of the expression. A conscious contrast can be established between the present colon and 4_{5A} where there is mention of the fact that Zion's children were used to eating the best of food. Now the גֶּבֶר is forced to eat nothing but bitter herbs. Once again we are confronted with profound disparity. A number of indications suggest that the eating of bitter herbs took place under pressure from the severest hunger. In the light of 2_4 and 3_{12}, YHWH's arrows in 3_{13} also turned out to be arrows of hunger. At the same level within the songs we can also point to associations with 1_{6bc} and 5_6 (with the same verb: [ל]שׂבע [לָחֶם]). The primary point of reference, however, is 4_{3-5}. As we shall see, the relationship between the present colon and these verses in the fourth song

[86] For נְגִינָה as 'mocking-song' cf Ps 69_{13} and Job 30_9.
[87] Cf, for example, TWAT V 17 (Ringgren).

extends beyond the aforementioned contrast. When there is a scarcity of food, people try to satisfy their hunger with what is at least edible.[88] Bitter herbs, a minor constituent of the Passover meal (Ex 12_8, Num 9_{11}), were apparently still available. As such they were the only type of food which could provide a feeling of satisfaction, although at the cost of tasting much bitterness which naturally had its effect in the frame of mind of those who had to resort to them for nourishment. Bitter herbs are not the kind of food which cheers the heart. It is not for nothing that Lady Jerusalem's lot is described in 1_{4cB} as one of 'bitterness'.

15B *gives me bitterness to drink.* הִרְוַנִי לַעֲנָה

Thirst is a judgement from God.[89] Although less is said of thirst than of hunger, the latter is explicitly mentioned nevertheless in 4_4 while 5_4 clearly states that water was only to be had at a price. Given the circumstances, it is not beyond the bounds of possibility that the inhabitants of Jerusalem and Judah endeavoured to lessen their thirst by drinking a (bitter) plant extract. The term לַעֲנָה is traditionally translated as 'wormwood'/'absinthe' but this is probably inaccurate. Worm-wood or absinthe is a drink made from the buds of *Artemisia absinthum* which, in spite of its extremely bitter taste, served in small quantities as a restorative for the stomach. If one were to employ לַעֲנָה to lessen one's thirst, however, the result would be serious poisoning. The question remains open, therefore, as to whether we ought still to identify לַעֲנָה in this way.[90] In spite of the fact that HAL 506 ascribes an exclusively metaphorical interpretation to the term, the image itself must be rooted in some reality or other. It is quite possible that the severity of their thirst forced the people to drink the sap of plants in spite of their bitter and poisonous taste. As such, the image can continue to function well in the context of an announcement of judgement (cf Jer 9_{15} [MT 9_{14}]). It is not impossible, furthermore, that the constant use of bitter herbs and plant juice led to kidney problems, whereby an associative link is established with 3_{13}. The entire picture turns out to be far more realistic than it first appeared to be. At the same time, the choice of words makes it clear that the experience is to be interpreted as the fulfilment of a prophecy of doom and disaster (cf Jer 23_{15} and the explanation of 3_5).

---

[88] Cf $1_{11b,19c}$, $2_{11f,20}$.

[89] Cf Am 4_8, Isa 5_{13}, 65_{13}, Hos 2_3 (MT 2_6).

[90] Cf TWAT IV 587 (Seybold) and WMcKane, 'Poison, Trial by Ordeal and the Cup of Wrath', VT XXX (1980), 483f.

16A *He makes me grind my teeth on gravel,* וַיַּגְרֵס בֶּחָצָץ שִׁנָּי

Kraus, followed by a number of others, considers the present text to propose the image of YHWH as a cruel innkeeper who ridicules the regulations governing oriental hospitality by giving his guests stones to eat instead of bread (cf Mt 7_9). A rather far fetched exegesis, in my opinion. Given 3_{15}, any explanation will have to honour the relationship with 4_{5bB}: 'and they cling to ash heaps'. In their dreadful hunger, the people would have rummaged for morsels of (half burned) food which might have fallen into the ashes during preparation. On occasion they would have thought they had found something to eat only to find that their teeth encountered nothing but cinders or stones. Prov 20_{17} and Ps 102_{10} support such an interpretation of the text. The root גרס is only found elsewhere in Ps 119_{20} (as a metaphor for the consumption of the נֶפֶשׁ). The present translation 'gravel' is derived from the context.

16B *he presses me down in ash.* הִכְפִּישַׁנִי בָּאֵפֶר

The גֶּבֶר is portrayed here as a child of Zion clinging to the ash heap (4_{5bB}), albeit involuntarily. Such is not his own choice; he is driven to it by hunger. The real reason behind his actions is YHWH who has forced this hunger upon him. The translation of √כפשׁ as 'to press down' is uncertain since the verb is a *hapax.*[91] The Ugaritic term *kpṯ* 'earth' (UT nr 1291a) and the related √כבשׁ 'to press down (to the ground)', however, both support our translational option (cf HAL 439).

The unusual spelling of אֵפֶר, a synonym of עָפָר 'dust' (in the latter form in 2_{10} and 3_{29}), suggests a slight difference in meaning here. Besides meaning '(ground) dust', אֵפֶר can also mean 'ash' (cf Num 19_{9f}, Ezek 28_{18}). In light of the concatinative connection with 'ash heaps' in the parallel verse in Lam 4_5, therefore, we translate אֵפֶר in the present context as 'ash'. At the same time, however, there is also an echo of the usual meaning of עָפָר 'dust' in the sense that the starving children of Zion lie close to death in the dust covered ash heaps. Thus in the central strophe of canto I we once again (contra Westermann) find a connection with the dirge. For further discussion of the term עָפָר as well as the realm of the dead cf the explanation of 2_{10bc}. The same connection is indicated within sub-canto I (3_{1-21}) via the inclusion כְּמֵתֵי עוֹלָם (3_{6B}) // בָּאֵפֶר (3_{16B}). It was characteristic of ancient Israel that in death a person considered him/herself cut off from YHWH.[92]

[91] Cf HAL 471.

17A *Cast out from peace is my soul,* וַתִּזְנַח מִשָּׁלוֹם נַפְשִׁי

As is evident from our structural analysis, 3_{17} is one of the two nuclear verses of the book of Lamentations. Together with the canto response 3_{50}, these verses constitute the primary theme of the songs as a whole, a theme which includes affliction, distress and the residue of the people's expectations rolled into one, a theme which is echoed throughout the remaining songs.[93]

The present verse is clearly formulated as a fundamental idea. The term נֶפֶשׁ implies more than just the גֶּבֶר's personal strength or vigour (as in $1_{11,16,19}$, $2_{12,19}$), it refers to the גֶּבֶר rather as a living, vital subject. In this canticle, the גֶּבֶר's נֶפֶשׁ is wedged symmetrically between his heart and his kidneys: כִלְיוֹתָי (3_{13A}) // נַפְשִׁי (3_{17A}) // לִבִּי (3_{21A}). If one were to place accents, then one might legitimately characterise the kidneys as the seat of human emotions. The heart is likewise the seat of emotions but has the added dimension of being the locus of mind and reflection. The נֶפֶשׁ, however, includes all of the aforementioned aspects and stands for the intensity and vitality of the self in its orientation towards life. Without such an orientation a human person ceases to be a human person. Translation with the term 'soul' is perhaps the most effective way of rendering נֶפֶשׁ in our modern idiom, [94] although we must be careful to avoid being drawn into the Greek dichotomy of soul and body. The human person does not have a soul, he or she is a soul.[95]

With every fibre of his being the גֶּבֶר experiences himself cast out from the שָׁלוֹם. The term שָׁלוֹם is most frequently translated with the general concept 'peace' and it remains difficult to find another option. In the present context, however, receptor and donor languages do not completely correspond and further explanation is necessary to more fully describe the content of the term. Gerleman correctly endeavoured to understand the concept based on the fundamental meaning of the verb שלם, namely 'to pay' or 'to obtain abundant satisfaction'. שָׁלוֹם also implies: 'having all one's needs richly provided for', that which satisfies and fulfils a person in the positive sense of the term.[96] The fact that the גֶּבֶר's נֶפֶשׁ no longer

---

[92] Cf Ps $88_{5f,11ff}$; GvRad, *Theologie des Alten Testaments, Band I, Die Theologie der geschichtlichen Überlieferungen Israels*, München 1966[5], 401; KSpronk, *Beatific Afterlife in Ancient Israel and in the Ancient Near East*, AOAT 219, Neukirchen-Vluyn 1986, 272 and the explanation of 3_6.

[93] Cf the introduction to the present canticle above.

[94] Cf THAT II 79 (Westermann).

[95] Cf THAT II 84 (Westermann) and TWAT V 543–546 (Seebass).

experiences any שָׁלוֹם means that there is no sense of satisfaction in his existence. In every dimension of his life he is confronted with profound disappointment. His anguish is clearly no mere triviality. The גֶּבֶר did not lose his שָׁלוֹם step by step, he was cast out from שָׁלוֹם in one fell swoop. The author(s) employ the √זנח II to express this 'casting out', a verb which is only found elsewhere in Lam 2_7 (song-response at the canticle level) where YHWH is described as having 'scorned' his altar in destroying it. Here too YHWH's presence as subject is implied although not at the grammatical level. וַתִּזְנַח (from √זנח II) can be translated in two different ways: (with a different vocalisation) as a *niph'al* imperfect 3f sg, whereby the passive subject is understood as the soul of the גֶּבֶר[97] or as a *qal* imperfect 2m sg with YHWH as subject: "You have cast my soul out from the שָׁלוֹם".[98] The *niph'al* interpretation seems preferable since we would otherwise be left with a direct address to YHWH in contrast to the fact that the entire summing up of complaints in 3_{1-21} consistently speaks of YHWH in the third person.

Abruptness appears to be a distinctive feature of the verb זנח II. Its appearance at the same level in the second song – also in the third canticle (2_{6-7}) – provides וַתִּזְנַח with the character of a song reponse. This leads us to assume that the גֶּבֶר's deep sense of frustration is primarily rooted in the fate of altar, temple and worship (cf the explanation of 2_7). By scorning and rejecting his altar, YHWH has cast out the גֶּבֶר's soul from the שָׁלוֹם. At the same time, therefore, it becomes clear that the notion of שָׁלוֹם is not theologically neutral. It is rather a situation of well-being given and guaranteed by YHWH himself. Its removal is his judgement. Inversely, it became possible to proclaim the restoration of YHWH's covenant of peace with his people after the exile.[99]

17B *I am forced to forget good things.* נָשִׁיתִי טוֹבָה

טוֹבָה is a substantivised adjective, the feminine form of which suggests a collective interpretation "all good things".[100] Internal parallelism reveals that the 'good things' in question point to the גֶּבֶר's lost שָׁלוֹם referred to in the first colon. The parallel expression שָׁלוֹם // טוֹב is also to be found in Jer 8_{15} and 14_{19}. The new element in the present context is the verb

[96] Cf TWAT II 922f, 927f.
[97] Cf Syriac, Vulgate, HAL 265.
[98] Cf Rudolph, Gottwald, Kraus etcetera.
[99] Cf Isa 54_{10}, Ezek 34_{25ff}, 37_{26}.
[100] Cf GES-K § 122s.

נשה 'to forget' which only appears five times in the OT as a whole.[101] The noun נְשִׁיָּה 'forgetfulness' appears on one occasion in Ps 88_{13}, a Psalm which already disclosed connections with the present text, especially at the level of context. The concluding cola of the first and last bicolon of the present strophe are redolent with the realm of the dead: (incl) בָּאֵפֶר (3_{16B}) // תּוֹחַלְתִּי מֵיְהוָה ... אָבַד (3_{18B}), dust and the absence of hope. It is probable, therefore, that we should understand the forgetting of good things by the גֶּבֶר in such a context. Thus 'to forget' does not mean to have lost one's memory of the good things one once had, a situation which would hardly induce the kind of pain the גֶּבֶר is enduring; it means rather to be so far gone that one resembles those in the realm of the dead for whom the experience of good things – while still possible to imagine – has become impossible. In this sense the realm of the dead is truly the 'land of forgetfulness' and the place of 'no remembrance'. Cf Ps 6_6, 88_{12f} and Keel: "Das Schweigen der Totenwelt ist in den Pss die Folge davon, daß Jahwe der Totenwelt, wo Kraftlosigkeit und Dunkel herrschen, fern ist. Die Verstorbenen sind von seinem kraftvoll wirkenden Arm gescheiden. Er erinnert sich ihrer nicht mehr (88,6b). Sie sind Vergessenen (31,13), das Totenreich ist das Land der *Vergessenheit* (88,13)."[102] The reverse is to be found in Ps 103_{4f} where the poet confesses that YHWH redeems his life from the realm of the dead (the Pit) and fills his soul with good things.

If one were to suggest a concrete interpretation of that which the גֶּבֶר is being forced to forget then the song-response 2_{6b} might provide an answer via the complaint that YHWH has caused sabbath and festival to be forgotten in Zion. One is reminded in turn of the expression of trust in Ps 65_5: "we shall be satisfied with the goodness of your house, your holy temple".[103] The גֶּבֶר must now forget such things.

18A *And I said, "Ravaged is my splendour,* וָאֹמַר אָבַד נִצְחִי

The גֶּבֶר surveys what is happening to him and summarises his situation: his נֵצַח has faded. Commentators differ on their interpretation of the noun in the present text: 'splendour' or 'length of time/duration'.[104] Keil opts for the latter interpretation, albeit in a derived form: "vom Grundbegriffe

101 Also in Isa 44_{21} (*niph'al*), Gen 41_{51} (*pi'el*), Job 11_6 and 39_{17}; cf TWAT V 663f (Ringgren).

102 In OKeel, *Die Welt der altorientalischen Bildsymbolik und das Alte Testament*, Zürich-Einsiedeln-Köln-Neukirchen-Vluyn 1977[2], 59.

103 Cf Ps 128_5 and Jer 31_{14}.

104 Cf HAL 676.

des Festen, der Dauer ausgehend bed. nach traditioneller Erklärung *vigor* Lebenskraft, dann übertragen auf den Lebenssaft, *vis vitalis*, Jes $63_{3,6}$." The duration of the גֶּבֶר's existence is lost; he has become a fragile and vulnerable human person. While Gottwald, Weiser and Gordis follow a similar line of thought, an explanation based on the interpretation of נֵצַח as 'splendour' would appear to deserve preference.

נֵצַח as 'splendour' serves as an adjective with respect to YHWH: he is Israel's 'splendour'.[105] Kraus opts for such an interpretation of the present text: the גֶּבֶר is stating that YHWH (for him) has been lost. From a theological perspective, however, Kraus' explanation of the text is unworkable since the use of the root אבד stands in opposition to it. One cannot say that one's 'splendour' – and thus YHWH himself – has perished. The root in question is often used, in fact, to express the opposite intention: YHWH being the one who ruins.[106] The verb אבד functions in the same way here: the גֶּבֶר is undergoing YHWH's judgement. He feels himself pressed down in the ashes (3_{16B}).

The 1st sg suffix of נִצְחִי calls for a more direct interpretation: it refers to the 'splendour' of the גֶּבֶר. While it is true that the notion 'splendour' is not usually related to human persons in such a direct fashion, indirect association is not unrepresented in the bible. In I Chron 29_{11}, for example, the praises are sung of YHWH's נֵצַח (splendour) as well as his תִּפְאֶרֶת (glory). This is reminiscent of Lam 2_{1bB} in which the expression תִּפְאֶרֶת יִשְׂרָאֵל is apparently used to imply the heavenly glory of YHWH which radiates forth upon his earthly sanctuary and thus becomes Israel's 'possesion'. By analogy, the present text would appear to be referring to God's splendour as it radiates forth upon the children of Zion (cf Ps 89_{18}). Just as YHWH has removed his תִּפְאֶרֶת from Israel, so he removes his splendour which once radiated upon the גֶּבֶר. The theological context of נֵצַח is also supported by internal parallelism in the bicolon (נִצְחִי // תּוֹחַלְתִּי מֵיְהוָה). Israel's glory, elaborated in the description of the destruction of temple and cult in the parallel canticle of the second song (2_{6-7}; cf 2_{9a}), has also been thrown off.

The analogy with Israel's תִּפְאֶרֶת thrown down in 2_1, however, extends a great deal further. While the 'throwing down' of Israel's glory manifested itself in the destruction of the temple, the removal of the גֶּבֶר's splendour is made visible in his own personal destruction (3_{11B}), emaciation ($3_{4A,15,16}$)

---

[105] Cf I Sam 15_{29}, I Chron 29_{11}.

[106] Cf TWAT I 21ff (Otzen).

and brokenness (3_{4B}). Measured against the Psalms, all of this serves to underline a profound contrast. Indeed, when YHWH is near, he satisfies his people (Ps 145_{15f}) with good things (Ps 103_{5}) as with rich foods (Ps 63_{6}); there is no longer want (Ps 34_{10f}), and he protects the bones of the righteous (Ps 34_{21}). This contrastive connection reveals the link with the ז-strophe in the fourth song (4_{7}) where there is mention of the former radiance and splendour of Jerusalem's nobles followed by a horrendous portrayal of the ultimate loss of all their magnificence (cf 4_{8}).

18B *my expectation from* YHWH." וְתוֹחַלְתִּי מֵיְהוָה

As was the case with נִצְחִי, וְתוֹחַלְתִּי is the passive subject of the verbal form אָבַד. We translate it as 'expectation', not in the general sense of hope for the future but in the specific sense of the גֶּבֶר's expectations of YHWH, based on the latter's association with Zion. YHWH's deeds of liberation, comfort, forgiveness, salvation etcetera can all be placed within such a framework.[107] It is stated in the parallel 2_{6} that YHWH has broken his relationship with Zion (cf also the explanation of 2_{9a}). The same notion resonates here in the גֶּבֶר's ravaged expectations of his God. Internal parallelism תוֹחַלְתִּי // נִצְחִי – cf the relationship with YHWH's תִּפְאֶרֶת referred to in the explanation of the first colon – likewise supports our interpretation.

Bearing in mind the imperative in the following verse (3_{19}) it is important that we have a clear understanding of the present colon. The suggestion is not that the גֶּבֶר – in all his frustration and affliction – has lost his faith and given up hope nor that he has actively come to the conclusion that he has nothing left to believe in or hope for. If this were true then the following imperative would indeed be incomprehensible: how can someone who has no further expectations from YHWH still call upon him to observe the affliction he is being forced to endure? The error of logic involved in such an understanding of the text is that one makes the abandonment of hope dependant on the frame of mind of the גֶּבֶר while it ought in fact to be related to God's unwillingness to assist. Once again the song-response 2_{6} sheds some light on the present text: YHWH himself has destroyed Zion and in so doing he has also destroyed the faith and expectation associated therewith.

As we already mentioned in connection with 3_{16B}, the present strophe (cf also 3_{6B}) is redolent with the realm of the dead. Although YHWH still

[107] For Zion as the 'Sitz im Leben' of the theology of the Psalms cf 1983, 284f and HSpieckermann, *Heilsgegenwart. Eine Theologie der Psalmen*, Göttingen 1989.

exercised power over the שְׁאוֹל,[108] Israel considered herself cut off from him in the kingdom of the dead (cf Ps 6_6, 88_{12f}). The reality of the גֶּבֶר is the realm of the dead (cf once again הִכְפִּישַׁנִי בָּאֵפֶר in 3_{16B}) and this leads him to the conclusion that he can no longer count on YHWH's help. Indeed, his actual experience matches his conclusion: his cry of distress and appeal for help have gone unanswered (3_8). Yes, YHWH himself has cast the גֶּבֶר's expectations in the saving God of Zion to the ground. Thus his hope has departed him. He wants to have hope but it is no longer possible. It should be noted that the divine name 'YHWH' is used here for the first time in the third song.

19 *Realise my affliction and wandering,* זְכָר־עָנְיִי וּמְרוּדִי
bitterness and poison. לַעֲנָה וָרֹאשׁ

The imperative זְכָר is directed to YHWH and amounts to a prayer that he will realise the extent of the affliction which has overcome the גֶּבֶר; the longing to be saved by YHWH is clearly contained therein.[109] It is characteristic of the Psalms that the imperative in question is used exclusively in prayer to YHWH.[110] The same association is evident here also but indirectly: although belonging to the previous strophe, the name of YHWH still directly precedes the imperative זְכָר in the text.

We already indicated our reasons for maintaining the present imperative reading of זְכָר in our explanation of the preceding colon.[111] The efforts of Rudolph, Kraus, Hillers and Kaiser to read an infinitive or a 1st person singular (cf also LXX) fail to convince. In contrast with the imperative of זְכָר, no infinitive of the root can be found in Psalms in a similar context.

Although it might seem illogical to read an imperative at this point in the text, the fact that, while he still draws breath, the גֶּבֶר continues to hope even against his better judgement remains an exceptionally human reaction. As a matter of fact, such imperatives are not unusual within the songs as a whole. While the same opening זְכֹר can be found in the prayer of Lam 5_1, on several occasions we also hear Lady Jerusalem turn to YHWH with similar cries of distress using the imperative of רְאֵה (cf $1_{9,11}$). Thus, with an equally sudden outburst, the גֶּבֶר anticipates his imminent

108 Cf KSpronk, *Beatific Afterlife in Ancient Israel and in the Ancient Near East*, AOAT 219, Neukirchen-Vluyn 1986, 281f.

109 Cf Ps 9_{13}, THAT I 514 (Schotroff) and TWAT II 578 (Eising).

110 Cf Ps $25_{6,7}$, $74_{2,18,22}$, $89_{48,51}$, 119_{41}, 132_1, 137_7.

111 Cf also Albrektson, Gordis, Van Selms.

transformation from bitter disappointment in YHWH to renewed faith and hope in his God (3_{22-33}).

In the short and somewhat abrupt supplication of 1_{9cA}, Lady Jerusalem calls upon YHWH to look upon her affliction. Within the third canticle of Lam I (1_{7-9}) this 'affliction' constitutes an inclusion: עָנְיִי (1_{9cA}) // עָנְיָהּ וּמְרוּדֶיהָ (1_{7aB}). The latter colon (1_{7aB}) provides exactly the same description of Lady Jerusalem's affliction as 3_{19A} does of that of the גֶּבֶר. The meaning is clear: Lady Jerusalem's affliction and that of the גֶּבֶר are one and the same. As we already noted, the imperative use of √זכר in the present context does not suggest 'remembering' but rather 'realisation', 'being aware of'.[112] The implication behind the term מָרוּד suggests both the notion of 'homelessness' (cf 1_{7a}) as well as the derived meaning 'to wander'. The 'homelessness' dimension is illuminated via the song-response with 2_7: Lady Jerusalem has lost her temple and the גֶּבֶר his home. Without Zion's safeguarding walls (2_{7b}) and the protection of YHWH's anointed, the גֶּבֶר is nothing more than a transient outlaw. Thus the 'wandering' aspect of מָרוּד is illuminated via the canto-response with 3_{52} in which the גֶּבֶר refers to his being hunted down by the enemy.[113]

20A *My soul is abundantly aware of it...* זָכוֹר תִּזְכּוֹר וְתָשִׁיחַ

The translation provided here does not correspond exactly with the Hebrew. The constraints of modern English force us to bring forward the subject נַפְשִׁי from the second colon.

Both Gottwald and Albrektson accept the tradition that we are dealing here with one of the *tiqqunê soferim*, the 'corrections of the scribes',[114] according to which the original reading was נַפְשְׁךָ, that is to say YHWH's soul, which would thus render the translation: 'your soul surely remembers and bows down on my account'. Such an interpretation is unacceptable for three reasons: (a) YHWH's נֶפֶשׁ is almost never spoken of in the OT;[115] (b) the tradition of scribal emendation with regard to this text is extremely questionable;[116] (c) one can object at the level of content that if the

[112] Cf HAL 259 and the explanation of Lam 1_{7a} (also for עָנְיִ [cf 3_{1A}]).

[113] For רֹאשׁ cf the explanation of 3_{5B} and for לַעֲנָה the explanation of 3_{15B}.

[114] Cf text critical apparatus BHK and BHS.

[115] Cf THAT II 91 (Westermann) and TWAT V 551f (Seebass).

[116] Cf Hillers, Gordis, Gottlieb, CMcCarthy, *The Tiqqune Sopherim and Other Theological Corrections in the Masoretic Text of the Old Testament*, Göttingen 1981, 120–123 and ETov, *Textual Criticism of the Hebrew Bible*, Assen/Maastricht, 1992, 64–67.

reading נַפְשֶׁךָ is correct, then the גֶּבֶר is either speaking of an apparent turn around on the part of YHWH or he is stating that YHWH is also weighed down by his suffering. Clearly the preceding verses give witness to the fact that YHWH has not had a change of heart, while the notion of YHWH himself being burdened by the suffering of the גֶּבֶר lacks echo in any part of Lam III. For this reason, it appears most likely that MT contains the original reading. Parallels with Ps $42_{6,7}$ and 43_5 further support such an option.

The present bicolon functions as the premise for the imperative in 3_{19A}: YHWH must realise the extent of the גֶּבֶר's affliction. He himself is intensely aware of his pain at every moment and cannot escape it. We understand the emphasis brought about by the paronomastic infinitive as intensive and translate with the term 'abundantly'. The subject of תִּזְכּוֹר (*qal* 3f sg impf) is the soul of the גֶּבֶר. For נֶפֶשׁ as a reference to the entire person of the גֶּבֶר see 3_{17A} above. What these verses are making clear is that the גֶּבֶר is constantly and profoundly aware of the affliction and homelessness confronting him as a consequence of YHWH's judgement (cf the already mentioned לַעֲנָה וָרֹאשׁ, the 'bitterness and poison' of 3_{19B}).

20B *... and it pities me.* עָלַי נַפְשִׁי

Commentators frequently substitute the *k^e^tîb* תָשִׂיחַ for the *q^e^rē* תָשׁוֹחַ.[117] The root שחח means 'to bow down' and the expression is thus translated: 'my soul bows down within me', that is to say it is weighed down. This was my own option in 1983.[118] Having thought the matter through once again, however, I now consider it more appropriate to opt for an alternative solution. The problem confronting my 1983 exegesis remains the suffixed preposition עָלַי which usually means 'over me' or 'concerning me' rather than 'within me'. It is possible, nevertheless, to speak of נֶפֶשׁ in such a way that a person is portrayed in a relationship with him/herself (his/her נֶפֶשׁ). One can call upon one's נֶפֶשׁ, for example, to offer praise to YHWH.[119] The נֶפֶשׁ itself can also be the subject of an action[120] as well as being flushed with emotion such as bitterness.[121] In this sense it would appear that the *k^e^tîb* can be retained, with תָשִׂיחַ understood as a *qal* 3f sg impf of √שיח = 'to occupy oneself with lamenting'. The 'lament' interpretation

[117] Cf text critical apparatus BHS and KBL 960 sv שחח and 965 sv שיח.
[118] Cf 1983, 299f.
[119] Cf Ps $103_{1,2,22}$ etcetera.
[120] Cf Ps $42_{2f,6f}$, 57_2, 62_2, $63_{2,9}$ etcetera.
[121] Cf I Sam 1_{10}, Job 7_{11} etcetera; cf also TWAT V 545f (Seebass).

can also be found in Ps 55_{18}, Job 7_{11} (+ נַפְשִׁ!). The substantive form can also signify 'lament': Ps 55_3, 64_2, 102_1, 142_3.[122] Thus the גֶּבֶר is on the point of sinking into the depths of self-pity.

21 *(But) this I shall once again take to heart,* זֹאת אָשִׁיב אֶל־לִבִּי
therefore I still hope: עַל־כֵּן אוֹחִיל

It is almost as if the גֶּבֶר is suddenly shocked by the possibility that self-pity might turn out to be his sole and final perspective. A supplementary reading of the צ-strophe (3_{52-54} [canto-response]), nonetheless, reveals that this is not his only response. In 3_{52-54} the גֶּבֶר offers an alternative rendering of his present affliction, particularly in 3_{54B} where he announces: "I thought, I am lost" (see the exegesis below). This statement is quite relevant to the present verse because it clearly provides a reason for the גֶּבֶר's renewed hope. The גֶּבֶר is afraid that the ongoing affliction and persecution he is being forced to endure will eventually get the better of him and that he will no longer be able to survive under his own steam. He is also aware, however, that there is an alternative, something which might provide the foundation for renewed hope, something he had experienced before as a constituent of his גֶּבֶר-ness. This aspect is missing from the LXX which reads אָשִׂים (√שׂים I, 'to place') while MT reads אָשִׁיב (√שׁוב I, *hiph'il* impf 1 sg 'to bring back'): he shall 'bring it back' to his heart. This means, of course, that something has disappeared from his heart, that he is a believer whose hope and trust have been taken from him (cf 3_{17f}). Nevertheless, the גֶּבֶר does not allow his condition to get the better of him. Even without hope he continues to trust in YHWH. Thus, in spite of everything, the גֶּבֶר makes his transition from profound lament to renewed hope.

Texts which employ √יחל 'to wait'/'to hope' usually also provide an object of hope or an indication of the length of time a person is expected to wait. Both elements are evidently absent from the present text, giving rise to the possibility of an absolute use whereby, according to Barth "die Haltung des Wartens-an-sich..." finds itself "...in den Mittelpunkt des Interesses."[123] If it is true that the גֶּבֶר's 'waiting' stance is thus the focus of attention, it is equally clear that his hope is directed towards YHWH.[124]

The foundation of the גֶּבֶר's hope is elucidated in what follows. It is clear, therefore, that this concluding bicolon of the first sub-canto (3_{1-21}) exer-

---

[122] Cf HAL 1230.
[123] In TWAT III 606.
[124] Cf 3_{24B}; see also 3_{18B} where the גֶּבֶר mentions his (impossible) hope in YHWH.

cises a connective function at the level of content. In the following sub-canto (3_{22-33}) the picture changes: the גֶּבֶר's perspective is no longer determined by bitterness, pain and sorrow; his attention now turns to the חַסְדֵי יְהוָה.

Sub-canto II (Lam 3_{22-33})

In the present sub-canto the devout one speaks of the why's and wherefore's of his renewed trust in YHWH. He is suddenly aware of unexpected survival (3_{22}) which he views as a manifestation of YHWH's fidelity (3_{23}) and goodness (3_{25-27}). It is evident that YHWH has not turned away from his people for good. Thus, in the second and last canticle (3_{28-33}) the possibility of restored hope becomes the focus of the text (3_{29}). In perseverence and humility (3_{28-30}) one must await the salvation of YHWH (3_{26}). The canticle/sub-canto/canto concludes with further reason to hope which the גֶּבֶר discerns in the fact that, given past experience, rejection by YHWH does not last forever. It is in line with this awareness that the devout one experiences the tension between the distress which has overcome him and the essence of YHWH in his orientation towards humanity. By allowing this to happen, YHWH is going against himself: it is not his way. The question remains as to whether YHWH desires to continue in this tension.

Canticle I (3_{22-27})

Content/theme: *In spite of everything, the devout one can still speak of* YHWH*'s evident fidelity*

Literary argumentation:

inclusions:	חַסְדֵי יְהוָה (22A) // טוֹב (יְהוָה) (27A)[125]
	כִּי (22A) // כִּי (27A)
	אֱמוּנָתֶךָ (23B) // תְשׁוּעַת יְהוָה (26B)
	יְהוָה (24A) // יְהוָה (25A)
	נַפְשִׁי (24A) // לְנֶפֶשׁ (25B)
responses:	חַסְדֵי יְהוָה (22A) // טוֹב יְהוָה (25A)
ext par:	אוֹחִיל (24B) // וְיָחִיל (26A)
concat:	אוֹחִיל (24B) // לְקֹוָו (25A)
	נַפְשִׁי (24A) // לְנֶפֶשׁ (25B)

[125] Cf, for example, Ps 23_6.

From the stylistic perspective, the multiple use of the divine name YHWH is quite striking in comparison to the previous sub-canto. There is little doubt that this is due to the mention of YHWH's חֶסֶד. At the level of content, preceding canticles tended to focus on God's consistently unfavourable deeds, thus preventing the גֶּבֶר from attaching YHWH's name thereto. Now that the גֶּבֶר has turned his attention to the more positive dimensions of his present situation, YHWH's name can ring out loud and clear.

The ח-strophe (3_{22-24}) is missing from the LXX, undoubtedly as a result of *homoioteleuton*. See אוֹחִיל (3_{21B}) and אוֹחִיל לוֹ (3_{24B}).

22A *It is (due to) the favours of* YHWH... חַסְדֵי יְהוָה

The restoration of the גֶּבֶר's hope is rooted in his renewed consciousness of the good favours of YHWH, which the construct plural clearly suggests are manifold. What does the author mean by YHWH's good favours? Kraus takes Glueck's (1927) position[126] as his point of departure, arguing that the exercise of חֶסֶד should be considered a covenant obligation. In the present context, such an approach to the term would imply that YHWH has upheld his covenant with Israel in one way or another and that this is the basis of the גֶּבֶר's hope. Such an exegesis of the text, however, is difficult to endorse. The downfall of the city and the land together with the extreme affliction and distress which has overcome the population can only lead us to one conclusion: the covenant between YHWH and his people has been broken. The very articulation of the horrors facing the people provides a literal reminder of the punitive sanctions associated with the breaking of the covenant. This same idea is expressed within the songs in the confessions of sin and guilt.[127] Even the new covenant after the exile (Jer 31; Ezek 26) points to the fact that the old covenant was in tatters.

In light of what we have said, it becomes impossible to interpret the חֶסֶד to which the גֶּבֶר refers in the context of the covenant between YHWH and his people. What then might the appropriate interpretative context be? The concept is employed to refer to a particular mode of interpersonal association. When people show each other חֶסֶד, their actions imply mutual warmth and affection, congeniality and fidelity to which there is no binding obligation. At the same time, however, one can oblige oneself to

[126] NGlueck, *Das Wort hesed im alttestamentlichen Sprachgebrauch als menschliche und göttliche gemeinschafts-gemäße Verhaltungsweise*, BZAW 47 (1927).

[127] See Lam $1_{5,8,14,22}$, 2_{14}, $3_{39,42}$, $4_{6,13}$, 5_{16}.

such actions in the form of a בְּרִית. The translation 'favour' does justice to the non-binding dimension of חֶסֶד. The same translational term also incorporates the practical aspect of חֶסֶד which not only implies an inclination towards such interpersonal association but also includes actual deeds which flow therefrom. A third characteristic of חֶסֶד is 'durability', an aspect which is best rendered with the notion of 'fidelity'. A single translational term which includes all three dimensions of חֶסֶד is extremely difficult to find.

The term חֶסֶד is also used to express a particular form of association between God and human persons. Besides a number of more permanent aspects, the theological use of the word also implies something of shift. What remains is the goodness and warmth, affection and fidelity which God gives to those who know his fellowship. Likewise, the practical dimension of חֶסֶד is also preserved: God's goodness and kindness express themselves in actual deeds to the benefit of both individuals and the people as a whole. God's חֶסֶד takes the form of blessing, well-being, divine contrition, redemption, wonderous deeds, God's goodness and fidelity towards the house of David, etcetera.[128] The mutuality which characterises חֶסֶד-filled relationships between human persons, however, fades into the background in the theological context: the human person is able to receive God's חֶסֶד but he or she cannot return it.[129] It is evident that the practice of חֶסֶד goes beyond obligation. Nevertheless, the favours of YHWH mentioned here do require further elucidation. Since his people have proven themselves disobedient, YHWH has been released from his covenant obligations in Israel's regard. For this reason the גֶּבֶר does not build his hopes on covenant obligations but rather on the expressions of YHWH's goodness to which he has no obligation, acts of kindness which he continues to reveal nevertheless.

22A ... *that we do not perish,* כִּי לֹא־תָמְנוּ

We must continue to focus here on the pragmatic character of YHWH's favours, a dimension which is missing from interpretations which would emend תָמְנוּ[130] to read תַּמּוּ.[131] By changing the text in this way, YHWH's favours become the subject of the verb: 'they do not cease (to happen)',

[128] Cf, for example, Ps 107_{43}.

[129] For a more detailed and well-argued description of the content of חֶסֶד cf TWAT III 48–71 (Zobel) and THAT I 600–621 (Stoebe).

[130] This is pf 1 pl of √תמם; for the form see GES-K § 67e and Jer 44_{18}.

[131] A pf 3 pl; cf BHK, BHS and a multitude of exegetes.

an idea which is fully in harmony with the confession that God's חֶסֶד is eternal: Ps 106_1, 107_1 etcetera. The question arises, therefore, whether the גֶּבֶר is not basing his hope on some ancient confession,[132] traces of the reality of which are not to be found in his current situation. After making so much of the affliction facing the גֶּבֶר and his people, however, it comes accross as somewhat unbelievable and unrealistic to suddenly begin to speak of YHWH's favours if they are not actually in evidence. Such lack of realism is also difficult to reconcile with the pragmatic character of YHWH's חֶסֶד. The question also remains as to the credibility of the גֶּבֶר's sudden appropriation of a credo. The fact of the matter is that the גֶּבֶר has had to face disappointment of the severest nature because another credo – that of YHWH's promised protection of Zion – has been called into question (cf 4_{12}).

The reading of the MT, on the other hand, points to the evidently pragmatic nature of YHWH's חֶסֶד. Although the downfall of land and city is an incontrovertable fact and YHWH's judgement has reached its fulfilment, this does not imply that all human life itself is at an end. It is here that we see evidence of YHWH's merciful favour: no matter how dreadful the גֶּבֶר's suffering, no matter how freely death and destruction hold sway and YHWH's judgement is complete, in the face of all such horror the גֶּבֶר realises that survival is still a possibility. This is true not only for the גֶּבֶר but for all those other survivors who confirm his realisation.

Commentators have challenged the reading of MT, תָמְנוּ, on the basis of the fact that it would imply that the present text was an individual lament and that the גֶּבֶר was, of necessity, speaking for himself alone. We already noted, however, that such a determination of genre is inadequate to the context (cf the introduction to this song). The גֶּבֶר also calls others to renew their faith and trust in YHWH (cf 3_{40ff}). The plural forms in Lam III, therefore, are an indication of the fact that he is including his fellow survivors in his thoughts and reflections. One might well ask oneself if such bare survival, such existence on the edge, surrounded by a social wasteland and threatened by starvation and death, ought to be understood as evidence of YHWH's חֶסֶד. That this is indeed the case becomes apparent from a comparison with prophecies of doom directed against Israel in which Israel's end (= קֵץ) is announced on account of her sin. This finds its most pointed expression in Am 8_2, taken over by Ezekiel within the framework of his יוֹם יְהוָה-preaching.[133] In the narrative of the flood, קֵץ is

[132] Cf Ex 34_6, Jona 4_2 etcetera; cf also TWAT III 64 (Zobel).

used to proclaim the final end of all living things (Gen 6_{13}). The prophets also directed such words of total destruction against Israel. The גֶּבֶר realises that this final end – which YHWH had the right to inflict upon his people (cf 1_{18}) – had not become a reality understood as the end of all life (cf 4_{18} [song-response]). The fact that there are still survivors, including those to whom his words are addressed, the גֶּבֶר ascribes to the non-obligatory favour and grace of YHWH (cf Gen 6_{8}). Since there are still survivors the גֶּבֶר can (still) hope. It remains an extreme form of survival, nevertheless, as is evident from the parallel with 3_{55} from the second canto of Lam III where there is mention of בּוֹר תַּחְתִּיּוֹת, 'the depths of the pit' or, in other words, the very edge of the realm of the dead. It is from here that the גֶּבֶר appeals to YHWH for liberation. The aforementioned canto-response supports our understanding of the continued survival of the גֶּבֶר and others as a sign of God's favour. The use of √כלה I in the following colon also points in this direction.

22B *for his mercy never ceases.* כִּי לֹא־כָלוּ רַחֲמָיו

The *plurale tantum* רַחֲמִים suggests feelings of compassion and mercy rooted in love, the compassion of a mother (רֶחֶם = womb) for her child (cf Isa 49_{15}) as well as that of a father (cf Ps 103_{13}). God's רַחֲמִים for Israel far surpass those of human parents towards their children (cf, once again, Isa 49_{15}). It is because of his mercy that YHWH continues to show favour. Aware that he is still alive, the גֶּבֶר realises that YHWH (still) has compassion for him and that this compassion is ongoing. Thus the confession of Ps 25_{6} remains in effect: God's favour and mercy are eternal (thus God's חֶסֶד endures).

There appears to be an example of word-play between √תמם and √כלה I. Lam 3_{22} reveals a clear chiastic/concentric structure: חַסְדֵי יְהוָה // רַחֲמָיו and כִּי לֹא־כָלוּ // כִּי לֹא־תָמְנוּ (the latter being supplementary parallelism).[134] The verb כלה I with YHWH as subject is frequently employed in prophecies of doom where it means: 'to raze to the ground'/'to destroy'.[135] In addition, however, there remains a sense that YHWH will not make an absolute and final end of Israel.[136] His judgement is intended to confront Israel with her guilt (cf Jer 5_{19}), an insight which will have a role to play later on in Lam

133 Ezek 7; cf WZimmerli, *Ezechiel 1–24*, BKAT XIII/1, Neukirchen 1979^2, 168ff.

134 For the combination of חֶסֶד with רַחֲמִים see Ps 25_{6}, 40_{12}, 103_{4}, Jer 16_{5} etcetera.

135 Cf Jer 9_{16} (MT 9_{15}), 14_{12}, Ezek 20_{13} etcetera; see also TWAT IV 170f (Helfmeyer) and compare the echo thereof in Lam 2_{11a} and 2_{22c}.

136 Cf Jer 5_{18}, 30_{11}, 46_{28}.

III (cf 3_{39-41}). In the post-exilic period, we find grateful recognition that God in his infinite mercy did not count his people's guilt against them for good (cf Neh 9_{31}). It would appear then that the present verse has its roots in such an insight. YHWH has not destroyed his people for ever because his רַחֲמִים are never ending. In spite of the confession that YHWH's mercies are everlasting, the author of Ps 77_{10} appears to have accounted for the possibility that YHWH's wrath (אַף) might exclude his רַחֲמִים. In the present text, however, the גֶּבֶר is not forced (not yet, cf 5_{22}) to draw such a conclusion. In spite of everything, YHWH still has compassion.

23A *New (signs of favour) every morning;* חֲדָשִׁים לַבְּקָרִים

Keil is correct in proposing that the plural חֲדָשִׁים should be related adjectivally to YHWH's favours and not to his 'compassion'.[137] YHWH's feelings of compassion and mercy are constant; the favours which flow therefrom have a practical character. Under the present circumstances, YHWH's various deeds are what makes survival possible: at least there is some protection from the enemy, at least some food to eat and water to drink. Such deeds, however, are not evidently ongoing. The fact that there is something to eat today does not guarantee that there will be something to eat tomorrow. On the contrary, the גֶּבֶר considers it a miracle that there are still enough provisions for survival at all. This can be determined from the use of the word חָדָשׁ. What does it mean in the context that there are new favours with each new morning? Compared with modern usage of the term 'new' (in compound forms) in a contemporary society in which things do not tend to endure for long, the √חדש (and its derivatives) turns out to be something of a rarity in Hebrew.[138] Where √חדש is employed elsewhere there is usually something unique and special at hand: a new and hitherto unheard of deed of YHWH, for example, which gives rise to a new song. If the poets refer to YHWH's favours as new, then they are implying that they manifest themselves in unexpected and unanticipated ways. The additional temporal indicator 'each morning' underlines and elucidates this in a unique way. According to Ziegler,[139] the morning is YHWH's preferred moment for coming to the aid of his people. However

137 Cf THAT I 529 (Westermann) and TWAT II 773 (North).

138 Cf also 5_{21B} and THAT I 526 (Westermann) who wrongly understands the present text as suggesting an analogy with a new harvest or a new garment; the novelty or originality suggested here, however, does not possess the familiar continuity of repetition.

139 JZiegler, 'Die Hilfe Gottes "am Morgen" ', Fs FNötscher, 1950, 281–288.

YHWH is certainly not bound to a specific time of day for doing so (cf also Ezek 32_{7f}),[140] although it is possible that in synchretistic Judah prior to the downfall of 587 connections were made between the dawn and rising sun as appearance of the deity.[141] If one were to take the human person as point of departure – the גֶּבֶר is speaking here from his own experience – then the morning is the moment par excellence to face the questions and possibilities presented by a new day and by extension the best moment to pray for YHWH's blessing and favour for the hours ahead.[142] Living from day to day with affliction and uncertainty, the גֶּבֶר is aware nonetheless that unexpected things happen, unforeseen things which continue to make life possible.

23B *manifold is your faithfulness.* רַבָּה אֱמוּנָתֶךָ

אֱמוּנָה, 'faithful', portrays a characteristic of God in relationship with human person made manifest in his deeds. Characteristics of such fidelity are consistency, stability, truth and permanence.[143] YHWH's אֱמוּנָה was something to be relied upon. The given circumstances which allow the גֶּבֶר to survive cannot be written off by him as a mere accident of fate. The consistency apparent in unexpectedly receiving what was necessary for survival day after day could only be ascribed to YHWH's ongoing fidelity, a fidelity which the poets describe as רַבָּה. This latter term can be translated as 'great' or 'extensive' but such an interpretation might give the impression that YHWH's fidelity might on occasion be small or less extensive. Any change in the extent of YHWH's fidelity, however, is a *contradictio in terminis.* In the first instance, רַבָּה means 'many'/'numerous' (and only in derivative form 'great' or 'extensive') and ought to be related to the (manifold) manifestations of YHWH's fidelity. There is clear internal parallelism at work here: YHWH's aforementioned favours are, in equal number, also signs of his fidelity; his fidelity is the source of his favours. Thus his favours are not simply a bunch of unrelated acts of mercy, they are to be understood as a consistent expression of YHWH's אֱמוּנָה.

The change of suffix (2m sg instead of 3m sg) in the present colon is worthy of observation. Up to this point the גֶּבֶר has spoken about YHWH in the third person, now he addresses him directly with words of praise:

---

[140] For further objections to such a position see TWAT I 751f (Barth).

[141] Cf II Kgs $23_{5,11}$; THAT II 996 (Hartmann) and HSpieckermann, *Juda unter Assur in der Sargonidenzeit*, FRLANT 129, Göttingen 1982, 257–273.

[142] Cf Ps 5_4, 88_{14}, 90_{14}, 143_8, Isa 33_2.

[143] Cf TWAT I 343f (Jepsen).

"your faithfulness". In the midst of all his affliction and distress he still experiences the vestiges of an 'I - Thou' relationship. The illuminating effect of his experience, however, is unique here. He does not repeat his claim nor further embellish his praise. The גֶּבֶר's renewed faith in YHWH remains fragile and tender indeed. At the end of the second canto we hear 'Thou' resound once again, this time in broader fuller tones, as if the גֶּבֶר's trust has grown all the stronger in the midst of his affliction and reflections thereupon.

24A *"My portion is* YHWH*",* חֶלְקִי יְהוָה

The most fundamental meaning of חֵלֶק, 'portion', is made evident when the term is applied to the possession of a piece of the arable land surrounding a city or a village. Such land ownership constituted the very basis of human survival and as such, the term is often found in parallel with 'heritage' which was considered to be inalienable. As 'owner' of the land, YHWH had given the Israelites their portion.[144] Possessing a portion of YHWH's land, therefore, could be translated as participating in YHWH, having one's portion in him. As we can read in Jos $22_{25,27}$, the Levites did not possess their own portion or their own territory, but YHWH himself was their portion.[145] For practical purposes this meant that the Levites received a portion of the sacrificial gifts offered by the Israelites as their due. All this does not necessarily suggest that the גֶּבֶר was a Levite. The idea that YHWH was the Israelite's only Portion is expressed in the personal name 'Hilkiah',[146] but it is not necessarily evident that the persons mentioned in connection with this term were Levites. The name can imply a kind of personal piety which considered YHWH as the human person's only possession, the unique ground of his or her existence. This is certainly the case where a number of the Psalms are concerned[147] and it is especially striking that the confession of such piety is sometimes found in the context of a life threatening crisis (Ps 73_{26}, 142_{6}). In the midst of extreme danger, at his or her moment of greatest need, the human person is thrown back on YHWH as his or her only possession. To paraphrase Miskotte: 'this God is their lot'.[148] It is in such a spirit that the גֶּבֶר can adopt this confession

[144] Cf also the explanation of 5_2.
[145] Cf Num 18_{20}, Deut 10_9 etcetera.
[146] חִלְקִיָּהוּ; cf II Kgs 18_{18}, Isa 22_{20}, Jer 1_1, 29_3.
[147] See Ps 16_5, 73_{26}, 119_{57}, 142_6.
[148] KHMiskotte, *Als de goden zwijgen. Over de zin van het Oude Testament*, Haarlem 1966, 358.

as his own. It would be wrong to imagine in the present context, however, that the גֶּבֶר has emerged at this point from some kind of psychological process in which he had successfully enaged in a spiritual struggle to free himself from his negative defeatism and was now in a better position to see the positive aspects of his existence. The literary structure of the songs as a whole runs counter to such an interpretation. While it was apparent elsewhere that the גֶּבֶר's laments conform with one another at the same levels in the various songs, it is equally evident here that the ח-strophe is in sharp contrast to its corresponding strophes in the other songs. Elsewhere, the ח-strophe speaks of scorn and contempt (1_8), the destruction of Zion (2_8), the perishing of her inhabitants (4_8) and oppression at the hands of slaves (5_8). In the middle of such real and actual affliction, the גֶּבֶר utters his confession and affirms that he considers YHWH to be his possession; YHWH who alone can save.

24A *says my soul,* אָמְרָה נַפְשִׁי

As with the previous colon it is important that we avoid interpreting these words as an expression of victory after a spiritual crisis. It would be wrong to imagine that the גֶּבֶר's struggles are all behind him. Even at the level of content, the antithetical relationship between the two sub-cantos (3_{1-21} \\ 3_{22-33}) strongly suggests otherwise. It is not a question of renewed faith after the attack but of faith regained in the midst of the attack. Indeed, it is the גֶּבֶר's very faith in YHWH which is under attack. He can call his basic survival a sign of YHWH's favour and fidelity but in the eyes of his fellow Israelites such a notion is hardly worth mentioning (cf the explanation of 3_{14}). The גֶּבֶר's faith is not held up by unassailable evidence and established, observable proof, rather it is one of deep interior conviction. Such a truth is eloquently expressed in the simple phrase אָמְרָה נַפְשִׁי. It is the גֶּבֶר's soul which speaks, that is to say: with his entire existence and every fibre of his being he is convinced of what he says.[149]

24B *therefore I will hope in him.* עַל־כֵּן אוֹחִיל לוֹ

The present colon is almost a repetition of 3_{21B}, the only difference being the addition of the suffixed preposition which serves here as an accusative of object[150] and functions to firmly underline the fact that YHWH is the

[149] Cf the explanation of 3_{17A} for the idea of נֶפֶשׁ as the embodiment of the גֶּבֶר's very being.

[150] Cf GES-K § 117*n*.

one in whom the גֶּבֶר now places his hope. The repetition stands as an affirmation of the גֶּבֶר's continued hope. Although he expresses his realisation that he has benefited from the favours of YHWH, it would be wrong to imagine that a new situation of well-being and salvation has come into existence and that his hope has been fulfilled. On the contrary, the ongoing presence of affliction and distress simply serve to stimulate the גֶּבֶר's hope in renewed help from YHWH (cf חֲדָשִׁים in 3_{23A}).

By expressing the גֶּבֶר's hope in this way, the poets lead us from one extreme to the other in the present song. Where the first sub-canto is characterised by bitter accusations, the second procedes nevertheless with unconditional faith in God. Although such a radical change of attitude might seem, at least at first sight, rather difficult to understand, the extremes in question are not so far apart as we might be inclined to imagine. Even in his accusations, the גֶּבֶר never speaks in detachment from YHWH. It is no longer a question of indifference, the גֶּבֶר's accusations against YHWH have their roots in wounded love. His very self-depiction betrays his position: he, the devout one filled with faith and trust in God, is forced to undergo all of this affliction at the hands of YHWH (cf the exegesis of 3_{1A}). Where an intimate relationship is concerned, the emotions are always stronger and the pain more unbearable than in a situaton bereft of commitment. Wounded love, however, longs for nothing less than healing and restoration. Such is the deepest intention of the גֶּבֶר's words (cf 3_8).

25A YHWH *is good...* טוֹב יְהוָה

Once again the גֶּבֶר employs language from Israel's most ancient confessions. What exactly is implied, however, by the expression 'YHWH is good'? YHWH is the personification of all good; he is Goodness itself, and as such the source of all the good things which people encounter (cf the concise confession of YHWH's goodness in Ps 119_{68} preserved even after the exile: טוֹב־אַתָּה וּמֵטִיב).[151] It is impossible to think of YHWH's goodness without also thinking of human experiences thereof, a fact succinctly formulated in the hymnic confession 'praise the Lord for he is good'.[152] The occasions which stimulated such praise of YHWH are related to his concrete deeds on behalf of individuals and his people as a whole, actions which are given form in blessings, interventions in history[153] and in drawing near to

[151] Cf also Hos 3_5, Neh 9_{25}.
[152] Cf Ps 106_1, 107_1, 118_1, 135_3, 136_1, Jer 33_{11}, I Chron 16_{34}, II Chron 30_{18}; cf also Ps $25_{7,8}$, 27_{13}, 34_9, 52_{11}, 54_8, 73_1, 86_5, 100_5, 145_7 etcetera.
[153] Cf Ps 68_{11}, 104_{28}, 145_9, Nah 1_7.

his people in both temple and liturgy.[154] In the present context, only those deeds which make it possible for him to continue to survive are the focus of the גֶּבֶר's praise. The גֶּבֶר confesses that goodness is also a characteristic of God and that one might look forward to its future manifestation. Such a privilege is not open to all, however, as we can see from the following colon.

25A ... *to those who wait intently for him,* לְקֹוָו

The גֶּבֶר considers the tangible signs of YHWH's goodness to be profoundly related to human expectation thereof. On the one hand, this implies limitation: not everybody (still) shares the גֶּבֶר's faith and trust in God. On the other hand, however, there is also an implication of openness: the גֶּבֶר does not reserve his experience of God (his experience of YHWH's favours) to himself. The awareness of God's ongoing kindness is available to others also and they can experience it as such in their continued survival (cf 3_{22A} and 3_{39}). Up to this point, the גֶּבֶר has not been ashamed of his hopeful expectation of (new) favours from YHWH. At the same time, all those around him are free to nourish that hope once again if they wish. While the *q^e^rē* (pt pl st cs + sf 3m sg) renders the pluralist understanding of the text quite literally, the *k^e^ṯīḇ* (pt sg) can still be upheld (cf also the singular נֶפֶשׁ in the following colon) since an undefined singular can be understood as a collective ('one'). To express the גֶּבֶר's expectation the poets employ the root קוה I, used earlier in Lam 2_{16} (in a profane context) for the enemy's long (yet futile) wait for the downfall of Jerusalem. The present context uses the term for the idea of 'waiting for YHWH', a theological contextualisation of √קוה I most frequently used in the expressions of trust found in the Psalms which confess YHWH as the only ground for hope.[155] The reasons for our insertion of the adverb 'intently' in our translation are twofold. Firstly, it would seem to be etymologically possible to assume a connection between √קוה I and the noun קָו (measuring line), understanding the former to be a derivative of the latter. The basic meaning of √קוה I thus suggests itself in the translation 'to wait intently (literally 'stretched out') for something.[156] The same connection between noun and verb can be found in a response between the fourth canticles of the second and third songs: קָו (נָטָה) (2_{8bA}) // (לְ)קֹוָו (3_{25}). Secondly, √קוה I always implies

---

[154] Cf TWAT III 335f (Höver-Johag) and Ps 35_9, 52_{11}, 54_8, 86_5.

[155] Cf THAT II 624ff (Westermann) and TWAT VI 1232f (Waschke).

[156] Cf KBL 830f, THAT II 619 (Westermann), TWAT VI 1225f, 1229 (Waschke) and HAL 1011.

an intense sort of hope and expectation, one which is not inappropriate in a context filled with negative experiences and disastrous situations from which those who are suffering long to be liberated.[157] The aforementioned response makes it clear that the גֶּבֶר does not present a prettier picture to his possible followers than reality permits: their expectation implies an intense period of waiting for YHWH, for the very one who stretched out the measuring line to determine the extent of the devastation they would have to face. Their hope is a hope in Him, in the one who has devastated and continues to devastate all around them.

25B *to the soul that seeks him.* לְנֶפֶשׁ תִּדְרְשֶׁנּוּ

The גֶּבֶר's orientation towards YHWH is repeated in the present colon with a development from passive waiting to active trust in Him. It is unlikely that the expression דרשׁ יְהוָה stands for the institutional questioning of YHWH – via a prophet in a cultic context – by people suffering affliction, as was commonly the case prior to the exile. It is clear from the present context that the prophets have ceased to function (2_{9c}) while the destruction of the temple has made any kind of cultic activity impossible (2_{6}). The expression appears to be employed here rather to refer to the intention lying behind the institutional, cultic use thereof, being applied as such to the human person in need who longs for YHWH's liberation.[158] Such an intention appears, in fact, to be sufficient both here and elsewhere (even outwith the liturgical context footnoteCf Ps 51_{18f}; cf also Lam 2_{18a} and 3_{55-66}.), implying a longing for YHWH which is rooted in the very fibre of a person's existence (נֶפֶשׁ, cf Lam 3_{17A}). Westermann is of the opinion that we are already dealing here with a general dictum of faith.[159] The context of severe affliction, however, remains undeniable.

26 *Good is he. May one quietly wait* טוֹב יוֹחִיל וְדוּמָם
for YHWH*'s help.* לִתְשׁוּעַת יְהוָה

A detailed discussion of the various possibilities and impossibilities with regard to the multitude of readings and interpretations of the difficult Hebrew expression טוֹב וְיָחִיל וְדוּמָם can be found in Albrektson and Gottlieb. We must limit our discussion here to the following: (I) the unfamiliar verb form (וְ)יָחִיל and (II) the copulative ו preceding דוּמָם which disrupts the

[157] Cf TWAT VI 1229 (Waschke).
[158] Cf THAT I 463ff (Gerleman).
[159] CWestermann, 'Die Begriffe für Fragen und Suchen im Alten Testament', in: *Forschung am Alten Testament*, ThB 55, München 1974, 185ff.

flow of the sentence.[160] Most exegetes are inclined to emend the text, the least intrusive and radical being that of Budde[161] who reads: וְיוֹחִילוּ דוּמָם, the ו preceding דוּמָם being understood as part of a verbal form of √יחל (*hiph'il* impf 3m pl) '...it is good that they (namely the קֹוָו of 3_{25}) hope in silence...'. While Gordis and Haller follow a similar line of thought, the argumentation remains unconvincing given the fact that the plural of 3_{25} does not appear to be original.

In place of the unfamiliar וְיָחִיל we assume an original יוֹחִיל, the *hiph'il* impf 3m sg of √יחל ('to hope'). In ancient Hebrew the consonants ו and י are very similar and are frequently confused and interchanged.[162] As a consequence, a copyist's error may have led to the metathesis of the much more frequent consonantal sequence וי of the *imperfectum consecutivum*. An additional suggestion offered by Gottlieb sheds further light on the situation. He proposes that our translational problems have emerged from the fact that we assume וְיָחִיל וְדוּמָם to be the subject of a nominal clause introduced by טוֹב (that is 'Good is...'). A significant difference is made, however, if one understands טוֹב to be the predicate of YHWH as in 3_{25}. Gottlieb contends, therefore, that we should read וְיָחִיל וְדוּמָם via the ו as an asyndetic circumstantial clause: 'good is He, when one waits in silence...". The difficulty remains, however, that such a solution fails to explain the unfamiliar verb form וְיָחִיל. We suggest that the text should be read as יוֹחִיל וְדוּמָם, understood as a jussive and interpreted as a circumstantial clause with an undetermined subject.[163] In addition, the ו preceding דוּמָם ought to be understood as explicative.[164] By rendering דוּמָם adverbially as 'quietly',[165] we obviate the need to provide a translation of the ו. The Peshitta follows a similar approach as does Ehrlich. Wiesmann offers an alternative translation in line with what we have suggested. The explicit mention of YHWH's name at the end of the colon need not be understood as a counter argument to our proposal (cf Lam 3_{66}).

Whatever the problems existing at the linguistic level, the meaning and content of the text remain unobscured. The idea of hoping in silence for

160 Cf Keil's translation: "und zwar schweigend."

161 Cf KBL 378.

162 Cf EWürthwein, *Der Text des Alten Testaments*, Stuttgart 1973⁴, 104, 205 and ETov, *Textual Criticism of the Hebrew Bible*, Assen/Maastricht, 1992, 246f.

163 Cf Brockelmann § 159a and GES-K § 141*e*, § 142*d*; with regard to the undetermined subject cf GES-K § 144*d*.

164 Cf HAL 248 sv ו (5) and GES-K § 154a note 1(b).

165 For the form cf BL 504*k*.

salvation from YHWH is not unusual in the OT.[166] What is new in the present context is the notion of 'being silent'. In the light of 2_{10}, however, such 'being silent' ought to be understood as more than simply sitting in a sort of paralized amazement. The present text speaks rather of a tenacious intensification of 'being silent', of a conscious option for remaining silent. Whether such an attitude is inspired by the expectation of a change for the good[167] remains open to question and is far from certain (cf 3_{29}). The theme of Ps 39 would appear to be closer to the point: because of the affliction he has suffered, the poet has difficulty in restraining his tongue. At the same time, he is aware that the use of rebellious and reproachful language towards YHWH is inappropriate for a human person and is certainly no preface to divine intervention.[168] We are thus reminded of 3_8 which forms an antithetical inclusion with 3_{26} within the first canto. In 3_8, prayer, in the form of a cry of distress and an appeal for assistance, is looked upon with disdain and rejected by YHWH. Silence, however, stands in sharp contrast to the somewhat hazardous and reproving images of the great Enemy in the first sub-canto. In the present context, the גֶּבֶר now calls for an alternative aproach: silence in the midst of affliction. In remaining silent a person surrenders him or herself completely, trusting in YHWH alone and waiting in hope for his salvific intervention.

Unique to the concept תְּשׁוּעָה – as salvation from YHWH – is the fact that it implies a sort of miraculous intervention on the part of the deity.[169] Such an intervention is clearly necessary given the hopeless situation in which the גֶּבֶר and his compatriots find themselves. The parallel colon in 1_{9bA} contrastively depicts the same situation in terms of an equally extraordinary collapse (וַתֵּרֶד פְּלָאִים). The restoration of city and land calls for a further miraculous intervention on the part of YHWH (cf the explanation of 5_{21B}).

27 *He is good to a devout one when he must bear a yoke in his youth.* טוֹב לַגֶּבֶר כִּי־יִשָּׂא עֹל בִּנְעוּרָיו

Our translation here deviates from the most frequent rendering: 'it is good for a גֶּבֶר that he bears a yoke in his youth', the accuracy of which we have already called into question elsewhere.[170] The present translation follows

166 Cf Ps 37_7, $39_{3,8}$, $62_{2,6}$, Isa 30_{15}.
167 Cf TWAT II 282 (Baumann).
168 Cf NHRidderbos, *De Psalmen I*, KV, Kampen 1962, 424.
169 Cf Ps 33_{16}, Hos 1_7, Isa 30_{15}, THAT I 790 (Stolz) and TWAT III 1051ff (Sawyer).
170 Cf 1983, 301.

the Peshitta, Wiesmann and Gottlieb, taking טוֹב to be a predicate of YHWH.[171] In addition, we understand כִּי to be conditional[172] and take YHWH to be the subject of the nominal clause ל... טוֹב. From the literary perspective, the fact that the same construction ל... טוֹב is used in the first and last bicola of the present strophe confirms our position. The frequently evident concentric structure at the strophic level (cf, for example, 3_{31-33}) allows us to postulate a parallel between both bicola.

From the perspective of content, the traditional translation presents a major difficulty: it presumes the (wisdom) insight that a human person becomes spiritually stronger if he or she has already learned to overcome difficulties in his or her youth. With respect to the affliction outlined in the book of Lamentations, however, such an idea is not only repugnant, it is quite misplaced. Divine pedagogy of this type is clearly due to later interpolation. It cannot be denied that YHWH has permitted his people to be confronted with great affliction, but the idea that he may have done so as a means towards their greater spiritual maturity is far from evident. In any event, what it does lead to is an awareness of guilt.[173] A further difficulty lies in the fact that the notion of purification brought about by trial and tribulation can only be realised in hindsight. In the present circumstances such hindsight cannot apply since many have not survived the 'lesson' and those who are still alive continue to face unabated death and destruction.[174] The difficulties facing the גֶּבֶר have clearly not been overcome and the question remains as to whether his renewed faith and trust in God will be vindicated or not (cf 3_{29} and 5_{22}). A third problem emerges from the fact that a traditional translation of this verse impedes the proper functioning of the bicolon at the level of content. It is clear that the גֶּבֶר wishes to move others to share in his renewed faith. As such, the argument that YHWH is a God who desires to make his people wiser by afflicting them with famine and death is hardly convincing. Finally, the content of the second colon also runs counter to the usual interpretation of the verse. It became apparent in our exegesis of 1_{14a} that the term עֹל implied a yoke intended specifically for beasts of burden. If human beings were to have such a yoke placed on their shoulders, the load would be too great and they would collapse under it – just as Lady Jerusalem almost collapsed under her yoke – learning nothing from the experience.

171 For the interpretation of √נשׂא as 'to bear' cf HAL 683f.

172 Cf HAL 449 sv כִּי II (11).

173 Cf Jer 5_{19}, Lam 1_{18}, 3_{40-42}.

174 See 1_{20c}, $2_{4,12,20}$, 4_9 etcetera.

The poets, however, have made the contrast even more acute. While in Isa 47_5, the inhumanity of Lady Babylon is illustrated by her application of the same type of yoke to the naturally weak and elderly, the present text employs the young people of Jerusalem to further sharpen the contrast. If adult men in the fullness of their physical powers are unable to bear such a yoke, how then can the young be expected to do so? Given the use of גֶּבֶר side by side with נְעוּרָה, however, it is evident that the primary poetic concern is one of contrast rather than one of age.

Our position on this text stands in line with the belief that YHWH does not put to shame those who must count on his help in time of need,[175] a belief which has validity in the context of a relationship of faith in God. Such a relationship is also assumed here. Indeed, the גֶּבֶר does not say that YHWH is good to everyone, only to those who themselves are גְּבָרִים. In so doing he does not focus attention on himself but rather on the faith relationship with YHWH which is characteristic of a גֶּבֶר (cf the explanation of 3_{1A}).

Besides the aforementioned considerations, the literary structure of the second sub-canto and indeed of the third song as a whole calls for further examination. Within Lam III, the ט-strophe (3_{25-27}) and the כ-strophe (3_{31-33}) do not only begin with three times the same letter but also, strikingly enough, with three times the same word! Thus within sub-canto 3_{22-33}, the כ-strophe assumes a responsive character in relation to the ט-strophe. From the perspective of content, the response in question has the following structure:

טוֹב ... כִּי ...: good is He... for...

This remains a familiar structure even although the expected call to praise is missing from 3_{22-33} (cf the colometric sequence of Ps 136_1 together with the frequent use of כִּי and the clusters with YHWH's חֶסֶד at the beginning of the sub-canto [חַסְדֵי יְהוָה, 3_{22A}] and כְּרֹב חֲסָדוֹ[!] in 3_{32B}). In similar fashion, 3_{31} can be read in sequence with 3_{25}: 'good is he for those who wait intently for him... for he does not reject forever'. At the same time, 3_{32} can be read in sequence with 3_{26}: 'good is he, may one quietly wait for YHWH's help... for whenever he has caused much grief, he has compassion according to his many favours'. Following the same structural sequence, therefore, we can understand 3_{33} as supplementary parallel to 3_{27}: 'Good is he for a גֶּבֶר, when he must bear a yoke in his youth... for the oppression and grieving

175 Ps 22_6, 25_3; cf Ps 130_{5-8}.

of human persons does not conform to his heart'. The latter sentiment expressed in 3_{33} which firmly states that oppression does not conform to YHWH's heart is clearly in contradiction with any wisdom interpretation which might suggest that Adonai afflicts people with dreadful need and misfortune in order to educate them. In other words, the pedagogy of the wise teacher whose concern for his children leads him to intentionally afflict them with difficulties in order to teach them wisdom can and indeed must not be projected onto YHWH in the present text.

The diptych structure of Lam III in which the ט-strophe (3_{25-27}) constitutes a canto-response with the ר-strophe (3_{58-60}) also supports our proposed interpretation of the text. In the same way as 3_{17} can be read side by side with 3_{50}, it is possible to read the ט-strophe side by side with the ר-strophe. Thus the expressions of trust found in the ר-strophe constitute fitting responses to the טוֹב-statements: 'Good is YHWH... for he saves'; 'good is YHWH, may one quietly wait... for he sees the injustice done'. Against the background of such supplementary canto-responses, therefore, it becomes possible to read 3_{27} in the light of 3_{60}, a reading which only makes sense in the context of our proposed interpretation: 'good is YHWH for a גֶּבֶר... for He sees all the malice and the plots directed against him'.

Thus the ט-strophe concludes with new and encouraging insight: where YHWH's faithful are threatened with burdens they cannot endure he is at their side.

Canticle II (3_{28-33})

Content/theme: *Perhaps there is hope, for* YHWH*'s wrath does not endure forever; thus one must bear one's fate in silence.*

Literary argumentation:

inclusions:	כִּי (28B) // כִּי (33A)
	נָטַל עָלָיו (28B) // עִנָּה (33A)
	חֶרְפָּה (30B) // יִזְנַח (31A)
incl/resp:	תִּקְוָה (29B) // חֲסָדוֹ (32B)
responses:	כִּי (28B) // כִּי (31A)
	בֶּעָפָר פִּיהוּ (29A) // הוֹגָה (32A)
	תִּקְוָה (29B) // וְרִחַם (31A)
	נָטַל עָלָיו (28B) // יִזְנַח (31A)
	לְמַכֵּהוּ לֶחִי (30A) // עִנָּה (33A)
	יִשְׂבַּע בְּחֶרְפָּה (30B) // וַיַּגֶּה (33B)

In this final canticle of the present (sub-)canto the first strophe focuses on the attitude of a wretched man who has been smitten by YHWH's judgement. This attitude can be characterised as an attempt at self-resignation, acceptance of the fact that YHWH is the one who has placed this burden upon him. Outspoken complaint in the face of humiliation and affliction is replaced by quiet forbearance. The final strophe presents arguments in support of such an attitude: God's wrath does not endure forever nor is the oppression of human persons according to his nature.

28A *May he sit down alone and be silent,* יֵשֵׁב בָּדָד וְיִדֹּם

The subject here is the undetermined גֶּבֶר already mentioned in 3_{27A}: the גֶּבֶר (of 3_1) offers advice to any גֶּבֶר. Within the book of Lamentations as a whole, the image of sitting alone (ישב בָּדָד) has its parallel in 1_{1aA} in which Lady Jerusalem is portrayed as sitting alone in a context of leprosy and mourning. The repetition of the same word combination in the present colon is far from accidental. As Lam I begins with desolate prostration so the first canto of Lam III ends with it. The significance is quite clear: the fate of Lady Jerusalem is the same as that of her inhabitants. The appeal for silent endurance of that fate, however, is new here (cf the explanation of 3_{26}). A further parallel exists – at precisely the same level – with 2_{10a} (song-response) in which the elders prostrate themselves in mourning over their own fate and that of the city. The parallelism implies that the גְּבָרִים are being called upon to prostrate themselves in the same way as the elders of 2_{10a}. Not only must they share their physical state, however, they must also share their silence, albeit now in the form of humble resignation in spite of the context of affliction and death. Striking correspondences with the fate of the גֶּבֶר are quite in evidence. Within the canto's concentric structure, 3_{28} corresponds with 3_6 (cf the corresponding √ישב) in which the גֶּבֶר complains about the circle of death, loneliness and abandonment in which YHWH has placed him. He is not alone in this circle, however. He is joined by other whom he adjures to accept their fate.

28B *for He has imposed it on him.* כִּי נָטַל עָלָיו

The verb נטל is only found in three other places in the OT. In II Sam 24_{12} (// I Chron 21_{10}) it is employed for the imposition of a punishment. The translation 'to bear' also appears to be possible.[176] LXX, Peshitta and Targum (followed by Gordis among others) all understand the afflicted

[176] Cf Isa 63_6; the meaning and derivation of יִטּוֹל in Isa 40_{15} is disputed.

one to be the subject and not YHWH: 'when such a one takes up/bears his yoke'. Such an interpretation appears to assume a degree of free will, however, as people were free to submit themselves to the great affliction or to choose to avoid it. Given our explanation of the previous colon, the idea of free will is clearly out of the question. What was implicitly present in the previous colon – namely that a person must submit to this judgement, placed like a yoke on his or her shoulders by YHWH – now becomes more explicit. For this reason we opt for the translation 'to impose' (cf II Sam 24_{12}) with YHWH as subject, the yoke (עֹל) from 3_{27B} as object and the afflicted one as dative. The yoke to which the גֶּבֶר refers is, of course, reminiscent of the yoke fastened about Lady Jerusalem's neck with her sins in 1_{14}. The connection with 1_{14} is important here: it should be clear that the yoke imposed by YHWH is not a meaningless burden. The yoke imposed by YHWH is not the result of arbitrary and convoluted divine creation but a consequence of Lady Jerusalem's sins with which YHWH is ultimately forced to confront her.

The present judgement raises questions concerning collective punishment and the individual's part in the transgression. In other words: should the devout be forced to suffer along with the guilty? Jer 45 offers something of an answer to the problem. In the context of judgement – which is even hurtful to God himself – Baruch must not expect to be treated as an exception. Nevertheless, he is promised that YHWH will give him his life as a prize of war. Corresponding elements are also present here. YHWH's faithful see themselves confronted with his judgement against Judah and Jerusalem (cf Jer 49_{12}) under which they too are forced to suffer the most unbearable affliction. How can such an awareness be reconciled with the 'God is good' expressions of the previous strophe? No matter how far it remains from his heart, YHWH's judgement has become inevitable, even for those who continue to have faith in him. In the context of that judgement, however, he can do nothing more than sustain them in life. Such is their prize of war, their booty. This is precisely what the גֶּבֶר has experienced so far. It is in the very fact that he is still alive that YHWH manifests his goodness (cf the explanation of $3_{22,23,25-27}$). In addition, it should be noted that Baruch is oblivious of any guilt in Jer 45. The גֶּבֶר, on the other hand, confesses on his own behalf and that of his compatriots that they have sinned and have acted defiantly (cf 3_{42}).

29A *May he press his mouth to the dust,* יִתֵּן בֶּעָפָר פִּיהוּ

There appears to be a certain logical progression at work here. The person who sits down with the burden of a heavy yoke upon is shoulders is unlikely to be able to stay upright, his back gradually bending over as he succumbs to the load. The גֶּבֶר adjures no resistance. As he folds under the weight of his yoke, he eventually finds his face pressed to the ground and his mouth in the dust. The image is reminiscent of that of a defeated enemy who is expected to serve as a footstool for his victorious enemy.[177] The triumphant victor would also place his foot on the neck of his prostrate captive as a sign of ultimate humiliation.[178] In such circumstances the captive's mouth was driven into the dust.[179] A certain amount of this kind of behaviour was voluntary, however, particularly when an enemy was seen to throw himself to the ground before his captor, kiss his feet and lick the dust before him.[180] The present text also suggests something of a reversal of fortunes: at one time this humiliation had been the fate of Israel's enemies but now it is Israel's turn to submit. Lam 3_{34} also presents an image of being trampled under the feet of the enemy. The גֶּבֶר calls upon his people to endure the humiliation.

We already noted connections between this colon and 2_{10c} where the young girls of Jerusalem are portrayed as lying face down on the ground, finding themselves thus in the dust and in the realm of death and mourning. Such a display of grief served as an expression of submission before YHWH. A similar sort of submission is being called for here. In light of the agreement between the present text and 3_{16B} where the גֶּבֶר is pressed down in the dust/ash, it seems possible that the authors may be referring to the actual lot of the גֶּבֶר himself (compare Ugaritic *kpṯ*, 'earth' UT 1291a).

29B *perhaps there is still hope.* אוּלַי יֵשׁ תִּקְוָה

The present colon anticipates the following כ-strophe in which arguments are offered in support of maintaining a sense of hope and reason is given for the called for resignation and aquiescence.

תִּקְוָה is closely related to the root קוה I (cf 3_{25a}) and suggests a sense of anticipation. The hope implied in these words is that YHWH will intervene and bring about a change in the people's fortunes (cf Ps 62_6, 71_5). Westermann[181] wrongly proposes that there is no question of hope in YHWH

[177] See I Kgs 5_3 (MT 5_{17}), Ps 110_1 and figures 341 and 342 in OKeel, *Die Welt der altorientalischen Bildsymbolik und das Alte Testament*, Zürich-Einsiedeln-Köln-Neukirchen-Vluyn 1977², 232f.

[178] Cf Jos 10_{24}, Ps 18_{39}.

[179] See Keel, 276, figure 404.

[180] Cf Ps 72_9, Mic 7_{17}, Isa 43_{23}.

contained in these words. The entire context, however, would appear to suggest the opposite. Our translation with 'there is still hope' is based on the frequently negative context of the root קוה I: "Es muß auffallen, daß vom Hoffen so überwiegend negativ gesprochen wird...; das Hoffen muß also besonders dort bewußt geworden sein, wo das Erhoffte nicht eintrat. Es macht sich dort bemerkbar, wo es sich lange hinzieht, ohne Erfüllung zu finden." [182] Of course, a sense of resignation is also unmistakably present here. There is certainly no suggestion of joyous and open-hearted expectation. Instead, the authors paint a picture of wavering anticipation which, in the climate of otherwise total hopelessness which held sway after the fall of the land and the city, has to be expected, at least from the human perspective. The people complain in Ezek 37_{11}: "Our bones are dried up, and our hope is lost; we are cut off completely." Hesitation is also evident in the term אוּלַי 'perhaps' which, no doubt, the poets employ as a means to respect the sovereignty of YHWH in the same way as the prophets did when they spoke of the possibility of being spared on the day of YHWH's judgement.[183] At the same time, however, the term also contains a sense of hesitation and uncertainty with respect to the positive outcome of the present circumstances.[184] Thus the text contains no suggestion of certainty in faith (Heb 11_1). What is evident is the fidelity of a faith under challenge (Mk 9_{24}).

If one turns a blind eye to the context of immense affliction and suffering then such an unsure faith becomes all the more difficult to understand and accept, a fact to which the text tradition of this verse is witness. LXX drops the verse completely, perhaps due to haplography in light of the identical introductory terms of 3_{29} and 3_{30}. Given the regular order of three times the same opening letter, however, haplography would appear to be an unlikely cause. The Syriac and the Peshitta translate with אוּלַי 'because' (there is hope). Albrektson is correct in discerning 'a dogmatic flavour' in such an emendation.

30 *May he turn his cheek to the one who strikes him,*	יִתֵּן לְמַכֵּהוּ לֶחִי
may he be filled with insults.	יִשְׂבַּע בְּחֶרְפָּה׃

The person at prayer in Ps 3_8 gives thanks for the fact that YHWH has struck his enemy on the cheek/jaw. The one who delivers such a blow

---

181 See THAT II 620.
182 Cf THAT II 622 (Westermann).
183 Cf Am 5_{15}, Zeph 2_3; cf also Jer 21_2 and Jonah 1_6.
184 Cf 1983, 308.

demonstrates great superiority. To slap someone on the cheek is an act of scorn and a sign that one no longer has the slightest respect for the person one strikes. Such behaviour affects the humiliated party at the very core of his/her existence.[185] It appears in ritual form as part of the Babylonian *akîtu*-festival during which the priest was seen to strike the king on the cheek and pull at his beard. Specific contexts of this type are absent from the OT although the universally human aspect of such treatment is attested.[186]

In our explanation of 2_{11c} we pointed to the connection between שֶׁבֶר 'break'/'rupture' and √נכה with respect to the immense catastrophe which has confronted Israel, humiliation and derision at the hands of the enemy being part of the same picture (cf 2_{16}). In the present context such humiliation is indicated by the term חֶרְפָּה (basic meaning: 'sharp', 'keen', 'acute') in which the might of the one perpetrating the humiliation rings through loud and clear. One should not only think here of objective humiliation, however, in the sense of the derision of others. The text also implies subjectively endured humiliation in the sense of the shame caused thereby. Such derision always hits home and always hurts. In its broadest sense, the humiliation in question here concerns the horrendous downfall of the city and the land, a fact which has pierced everyone to the core (cf the explanation of 5_1), although – from the perspective of 1_{10} – it is possible that the more specific humiliation of having pagans in the sanctuary may be closer to the authors' intention.

The גֶּבֶר appeals to his audience to endure the shame confronting them because it is YHWH's judgement. In the concentric structure of the first canto (3_{1-33}), this verse is related to 3_4. In terms of content, the relationship between both verses is quite clear. In 3_4, the גֶּבֶר is left emaciated by (the sword of) hunger (see 2_{12bA} and 4_{9aB}); here he is offered nothing other than piercing humiliation to satisfy his hunger. In 3_4, YHWH makes a broken man (√שבר) of the גֶּבֶר; here his blows strike (√נכה) to the גֶּבֶר's very being. In real terms the גֶּבֶר's suffering remains the same, although the disposition with which it is endured has to change: no more blind rebellion, only acceptance that God must place this burden on his shoulders and those of the people. The continued awareness that God is good, however, sustains an element of hope that things will change for the better. The following strophe expresses this hope more explicitly.

---

[185] Cf TWAT V 447 (Conrad).

[186] Cf I Kgs 22_{24}, Job 16_{10}; cf also Isa 50_6.

31 *For he does not reject forever,* כִּי לֹא יִזְנַח לְעוֹלָם
Adonai. אֲדֹנָי

In the final strophe of the present (sub-)canto/canticle, the poets render account of their reasons for hope, taking 'rejection' by YHWH as their point of departure. The two earlier uses of the root זנח II can help shed some light on what they mean by 'rejection'. In 2_{7aA} the term refers to the rejection of the altar (and, by implication, the priests) which can be understood as a chiffre for the rejection of the cult. Such rejection echoes loud in the suffering of the גֶּבֶר[187] although it is also experienced by others. The present verse now indicates the limited duration of YHWH's rejection.

What makes it possible for the poets to arrive at such an insight? Any analysis of the use of √זנח II will reveal that rejection on the part of YHWH is nowhere understood as, per definition, a temporary matter. It remained part of their experience, nevertheless, that after a period of rejection, YHWH once again offered a helping hand to his people (cf Ps 60, 108_{12}). The fact that such a turn of events was not considered a foregone conclusion, however, is evident in the question whether YHWH might reject (his people) forever.[188] We can deduce from Ps 74_1 and Zech 1_{12}, that the long duration of the exile had led some to think that rejection by YHWH could last for a very long time indeed. At the same time, both Zech 1_{12} and Ps 74_1 offer something of a key to the understanding of our present verse in the very fact that such a lengthy period of rejection was considered absurd and irreconcilable with God's mercy. Moreover, both texts establish a relationship between rejection by YHWH and YHWH's anger, the former being the consequence of the latter. Israel was fundamentally aware that YHWH's wrath was short lived (cf the explanation of 5_{22}). Ps 103_{8f} is similarly enlightening with its striking terminological affinities with the present text and context (cf: רַחוּם [103_8] // √רחם [3_{32}]; וְלֹא לְעוֹלָם יִטּוֹר [103_9] // כִּי לֹא יִזְנַח לְעוֹלָם [3_{31}]; וְרַב־חָסֶד [103_8] // כְּרֹב חֲסָדוֹ [3_{32}]). The affirmation that God does not maintain his anger forever (Ps 103_9) is parallel, in a certain sense, with the present verse (3_{31}): YHWH does not reject forever. Why this is so remains unspoken. Indeed, if one accepts a causal relationship between YHWH's anger and his rejection then there is no need to offer further explanation since Israel was totally convinced of the fact that in principle YHWH's anger was short lived. In addition, one is reminded of the appendix to the second commandment in which there is an enor-

187 Cf the exegesis of the core verse 3_{17}.
188 Cf Ps 44_{24}, 77_8.

mous difference in duration between YHWH's wrath and his compassion and mercy as well as of the fact that no human person can survive God's anger for long.[189] Rejection as a consequence of God's wrath, therefore, can only endure as long as the wrath itself endures (cf, once again, the explanation of 5_{22}).

Given the shortness of the second colon (with אֲדֹנָי alone) it is assumed that a verb form has fallen out of the text.[190] Any proposed synonymous reconstruction, however, remains guess work and is, in fact, unnecessary since the textual tradition offers no alternative indications and a short colon is not outwith the bounds of possibility.[191]

32A *Whenever he has grieved, he has compassion...* כִּי אִם־הוֹגָה וְרִחַם

The present colon constitutes a more detailed explication of that which precedes it. In the context, כִּי אִם means 'when'/'whenever'.[192] For the significance of הוֹגָה (*hiph'il* pf with YHWH as subject) see the explanation of 1_{4cA} (the young girls of Jerusalem) as well as the following bicolon. In 1_{5bA} and 1_{12cA} Lady Jerusalem is the object of grief, and thus, by extension, her population. The same is implied here also: the גֶּבֶר reflects on the profound sorrow felt within the city. After causing such grief YHWH has compasssion. The root רחם (*pi'el*) is closely related to the term רֶחֶם 'womb' and suggests the natural, affective relationship existing between a mother and her child, an affection which she makes concrete in her deeds of love. Use of the term elsewhere in the OT shows that such a specific context cannot always be assumed. The exercise of compassion also implies affectivity within other relationships whereby the 'performative' character is still preserved. In addition, compassion always has its place in a movement between someone superior and someone inferior, between an adult and a child, between God and human persons, but never the other way round.[193] If one respects all of these ideas surrounding the notion of compassion then the compassion implied in the present text suggests a complete restoration of everything that has been destroyed as a consequence of YHWH's anger.[194]

189 Cf Ps 90_7, 102_{10-12}, Ex 33_{10-12}, Nah 1_6.

190 Cf text critical apparatus BHS.

191 See MCAKorpel – JCdMoor, 'Fundamentals of Ugaritic and Hebrew Poetry', in: *The Structural Analysis of Biblical and Canaanite Poetry*, (eds WvdMeer and JCdMoor) JSOT suppl series 74, Sheffield 1988, 4–14, and only אֲדֹנָי gives emphasis.

192 Cf HAL 449 sv כִּי אִם.

193 Cf THAT II 763f (Stoebe).

194 Cf THAT II 766 (Stoebe).

Once again the question arises as to how the poets have been able to arrive at such an insight. In the context of √יגה I with YHWH as subject, one never finds his impending compassion mentioned in opposition to his causing of grief, either conditionally or unconditionally. If one examines the arguments given elsewhere for YHWH's merciful intervention then we frequently find (the hope) that YHWH has compassion because people have changed and evil is removed or likewise that there is no compassion because injustice is still present.[195] A connection of this kind, however, is not always part of the context. God's mercy is also mentioned without talk of (prior) conversion,[196] and in some circumstances it is simply his good will which stands at the roots of his compassion (Isa 60_{10}). It would appear, therefore, that a unequivocal relationship between God's mercy and human conversion is difficult to establish. The fact of conversion would also appear to be absent from the present context, being reserved for the following canto, in 3_{40}. For this reason we must seek our explanation in the relationship with YHWH's anger (cf the explanation of 3_{31}). Not only rejection emerges as the consequence of such anger but oppression as well, the kind of oppression which leaves human persons wretched and lost. In precisely this state – having endured his wrath – human persons arouse YHWH's mercy and compassion.[197]

32B ... *according to his many favours.* כְּרֹב חֲסָדוֹ

For the full meaning of חֶסֶד see the exegesis of 3_{22A}. The content and structure of Ps 77 is germane to our understanding and explanation of the partitive genitive כְּרֹב חֲסָדוֹ. In the first part of the psalm we hear the fearful question whether YHWH will reject forever and whether his anger will obliterate his mercy (Ps 77_{8-10}). The same question clearly preoccupied the poets of Lamentations. The author of Ps 77 sought his answer in Israel's history, in the many examples of God's powerful liberation (77_{12-21}). The fact that the poets of Lamentations follow a similar line is evident in the present colon: 'in accordance with his many favours' (read the *qᵉrē*). The use of the term רֹב 'multitude', however, makes it clear that their view of YHWH's favours, includes more than the חַסְדֵי יְהוָה mentioned by the גֶּבֶר in 3_{22A}.[198] Their understanding includes the many favours per-

[195] Cf II Chron 30_9, Deut 4_{30ff}, 13_{17}, 30_{2f}, Isa 9_{16}, 27_{11}, 55_7, Jer 13_{14}, 21_7, Joel 2_{13}, Hos 2_6.

[196] Cf Ps 78_{38f}, 103_{8f}, Neh 9_{17}, II Kgs 13_{23}.

[197] Cf Ps 103_{8-11}, Isa $54_{7,8}$.

[198] For the translation of the preceding כְּ cf HAL 433 sv כְּ (3).

formed by YHWH in the course of history on behalf of his people, the Davidic king and, indeed, many an individual Israelite. For examples of the favours which YHWH has shown to Israel throughout her history see Gen 32_{11}, Ps 25_6, $89_{2,50}$, 106_7, 107_{43}, Isa 63_7, together with the places where YHWH's חֶסֶד appears in the singular[199] among which the lasting character of the חֶסֶד is not infrequently rendered by the term עוֹלָם: Ps 25_6, 106_1, 107_1, 117_1, Isa 54_8. חֶסֶד thus proves to be the implicit antithesis of God's (short-lived) anger (cf 3_{31}). Israel's history has revealed God's salvific concern so often, in spite of her manifold disobedience. Why then should the present situation constitute an exception?! This is the hope of the poets, even although their extrapolation of salvation history does not offer them any certainty. Why should it? The disaster confronting them is of such enormous proportions (cf 2_{13c}). Heaven forbid that YHWH's favour should come to an end now (cf 3_{29B} and 5_{20}).

33 *For it does not conform to his heart: oppression* — כִּי לֹא עִנָּה מִלִּבּוֹ
and grieving of human persons. — וַיַּגֶּה בְּנֵי־אִישׁ

Inclusion at the strophe level is immediately evident in the Hebrew between the present text and 3_{31A}: כִּי לֹא (3_{31A}) // כִּי לֹא (3_{33A}). At the level of content there is also evidence of supplementary parallelism, the expression '...does not reject forever' in 3_{31} being provided here with further motivation. Where the preceding statements concerning God's merciful favours could only find a basis in the limited duration of God's anger, here, at the end of the canto, the concept is given much firmer roots in very fundamental theology: the poets speak of the very essence of God. As a matter of fact, here in the middle of the third song and simultaneously – at the literary-structural level – in the centre of the five songs as a whole, we find the very basis for all the sighs and laments, prayers and pleadings, hopes and expectations we have encountered so far from the poets and their sympathisers: they know that all of this does not conform to the essence of God. What they have been forced to endure is clearly against God's nature. In expressing this awareness they employ the metaphor of God's heart. By analogy with human beings (cf the explanation of 1_{20bA}), God's heart is the centre of his emotions (cf Gen 6_6); he takes cognisance of things with his heart (Jer 44_{21}, Job 7_{17}); his heart is the place where he ponders things and comes to decisions (cf Job 36_{5ff} [כֹּחַ לֵב] and Gen 8_{21} [אֶל־לִבּוֹ]). In Gen 8_{21} we are told how God distanced himself from the

[199] Cf TWAT III 61ff (Zobel).

great judgement of the flood. Jeremiah is also aware that the horrors of child sacrifice did not come forth from God's heart.[200] God's heart is the ultimate source of his compassion for Israel (Hos 11_8), it is filled with kindness towards human persons.[201] Given the diffusion of this aspect of the knowledge of God throughout the various traditions of the OT, it is clear that we are dealing with an insight which was far from limited. Israel's experience was unequivocal: this was the language of God's heart and none other.

It is equally evident, however, that present experience and theological insight were at odds with one another. Faced with the dreadful affliction God had imposed on his people, the poets had been obliged (via the גֶּבֶר) to speak quite differently in the first sub-canto (3_{1-21}). They now summarise their earlier thoughts in the form of two concepts. Firstly, they employ the root ענה II (*pi'el*) 'to oppress', which means the humiliation of a human person by way of physical and spiritual violence. "Wer "unterdrückt, vergewaltigt, erniedrigt, demütigt", gebraucht seine Macht gegen bestehendes recht"; the status of a human person or of a people is negatively altered by such oppression.[202] The verb in question can be employed in a great variety of contexts and thus lends itself to expansion, *in casu* for the detailed description of the affliction related in the five songs as a whole. If one reflects on the notion of a negative change of status, included among the aspects of such a change is the loss of election (cf the explanation of 4_2). In addition, elements such as the break-down of norms and the overstepping of boundaries are included in the semantic field of √ענה II. Oppression in itself is an extreme, a fact which is no less valid when God is the oppressor.[203] For this reason √ענה II, with YHWH as subject, constitutes, in fact, a *contradictio in terminis*. For God, oppression is an *opus alienum*.[204] At the same time, oppression as such provides an appropriate basis for Israel's appeal for restoration and justice. The second concept employed by the poets offers something similar: √יגה I,[205] 'to grieve', brought about by God's negative disposition which brings sorrow and heartbreak to his people. The extent to which the other songs expand on this concept

---

[200] Cf 7_{31}, 19_5, 32_{35}.
[201] Cf TWAT IV 448f (Fabry).
[202] Cf TWAT VI 253f (Gerstenberger).
[203] Cf Ps 88_8, 90_{15}, 102_{24f}.
[204] Cf JJeremias, *Die Reue Gottes*, Neukirchen 1975 and GGerstenberger–WSchrage, *Leiden*, Stuttgart 1977, 85–89.
[205] For the form cf BL 220*n*; GES-K § 69*u*.

needs little explanation.[206] Such ‘grieving’ is equally alien to the essence of God, not according to his heart. The term should be read, in the first place, alongside the central song-response in 1_{12} in order to bring the contradiction in YHWH’s heart – brought about by his deeds of judgement – into sharp relief: כְּמַכְאֹבִי ... אֲשֶׁר הוֹגָה יְהוָה (1_{12bc}) \\ כִּי לֹא עִנָּה מִלִּבּוֹ וַיַּגֶּה בְּנֵי־אִישׁ (3_{33}). He does not delight in such deeds. The inclusive expression ‘human person’ at the conclusion of the bicolon indicates the extent to which the poets are dealing with a characteristic of God which touches all human beings, even Israel’s enemies (cf the explanation of the concluding strophe of the parallel canto 3_{64-66}).

The גֶּבֶר looks around him and sees enemies within the gates of Jerusalem and the smoking ruins of the temple and the city. He sees harassed, hungry people and starving children; death and decay are everywhere. He is aware of his exhausted body and tormented spirit and he is convinced that none of this is according to the heart of God. In spite of the immensity of the catastrophe confronting the people, the poets hold fast to this essential insight. No matter how necessary YHWH’s judgement against Israel is, he does not carry it out willingly because it does not belong to his nature to do so. Thus the poets recognise a conflict in the very heart of God and such an awareness is far from insignificant. The realisation that, in the midst of this disaster, God has actually turned against himself, begins to feed their hope that he will finally turn their sorrow and affliction around. Patient anticipation of such a change is not without reason, even although there can be no absolute certainty (cf 5_{22}).

At the end of the first canto it would appear that the גֶּבֶר has said his piece. His unfathomable suffering, his great affliction, his rebellious complaints, his interrogation of God, his struggle to renew his faith in God and the foundations of his ongoing hope in YHWH’s salvific intervention have all been put into words. His intention in all this is not personal catharsis, however, but rather an endeavour to recruit others, to have them follow him in his path away from self-pity to renewed hope and expectation.

Canto II (Lam 3_{34-66})

The second canto represents the same structure as the first. The first sub-canto (3_{34-54}) contains the complaints of the גְּבָרִים directed against YHWH, with a word of opposition from the גֶּבֶר himself (3_{34-39}). The גֶּבֶר’s

[206] Cf also the occurence of the verb in $1_{4c,5b,12c}$, and in the preceding bicolon.

subsequent appeal for conversion is followed by prayers of lament over the behaviour of the enemy (3_{46-48}, 3_{52-54}). The second sub-canto (3_{55-66}) consists of the גֶּבֶר's prayer to YHWH filled with confidence that He will save.

Sub-canto I (Lam 3_{34-54})

A review of the content of the preceding canto will reveal that the גֶּבֶר himself was the speaker. He let it be know that he had moved away from rebellion against YHWH and arrived at acceptance and renewed faith in God. In the light of 3_1 – the גֶּבֶר's personal introduction – it is clear that the first canto was declared in the presence of others. It now becomes evident that in the midst of all this injustice, yet other גְּבָרִים continue to rebel againts YHWH's distant aloofness. YHWH seems unwilling to look upon the violence of the enemy and human beings are left to suffer great affliction at their hands. The ongoing alphabetic acrostic carries precisely this meaning: the affliction continues to manifest itself unhindered. What is at stake here at the opening verses of the second canto is thus identical with what was at stake at the beginning of the first. As a matter of fact, 3_{34-36} provide a compact summary of the גֶּבֶר's bitter complaints as they were expressed in 3_{1-20}.

In the strophes which follow we encounter a further element of association with the first canto, namely the transition from murmuring to humility before YHWH. The devout גֶּבֶר endeavours to move other, still rebellious, גְּבָרִים to follow this same course of action, to do what he himself has done by critically questioning the origins of the evil which has fallen upon them (3_{37}). The answer is clear: they themselves are the cause of their own grief, not YHWH. Accusations laid at YHWH's door are inappropriate and conversion should take their place (cf 3_{40ff}). Confession, humility, sincere lament and prayer make up the remainder of the sub-canto. The poets hope that all of this will move YHWH to look down on his people and save them. In appealing for a change of heart and in taking the lead in allowing himself to be changed, the גֶּבֶר once again articulates his own conversion and his renewed faith in YHWH as he did in the first canto.[207]

Canticle I (3_{34-39})

Content/theme: *Complaint concerning the calamities not wrought by* YHWH

[207] More on the structure of the canto can be found in the exegesis of 3_{36B}.

Literary argumentation:

inclusions:	(39B) חֲטָאוֹ // (34A) לְדַכֵּא תַּחַת רַגְלָיו
	(39A) יִתְאוֹנֵן // (34B) אֲסִירֵי
	(37B) אֲדֹנָי לֹא צִוָּה \\ (36A) לְעַוֵּת אָדָם בְּרִיבוֹ
	(37B) אֲדֹנָי לֹא צִוָּה \\ (36B) אֲדֹנָי לֹא רָאָה
incl/resp:	(38B) הָרָעוֹת // (35A) לְהַטּוֹת מִשְׁפַּט־גָּבֶר
	(38A) מִפִּי עֶלְיוֹן // (35B) פְּנֵי עֶלְיוֹן
responses:	(37B) אֲדֹנָי לֹא צִוָּה \\ (34A) לְדַכֵּא תַּחַת רַגְלָיו
	(39A) אָדָם // (36A) אָדָם
ext par:	(39B) גָּבֶר // (35A) גָּבֶר
concat:	(37B) אֲדֹנָי לֹא // (36B) אֲדֹנָי לֹא

The above literary argumentation clearly indicates a close relationship between the ל-strophe and the מ-strophe, an association which ought to be respected in the exegesis of the difficult – with respect to content – verses 3_{34-39}. As far as possible, the explanation of the individual cola will be related to the other expressions in the canticle. In addition, the concentric structure of the first sub-canto (3_{33-54}) is also important for a correct explanation of the ל-strophe (3_{34-36}), the latter constituting an inclusion with 3_{52-54}. The same verses, moreover, constitute an inclusion with 3_{46-48} within the eighth canticle. Such an inclusion suggests that the strophes in question all deal with enemy oppression which still continues to be the lot of the גָּבֶר.

34 *To be trampled under (the enemy's) foot* — לְדַכֵּא תַּחַת רַגְלָיו
serve all the prisoners of the land; — כֹּל אֲסִירֵי אָרֶץ

The infinitive + לְ usually serves to provide direction/intention to the verbal root.[208] The *pi'el* of √דכא means 'to trample'/'oppress (to the point of death)'.[209] The colon literaly states the following: 'to trample under his foot serve all prisoners in the land'. It is clear that the suffix of רַגְלָיו refers to the subject of דַכֵּא, but who is intended thereby? Lindström suggests the sins of the people are described here. He offers an exegesis of the present text running on from 3_{33}: the Lord does not oppress without reason (= in his opinion לֹא ... מִלִּבּוֹ); since the people have maltreated the poor and the needy there is a reason for this present punishment; it would be wrong to suggest that the Lord did not notice such oppression, leaving it

[208] Cf GES-K § 114g.
[209] Cf Ps 72_4, 89_{11}, 94_5, 143_3, Job 6_9, Isa 3_{15}.

unpunished.[210] The structure of the songs as a whole, however, including external parallelism and operative idiom, suggest otherwise. In contrast to a review of the people's former sins, the infinitives + לְ point to current behaviour. External parallelism confirms this. In the song-response 4_{12B} the enemy is mentioned directly: they are the צַר וְאוֹיֵב who, counter to all (pious) expectations, have penetrated the gates of Jerusalem and are now in control on the very spot where justice ought to be administered. In the fifth song, we encounter a song-response with a similar suffix (cf תַּחַת רַגְלָיו [3_{34aA}] // בְּיָדָם [5_{12A}]). The same enemy is (are) intended and the parallelism is clear: trampled under enemy feet and strung up by enemy hands.

The parallel with 5_{12} offers additional clarification: the elders in the captured city gates are being offered no respect. The context of the remaining song-responses offers further details: the women of Zion and the young girls of the cities of Judah are being raped (5_{11}). The starvation of mothers and their children in 2_{12} is partly due to the cruelty and ruthlessness of the enemy (cf $5_{5,6,9,10}$). While Lady Jerusalem laments over her incomparable affliction in 1_{12}, there are deeds taking place in the countryside (cf 1_{3b}) which will bring 'widow Judah' just such heart-rending suffering. The fifth song, in addition, mentions the forced labour inflicted on the people (5_5), a detail which is already mentioned in $1_{1,3}$ (מַס and רֹב עֲבֹדָה). The entire country is suffering under hostile enemy exploitation and persecution. "All the prisoners of the land" does not only refer to those who have been forced into slavery, it is an assertion concerning the status of the entire population. An אָסִיר is a prisoner who was forced to perform all sorts of tasks (cf HAL 71). When one looks at the various contexts in which the term is employed, however, one encounters something of a contrast: the Psalms, for example, sing of the fact that a prisoner can count in advance on YHWH's help.[211] At one time YHWH took the side of those trampled under foot and oppressed (Ps 72_4, Isa 3_{15}), but now?

35 *to be subverted (serves) the right of a devout one* לְהַטּוֹת מִשְׁפַּט־גָּבֶר
before the presence of the Most High; נֶגֶד פְּנֵי עֶלְיוֹן

Once again we have an infinitive + לְ at the beginning of the bicolon. The lament of the previous bicolon is sharpened in the present and intensi-

[210] FLindström, *God and the Origin of Evil. A Contextual Analysis of Alleged Monistic Evidence in the Old Testament*, Coniectanea Biblica, Old Testament Series 21, Lund 1983, 214–236.

[211] Cf Ps 68_7, 69_{34}, 146_7.

fied. A גֶּבֶר enjoyed a unique relationship of trust with God (cf 3_{1A})! It would be only reasonable to expect, therefore, that a God who was already on the side of the powerless and the oppressed would be even more inclined to come the aid of those who must have been especially close to his heart. The expression 'to subvert the rights of…' (הִטָּה מִשְׁפָּט *hiph'il*) is found elsewhere in a number of places[212] where it refers to the violation of fundamental rights, particularly of those who can barely, if at all, defend themselves, namely the poor and the foreigner, the widow and the orphan.[213] The subvertion of a person's מִשְׁפָּט ultimately constitutes an attack on that person's שָׁלוֹם.[214] Indeed, in such a circumstance, it was not simply a matter of a single right; the subversion of a person's just claims was in fact an attack on his or her entire existence. The aforementioned elements are also part of the present context: defencelessness, since the enemy is extremely powerfull (cf 1_{9c}) and murders at will (2_{12}); in 3_{17} the גֶּבֶר laments that he as been robbed of his שָׁלוֹם.

The present complaint is clearly pointed in YHWH's direction. Indeed, in the ancient book of the covenant he had promised that he would not subvert the rights of his people.[215] In fact, his prophets, both early and late, challenged every violation of such rights.[216] In the present circumstances, however, he himself is permitting the subversion of the rights of his people, of people, *nota bene*, who are bound to him in a special way. The גֶּבֶר knows what he is talking about (cf the introduction to the present canticle). It is not without reason that his lament includes the divine name עֶלְיוֹן 'Most High'. It's use betrays bitter disappointment. Indeed such a title is normally employed to confess YHWH's superiority. He is the creator-God of heaven and earth and as such he reigns over all peoples. His being judge of the earth guarantees the שָׁלוֹם – an idea which had a particular place in the Jerusalem tradition.[217] Confronted with such injustice (נֶגֶד פְּנֵי עֶלְיוֹן), however, what does the Almighty do?

36A *human persons (serve) to be agrieved in their rights,* לְעַוֵּת אָדָם בְּרִיבוֹ

The present colon is much more general than those preceding it since it does not refer to those גְּבָרִים who have a special relationship with God

212 Cf Ex $23_{2,6}$, Deut 16_{19}, 24_{17}, 27_{19} etcetera.
213 Cf TWAT V 414 (Ringgren).
214 Cf THAT II 1001ff (Liedke).
215 See Ex $23_{2,6}$! Cf also the texts mentioned above.
216 Cf, for example, Am 2_{4-7}, 5_{12}, Mic 3_{11}, Isa 1_{17}, Zeph 3_3, Jer 7_6, Ezek $22_{25,27}$.
217 Cf THAT II 1002 and 1007ff (Liedke), TWAT VI 145–151 (Zobel) and 1983, 304.

but to the violation of the rights of human beings as such. One might think of the prisoners referred to in 3_{34}. At the same time, the term רִיב should not be placed in the specific context of a legal battle. The enemy are clearly not concerned with Israel's prevailing jurisprudence (cf 5_{12}). רִיב here should be understood as a non-judicial, disproportionate struggle between the crushing/trampling enemy and the people whose rights they agrieve, a struggle which in practical terms amounts to subjection.[218] We have somewhat freely translated the infinitive *pi'el* of √עות as 'to agrieve'. The term actually means 'to subvert'/'to bend' but can also be used figuratively to mean 'to tamper with...' (cf HAL 760). The poets have set their minds on the mindless deeds of the enemy against all the people in the land, including those who have remained faithful to God.

36B *and Adonai does not want to see it!* אֲדֹנָי לֹא רָאָה

Our translation of this colon deviates from the prevailing rhetorical question 'does the Lord not see?' which many exegetes and several translations[219] tend to follow. Even the preceding ל of the infinitives is thereby treated differently, namely as an emphatic: 'that they are trampled...' etcetera.[220] Provan suggests an alternative approach, however, paraphrasing לֹא רָאָה as: 'the Lord does not approve'.[221] At the level of content, such a translation is in accord with the traditional rhetorical question, and understandably so, since a linear reading of the text would make it difficult to believe that we had returned to profound lament after the fine and encouraging words of the previous verses. It is for this reason that commentators expect to read the same thing in 3_{34-39} as they read in 3_{22ff}, and they proceed by formulating the present colon as a rhetorical question which must clearly demand a positive answer: 'YHWH does see the oppression of his people and he will ultimately bring it to an end; in the meantime they must endure the affliction without complaint'. Following this scenario, either the transition from positive to negative then takes place between 3_{42} and 3_{43} or one has to consider the entire song as a retrospective reflection in which the גֶּבֶר looks back at his people's affliction in order to call to mind his prayer and its answer. Such an understanding of the text, however, is difficult to reconcile with the cohortatives in $3_{40,41}$, the prohibitive אַל־תַּעְלֵם אָזְנְךָ in 3_{56}, the imperfects in 3_{64-66}, the conclusion

218 Cf THAT II 772f (Liedke).
219 See, for example, SV, NBG, NEB, NRSV.
220 Cf ThFMcDaniel, 'Philological Studies in Lamentations II', Biblica 49 (1968), 207f.
221 Cf also BJohnson, 'Form and Message in Lamentations', ZAW 97 (1985), 66.

of the remaining songs and the tenor of the book of Lamentations as a whole. Even from a grammatical perspective, the aforementioned solution comes across as rather diffident. The most obvious explanation, therefore, is to let 3_{36B} be dependant on the infinitives of the preceding cola.[222]

Further, more weighty arguments also lead us away from the prevailing approach to this text. First of all we have to consider the results of structural analysis which show the third song to possess a diptych structure.[223] Our analysis revealed that both cantos of Lam III exhibit a degree of mutual independence but have to be read in a responsive relationship with one another because their strophes frequently constitute canto-responses. It was noted, in addition, that, in itself, each canto had the same structure as the other songs taken as a whole: beginning with laments and concluding with prayers and expression of hope. In Lam III, the same division coincides, at the content level, with the sub-cantos: the larger sub-cantos I (3_{1-21} and 3_{34-54}) containing the laments, the smaller sub-cantos II (3_{22-33} and 3_{55-66}) the expressions of trust. Thus the beginning of the second canto, by analogy with the beginning of each individual song, is not dominated by a portrayal of trust, but rather by expressions of lament. The present text, therefore, depicts exactly the same transition from trust/prayer to renewed depiction of distress as we find between one song and the next.[224] Such a transition is also evident at the level of content between the first and the second canto of Lam III. When one is able to avoid conceiving an absent interrogative particle here then the clause אֲדֹנָי לֹא רָאָה has to be translated *'The Lord does not see (it)'*. In order to bring the perfect רָאָה in line with the use of the imperative of √ראה in the remainder of the songs, we are obliged once again to translate it in the present tense.[225] The imperative in 1_{11cA} – just as the one preceding it in 1_{9cA} and the one following it in 1_{20cA} – is emphatically directed towards YHWH and has to do with the primary theme of the book of Lamentations as a whole: 'whether YHWH will finally pay heed to his people's affliction'.[226] It is possible to conjecture, of course, that the גֶּבֶר has now become convinced that YHWH does indeed see the injustice being done and thus he can speak of His favours and kindness. In this case it would be correct to interpret

222 See also Rudolph.

223 See page 336 and 1988, 331ff.

224 Cf 2_1, 3_1, 4_1 and 5_1.

225 Cf the core of the first song with its double imperative רְאֵה יְהוָה וְהַבִּיטָה (1_{11cA}).

226 Cf also the double imperative הַבֵּיט וּרְאֵה at the beginning to the great concluding prayer of Lam V.

the present colon in a positive manner, 'YHWH sees (the affliction)', and the negative לֹא can stay where it is as part of the formulation of a rhetorical question. Such an approach, however, would establish a procedure which is not evident in the remainder of the songs. Although the גֶּבֶר is indeed capable of expressing his own situation in positive terms, this does not imply that the people's incomparable suffering is thereby reduced in reality. Any sign of relief in the present affliction is not yet evident. Indeed, such is the very paradox confronting the גֶּבֶר. Rudolph rightly refers to the ל-strophe as a "Gegenrede ... die die vorgetragene Trostgedanken zurückweist." [227] Even Calvin followed a similar line of thought, suggesting that this is a complaint of 'unbelievers' that YHWH disregards the people's affliction: "Ego itaque existimo referri impias eorum voces, qui Deum queruntur non moveri ulla misericordia." [228] The outcry of these 'unbelievers' appears to be justified: they find themselves in the deepest misfortune which is showing no signs of letting up. At the same time, however, the גֶּבֶר does not deny this fact. Once again we are brought face to face with the significance of the ongoing acrostic: in spite of the גֶּבֶר's renewed faith, misery and affliction continue to prevail in the land and there is no sign of even the first step towards salvation by YHWH. According to Vetter: "Die Geschichte der Rettungen im AT beginnt damit, daß Jahwe das Elend der Bedrängten »sieht«...".[229] For the moment, however, YHWH does not 'see', and the outcry in Lamentations continues to be an outcry emanating from the depths and oriented towards God. This is evident from the central verse of the canto in 3_{50}: the גֶּבֶר shall continue to display his tearfull suffering until YHWH looks down from heaven and sees his affliction. That fact that there are those who intend to follow the גֶּבֶר in his determined wait is made clear at the beginning of the fifth song with a return to the imperative רְאֵה directed to YHWH (5_{1B}) together with the suffix נוּ. This frequently repeated and urgent appeal to YHWH to look down and see his people's affliction implies, in fact, that he has not done so up to the present moment. It would appear that he does not want to see, that he has become estranged from his people (cf $3_{8,44}$). Expressions of trust and expectation are thus wedged between laments and descriptions of terrible affliction. Indeed, the entire book of Lamentations begins with mourning (1_1) and ends with insecure hope (5_{22}). The same thing can be found here in a nutshell in the antithetical transition between

227 Cf also GFohrer, *Geschichte der israelitischen Religion*, Berlin 1969, 315f.

228 JCalvin, *Lamentationes Ieremiae*, in: OC 38, 586.

229 In THAT II 696; cf Ex 3_7.

the central strophes of Lamentations (3_{33} and 3_{34}). The גֶּבֶר's faith-filled expectations stand in sharp contrast to the affliction which continues to prevail all around him. Thus, it would appear that the structure supports the complaint character of the ל-strophe.

We now turn to the question of the speaker and address a number of possiblities. One might imagine a reversion to the גֶּבֶר himself or to other individuals who oppose his words. It is even possible to imagine that the גֶּבֶר is actually quoting the complaint of such individuals in the present text. In addition, a combination of voices is quite conceivable: the גֶּבֶר relapses into lament with which he simultaneously translates the feelings of his people. Even resignation on the part of the גֶּבֶר himself is not beyond the bounds of possibility. It is surely part of the human condition that in the midst of new hope despair once again begins to take hold. The trials and tribulations of the גֶּבֶר, however, have already been elaborated in some detail at the beginning of the first canto where a first person formulation was employed with purpose (cf 3_{1ff}). Such an intended emphasis on the person of the גֶּבֶר is missing from the present text, indeed its presence would constitute an unnecessary repetition. What is striking is the inclusive formulation by way of the undetermined גֶּבֶר (3_{35}) and אָדָם (3_{36}). The lament has to do with the suffering of the people in the land. At the level of content, this is diametrically opposed to the concluding statement of the גֶּבֶר at the end of the first canto: YHWH does not enjoy oppressing humankind (even generally). We are led to the conclusion that the גֶּבֶר is either referring to the people's objection (cf Calvin) or that we are actually hearing the people's dissent as such (Rudolph). The quotation-like character of the song-response in 2_{12} in which the poets cited the words of the pining children supports the latter interpretation: here they cite the words of those who have been trampled in the land. In the song-response in 4_{12} the poets likewise convey the insights of others. From a variety of perspectives it would appear that the second canto opens with the quotation of a complaint: YHWH does not wish to look on the affliction of his people. The similar structure and language of Ps 94_{5-7} with its quoted(!) lament further supports this position: יְדַכְּאוּ ... לֹא יִרְאֶה־יָּהּ.

37A *Who spoke, that such a thing should happen?* מִי זֶה אָמַר וַתֶּהִי

The present bicolon (3_{37}) contains the frequently used verbs √אמר I, √היה and √צוה, but the combination found here is very unusual and appears in only one other place in the OT, namely in Ps 33_9, in the context of God's 'good' creation which he had summoned into existence with his word. The combination of √אמר I and √היה is also familiar from Gen 1$_{4,13,18,21,25,31}$, in the refrain in which God sees his creation and finds it good. Thus the aforementioned verbs are clearly used as specific terminology for God's creative activity. Furthermore, in Lam 3$_{35}$, as well as in the following verse (3$_{38}$), the poets employ the divine name עֶלְיוֹן, a title which is expressly associated with the confession that YHWH is the creator of heaven and earth.[230] That precisely this terminology is employed in the present context is an indication that an aetiological question is being asked here. With regard to the origins of what? A very substantial number of exegetes think that the origin of evil in general is being explored in these verses since the OT is not dualistic and everything must ultimately be resolved into YHWH.[231] There is no immediate reason, however, to suddenly assume some kind of theological reflection on monism or dualism. It seems quite obvious that the evil in question is the great affliction which has fallen upon the land.[232]

וַתֶּהִי is an impf cons 3f sg.[233] The feminine form can be used to suggest a collective[234] which stands for 'evil things', that is הָרָעוֹת of the following bicolon (3$_{38B}$). Who lies behind this horrendous evil? Such is the question at hand. In terms of content it is a logical response to the complaint of 3$_{36}$: God does not wish to see the affliction of his people. On the contrary, he tolerates the fact that people are trampled under foot even although he has the power to prevent it. The complaint of 3$_{36}$ leaves open the possibility that YHWH himself is the ultimate offender, the guilty party, because his blindness is tantamount to his permission. The גֶּבֶר counters such an idea by explicitly raising the question of the ultimate cause of this great evil which is now confronting both land and people. The response in the following colon will insist that others, not YHWH, are the guilty party. At first sight, it might be objected that the terminology employed here is so exclusive to God that he alone must be the implied subject. In other words, we are dealing with a question which already contains its own answer and which justifies the classical translation of the verse as a rhetorical question with the response that God created all things

230 Cf Gen 14$_{19,22}$, TWAT VI 145f (Zobel) and 1983, 304.

231 Keil, Oettli, Löhr, Knight, Rudolph, Weiser, Kraus, Plöger, Fuerst, Hillers, Kaiser, Boecker etcetera, follow this line of argument.

232 Cf FLindström, *God and the Origin of Evil. A Contextual Analysis of Alleged Monistic Evidence in the Old Testament*, Coniectanea Biblica, Old Testament Series 21, Lund 1983, 214–236.

233 For our translation cf GES-K § 111*i*.

234 See GES-K § 145*k*

including evil. Quite a powerful argument! It loses impetus, however, when one discovers that in answering their own question the poets were not thinking of random individuals but rather of the prophets of Jerusalem who thought they were speaking God's word. This will become clear below in the exegesis of 3_{38B}.

37B *Adonai did not command it!* אֲדֹנָי לֹא צִוָּה

Classical exegesis proposes a rhetorical question for the present colon also: 'did not the Lord command it?', [235] an explanation which points to the necessity for acquiescence: human persons have to accept both the good and the bad which God has created for them (cf Job 2_{10}). To interpret this colon in the same way, however, would be to misunderstand the creation terminology employed in the strophe. When God creates something, then it is always good or part of 'the good'. God neither creates nor commands evil. For the use of √צוה in the creation context see Ps 33_9, 148_5; cf 147_{15-18}. In addition see Isa 45_{12}, a text which has clear associations with Gen 1.[236]

Two texts in the OT, Ezek 20_{25} and Isa 45_7, would appear to counter such an interpretation. With respect to the former text, however, the terminology of creation is absent, while the creation of רָע in the latter text refers to the achievement of Babylon's downfall at the hands of Cyrus and not to absolute evil in the ethical sense of the term.[237]

Nonetheless, the perpetration of רָע by YHWH against human persons remains quite unusual and theologically strained (cf 1_{21b}), an indication of the difficulty with which he permits himself to be associated with such evil/calamity. Our colon does not focus primarily on YHWH's peremptory power throughout history, however, but rather on the fundamental question of the origins of the evil with which Judah is currently being confronted.[238] The use of creation terminology points precisely in this direction, and necessarily so, since, if one were to place the present statement next to 1_{17bA} (which likewise uses √צוה), then one would be left with a contradiction. 1_{17bA}, however, speaks of YHWH's power to command the nations. In other words, it may be true that YHWH has afflicted his people by abandoning them (5_{20B}) and leaving them at the mercy of the enemy,

235 See the exegesis of Löhr, Haller, Rudolph, Kraus, Plöger, Van Selms, Brandscheidt, Kaiser, Boecker, Provan, NBG etcetera.

236 Cf TWAT IV 955f (García López).

237 Cf JLKoole, *Jesaja II, deel I Jesaja 49 tot en met 55*, Kampen 1985, 328.

238 See the song-responses with 1_{13}, 2_{13} and 5_{13}.

but the reason for such actions was not created by him nor should it be sought at his door.

The verbal form צִוָּה has an additional function in the present text. Not only is there an association with YHWH's vital creative activity, the verb is also used specifically for his command to the prophets to speak their prophetic message.[239] Jer 23_{32} is of particular interest here because it employs the same combination √צוה + לֹא and pertains to the so-called false prophets whom YHWH has not commanded to speak. By speaking in his name nonetheless, they have brought about the evil with which Israel is confronted while 'the burdens' they pronounced over the peoples have become Israel's burdens (Jer 23_{33-40}). Once again we are referred to song-responses in the neighbouring songs at both the strophe and canticle level. In 2_{14}, there is mention of hollow and empty prophecy which is not authorised by YHWH and of the fact that the errant prophets of Jerusalem had withheld the opportunity from the people to change their ways and thereby avoid ultimate downfall. The first canticle of the second sub-canto of the fourth song (4_{12-13}) reveals exactly the same set of connections. The first strophe (4_{12}) observes that the unbelievable has in fact happened: enemies have forced their way through the gates of Jerusalem, while the second strophe (4_{13}) names the priests and the prophets as the principal offenders lying behind this disaster. Thus, in the present text, it is not YHWH but the prophets of Jerusalem who are primarily responsible for the advance of the enemy (and the oppression portrayed in 3_{34-36} and corresponding song-responses which is its consequence). The following verse confirms this hypothesis in its own unique fashion.

38 *From the mouth of the Most High come not* מִפִּי עֶלְיוֹן לֹא תֵצֵא
evil words, but the good! הָרָעוֹת וְהַטּוֹב

This bicolon also possesses a double significance. Firstly, as with the preceding bicolon, we hear once again the echo of creation terminology. When the Most High speaks his creative word then only the good comes into existence and not evil. As is evident from the translation, we render the ו preceding הַטּוֹב as adversative. See once again Gen 1 for the ultimate good outcome of YHWH's creative utterances. Everything is טוֹב. Thus when something glistens then it must be gold (cf 4_{1aB} [הַכֶּתֶם הַטּוֹב]), and שָׁלוֹם is in the air (for the reverse see 3_{17}). Evil does not come about via God's creative utterances. Thus the text states once again that YHWH is not

[239] Cf Jer $1_{7,17}$, 13_{5f}, 14_{14}, 23_{32}, $26_{2,8}$, 29_{23}, THAT II 533, 535 (Liedke).

the cause of Israel's misfortune. The formulation of the bicolon is unusual, even to the Hebrew ear, particulary in the use of the plural הָרָעוֹת. Gordis is led to emend the text here, reading הָרָע אֶת הַטּוֹב, that is both singular and both in agreement with the 3f sg תֵצֵא. Such an emendation, however, remains without text critical foundation. At the grammatical level, the text is acceptable as it stands if one interprets the plural הָרָעוֹת as a *pluralis intensivus*[240] which one might then render as 'evil itself'. Nonetheless, the plural continues to be unusal. In our opinion, this has to do with the second meaning which the poets wished to express here at the same time as the first. The poets achieved their purpose by employing the metrical foot מִפִּי עֶלְיוֹן, a unique expression made up of a combination of √אמר and עֶלְיוֹן, יְהוָה and (מִ)פִּי. Such an amalgamation of terms simultaneously brings both God's creative utterances and the utterances of the prophets to the fore. Where prophetic utterances are concerned the expression (מִ)פִּי יְהוָה is in frequent use.[241] In Am $3_{7,8}$, for example, YHWH's words and deeds have no effect beyond his prophets; they stand in his council. One particular text from Jeremiah's critique of the 'false' prophets deserves special attention in this regard, namely the conclusion to Jer 23_{16}: חֲזוֹן לִבָּם יְדַבֵּרוּ לֹא מִפִּי יְהוָה, 'they speak the vision of their own heart, not from the mouth of YHWH.' Such prophets were not a part of YHWH's council yet they spoke in his name nevertheless (cf Jer 23_{18}). Once again we find ourselves in the context of 'false' prophecy which clearly reveals the connection with the concatenative parallel strophe 2_{14} where √חזה is also employed. The prophets of Jerusalem uttered hollow words, and it is clear that the plural הָרָעוֹת (the evil words) has this significance: מַשְׂאוֹת שָׁוְא וּמַדּוּחִים, the baseless but alluring prophecies of salvation uttered by the prophets of Jerusalem[242] which brought even the גֶּבֶר nothing but רֹאשׁ וּתְלָאָה and לַעֲנָה, poison, hardship and bitterness.[243] Their conceited use of God's name, their unauthorised divine word created the present evil now confronting the people. Micah (3_{12}) as well as Jeremiah (14_{15f}) were already aware that faith in false prophecy brought judgement upon Jerusalem (see, in addition, 2_{14}).

The fact that the poets so explicitly allude to 'false' prophecy makes it clear that, after the fall of Jerusalem, probing questions were asked with regard to the oracles of those prophets which were to be heard in Jerusalem

240 Cf GES-K § 124a.
241 Cf Hos 6_5, Jer 15_{19} and TWAT VI 531–533 (García López).
242 Cf also the song-response 4_{13} with מֵחַטֹּאת נְבִיאֶיהָ (plural).
243 Cf the explanation of the canto-response in 3_5.

only a short time prior to these disastrous events. It does not seem imaginable, however, that those who had remained faithful to YHWH were contested with the obvious fact that he could not fulfill his own words. On the contrary! Although the prophets had spoken with uncontested authority, nothing had come true of their comforting and hope-giving words! Their visions had caused nothing than false security The poets defend themselves against this complaint by proposing in 2_{14} that the prophets of Jerusalem had forsaken their duties and had offered their people nothing more than empty prophecy. In the present text, the poets supplement this by pointing out that such misleading and evil-inducing words could not have come from the mouth of the Most High. They originated in the hearts of these particular prophets. The only true prophetic word, spoken at YHWH's command, is ultimately good and brings about good. Such an awareness is at its most valid with respect to YHWH's prophecies of doom which do not have judgement as their primary intent but rather conversion and life for human persons and nations.[244]

39A *Why then should a survivor grumble,* מַה־יִּתְאוֹנֵן אָדָם חָי

The internal parallelism between אָדָם and גֶּבֶר in this bicolon makes it clear that we are not dealing with scepticism here but with the recalcitrance of the faithful.[245] The גֶּבֶר knows what he is talking about. He too once grumbled and moaned (cf 3_{1-20}). Other people, however, who in one way or another still see themselves in association with YHWH, continue to have most profound difficulty with the paradox of their downfall. Why did the words of hope offered by Jerusalem's prophets not come true? The unacceptability of this fact is evident in the use of יִתְאוֹנֵן, *hithpolel* of √אנן 'to murmur'/'grumble'. The verb is only found elsewhere in Num 11_1 where it points to rebellious complaint resulting from problematic situations which were considered to be the fault of others (YHWH, Moses). Present usage should not be understand as a prayer of complaint to YHWH as Westermann assumes it to be.[246] Note should be taken of the correspondence with תְּלָאָה, the tribulations of Israel's sojourn in the wilderness (Ex 18_8, Num 20_{14}) mentioned in the parallel strophe in the first canto (cf 3_{5B}). After the downfall of Jerusalem and Judah such grumbling and complaint was to be heard throughout the city and the countryside. The גֶּבֶר in-

[244] Cf Ezek 18_{32}, Jer 18 and the bookmark of the prophets: Jonah.

[245] For the meaning of גֶּבֶר see 3_{1aA}.

[246] CWestermann, *Die Klagelieder, Forschungsgeschichte und Auslegung*, Neukirchen-Vluyn 1990, 26.

sists, however, that this is unjustified. One cannot accuse God of having caused this calamity. Furthermore, such complaining tends to miss out on the fact that it could have been a great deal worse. There are survivors! The precise positioning of חָי immediately after אָדָם emphasises this fact with some force,[247] as Kraus correctly points out. It would be incorrect, therefore, to translate חָי as an adjective ('a living person') but better to render it as an attributive clause. The גֶּבֶר is not referring here to the slender comfort that people have escaped with their lives. Sometimes life can be worse than death while a quick death can often be preferrable to prolonged suffering as the poets state quite literally in 4_9. Without doubt the גֶּבֶר's words should be seen in the same theological context of 3_{22A}. The fact that there are those who have survived the calamity deserves to be understood as a sign of YHWH's favour (cf חַסְדֵי יְהוָה, 3_{22A}; see also the antithesis in the canto-response between אָדָם חָי [3_{39}] and כְּמֵתֵי עוֹלָם [3_{6B}]). If YHWH is not the cause of Israel's downfall but is punishing her nonetheless – although not with death – then there is something more at hand than an incomprehensible action on behalf of the Most High which brings suffering to his people. A person who is given the chance to live should not grumble but should search for the true cause of his or her suffering.

39B *a devout one concerning his sin-fate?!* גֶּבֶר עַל־חֶטְאוֹ

If one maintains the MT here then יִתְאוֹנֵן also verbally determines the second colon. One is then left with the question as to the meaning of חֶטְאוֹ in such an instance. As a matter of fact, √אנן is oriented, by definition towards another – in this case the Most High – and one cannot grumble about one's own sins! It is common practice to see the present colon as antithetical, whereby the meaning 'to grumble' is interpreted as 'to complain': if a person must complain, rather he complain about his own sin than about God. At the level of content, however, such an interpretation is impossible. Rudolph offers an alternative solution. He emends the text here to read יְהִי גְבִיר, that is: 'let him be master over his sin',[248] a suggestion which ultimately boils down to an appeal for conversion but in the most uncommon terms. Conversion is called for in the following colon in much more appropriate terminology. One can maintain MT if one interprets חֶטְאוֹ not as sin but as the 'consequence of sin'. In this event, the *k^e^t̲īḇ* (חֶטְאוֹ) together with LXX (τῆς ἁμαρτίας αὐτοῦ), rather than the plural *q^e^rē* (חֲטָאָיו) would appear to be correct. The authors are not speaking

[247] Cf Gen $43_{7,27,28}$, $45_{3,26,28}$; 46_{30}, I Sam 20_{14}, Job 19_{25}.
[248] Cf also text critical apparatus BHS.

here of the multitude of the people's sins but of the single fate which is their consequence, of the affliction and misfortune which befall a human person as a result of his or her sin (or that of others). The relationship between sin and the misfortune arising therefrom is strongly associated with the notion חֵטְא.[249] According to Koch, חֵטְא means: "eine die einzelnen Taten übergreifende, unvergebbare Sündenlast (...) die aufgrund des Tun-Ergehen-Zusammenhang unweigerlich zum Tode führt."[250] For the aforementioned association between חֵטְא and death see Ex 10_{17}, although it would also appear from the text in question that it is ultimately YHWH who either brings this association about or does not. It is important to note, furthermore, that חֵטְא can be perpetrated unconsciously (cf Gen 20_9) and that it can overcome one via others.[251] If one respects such nuances then the colon is not as difficult as it would seem. חֵטְא need not only imply personal (conscious) sins; the concept can also refer to the fate of someone who has been affected by the sins of others. In such an event, bitterness is not out of place and grumbling is not only appropriate, it is in agreement with 2_{14} and 4_{13}: the prophets are the chief culprits and because of their sin – wrongful prophecy – the sin of the people has come to this. It could have been otherwise, however! Their fate could have been turned around (cf 2_{14b}). A concretisation of the consequence of sin consists of the abuse and pernicious plots of the enemy (cf 3_{61}) whereby an inclusion is formed within the canto (3_{33-66}).

The גֶּבֶר understands well that a גֶּבֶר might rebel against such a notion, after all, he himself had experienced such rebelliousness at its most acute (cf 3_{1-20}). Indeed, it once appeared to be justified! Those who had remained faithful to YHWH ought surely to have expected different treatment because of their special relationship with him.[252] Surely they should have been able to experience YHWH's desire to save, whereby he draws a veil over sin and does not impute injustice.[253] Such an appeal was to no avail (cf 3_8). God is not moved by murmuring! For this reason the גֶּבֶר calls on other גְּבָרִים to cease their grumbling since it has no place in their relationship with YHWH. They must choose a different path.

A quick look back at the opening canticle of this chapter (3_{1-6}) might be interesting. At that point the גֶּבֶר himself was still grumbling over his

249 For the full meaning cf 1_{8aA}.

250 Cf TWAT II 864; cf also the exegesis of 1_{14bB}.

251 Cf Ex 32_{21}, Jos $7_{11,20}$.

252 Cf Ps 34_9, 37_{23f}.

253 Cf Ps 32_2; TWAT II 862 (Koch).

tribulations (cf רֹאשׁ וּתְלָאָה and לַעֲנָה, 3_{5B}) just as the other גְּבָרִים are doing here. The way in which he now encourages the sceptics and distraught faithful among his people to see their fate in a different light and to think differently about YHWH is evidence that the new start he was able to make was not in vain. On the contrary, the murmurer and accuser has become a defender.

Canticle II (3_{40-45})

Content/theme: *Conversion is necessary because* YHWH *has not forgiven their sins*

Literary argumentation:

inclusions:	בַּשָּׁמָיִם (41B) // בֶעָנָן (44A)
	מָרִינוּ (42A) // אַף (43A)
	אַתָּה לֹא סָלָחְתָּ (42B) // הָרַגְתָּ לֹא חָמָלְתָּ (43B)
incl/resp:	נִשָּׂא לְבָבֵנוּ אֶל־כַּפָּיִם (41A) // תְּפִלָּה (44B)
response:	לֹא סָלָחְתָּ (42B) // סְחִי וּמָאוֹס תְּשִׂימֵנוּ (45A)
incl/concat:	by way of the suffix נוּ
concat/asson/allit:	אַתָּה לֹא סָלָחְתָּ (42B) // הָרַגְתָּ לֹא חָמָלְתָּ (43B)

The preceding canticle ended with the גֶּבֶר's appeal to cease from grumbling about the trouble and affliction which is confronting his people, a path which ultimately leads nowhere because God is not to blame for the situation. Thus the גֶּבֶר suggests and alternative path, one which does indeed offer some perspective, the path of self-examination and conversion.

40A *Let us search and scrutinise our ways,* נַחְפְּשָׂה דְרָכֵינוּ וְנַחְקֹרָה

Compared with the previous canticle, the opening of the present canticle is striking for its transition from singular to plural. Van Selms fails to appreciate the poet's skill in his suggestion that the נ-strophe forced them to continue in the style of a collective song of lamentation. The poets were not restricted by language, their thoughts and ideas determined the form. For that matter, a change in the sense that the גֶּבֶר is now suddenly introducing others into his considerations is quite out of the question. His appeal is turned directly towards those to whom he had made clear in the previous canticle that they should not ascribe the blame for their situation to the Most High.

Even although the גֶּבֶר has already made himself clear in the matter of guilt, this does not imply that the affliction confronting the people has come to an end. On the contrary, the oppression and subjugation of human persons continues unabated and YHWH still does not give it his attention. His aloofness remains fatefully tangible. In the shared wisdom of the Ancient Near East national affliction was the consequence of the wrath of the gods. Even Israel ascribed her present state to the anger of YHWH which she considered to have been aroused by the sin of the people. The relationship between affliction and YHWH's anger is established in the punitive sanctions associated with the covenant and in the prophetic announcement of judgement (cf Am 4_6–5_3). Even the Judges cycle reflects this theological vision of things.[254] The fact that YHWH still holds himself aloof can only be explained by his ongoing anger at the people's unrepented sin. On this very question, however, a new difficulty now emerges: neither the גֶּבֶר nor the people are completely clear on what precisely is wrong. In our explanation of the previous strophe it became apparent that חֵטְא could stand for sin committed without being aware of it. The opening of the present canticle links up with this idea. Since there remains (partial) uncertainty, self-examination is required. Indeed, if the people want to avert YHWH's anger then they have to get rid of whatever it is he is refusing to endure (cf Num $25_{4,11}$). Silence and trust alone, to which the גֶּבֶר has already called the people (3_{28-30}), are not enough, conversion must be part of their response also (cf Isa 30_{15}). Conversion is only possible, however, if one is aware of what it is one must convert from. At this point in the book of Lamentations sin is under discussion, but in most cases – including that of the preceding bicolon – this has more to do with its consquence rather than its nature (cf $1_{5b,8a,14a}$). It is true that the sins of Jerusalem's prophets are described with more clarity, as is evident from the song-responses 2_{14} (strophe level) and 4_{13} (canticle level). They had spilled the blood of the righteous and covered-up the sins of the people. It is evident from 1_{18a} that the warnings of others besides these temple prophets were simply disregarded, with the current situation as a consequence (cf √מרה in the last bicolon of this strophe). For this reason, the people's עָוֹן – including that of the גֶּבֶר – must now be brought into the open. The formulation of the text shows that this must be performed with thoroughness. The *qal* of √חפשׂ implies intensive scrutiny (cf Prov 2_4, 20_{27}), the object of which is to be 'their ways'. דֶּרֶךְ means the way one conducts one's life, one's successes and failures[255] but also includes the disposition with which one engages in life in all its aspects. The latter

[254] Cf, for example, Judg 10_{6-16}.
[255] Cf TWAT II 303 (Koch).

aspect is evident from the cohortative וְנַחְקֹרָה from the root חקר which can likewise have to do with an inquiry into a person's disposition.[256] Tsevat suggests 'to split' as the possible basic meaning of √חקר.[257] Even if the sin is well hidden it must still be brought into the light (cf Job 28_3). Of course, such scrutiny cannot take place without a frame of reference. The גֶּבֶר focuses first, however, on the people's willingness to examine themselves. The aforementioned frame of reference only appears in 3_{42}.

40B *and return to* YHWH! וְנָשׁוּבָה עַד־יְהוָה

Once again the גֶּבֶר speaks in inclusive terms. If one pays due attention to the parallel strophe from the first canto (3_{7-9}), however, one will note that there is both similarity and difference. There is agreement in the גֶּבֶר's turning to YHWH, even although he was aware that his prayer was rejected. The difference is also quite apparent: at that time the גֶּבֶר himself was still going through a phase of bitter rebelliousness but now he appeals to others to return to YHWH. Such an appeal requires a completely different disposition on the part of the גֶּבֶר. Undisguised complaint must now give way to self-criticism and recognition of one's shortcomings with respect to YHWH. It is quite unnecessary to see specific deuteronom(ist)ic terminology in the combination שׁוב + עַד, as Albrektson does. The expression is also to be found in Amos and Isaiah.[258] Given the further examples of association with these prophets throughout the book of Lamentations[259] it seems more reasonable to assume that poets were also inspired in the present colon by their prophecies. Indeed, the current affliction is reminiscent of the disasters foretold by Amos which had Israel's refusal to change her ways as their origin. Amos' accusation returns repeatedly in a refrain like censure (cf Am 4_{6-11}). Van Leeuwen[260] points out, in addition, that in contrast to Lev 26, Deut 28 and I Kgs 8 (the latter two having certainly undergone deuteronomistic reworking) only in Am 4_{11} is allusion made to the conversion of Sodom and Gomorrah, a motief which resonates profoundly in Lamentations (cf $1_{13a,20b}$ and 4_6). This betrays influence on the part of Amos rather than on the part of the deuteronomist.

Apart from this, it is important to guard against viewing such associations too exclusively. This is underscored by the agreement with Hos 14_{2f} and

---

256 Cf I Sam 20_{12}, Ps $139_{1,23}$; cf also HAL 334.
257 Cf TWAT III 157f.
258 Cf Am 4_{6ff}, Isa 9_{12}, 19_{22}.
259 Cf 1983, 262–266.
260 CvLeeuwen, *Amos*, Nijkerk 1985, 154f.

Joel 2_{12} – both of which include the combination שׁוּב + עַד as well as terms such as ‘to be rebellious’ (√מרה), ‘injustice’ (עָוֹן), ‘heart’ (לֵב) etcetera. The poets did not only turn to one pre-exilic prophet for inspiration but to several. With reference to Hos 14_2, Isa 9_{12}, Deut 4_{30} and 30_2, Wolff expresses the opinion that שׁוּב + עַד was primarily used for a return from the service of alien gods to the service of YHWH, but his proposal seems to be too constrictive.[261] Indeed, the context of Isa 9_{12} points to other possible transgressions beyond idol worship. The people's examination and scrutinisation of their ways will certainly include the other complaints of the prophets and not be as restricted as Wolff might suggest. Van Leeuwen draws attention to the distinction between שׁוּב + אֶל and שׁוּב + עַד, whereby the former refers more to the liturgy and the latter to one's interior relationship with YHWH.[262] The following bicolon confirms this distinction.

41 *Let us lift up our heart along with our hands*	נִשָּׂא לְבָבֵנוּ אֶל־כַּפָּיִם
to God in the heavens.	אֶל־אֵל בַּשָּׁמָיִם

נִשָּׂא is a *qal* impf 1 pl and, in spite of the omission of the final ה,[263] ought to be understood as a cohortative. The expression itself is reminiscent of 2_{19c} (נָשָׂא כַּף) where the spirit of prayer had more to do with the desire to receive. The opposite is true in the present circumstances: hands are not raised to receive but to give. The גֶּבֶר appeals to his listeners not to let the raising of their hands remain a mere gesture but to let it come from the heart.[264] לֵב/לֵבָב stands for interior surrender and dedication of an individual's true self, without any form of reservation. Once again we are reminded of Hos 7_{14}: “they do not cry to me from their hearts...”, a divine accusation which is taken seriously in the present bicolon.

The preposition אֶל in אֶל־כַּפָּיִם is considered problematic by a number of commentators, certainly if one understands it to mean ‘to’ or ‘towards’. Some have been tempted, therefore, to emend the text to עַל, whereby the people's hearts are seen to be raised up ‘upon’ their hands (cf LXX: ἐπὶ), but we are left, nevertheless, with a rather unusual image. An alternative possibility is proposed by Kraus and Gordis, for example, who do not vocalise אל as a preposition but read it rather as a negation וְאַל: ‘let us lift

---

261 HWWolff, *Dodekapropheton 2, Joel und Amos*, BKAT XIV/2, Neukirchen–Vluyn 1969, 260.

262 Van Leeuwen, 154.

263 Cf König § 197*b*.

264 לֵבָב is singular but should be understood collectively.

up our hearts, and not our hands' (cf Joel 2_{13}). Albrektson clearly offers the correct solution to the problem by referring us to Lev 18_{18} where the preposition אֶל means 'together with', an appropriate solution here also since the expression נָשָׂא כַּף as a gesture of prayer is evidently established via 2_{19c} (cf also Gottlieb). The fact that the same preposition is used in the second colon with a different meaning need not be a problem since it is mostly the context which determines the actual meaning of the term under dispute. The presence of the divine name אֵל, furthermore, establishes alliteration with the preposition אֶל. In terms of content, this name is primarily used to indicate God's divinity.[265] In this sense Lamentations emerges as strikingly 'monotheistic': other gods are nowhere to be found.

42A *We, we sinned and were rebellious!* נַחְנוּ פָשַׁעְנוּ וּמָרִינוּ

Prayer, made evident in the direct address of YHWH in the following colon (אַתָּה), follows immediately upon the גֶּבֶר's appeal. The subject is given further emphasis via the addition of the pronoun.[266] Who then is the speaker: the גֶּבֶר or those to whom he has addressed his appeal? A number of exegetes, inspired by the plurals of this colon, have interpreted these words as the opening of a collective lament,[267] thus forcing us to assume that Lamentations had a liturgical context at its foundation, during which the community would have sung or recited this part of the song. In terms of the original 'Sitz im Leben', however, such an interpretation is difficult to imagine in the context of an organised liturgy.[268] Throughout the book of Lamentations as a whole, the poets themselves point out that liturgy as such has come to an end (1_4, 2_6, 5_{15}). Moreover, given a liturgical setting, one would have to accept that 'community's' endorsement of the גֶּבֶר's appeal must have been almost instantaneous. Since the גֶּבֶר's own conversion only took place after an entire sub-canto (3_{1-20}), is it likely, then, that that of the 'grumblers' of $3_{34-36,39}$ would be complete in the space of a single strophe thus allowing them to participate in the liturgy? For two reasons, therefore, we assume that the גֶּבֶר is still speaking at this point in the song, albeit in the form of a prayer for others (and perhaps with others, however reluctantly). First of all, the plural cohortatives employed in this appeal are not out of place on the lips of an individual. Our sec-

[265] JCdMoor, *The Rise of YAHWISM. The Roots of Israelite Monotheism*, Leuven 1997[2], passim.

[266] Cf Brockelmann § 34a.

[267] Cf, for example, Kraus, Lamparter, Hillers etcetera.

[268] Cf Introduction III.3.

ond reason is found in the remainder of the song, namely in the sudden transition from plural to singular between 3_{47} and 3_{48}, i.e. within one single strophe. Such a transition is difficult to explain unless one imagines a situation in which a choir of voices alternates with a solo voice; but this, once again, is not easy to accept. Within a single prayer, it is possible for an individual to present both personal and collective need to God side by side. The conclusion of the song (3_{55-66}) is also formulated in individual terms and offers, in fact, an elaboration of the ח-strophe (3_{22-24}) in which the גֶּבֶר professes that YHWH is his 'portion'. The prayer of an individual need not imply isolation. Indeed, the cohortatives suggest the very contrary to be the case. Thus, the image presented focuses first on a lonely, devout individual (cf 3_{14}) who enters into dispute with his recalcitrant fellow Israelites – in the squares of the city? –, endeavours to guide them onto the right path, is their leader in prayer and ultimately continues the search for YHWH, their God, because the affliction is so great.

The גֶּבֶר's change of tone is made evident in a completely different line of attack. No more bitter complaints concerning the affliction endured (cf 3_{1ff}) but a first step towards humility before God, something which the human person must learn by turning to him. What follows is a confession of guilt: 'we, we have sinned and have been rebellious'. Such a confession functions as the basis of an appeal in the context of prayer.[269] The independent personal pronoun נַחְנוּ points with some emphasis to the individuals themselves, hence the double 'we' in the translation. The root פשׁע does not refer so much to sinful inclination as to actual, concrete violations of a given order. As a matter of fact, it is employed to signify 'sinning' at its most serious (cf also 1_{5bB}). The noun פֶּשַׁע – on combination with the 'yoke of transgression' – is employed in the song-response 1_{14}. After the admission of sin follows a confession of past rebelliousness. The poets already used the root מרה (+ פֶּה) in 1_{18a} and in 1_{20b} with reference to the people's resistance to the prophetic announcements of judgement. The same is implied in the present colon. It is evident that the poets were aware of differences among the prophets on this matter. Indeed, in the song-response of 2_{14} they accuse the prophets of Jerusalem of not disclosing their own lack of righteousness. The use of √מרה, however, reveals that the poets remember other prophetic voices (cf also 2_{17}!). The גֶּבֶר now confesses that the call of these 'other' prophets to return to the order established by YHWH was ignored. In light of the call to self-

269 Cf NHRidderbos, *De Psalmen I*, KV, Kampen 1962, 23.

interrogation (3_{40}), one should not be tempted to conclude that the people had a clear image of the sins they had committed (cf the 'exposure' of 2_{14b}). In line with the declaration of intention in 3_{41}, a recognition of Israel's guilty status before God, brought about by her refusal to listen to his 'true' prophets, would seem a more fitting interpretation. The גֶּבֶר does not come to this awareness by way of a (complete?) analysis, but by way of the consequences brought on by sins which remain unforgiven, which have not been cast into the depths of the sea (Mic 7_{19} \\ Lam 2_{13c}). Such transgressions cry out for YHWH's repressive response (cf 1_{5b}).

42B *You, you have not forgiven!* אַתָּה לֹא סָלָחְתָּ

The double 'you' in the translation is intended to recognise the independent personal pronoun אַתָּה which introduces this colon and emphasises the fact that it is YHWH himself who has not forgiven. Even at the level of content there is evidence here of profound disappointment contained within the significance and context of √סלח in the OT. The combination with the noun פֶּשַׁע is frequently found with YHWH alone as subject of forgiveness. Indeed, the verb is not used for mutual forgiveness between human persons; סלח, 'to forgive' is specifically God's work, and to such an extent that the 'forgiving disposition' can be referred to as a divine characteristic.[270] God forgives with pleasure[271] and it is a rare (and mostly late) occasion, therefore, that we find mention of his apparent refusal to forgive.[272] The present colon is one of those rare examples. Its very absurdity gives us a further taste of the גֶּבֶר's sorrow: 'You, who desire so much to forgive, have not forgiven.' Thus the גֶּבֶר turns in profound despair to YHWH. One might venture to suggest that the גֶּבֶר is playing YHWH off against himself. His basis for confronting YHWH with his refusal to forgive can be found in 3_{33}, 'the oppression of human persons is not according to YHWH's heart' (cf the exegesis of said verse). The fact that YHWH has in truth withheld his forgiveness is signalled in the 'yoke of transgression' which must now be borne (cf the song-response 1_{14}), as well as in the prophets and priests who wander blind and blood-stained through the city streets (cf song-response 4_{14}).

It is important to note here that the גֶּבֶר's prayer marks the transition from humility and confession of sin to complaint once again. The return to complaint reflects a different tone, however, to that of the first sub-canto

[270] Cf TWAT V 863f (Hausmann).

[271] Cf Ps 86_5, 103_3, 130_4, Isa 55_4.

[272] Cf Deut 29_{19}, II Kgs 24_4, Jer 5_7; cf also TWAT V 861 (Hausmann).

(3_{1-18}) where the גֶּבֶר addressed his fierce complaints concerning YHWH's behaviour to a third party. In the present context the complaints are addressed to YHWH himself with the intention of eliciting his favourable intervention. Exegetes who are unaware of this fact tend to have problems understanding the structure of the song because they find themselves confronted with a number of complex and incomprehensible transitions from hope to lament and back again.

43A *You cover yourself with anger and pursue us!* סַכֹּתָה בָאַף וַתִּרְדְּפֵנוּ

For the present tense translation of the perfect in the second colon see 1_{1a}. YHWH does not only withhold his forgiveness, his anger continues unabated and affliction follows in its wake. The ongoing character of YHWH's anger is rendered in an unusual manner via the root סכך I. In the *qal* this root means 'to provide protective cover' (cf HAL 712) and can be found in a positive sense in Ps 140_8 with YHWH as subject: YHWH protects in the day of battle. The same is true of Job 1_{10} where Satan refers to YHWH as Job's 'protector' or 'patron'. Thus it would appear that such protection was considered part of God's nature.[273] While the verb in question is always used in a transitive manner, that is: YHWH protects others, not himself, the latter option appears to be in effect in the present text and constitutes an unlikely scenario for many. Thus Gottlieb and Hillers take the 1st person plural suffix of וַתִּרְדְּפֵנוּ as the object of סַכֹּתָה: 'You have covered us with anger.' Given that the verb is rare, it remains difficult to draw hard and fast conclusions with respect to its use. In light of the following bicolon (3_{44}), however, a reflexive interpretation does seem at least possible. Thus we are confronted here with the same contradiction as we were with YHWH's forgiveness in 3_{42}: YHWH, who always protects with care, now covers himself with anger. Such a thing also runs counter to his nature. The present text refers in fact to the thematic introduction to the second song.[274] If our interpretation is correct, then we can assume the presence here of an image derived from theophany. Colossal clouds, blinding light and fire, were all associated with YHWH's appearance; then he would turn his anger against Israel's enemy and attack them with his arrows.[275] Now the same thing is happening to Israel and the גֶּבֶר. If one reads the parallel strophe from the first canto (3_{7-9}) side by side with

273 Cf TWAT V 843 (Kronholm).

274 Cf 2_{1aA}; for אַף as 'scorching anger' cf 1_{12cB}.

275 For a more detailed description of theophany cf Ps 18_{7-20} and JJeremias, *Theophanie*, WMANT 10, Neukirchen 1977².

the present strophe then one would not be surprised to learn that the גֶּבֶר speaks of being pierced by YHWH's arrows, words which in turn constitute a reference to the destruction of Zion and her children in the second song (cf the arrows and flaming fire spoken of in $2_{3,4}$).

The aforementioned contrastive use of √סלה and √סכך I also appears to apply to the present use of √רדף. Persecution by the enemy constitutes a stereotypical psalm-lament,[276] suggesting that those under attack are aware that YHWH alone is willing and powerful enough to liberate them from their persecutors.[277] The same YHWH, however, is now confronted with the fact that he is persecuting his own people, once again a fact which runs counter to his nature. There is mention of enemy persecution in $1_{3c,6c}$, 4_{19} and 5_5, but in their persecution YHWH's persecution is made manifest.

43B *You kill and have no mercy!* הָרַגְתָּ לֹא חָמָלְתָּ

The second colon of this verse is a contraction of 2_{21c}. For the meaning of √חמל see the exegesis of $2_{2a,17b}$. Death at the hands of YHWH was also discussed already in the exegesis of $2_{4b,20}$. The use of √חמל + לֹא does not introduce a contradiction with the expectations found in the Psalms because the verb as such does not appear there. One does find hymns in which the root הרג has YHWH as subject, in which he is lauded for having once killed mighty kings who tried to hold back his salvific will for Israel (cf Ps 135_{10}, 136_{18}). In the present text it is Israel herself who is being killed and the poets are painfully aware of unforeseen yet valid prophecy (cf Am 9_{1-4}).

44 *You wrap yourself in a cloud,* סַכּוֹתָה בֶעָנָן לָךְ
inaccessible to prayer! מֵעֲבוֹר תְּפִלָּה

According to KBL 657, סַכּוֹתָה is derived from one of the סכך roots and means 'to be impenetrable'. HAL 712 distinguishes three verbs with the root and derives סַכּוֹתָה from √סכך III which means 'to conceal'. Kronholm, however, calls the very existence of a √סכך III into question, given that the meaning is so close to √סכך I.[278] Van Selms' suggestion that the different spellings indicate the existence of different verbs remains unconvincing.[279]

276 Cf Ps 7_2, 142_7, 143_8.
277 See Ps 31_{16}, $35_{3,6}$, Jer 20_{11}.
278 See TWAT V 844.
279 Cf the alternating spelling of א(ו)יב throughout the songs: $1_{2,5,9,16,21}$ etcetera.

It is possible that an auxiliary vowel was introduced here to avoid confusion between the sentences. The reflexive character of the expression is evident from the supplementary *dativus ethicus*.[280] Brandscheidt is perhaps correct in suggesting that there was no room for such a dative in the preceding bicolon.

The image in this verse is much better known. The darkness of clouds is mentioned in many descriptions of theophany.[281] The pillar of cloud which concealed YHWH is also to be found in Ex 14_{19f}, for example, with its dark, threatening side turned towards the pursuing Egyptians. In addition, the metaphorical dimension of an impenetrable fog also has a role to play here (cf Ezek $38_{9,16}$). It is in this sense that YHWH has become inaccessible to prayer.[282] For the meaning of תְּפִלָּה see the explanation of the canto-response 3_8. Inaccessability to prayer joins the line of contradictions evident in these verses. In Ps 65_3, the God of Zion is referred to as 'you who answer prayer' and elsewhere in the Psalms the faithful frequently give thanks to YHWH for having heard their prayer.[283] The spurning of prayer is a rare occurence (cf Ps 80_5). Such refusal to listen to his people's prayer is not according to the divine nature. Within the concentric structure of this canto, the antithetical inclusion with 3_{56}: 'You hear my voice...' is also worthy of note in the present context.

45A *You make us into filth and rubbish...* סְחִי וּמָאוֹס תְּשִׂימֵנוּ

The noun סְחִי is a *hapax legomenon*, to be derived from the root סחה (cf HAL 707) which is itself a *hapax*. In Ezek 26_4, the *pi'el* of סחה must mean something similar to 'to wipe away'; hence the translation with the noun 'filth'. מָאוֹס is a substantivised infinitive of √מאס I, 'to reject'/'to throw away'.[284] With YHWH as subject, this verb has a place in the prophecy of judgement, indicating God's analogous reaction to Israel's scorn and contempt for his covenant (rules).[285] In Am 5_{21} the verb is coupled with the devine emotion of abhorrence and scorn.[286] Once again the contradiction implied in these words is crystal clear as Wagner states: "Daß JHWH als

280 Cf GES-K § 119*s* and § 135*i*.

281 Cf JJeremias, *Theophanie*, WMANT 10, Neukirchen 1977², 28ff; Zeph 1_{15}, Nah 1_3, Ezek $3_{3,18}$ etcetera.

282 Cf TWAT VI 272f (Freedman).

283 See, for example, Ps 6_{10}, $66_{19,20}$; cf 69_{34}, 102_{18}.

284 Cf HAL 513 and BKWaltke – MO'Conner, *An Introduction to Biblical Hebrew Syntax*, Winona Lake, Indiana 1990, § 35.3.3*b*.

285 Cf Hos 4_6, Jer 8_9 and TWAT IV 623 (Wagner).

286 Cf, in addition, Jer 6_{30} and 7_{29} (with עֶבְרָה); see Lam 3_1!

Subjekt einer *m's*-Tätigkeit vorgestellt wird, gehört eigentlich zu seinen opera aliena, sein opus proprium besteht im *lo' ma'as*." [287] Wagner bases this in the theology of creation: God does not reject what he has created. It would be more appropriate at this point, however, to envisage a contrast with the election of Israel: God is not inclined to reject what he once chose (see the following colon and compare with the integration of this theme in Deutero-Isaiah, Isa 41_9).

If we place this verse side by side with the song-response 2_{15} then the connection between the two becomes clear, even with respect to terminology (cf, once again, the description of the fall of Tyre in Ezek 26_4, 27_2). The song-responses Lam 2_{15} and 3_{45} contrastively complement one another: the exalted, 'divine' (see exegesis) beauty of Jerusalem was once a source of wonderment to all, but now her inhabitants – upon whom YHWH's glory once radiated – are mere filth, rejected by him before the peoples. The profound contrast is reminiscent of the 'then-now' antithesis of the funeral dirge. In 4_{15}, the priests and prophets take their turn as 'unclean' individuals to be driven away.

45B ... *in the midst of the peoples!* בְּקֶ֫רֶב הָעַמִּים

The present colon also establishes a point of contrast between the present situation and YHWH's erstwhile election of Israel from among the nations.[288] Once again, there is no need to propose the presence of deuteronomic theology here. Indeed, the context suggests that an older and more widespread datum of faith is involved. Seebaß concurs: "Sobald die Volkserwählung zum erstenmal unter der Vokabel בחר greifbar wird – und das ist im dtn/dtr Schriftenkreis der Fall –, wird sie so beiläufig und unbetont erwähnt, daß sie unmöglich als dort ersonnen und proklamiert gelten kann." [289] The nations mentioned need not be seen as a reference to the exile, but as was the case with 1_{3bA} (בַגּוֹיִם), the surrounding peoples prove to be more appropriate candidates (cf also כָּל־עֹבְרֵי דֶרֶךְ in 2_{15aB}). In the present colon, the nations serve as a contrast motief: once chosen by YHWH from among the nations, now rejected by him among the nations.

If we look back as we approach the end of this canticle, it becomes evident that the גֶּבֶר's prayer was one of antitheses. He points to the contrast between God's actual deeds and intentions towards Israel and the current

[287] Cf TWAT IV 630 (Wagner).
[288] Cf Deut 7_6, 10_{14f}, 14_2.
[289] In TWAT I 603.

affliction which he allows to befall his people. The situation, in fact, is not the way God would want it to be. The גֶּבֶר confronts YHWH with his actions as in conflict with his nature. Thus he humbly plays God off against himself. The basis of such prayer is his conviction that such oppression is not according to the heart of YHWH (cf 3_{33}).

Canticle III (3_{46-54})

Content/theme: *Tormented, until* YHWH *looks down...*

Literary argumentation:

inclusions:	עָלֵינוּ (46A) // עַל (54A)
	פִּיהֶם (46A) // רֹאשִׁי (54A)[290]
	וָפַחַת (47A) // בּוֹר (53A)
	וְהַשָּׁבֶר (47B) // וַיַּדּוּ־אֶבֶן בִּי (53B)
	עֵינִי (49A) // עֵינִי (51A)
incl/asson/allit:	פָּצוּ (46A) // צָפוּ (54A)
responses:	כָּל־אֹיְבֵינוּ (46B) // אֹיְבַי (52B)
	פַּלְגֵי־מַיִם (48A) // צָפוּ־מַיִם (54A)
	עֵינִי (48A) // עֵינִי (51A)
	בַּת־עַמִּי (48B) // בְּנוֹת עִירִי (51B)
	שֶׁבֶר בַּת־עַמִּי (48B) // אָמַרְתִּי נִגְזָרְתִּי (54B)
	לְנַפְשִׁי (51A) // עַל־רֹאשִׁי (54A)

This central canticle of the second canto (and final canticle of the first sub-canto) portrays, among other things, the suffering brought about by the enemy. The גֶּבֶר makes it clear that he will not cease to bring this suffering to YHWH's attention until he intervenes to save his people. His attitude is ultimately supported by the insight that – sooner or later – YHWH will permit himself be moved to mercy by human persons in need.

From the stylistic perspective, the change of number in 3_{48} is worthy of attention: no longer 'we/us' but again the גֶּבֶר's personal complaint. At the end of the פ-strophe (3_{46-48}), there is a certain sense of conclusion present in the mention of the summarizing noun שֶׁבֶר 'disintegration'. The same substantive is also used in the preceding bicolon in which the plural is heard for the last time (cf 3_{47B}). A survey of 3_{42-47} reveals that all the elements of the present affliction are present: guilt (3_{42}), YHWH's wrathful judgement (3_{43}), his imperviousness to prayer (3_{44}), his rejection of

290 For the word-pair פֶּה/רֹאשׁ cf Ps 133_3, Prov 10_6.

Israel as filth (3_{45}), humiliation by the enemy (3_{46}) and the summary 3_{47} including panic, pitfall, destruction and disintegration. The גֶּבֶר's prayer of intercession concludes the survey.

The גֶּבֶר's tearful suffering makes it clear that there can be no talk of giving up his prayer. The cause of his sorrow is the continuation of the affliction (3_{51}). He states the intention of his prayer of tears in 3_{50} – a consciously demonstrative element in this central verse of the book of Lamentations – either in the midst of or in front of a community (cf the cohortatives in 3_{40-42}). Thus the intimacy of the personal 'I—Thou' relationship is transcended. Those who surround the גֶּבֶר are made participants in his intercession. Clearly his purpose in so doing is to have them share in his intention and follow him in his prayer. It becomes possible, therefore, to understand 3_{48-54} as both introduction and argument for the גֶּבֶר's ongoing, personal prayer which is intended to have exemplary significance for those who are confronted with the same affliction as he.

46 *They open wide their mouths about us,* פָּצוּ עָלֵינוּ פִּיהֶם
all our enemies! כָּל־אֹיְבֵינוּ

This bicolon is almost identical to the song-response 2_{16a}, although the single difference between the two is quite significant. Whereas the 1st person singular suffix in 2_{16} referred to daughter Jerusalem, the present suffix נוּ has to do with the גֶּבֶר and the people for whom he speaks. Thus the mockery of the enemy which so disturbed daughter Jerusalem, also effects the גֶּבֶר and those around him. The convergence of identity seems clear. The mockery in question is found in Lam II in the final canticle (2_{6-17}) of sub-canto 2_{11-17}, while in the present context, the poets have situated it in the centre of the second canto (3_{34-66}), thus accentuating it (cf the exegesis of 2_{16}). Who is the addressee of these words? Clearly YHWH, since it is obvious that the accusatory prayer of 3_{45} runs on into 3_{46}. The גֶּבֶר's prayer continues with complaints concerning the suffering brought upon him and his fellow Israelites by the enemy.

47A *Panic and pitfall come upon us,* פַּחַד וָפַחַת הָיָה לָנוּ

The word-pair פַּחַד וָפַחַת is characterised by both alliteration and assonance.[291] The combination is found in two other places in the OT: Isa 24_{17} and Jer 48_{43}. The latter text is certainly older than Lam 3_{47} and is located in the context of a prophecy of judgement (against Moab). Both

---

[291] Cf idem תַּאֲנִיָּה וַאֲנִיָּה in 2_5; cf also Ps 14_5.

texts, moreover, are more extensive, with alliteration and assonance further developed via the noun פַּח, 'the snare of the bird-catcher'. Given the fact that the image of bird catching appears in the third strophe of the present canticle (3_{52}) we can certainly speak here of a degree of association with the fuller expression. We are presented with a hunting scene: the hunters raise the game which runs off without paying attention to the hidden snares in its path, behind which might lie further nets and traps intended for animals able to avoid the initial traps or even climb out of them.[292] פַּחַת suggests a kind of fall-trap or pit while פַּחַד suggests 'sudden terror' or 'panic'. Interestingly enough, פַּחַד, with one exception (Job 39_{25} [MT 39_{22}]), is never used for animal terror. The noun is primarily employed to designate the terror brought about in human persons by God's less positive interventions[293] or by his theophany.[294] Thus the poets do not only call to mind the world of the hunt, they also draw our attention to the angst and terror brought about by YHWH's more hostile appearances. See especially Isa 33_{14} – the judgement of the sinners in Zion in which YHWH is described as a devouring fire. See Lam 2_{3c} as well as the echoes of theophany in the preceding strophe, 3_{43-45}. Once again we have the reversal of a theological motief from Israel's salvation history: whereas YHWH once overcame Israel's enemies with his terror,[295] now that same terror overcomes his own people.

47B *the devastation and the disintegration!* הַשֵּׁאת וְהַשָּׁבֶר

The noun שֵׁאת is a *hapax*. Indeed the root שׁאה from which it is derived is also quite rare: Isa 6_{11} (2x), 37_{26} (// II Kgs 19_{25}), both texts stemming from the context of the prophetic announcement of judgement. The context of both texts makes it clear, in addition, that they have to do with the devastation of cities and (agricultural) land. In Isa 6_{11} the root שׁאה I is parallel with the noun שְׁמָמָה thus placing devastation side by side with the disappearance of inhabitants. The same motifs can also be found on this level in the songs of Lamentations: devastation, mentioned in the song-response 1_{16c} (= sub-canto response with 1_{13c}) and dispersal of inhabitants, mentioned in song-response 4_{16a}

[292] Cf Jer 48_{44} and Isa 24_{18}; cf also figures 110–120 in OKeel, *Die Welt der altorientalischen Bildsymbolik und das Alte Testament*, Zürich-Einsiedeln-Köln-Neukirchen-Vluyn 1977².

[293] Cf Ex 15_{16}, Isa 19_{16}, 33_{14}, Mic 7_{17}, Jer 49_{5}.

[294] Cf Isa $2_{10,19,21}$ etcetera; cf also THAT II 412f (Stähli).

[295] Cf Ex15_{16}, II Chron 14_{13}, 17_{10}, 20_{29}; cf also Deut 2_{25}, 11_{25}, Judg 7_{16ff}. This in conjunction with the 'holy war'; cf TWAT VI 557f (Müller).

The present formulation draws particular attention to the definite articles attached to both הַשֵּׁאת and הַשָּׁבֶר, a usage alien to pre-exilic prophecy where שֶׁבֶר is always spoken of undefined (for its meaning cf 2_{11bB}). The use of the definite article here not only defines the term, it also possesses a demonstrative value: this devastation and this disintegration. The same is true of Isa 51_9, the only other place in the OT where שֶׁבֶר appears with the definite article and in which clear reference is being made to the fall of 587. Thus it is clear that the poets are not referring here to devastation and disintegration in general but to the particular devastation and the particular disintegration predicted in pre-exilic prophetic announcements of judgement. There is an evident relationship, therefore, with 2_{17ab}: 'YHWH has consummated his word' as well as with 1_{21a}: 'You brought on the day you had announced'. Thus the poets endorse once again the realisation of a former prophetic announcement of judgement.

48 *My eye flows with torrents of water* פַּלְגֵי־מַיִם תֵּרַד עֵינִי
because of the disintegration of my daughter, my people. עַל־שֶׁבֶר בַּת־עַמִּי

For the transition from third to first person see the introduction to the present canticle. The גֶּבֶר's intercessory prayer comes to an end but – given the enormity of the affliction – to stop praying altogether would have been out of the question. His tearful agony is and remains the justification of his ongoing prayer. This verse is closely related to 1_{16} and 2_{18} which depict the tearful sufferings of daughter Zion/Jerusalem. As she weeps and can do nothing more than weep, so the גֶּבֶר weeps. In so doing he is responding to the call to daughter Jerusalem to let tears flow like a river: הוֹרִידִי כַנַּחַל (2_{18bA}) // פַּלְגֵי־מַיִם תֵּרַד. תֵּרַד = 3f sg *qal* impf of √ירד, the subject being עֵינִי (sg + sf 1 sg). פֶּלֶג is used to designate canals dug out for the purpose of irrigation (cf HAL 877) and can be used in a figurative sense (Prov 21_1; cf Job 29_6). In the present context, the metaphor clearly indicates tears of great intensity. Weeping of such a nature and intensity is more than just an expression of human sorrow, it has its proper place in the context of prayer (likewise in $2_{18,19}$) and is ultimately directed towards YHWH (2_{20ff}).

With the expression עַל־שֶׁבֶר בַּת־עַמִּי the גֶּבֶר repeats the words of 2_{11bB}, the same words once used by Lady Jerusalem to pour out her lament. Their suffering is identical: the disintegration of their people. The significance of the formulation (cf 2_{11bB}) would appear to suggest that such lament reflects the acknowledgement of a prophetic announcement of judgement, thus bringing the present bicolon into line with that preceding it. Here in

3_{48} the expression has a certain summarising quality, similar in fashion to 3_{42-47} which depicts the primary elements of the (cause of) the people's affliction.

49 *My eye gushes with water, restless,* עֵינִי נִגְּרָה וְלֹא תִדְמֶה
without sleeping, מֵאֵין הֲפֻגוֹת

The present strophe is connected to what precedes it by way of concatenation: עֵינִי ↔ עֵינִי. Besides this literary dimension, however, there is also an element of continuity at the level of content. A quite sold literary association is evident with 2_{18}: עֵינִי // עֵינֵךְ; אַל־תִּדֹּם // וְלֹא תִדְמֶה and אַל־תִּתְּנִי פוּגַת // מֵאֵין הֲפֻגוֹת. The גֶּבֶר responds in obedience to the appeal directed to Lady Jerusalem as she herself had done in 2_{20-22}.

Where the preceding strophe emphasised the intensity of the weeping, the present strophe focuses on its duration via the underlying meaning of √נגר (cf HAL 632f). 'Duration' is inherent in the idea of flowing/gushing. The verb is found in one other place in II Sam 14_{14} (also in the *niph'al*) where it refers to water which has been discarded and which disappears as it flows away, being absorbed into the ground. The element of 'waste' is likewise present in this bicolon: the eye wastes away with tears. Daughter Jerusalem utters similar expressions in 2_{11aA} (and cf 2_{18b}), yet in spite of being 'blinded' her eyes do not cease to run with tears: לֹא תִדְמֶה, from the root דמה II *qal*, literally 'it does not rest' (cf HAL 216). The incessant character of the גֶּבֶר's weeping does not detract from its intensity; at least that is how we understand the noun הֲפֻגָה (*hapax*), derived from √פוג 'to get weak'; here in the plural form הֲפֻגוֹת, 'weakenings' (different HAL 243); cf 2_{18c}). מֵאֵין means 'without' (cf HAL 41 sv אַיִן IB (2b). There is no point at which the גֶּבֶר's tears are even slightly diminished.

50 *until he looks down and sees,* עַד־יַשְׁקִיף וְיֵרֶא
YHWH *from the heavens.* יְהוָה מִשָּׁמָיִם

The second core verse (cf 3_{17}) – encircled by the clear inclusion עֵינִי (3_{49A}) // עֵינִי (3_{51A}) – reveals the presence of a skillfully constructed chiasm: שקף // מִשָּׁמָיִם ⟺ יְהוָה // ראה. Here we see the most profound intention behind all the laments, appeals and prayers: it is directed to YHWH.[296] The present canto opened with the realisation that the Most High did not want to look down upon the affliction of his people (3_{36B}). In contrast to this, however, the גֶּבֶר presents his complaints, with bitter, unremitting

[296] Cf $1_{9c,11c,20-22}$, $2_{10,18-22}$, 3_{41-66}, 5_{1-22} etcetera.

and long-sustained tears, until YHWH is moved by his people's affliction and looks down upon it.

The root שקף means 'to look down from above at something below'. It is employed with YHWH as subject in Ex 14_{24} (consequence: confusion among the Egyptians), Deut 26_{15} (consequence: blessing for Israel), Ps 14_2 (=53_3 [in order to inquire into the human person]) and in Ps 102_{20}. The latter text is post-exilic and implies that the prayer of Lamentations has been heard. In itself the verb has neither positive nor negative significance; its purpose is to indicate the superior position from which YHWH looks down (מִשָּׁמַיִם). The root with YHWH as subject, however, does not simply constitute a neutral observation but implies rather an activity (cf Ps 104_{32}). "»Gott sieht« drückt aus, daß Jahwe auf die Geschehnisse eingeht." If he looks down on people in need then he sets to work as a liberator. This is in fact a fundamental tennet of Israel's faith: "Die Erfahrung, daß der erhabene Gott »in die Tiefe sieht«, ist zur Grundaussage des Lobes in Israel geworden (Gen 29,32; Ps 33,13; 113,6; vgl. Ps 9,14; 138,6)".[297]

It is clear that at this point in time YHWH is not looking down, does not see the affliction of his people and has not set them free. The גֶּבֶר, however, does not give in. He has already stated that YHWH's refusal to look down and to liberate are not according to his heart. Thus he is aware that it must pain YHWH to maintain such a stance.[298] With his incessant prayer of tears he endeavours to raise this painful tension in YHWH's heart to such a pitch that it becomes unbearable and he looks down and acts to save his people. Take note of the use of the tetragrammaton here, clearly intended to make the גֶּבֶר's appeal all the more persuasive: after all, He, YHWH, is their God from of old! (cf 5_{19ff}). The third person singular formulation employed here together with the mention of praying to YHWH points to the exemplary character of the גֶּבֶר's prayer of tears. The formulation also associates this verse with 3_{17}, the other core verse. Thus both core verses render the central theme of the songs as a whole.

51A *My eye causes me deep pain...* עֵינִי עוֹלְלָה לְנַפְשִׁי

The repetition of עֵינִי at the beginning of this bicolon (also in 3_{49aA}) reveals the concentric structure of the ע-strophe as well as the central positioning of the preceding bicolon (3_{50}). Before making the origin of his sorrow more concrete, the גֶּבֶר indicates the depth at which his suffering has touched

297 Cf THAT II 696f (Vetter); cf also the exegesis of $1_{9c,11c}$.

298 Cf the exegesis of 3_{33} and cf also Judg 10_{16}, Isa 30_{18}, 42_{14}, 54_7.

him. עֵינִי is the subject of עוֹלְלָה (=√עלל I *po'el* pf 3m 3g); the masculine form is somewhat surprising given that 'eye' is feminine.[299] The verb in its present form clearly carries the notion of 'to cause pain'/'to hurt'. It is used elsewhere in Lamentations in $1_{12,22}$ (2x) and 3_{20}. See the exegesis of 1_{12bB} for further details on the significance of this root. The גֶּבֶר literally says: 'my eye causes pain to my soul'. For the significance of נֶפֶשׁ see the explanation of the canto-response 3_{17A} and the exegesis of 3_{20}. What the גֶּבֶר sees causes him intense pain which touches the very depths of his being.

51B ... *because of all the daughters of my city.* מִכֹּל בְּנוֹת עִירִי

This colon is often considered corrupt and fit for emendation. Perhaps the most radical change is the proposed rearrangement of the sequence of bicola in the strophe into 51, 49, 50, in addition to which בְּנוֹת is emended to read בְּכוֹת (the infinitive construct of √בכה 'to weep') and עִירִי (my city) is read as a scribal error for עָנְיִי (my affliction). We are then left with the translation: 'my eye hurts from weeping' which is followed by Rudolph and in a similar vein by Haller, Weiser, BHS, together with Kraus, Kaiser, Boecker, Groß etcetera, who drop the rearrangement of the verses but maintain the infinitive בְּכוֹת. Older exegesis (Blayney, Ewald, Löhr) reads 'the daughter cities' of Jerusalem, referring for support to Jer 44_2, Ezek 16_{14ff} and Ps 48_{12} but the idiomatic usage does not agree. Aalders, Meek, Albrektson, Gordis and Provan rightly maintain the MT. Objections to the MT suggest, among other things, that 3_{48} already constituted something of a closure and that a specific lament concerning the women of Jerusalem would be a little behindhand at this stage. For the same reason, commentators give 3_{51} a general significance. Van Selms maintains עִירִי, but purports to deduce therefrom that the גֶּבֶר must have been a Davidite since such and such alone would have been able to refer to Jerusalem as 'my city'. The general usage of עִירִי, however, can be found in Deut 19_{12}, II Sam 17_{23}, 19_{37} (MT 19_{38}) etcetera. Thus, in the present context, the גֶּבֶר is naming his own city and it is evident that he is being portrayed as an inhabitant of Jerusalem.

It is quite understandable that the present colon has set exegetes on the wrong path when one is aware of their lack of familiarity with the concentric structure of the larger and smaller units within the songs and of their mutual cohesion. It is equally clear that the rearrangement of verses

299 Cf, however, GES-K § 122*n* and Zech 3_9.

would lead to a disturbance of said structure. Commentators are perhaps correct in suggesting that 3_{48} provides a certain element of closure (cf the introduction to the present canticle) but, at the same time, the גֶּבֶר assures us that he intends to press on with his prayer of tears (3_{49-50}), and this would have little meaning if there was not also a continuation of need and affliction. It is apparent from the concentric structure of this strophe, together with the transition from 3_{48} to 3_{49} that the affliction and need refer to the people as a whole. The same affliction and need continue undiminished. As a consequence, the גֶּבֶר specifies two aspects thereof which pain him the deepest: the unique affliction of the women of Jerusalem and his own persecution and imprisonment in a hellish pit (3_{52-54}). When one reads the third song by itself then the mention of the בְּנוֹת עִירִי does indeed come across as rather sudden and perhaps even incidental given the lack of a clear and direct relationship with the context. Wiesmann also argues: "Daß die Frauenwelt Jerusalems gemeint sei, ist höchst unwahrscheinlich; denn sie wird in der Dichtung (vgl. 1:4,18; 2:10,21) nirgends allein betrauert".[300] Nevertheless, the affliction of the בְּנוֹת צִיּוֹן as a distinct theme within Isaiah's prophecy of doom[301] is not alone in leading us to suspect Wiesmann's vision of inaccuracy. Even within the book of Lamentations itself, the affliction of the women appears to have a much more central place than many exegetes suggest. Indeed, structural analysis provides a plethora of arguments to back this up. We noted elsewhere that central strophes are used to create enveloping inclusions with respect to adjacent cantos of neighbouring songs.[302] One might argue that the same is also true between 3_{49-51} (central strophe of the second canto) and the second canto of Lam II in the first and last canticle of which the women of Jerusalem are powerfully featured. In 2_{12} we are confronted with the mothers of starving children while 2_{20} depicts the horrible scene of women driven by hunger to eat the flesh of their dead offspring. The latter image is repeated once again in 4_{10} while 4_2 (inclusion in sub-canto 4_{1-11}) considers their children as equal in value to mere potsherds; 5_{11} relates the rape of the women of Zion while in 1_{10}, the centre of the first song, the poets tell us of the theft of their jewels. All of these instances of the horrendous affliction confronting the women of Jerusalem and the specific places they are to be found within the songs – namely at the beginning and end or in the centre of the relevant cantos or songs – indicate how this

300 HWiesmann, *Die Klagelieder übersetzt und erklärt*, Frankfurt–Main 1954, 190.
301 Cf Isa 3_{16-24} and HWildberger, *Jesaja 1-12*, BKAT X/1, Neukirchen 1972, 135–145.
302 Cf 1988, 346 and the explanation of 2_{10a}.

aspect in particular of the calamity facing the people made an extremely profound impact. Of course, this is hardly surprising, given the content of the first (2_{11-13}) and last (2_{20-22}) canticles of canto II of the second song. In the present core strophe, the גֶּבֶר expresses his deep consternation and horror at such events: his eyes cause him pain when he comes face to face with such dreadful scenes between mothers and their children.[303]

52 *They hunted me like a bird,* צוֹד צָדוּנִי כַּצִּפּוֹר
my enemies, without reason. אֹיְבַי חִנָּם

Besides the affliction of the women of Jerusalem we also have the personal affliction of the גֶּבֶר which he depicts using the imagery of the hunt. This is not without significance given that the same imagery was used at the beginning of the present canticle with reference to the suffering and need of the people (cf 3_{47A}). By placing solidarity in affliction in first position, the גֶּבֶר draws attention to the way he has chosen to escape this misfortune with the background intention of recruiting others to follow him.

The first bicolon of the צ-strophe employs the metaphor of bird-catching or fowling, a practice common in Israel. Texts and images reveal great ingenuity in the various techniques employed to catch birds in the Ancient Near East.[304] One would be mistaken if one were to imagine a well constructed snare[305] in the present context. Birds were also caught by throwing a sort of boomerang at them[306] or with a bow and arrow, the birds being first chased from their cover and then shot at (cf Ps 11_{1-2}). The latter form of fowling appears to be the metaphor serving here since both elements are found in the text and the context. Of course, it is no accident that the song-response 4_{18} – using the same verb צוד – likewise speaks of the hounding of human beings through the squares of the city. Indeed, it is in the self same place that the children waste away and die of hunger (cf 2_{11c}, the beginning of canto II of Lam II). The same theme is evident in the beginning of canto I of Lam III (2_{11c} // 3_{4c} = response at canto level): the wasting away of the גֶּבֶר. Such additional indications serve to sharpen the present image: weak and emaciated, the גֶּבֶר is hounded into

303 The prepostion מִן before כֹּל in the present colon should be understood as causative; see HAL 566 sv מִן (4).

304 Cf AvDeursen, *De achtergrond van de Psalmen*, Baarn (undated), 128–135 and OKeel, *Die Welt der altorientalischen Bildsymbolik und das Alte Testament*, Zürich-Einsiedeln-Köln-Neukirchen-Vluyn 1977², 78–84.

305 Cf Ps 141_9, Am 3_5, Qoh 9_{12}.

306 Am 3_5; cf Keel, 84.

flight by his enemy as a bird chased from its hiding place. There is also a possible association with the bow and arrow (used in this form of hunting) mentioned in $3_{12,13}$, the converse canticle in the first canto, in which the גֶּבֶר complains that he has been shot and pierced by the arrows of his Enemy. Furthermore, in the canto-response with 3_{19} there is mention of the גֶּבֶר's 'meandering about' which corresponds well with the image of being hunted.

The enemies in question is the same as those mentioned in 3_{46} and 2_{16}. One is also reminded of the terror mentioned in 1_{10} and 5_{12}. The term חִנָּם 'without reason' should not be seen as a judgement on the deserved or undeserved character of the גֶּבֶר's fate. Rudolph suggests that it refers to the sinlessness of the one being chased but this does not square with the plural confession of sinfulness in 3_{42}. The term really points to the arbitrariness with which the enemy abuse both the people and the גֶּבֶר.[307] The enemy makes no distinctions and is no respecter of persons.

53A *They let my life waste away in a pit...* צָמְתוּ בַבּוֹר חַיָּי

The poets present us here with a change of image, although the גֶּבֶר used the same image in the first canto. Once again, there is a possibility that the גֶּבֶר's audience will identify with his imprisonment, as the inclusion between the ל-strophe and the צ-strophe within this sub-canto (3_{34-54}) makes clear, namely אָסִיר (3_{34B}) // בּוֹר (3_{53A}). The combination of בּוֹר 'pit' and אָסִיר 'prisoner' can also be found in Isa 24_{22} (cf Ps 107_{10}). The *qal* of the root צמת is unique here. Two possible meanings are suggested in HAL (970) on the basis of similarities with cognate languages: 'to destroy' or 'to silence', but neither fits the context well. The *niph'al* is used in Job 6_{17} with reference to streams which disappear during the dry season. As such streams dry up it looks as if the water is disappearing into the ground. In similar fashion, the enemy cause the גֶּבֶר's life to disappear into a pit. The hunted is taken prisoner and locked away in the classical fashion, namely in an empty cistern (בּוֹר), an underground reservoir for water which was hewn from stone in the form of a vertical pitcher (Deut 6_{11}, Jer 2_{13}). The form itself is the same as that of a carved out grave,[308] and whoever found himself in such a place knew his death was not far off.[309] Escape was impossible because their was nothing on the concave

---

307 Cf 3_{34-36} and 4_{16}; cf also Ps 35_7 which likewise employs the imagery of the hunt.

308 Gen 37_{22ff}, 41_{14}, Isa 14_{15}, 38_{18}, Ezek 26_{20}, $31_{14,16}$, 32_{18},Ps $88_{5,7}$ etcetera.

309 Cf Ps 79_{11}, 107_{10}.

walls to grab hold of in order to climb out of such a pit.[310] To find oneself in such a place was a death sentence (cf Jer 38_9).

53B *... and have thrown stones upon me.* וַיַּדּוּ־אֶבֶן בִּי

The throwing of stones should not be seen as a part of the hunt at which the captive animal is stoned to death while caught in the net (cf Brandscheidt). It likewise has nothing to do with the stoning of the גֶּבֶר as Aalders would suggest, referring to II Sam $16_{6,13}$.

The following bicolon (3_{54}) continues the image of the pit and this must determine our understanding of stone throwing in the present context. The narrow opening of a cistern was closed of with (piled up) stones which were too big to fall into the pit (see the aforementioned drawings in Keel). Such stones prevented dust from blowing into the cistern as well as animals and humans from falling into it.[311] Large and therefore heavy stones made the pit inaccessible.[312]

Where the pit also served as a prison cell, the prisoner felt himself even further shut in as he or she saw and heard the stones being thrown over the opening making the daylight gradually disappear. In such darkness one might imagine that one was already in the grave. The first canticle of the first canto (3_6) where the גֶּבֶר complains that he is fated to live in 'dark places like the dead of long ago' echoes clearly in this image. Once again the גֶּבֶר's affliction continues unabated.[313]

54A *Water flows over my head;* צָפוּ־מַיִם עַל־רֹאשִׁי

We remain with the image of the pit. Cisterns were dug in lower places where rainwater collected in large quantities. When there was a heavy rainstorm the water flowed through the covering stones into the pit and where the pit was in use as a prision it dripped from the walls onto the head of the prisoner. If the water level was rising fast then there was a real threat of drowning. On top of this, rain softened the sediment at the bottom of the pit causing the prisoner's feet to sink into the mud and, apparently, causing the water level to rise even faster.[314] Really a dreadful experience.

---

310 Cf the images 78 and 79 in Keel, 60–63.

311 See Ex 21_{33}, Lk 14_5.

312 Cf Gen 29_2, Ps 69_{16}.

313 For the form וַיַּדּוּ cf GES-K § 69*u*.

314 Cf Ps 69_{2f}, Jer 38_6.

54B *I thought, 'I am lost.'* אָמַרְתִּי נִגְזָרְתִּי

The root גזר is employed to signify the cutting off of a person's life.[315] Ezek 37_{11} offers a good illustration with the people's complaint 'we are done for' (נִגְזַרְנוּ לָנוּ). As the water rose steadily in the pit, the גֶּבֶר drew the obvious conclusion: he is not going to survive this ordeal. The question remains, of course, as to whether we are dealing here with literal or figurative language, image or real experience. Given the frequent use of the image of the pit as a prison, together with the distinctive character of the גֶּבֶר's affliction, it has to be accepted that the present text is based on a well-know image (cf the quotation from Keel in the introduction to Lam III) although one which need not necessarily represent actual experience. Nevertheless, it constitutes an image which effectively depicts the גֶּבֶר's present, real and mortal despondency. Once again it is important to note that the horrendous situation is not depicted as having passed. The only element of this colon which offers any future perspective is אָמַרְתִּי, 'I thought', since it reminds us of the fact that the גֶּבֶר had apparently found an alternative possibility of obtaining salvation. As a matter of fact, we already encountered this perfective conclusion on the part of the גֶּבֶר in the parallel canticle of the first canto, 3_{13-21}: In 3_{18} we find a corresponding expression likewise employing the root אמר I: 'and I said: Ravaged is my splendour, my expectation of YHWH.'

It is striking how both canticles – in keeping with the responsive diptych structure – also agree with one another at the level of content. The complaints mirror one another: arrows and enemies, derision and terror, bitterness and tears, absence of good and absence of YHWH, wandering and being hounded, lament of the captive and the pit. While it is true that the גֶּבֶר has now turned his gaze towards YHWH and placed his hope in Him, there is still no mention of salvific intervention on the part of YHWH. The difference remains, however, that in the present canto, the גֶּבֶר – in accordance with his regained faith (3_{22-33}) – now turns quite expressly to YHWH, not in blind rebellion, but in recognition of guilt and with an appeal to YHWH's heart.

Sub-Canto II (Lam 3_{55-66})

The present canto constitutes the גֶּבֶר's final prayer running parallel with the final prayers of Lady/daughter Jerusalem in Lam I and II. The first canticle (3_{55-60}) consists of expressions of trust in YHWH: YHWH is a

[315] Isa 53_{8}, Ps 31_{23}, 88_{6}.

God who hears, who is close-by, who is just and who redeems. He sees the revengeful plans of the enemy, concocted against his devout one. The concluding canticle (3_{61-66}) details the גֶּבֶר's hoped for liberation in the form of revenge dealt out against the mockery and wicked deeds of the enemy.

Canticle IV (3_{55-60})

Content/theme: *Prayer to* YHWH

Literary argumentation:

inclusions:	(60A) רָאִיתָה // (55A) קָרָאתִי שִׁמְךָ יְהוָה
	(58A) רַבְתָּ // (57A) קָרַבְתָּ
	(58B) גָּאַלְתָּ חַיָּי // (57B) אָמַרְתָּ אַל־תִּירָא
incl/resp:	(59B) רָאִיתָה // (56A) קוֹלִי שָׁמָעְתָּ
	(59B) שָׁפְטָה מִשְׁפָּטִי // (56B) לְשַׁוְעָתִי
response:	(58B) גָּאַלְתָּ חַיָּי // (55B) מִבּוֹר תַּחְתִּיּוֹת
ext par:	(59A) יְהוָה // (55A) יְהוָה
incl/resp/concat:	via 2m sg suffixes

Plöger is of the opinion that 3_{55-66} of the third song have the basic characteristics of a song of thanksgiving, although not entirely since "ein Eintreten Jahwes in Umrissen und partiell bereits erkennbar ist, allerdings die endgültige Restitution noch aussteht."

Rudolph changes the imperatives and imperfects of 3_{64-66} into perfects and considers the entire piece to be an erstwhile thanksgiving song of Jeremiah on the occasion of an act of salvation by YHWH, the salvation in question functioning here as a sign of the future salvation of the people. Kaiser, Brandscheidt and Boecker also tend to presume the presence of a song of thanksgiving.

However, an essential element of the song of thanksgiving is missing. One cannot find the announcement of praise together with the accompanying grounds thereto.[316] A further essential component of the song of thanksgiving is the actual experience of salvation and restoration. There is clearly no mention of such a component here. The present sub-canto is nothing more than a prayer for intervention addressed to YHWH. What follows the

[316] Cf Ps 9_{2f}, 18_4, 30_{2-4}, 34_{2-6}, 40_{2-4}, 66_{17}, 103_{1ff}, 118_{1-4}, 138_{1-3}; cf 13_6, 22_{23-32}, together with HGunkel – JBegrich, *Einleitung in die Psalmen*, Göttingen 1975[3], 267ff.

third song – namely the complaints of Lam IV – reveals that YHWH has not yet granted actual restoration to his people, just as the conclusion of Lam V. Indeed, such a restoration is absent from the five songs as a whole. Only the very fact of his ongoing survival in the midst of judgement is considered by the גֶּבֶר as a favour from YHWH (cf 3_{22ff}).

In consideration of these facts, it would be wrong to view this part of Lam III as a (partial) song of thanksgiving. While it is true that the גֶּבֶר has so far survived the disaster and as such has not yet reached his final end (3_{22}), the water is still up to his neck and there appears to be little chance of escape (3_{54B}, 4_{18b}). One should not be misled, therefore, by the perfects in 3_{55-63} and interpret the liberation as (at least partially) a thing of the past as do LXX and Peshitta.[317] Indeed the perfects in the present text can just as well signify present meaning (see the exegesis), allowing us to understand the entire text as a prayer beginning with expressions of faith on the basis of which the גֶּבֶר has consistently appealed to the heart of YHWH. He is confident that YHWH will hear, see and save.

The understanding of this part of Lam III as a song of thanksgiving is quite understandable, however, given the close idiomatic connections with the corresponding genre in the Psalms.[318] The relationship not only points to the language of the song of thanksgiving but just as strikingly to that of the prayer of supplication found in Israel's liturgy. Such associations, however, need not undermine an interpretation which departs from the concrete horrific circumstances in which the גֶּבֶר finds himself. Once again the community is able to hear her actual experience translated into more classical terminology since the language of the liturgy is, by its very nature, more open to such use.

55 *I call upon your name, O* YHWH, קָרָאתִי שִׁמְךָ יְהוָה
from the depths of the pit. מִבּוֹר תַּחְתִּיּוֹת

A quite understandable continuation of the complaint in 3_{52-54}! The גֶּבֶר, who thought that all was lost, realises that there is one and one alone who can save him from his misfortune: YHWH. The same notion has found new life in him (cf 3_{21}) and his recovered faith is expressed in the language of erstwhile confessions of YHWH's already substantiated power and fidelity in similar situations. Such language is to be found in the songs of

[317] Cf also Plöger, Löhr, Haller, Wiesmann, Meek, Gottwald, Weiser, Kraus, Kaiser, Groß etcetera.

[318] Cf the survey in 1983, 230f.

thanksgiving in the Psalms. It is precisely here that we find that YHWH drew his supplicants from the pit and thereby saved them from the power of the kingdom of death.[319] The גֶּבֶר now appeals to that same desire to save. He turns to YHWH who is able to look into the depths from on high and raise up the poor from the miry pit (cf Ps 113_7). For the present tense interpretation of the perfects, with which the גֶּבֶר's already initiated prayer continues, see GES-K § 106g and Ps 17_6, 88_{10}, 119_{145}, 130_1, 141_1. Keil, Albrektson and Gordis are likewise correct in interpreting the present text in the present.[320] The word combination בּוֹר תַּחְתִּיּוֹת signifies the deepest part of the pit and is only found elswhere in the OT in Ps 88_7 (cf, however, the combination of תַּחְתִּיּוֹת with Sheol (שְׁאוֹל) in Ps 86_{13} and Deut 32_{22} as illustrative of the atmosphere.

56A *You hear my voice, do not close your ear...* קוֹלִי שָׁמָעְתָּ אַל־תַּעְלֵם אָזְנְךָ

The meaning of the perfect שָׁמָעְתָּ has recently been called into question once again by Provan.[321] He too is right in assuming that there is only one situation of need being treated in the present context: the current misfortune of the גֶּבֶר. As a consequence he sees the perfect tense as a problem if one is inclined, of course, to translate it as a perfect. One is then left with the somewhat illogical: 'You have heard my voice, do not hide your ear', whereby Provan comments: "In no other address to God in the OT of which I am aware, however, is a statement that he has heard (*šm'*) a petition followed by a citation of that petition." (171). For that reason the perfect שָׁמָעְתָּ must have something to do with a prayer for redemption: "...for the two parts of this line are best understood, if they both refer to the future, as strictly parallel." His translation, therefore, runs as follows: "hear my plea; do not close your ear to my cry for help" (173). What we now have appears to be an imperative but Provan does not understand it as such. He considers the text to be proof par excellence for the existence of a so-called precative perfect or the 'perfect of entreaty'. Thus, by way of clarification, we might paraphrase Provan's translation as: 'I beg you, listen to me!' Sadly, Provan's understanding of the text remains unconvincing. One might ask why, in the depths of

319 Ps 30_2, 40_{2-4}; cf Ps 18_{4-20}, 103_4; cf also KSpronk, *Beatific Afterlife in Ancient Israel and in the Ancient Near East*, AOAT 219, Neukirchen-Vluyn 1986, 283f.

320 Cf also the detailed explanation of HGottlieb, *A Study of the Text of Lamentations*, Acta Jutlandica XLVIII, Århus 1978, 57–60.

321 IWProvan, 'Past, Present and Future in Lamentations iii 52–66: the Case for a Precative Perfect Re-examined', VT XLI (1991), 164–175.

such misfortune, the poets would have employed a weaker precative perfect instead of an imperative שְׁמַע which would have been stronger, much more appropriate in the context of need and consistent with the following prohibitive אַל־תַּעְלֵם אָזְנְךָ. Likewise, the use of the imperative – in similar contexts – is also quite common in the Psalms.[322] If one were to understand 3_{55-66} as nothing other than a prayer of supplication on the basis of assumed precative perfects then one would run the risk of ignoring something very important: the גֶּבֶר's experience of the חַסְדֵי יְהוָה which stands in parallel with the present prayer in the first canto (3_{22}). In fact the whole sub-canto 3_{22-33} consists of the גֶּבֶר's expressions of trust which form the basis for the given concretisation of the help he expects from YHWH. Up to the present, the גֶּבֶר's experience as led him to the insight that YHWH has not yet abandoned him and his people altogether. In, and in spite of, the enormity of his affliction he experiences God's fidelity (cf the explanation of 3_{23}). In this situation, therefore, a present tense translation of the perfect שָׁמָעְתָּ would seem the most appropriate, indeed, the Hebrew syntax does not stand in the way of such an interpretation.[323] A further example of the same thing can be found in Ps 10_{17}.[324] YHWH does actually hear the גֶּבֶר's appeal. Thus we might paraphrase the text as follows: 'You do indeed hear me'. The גֶּבֶר is aware that his trust is articulated in Israel's most fundamental confessions which he considers to be valid still: YHWH always hears the cry of a person in need.[325] Nothing escapes him. If YHWH does not hear then it is not because he cannot but because he does not want to hear.[326] Thus – contra Provan – one should not simply interpret אַל־תַּעְלֵם אָזְנְךָ as a repetition of קוֹלִי שָׁמָעְתָּ. Hearing need not mean the same thing as 'listening' which in YHWH's case ultimately boils down to salvific intervention. The prohibitive constitutes an appeal to YHWH – expressed in anthropomorphic terms – not to stop his ears and cut himself off from the appeal for help which he actually hears. This is how we understand √עלם I *hiph'il* impf.[327] Indeed the prohibitive formulation likewise militates against a preterite interpretation of the preceding perfect.

The anthropomorpic language used here is quite striking in its uninhibited reference to YHWH's ears and ability to hear. There is no system at the

[322] Cf Ps 27_7, 30_{11}, 54_4, 64_2, 143_1.
[323] Cf JOÜON–MURAOKA § 112*f*.
[324] Cf GES-K § 106*n* which speaks of a *perfectum confidentiae*.
[325] Cf Gen 16_{11}, Ex 22_{26}, Ps $34_{16,18}$.
[326] Cf Isa 1_{15}, 59_{1f}, Jer 14_{12}.
[327] Cf TWAT VI 164 (Locher).

root of such anthropomorphisms nor a divine type, but they are characterised by a certain nimbleness and vivacity: "Weil das AT in Anthropomorphismen von ihm redet, deshalb steht sein Gott als der persönlichen und lebendige Gott vor den Menschen...".[328]

Of further interest is the contrast between the present verse and 3_8 (antithetical inclusion at the song level) and 3_{44} ([תְּפִלָּה], antithetical inclusion in the second canto). If one were to compare 3_{56} with $3_{8,44}$ then one might well ask why the גֶּבֶר now seems to think that YHWH desires to hear him. This can only be explained on the basis of the changes which have taken place within the גֶּבֶר himself. After 3_{18} his attitude and tone were modified. While he once stated that YHWH was his relentlessly cruel guard, he can later confess that YHWH is his portion (3_{24}). The גֶּבֶר humbles himself and desires to be converted. Only then can he entertain any hope that YHWH will attend to his affliction, for He never despises a broken and contrite heart (cf Ps 51_{19}).

56B ...*to my gasping and crying for help.* לְרַוְחָתִי לְשַׁוְעָתִי

Most exegetes consider this second colon to be corrupt in some way.[329] Many find it too long and assume לְשַׁוְעָתִי to be secondary[330] while others prefer to scrap לְרַוְחָתִי;[331] one being understood as an explanatory gloss for the other. Those who find the verse too long, however, must base themselves on the (not so substantial) presupposition of the presence of a strict metre. Objections on the basis of length are hard to maintain, moreover, if one were to take אַל־תַּעְלֵם as one beat and join it to the first colon. In addition, the poets are not unfamiliar with the use of word pairs.[332] The structure of the song as a whole also argues against the elimination of לְשַׁוְעָתִי. At the song level, 3_{56} constitutes an inclusion with 3_8: לְשַׁוְעָתִי // וַאֲשַׁוֵּעַ. Elimination of לְשַׁוְעָתִי, therefore, would also eliminate this decidedly intended external parallelism. At the same time, however, it is equally unacceptable that לְרַוְחָתִי should be considered secondary since it is a relatively rare noun and any scribal error would be hard if not impossible to explain. Thus we maintain the text as it is.

---

[328] So LKöhler, *Theologie des Alten Testaments*, Tübingen 1966[4], 6; cf THAT I 97 (Liedke) and the explanation of MCAKorpel, *A Rift in the Clouds*, Münster 1990, 614–637.

[329] Cf also Robinson in text critical apparatus of BHS.

[330] Cf Aalders, Haller, Rudolph, Albrektson, Kraus, Gordis, Kaiser.

[331] Cf Ehrlich, Wiesmann, Brandscheidt.

[332] Cf 1_{7aB}, $2_{5cB,22bB}$, 3_{47A}.

The meaning of רְוָחָה is not simple to ascertain. The noun can be found in one other place (Ex 8_{15} [MT 8_{11}]) where it clearly has something to do with 'respite' but such an interpretation does not fit the present context. A parallel or synonym of שַׁוְעָה 'call for help' would seem more appropriate. Based on the root רוח 'to make spacious' (HAL 1115), which can also apply to the lungs/thorax, we understand the term to have to do with 'breathing', an interpretation which might also explain the association with 'respite' in the text from Exodus as a sort of 'relief' following deep breathing (cf also Job 32_{20}). The translation of NBG suggests 'to sigh', but it is quite clear from the מְבוֹר תַּחְתִּיּוֹת from the preceding bicolon that the image of the cistern is still operative here and still determinative of the idiom. As the water pours in up to his lips, the גֶּבֶר finds himself profoundly cramped in his narrow and dark pit. Breathing becomes difficult and quite audibly so. Thus the term רְוָחָה in the present context must signify a sort of longing to be able to breath freely and unhindered, hence our translation: 'gasping'.[333] שַׁוְעָה (from √ שׁוע, cf 3_{8}) suggests an (articulated) cry for help, an appeal which, it should be noted, is always directed towards God. Ps 40_{2} is closely related.

The 'cry for help' has its origins in the very beginning of the history of YHWH's relationship with Israel, Ex 2_{23}, as he turned his attention to the appeal of the Israelites for help in Egypt. After this, the awareness remained strong that YHWH would respond to his people's cry.[334] If he did not then they feared that he had abandoned Zion.[335]

57A *You are near on the day I call to you;* קָרַבְתָּ בְּיוֹם אֶקְרָאֶךָּ

The aforementioned fundamental dimension of Israel's faith is here further articulated: YHWH is close to those who fear him and call upon him in their need. One is reminded of Hagar's unmentioned yet still heard affliction in Gen 16_{11}.[336] It is part of God's nature to be mindful of those who so confess. The present appeal to YHWH is not couched in a liturgical context but constitutes a simple appeal in a situation of need. √קרא is also used in such circumstances.[337] Even outside Zion YHWH is ready to

333 Cf the expression of trust: "O God, you gave me room when I was in distress" in Ps 4_{2}.

334 Cf Ps 18_{7}, 34_{16}, 39_{13}, 145_{19} and WZimmerli, *Grundriß der alttestamentlichen Theologie*, Stuttgart Berlin Köln Mainz, 1972, 17f.

335 Cf Jer 8_{19}; cf also ARHulst – CvLeeuwen, *Bevrijding in het Oude Testament*, Kampen 1981, 74–83.

336 Cf also Gen 21_{17}, Deut 4_{7}, Isa 50_{8}, 55_{6}, Ps 34_{19}, 145_{18} together with the גֶּבֶר's confession חֶלְקִי יְהוָה in the opposite bicolon (3_{24A}).

save and liberate. In spite of the enormity of his affliction, the גֶּבֶר has never given up on this fundamental aspect of his faith. It is, in fact, a necessary presupposition for his prayer.

57B *you say: "Fear not!"* אָמַרְתָּ אַל־תִּירָא

The expression אַל־תִּירָא can be found in a variety of contexts in the OT. In difficult situations, for example, people can use it to encourage or give heart to one another.[338] It is employed elsewhere as a sort motivation prior to the commencement of a battle, expressing YHWH's support.[339] According to Begrich,[340] the formula had a fixed place in the so-called priestly oracle of salvation in which the priest – after sacrifice and prayer – was at liberty to promise the petitioner God's assistance.[341] It is more likely, however, that the formulation came from a prophet active in the cult since priestly oracles via Ephod and Urim and Tummim were only known in very ancient times in Israel and only provided either a 'yes' or a 'no' in response to a petition. Emerging prophetism provided more nuanced answers and was also more in harmony with the formulation in question.[342]

Given the גֶּבֶר's situation, however, אַל־תִּירָא can hardly be a prophetic response in the present context. The crisis in which Jerusalem's prophets found themselves at that moment (cf 2_9 and 4_{13}) together with the pit in which the גֶּבֶר had been imprisoned – in which there were no prophets – make such an interpretation highly unlikely. The authors must have intended us to understand these words as spoken by an interior voice in the mind of the גֶּבֶר, words he had frequently heard in the temple liturgy when God's salvation and liberation were promised to the petitioner. The expression 'fear not' always went hand in hand with a promise of salvation to which YHWH obliged himself.

It is not impossible that the present אַל־תִּירָא simultaneously echoes a different context, namely that of YHWH's struggle against the enemies of his people,[343] given that in the formulation of his expectations, the גֶּבֶר sees

[337] Cf for the present meaning: Deut 15_9, 24_{15}, Judg 15_{18}, 16_{28}, Jonah 2_3, Ps 28_1, 50_{15}, 57_3, 86_7, 88_{10} etcetera.

[338] Cf Gen 35_{17}, Judg 4_{18}, Ruth 3_{11} etcetera.

[339] Ex 14_{13}, Deut 1_{21} etcetera.

[340] JBegrich, 'Das priesterliche Heilsorakel', ZAW 52, 1934, 81–92; idem, *Gesammelte Studien*, ThB 21, München 1964, 217–231.

[341] Likewise Stähli, THAT I 772f and Fuhs, TWAT III 884f.

[342] Cf JCdMoor, *De tijd van het heil*, Kampen 1970, 14–19.

[343] Cf Ex 14_{13}, Num 14_9, 21_{34}, Isa 7_4 etcetera; cf also Fuhs, TWAT III 883f.

YHWH taking a stance against the enemy on his behalf (and that of his people). This becomes apparent in the following verses.

58A *You, Adonai, battle always for my soul,* רַבְתָּ אֲדֹנָי רִיבֵי נַפְשִׁי

This expression of trust in God establishes a significant contrast with the complaints and laments of the opening strophe (3_{34-36}) of the present canto in which YHWH is accused of not seeing that the rights of his people are being violated. Here as well as in 3_{34-36}, however, there is no mention of a juridical context. It has to do, rather, with an unjust and uneven struggle, namely the oppression experienced by the גֶּבֶר at the hands of the enemy in which his life is placed in danger. Surrounded by such danger, he puts his trust in YHWH his God who alone can take his side and protect his life. He knows that YHWH has done this in the past (see explanation of 3_{22}) and he trusts that he will do it again in the future (for the present tense translation see 3_{55}). Thus, we should understand the רִיבֵי נַפְשִׁי as 'the struggle to protect my life' (cf Ps 119_{153f}).

The final י of רִיבֵי constitutes something of a problem for our interpretation, however. The Masoretic vocalisation reads a construct plural, literally: 'the (legal) matters of my soul' which is only found elsewhere in Ps 18_{44} (= II Sam 22_{44}). Commentators such as Hillers, Kaiser, Brandscheidt and Groß, among others, read a 1st sg suffix and offer a more direct translation: 'You wage my war', but thereby lose the parallel with the second colon. The plural is supported by LXX and should be maintained.[344] A translation which only employs the collective 'battle' does make the problem invisible but nevertheless includes the notion that Adonai intervenes on the גֶּבֶר's behalf at those crucial moments when his life is in the balance (נַפְשִׁי // חַיָּי). The translation attempts to include this element in the term 'always'. It is not for nothing that the name אֲדֹנָי is used at this point in the text. The power, authority and exaltedness implied thereby clearly suggests that the enemy should 'back off'.[345]

58B *you free my life.* גָּאַלְתָּ חַיָּי

The second colon of 3_{58} is a summary of the first. The root גאל with YHWH as subject is found in juridical contexts such as Prov 23_{11} in which he presents himself as defender of the orphan and the widow. The nuance of its use in Ps 72_{14}, however, seems closer to the present meaning[346]:

344 See also Albrektson and Gottlieb.

345 Compare the explanation of 1_{14c}.

346 Cf also the remaining agreement with Ps 72_{12-14}.

as YHWH's representative on earth, the king will come to the aid of the oppressed and set them free. In the parallel strophe of the fourth song (4_{20}), however, one reads that no assistance can be expected from the king since he himself has been taken prisoner by the enemy. This explains why the גֶּבֶר already turns his attention directly to אֲדֹנָי with a prayer that might also have been adddressed to the king. The prison context suggests that we give preference to the translation 'to free' over that of 'to redeem' although the notion of 'redemption' is also present. The object of גאל is the life of the גֶּבֶר who does not only find himself locked up in a prison but is in danger of drowning in a cistern which is steadily filling with water. The combination √גאל + חַי can also be found in Ps 103_4 (context: 'from the grave').

59 *You see, O* YHWH, *my oppression,*	רָאִיתָה יְהוָה עַוָּתָתִי
do me justice.	שָׁפְטָה מִשְׁפָּטִי

We now come to the point of transition from 'hearing' to 'seeing' whereby a link is established with the imperatives of ראה in the parallel verses 1_{20aA} and 2_{20aA}. רָאִיתָה is a *qal* pf 2m sg, *scriptio plena.*[347]

One can also offer a paraphrase of this expression of faith: 'You do indeed see me' (cf 3_{56A}). The fact that up to this point YHWH has paid no attention to the גֶּבֶר's affliction does not have its roots in any inadequacy on YHWH's part but in his unwillingness to do so. The גֶּבֶר aims these words of trust and faith at God's heart in the hope that he will conquer his reluctance. After all it is part of YHWH's nature to attend to the poor and the oppressed and to take their side.[348] Israel had long held the conviction that the very combination of YHWH's 'seeing' and the affliction of his people would bring about incredible unease in YHWH (compare 3_{33}). The גֶּבֶר stands firm in this ancient tradition of his people. One is reminded of the eponymous confession of Hagar אֵל רֳאִי. See Gen 16_{13f}.

The object of YHWH's 'seeing' is עַוָּתָה, a *hapax* derived from the root עות: 'to bend'/'to make crooked' (cf HAL 760). It is used in a figurative sense with מִשְׁפָּט in Job 8_3 and 34_{12} which, given the מִשְׁפָּטִי in the second colon, provide something of a clue to the interpretation of the present verse. The terminology as a whole varies slightly from that found in 3_{35-36}: the 'subversion of right' (מִשְׁפָּט) and the 'aggrieving of human persons in their rights' (רִיב). The oppression of the גֶּבֶר in the present context refers to

347 Cf GES-K § 44g.

348 Compare the explanation of √ראה in 3_{50}!

the 'distortion' of his מִשְׁפָּט, whereby his שָׁלוֹם is adversely affected (cf the explanation of 3_{35}). The verbal root שׁפט with the substantive מִשְׁפָּט as subject means 'to do justice/right'.[349] Given the *qal* imp 2m sg here, it is evident that the גֶּבֶר is not expressing his trust in God but rather offering a prayer. The *qal* imp 2m sg can be maintained.[350] With an urgent prayer, the גֶּבֶר calls upon YHWH to restore him in his מִשְׁפָּט. It is important here also to avoid making sharp juridical distinctions since the appeal might also imply the rule of a salvific judge/king.[351] Indeed, the גֶּבֶר's prayer can be quite easily understood in such a manner. Where the מְשִׁיחַ יְהוָה has vanished (4_{20}), YHWH alone can restore מִשְׁפָּט.[352] The royal judgeship of YHWH implied in the confession found in the parallel verse 5_{19} is also worth noting: 'Your throne endures for eternity'.

60A *You see all their malice,* רָאִיתָה כָּל־נִקְמָתָם

If one were to place 3_{60} side by side with Jer 11_{18-20} and $20_{10,12}$ then the fact that commentators discern the voice of Jeremiah in this verse would become quite understandable (cf Rudolph). Since Baumgartner, however, it has become clear that in his laments Jeremiah employed existing, classical idiom.[353] We have no real basis, therefore, for concluding that there is evidence of dependence here. In addition, the historical context differs quite considerably: the prophets enemies are among his fellow Israelites and he comes under threat prior to the fall of Judah and Jerusalem while the גֶּבֶר endures his affliction at the hands of external enemies after the said event.

One can deduce from the term נִקְמָתָם, 'their malice', that the context in which the גֶּבֶר finds himself is more clearly indicated than is apparent at first sight. The 3m pl suffix has no antecedent within the canticle, although it doubtlessly refers back to the enemy mentioned in $3_{46,52-54}$. The גֶּבֶר is thus referring to the malice of the enemy. נְקָמָה, in the first instance, implies some sort of revengeful behaviour in response to already endured loss or damage,[354] an act of wrath against those who caused the damage. What destructive behaviour is implied here and who are its avengers? There is reason not to suspect a destructive behaviour of the גֶּבֶר himself. In

349 Cf Deut 16_{18}, I Kgs 3_{28}, Jer 5_{28} etcetera.
350 Contra Robinson in text critical apparatus of BHS; see Albrektson.
351 Cf THAT II 1003ff (Liedke).
352 See Ps 67_5, 96_{13}, 98_9.
353 WBaumgartner, *Die Klagegedichte des Jeremias*, BZAW 32, 1917.
354 Cf TWAT II 106–109 (Sauer).

3_{52B}, in contrast, he speaks of being 'hunted down without reason'. √נקם, in addition, is often used to refer to something that happened between two collective entities, for example between Israel and her enemies.[355] It is clear that when one thinks of the enemy in Lamentations one must include both the Babylonians and the neighbouring peoples they had mustered at their side.[356] It is equally clear that one of the nations is always given particular mention, namely Edom, a nation under which Judah suffered terribly, particularly after her fall. Refer, once again, to Lam 1_{2c} where we noted that the memory of the abhorrent behaviour of the Edomites echoes strongly throughout the OT.

We still do not have reason to assume that the present text constitutes just such an echo. Nevertheless, there remain two compelling reasons for associating these verses with Edom's vindictiveness. Firstly, we have the practical parallel with 4_{21} where Edom is the only enemy mentioned by name in Lamentations as a whole. The second reason is to be found in Ezek 25_{12-17} which is unique in mentioning Israel's vindictive enemies, specifically naming Edom's revenge against Judah in 25_{12} with √נקם! Given the Edomites' past experience with Israel and Judah, a high degree of rancour on their part is quite understandable.[357] An entire nation is hardly likely to forget such matters; cf Am 1_{11} and Ezek 35_5. Wherever Edom was able it tried to regain its influence in the region.[358] It is evident from Ps 137_7 and Ob $_{11,13f}$ that Edom had cooperated wholeheartedly in the destruction of Judah and in the 'Day of Jerusalem'.

Edom's revenge, however, has gone beyond the bounds of restitution and degenerated into malevolence. Retribution has evolved into a craving in which all reason has been swamped by jealousy and hatred.[359] It is true that Ezekiel also mentions the vindictive behaviour of the Philistines,[360] but given the special mention of Edom in Lam 4_{21}, it would seem more reasonable to assume that it was the implacable behaviour of the Edomites which the poets had in mind. Expressing his conviction that YHWH sees

---

355 Num 31_2, Josh 10_{13}, I Sam 14_{24}; cf Jer 50_{15} and THAT II 108 (Sauer).

356 Compare the explanation of 1_{2c}.

357 Cf I Sam 14_{47-48} and compare JRBartlett, *Edom and the Edomites*, JSOT suppl series 77, Sheffield 1989, 103f); II Sam 8_{13f}, cf I Kgs 11_{14-16}; I Chron 18_{12} and Ps $60_{1,2}$ and compare Bartlett, 104–107; II Kgs $14_{7,10,22}$, cf II Chron 25_{5-13}, particularly 25_{12} and see Bartlett, 122–124.

358 Cf II Kgs 16_6 and II Chron 28_{17}.

359 Cf Prov 6_{34} and Ezek 35_{11}.

360 Ezek 25_{15-17}; cf WZimmerli, *Ezechiel 25–48*, BKAT XIII/2, Neukirchen 1969, 598f.

their malice and supported, perhaps, by familiar prophecies against Edom from Jeremiah and Ezekiel (cf 4_{21}), the גֶּבֶר is confident that YHWH will intervene to redeem and liberate.[361]

What has been stated above is important for the explanation of the canto as a whole. From 3_{52} onwards it would appear, in the first instance, that we are dealing with the personal experiences of the גֶּבֶר, but these are not limited to him alone. His personal experience is that of the affliction which the enemy have brought upon the entire people. His affliction is the same as that of his people and his expressions of suffering are exteremely familiar to them. The individual formulation of the גֶּבֶר's prayer, however, makes his function as 'spokesman/leader' quite clear.

60B *all their plots against me.* כָּל־מַחְשְׁבֹתָם לִי

The noun מַחֲשָׁבָה and the verb חשׁב 'to calculate', 'to contrive', 'to devise' (cf 2_{8aA}) are found in a variety of contexts: "Eine spezielle Bindung an eine literarische Gattung ist nicht feststellbar. Nicht gattungsgebunden, aber sehr häufig erscheint die Wortgruppe als Feindtopos in den Psalmen."[362] Seybold notes with at least 20 references, including Ps 10_2, 21_{12}, 44_{23}, 56_6, 88_5. It is used here with the same negative significance. One should not understand the לִי 'against me' in an isolated, individualistic way. It is obvious that the expression refers to the enemy's plan to profit as much as possible from the defencelessness of the inhabitants of Judah and the citizens of Jerusalem, the גֶּבֶר among them. See 1_{22a} where there is mention of all the wickedness of the enemy.[363] What the גֶּבֶר formulates in his own regard is equally applicable to his fellow citizens.

The fact that YHWH sees these plans need not be a cause for surprise. It is not only true that YHWH looks down on humanity from the heavens and that he knows what is in their thoughts,[364] but it is possible to discern the wicked plans of a person in his or her particularly negative attitude (cf Ps 41_8). √חשׁב can also imply 'contempt/disdain'.[365] The גֶּבֶר is convinced that YHWH is aware of what is going on and attempts to move him to action by his expression of trust.

---

361 For the significance of √ראה with YHWH as subject see the exegesis of $1_{9c,11c}$; $3_{36B,50}$.

362 Seybold, TWAT III 252.

363 Cf also $5_{4f,8}$.

364 Cf Ps 11_{4f}, 14_2, 139_{1-4} together with the explanation of 3_{63}.

365 Gen 35_{15}, I Sam 1_{13}; cf TWAT III 249 (Seybold).

Canticle II (3_{61-66})

Content/theme: *Prayer for retribution*

Literary argumentation:

inclusions:	חֶרְפָּתָם (61A) // אַף (66A)
	יְהוָה (61A) // יְהוָה (66B)
	שִׁבְתָּם וְקִימָתָם (63A) // כְּמַעֲשֵׂה יְדֵיהֶם (64B)
incl/resp:	קָמַי (62A) // לֵב (65A)
responses:	יְהוָה (61A) // יְהוָה (64A)
	כָּל־מַחְשְׁבֹתָם (61B) // מַעֲשֵׂה יְדֵיהֶם (64B)
allit:	שִׁבְתָּם (63A) // תָּשִׁיב (64A)
	מַנְגִּינָתָם (63B) // מְגִנַּת (65A)
incl/resp/concat:	via 3m pl suffixes ם, עַל and לָהֶם

The previous canticle placed the emphasis firmly on the גֶּבֶר's expressions of trust in God as the basis of his prayer for redemption. In the final bicolon (3_{60}) a turn was made (via concatination) towards the concretisation of his longed for liberation which stands at the heart of the canticle, the necessity of which was underlined with reference to the enemy's hostile behaviour. In the first strophe of the present canticle, the גֶּבֶר draws YHWH's attention to the enemy's transgressions with great insistance (cf the consistent use of 3m pl suffixes). This ultimately constitutes the basis of his prayer in the final strophe: whether YHWH will repay his enemies for their evil deeds. Where the preceding canticle had already, to some degree, singled out Edom among Israel's enemies, this final canticle sees the poets turn their full attention to the Babylonians. It is interesting to note the somewhat concealed manner in which this is done, namely via word-play. The same covert approach is also to be found in Jeremiah's prophecy against Babylon (Jer 51; cf the explanation of 3_{65B}).

61 *You hear their taunts, O* YHWH, שָׁמַעְתָּ חֶרְפָּתָם יְהוָה
all their plots against me, כָּל־מַחְשְׁבֹתָם עָלָי

This colon is very akin to that which precedes it. Rudolph thus considers it a 'non-original repetition' and emends the text to read מַלְשְׁנָתָם from √לשן 'to insult'/'defame'.[366] Textual surgery of this kind, however, is difficult to justify. Marked concatination between the canticles of Lam III tends to support the MT.[367] While there is clearly a level of repetition it is

[366] Cf HAL 510 and KBL 487.

certainly not without meaning since the first reference (3_{60}) focuses on 'seeing' while the present verse supplements this with 'hearing'. Indeed, the גֶּבֶר brings every aspect of the enemy's hostility before YHWH: their thoughts, their words, and their deeds.[368] A new and as yet unmentioned element of the גֶּבֶר's complaint emerges here: YHWH also hears the insult and abuse hurled by the enemy.[369] The enemy's invictive is presented with considerable emphasis in this strophe given that it returns in each of the three bicola with only minor variance: חֶרְפָּתָם // הֶגְיוֹנָם // מַנְגִּינָתָם (see further below). The preposition is certainly correct (cf LXX with κατ' ἐμοῦ and Albrektson) and is determined by √שׁמע. YHWH not only sees the wicked plans being hatched against the גֶּבֶר he also hears the enemy's mutual deliberations to this end. Once again we should not understand this text in an individualistic way (cf the remark on לִי, 3_{60B}).

62 *the whispers of my adversaries and their jeers* שִׂפְתֵי קָמַי וְהֶגְיוֹנָם
over me, all day long. עָלַי כָּל־הַיּוֹם

שִׂפְתֵי = pl st cs 'lips' and stands for 'whispers'[370] which, given the context, the poets doubtlessly intend to be understood as 'harmful whispers'. √קום + the preposition עַל means 'to rise up against someone' and is likewise found with exclusively adverse significance. Parallel concepts include 'violence' (II Sam 22_{49}) and 'to hate' (Deut 33_{11}, Ps 44_{8}). קָמַי is a substantivised plural participle with a 1st person sg suffix: 'my adversaries'.[371] It is worth noting that the expression can be found in related songs such as Ps $44_{6,8}$; 74_{23}. There appears to be a special relationship with Jer 51_{1} (see the conclusion of the exgesis of 3_{65B}). קָמַי functions as a synonym: the adversaries in question are the enemies of the גֶּבֶר and their 'verbal abuse' is equivalent to the 'whispers' they utter.

The meaning of הִגָּיוֹן, a derivative of √הגה I: 'to think over', 'to read quietly', 'to ponder'[372] is unclear and has led to a variety of translations such as 'murmuring' (NBG NRSV). Such an interpretation does not seem appropriate if one considers the fact that the enemy's loud victory celebrations (2_{7c}), their wide open mouths (2_{16}, 3_{46}) and their joyful gestures

367 Cf 1988, 329f.
368 With respect to YHWH's 'hearing' compare 3_{56A}.
369 Zeph 2_{8}; cf Ps 31_{18f}; for the significance of חֶרְפָּה see the explanation of 3_{30B} and compare 2_{16}, 3_{46}.
370 Cf Gen $11_{1,6f,9}$, Isa 19_{18}, Ps 81_{6}.
371 Cf Ex 15_{7}, 32_{25}, Deut 33_{11}, Ps $18_{40,49}$.
372 Cf KBL 224 and HAL 228.

(1_{21b}, 4_{21a}) are variously mentioned elsewhere. The root הגה I can also mean ‘to wail’ (cf Isa 16_7, Jer 48_{31}), and ‘to make a sound’, ‘to speak’/‘to report’ (cf Ps 35_{28}, 115_7). In Ps 92_4 הִגָּיוֹן means ‘the sound of a stringed instrument’. A combination of the tonal elements of ‘wailing’ and ‘stringed instruments’ together with wide open mouths and the excited state of the enemy leads us to the translation ‘jeer’. This is further supported by the preceding חֶרְפָּתָם and ‘their mocking-song’ (מַנְגִּינָתָם) in the following verse. The ו preceding הִגָּיוֹן should be understood as a ו-explicativum[373] relative to שְׂפָתֵי.

63 *Their sitting and rising you observe;* שִׁבְתָּם וְקִימָתָם הַבִּיטָה
I am their mocking-song. אֲנִי מַנְגִּינָתָם

שִׁבְתָּם is a substantivised *qal* infinitive of √שׁבת + 3m pl suffix. The *hapax* קִימָה (= substantivised infinitive of √קום[374]) + 3m pl suffix means ‘their rising’. The first colon is reminiscent of Ps 139_2 which alone shares the same word combination of ‘sitting’ and ‘rising’ with the present text. The context of Ps 139_2 further elaborates the meaning of the expression via ‘you search my path and my lying down’ (139_3). One can conclude that the one praying in Ps 139 is also ultimately confessing that YHWH is completely familiar with his ways and his thoughts. The same is implied here in Lam 3_{63}, but with the focus turned on the enemies of the גֶּבֶר. The combination of ‘sitting’ and ‘rising’ suggests an established expression similar to ‘comings and goings’. Every action, thought and word of the enemy is familiar to YHWH. It is not without reason that the poets employ the root נבט here in the final canticle of Lam III. Together with the ראה in the first canticle (3_{1A}) both verbs establish an inclusion using the core theme of Lam I. We already noted with respect to the exegesis of 1_{11c} that √נבט indicated a more penetrating visual observation than √ראה. At the same time, connections with Habakkuk were discussed, a prophet who was quite familiar with the unease engendered in YHWH by the sight of evil: “Your eyes are too pure to behold evil, and you cannot look upon (√נבט) wrongdoing” (Hab 1_{13}). It is this unbearable tension between YHWH’s ‘seeing’ and the enemy’s wrongdoing which the גֶּבֶר wants to stimulate. The very wrongdoing which YHWH cannot bear to look upon is still there for him to observe: he sees all the evil deeds (cf 1_{22a}), lust for revenge and wicked schemes being brought by the enemy against the גֶּבֶר. Can he really bear to look upon such things? The question becomes all the more

[373] Cf GES-K § 145a note 1.
[374] Cf BL 452*q* and HAL 1025.

acute when one realises that the enemy is not bent upon treating some godless individuals in this manner but YHWH's very own גֶּבֶר. The latter now focuses attention on himself via the personal pronoun אֲנִי.[375] He is the one who is suffering thus and his change of attitude, therefore, has to be taken into account. After a time of bitter complaint he confessed his guilt and placed his trust fully in YHWH. All of this marks him out as one whose heart has been broken and it is not in God's nature to scorn the broken hearted. See Ps 51_{19}.

In spite of everything, the גֶּבֶר still suffers profoundly under the abuse and mockery of his enemies; he is their mocking-song. The noun מַנְגִּינָה (*hapax*) is derived from the root נגן, which means 'to play a stringed instrument'. The variant נְגִינָה in 3_{14b} has a similar turn of meaning. Perhaps the orthographic variation between the two has to do with variation in subject: in 3_{14} the גֶּבֶר is mocked by his own people, here in 3_{63} he is mocked by his enemies. Given its fixed shape and repetitive character, the mocking-song is much sharper and more insulting than simple verbal mockery. Mocking humiliation and abuse are an aspect of YHWH's judgement and are found as such in the context of the metaphor of the poisoned cup.[376] Via this theme there appears to be a connection at the song-response level with Lam 2_{21} and 4_{21}.

64A *You shall pay them back, O* YHWH, תָּשִׁיב לָהֶם גְּמוּל יְהוָה

Having affirmed YHWH's hearing and seeing of the misdeeds of the enemy, the גֶּבֶר now assumes that he will intervene in some powerful and concrete way against them. He asserts his belief in expressions of trust which are simultaneously prayers. Thus he has confidence that YHWH will repay the enemy for their deeds. Between human persons, the root גמל suggests reactive behaviour: repaying someone both in the negative and the positive sense. The noun גְּמוּל "bezeichnet demnach das dem Mitmenschen mit Absicht und Bedacht zugewandte, engagierte Handeln, das dieser als gut und förderlich oder als schädlich und böse erfährt und beurteilt." [377] In theological contexts, God's reactive behaviour is determined by the divine subject and thus more abstractly applied.[378] See, for example, Jer 51_{56}, where God is referred to as a 'God of recompense'.[379] The fact that YHWH

375 See also the opening of Lam III.
376 Cf Jer 49_{13}, Ezek 23_{32}.
377 Seybold in TWAT II 29.
378 Cf TWAT II 32f (Seybold).
379 אֵל גְּמֻלוֹת; cf Deut 32_{35}, Jer 51_{6}.

is part of the conflict is evident from the use of the verb שׁוב *hiph'il*, 'to cause to return', which means that YHWH allows people to reap the fruits of their own deeds. Seybold is unaware, however, of an important aspect of divine recompense, namely that God intervenes in fact as a third party when he takes inter-human repayment or retribution upon himself: where people treat others wickedly, God can repay them for their wickedness. God comes between the two parties where the one affected is powerless to repay what has been done to him (Ps 28_4, 94_2). The expression 'God of recompense' implies that God is guarantor of the dispensation in which good and evil will ultimately have their reward.[380] This theological element partly constitutes the basis for the גֶּבֶר's trust and supplication.

64B *according to the work of their hands.* כְּמַעֲשֵׂה יְדֵיהֶם

There can be little doubt that the poets are referring here to the negative and injurious deeds of the enemy. While the immediate context of mocking-song, insult and wicked scheming directed against the גֶּבֶר confirms this fact, it tends to focus on thoughts and words, whereas the present text turns its attention to actual deeds: מַעֲשֵׂה יְדֵיהֶם. That we should understand such deeds in a negative light is underlined by the song-response in 1_{22A} and the parallel expression 'all their evil' (כָּל־רָעָתָם).[381] Whereas the conclusion to the first and third songs are synonymous at the level of content, the relationship between the final passage of the second song and that of the third is more antithetical: YHWH is ultimately responsible for bringing about this great affliction and the enemy is simply his instrument. In such a light, a prayer that YHWH should repay the enemies for their deeds would appear to be somewhat paradoxical: why should YHWH punish them for what they did on his behalf? We cannot blame the poets for apparently allowing such an evident inconsistency. The גֶּבֶר's appeal remains quite meaningful if one views it against the background of the poets awareness that the enemies have gone far beyond the mandate they received from YHWH. Indeed the concluding supplication of Lam II confronts YHWH with the very absurdity of the deeds he appears to be permitting. The fall of Jerusalem and her temple together with the loss of her princes and the deportation of her population constituted the fulfilment of the prophecy of doom announced against her.[382] Yet her citizens

---

[380] Cf also the use of √שׁלם *pi'el* which is used in parallel with גְּמוּל, particularly in Ps 94.

[381] Cf also עֲוֹנֵךְ and חַטֹּאתָיִךְ in 4_{22b} (song-response).

[382] Cf תַּם־עֲוֹנֵךְ בַּת־צִיּוֹן in 4_{22aA} and its explanation.

must still endure exploitation and abuse. It is thus the enemies protracted wicked behaviour which makes them guilty before YHWH.[383]

With reference to the content of this supplication Haller remarks: “So endet auch dieser individuelle Klagepsalm ... mit einem für den Christen beinahe unerträglichen Mißton.”[384] In his explanation of 3_{64}, Kaiser makes reference to Christ's prayer for his enemies (Lk 23_{34}) although he is not completely justified in doing so since Christ's enemies did not know what they were doing, which is something we cannot say of the גֶּבֶר's enemies (cf 2_{16}). If one were to understand the expressions in this final strophe as a call for actual vengeance then there might be reason to expect an amount of theological criticism, even although the immense restraint seems quite appropriate. With reference to Haller's comments, Gordis keenly remarks: “This in a commentary published under Hitler in Nazi Germany in 1940, with the stench of the crematoria filling the land.” His references to Job 13_5 and Mt 7_4 are very understandable.

The aforementioned theological criticism, however, tends to reveal that the exegesis which lies behind it is more determined by the emotional value of the words in their modern idiom than by the significance of the Hebrew words employed in the context. A closer examination of the Hebrew text shows that we are certainly not dealing with a (senseless) desire for vengeance. In order to correctly understand the expressions employed here it is first necessary to examine the parallel strophes in the other songs. Lam 1_{22}, in fact, provides the basis for our exegesis of 3_{64}. Lady Jerusalem's prayer is identical in terms of content to that of the גֶּבֶר. The *hubris* of the enemy has resulted in excessive suffering. Their wicked deeds (כָּל־רָעָתָם [1_{22a}] // מַעֲשֵׂה יְדֵיהֶם [3_{64B}]) are no longer in proportion to YHWH's justified punishment. Thus YHWH – who is just (1_{18a}) – ought to punish their wickedness just as he has punished the sins of his own people. As a consequence of such punishment, the enemy's stranglehold would be weakened.[385] This aspect of the גֶּבֶר's immense affliction was treated in 3_{46-54}. A new element with respect to the first song is the גֶּבֶר's conversion and his renewed trust in YHWH. This must make the ongoing hostilities towards him unbearable in the eyes of YHWH. The deepest intention of the גֶּבֶר's prayer is that YHWH would intervene to liberate him from such hostility.

---

[383] See also the explanation of 1_{22a}.

[384] Cf also Van Selms with reference to 1_{21}.

[385] Cf also the contrasting בַּת־צִיּוֹן \\ בַּת־אֱדוֹם in 4_{22} with √ פקד, the visitation of Edom's iniquity.

Even in its widest sense we can understand a prayer for the redress of evil as a genuine prayer which people of any age can share, albeit that one might ascribe a different fate to one's enemies in the post-Christian era than one might naturally have preferred (see Mt 5_{43ff}).

65A *You shall give them an anguished heart,* תִּתֵּן לָהֶם מְגִנַּת־לֵב

The meaning of the Hebrew text here is difficult to understand and equally difficult to provide with an adequate translation. Whatever the case, at first sight the text gives a somewhat negative impression which is not intended. Our explanation will endeavour to correct any misunderstanding.

The precise meaning of the *hapax* מְגִנָּה is difficult to determine. The most commonly suggested root is גנן, 'to shelter', 'to cover' (HAL 91), to be understood here as 'covering of the heart', which is explained as 'hardening',[386] or 'clouding of the mind'.[387] Neither explanation is convincing. Hardening of the heart is usually expressed with the root אמץ I which is not surprisingly absent from the present context since it would ultimately imply a continuation of enemy oppression which the גֶּבֶר clearly does not desire. With respect to 'blinding of the mind' Kraus refers to Gen 19_{11} and II Chron 6_{18} but both these texts seem to refer to physical blindness. Job 17_4 appears to be close to the present text although agreements in terminology are only very partial.

Once again external parallelisms suggest an alternative meaning for the text. Parallels with לֵב, for example, establish a song-response with 1_{22}: וְלִבִּי דַוָּי 'my heart is sick' // מְגִנַּת־לֵב (3_{65A}). The somewhat rare expression וְלִבִּי דַוָּי is also to be found in Jer 8_{18} where it is parallel with יָגוֹן, 'grief', 'distress', a term derived from the root יגה I 'to grieve'/'to afflict'. It is certainly no accident that the same verb is used in Lam $3_{32,33}$, the last strophe of the first canto.[388] The noun יָגוֹן is to be found in a number of striking word-pairs: with אֲנָחָה 'sigh', for example,[389] and with רָעָה in Ps 107_{39} (cf כָּל־רָעָתָם in Lam 1_{22a}). In light of all this we are inclined to believe that מְגִנָּה is related to the noun יָגוֹן and is likewise to be derived from √יגה I, with the preformative מ constituting an indicator of action, result or place,[390] which always follows in cases with לֵב.[391] Hense our translation

[386] So Albrektson, Kaiser, Plöger, Stoll, Westermann, Provan.

[387] So Aalders, Weiser, Kraus, Brandscheidt etcetera.

[388] Cf also the centre of the first song, 1_{12c}!

[389] Cf Isa 35_{10}, 51_{11}; see also, however, Lam 1_{22c} (אַנְחֹתַי).

[390] Cf GES-K § 85*e–m*; Lett § 22*i,3* and § 44*t*.

[391] For possible formation of the term see BL 494*f* (// מַנְגִּינָתָם from Lam 3_{63}!).

'anguished heart' which is parallel with the 'sick heart' of Lady Jerusalem in 1_{22cB}. The enemy's initial joy (2_{17}) will turn into sorrow (the reverse of Jer 31_{13} with [מִ]יגוֹנָם and √שׂמח). Their hubris will ultimately bring them disappointment and grief. The parallel contexts of the remaining songs offer some indication as to the roots of this enemy grief. It is striking that Jer 25 employs the same expression as we find here in Lam 3_{64}, namely 'the repayment of the work of their hands' (וּכְמַעֲשֵׂה יְדֵיהֶם). Jer 25_{15} follows up with the implementation of this repayment via being forced to drink from the cup of YHWH's judgement. In an image of the destruction and misfortune about to overcome her, Lam 4_{21} states, in so many words, that daughter Edom will also drink the cup. Thus the anguished heart of the גֶּבֶר's enemies has its ultimate origins in their drinking the cup of YHWH's judgement. It would appear, therefore, that in the present ת-strophe, the faith-filled expectations of the גֶּבֶר constitute an interpretation of the supplication of Lady Jerusalem: 'let them become as I am' (וְיִהְיוּ כָמוֹנִי [1_{21cB}]). The גֶּבֶר places his hope in the consistency of YHWH's actions: equal measure from His cup of judgement.[392]

This and the following colon have also given rise to theological criticism (cf 1_{21c}). To wish someone the same dreadful fate as one's own does not comply with the command to love one's enemy. Once again, however, it is important to note that the גֶּבֶר's supplication does not have its roots in the *ius talionis* but rather in the desire to see a return to better times and the relief of his and his people's affliction (cf 5_{21B}). Nevertheless, it seems unavoidable that the enemy would endure great suffering if the גֶּבֶר's wish were to be fulfilled. From a New Testament perspective one is likely to be confronted with the question whether this is according to God's nature (cf Mt 5_{44f}). The diptych structure of Lam III, however, reveals the premature character of such an objection. The fact that the poets themselves have thought this question through from the theological perspective is clear from the supplementary canto-response evident in the final canticles of both cantos: the realisation of the desire for emancipative restitution remains limited in the damage that can be done. One should read 3_{31-33} side by side with 3_{64-66}: YHWH does not reject forever and grieving others is not according to his nature. The formulation of 3_{33} is general and applies to all human persons – בְּנֵי־אִישׁ – including Israel's enemies. It would also seem that there is something of a prophetic echo hidden within 3_{31-34} since it is not uncommon to find a prediction at the

392 Cf the explanation of 1_{21f} and 4_{21}.

conclusion to an announcement of judgement against the foreign nations that YHWH will ultimately turn their lot around (Isa 19_{21ff}, Jer 48_{47}, $49_{6,39}$, Ezek 29_{14}; cf Ezek $16_{53,55}$), even although such a turn need not imply the restoration of political power nor exclude the definitive removal of the source of Israel's hostile treatment.[393] The song-response with $5_{21,22}$ shows that the poets fervently hope that YHWH will also bring about a turn in the lot of the people and at the same time betrays a longing for the restoration of the kingdom (see the explanation of 5_{21B}).

65B *your curse upon them.* תַּאֲלָתְךָ לָהֶם

A number of interesting remarks can be made with respect to the terminology of this colon. The association between תַּאֲלָה (curse) and תְּלָאָה (hardship) in 3_{5B} where it combines with רֹאשׁ (poison) appears to play a role in the present image via the drinking of the 'cup of poison' in 4_{21} which ultimately brings about the enemy's מְגִנַּת־לֵב.[394] The Septuagint and the Targum even read תְּלָאָה instead of תַּאֲלָה,[395] an error to be explained by metathesis together with the evident association between the two terms. The MT is to be preferred, therefore, especially if one considers the fact that the poets frequently and quite deliberately use forms which only differ from one another by metathesis.[396] The verbal form תִּתֵּן also has a determinative influence on the second colon. The heart of Lady Jerusalem has grown sick at the loss of her children, her home, her land and at the continual torments of her enemies.[397] Given the fact that the גֶּבֶר shares in Lady Jerusalem's 'incomparable suffering' (1_{12b}, 2_{13}) there is certainly nothing inhuman about his present imprecation (compare Job 31_{29f}).

The גֶּבֶר's supplication does not mean, however, that he wishes divine malice upon his enemies as LXX appears to suggest via μόχθον σου ('your hardship'; likewise the Vulgate's *laborem tuum*). The use of the noun תַּאֲלָה 'curse'[398] which is related to the noun אָלָה, both being derived from √אלה I (HAL 49), suggests that nothing more is being implied here beyond the loss of that which was unjustly appropriated. The verb in question signifies the utterance of a particular sort of curse or oath. Thus the text

393 Cf Isa 13_{20}, Jer $49_{13,15}$, Ezek 25_{7}, 29_{15}, 35_{9}, Ob $_{2,10}$.
394 See also the associations with Jer 25_{14}.
395 Cf text critical apparatus BHS.
396 Cf, for example, the inclusion between 3_{46} and 3_{54}: פָּצוּ // צָפוּ; see the literary argumentation for the second (3_{7-12}) and the eighth canticle (3_{46-54}).
397 See the explanation of 1_{22c} and cf Isa 1_{5}.
398 See for the form see BL 494*h*.

here does not imply curse or imprecation as a mere expression of negative desire but means rather "nur bedingte Flüche, die man über andere oder sich selbst ausspricht, um Rechtsgüter oder religiös-sittliche Ordnungen zu schützen."[399] At the same time one would be incorrect to read an element of magical effect into the expression since it has to do with a word of power uttered with respect to a human person, sanctioned by YHWH and intended to restore justice. Where there was innocence the 'word' brought acquittal, but where there was guilt divine judgement was its consequence.[400] Such a curse was especially useful in restoring stolen property to its rightful owner (see Judg 17_2). When uttered publicly, a thief or his fence would have been unable to contradict the curse to his own detriment.[401] The root אלה can also have a function within a בְּרִית (covenant), ratifying its provisions.[402] Scharbert places Lam 3_{65} in this same context: "Das Nomen תַּאֲלָה in Kl 3,65 ist das ganze Unheil das auf Grund der alle Übeltäter bedrohenden, das Bundesgesetz schützenden über die Bösen hereinbricht."[403] but in so doing he misunderstands the text and does not account for the antecedent of the 3m pl suffix. It is not a matter of evildoers among the people of God who are violating the provisions of the covenant but rather of a foreign enemy which has assaulted YHWH's people and land. Thus there cannot be question of a covenant relationship.

The explanation of this colon must take the protection or restoration of righful ownership via the utterance of a תַּאֲלָה as its point of departure (see again Judg 17_2). In this event, a connection becomes apparent with Lam 5_{2-4} where it is lamented that hostile foreigners have not only appropriated inheritence, cities and houses but even drinking water and wood have to be paid for by their rightful owners. This inheritence was given to Israel by YHWH as inalienable property for which He himself, as a living testator, would stand guarantee.[404] The Edomites were among the foremost culprits in alienating such property. Only YHWH's curse, therefore, would be able to expose such theft and force Edom to return Israel's inheritence. Take note of the parallel expressions in Lam IV (visitation and disclosure of Edom's sin, 4_{22}) and Lam V (prayer for the resoration of former times). The גֶּבֶר's longing to hear YHWH's curse uttered against his

399 Cf Scharbert, TWAT I 280.

400 Cf, for example, Num 5_{11-31}.

401 See Lev 5_1, and Prov 29_{24}.

402 Cf TWAT I 282f (Scharbert).

403 Scharbert, 283.

404 Cf the explanation of 5_2.

enemies, therefore, should not be understood as an inappropriate desire for revenge but as a prayer for the restoration of rightful ownership with reference to houses and land.

It would be quite reasonable to accept, however, that the גֶּבֶר's prayer extended beyond the return of property to include, among other things, the return of the children of Lady Jerusalem who were deported as slaves by the Babylonians.[405] Thus the parallel supplication in 5_{21} (הֲשִׁיבֵנוּ) likewise becomes an implicit appeal for the return of the exiles, and quite appropriately, given that the Baylonians are also covertly identified in this canticle as enemies over whom – the גֶּבֶר hopes – YHWH will utter his תַּאֲלָה.

A final remark on the present colon. It is somewhat surprising that the Edomites are the only people explicitly named in Lamentations (in 4_{21}) as enemies. In spite of their deeply rooted ill-will towards Israel (cf כָּל־נִקְמָתָם [3_{60A}]), it would be wrong to characterise them as Israel's primary enemy at the time of the fall of Judah and Jerusalem. The Babylonians alone deserved that title. Indeed, the Edomites were only able to operate with Babylonian permission. Thus it is odd that Edom is mentioned here and not Babylon. While this is true, Babylon does manage to get a mention if only in a somewhat hidden manner. The inclusion in the present canticle between קָמַי (3_{62A}) and לֵב (3_{65A}) can also be found as a word-pair in Jer 51_1, לֵב קָמָי, where we have to do with a transposition of the word כַּשְׂדִּים, the Chaldeans, an alternative term for the Babylonians. The transposition takes place according to the so-called *atbas*-method, whereby a Hebrew letter is replaced by its opposite counterpart in the Hebrew alphabet: א for ת and ב for ש etcetera. Thus the term Šēšach (שֵׁשַׁךְ) implies Babel (בָּבֶל; Jer 25_{26}, 51_{41}).

What might such a covert indication mean? It is possible that Lamentations was written at a time when the Babylonians were still breathing down the necks of its authors. In this case they would have been forced to watch their words and opt for the timeless procedure of creating and using a pseudonym.

66 *You shall pursue them in anger and destroy them,* תִּרְדֹּף בְּאַף וְתַשְׁמִידֵם
from under the heaven of YHWH. מִתַּחַת שְׁמֵי יְהוָה

This expression of trust/supplication is also based on the expectation that YHWH ought to be consistent in his restoration of justice. Lam 3_{43} states that YHWH himself has persecuted and put to death his own people on

[405] See Lam $1_{5c,18c}$; cf Ob $_{14}$.

account of their sins (3_{42}). One can expect, therefore, that the enemy will meet a similar fate on account of their evil deeds.[406] In his anger at their wickedness[407] YHWH will hound them down and repay them just as he allowed his own people to be persecuted[408] and put to death.[409] Thus the persecuters become the persecuted and YHWH saves his people from their power.[410] The 3m pl suffix of תַּשְׁמִידֵם is also the object of the verbal form תִּרְדֹּף. The addition of αὐτους in LXX is a correction.

Once again this appeal for destruction does not have its roots in a desire for revenge. It constitutes rather a return to the ancient tradition of YHWH's gift of the land to Israel and provides a more detailed elaboration of the 'curse' mentioned in 3_{65B}. The root שׁמד in the *hiph'il* means 'visible extermination'.[411] The term has its 'Sitz im Leben' in the so-called 'ban': "Sie entspricht dem Banngebot, das von der Kultgemeinschaft die physische Vertilgung (שׁמד hif.) des Gebannten (חֵרֶם) aus ihrer Mitte (Jos. 7,12 fordert."[412] Within the tradition of YHWH's gift of the land, its original inhabitants were placed under the ban according to the extent of their iniquity (Gen 15_{16}). Such were the origins of their destruction, whereupon their land was handed over to Israel.[413] Extermination also had its place with respect to sins which threatened the community[414] although these also related to over-confident earthly kings and kingdoms.[415] For √שׁמד with respect to the Edomites see Jer 49_{10}.

Some of the aforementioned comments appear to enjoy a particular echo in the present context. Thus the authors are probably alluding to erstwhile destruction, prior to the giving of the land. In this context, the formulation of Deut 7_{23f} is of particular interest given the corresponding expression מִתַּחַת הַשָּׁמָיִם. In addition, the destruction mentioned here in Lam 3_{66} refers to injustices already perpetrated (cf 4_{22}) and hubris already made evident (cf 1_{22a} and 3_{64}). If the call for YHWH's 'curse' was a prayer for the restoration of rightful ownership, the גֶּבֶר's present prayer for the obliteration of the enemy ultimately calls upon YHWH to attend to

406 Cf כָּל־רָעָתָם in 1_{22a} and עֲוֹנֵךְ/חַטֹּאתָיִךְ in 4_{22b}.
407 For אַף see 1_{12c}.
408 Cf $1_{3c,6c}$, 4_{19}, 5_6.
409 See $2_{4b,20c,21c}$, 3_{43a}; for √הרג // √שׁמד cf Est 3_{13}, 7_4, 8_{11}.
410 Cf Ps 31_{16}, $35_{3,6}$ etcetera.
411 Cf Deut 4_{26}, 6_{15}, Judg 21_{16}.
412 According to Vetter, THAT II 964.
413 Cf Deut $2_{12,21,23}$, $7_{2,24}$, 9_3, 33_{27}, Jos 9_{24}, Am 2_9 etcetera; cf also Ps 106_{34ff}.
414 Cf Deut 6_{15}, 7_4, I Kgs 13_{34}, Am 9_8.
415 Cf Isa 14_{23}, Ezek 25_{6f}!

their *hubris* and injustice, expel them from the land of Israel and return it once again to his people so that he can reside there anew (cf 5_{21} כְּקֶדֶם).

A number of exegetes find it necessary to emend the final colon of 3_{66} to read שָׁמֶיךָ 'your heaven', thereby assuming the tetragrammaton to be a vocative (cf also the Peshitta). From a text critical perspective, however, the support for emendation is not strong. The understanding of שְׁמֵי as a pl st cs, namely 'the heavens of YHWH' would seem to be unusual in the context of a direct address. The solution to the problem proposed by Ehrlich and Albrektson, who read שָׁמַי as 'my heavens', whereby the suffix refers to the גֶּבֶר and not to YHWH and the divine name is once again understood to be a vocative, is likewise unconvincing. Indeed, Gottlieb is correct in objecting that one never finds the expression 'my heaven(s)' on the lips of an Israelite. The MT of Deut 33_{28} offers a more acceptable solution: Jacob's land of 'grain and wine' is paralleled with 'his' heavens (שָׁמָיו) which 'drop down dew'. To whom then does the suffix attached to 'heavens' apply: YHWH or Jacob? The context leads one to suspect YHWH. It is he who gives the land together with his blessing to Jacob (cf Deut 33_{26}). The land of Israel lies under YHWH's heaven. Thus the suggestion of expulsion from the land simultaneously implies expulsion from under YHWH's heaven. We understand שְׁמֵי, therefore, to be a plural *status constructus.*[416] In our modern languages it might come accross as strange that YHWH's name can be mentioned in this fashion in a direct address but such is not the case for Hebrew. Lam 2_{22ab} provides a clear example where the day of YHWH's anger is spoken of in his direct presence.[417]

To conclude, it is not without significance that this central song ends with the divine name YHWH. It started with the complaining גֶּבֶר who refused for a long time even to utter the tetragrammaton (3_{18}). It concludes with the same individual praying with hope and trust to YHWH whose divine name is his final word. Thus even the last word is indicative of the turnabout which has taken place in this third song.

---

[416] Cf GES-K § 96.

[417] Cf Gottlieb and also on this subject HWWolff, *Dodekapropheton 1, Hosea*, BKAT XIV/1, Neukirchen 1965², 16f.

Hermeneutical Epilogue

The reader of this commentary will have noted that in a number of places the author has insisted that perfects should be read as presents. Indeed, from the very first verse (1_{1a}) it would appear that a present tense translation of the Hebrew perfect is most appropriate. Thus, at the beginning of the third song, we opted for a translation which described the גֶּבֶר as 'seeing'/'undergoing' affliction rather than having seen affliction. Grammatical flexibility allows for such translational options. As we know, the Hebrew perfect and imperfect forms do not exhibit a strictly determined temporal aspect. In other words, perfects need not always have to do with the past nor imperfects with the present or the future.[418] Any reading of our translation of Lamentations would make it impossible to miss its 'present' character. The songs as such do not intend to provide a retrospective glance from a later perspective of restoration. It is the intention of the poets rather to provide an actual account of the affliction and tribulation of those people who experienced the fall of Judah and Jerusalem, temple and palace, people who knew what this disaster was really all about. Lamentations offers no reason to doubt that the poets themselves actually lived through the events they describe and actually experienced the spiritual crisis which was their consequence.[419]

Of course, the unavoidable question remains as to whether, with its transitory present, Lamentations does not imply that the affliction endured and described does not inevitably suggest that the spiritual actuality of the songs is, by its very nature, dated. The same question remains whether we translate the perfects in the present or as (complete) action in the past: the time during which all these events took place has passed. Jewish liturgical usage, wherein the songs only function with respect to the memorial of the destruction of the temple, clearly points to this 'dated' nature of the material. Such liturgical reminiscence would be truly meaningful had YHWH's temple been rebuilt and its erstwhile destruction illuminated by the later grace of its restoration. For the last two thousand years, however, this has not been the case and present day (annual) remembrance of the destruction of the temple has in fact become something of a liturgical fossil, unless, indeed, one experiences it as an existential extension of YHWH's judgement. The fact that connection is made between the 9th of Ab and not only the destruction of the first temple but also that of the second, the

[418] Cf GES-K § 106g and Rudolph.

[419] Cf also, the explanation of Lam 2_{20b} and 3_{51}.

termination of the Bar-Kochba revolt and the expulsion of the Jews from Spain in 1492 certainly points in that direction. Obviously, Lamentations has nothing to do with the latter three events. Even the content of the songs denies any suggestion that the poets intended them to be memorial songs on the occasion of the fall of the first temple, no matter how much that event constituted a profound element of their sorrow. Not one single aspect of the songs leads us to conclude that they were put together in the light of any kind of restoration. Likewise, it was certainly not the poets' intention to provide a moment of existential reflection on YHWH's judgement. The intention (and conclusion) of the songs is and remains a prayer of hope(lessness) uttered by broken believers longing for YHWH's salvific intervention in their dreadful present existence.[420]

The cohesive relationship between all five songs is what points us to the hermeneutic significance of the present tenses. It is clear that Lamentations is dealing with a very specific and clearly datable disaster, namely the fall of Judah in 587: the destruction of Jerusalem and the temple, the dissolution of the Davidic dynasty and all the actual affliction resulting from the events in question. This, however, is only one side of the disaster. Prior to and during the fall of Judah, the true significance of Jerusalem, temple and king was unimaginable without the essential religious categories which pertained thereto. What the people endured at that moment was, by definition, divine gift and a sign of their relationship with YHWH and his nearness to them. Thus the fall of Judah and Jerusalem had an almost ruinous effect on Israel's faith.[421] It is extremely interesting to note how the external facts of the fall are rendered in the third song in terms of the personal experience of a devout man who must undergo this immense torment. In the description of his affliction, the presentation of the actual devastation in the other songs is replaced by an (impressionistic) study of the גֶּבֶר's suffering. Closer exegetical exploration, however, has established a fairly undeniable link between the גֶּבֶר's suffering and the affliction in the land. This stylistic change reveals the poets' firm hermeneutical 'Anliegen', likewise made clearly evident in the third song. They are not particularly interested in describing the disaster as such, but in the people who are having to endure it and who are in danger of losing their relationship with God or have already lost it. Such people are ulti-

420 Compare, particularly, the explanation of 5_{19-22}.

421 See, for example, the explanation of 3_{14} and the association with elements of the funeral dirge.

mately able to recognise themselves in the poets' portrayal of the גֶּבֶר: in his affliction and disputation, in his rebelliousness and accusatory stance towards God, in his (almost) lost faith, all of which pushes to the very limits of what a human person can possibly endure. If such a tormented and defeated individual can return to his relationship with God in spite of the immense and very real affliction he is being forced to endure and, in spite of everything, trust once again in YHWH his God, what else remains for those who identify with the גֶּבֶר? The poets' primary purpose is to affect a similar transformation in their audience by way of the גֶּבֶר's example: follow the גֶּבֶר!

The poets, however, have clearly set their sights on a great deal more. Their consciously personal yet impressionistic style in which actual affliction is described from a certain distance does not only confront the generation which experienced the fall of Judah with the way of the גֶּבֶר. Significant associations with the genre of the individual lament in the Psalms indicate that at different times in Israel's history people had found themselves in similar situations of need and that the same was likewise possible for future generations, need and affliction immense enough to undermine their relationship with God. The authors of Lamentations were aware that the literary establishment of the way of the גֶּבֶר from affliction to renewed faith and trust in God could have meaning for future generations if their description of his misfortune and challenge could be portrayed in a manner they themselves might recognise.

It is clear that a precise, perfect tense, retrospective portrayal of the גֶּבֶר's misfortune would stand in the way of such self-identification because it creates distance and thus dissociation: it all happened too long ago! The interpretative flexibility of the poets' more expressionistic style, in contrast, is particularly appropriate in that it creates the possibility of recognition by future generations and identification of their distress with that of the גֶּבֶר even although they need not be identical in terms of content and extent. Perhaps this partly explains the somewhat reserved portrayal of sin found in the songs. Indeed the content of the sins committed by the people is never made concrete. We already noted our suspicion, on the basis of 3_{40}, that for the generation which experienced the fall of Judah and Jerusalem it was not entirely clear what was sinful and what was not in their relationship with YHWH.[422] One must take care, therefore, not to give in to the temptation to project back all sorts of later deuteronomistic

[422] Cf 'unveiling' in 2_{14}.

redactional clarity concerning Israel's sins in the national awareness in the period of the kings. At the same time, one cannot deny that the poets themselves had reliable knowledge of admonishing prophetic voices, insurgent behaviour and actual offence. Nevertheless, it is evident from the hermeneutical perspective, that such facts were not of sufficient importance to warrant detailed description. Stark contrast in the actual sins committed would have hindered the self-identification of future generations with their counterparts from $\pm$587. On the other hand, the emphasis on being (or having been) sinful, with the accent on personal failure regardless of the nature of the offence, can create a point of recognition for future generations because their specific faults and the actual shortcomings in their relationship with God do not then have a role to play in the process of recognition. In the same way, a present tense rendering of the גֶּבֶר's affliction can establish an immediate and direct relationship. The more so, given that the remaining songs, with their mostly factual treatment of the disaster, portray a not uncommon existential calamity which can be recognised by all ages.

Self-identification via the portrayal of גֶּבֶר then should not be limited to individual alone. It is not simply a question of an individual's particular religious response in time of need, motivated or not by personal guilt. Such an interpretation would betray a misunderstanding of the relationship between the third song and the remaining songs. The גֶּבֶר does not see the affliction about which he laments as his own personal misfortune. His perspective is one of collective affliction, of which his personal distress forms only a part. This means, therefore, that his complaints and his prayers are not merely intended for his own salvation but for that of the entire people. The same is evident here at the end of the third song. Thus his supplication is simultaneously a prayer of intercession on behalf of his society in crisis, for those who must suffer in innocence ($2_{11-12,18-19}$), for the children and their mothers, for the displaced, for the women and their young girls, for the young and the old, for those whose lives are on the point of yielding to violence and distress.

The fact that, in practical terms, the poets have succeeded in their intentions can be established from the 'Wirkungsgeschichte' of their work. Although it is difficult to verify, one can accept, nevertheless, that the third song (with its various contexts of affliction and distress) of the book of Lamentations has been at the centre of (homiletic) attention throughout the course of its history. At the same time, it cannot be denied that the conclusion of the first canto, namely sub-canto 3_{22-33}, constitutes a point of climax within the songs as a whole. This does not imply that we can read this part of Lamentations in isolation from the rest, as commentators frequently do. If one wishes to have a reliable insight into the real tensions to which the גֶּבֶר was exposed, this can only be achieved in the context of the immense distress which held sway in Judah and Jerusalem during and after their downfall as portrayed in the entire book of Lamentations which, as Moore correctly notes,[423] affected every level of society. Nevertheless, much of the human distress of those days is still recognisable today and still experienced by many of our contemporaries. The dreadful reality of former times included famine, sickness and death, suffering women and dying children, human failure, devastation, murderous enemies, abuse and oppression, and in the midst of such injustice, violence and evil, faith in God faded and vanished. Nothing has changed! In contrast to all this, however, the voice of the גֶּבֶר still resounds, the voice of a devout one who had known the height of affliction yet still warned against the very defeatism and fatalism which gnawed at his own heart. The same גֶּבֶר called for self-examination and proposed that all the terrible things we ascribe to God were never according to his nature nor at home in his heart. This very fact provides firm ground for not abandoning one's faith and trust. At the same time, it offers the occasion to keep on hoping in Him in spite of appearances. In concrete terms, the גֶּבֶר's appeal invites us to employ the living language of lament to express our grief before God for those in distress and to pray, especially for those who must suffer in silence, for a better life and for better times. Thus, while the need remains, the canon allows the voice of the גֶּבֶר to echo through history's moments of great affliction, times which ultimately obscure the face of God.

[423] MSMoore, 'Human Suffering in Lamentations', RB 83 (1990), 538–555.

Lamentations IV

Sub-canto I (4_{1-11})

1 א *Ah, how the lustrous gold has grown dim,*
that pure gold.
Scattered, lie the sacred stones
at the corner of every street.

2 ב *The precious children of Zion,*
once deemed more valuable than fine gold,
ah, how they are now reckoned as shards of clay,
the work of a potter's hands.

---

3 ג *Yes, wild animals offer the teat,*
they nurse their young;
but my daughter, my people, is as pitiless
as ostriches in the wilderness.

4 ד *The tongue of the infant cleaves*
to the roof of his mouth from thirst.
Children ask for bread,
no one gives it them.

5 ה *Those who once ate delicacies,*
(move) emaciated through the streets;
those once cared for in scarlet
now cling to the ash heaps.

---

6 ו *Yes, greater is the iniquity of my daughter, my people,*
than the sin of Sodom,
that (city) overthrown as in the wink of an eye,
without the agency of (human) hand.

---

7 ז *Once were her nobles purer than snow,*
more lustrous than milk,
red as coral (their) bones,
as azure their countenance.

8 ח *Now blacker than soot is their appearance;*
they are unrecognisable in the streets.
Their skin lies shrivelled on their bones,
dried up, become as wood.

9 ט *Those pierced by the sword were better off*
than those pierced by hunger,
than those who waste away, brought down
by cropless land.

---

10 י *The hands of tender-hearted women*
boil their children.
They have become their food of solace
in the destruction of my daughter, my people.

11 כ YHWH *has quenched his inner wrath,*
he poured out his burning anger.
He kindled fire in Zion
that devoured her foundations.

Sub-canto II (4_{12-22})

12 ל *The kings of the earth did not believe,*
nor did the inhabitants of the world,
that adversary or enemy could enter
the gates of Jerusalem.

13 מ *On account of the sins of her prophets*
and the iniquities of her priests,
who spilled in her midst
the blood of righteous ones, (this happened).

---

14 נ *Blind, they falter through the streets,*
smearing themselves with blood.
Things forbidden to them,
they touch with their clothing.

15 ס *"Make way! Unclean!",*
people give warning concerning them.
"Make way! Make way! Do not touch!"
Yes, they make way and wander around;
it is said among the nations:
"they can no longer stay here!"

16 פ *The countenance of* YHWH *scatters them;*
he no longer regards them.
the face of the priests they do not honour
and for the elders they have no respect.

---

17 ע *Our eyes yearn continually*
for help, (but) in vain.
On our vantage points we look out
for a nation that does not save.

---

18 צ *They hem us in with every step,*
we cannot show ourselves in the open!
Our end is near,
our days are running out,
yes, our end has come!

19 ק *Our pursuers are faster*
than eagles in the heavens!
Fired up, they hunt us on the mountains,
in the wilderness they lie in wait for us.

20 ר *Our life's breath,* YHWH*'s annointed,*
is imprisoned in their pits,
he, of whom we thought:
in his shadow we shall live in the midst of the nations.

---

21 ש *Rejoice and be glad, daughter Edom,*
you, inhabitant of the land of Uz!

To you also shall the cup pass
and you shall drink and uncover yourself!

22 ת *Your iniquity has amplified itself, daughter Zion!*
He has completed your exposure!
He shall visit your iniquity, daughter Edom!
Your sins he shall uncover!

* * *

LITERARY STRUCTURE OF CANTO LAMENTATIONS IV

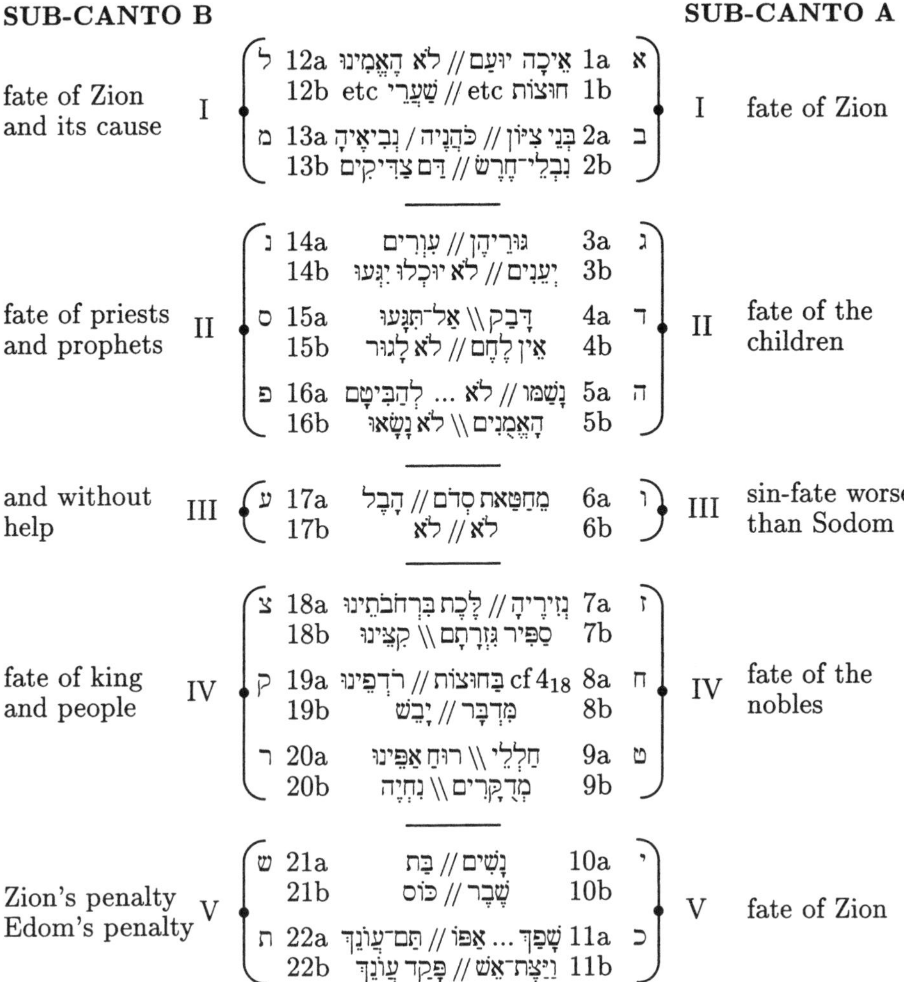

Remark: the literary similarities between both sub-cantos are also rendered on the level of the canticles; see further 1988, 334–346.

figure 4

Essentials and Perspectives

It is not surprising that in the heyday of literary criticism Lamentations was seen as a collection of independent and very different songs. After the expressions of faith and trust which conclude the third song, one enters into a completely different world at the beginning of the fourth song, or so it would seem at first sight. Trust appears to have been forgotten and one is confronted with nothing more than lament and dismay, witness the twice repeated 'ah!' of the dirge form ($4_{1A,2B}$). Such an evaluation of Lam I-IV has its roots in a reading of the text from within a chronological, linear framework whereby one creates a 'one after the other' perspective on the songs when one ought in fact to see them 'side by side'. At the same time, the devout one's faith and trust does not begin after a time of affliction but precisely in the midst of it, as is apparent from the fact that the third song is enclosed between the second and the fourth, the latter being a description of no other affliction than that described in the remaining songs, albeit in Lam IV's own unique fashion.

The final part of Lam IV is somewhat unusual, at least when one compares it with the conclusions to each of the other songs. The prayers and expressions of trust which round off Lam I–III and Lam V are completely lacking in Lam IV. Only one element of trust is present and to be found in the final canticle (4_{21-22}): like Judah, hostile Edom will likewise have to drink the cup of YHWH's judgement. The prayers lacking in Lam IV, however, follow directly in the fifth and final song, pointing to a strong relationship between both songs which allows the conclusion that the final song functions as an extended concluding prayer to the fourth.

Awareness of the aforementioned relationship helps provide a clearer explanation of Lam IV: its primary intention is to describe the affliction which the people in Judah are enduring. Their existence is one of death and destruction. The powerful introduction with its double 'ah!' certainly points in this direction and indicates that these words are an expression of personal affliction and sadness. Such realisation of personal affliction, together with the awareness of YHWH's involvement ($4_{1,11}$) and its justification (4_{21-22}), serves as a preparation for the great concluding prayer of the final song in which the same affliction is once again repeated before

YHWH. Like Lam III, the literary structure of Lam IV – which once again conveys the main features of our exegesis – is composed as a responsive diptych, both panels being characterised by unusually impressive concentricity. The central strophes 4_6 and 4_{17} together convey the powerful thematic tension present in this song: Judah's fate is worse than that of Sodom and there is no sign of help. The first panel, sub-canto I (4_{1-11}), further elaborates the thematic strophe 4_6 via two additional themes: the destruction of the temple and the destruction of the children of Zion, that of the former being mentioned first and last and thereby enclosing that of the latter. Thus the destruction of Zion includes the destruction of her children.

Both 'destructions' are already placed in parallel in the first canticle (4_{1-2}). Exegesis shows that the first strophe has to do with the destruction of the temple, revealing a degree of 'personalisation' of the divine dwelling. The greatest extremes possible are used to represent the depth of Zion's fall: the golden lustre of the temple has lost its brilliance. The casting off of Israel's adornment first mentioned in 2_1 is hereby repeated. Indeed her children, once set beyond price, are now worth nothing more than mere potsherds.

The second canticle (4_{3-5}) reveals the worthlessness of Zion's children to be a result of their starvation. The hunger of the (small) children is central to the canticle, young people ignored by those around them. Three points of contrast highlight the poignancy of this situation: wild animals suckle their young (4_3) while human offspring languish from thirst; lack of human parental care is even worse than that of the ostrich which is well known for its lack of interest in its young; contrast between the once luxurious existence of Zion's indulged and spoiled children who are now despised and forced to rummage in the ash-heaps in the hope of finding something edible.

The thematic centre and mini-canticle 4_6 compares the fate of the people with that of Sodom. The difference between the two lies in that fact that while the fall of Sodom was quite violent it was, nevertheless, over in a moment. Judah, in contrast, has been plunged into a long and horrendous time of suffering, constantly menaced by a hostile enemy. The comparison is important because it indicates the extent to which Judah's present punishment seems to go far beyond that of the 'city of sin' par excellence. The ongoing attacks of the enemy implicitly call the relationship between sin and punishment into question.

The fourth canticle (4_{7-9}) returns to the theme of starvation, focusing now on the hunger of the most distinguished elders rather than on the smaller and smallest children. The loss of their radiant beauty and prominent status together with their physical deterioration is described in detail. The picture of those who are left to waste away and die a slow death from hunger leads to the conclusion that those who died from the sword were ultimately better off.

The final canticle (4_{10-11}) offers a striking analogy related to the starvation of the people: just as the women of Jerusalem were forced by hunger to eat the flesh of their own beloved children so YHWH has been forced to destroy his own sanctuary by fire. In its own way, the analogy in question reveals the extent to which YHWH has been forced to act against his own nature and how the consequences of human sin also touch His heart.

Sub-canto II (4_{12-22}) repeats and particularises the first. In addition — as with canto II of Lam II — we are once again confronted with the question of guilt. Sub-canto II attaches itself to the preceding sub-canto by emphasising the unbelievable nature of Zion's downfall.

In terms of content, both strophes of the first canticle (4_{12-13}) exhibit the same relationship as the parallel strophes in the third song (3_{34-36} and 3_{37-39}). 4_{12} boldly states that what everyone thought impossible has actually happened: the enemy has entered into Zion's gates. The question unavoidably arises as to why YHWH has permitted this to happen. 4_{13} plainly responds: because of the sins of the priests and the prophets. The poets take things a step further here when compared with 2_{14}: the prophets not only uttered empty prophecies and neglected their actual duties, they also made themselves guilty of the spilling of innocent blood hand in hand with the priests.

The second canticle (4_{14-16}) once again describes the fate of Zion's children, in this instance that of the aforementioned priests and prophets. Alongside the population in general they too are forced to bear the consequences of their sins, and how! Those who were once respected prophets and seers of old now wander like blind men through the streets of the city and together with the priests they make themselves impure by smearing themselves unawares with the blood and excrement of those who lie crushed in the streets. Thus the very ones who were so careful with respect to their cultic purity have become like lepers. A further twist of fate still awaits them: those who once ordered others to announce their impurity before them as a warning are now confronted with people who warn them to depart because they themselves have become impure. As a consequence they are considered as outcasts with nowhere to call their own, untouchables doomed to wander homeless. Their situation is the result of God's judgement and they no longer deserve nor receive any respect.

The thematic centre and mini-canticle 4_{17} reports the painfully human desire for help in affliction. It would appear thereby that even after the fall of Zion a degree of hope continued to be fostered that Egypt might intervene as a helper. At the same time it is reported that no such help was forthcoming. Egypt cannot save. Indeed, the very concept of salvation is expressed in terms which apply only to YHWH. Since Egypt cannot save, the people are thrown back on the only one who can, upon YHWH. Implicit reference is thereby made to the גֶּבֶר who, in the parallel section of the third song, announces that he intends to weep until YHWH looks down, that is until YHWH saves.

The last canticle but one (4_{18-20}) renders the impression of helplessness via the theme of hostile enemy persecution which also includes the imprisonment of the king among its consequences. The terminology employed points to the great import of the laments. Much of what has happened is seen as the judgement due on the day of YHWH, a day which spells the end of a once advantaged existence in Zion under the protection of God and his king.

The final canticle (4_{20-22}) portray's the totality of YHWH's judgement. The completeness of her downfall makes it clear that daughter Zion has been forced to drink the cup of his wrath to its very dregs. Everything the prophets once predicted in this regard has come true, up to and including the destruction of the temple, the final act whereby YHWH has brought the destruction of Zion to its completion. The poets can offer but one consolation: the prophet who foretold that Judah would drink the cup of YHWH's judgement also foretold that her enemies would have to do the same, the very ones who now indulge their vindictiveness at Israel's expense, the Edomites. They may be able to rejoice for a while at the misfortune of daughter Zion but they will ultimately have to face the same fate. While it is true that such a fate implies the cessation of their hostilities, up to this point there is no cessation in sight. For this reason the fifth song urgently reiterates Zion's affliction and desperate need before YHWH in the hope that he will keep to his word and bring liberation.

Lamentations IV
Scholarly Exposition

Introduction

The expressions of trust and prayers of the גֶּבֶר at the end of the third song are directly followed in the fourth song by the reappearance of the 'ah!' of the funeral lament. The extent of the transition from trust to lament leads one to question whether the גֶּבֶר himself may still be considered the speaker. While it is true that in any human life, moments of hope and despair suddenly come and go, we assume that the poets have only allowed the גֶּבֶר to speak as an individual in Lam III. The inclusion at the canticle level between אֲנִי (3_{1A}) // אֲנִי (3_{63B}) certainly points in this direction. Given its line of attack, Lam IV does not appear to be about the גֶּבֶר and him alone. Indeed, besides the singulars found in 4_3 and 4_6, there are also first person plurals to be found in 4_{17-20}. This is quite explicable if one recognises the voice of a collective in these verses. One should consider $4_{1-6,10-11}$, therefore, to be the words of Lady Jerusalem and 4_{7-9} as the direct speech of the poets.[1] The poets can also be considered the speakers in 4_{12-22} [2] although, at the same time, they employ the 'we-form' to give voice to the sense of defeat which holds sway among the population (4_{17-20}).

It is primarily the suffering of the explicitly named children of Zion (בְּנֵי צִיּוֹן in 4_{2a}) which constitutes the focus of Lam IV. It is striking that the poets always begin each of the songs with an indication of its primary subject.[3] The affliction of Zion's children is chiefly rendered in terms of great hunger. While the descriptions are different they remain a thematic repetition, although not without reason. Indeed, the גֶּבֶר's restored faith

[1] Cf the 3f sg suffix in 4_{7aA}.
[2] Cf 3f sg suffixes in 4_{13}.
[3] Cf הָעִיר the city, 1_1; בַּת־צִיּוֹן, daughter Zion, 2_1; אֲנִי הַגֶּבֶר the devout one, 3_1; בְּנֵי צִיּוֹן the inhabitants of Zion, 4_2; לָנוּ the praying inhabitants of the land, 5_1.

in God is introduced into the prevailing situation of great need: he is one among Zion's children (cf 3_{1A}) and their affliction is identical and concurrent with his. The main purpose of the literary structure of the book as a whole is thus clear: the third song which includes the גֶּבֶר's change of heart, is wedged in between the other songs which echo and supplement one another as they relate their tale of affliction, not as past history, but as oppressive and suffocating present. We already noted the extent to which the second and fourth songs which frame the third exhibit many levels of correspondence. Even in the heyday of literary criticism, these two songs were ascribed to the same author.

It is important to pay careful attention in this regard to the final canticle of Lam II and the opening canticle of Lam IV. At the literary level one can observe the following parallels:

בְּמִקְדַּשׁ (2_{20cA}) // אַבְנֵי־קֹדֶשׁ (4_{1bA})
בְּמִקְדַּשׁ (2_{20cA}) // צִיּוֹן (4_{2aA})
לָאָרֶץ חוּצוֹת (2_{21aA}) // בְּרֹאשׁ כָּל־חוּצוֹת (4_{1bB})
עֹלֲלֵי טִפֻּחִים (2_{20bB}) // בְּנֵי צִיּוֹן הַיְקָרִים (4_{2aA})

Agreement is also quite evident at the level of content: both deal with the destruction of Zion's children, while the affliction with which the second song ends is the same as that with which the fourth song begins. Thus the witness of the גֶּבֶר resounds in the heart of the godforsakenness and horror which threaten the land and its inhabitants. His faith and his prayer arise from the very depths in which Zion's children now find themselves.

Levels of conformity with the second song need not imply that the fourth is nothing more than repetition. New dimensions and comparisons emerge here also as we shall see below. An important distinction at the level of content lies in the fourth song's focus on the fate of human persons while the second song tends also to shed ample light on Zion's material destruction. The latter dimension is barely present in the fourth song, except with regard to the temple. What distinguishes the fourth song, therefore, is the fact that it does not speak of the temple's destruction as an independent theme but parallels it rather with the destruction of the inhabitants of Zion, thereby giving it a personal aspect (cf, especially, the exegesis of $4_{1,2}$ and $4_{10,11}$).

Structure and Genre

From the literary perspective, the fourth song distinguishes itself from the second by way of its shorter strophes which consist of two instead of three cola and are in harmony with the structure of the *qinah*-rhythm. The fourth song is therefore substantially shorter than the first three and appears to consist of only one canto. Being constructed out of two sub-cantos which mirror one another in a variety of responses, it shares the diptych structure of the third song. Thus a number of external parallelisms offer new perspectives on our interpretation of the text.

Compared with the remaining songs, Lam 4 exhibits a noteworthy difference: it contains no prayer for help (with the minor exception of the faint echoes of the גֶּבֶר's renewed faith and trust in 4_{21}). This can only be explained if one assumes a close relationship with the final song which, unlike the other songs, opens with prayer (see 5_1). The fifth song functions as an expansion of the prayers (at the end) of the first three songs and at the same time provides a prayer supplement to the fourth. What appears to be missing at the end of Lam IV is thus roundly expressed in Lam V. Taken together, both songs amount to the same as each of the other three songs taken seperately. Evidence once again of the poets' endeavour to establish balance at the higher levels of the composition.

The aforementioned cohesion between Lam IV and the final song sheds some light on the former's ultimate function: as 'Wir-Klage', its account of the horrendous situation holding sway in the city is implicitly aimed at YHWH and serves as such as a preparation for the great final prayer for restoration in Lam V. Further information on genre can be found in the introduction (III.2) and our remarks on the question in the introductions to Lam I and III. The present song also exhibits the same characteristic association of lament with the dirge or funeral lament (cf the introductory אֵיכָה [2x in the first canticle]), a characteristic similarly manifest in the contrast between former glory and present misfortune.[4]

Sub-canto I (Lam 4_{1-11})

Judging by its considerable number of inclusions, the present sub-canto exhibits a strongly concentric structure.[5] If one remains unaware of this and considers the text to follow a linear sequence then one will be forced to conclude that one is dealing with a rather discordant whole.[6] If, however, one respects the concentricity introduced by the poets (at the canticle

4 Cf CWestermann, *Die Klagelieder, Forschungsgeschichte und Auslegung*, Neukirchen-Vluyn 1990, 165.

5 For more detailed argumentation concerning the literary structure of the fourth song see 1988, 341–346.

6 Cf Westermann, 163–166.

level), then the structure becomes clear. The sixth strophe 4_6 (simultaneously the central canticle) stands at the centre of this sub-canto and expresses its thematic core: the people's sin is greater than that of Sodom and its consequences more grave. Throughout the present sub-canto, this essential theme is primarily related to the destruction of Zion and her children made physically visible in the horrendous hunger which spares no one. The same theme was always dealt with more or less in passing in the earlier songs,[7] although the most detailed description remains that of the starvation of Jerusalem's infant children at the beginning of canto II of the second song. Here, however, the sub-canto is devoted for the most part to the devastating hunger confronting the people. The poets have introduced a further theme side by side with that of starvation: the fact that YHWH has been forced to destroy his Zion. Indeed, in so doing, they introduce a remarkable parallel between the destruction of Zion and that of her children. The opening and closing canticles (4_{1-2} and 4_{10-11}) underline this fact, the latter revealing that the poets are aware of YHWH's sadness at Zion's downfall made manifest in the analogy they see between His destruction of Zion and the tender-hearted women of Jerusalem who, driven by hunger, are forced to eat their own children.

Canticle I (4_{1-2})

Content/theme: *The fate of Zion and her inhabitants*

Literary argumentation:

inclusions:	אֵיכָה (1aA) // אֵיכָה (2bA)
	אַבְנֵי־קֹדֶשׁ (1bA) // הַיְקָרִים (2aA)
responses:	זָהָב / הַכֶּתֶם הַטּוֹב (1a) // הַיְקָרִים ... בַּפָּז (2a)
	תִּשְׁתַּפֵּכְנָה אַבְנֵי־קֹדֶשׁ (1bA) // לְנִבְלֵי־חֶרֶשׂ (2bA)
	רֹאשׁ (1bB) // יְדֵי (2bB)

1a *Ah, how the lustrous gold has grown dim,*
that pure gold.

אֵיכָה יוּעַם זָהָב יִשְׁנֶא
הַכֶּתֶם הַטּוֹב

By way of the initial אֵיכָה, the poets reconnect us with the world of the funeral lament. Compared with Lam 1_1 and 2_1, however, the present verse is strikingly different. In 1_1 the אֵיכָה had to do with 'widow Jerusalem' and in 2_1 with 'daughter Zion'. Here in 4_1, by contrast, there is no such personification present. Indeed, the lament as such is raised over the fall

[7] Cf $1_{6c,11a,19bc}$, $2_{4,12}$, $3_{15,16}$.

of a building, in this case the temple. This is quite unusual and, in fact, unique in the OT. The fall of the temple is placed in a personal context and as such it has to do with a living entity and not a thing. It will be apparent from the exegesis of $4_{10,11}$ that this is no accidental detail (cf also 2_{7a}).

Contrast, so characteristic of the funeral lament, confronts us immediately: the once lustrous gold has vanished/been covered. In light of the significant variety in meaning, GES-B (601) and KBL (715) distinguish two distinct verbs with the root עמם. HAL (800f), on the other hand, proposes one single root עמם with the basic meaning 'to cover'. The present text employs the *hoph'al* impf: 'to be covered'. The passive subject of יוּעַם is 'the gold' which is qualified by יִשְׁנֶא, from the root שׁנא meaning 'to gleam'/'to shine' (cf Qoh 8_1) and should be translated as an attributive subordinate clause: 'the gold that gleams'/'the lustrous gold' (cf HAL 1474). An alternative reading is proposed by some, namely that we emend יִשְׁנֶא to יִשְׁנֶה from the root שׁנה I meaning 'to change', attach it to the second colon with הַכֶּתֶם הַטּוֹב as its subject and translate the whole as follows: 'ah how the gold has faded, the pure gold changed'. While it is true that such a reading is grammatically attractive since it obviates the need to ascribe an adjectival meaning to the verbal form יִשְׁנֶא, it still does not have our preference for a number of reasons. Firstly, such an emendation would imply a $2+3$ rhythm whereas the *qinah*-form is strong in these verses (cf the double אֵיכָה in the present canticle) and a thus a $3+2$ rhythm would be more appropriate. The necessary textual emendation provides a second counter argument even although the LXX and a number of Hebrew manuscripts support it.[8] The LXX-reading appears to be inspired by its translation of כֶּתֶם as ἀγρύριον, 'silver' which does indeed change over time and lose its lustre due to oxydation while gold, in contrast, does not. כֶּתֶם, however, clearly means fine, high quality gold.[9] The second colon draws our attention to the lustre of the gold by focusing on its quality. It was not inferior gold, mixed with all sorts of impurities which would ultimately casue it to lose its gleam over time. On the contrary, it was the purest gold, superior in every way.

The question remains, however, as to what this 'pure gold' refers. Our explanation of the present verses is essentially determined by a new element thus far in the exegetical discussion, namely the strongly concentric

[8] Cf text critical apparatus BHS.

[9] Cf Job $28_{16,19}$, 31_{24}, Ps 45_{10}, Prov 25_{12}, Song 5_{11}, Isa 13_{12}.

structure of the first sub-canto (4_{1-11}) in which the first canticle (4_{1-2}) and the last (4_{10-11}) constitute an inclusion. Concentricity is even evident at the strophe level, whereby 4_1 corresponds with 4_{11} (via the inclusion תִּשְׁתַּפֵּכְנָה [1bA] // שָׁפַךְ [11aB]), and 4_2 with 4_{10} (cf the inclusion בְּנֵי צִיּוֹן [2aA] // יַלְדֵיהֶן [10aB]). 4_1 and 4_{11}, therefore, also correspond at the level of content. 4_{11} deals unambiguously with the total destruction of Zion by the fire which YHWH has kindled in her midst. At the same time, it is important to note the presence of a (sub-canto) response with 4_{12} where the unimaginable dimension of Jerusalem's downfall is underlined. 4_{11} and 4_{12}, therefore, are mutually determinative for the interpretation of 4_1 and all those exegetes who interpret the metaphors in these strophes as referring to the children of Zion are mistaken. Calvin and Kraus (as one of the few modern exegetes) correctly draw a connection with the destruction of the temple. Kraus, in addition, rightly points to the connection with תִּפְאֶרֶת in 2_1, envisaging thereby the splendour of Zion. A direct connection between תִּפְאֶרֶת and זָהָב in the context of the temple can be found in II Chron 3_6. In Ps 78_{61} we even find תִּפְאֶרֶת used for the ark pure and simple while the presence of gold can be assumed from the fact that, according to tradition, the ark was covered with the said precious metal.[10] This notion is supported by the song response with 2_{1c} where there is mention of 'his footstool', a reference to the ark. One might also picture the golden vessels/utensils employed in the temple as the referent (cf II Kgs 7_{48-50}) although it is hard to see how these could have been 'covered over' since they had already been carried off to Babylon as booty.[11] It is apparent from Jer 27_{18-21}, however, that Nebuchadnezzar did not plunder the entire contents of Jerusalem's temple in 597 and one can assume that an effort was made after 597 to make up for the scandal of what he did remove by replacing it as far as was possible (cf I Kgs 14_{26}). Second time round (587), however, it is clear that everything of value was taken (cf II Kgs 25_{13-17}).

The fact that there is no mention of the ark being included among the treasure pillaged in 587 suggests that it was left untouched. Given I Sam 5, the historiography of Israel would have had no reason to alter such an important detail. III Ezra 1_{54} does state that Nebuchadnezzar took the ark with him to Babylon but the report stands on its own and shows every sign of being a later addition. Had the ark been removed one might

[10] Cf Ex 25_{10-22}, 37_{1-9}.
[11] See 1_{10a} and cf II Kgs 24_{13}, Jer 28_{13}.

have expected a greater and more immediate response. It would seem reasonable to assume, therefore, that a common tactic, familiar to every period of history, was employed to hide the precious ark (cf the meaning of √עמם 'to cover') while the remaining temple gold was allowed to make its way out of the temple in the hands of the Babylonian plunderers. Whatever may have happened, the present text remains unclear about it. If it is true that the ark was indeed hidden then the lack of clarity in the text may be quite intentional. We must satisfy ourselves with the impression left by the text. In any case, the following bicolon seems to point in the direction of the destruction of the temple which, according to tradition, was set on fire.[12] The blackened, sooty ruin which once glistened with gold inside and out has inspired to the poets to lament that its gold is now covered and its lustre hidden. Whether or not the gold in question was still there is not really the point.

1b *Scattered, lie the sacred stones* — תִּשְׁתַּפֵּכְנָה אַבְנֵי־קֹדֶשׁ
at the corner of every street. — בְּרֹאשׁ כָּל־חוּצוֹת

תִּשְׁתַּפֵּכְנָה is a *hithpa'el* impf 3f pl of the root שפך 'to throw/pour out'. The אַבְנֵי־קֹדֶשׁ constitute the passive subject with קֹדֶשׁ understood as an adjective: 'sacred stones' or more literally: 'stones of the sacred'.[13] What the authors intend by these 'sacred stones', however, is the subject of some dispute. A significant number of exegetes propose that, by analogy with the following strophe (4_2), they should be understood as the children of Zion.[14] Others suggest that the stones in question are those of the sanctuary,[15] while others still are inclined to think of the precious stones used in the manufacture of priestly vestments or amulets.[16] HAL (8) offers the additional possibility of 'sculptures'/'stone idols'.[17] The two latter suggestions appear to me to be quite unlikely given that, at its deepest, the image ultimately implies a lament in the presence of YHWH (cf 5_1).

One objection raised against the idea of sanctuary stones is the additional description of them being scattered around at the corner of every street (בְּרֹאשׁ כָּל־חוּצוֹת). This location is employed elsewhere in the songs

[12] Cf II Kgs 25_9 as well as the explanation of 1_{4c}, $4_{11b,22b}$.
[13] Cf אַבְנֵי־צֶדֶק in Lev 19_{36} for a comparable construction.
[14] Cf Ewald, Löhr, Aalders, Haller, Wiesmann, Rudolph, Weiser, Gordis, Plöger, Gottlieb, Kaiser, Boecker.
[15] Calvin, JWellhausen, *Skizzen und Vorarbeiten V*, Berlin 1893², 184, Kraus, cf TWAT I 53 (Kapelrud).
[16] Cf Emerton (see below) and Hillers.
[17] Cf Jer 2_{27}, 3_9, Ezek 20_{32}.

to indicate the place where Zion's children and inhabitants lay down to die (2_{19d}) and might thus support the identification of the sacred stones with the children of Zion. A further argument in favour of such an interpretation is drawn from the expression אֶבֶן יְקָרָה[18] meaning 'precious stones' which would introduce a strong comparison with the first colon of the following verse: (א)בְּנֵי (צִיּוֹן) הַיְקָרִים (4_{2A}). This gives the impression that the 'sacred stones' are identical with the 'precious children' of Zion, a possibility underlined by the fact that קֹדֶשׁ not only means 'sacred' but can also mean 'precious'[19] (on the basis of the latter meaning of √קדש in East Semitic languages). Indeed, within the OT itself, the metaphor of precious stones for the children of Israel would appear not to be unique (cf Zech 9_{16} [אַבְנֵי־נֵזֶר]).

The aforementioned argumentation remains, nevertheless, unconvincing. Our own approach takes the already indicated association between the first and the final canticles as its point of departure and assumes that the present reference is the destruction of the temple. We already noted the fact that the first and last canticles of this sub-canto parallel the destruction of Zion with that of her children. Given the strong similarity between 4_1 and 4_{11}, therefore, we propose that the 'sacred stones' be understood as the stones of the sanctuary ("אֶבֶן wird fast immer von wirklichen Stein benutzt").[20] YHWH has poured out his burning wrath and kindled a fire which has razed Zion to her foundations. The very correspondence between שָׁפַךְ (4_{11aB}) // תִּשְׁתַּפֵּכְנָה (4_{1bA}) permits us to see how the sacred stones were 'poured out' by the 'pouring out' of YHWH's burning wrath (cf 2_{4c}). It is clear, therefore, that the reference here is to the stones of the temple. It is perhaps true that the scattering of these stones throughout Jerusalem is not immediately explicable, yet closer inspection shows that it is not so surprising. The city was badly damaged by siege and enemy plunder/deportation. It seems obvious that the remaining inhabitants would have taken any still usable and once valuable building materials from the ruined temple to try to repair their own houses. Indeed, their disappointment in YHWH would have left them without inhibition in this regard (cf 3_{14}). There is no need, therefore, to offer further explanation as to how stones from the temple complex found their way into every corner of the city. The evidently intentional parallel between √שפך and √הפך (4_6;

[18] Cf II Sam 12:30; I Kgs 5_{31}, $10_{2,10f}$, II Chron $9_{1,9,10}$, Ezek 28_{13}.

[19] See JAEmerton, 'The Meaning of אבני קדש in Lamentations 4,1', ZAW 79 (1967), 233–236.

[20] Cf TWAT I 52 (Kapelrud).

cf 3_3 and 1_{20bA}) is also informative: the destruction of the city being the consequence of YHWH's 'turn around'.

2a *The precious children of Zion,* בְּנֵי צִיּוֹן הַיְקָרִים
once deemed more valuable than fine gold, הַמְסֻלָּאִים בַּפָּז

In light of the already noted connection between (א)בְּנֵי (צִיּוֹן) הַיְקָרִים and the אַבְנֵי־קֹדֶשׁ, it is not completely incomprehensible that Robinson suggests in the text critical apparatus of BHS that we read אַבְנֵי (stones) instead of בְּנֵי (sons). Nevertheless, such an emendation must be rejected on the grounds that it upsets the evident alphabetic acrostic. In addition, the suggestion is not supported by a single textual witness. Although there is a tonal association with 'precious stone',[21] it remains clear that the reference is to Zion's children, given the general introduction: inhabitants of Zion/inhabitants of Jerusalem (cf Ps 149_2). One might ask why they are referred to here as precious? Wagner suggests that election by YHWH is the reason.[22] The use of the adjective יָקָר certainly points in that direction. It is used in a similar context in Jer 31_{20} where Ephraim is spoken of as YHWH's precious son. Isa 43_{3f} follows a matching line of thought: YHWH sees Jacob as precious, pays a considerable כֹּפֶר (ransom) for him and loves him (with √אהב). Genuine love is irreplaceable and surpasses every treasure (Song 8_7). The verb סלא (*pu'al* part) should not be understood here in its usual meaning 'to pay'.[23] It has to do, rather, with the determination of the exchange value of extremely valuable things which are actually beyond price (Job $28_{16,19}$). Our translation 'more valuable than' is based on the possible use of the preposition בְּ (before פָּז) to express the comparative.[24] With respect to content, the parallel with 1_2 supports this translation: Lady Jerusalem's lovers who once held her dear have decieved her pitilessly and abandoned her. Besides the political dimension, however, there is also a theological dimension: Lady Jerusalem's widow status implies that her 'husband' YHWH has left her, taking with him the very sign of their union, that priceless jewel, the temple (2_{1b}). Thus, at this level, the first songs do indeed suggest that we should think of forfeited election. Clearly Jerusalem's lovers are not the only ones to have rejected her nor the most significant: YHWH himself has turned his back on her (cf 3_{45}).

---

[21] Cf also סַפִּיר in 4_{7bB}.
[22] See TWAT III 864.
[23] As does HAL 714.
[24] Cf HAL 101 sv בְּ (14); Ps 89_3, 119_{89} and Prov 24_5.

2b *ah, how they are now reckoned as shards of clay,* אֵיכָה נֶחְשְׁבוּ לְנִבְלֵי־חֶרֶשׂ
the work of a potter's hands. מַעֲשֵׂה יְדֵי יוֹצֵר

What is typical of the dirge or funeral lament is the portrayal of the loss of election via enormous contrast: here from priceless to worthless; cherished, priceless gold and precious stones devalued to disgarded potsherds. This is how we interpret the combination נִבְלֵי־חֶרֶשׂ which others prefer to translate as 'earthen vessels'.[25] As we already noted, Robinson suggests in the text critical apparatus of BHS, that we read אַבְנֵי but this is simply not supported by textual witnesses. The resultant translation 'stones of earthenware' is likewise somewhat strange. There is little doubt that the term נֵבֶל I means a 'vessel' or 'pot' which is, by its very nature, made of earthenware.[26] חֶרֶשׂ is understood here as the material out of which pots are made although such an interpretation of the term is not found elsewhere. Indeed, on its own חֶרֶשׂ can mean a '(pot of) earthenware' (cf HAL 343). One is then left with a sort of tautology: 'earthenware pots of earthenware'. The second colon seems to confirm the first, however: the result of the work of the potter.

The question remains as to the correctness of such an interpretation. Although it might not be made of gold, an undamaged pot still had a certain value. The text, on the other hand, seems to suggest that נִבְלֵי־חֶרֶשׂ are of no value whatsoever. The contrast found in the dirge or funeral lament is always based on extremes. Thus the alternative meaning of חֶרֶשׂ 'potsherd' would appear to fit more appropriately in the context.[27] The sub-canto response נִבְלֵי־חֶרֶשׂ (4_{2b}) // אַשְׁפַּתּוֹת (4_{5b}) further confirms this since there is little doubt that potsherds would have ended up on the ash heaps.[28] Nevertheless, we are left with a degree of inconsistency with the second colon: 'the work of a potter's hands'. Clearly potters do not make shards!! Or do they? It is part of the work of the potter to select the pots which were of good quality and shape and smash up those which were flawed or of poor quality (cf Isa 30_{14}). Only undamaged pots were offered for sale. We assume that something similar is being suggested here. The use of root חשב + the preposition לְ points in the direction of evaluation.[29] For a negative interpretation of the term חשב with regard to persons, see the exegesis of $3_{60,61}$. We are faced, therefore, with material rejected by

[25] Cf Aalders, Rudolph, Kaiser, Boecker, Westermann etcetera.
[26] Cf Isa 30_{14}, Jer 13_{12}, 48_{12} etcetera; cf HAL 627.
[27] Cf Ps 22_{16}, Job 2_8.
[28] See once again Job 2_8.
[29] Cf the exegesis of 2_{8a}; cf also Job 35_2, 41_{19} (MT 41_{24}); HAL 346 sv √חשב (2).

the potter as unsuitable for sale. Since they were a poor advertisment for his skill as a potter, unsuccessful and damaged pots were destroyed. What were considered unworthy pots were condemned to be smashed into נִבְלֵי־חֶרֶשׂ, literally 'shards of clay'.

Of course, the acceptance or rejection of earthenware pots serves as a metaphor for the evaluation of the inhabitants of Zion: rejected. Thus their fate is sealed: to be smashed and thrown aside. The image of intentional and thorough shattering of earthenware in Isa 30_{14} serves as a metaphor in the context of the prophecy of doom: thus shall YHWH destroy his people. In our analysis of the literary structure of these verses we noted elsewhere that there was a close relationship between the fourth song and Isa 30, namely between Lam 4_{17} and Isa 30_{7} and between Lam 4_{6} and Isa 30_{13} etcetera.[30] We can now add the connection between the shattered pottery here and in Isa 30_{14} to our list of associations. Isaiah's prophecy of doom was to be taken up again by Jeremiah where we find the potter as a metaphor for YHWH (cf Jer 18_{1-6}) while the prophecy of the intentional destruction of the earthenware is elaborated in Jer 19_{1-15} (cf especially 19_{1} and 19_{10f}.) The poets now confirm that these prophecies of doom and judgement have become reality. Thus the subject of this act of contempt also becomes clear: YHWH, even although his contempt is only made visible in the actions of the enemy who have destroyed the temple and chased the population from house and land and left them to starve (cf the song-response with 5_{2}).

The disparaging of the children of Zion is thus made concrete in the events that overcome them. The second canticle (4_{3-5}) relates the horrors of famine. In addition to what we have said above, a number of song-responses are evident here. The verb שׁבר 'to break' in Isa 30_{14} and Jer 19_{11}, with YHWH as subject and the children/inhabitants of Zion/the land as object, resonates also in the lament of the גֶּבֶר in 3_{4B}: 'he breaks my bones'. In the beginning of the second song we hear that YHWH discards and annihilates (Lam 2_{1-2}). Jer 19_{11} draws exactly the same parallel between the fate of the people and city; both shall be shattered like an earthenware pot. Contempt for Zion's children takes its most abhorrent form in the cooking of their corpses; cf the inclusion within the sub-canto: נֶחְשְׁבוּ לְנִבְלֵי־חֶרֶשׂ (4_{2b}) // בִּשְּׁלוּ יַלְדֵיהֶן (4_{10a}).

If one reads 4_{2} side by side with 4_{13} in accord with the responsive diptych structure of the text then the same association emerges as in 2_{14}. The

[30] Cf 1988, 346.

word of judgement implied by the image of shattered pots did not become reality without reason; the sins of Jerusalem's prophets (and priests) are ultimately responsible for the fate of the children of Zion.

Canticle II (4_{3-5})

Content/theme: *hungry and thirsty children*

Literary argumentation:

inclusions:	תַּנִּין (3aA) // אַשְׁפַּתּוֹת (5bB)
	הֵינִיקוּ גּוּרֵיהֶן (3aB) // הָאֱמֻנִים (5bA)
	מִדְבָּר (3bB) // נָשַׁמּוּ (5aB)
	צָמָא (4aB) // לֶחֶם (אֵין) (4bA) [31]
responses:	חָלְצוּ שַׁד (3aA) \\ דָּבַק לְשׁוֹן (4aA)
	הֵינִיקוּ (3aB) // יוֹנֵק (4aA)
	בַּת־עַמִּי לְאַכְזָר (3aA) // פֹּרֵשׂ אֵין לָהֶם (4bB)
	מִדְבָּר (3bB) // אַשְׁפַּתּוֹת (5bA)
	עוֹלָלִים (4bA) // הָאֱמֻנִים (5bA) [32]
concatenations:	מִדְבָּר (3bB) // דָּבַק לְשׁוֹן (4aA)
	לֶחֶם (4bA) // הָאֹכְלִים (5aA)

The second canticle depicts and details the manner in which the inhabitants of Zion are humiliated. Two agreements with the second canto of the second song are worthy of note in this regard, namely starvation as the opening attack and the small children as it first victims (cf $2_{11,12}$). See also the emphasis placed on the latter in $2_{18,19,20}$ and the central verse 3_{51}. Once again the horror of this terrible suffering is underlined. Of course, starvation hit the elderly just as mercilessly as it did the children, but the affliction of small children is always more poignant than that of adults. In the present canticle, the poets portray the terrible situation of the hungry and thirsty children with the harshest of contrasts.

3a *Yes, wild animals offer the teat,*	גַּם־תַּנִּין חָלְצוּ שַׁד
they nurse their young;	הֵינִיקוּ גּוּרֵיהֶן

For the present tense significance of the prefect חָלְצוּ see 1_1. The SV follows the *k^e^ṯîḇ* תַּנִּין which it translates as a collective: 'sea calves'. In Gen 1_{21}, the תַּנִּינִם are considered to be sea animals while Ex $7_{9,12}$ and Ps 91_{13}

[31] Cf Isa 5_{13}, Am 8_{11}.
[32] Cf Lam 2_{20bB}.

use the term for (specific) types of snake which is Calvin's option here in 4_{3a}. Ezek 29_3 and 32_3 compare pharaoh with a powerful Nile crocodile (=תַּנִּים).[33] In Jer 51_{34}, תַּנִּין is seen as a dangerous animal ('dragon') and used as a metaphor for Nebuchadnezzar.[34] In Ps 74_{13}, Job 7_{12}, Isa 27_1, 51_9 תַּנִּין has mythical connotations.[35] Based on the context provided by Isa 13_{21f}, 34_{11f}, 43_{20}, Jer 50_{39} and Job 30_{29}, Margalith is of the opinion that תַּן suggests a kind of bird but he admits that it is difficult to see how a bird can 'offer the teat'![36] He refers, therefore, to the notion of the תַּן as a legendary snake with breasts, images of which can be found in the Canaanite temple of Beth Shean. It remains unclear whether he understands תַּן to be a bird or a snake. The various interpretations of the term seem difficult to reconcile, unless, and this is not uncommon, one pictures some sort of hybrid beast. Images of such beings can be found in Keel[37] presented as dangerous nocturnal beasts which have characteristics of the various aforementioned animals. He describes his figure 90 as follows: "Die Mischgestalt, die aus zwei Paar Menschenbeinen, einem Schlangenleib mit Menschenkopf, einem schnuppernden Schakalskopf, der den Schwanz bildet (...) und ein paar Geierflügeln zusammengesetzt ist." Keel notes in addition that the snake is the symbol of the sea.[38] In his book *Jahwes Entgegnung an Ijob*[39] he offers arguments for equating the 'twisting' Leviathan[40] with the similarly 'twisting' captive crocodile (תַּנִּים).[41] We are left with the impression that the term is (still) a (demythologised) chiffre for wild animals in general, the specific nature of which can only be discerned from the context or from prefixes (cf פֶּתֶן 'venomous snake' [fanged animal]). Because of this image of wild animals in general we do not agree with the usual interpretation which takes the *qᵉrē* תַּנִּים (plural of תַּן[42]) as its point of departure and translates 'jackal' (*canis aureus*: cf

[33] For the form cf WZimmerli, *Ezechiel 25–48*, BKAT XIII/2, Neukirchen 1969, 703.

[34] The LXX translates תַּנִּין in Lam 4_3 as δράκοντες.

[35] Cf CWestermann, *Genesis 1–11*, BKAT I/1, Neukirchen–Vluyn 1974, 190f; WZimmerli, 707f and JLKoole, *Jesaja II, deel II Jesaja 49 tot en met 55*, Kampen 1990, 140ff.

[36] OMargalith, 'Samson's Foxes', VT XXXV (1985), 227f.

[37] See OKeel, *Die Welt der altorientalischen Bildsymbolik und das Alte Testament*, Zürich-Einsiedeln-Köln-Neukirchen-Vluyn 1977[2], 67.

[38] Cf figure 36 + notes, figures 39–40 and the snake/dragon in figures 41 and 55.

[39] OKeel, *Jahwes Entgegnung an Ijob*, Göttingen 1978, 142f.

[40] See Job 3_8, Ps 74_{14}, 104_{26}; also referred to as a 'twisting' serpent in Isa 27_1; cf √לוה I 'to twist/coil'.

[41] Cf Ezek 29_3, 32_2.

[42] Cf, however, BL 565x.

HAL 1619). The 'jackal' is referred to in 5_{18}, however, where the term שׁוּעָל is used. The fact that גּוּר is not the specific term for a jackal's young but more of a general term for the suckling young of a large preditor such as a lion[43] further supports our interpretation. One is reminded of the גֶּבֶר's complaint in the (canticle level) parallel 3_{10} in which he speaks of the threat of wild animals and specifically mentions the lion.

Whatever the interpretation, תַּ(נִּי)ן are stereotypically present in prophecies of doom, especially in light of the biotope associated therewith. The territory of the תַּ(נִּי)ן is characteristically uninhabited, dry wasteland, with abandoned ruins constituting their preferred dwelling places.[44] Without doubt this explains why the authors opted for the present comparison. Ruined Jerusalem and the abandoned cities of Judah portray the fulfilment of such prophecies of doom. It is stated in parallel in the second song that Israel's horns have all been hacked off, which means that her fortress cities have all been destroyed. Such cities became the territory of the תַּנִּין; places of smoldering heat, hunger, thirst and abandonment, where wild animals, whose howling sounded like a funeral dirge for the dead (cf Mic 1_8), rummaged for something to suit their taste among the deserted rubbish heaps (cf the inclusion תַּנִּין [4_{3aA}] // אַשְׁפַּתּוֹת [4_{5bB}]).

The connection between 4_3 and the song-response 5_3 has a similar basis. In the latter text, a few remaining inhabitants lament over their abandoned cities[45] and not without reason. Their limited numbers no longer frighten off the the wild animals we have been describing. Comparison between human persons and animals in such places not only highlights the association between human funeral lament and animal howling, the poets are also aware of an acute contrast which extends far beyond the misfortune associated with prophecies of doom, made concrete in the difference in behaviour between female animals and human mothers. In spite of the harsh environment and the terrible lack of water,[46] female animals were still able to follow their natural instincts and suckle their young. Does this imply that the catch was sufficient and that others had fallen prey to preditors and not the גֶּבֶר (cf 3_{10})? In any case, when the poets see the young of the wild animals darting through the ruins, fit and playful, they are sure that their mothers have nourishment enough. The remaining

[43] Cf Gen 49_9, Deut 33_{22}, Ezek $19_{2f,5}$, Nah 2_{12}.

[44] Cf Isa 13_{22}, 34_{13}, Jer 9_{11f} (MT 9_{10f}), 10_{22}, 49_{33}, 51_{37}; cf Ps 44_{20}.

[45] Cf also the explanation of 5_{18B}.

[46] Cf Isa 35_7, 43_{20}, Jer 14_6.

children of Jerusalem, in contrast, fight for breath as they struggle with every move they try to make.[47]

3b *but my daughter, my people, is as pitiless* בַּת־עַמִּי לְאַכְזָר
as ostriches in the wilderness. כַּיְעֵנִים בַּמִּדְבָּר

The introductory בַּת־עַמִּי presents some difficulties. The expression 'daughter, my people' is a personification in which the entire people is presented as a woman (cf 2_{11b}). Nevertheless, it seems reasonable at first sight that the context of '(not) suckling' suggests that mothers with very young children (cf 2_{12a}) are intended here. For this reason, Robinson suggests [48] that we read בְּנוֹת־עַמִּי 'the daughters of my people'. Weismann, Rudolph, Kraus, Weiser, Brandscheidt and Westermann, among others, follow a similar line, supported by the LXX which translates θυγατέρες λαοῦ μου. The Greek reading, however, carries little weight because it appears to be a correction of the Hebrew text at hand. The Peshitta reads the same as the MT. In addition, the expression בַּת־עַמִּי seems to have a function within the literary structure of the fourth song.[49] Emendation, therefore, appears to be precluded. If the entire population is intended, both the men and the women, then the analogy with suckling animals should not be interpreted too strictly. The poets clearly have more than inadequately lactating mothers in mind; their reference is to the lack of parental care of the entire population. The strophe-response between 4_{3b} and 4_{4b} supports such an interpretation: heartlessness also manifests itself in the withholding of bread from the children. The lament is strongly reminiscent of that of daughter Jerusalem in $2_{11,12}$. It seems evident, therefore, that it is her voice that we hear in the present verse (cf the singular).

The precise translation of the ל preceding אַכְזָר remains something of a question. A number of exegetes opt for a ל-*emphaticum* [50] which is, however, barely recognisable in their translations.[51] Albrektson is inclined to see an analogy with (הָיְתָה) לְנִידָּה in 1_{8aB} with the 'silent' addition of the verbal form הָיְתָה, 'my daughter, my people has become heartless'. A corresponding construction can be found in Job 13_{12} and Dan 9_{16}. Although

[47] Compare the explanation of 2_{11c}.
[48] In his text critical apparatus to BHS.
[49] Cf 1988, 335f.
[50] Cf FNötscher, 'Zum emphatischen Lamed', VT III (1953), 372–380 and BKWaltke - MO'Conner, *An Introduction to Biblical Hebrew Syntax*, Winona Lake, Indiana 1990, § 11.2.10*i*.
[51] Gordis, Gottlieb and Westermann follow this option.

this solution is supported by the Syriac[52] it still appears to be an interpretation of the Hebrew text at hand. We understand the first colon to be a nominal clause and the ל as emphatic: 'so heartless'.[53]

The strophe concludes with a return to animal imagery. Within the strophe, the two animal metaphors constitute an inclusion. The image of wild animals suckling their young serves as a contrast while the behaviour of the ostrich is proposed as analogous with that of the people. It is also possible that the analogy is also related to the status of impurity (see below). Since the *k^etîḇ* כִּי עֵנִים is incomprehensible, the *q^erē* is universally accepted: כַּיְעֵנִים, plural of יַעֲנָה 'ostrich' (*Struthio camelus*; cf HAL 402) which likewise applies to the expression בַּת הַיַּעֲנָה (literally 'daughter of the wilderness') mentioned in Lev 11_{16} and Deut 14_{15}. There is a possible echo of the בַּת of בַּת־עַמִּי here. The preposition כְּ expresses comparison. Feliks rejects any identification with the ostrich on the basis of the fact that it does not dwell among ruins (BHH 1882f), and assumes that the term refers to some sort of owl. Keel, however, rightly points out: "Der Gegensatz ist nicht Stadt – Stadtruine, sondern bewohntes – unbewohntes Land."[54] On the basis of the comparison employed in this strophe we assume that the ostrich is the intended referent. Up to the beginning of this century, ostriches could be found in the desert regions of Palestine (cf BHH 1882f). The OT mentions the bird in a variety of places. The parallel with תַּן is striking since the ostrich also appears alongside the other wild animals in prophecies of doom: Isa 13_{21} (→ Babylon), 34_{13} (→ Edom), Jer 50_{39} (→ Babylon). Since it lives in uninhabited regions, the ostrich constitutes a sign of devastation and abandonment. See the song-response 5_3: cities are abandoned by their inhabitants.

The cry of the ostrich is quite similar to that of human lament (cf Mic 1_8 [אֵבֶל כִּבְנוֹת יַעֲנָה]), paralleling the howling of the wild animals. While it is clearly not the actual point of comparison, the fact that the ostrich is considered an impure animal may have a literary role to play. It is mentioned with some emphasis as such in Lev 11_{16} and Deut 14_{15}. The adjacent canticle of the second panel (Lam 4_{14f}) speaks of the impurity of the prophets and the priests. It seems reasonable to assume, therefore, that while the primary purpose of the comparison is to underline a similarity in behaviour between the inhabitants of Jerusalem and the ostrich, the bird's impure status also has some significance. A possible canticle response

[52] Cf text critical apparatus BHK.

[53] See HAL 485 sv לְ II.

[54] OKeel, *Jahwes Entgegnung an Ijob*, Göttingen 1978, 67 note 231.

might also be present here with 4_{5b} where the ash heaps (אַשְׁפַּתּוֹת) are scoured for food. The term אַשְׁפֹּת can also suggest the idea of 'dung'.[55]

While there may be a number of dimensions to the image employed here it is clear that the most important is the comparison in terms of behaviour, namely the presumed insensitivity of the ostrich. It is important, however, to view the comparison not from the perspective of the ostrich as a biological reality known to modern science but from the ancient understanding thereof (contra Van Selms) as we find it in Job 39_{16-21} (MT 39_{13-18}) which speaks of the female ostrich (= *רְנָנָה, derived from √רנן on the basis of the animal's mournful cry; cf 2_{19aA}). The ostrich is portrayed as an animal lacking in maternal love, which abandons its eggs in the sand and pays no attention to its chicks. Job 39_{19a} (MT 39_{16a}) leads us to the core of the comparison: at moments of danger, the ostrich deserts her chicks and runs away from them, probably in order to draw attention away from them and towards herself. The author of Job interpreted such behaviour as callous and insensitive. At the same time, however, since one cannot interpret the ostrich's flight in the face of danger as intentionally harmful, one must ajudge the not infrequent translation 'cruel' to be inaccurate.[56] The term is also used for lack of feeling and compassion.[57] Long term hunger can destroy a person's sensitivities even to the point of stifling their feelings towards their own children. It is evident from the following strophes that the same children have been abandoned to their own fate.

4a *The tongue of the infant cleaves* דָּבַק לְשׁוֹן יוֹנֵק
to the roof of his mouth from thirst. אֶל־חִכּוֹ בַּצָּמָא

It was evident at the end of the second song that many children had died of hunger. The surviving children are now tortured with severe hunger and thirst. Since many of the various scenes described by the poets may have taken place simultaneously, the present perfect (דָּבַק) need not be viewed as a retrospective glance (Van Selms) but can equally well be translated in the present.[58] The distressful situation, of which the גֶּבֶר is a part, continues unabated (see introduction). Thirst was already mentioned in the third song (3_{15B}) where the גֶּבֶר slaked his thirst with the sap of a poisonous plant. The same thirst now confronts the infants, the youngest group of children aged up to three years old (cf 2_{11cA} in which we find

55 Cf HAL 93 and Ezek 4_{12-15}.
56 Cf SV, NEB, and HAL 44.
57 See Job 30_{21}, Prov 5_9, Jer 6_{23}.
58 Cf 1_{1a} and GES-K § 106g.

the reverse order: first עוֹלֵל and then יוֹנֵק). The image of suckling infants is all the more intense when one realises that they depend for nourishment on their mother's milk. Their mothers, however, are physically no longer able to suckle them. The poets express their desperation more explicitly in $2_{11,12}$. In contrast with these verses, however, 4_4 expresses the element of (maternal) 'insensitivity' with greater emphasis (cf the preceding bicolon). While the mothers may (still) embrace their children in 2_{12} (see introduction to the said strophe), here hunger has robbed them of the last vestiges of their maternal instincts.

4b *Children ask for bread,* עוֹלָלִים שָׁאֲלוּ לֶחֶם
no one gives it them. פֹּרֵשׂ אֵין לָהֶם

The present bicolon is also reminiscent of 2_{12a} although one cannot uphold the suggestion that 4_{4b} is a contraction thereof. Both cola are more or less the same length and close comprison reveals significant differences between them. A certain vitality was still evident in 2_{12} in the appeal for corn and wine which emerged from the direct speech of the children. 4_{4b} speaks its own less vivid language. Hunger has driven off every last vestige of vitality. With their last breath, the children ask only for what matters, bread. The second colon depicts the apathy which has taken hold of every survivor. In normal circumstances no one would be able to resist the appeal of an infant for food but these are not normal circumstances and no one pays the slightest attention. In fact, no one cares about anyone beyond themselves. Young or old, parents or children, it no longer matters. Every man for himself! Such dreadful affliction can be found in pictorial form in Keel.[59]

5a *Those who once ate delicacies,* הָאֹכְלִים לְמַעֲדַנִּים
(move) emaciated through the streets; נָשַׁמּוּ בַּחוּצוֹת

מַעֲדַנִּים is a *plurale tantum*[60] 'delicacies', also found in Gen 49_{20}. The preceding preposition לְ serves here as an indication of the accusative.[61] The colon literally reads: 'the eaters (participle) of delicacies'. The extent of the famine is made explicit via the harsh contrast of the funeral lament, a further indication that the surviving children are very much a death's door. The poets juxtapose more pleasant former times with the horror of the

[59] Cf OKeel, *Die Welt der altorientalischen Bildsymbolik und das Alte Testament*, Zürich-Einsiedeln-Köln-Neukirchen-Vluyn 1977², figure 88 on page 66.

[60] GES-K § 124*f*.

[61] Cf HAL 485 sv לְ (21) and GES-K § 117*n*.

present situation: Zion's once pampered children (cf 2_{20bB}), once spoiled with the tastiest things, are now weary with hunger. Our translation of נָשַׁמּוּ requires some explanation. KBL 989 proposes the root √שׁמם (*niph'al* with human persons as subject): 'horrified' or 'bewildered', the cause of which can include destruction/divine judgement. It is clear that such an association is present in Lamentations (cf 1_{16c} and 3_{11B}), particularly in the present context. The primary focus here, however, is not the dreadful sight of devastation which can leave a person stunned and bewildered, but rather the physical concretisation of divine judgement, namely hunger and starvation. The locative designation 'through the streets' (בַּחוּצוֹת) anticipates the following bicolon and indicates movement: the emaciated children of Zion are no longer to be found in their homes. Hunger has driven them onto the streets, and ultimately towards the rubbish heaps, in search of food (cf 1_{19}). The poets depict this painful scene with further brutal contrast.

5b *those once cared for in scarlet* הָאֱמֻנִים עֲלֵי תוֹלָע
now cling to the ash heaps. חִבְּקוּ אַשְׁפַּתּוֹת

Niph'al and *hiph'il* forms of √אמן are relatively frequent although one can only find participial forms of the *qal*. The latter, moreover, appear to have a slightly different meaning, which is why HAL (62) takes √אמן II as its point of departure here: 'to be cared for' (by a wet nurse).[62] One might ask whether such an interpretation of the term justifies the acceptance of a √אמן II, given that one might include the notion of 'caring for' in the trust and constancy which is characteristic of √אמן I.[63] In any event, (הָ)אֱמֻנִים is a substantivised *qal* plural participle. It refers to the children of Zion who were once faithfully nursed and cared for with great luxury. Luxury is evident in the use of the term תוֹלָע or 'scarlet', a crimson red cloth with vivid and striking intensity.[64] Such material was extremely expensive, given the labour intensive collection of dye from the purple snail.[65] Women coveted it for dress making (II Sam 1_{24}, Jer 4_{30}). Evidently blankets and sheets were made of scarlet and the children were wrapped in them to be carried in the arms of their faithful nursemaids. עֲלֵי is an older, poetic form of the preposition עַל and can mean both 'on' and 'in'.[66] The

62 Cf Num 11_{12}, Ruth 4_{16}, II Sam 4_4, II Kgs $10_{1,5}$, Est 2_7, Isa 49_{23}.
63 See TWAT I 316 (Jepsen).
64 Cf Gen 38_{28}, Josh 2_{21}.
65 Cf RGradwohl, *Die Farben im Alten Testament*, BZAW 83, Berlin 1963, 73–78.
66 Cf BL 24 note 1 and HAL 780 sv עַל II (1a).

present situation, however, is one of the harshest contrasts: those once cared for are now abandoned; those once lovingly embraced now embrace the asheaps; those once spoiled with delicacies now rummage in the ashes for disgarded or half burnt leftovers; those once privileged in red, now pressed (cf 3_{16B}) into the gray ash. The גֶּבֶר faces the same fate. See the explanation of the song-response 3_{15f}; for the ash heaps see 4_{3b}.

Canticle III (Lam 4_6)

Content/theme: *Worse than Sodom*

Literary argumentation: In delimiting the second canticle we mentioned a number of literary arguments in support of the unity thereof. A first glance at Lam 4_6, however, introduces the temptation to review one's understanding of the boundaries of the preceding canticle. To be precise, בַּת־עַמִּי in 4_{6aA} is also found in 4_{3bA} and would appear to form an inclusion around a larger canticle running from 4_3 to 4_6. On closer inspection, however, a number of arguments emerge which run counter to this solution. In the first instance, given the numerous literary associations, there is clearly a very strong internal coherence between strophes 4_3 to 4_5 while 4_6 only has one single connection with the preceding strophe, namely בַּת־עַמִּי (4_{6aA}). Secondly, since there is clearly no allusion being made to the theme of the hungry and thirsty children of Zion, there is an evident distinction at the level of content. Thirdly, the expression בַּת־עַמִּי is also to be found in 4_{10bB} which creates the possibility that it functions at a higher level within the song as a whole. Finally, the following strophes reveal neither literary nor thematic associations with 4_6. For all these reasons, we are inclined to view Lam 4_6 as a strophe apart which functions, at the same time, as a so-called mini-canticle within the fourth song, a not unfamilair phenomenon in Hebrew poetry.[67]

The absence of literary and thematic associations with what precedes and follows this mini-canticle does not mean that coherence is absent at every level. On the contrary. In our literary analysis of the first canto we saw evidence that the sixth strophe stood at the heart of a concentric structure and provided the central formulation of the disaster which is further elaborated in the other canticles via a variety of concrete themes.[68]

---

[67] MCAKorpel – JCdMoor, 'Fundamentals of Ugaritic and Hebrew Poetry', in: *The Structural Analysis of Biblical and Canaanite Poetry*, (eds WvdMeer & JCdMoor) JSOT suppl series 74, Sheffield 1988, 43; WGEWatson, *Classical Hebrew Poetry. A Guide to its Techniques*, JSOT suppl series 26, Sheffield 1984, 162.

6a *Yes, greater is the iniquity of my daughter, my people,* וַיִּגְדַּל עֲוֹן בַּת־עַמִּי
than the sin of Sodom, מֵחַטַּאת סְדֹם

The root גדל together with the preposition מִן indicates comparison at the level of magnitude (cf I Kgs 1_{47}). The imperfect consecutive וַיִּגְדַּל connects verse 6 with the preceding canticle (4_{3-5}) since the comparison is related to the distress portrayed therein, expressed in the translation with the affirmative 'Yes'.[69] For the meaning of the term עָוֹן cf the exegesis of 2_{14b} and for the term חַטַּאת cf 1_{8a}. The particular form of the latter term is only found in the fourth song ($4_{6,13,22}$). Koch notes with respect to the different nominal forms derived from the root חטא: "Zwischen den einzelnen Formen dürften Bedeutungsdifferenzen bestehen, auf die bisher die Forschung noch nicht eingegangen ist."[70] Exegetes not infrequently give in to the temptation to substitute 'iniquity' and 'sin' with 'punishment' and 'lot' as more appropriate to the context. Van Selms, for example, proposes the following: "And the punishment which the daughter of my people had to undergo was worse than that which was inflicted upon Sodom." Thenius, Löhr and Gordis follow a similar line of thought. In terms of our understanding of the concepts in question, however, this approach implies a reduction in content: 'sin' and 'iniquity' can include the consequences thereof. See 3_{39B} and also Lam 5_7: 'bearing the עָוֹן of others' in which 'sin' is then the cause of distress and affliction.[71] The greater the sin the greater the affliction it brings about. In light of the following bicolon, it would appear that the accent in the present strophe is being placed primarily on the consequences of sin.

In order to reveal the magnitude of the disaster and its consequences, the poets employ the sin of Sodom and its consequences for that city as a comparison. In its later 'Wirkungsgeschichte', the sin of Sodom is primarily associated with homosexuality on the basis of Gen 19. A review of the content of the Sodom tradition within the OT alone, however, shows homosexuality to be an uncharacteristic and subordinate element. This in contrast to the many other motifs, such as the overthrow of the city, the hail of fire and brimstone and the subsequent cheerless and inhospitable nature of the salty and infertile territory around the Dead Sea, elements which constitute a stereotypical perspective of catastrophe within the con-

---

[68] For the literary analysis of the larger units in Lamentations cf 1988, 341–346.
[69] See for the comparative use of מִן GES-K § 133a.
[70] See TWAT II 859.
[71] Cf Ps 31_{11}, 38_{4-6}, 39_9, 40_{13}; cf also 1983, 268–270.

text of the announcement of judgement.[72] Such constitutive elements of the Sodom tradition are likewise to be found in Lamentations: for example the pouring out of fire ($1_{13,20}$) and the 'overthrow' mentioned here in 4_{6b}.

The prophecy of judgement also refers to the sin of Sodom, comparing it with that of Israel.[73] Wherever the comparison is made, it is clear that Sodom constitutes the lowest point of sin which Jerusalem and her prophets have managed to equal. Ezek 16_{47} is alone in accusing Jerusalem of having gone further in her sin than Sodom, the sins in question being characterised somewhat surprisingly as that of pride and social injustice (Ezek 16_{49}; likewise in Isa 1_{17} and 3_9 and the accusation of the prophets in Jer 23_{14}).

As we noted above with respect to Lam 2_{14}, for example, the influence of Ezekiel can also be presumed in the present accusation. The question remains, however, as to whether such influence simultaneously implies a confession of guilt on Zion's part in regard to social injustice. One cannot exclude this possibility, although 2_{14} (not disclosed) and 3_{40} (self-examination) would caution prudence in drawing any conclusions in this direction. Association with the following bicolon leads us to suspect that the poets are primarily interested in the fate of Sodom as the ground of their comparison rather than the content of her sin.

6b *that (city) overthrown as in the wink of an eye,* הַהֲפוּכָה כְמוֹ־רָגַע
without the agency of (human) hand. וְלֹא־חָלוּ בָהּ יָדָיִם

The standard expression for the destruction of Sodom is employed here, namely the 'overthrow' or 'overturn' (√הפך, part pass *qal*).[74] כְּמוֹ means 'as'; literally: 'the as in a wink of an eye overturned one',[75] focusing on the suddeness of Sodom's overthrow and destruction. This is expressed in Gen 19_{19} in the haste with which Lot and his family are forced to depart from the city. The term רֶגַע 'wink of an eye', however, is not used in Gen 19 and apart from its present use in Lam 4_6 it is to be found nowhere else in the Sodom tradition. The poets were thus able to use the 'instantaneous' notion of destruction/punishment in the present context because it is an inherent aspect of God's judgement.[76] Since Sodom was struck by God's

[72] Cf, for example, Deut 29_{22f}, Isa 1_9, 13_{19}, Jer 49_{18}, 50_{40}, Am 4_{11}, Zeph 2_9.
[73] See, for example, Isa 1_{10} (cf 1_{17}), 3_9, Jer 23_{14} (sins of the prophets[!]; cf 4_{13}).
[74] Cf Gen $19_{21,25}$, Deut 29_{22} etcetera.
[75] Cf Brockelmann § 109*e*.
[76] Cf Ex 33_5, Num 16_{21}, $16_{44,45}$ (MT 17_{10}), Ps 6_{11}, 73_{19}, Isa 47_9.

judgement this must have happened instantaneously, really in the 'wink of an eye'.

The meaning of the verb form חָלוּ in the second colon is the subject of some disagreement. Rudolph derives it from √חלה I 'to become weak', emends יָדַיִם (hands) to יְלָדִים (children) and translates: "ohne daß Kinder darin leiden mußten." His emendation, however, is difficult to defend. Kraus derives the form from √חיל I 'to tremble' and translates: "ohne daß Hände in ihm bebten.", to be understood as a further explication of רֶגַע: it all happened so fast that no one had time to be scared.

We opt for derivation from √חול, *qal* pf 3 pl, meaning 'to turn oneself against'[77] which fits well in the present context. From a literal perspective we are then left with the translation: 'did not turn herself against her hands', that is without human agency.[78] Reference is frequently made in this context to Dan $2_{34,45}$, 8_{25} (to which we can add Job 34_{20}). Understood thus, the text emphasises that the overthrow of Sodom was God's work alone. We are then confronted with a contrasting element with regard to the fate of Jerusalem which did not fall in an instant as a result of God's direct intervention but endured slow devastation at the hands of an (in)human enemy.[79] Jerusalem was not granted a sudden and merciful death but was forced to endure a long process of torture. Without mercy, her enemies left her to starve and, in light of the present sub-canto, it would appear that both the land and its inhabitants continue to suffer.[80] Jerusalem, whose sin was greater than that of Sodom (Ezek 16_{47}), must thus endure a fate worse than that of Sodom.

One might ask whether this is only an observation on the part of the poets or whether they actually experienced a contradiction in YHWH's behaviour. Does YHWH really take pleasure in attenuated suffering? The mention of such suffering suggests an implicit echo of 3_{33}: YHWH does not oppress and afflict human persons according to his heart. If it had been YHWH's sole intention to put an end to Judah's iniquity then a swift and merciful death such as that of Sodom would clearly have sufficed. On the other hand, this would have implied that the relationship between YHWH and his people had reached a final end. Evidently this was not (yet) the case! Such deferment was a source of hope (cf 3_{22}). The implicit question

[77] Based on its occurrence in II Sam 3_{29}, Hos 11_6, Jer 23_{19} and 30_{23}.

[78] Cf HAL 285 sv √חול and also Albrektson, Gordis and Kaiser among others.

[79] See 1_{7c} and compare II Sam 24_{14} (// I Chron 21_{13}).

[80] Cf also $5_{4,5,9}$ and 1983, 269f.

mark behind the seriousness of their suffering and YHWH's involvement therein is only made explicit in Lam V (cf, however, 2_{20-22}). In the meantime, however, the endurance of pain continues undiminished. In this light, one can then explain the parallel with 4_{17} from the second panel of the diptych where it is apparent that there is no help to be found in this greatest of afflictions.

Canticle I (4_{7-9})

Content/theme: *Starvation also affects the princes*

Literary argumentation:

inclusions:	נְזִירֶיהָ (7aA) // שֶׁהֵם (9bA)
	סַפִּיר — מִפְּנִינִים (7b) // טוֹבִים (9aA)
responses:	זַכּוּ (7aA) \\ חָשַׁךְ (8aA)
	נְזִירֶיהָ (7aA) // מְחֻלָלֵי רָעָב (9aB)
	חָלָב — שֶׁלֶג (7a) \\ שְׁחוֹר (8aA)
	עֶצֶם (7bA) // עַצְמָם (8bA)
concat:	גִּזְרָתָם (7bB) // תָּאֳרָם (8aA)
	יָבֵשׁ הָיָה כָעֵץ ... צָפַד עוֹרָם (8b) // מְחֻלָלֵי רָעָב (9aB)
	also via 3 m pl suffixes
asson/allit:	מֵחָלָב (7aB) // מְחֻלָלֵי רָעָב (9aB)

7a *Once were her nobles purer than snow,* זַכּוּ נְזִירֶיהָ מִשֶּׁלֶג
more lustrous than milk, צַחוּ מֵחָלָב

As part of the outcome of sin mentioned in 4_6, the poets refer once again to the consequences of the terrible famine which, having taken hold of the children (4_{3-5}), now reaches out to the aristocracy. Here too, the poets observe the sharp contrasts which the famine has brought about in their entire existence. The seventh strophe is entirely devoted to a description of the former splendour and magnificence of the nobles of the people.

We understand the term נְזִירֶיהָ as 'her nobles' with the suffix clearly referring back to בַּת־עַמִּי in 4_6. In the present context, it is unlikely that נָזִיר should be interpreted as 'Nazirean'.[81] Indeed the external splendour and magnificence portrayed here hardly befits a description of a 'Nazirean'. נָזִיר can also signify someone who holds high office.[82] Commentators most frequently translate the term with 'princes' or 'nobles'.[83] In line with

[81] Cf LXX and Peshitta.
[82] Cf Gen 49_{26} and Deut 33_{16} as well as KBL 604 and HAL 645 sv נָזִיר (3).

Ehrlich, however, Rudolph considers it improbable that the princes would have suffered so much from the famine that their appearance would fit that described in 4_8. He thus emends נְזִירֶיהָ to read נְעָרֶיהָ ‘her young men’ [84] but there are no textual witnesses to defend such an intervention in the text. Given the context of Lamentations as a whole, Rudolph's assumptions are clearly mistaken. Everyone, from king to infant, has been affected by this disaster (2_{9-11}) and no one has been able to escape the famine.[85] It is evident throughout the text that the poets are employing harsh contrasts as a means of describing this catastrophic situation and here is no exception. It even seems possible to identify the גֶּבֶר (at the literary level) with one of these נְזִרִים; see 3_{4A}. Hunger is the greatest equaliser. We opt, therefore, for the translation ‘nobles’. The poets' choice of words in this regard appears to exhibit a level of consistency within the songs at the level of content. They were unable to use שָׂרִים ‘princes’ because they had already been driven from the city (1_6), carried into exile (2_9) or even hanged (5_{12}).

The splendour and magnificence of these nobles was once pure and bright. זַכּוּ = *qal* pf 3m pl (cf BL 429 *k*) from √זכך = ‘to be bright/pure’, employed in Job 15_{15} and 25_5 for the brilliance of the heavens and the stars. Besides its external meaning the root also has an interior nuance: purity of heart and conduct.[86]

The comparison with the whiteness of snow reminds one of Isa 1_{18} and Ps 51_9 (both employing the same comparison) where the washing away of sins suggests inner purity. It does not seem accidental, therefore, that the song response in 2_{7aA} refers to the destruction of YHWH's altar, whereby the restoration of that purity was made an impossibility. The mention of ‘snow’ and ‘scarlet’ in Isa 1_{18} suggests the presence of a word-pair (indeed within this sub-canto תּוֹלָע (4_{5bA}) and שֶׁלֶג (4_{7aA}) constitute an inclusion. One can assume, therefore, that external purity and magnificence also had an interior dimension which was reflected in a person's appearance. All this was to a superlative degree since the brilliance and purity of the nobility was greater than that of snow. One is left with the question, therefore, as to whether this whiteness (only) had to do with their clothing. Apart from the fact that white is only mentioned late in the OT as the characteristic colour of festival clothing,[87] the already noted dimension

[83] See, for example, Albrektson, Davidson and Harrison.

[84] Cf text criticical apparatus BHS. See also Gross.

[85] Cf 1_{11aA} (כָּל־עַמָּהּ) and 1_{19b} (כֹּהֲנַי וּזְקֵנַי); cf also Jer 38_9.

[86] Cf Job 8_6, 11_4, 33_9, Prov 16_2, 20_{11}.

[87] See Qoh 9_8 and TWAT IV 453 (Ringgren).

of interior purity argues against such a notion as does the parallel with 'bones' in the following bicolon.

The phrase 'more lustrous than milk' repeats the first colon but adds a degree of warmth absent from the comparison with the cold purity of snow. Milk was also used to signify pure whiteness (cf Gen 49_{12}) and served in Song 5_{12} as a designation for the whites of the eye which fits with √צחח which stands for bright but warm shining (cf HAL 955). Similar terminology is used in Song 5_{10} in praise of the male lover (radiant [צַח] and ruddy [אָדוֹם, cf the following bicolon]).

7bA *red as coral (their) bones,* אָדְמוּ עֶצֶם מִפְּנִינִים

If one were to take the statement 'their bones redder than corals' literally then one is likely to be left somewhat nonplussed.[88] Of course, under normal circumstances bones cannot be seen. For this reason, therefore, we must understand עֶצֶם differently, namely as a reference to the whole person, as was also the case in 3_{4B}. Emendation – cf text critical apparatus BHK – is incorrect and unnecessary (cf the response with עַצְמָם in 4_{8bA}). How then should we understand פְּנִינִים? Most commentators opt for 'corals' although HAL 891 does not exclude the possibility that it might mean 'pearls'. The present circumstances, supported by the verb אדם, *qal*, 'to be red' and the parallel with Song 5_{10}, seem to call for the translation 'coral' (*plurale tantum*). Coral was considered particularly costly,[89] although the present comparison clearly focuses on impressions of colour rather than value: "אָדְמוּ bezeichnet hier (= Lam 4_{7bA}) das gesunde, gepflegte Aussehen eines Menschen (im Gegensatz zum kranken, ungepflegten), vielleicht helle, bräunlich-rötliche (natürlich nicht »rote«!) Hautfarbe. Dieser Teint galt zugleich als Merkmahl besonderer Vornehmheit, wohl weil er sich vom landläufigen dunkelbraunen, sonnenverbrannten der Hirten und Bauern (cf Cant 1:6) abhob...".[90] One might ask whether such a literal interpretation can be maintained in the remainder of the description.

7bB *as azure their countenance.* סַפִּיר גִּזְרָתָם

The meaning of גִּזְרָה is difficult to establish. The noun is derived from √גזר I which has the basic meaning 'to cut'.[91] In Ezek 41_{12-15} and $42_{1,10,13}$, it

[88] Cf the reading of the LXX which leaves עֶצֶם untranslated, a fact which supports the correctness of the MT.

[89] Cf Prov 3_{15}, 8_{11}, 20_{15}, 31_{10}, Job 28_{18}.

[90] Cf RGradwohl, *Die Farben im Alten Testament*, BZAW 83, Berlin 1963, 10.

[91] Cf I Chron 3_{26}.

indicates a 'seperate' (cut off) space (NRSV 'yard'). By inference, commentators suggest that גִּזְרָה has to do with contours, or where human persons are concerned, form or countenance.[92] Such an interpretation seems appropriate to the present context. It is clear that גִּזְרָה does not refer to distinct parts of the body or 'limbs' as Albrektson and Boecker, among others, would propose. Other commenators, such as Budde and Haller, suggest that we read the term in association with the blue colour of azure stone and see in it a reference to human veins. The relationship with √גזר I, however, would then become unclear (veins cutting through the skin?) and – although this might be subjective – one wonders what the beauty of such an image might be. From a physical perspective, 'blue' veins suggest old age. In the last analysis, the comparisons employed by the poets indicate that they have the entire person in mind.

The countenance of the nobility is characterised as סַפִּיר. This does not refer to saphire (according to the Graeco-Roman division), but rather to the softer *lapis lazuli*, a costly, transparent blue mineral in which golden yellow particles of pyrites could be seen.[93] The impression is one of brilliance and clarity. Once again the description of the male lover in Song 5 offers the closest parallels. See 5_{14}. In 5_{11} the terms כֶּתֶם and פָּז are also used in a comparison.[94] The number of points of contact between the present text and Song 5 suggests that the poets have borrowed from a classical description of beauty (of a lover) in order to indicate how magnificent the countenance of the nobility once was.

One might ask whether the comparisons employed constitute a literal reference to the former physical condition of the nobility. Aalders and Rudolph paraphrase here, suggesting the image of human(s) (cheeks of) 'milk and blood'. They are left with a problem, however, concerning the blue colouring of the סַפִּיר, which explains why they opt for the radiance of the סַפִּיר as the point of comparison. Such an option entails a degree of inconsistency with the use of the colours red and white in the preceding cola. It is possible that the bright blue colouring had to do with decorative pieces of clothing (cf, once again, Song 5_{14}). It is indeed possible to assume a similar usage to that of Song 5_{10-16} in which the countenance and physique of the male lover is described. Gerleman does not consider it possible that the lover himself was the actual physical model for the de-

[92] Thus, for example, Keil and Rudolph; cf Gordis and HAL 180.
[93] Cf Job 28_6 and HAL 722.
[94] Cf Lam 4_{1-2}; the difference between both types of gold is unclear.

scription. In his opinion, beauty is presented here in a stereotypical fashion according to concepts current in the artistic world of the time: “Die ganze Beschreibung, die in Bezug auf einem lebendigen Menschen unrealistisch und bizarr anmutet, wird auf einmal zutreffend und richtig, wenn wir sie als Schilderung eines Rundbildes lesen. Zwischen dem Jüngling und dem Beschreibungslied im Hohenlied steht die Menschendarstellung der bildenden Kunst, und zwar der Kunst Ägyptens.” [95] Statues and portraits in ancient art did not always conform to the human reality represented but were often rendered as aesthetic stereotypes. In Egyptian art, for example, old people were often presented as physically youthful.[96] Thus the present text is stating – no more yet no less – that the accepted extremes of beauty were once applicable to the nobles of Jerusalem. It is evident from the following strophe that the poets have chosen those comparisons from the stock available to them, which most lent themselves to portraying the contrast associated with the lament or funeral dirge.

8a *Now blacker than soot is their appearance;* חָשַׁךְ מִשְּׁחוֹר תָּאֳרָם
they are unrecognisable in the streets. לֹא נִכְּרוּ בַּחוּצוֹת

The poets portray an initial contrast by juxtaposing ‘present black’ and ‘former white’ in an antithetical response. תֹּאַר means ‘countenance’ or ‘appearance’ (cf HAL 1545). The term for black, שְׁחוֹר, is a *hapax legomenon* referring to charcoal black.[97] The verb שׁחר I ‘to become black’/‘to darken’ is a denominative of the noun (cf HAL 1359). With respect to the skin see Job 30$_{30}$ and the comparable text in Song 1$_{5,6}$ (שְׁחוֹרָה) with its (negative) reference to sun burned skin. Given the comparative usage, the noun שְׁחוֹר must stand for a sort of jet black material, often tentatively translated as ‘soot’. The idea of charcoal black would tend to support such a translation. The colour black applies to the ‘countenance’/‘appearance’ = תֹּאַר, the use of which in this context is already a *contradictio in terminis* since the term is almost always found in relation to exterior beauty. See Gen 29$_{17}$, 39$_{6}$, 41$_{18}$, Deut 21$_{11}$, I Sam 16$_{18}$, 25$_{3}$, I Kgs 1$_{6}$, Est 2$_{7}$. In the two remaining texts in which the term appears we are confronted with a different sort of exterior: Gen 41$_{19}$ (the thin, ugly cows) and Isa 52$_{14}$ and 53$_{2}$ (the hideous appearance of the עֶבֶד יְהוָה).

What might the cause be of this dark and repulsive exterior? In contrast to Song 1$_{5}$, the colouration of the nobility is due to hunger rather than

[95] GGerleman, *Ruth. Das Hohelied*, BKAT XVIII, Neukirchen-Vluyn 1965, 69.
[96] Cf Gerleman, 69–71 and 171–178.
[97] Cf LXX with ὑπὲρ ἀσβόλην and the Vulgata with *super carbones*; cf also HAL 1352.

the sun. One might then ask whether this state is the physical result of long term hunger and nothing more. Gradwohl's suggestion that the blackening of the skin is a symptom of undernourishment is not easy to accept.[98] While hunger (and illness) can make one appear dull and grey (cf Job 30_{30}), it certainly does not follow that one can become (charcoal) black from such a condition. Furthermore, the contrast being proposed by the poets has to do with the nobility's entire appearance not just the physical. In other words, their once well-tended and magnificent appearance has gone without a trace. Note the inclusion within the sub-canto between תּוֹלָע (4_{5bA}) // שֶׁלֶג (4_{7aA}), a fixed word pair judging from Isa 1_{18}. The children once splendid and clothed in scarlet now embrace the ash heaps (4_{5bB}). It would seem obvious, therefore, that besides the children and others, the nobility were also forced to comb the ash heaps for food. Rooting and grubbing around in ash has turned what was once pure and magnificent into something soiled and black. Given the images in 4_{4a} and 5_4 purification with water was clearly out of the question. Thus the nobility has become unrecognisable. Even in terms of appearance, hunger has made everyone equal (cf 1_{19bc}). They no longer stand out in the streets. The root נכר I (*niph'al* pf) employed here contains the idea of 'strangeness', 'foreignness'. The nobility of Judah and Jerusalem have become strangers to their compatriots.

8b *Their skin lies shrivelled on their bones,* צָפַד עוֹרָם עַל־עַצְמָם
dried up, become as wood. יָבֵשׁ הָיָה כָעֵץ

In the present bicolon the poets focus specifically on the physical results of hunger. √צפד is a *hapax* but its meaning is not unclear. Extreme weight less has made the very bones of these once healthy individuals visible for all to see and their withered skin is shrivelled together upon them. The singular + suffix 3m pl can be understood as a collective 'bones'.[99] It remains unclear, however, what one should consider to be the subject of the verbs היה and יבשׁ in the second colon. There are a number of possibilities: skin or bones; LXX suggests either the nobility or their bones (cf τὰ ὀστέα αὐτῶν) witness the plural forms ἐξηράνθησαν and ἐγενήθησαν, although this does not find support in the MT. Although it is possible to say that a person's bones are dried up,[100] the skin would appear to be the most appropriate subject in the present context, especially since

[98] Gradwohl, 53.
[99] Cf GES-K § 123a,*b*.
[100] Cf Prov 17_{22} and the lament of the people in Ezek 37_{11} (a metaphor for death).

the poetic description is focusing on exterior things. The image itself is not difficult to understand: hunger and thirst cause the skin to dry out and wither. Further support for this interpretation can be found in the identical complaint of the people in 5_{10} together with that of the גֶּבֶר in 3_{4A}. The latter agreement contributes to our belief that the גֶּבֶר does not only share the lot of the nobility, he is actually, at the literary level, one of their number.

9a *Those pierced by the sword were better off* טוֹבִים הָיוּ חַלְלֵי־חֶרֶב
than those pierced by hunger, מֵחַלְלֵי רָעָב

If a person's bones have become visible through their withered skin then it is evident that he or she has undergone a prolonged period of suffering and is close to death from starvation. The others, those who fell by the sword (cf 1_{20c} and 2_{21b}), were better off. It is a universal human belief that a quick death is to be chosen above a time of prolonged pain and suffering. The expression מֵחַלְלֵי רָעָב 'those pierced by hunger' is considered by some to be corrupt[101] since such a figurative use of the term is not found elsewhere. Van Selms follows a similar line of thought in this regard. Gottlieb is correct in pointing out, however, that the figurative significance of the expression is guaranteed by its parallel חַלְלֵי־חֶרֶב. One might point, in addition, to the figurative use of כֶּחָלָל in 2_{12b}, a text which Guillaume does not consider. For the comparative use of מִן see GES-K § 133a.

9b *than those who waste away, brought down* שֶׁהֵם יָזוּבוּ מְדֻקָּרִים
by cropless land. מִתְּנוּבֹת שָׂדָי

In relation to מֵחַלְלֵי רָעָב the present bicolon is also frequently viewed as corrupt.[102] The reason for this lies in the use of the root דקר. This verb means 'to pierce'/'to fell' and is generally used literally,[103] while here we are expected to read it in a figurative sense. For this reason Rudolph considers it to be a synonym of חַלְלֵי־חֶרֶב and understands it to refer to those actually felled by the sword whose sudden death constitutes the actual point of the reference. In order to arrive at this position, Rudolph has been forced to make substantial emendations to the text: שֶׁהֵם יָזוּ בִמְקֹר דָּמָם מֵתוּ בְחִשׁ ("weil jene, <den Quell ihres Blutes verspritztend, / schnell dahinstarben>."). The Masoretic text, however, can be allowed to stand as it is if one is

[101] Cf ACohen, 'Lamentations 4:9' AJSL 27 (1910/11), 190–191 and AGuillaume, 'A Note on Lamentations IV 9', ALUOS 4 (1962–63), 47–48.

[102] Cf text critical apparatus of BHS and the detailed discussion in Albrektson.

[103] Cf Num 25_8, Judg 9_{54}, I Sam 31_4, Zech 12_{10} etcetera.

willing to accept a figurative meaning for the verbs employed in this bicolon also. This is quite possible with the verb זוב which basically means 'to flow'.[104] יָזוּבוּ can then be seen to refer to those who died a slow death from starvation. שֶׁ serves as a conjunctive particle with 3m pl suffix (cf HAL 1271). In this case the *pu'al* participle מְדֻקָּרִים can also be understood in the same figurative fashion as חָלָל. Albrektson points to the parallelism between חֲלָלִים and מְדֻקָּרִים in Jer 51_4. Thus the מְדֻקָּרִים here in Lam 4_{9b} must correspond with the double חַלְלֵי in the preceding bicolon. The figurative meaning of the verb is thereby safeguarded (cf the verb 'fell' with similar possibilities of interpretation). The fact that the inhabitants of Jerusalem had no harvest (תְּנוּבָה) from the open fields – שָׂדַי includes fields, vineyards etcetera (cf Jer $40_{10,12}$ and HAL 1218f) – at their disposal, even after the fall of Jerusalem, has already been explained in our exegesis of 1_{11a}.

Canticle V (Lam 4_{10-11})

Content/theme: *The wasting away of both children and Zion*

Literary argumentation: Given the at first sight obvious thematic difference between the י-strophe and the כ-strophe it would appear that as such they do not belong together. As a cumulative description of the famine, 4_{10} fits better with the preceding and thematically identical verses 4_{7-9}. The theme of Zion's destruction in 4_{11}, on the other hand, seems to be an entirely different subject. Upon closer inspection, however, this appears to be something of an illusion since one can in fact speak of substantial agreement between the two verses. One literary indication that 4_{10} belongs to the present and not the preceding canticle can be detected in the alternation of subject. Lam 4_{7-9} focuses primarily on the nobility while 4_{10} turns to the mothers of Jerusalem. There is also an evident change of voice (cf בַּת־עַמִּי in 4_{10bB}). Given the association with the complaint in 2_{20b} it seems most likely that daughter Jerusalem is the speaker. In addition, there are no clear external parallelisms between 4_{7-9} and 4_{10}. The only literary connection between the strophes concerned consists of the concatenation הָיוּ (9aA) // הָיוּ (10bA). In contrast to this, 4_{10} and 4_{11} are evidently closely related to one another from the literary perspective:

inclusions: בְּשְׁלוּ (10aB) // וַיַּצֶּת־אֵשׁ (11aA)
בְּשְׁלוּ (10aB) // וַתֹּאכַל (11bB)

[104] Cf Jer 49_4 'ebbing away of power'.

responses: שֶׁבֶר בַּת־עַמִּי (10bB) // תֹּאכַל יְסוֹדֹתֶיהָ (11bB)
לְבָרוֹת (10bA) // תֹּאכַל (11bB)
עַמִּי (10bB) // צִיּוֹן (11bA)

Attention to the use of the verbs אכל and בשל makes the cohesion between the two strophes quite apparent at the level of content. The tenth strophe reports that the famine is so severe that even the tender-hearted women of Jerusalem are forced to eat their dead children. The eleventh strophe presents an analogous scenario in response: YHWH has set a fire in Zion, whom he loves, in order to devour her!

10a *The hands of tender-hearted women* יְדֵי נָשִׁים רַחֲמָנִיּוֹת
boil their children. בִּשְּׁלוּ יַלְדֵיהֶן

In similar fashion to the second song, the poets now turn their focus, here in the heart of the fourth song as a whole, upon the suffering of the women of Jerusalem as the lowest ebb in their experience of starvation. With the harshest of contrasts they describe the horrors of the event. At first the women are characterised as רַחֲמָנִיּוֹת 'tender-hearted', a fem pl of *רַחֲמָנִי, a *hapax* (cf HAL 1137). While it is true that the form only occurs here, associations with √רחם and רַחֲמִים are clear nevertheless. We are confronted with a group of women who are full of maternal feelings for their children. These very feelings, however, are the source of the enormous tensions set up by what the famine is forcing them to do: to cook the flesh of their dead offspring. Their revulsion at the deed they are describing (cf II Kgs 6_{29}) leads the poets to make the women's 'hands' the subject of בִּשְּׁלוּ and not the women themselves. Nowhere else in the OT can we find anything other than persons as the active subject of √בשל. By using יְדֵי, the poets render the mechanistic character of the women's actions: their hands are at work but they themselves are not really present. One might suggest that the form of the alphabetic acrostic forced the poets to use this formulation but one can also insist that there are many more words beginning with י. On the other hand, one can admire the poetic skill of those who were able to choose the precise form to express the feelings they desired to communicate. It is also apparent how the poets were able to add new accents to the thematic repetition of these verses. What is happening here in 4_{10a} was also related in 2_{20b}. Where 2_{20b} placed the accent on the once well-cared-for and even spoiled children of Zion who are now confronted with this dreadful hunger, 4_{10a} focuses on the emotions of their mothers and what they are forced by the same hunger to do to their dead children.

10b *They have become their food of solace* הָיוּ לְבָרוֹת לָמוֹ
in the destruction of my daughter, my people. בְּשֶׁבֶר בַּת־עַמִּי

(לְ)בָרוֹת can be understood in two different ways: as *pi'el* infinitive of √ברה I + preposition לְ with final meaning; translated: 'they are intended to be eaten as food of solace' (cf HAL 148 sv ברה I) or as a substantive derived from √ברה I[105] which is the alternative we opt for in our translation. The meaning becomes clear in II Sam $13_{5,6,10}$. It is a question of a type of food intended to build up the strength of a sick person or bring solace to someone who had endured great sorrow.[106] In addition to this, the serving of a meal was part of the ritual of condolence during which one provided support for the berieved by offering them the bread and the cup of consolation.[107] A combination of both elements appears to be present here: the only food of solace available was the flesh of the dead children, the loss of whom was the very source of their sorrow. In other words, the women ate their own sorrow, their only means of survival. A more tragic contrast is hard to imagine.

For the explanation of the second colon see 2_{11bB}. The fact that we have such a literal repetition here is not without meaning. If one were to take 4_{10ab} by itself then the poets' lack of emotion in portraying these horrendous events would be quite remarkable. Clearly there can be no talk of such a lack nor can one read anything into the reduction of one bicolon per strophe. Such ideas only make sense if one refuses to honour the interconnectedness of the songs as a whole. They disappear if one takes proper note of the relationship with 2_{11f} (song-response at the canticle level). 4_{10} does not report the death of the children in question, it presumes it. 2_{11f} points to the tragic entourage and the emotional chaos surrounding such events via the image of tear-blind and grief-torn daughter Jerusalem, whose heart is turned upside down in her midst at the sight of her emaciated children dying on the laps of their powerless mothers (cf also 2_{12c}).

11a YHWH *has quenched his inner wrath,* כִּלָּה יְהוָה אֶת־חֲמָתוֹ
he poured out his burning anger. שָׁפַךְ חֲרוֹן אַפּוֹ

YHWH's חֵמָה refers to his inner experience of anger (cf the exegesis of 2_{4cB}), stirred by human persons who oppose his being and violate his commandments. It constitutes his reaction to Israel's guilt.[108] The use of

105 Cf BL 505o; thus LXX: εἰς βρῶσιν.

106 Cf II Sam 3_{35}; cf also Ps 69_{22} and Jer 16_7.

107 Cf Jer 16_7, Ezek $24_{17,22}$, Hos 9_4; cf also HJahnow, *Das hebräische Leichenlied im Rahmen der Völkerdichtung*, BZAW 36, Giessen 1923, 7 and 31.

the root כלה I does not mean that YHWH has brought his חֵמָה to an end but rather that it has fulfilled the purpose for which it was stirred.[109]

YHWH quenches his inner חֵמָה by pouring out his burning anger. It is quite striking how the poets vary their use of terminology in this regard. The expression 'burning anger' (חֲרוֹן אַפּוֹ) is also be found in 1_{12c} (cf 2_{3a}). At the same time, the verb שׁפך with YHWH as subject can also be in 2_4 (object = חֵמָה) although the present text employs a different combination: √שׁפך + חֲרוֹן אַף. The additional determination 'as fire' (כָּאֵשׁ) in 2_{4c} portrays the realisation of YHWH's anger as a destructive fire, an image also evident in the following bicolon.

11b *He kindled fire in Zion* — וַיַּצֶּת־אֵשׁ בְּצִיּוֹן
that devoured her foundations. — וַתֹּאכַל יְסוֹדֹתֶיהָ

The poets now confront us with the concretisation of YHWH's anger. There can be little doubt that the present bicolon constitutes the theological explanation of the fact that YHWH's rain of anger manifested itself in the fire which had raged through the temple complex. In the inclusion in 4_{1a}, the poets speak of the decay of the temple's visible beauty while here they take things a step further by relating the fact that even the temple's invisble foundations have been destroyed by fire. Their portrayal of events is quite extraordinary and goes far beyond what had been foretold by the prophets.[110] In reality the foundations of a building are never affected by a fire since it cannot reach what is buried under the ground for lack of oxygen. Since this would also apply to the foundations of the temple, it is evident that the poets had something else in mind with these words.

At the literary level we can assume that the poets had total destruction in mind: the temple was completely ruined from top to bottom. The inclusion between 4_1 and 4_{11} certainly points in that direction. YHWH never does things by halves! His interventions are final. A number of texts[111] in which foundations are layed bare as a consequence of YHWH's radical destruction of the buildings upon which they rest support this perspective. The fact that the foundations are exposed but left undamaged in the aforementioned texts, however, underlines the contrast with the present

108 For the theological implications of God's anger cf 1_{12c}.

109 Compare Jer 23_{20}, 30_{24}; for the meaning of √כלה I see $2_{11a,22c}$ and also TWAT IV 172 (Helfmeyer).

110 Cf Jer 17_{27} and 21_{14} where we find the same word combination: אֵשׁ + בְּ + *hiph'il* √יצת.

111 Cf Mic 1_6, Ezek 13_{14}, Hab 3_{13}; cf also Ps 137_7.

state of affairs in which the foundations themselves are the very object of YHWH's destructive intervention. The frequently used translation 'to the ground' tends to ignore this fact.[112] Deut 32_{22}, in which the foundations of the mountains are devoured by YHWH's anger, is equally radical. YHWH alone can destroy such unshakeable foundations (cf Mic 6_2) because it was he who established them. The destruction of Zion's foundations can be understood in an analogous way. In light of the plural form in 4_{11}, Mosis is led to view the יְסוֹדֹתֶיהָ not only as a reference to the temple foundations but as metonymous for the entire building complex on Zion (cf Ezek 30_4).[113] Such an inclusive reference is clearly part of the text but the image presented here seems to speak of more than just the total destruction of a number of buildings. As a matter of fact, the use of יְסוֹדֹתֶיהָ 'her foundations' reminds one of the other OT appearances of the verb יסד I (and derivatives) in relation to Zion and with YHWH as subject. There is clear evidence of a unique relationship between YHWH and Zion as the place of his dwelling and throne, the place he chose as his sanctuary.[114] Indeed, YHWH created Zion.[115] He himself built his own sanctuary as the highest of the mountains (Ps 78_{69}) and established it thereby as unshakeable.[116] Indeed, his sanctuary is more robust than the mountains (compare Ps 46_3 with 46_6). Zion is his foundation[117] and he loves her.[118] The 'personal relationship' between YHWH and his sanctuary already signalled in 4_{1a} is clearly evident throughout the OT. The song-response in 3_{33} implicitly reveals the extent to which himself YHWH is affected by the destruction of his sanctuary since the ruin of Zion leads to the persecution of his people (cf 2_{8ff}, 3_{17f}).

Although human beings constructed the temple building, YHWH himself is its true builder. In accord with his creation of the world (Ps 75_4, 93_1) he thus provided the foundations of his sanctuary (Ps 125_1), foundations which human beings are unable to shake. YHWH alone has the power to do this (Job 9_6). It is clear from such theological presuppositions that no human enemy would have been able to destroy Zion by themselves, let

112 Cf Rudolph and Kraus.

113 See TWAT III 672.

114 See II Sam 24_{16-25} and HWHertzberg, *Die Samuelbücher*, ATD 10, Göttingen 1973, 341ff; Ps 78_{68} and I Chron 22_1.

115 See Ps 87_5 with *polel* of √כון; cf Ps 48_9 and THAT I 816 (Gerstenberger).

116 Ps 78_{69}, 125_1; cf Isa 14_{32}, 28_{16} (with √יסד I).

117 Ps 87_1 (יְסוּדָה).

118 Cf Ps 78_{68} (אֶת־הַר צִיּוֹן אֲשֶׁר אָהֵב).

alone her unshakeable foundations. Now that the enemy (Edomites?, cf 4_{22b}) has set Zion alight with fire, it is equally clear that YHWH alone must be responsible for setting that fire which would so fundamentally destroy his own foundation. The poets are quite aware that this fire has destroyed much more than the temple complex as such. Whatever the extent of the temple's physical destruction, the fact that YHWH no longer desires to be present in his divine dwelling (cf 2_1) implies that the very 'foundations' of Zion and her ancient faith have disappeared and her world is no longer stable (contra Ps 46_6).[119] It is evident that this non-physical understanding lies at the heart of the text and of the poets' intentions.

Given the analogy with 4_{10}, this fundamental destruction of Zion exhibits something of a divine tragedy. The poets clearly understood it as such: what YHWH himself has established and loved he must now devour (√אכל; cf Jer 45_4). This is not the first time that the poets of Lamentations have referred, albeit for the most part implicitly, to God's suffering and pain in their portrayal of events. The parallel in 3_{33}, however, represents an explicit and central statement of the fact that in the judgement of his people YHWH is forced to act against himself. Human sin pierces YHWH's heart. Indeed, the poets reveal the depths of that divine wound via the analogy of the intense tragedy of the women of Jerusalem who are driven in the depths of their hunger to devour what they had loved the most, their children.

In order to allow for the possibility of a new beginning[120] YHWH must sacrifice that which is closest to his heart. His ultimate readiness to go further than the abandonment of his earthly sanctuary is made evident in the Christ event, although this movement of his heart is already visible here in Lamentations.

Sub-canto II (Lam 4_{12-22})

The second sub-canto continues with the portrayal of disaster but, as in canto II of Lam II, introduces thereby the question of guilt. Helplessness now pushes hunger from centre stage. Given the 3f sg suffix in 4_{13} it would appear that the poets are once again the direct speakers of the canticle in question.

---

[119] Cf also 1983, 280–294.
[120] Cf Deutero-Isaiah and 1983, 325–331.

Canticle I (4_{12-13})

Content / theme: *The fall of Jerusalem was a result of the sins of her prophets and priests*

Literary argumentation:

inclusions: צַדִּיקִים (13bB) // √אמן (12aA)[121]
צַר וְאוֹיֵב (12bA) \\ נְבִיאֶיהָ ... כֹּהֲנֶיהָ (13a)[122]

responses: בְּשַׁעֲרֵי יְרוּשָׁלָםִ (12bB) // בְּקִרְבָּהּ (13bA)

Although concatenation is established with the preceding strophe (cf צִיּוֹן // יְרוּשָׁלָםִ) via the destruction of Zion, there is still clear evidence of a new canticle in verses 4_{12-13}. There is clearly a change of subject, but the two inclusions and single response noted above are the only literary connections we were able to observe. At the level of content, the combination of the ל-strophe and the מ-strophe into one canticle is also supported by the sixth canticle of the second song (2_{14-15}) where the same connection is made: the fall of Jerusalem is to be blamed, in the first instance, on the failure of her prophets. Moreover, the dismay of those who pass by is parallel with the disbelief of the kings of the earth.

12 *The kings of the earth did not believe,*	לֹא הֶאֱמִינוּ מַלְכֵי־אֶרֶץ
nor did the inhabitants of the world,	וְכֹל יֹשְׁבֵי תֵבֵל
that adversary or enemy could enter	כִּי יָבֹא צַר וְאוֹיֵב
the gates of Jerusalem.	בְּשַׁעֲרֵי יְרוּשָׁלָםִ

Once again the poets raise the question of Zion's inviolability. Prior to the fall of Jerusalem, belief that the city was impregnable was based on the presence of YHWH in his temple. As Lord and Mighty King (מֶלֶךְ רָב, Ps 48_3), he protected his city and thus transformed it into a powerful stronghold.[123] The poets are not quoting Judah's erstwhile confession of faith, however, but making reference rather to the former convictions of the kings and the inhabitants of the earth.

The root אמן (*hiph'il*) does not have a religious significance in the present text in the sense that the poets wish to present the kings and inhabitants of the earth as believers in YHWH. It is used here rather in its

[121] See Ps 15_2, 19_{10}, 40_{11} etcetera.
[122] Cf the explanation of the text.
[123] See Ps 46; cf 1983, 281–284, TWAT VI 1016–1018 (Otto) and HSpieckermann, *Heilsgegenwart. Eine Theologie der Psalmen*, Göttingen 1989, 186–196.

profane sense: 'to believe something possible'.[124] Perhaps the most thorough study of the term is that of Jepsen.[125] who notes that the profane use of אמן *hiph'il* has a negative resonance: "es gibt allzuviel Menschen und Verhältnisse, auf die man sich nicht verlassen, Botschaften, die man nicht für wahr halten kann." Gen 45_{26} offers an elucidative parallel. Jacob cannot believe (likewise *hiph'il* √אמן + לא) that Joseph is still alive let alone that he is ruler over the entire land of Egypt. Such a thing could not be possible. Thus, an enemy occupation of Jerusalem was viewed by the kings as ultimately impossible. One might ask oneself whether this was true in reality or whether it was a result of a former theological position concerning YHWH's kingship which the poets projected on the nations. Indeed, they proclaimed YHWH as king to be Lord over rivers and mighty water, symbols of the chaos powers and the enemy, and that nations and kingdoms recoiled before him.[126] Nevertheless, the text states that the kings themselves believed that Jerusalem was inviolable.

We posed the question elsewhere as to whether Judah's faith in the invincibility of Jerusalem had not been undermined in the course of time by historical reality. We noted in response, however, that history appeared to be a positive witness. Jerusalem had remained untouched for centuries. In spite of their many attacks upon her, the enemy often went home empty-handed, unable to penetrate her mighty walls. From the time of Solomon's construction of the temple to its destruction by the Babylonians it had remained intact, even although it was to endure moments of extreme trial.[127] This fact would certainly not have slipped the attention of the kingdoms surrounding Judah and would have convinced their rulers that Jerusalem enjoyed some kind of special protection. Of course, it is evident from the negative character of לֹא הֶאֱמִינוּ that Judah's neighbouring kingdoms were little pleased with Jerusalem's unique position. In fact, their belief in Zion's inviolability was a source of frustration. Thus Lam 2_{16c} – the centre of canto II – appears to resonate at the beginning of the present sub-canto: the enemy were aware that Judah's downfall was a vain hope.

Why then do the poets make reference to the 'faith' of the kings and the nations? No doubt they intend thereby to underline the incredibility of Jerusalem's downfall. Zion's belief in her own inviolability might still be

124 Cf I Kgs 10_7, Isa 53_1 and THAT I 189 (Wildberger).
125 See TWAT I 324f.
126 Cf Ps 46; 48 and 93 etcetera; cf also TWAT VI 1017 (Otto).
127 See 1983, 90–145 for a more detailed treatment of this topic.

written off as 'wishful thinking' but if even foreigners acknowledge it there can be no more doubts. It becomes all the more unbelievable when we are confronted with the fact that the enemy has penetrated the gates and the fall of the city is a reality. The connection with parallel verse 4_1 in the first sub-canto is quite clear: the destruction of Jerusalem and its temple are a consequence of the enemy invasion. Ob $_{11}$ names the Edomites as one of the hostile forces to break through Jerusalem's fortifications. An inclusion in the present sub-canto is thus made apparent: מַלְכֵי־אֶרֶץ ([// צַר וְאוֹיֵב 12bA] 12aA) // בַּת־אֱדוֹם (22bA).

13aA *On account of the sins of her prophets...* מֵחַטֹּאת נְבִיאֶיהָ

We are now unavoidably confronted with the question of guilty parties, those who contributed to this unbelievable fall and its dreadful consequences for the inhabitants of the city. This can be determined from the parallel within the diptych structure between 4_2 and 4_{13}. The same relationship can be found between 2_{13} and 2_{14}, the latter strophe likewise citing the failures of the prophets. Two additional elements are included in the second song: misplaced announcement of salvation and the covering up of Lady Jerusalem's iniquities. If we compare this with 4_{13} then it is striking that the portrayal of prophetic failure in 2_{14} does not employ a term for sin. Moreover, it was apparent in our explanation of these strophes that the prophets in question were to be considered blind in their actions, their failure inexcusable but nevertheless unintended. In the present text, however, the poets do not shy from employing a term for sin to depict the failure of the prophets, namely the noun חֵטְא.[128] Structural cohesion is evident with the central strophe 4_6 since the noun חֵטְא recurs in the enclosing canticles of the second sub-canto (4_{12-22}), here in 4_{13} (the sins of the prophets) and in 4_{22} (Edom's sin).[129] In the final strophe of the present song (4_{22}), daughter Edom's sin is set in parallel with her iniquity and that of daughter Zion. With respect to the exegesis of these verses, therefore, this means that the sin of the people also includes the sin of the prophets. Although this may seem obvious, it is still necessary to draw attention to the fact in order to avoid the impression that the fall of Jerusalem was the sole responsibility of prophets and priests as Kraus and Van Selms would have us believe. It is clear from $1_{8,18}$, 2_{14}, 3_{42} and 5_{16} that this is certainly not the authors' intention. Nevertheless, repeated reference to the part played by these prophets confirms the suggestion

[128] For the meaning of חֵטְא cf 1_{8a}.

[129] Cf 1988, 346.

that the poets considered them particularly reponsible for the disastrous turn of events. If they had done their job properly, then the sin of the people need not have led to the fall of the city (cf 2_{14}).

It was Jeremiah who chose the sin of Sodom as a metaphor for the sin of the prophets (Jer 23_{14}) and we can thus assume a certain Jeremian influence here. He not only reported the prophets for their misleading prophecy but also for their personal misconduct in the form of blasphemy, adultery, theft and lying. In spite of the metaphorical associations, the poets of Lamentations do not adopt Jeremiah's complaint in its entirety. While they go far beyond Jeremiah's accusations by stating that the sins of the prophets are greater than the sin of Sodom, they still do not detail those specific violations mentioned by Jeremiah. They do, however, mention another offence (corresponding to the superlative?): the spilling of the blood of the righteous (cf 4_{13b}).

13aB ... *and the iniquities of her priests,* עֲוֹנוֹת כֹּהֲנֶיהָ

Compared with 2_{13} the present colon introduces a completely new element. The only mention of the priests so far focused on their sad fate ($1_{4,19}$, $2_{6,20}$), but now we are confronted with priestly guilt brought about by their iniquities.[130] Once again it should be noted that as with the חַטֹּאת of the prophets the עֲוֹנוֹת of the priests echoes the central strophe 4_6: the iniquities of the priests are also a part of the iniquities of the people. For the third time, the priests are mentioned together with the prophets. Cf 2_9 [implicitly] and 2_{20}.[131]

In prophetic preaching, the priests are clearly reproached for their incompetence in giving judgement (Isa 28_7), their unjustified acceptance of payment for priestly teaching (Mic 3_{11}, cf Lam 2_{9b}), their failure to teach the Torah (cf Ezek 22_{26}), their personal violation of certain provisions thereof (Zeph 3_4, Jer 23_{11}, Ezek 22_{26}) or their lack of due attention to YHWH (cf Jer 2_8). In all these texts, however, there is never mention of the violation alluded to in the following bicolon.

13b *who spilled in her midst* הַשֹּׁפְכִים בְּקִרְבָּהּ
the blood of righteous ones, (this happened). דַּם צַדִּיקִים

The expression שָׁפַךְ דָּם always means 'to cause death by one's own fault', although it does not provide an indication of the manner in which death

[130] For the meaning of עֲוֹנוֹת cf 2_{14b}.
[131] See for the twin concept 'priest and prophet' the explanation of 2_{20}.

is brought about.[132] Kedar and Kopfstein likewise note: "Die Wendung שָׁפַךְ דָּם, 'Blut vergießen', wird gleichbedeutend mit 'Leben vernichten, töten, ermorden' (Gn 9,6; Ez 10,10 u.ö.) und wird damit synonym mit נֶפֶשׁ umbringen" and "Ein Menschenleben vernichten ist der größte Frevel." [133]

Jerusalem's prophets and priests have the death of righteous individuals on their conscience. Jer 26 provides a clue from within the OT tradition as to what is intended here. Jeremiah mentions both priests and prophets in the same breath in their attempt to censure the prophet for blasphemy. In so doing they are even confronted with the princes, elders and the people (Jer 26_{16f}). Jeremiah calls the implementation of their plan an assualt on innocent blood which will return upon Jerusalem and her inhabitants (Jer 26_{15}). Jeremiah escapes this fate with protective help from on high. The prophet Uriah, on the other hand, who prophecied in the same way as Jeremiah was killed (Jer 26_{20-23}). It seems clear from these events that the צַדִּיקִים mentioned here in Lam 4_{13} are people who conducted their lives in an upright manner.[134] Such righteous individuals examined the lifestyle of those who believed in Zion's protection and came to the conclusion that YHWH's fidelity and justice[135] found no echo in Zion.[136] On the contrary, the reproach for lack of justice and the accusation that Zion had been built upon innocent blood had already been heard,[137] and had been associated with an insistance on conversion. This in itself was still not considered blasphemous even although it was predicted that lack of repentance would lead to the destruction of Zion (cf Jer 26_9). This very aspect was removed from the context of complaint by the established clergy and consequequently viewed as an attack on YHWH's dwelling and, as such, on YHWH himself. This provided sufficient reason for the death penalty and, while Jeremiah was able to escape, others were not. The plural צַדִּיקִים suggests here that the prophet Uriah was not alone in being put to death for such 'blasphemy'. At the same time it is clear that the accusations of the צַדִּיקִים were thus emasculated and the people were not spurred on to self-examination. Thus 2_{14b} has an echo here in 4_{13}: 'they did not expose the iniquity of the people'.

---

[132] Cf HChrist, *Blutvergießen im Alten Testament*, Basel 1977, 26, 28ff, 147, and also THAT I 449 (Gerleman).

[133] See TWAT II 256f.

[134] Cf TWAT VI 917f (Johnson).

[135] See Ps 48_{10-12}, Zeph 3_5; cf Isa 1_{21}.

[136] Cf Ps 15; 24_{3-6}.

[137] See Mic 3_{11}; cf Hab 2_{12}, Ezek 22_2 and 24_{6-8}.

Once again such unqualified belief in Zion's inviolability speaks of a degree of ignorance given that it is not related to the proper response to YHWH's fidelity and justice. Ignorance, however, cannot absolve one of guilt.

Canticle II (Lam 4_{14-16})

Content / theme: *the fate of priests, prophets and elders*

Before proposing the limits and cohesion of the present canticle it is important that we first establish our preferred text. Counter to the suggestions made in the textcritical apparatus of BHK, BHS etcetera, it is our opinion that the Masoretic reading of 4_{14b} indicated by the *zāqēf qāṭōn* (בְּלֹא יוּכְלוּ), which gives יִגְּעוּ בִּלְבֻשֵׁיהֶם as the second colon, should be maintained. We propose, in addition, that 4_{15} should be seen as a longer strophe consisting of two tricola which are joined together in a chiastic structure via the exterior cola. Cf:

סוּרוּ טָמֵא   קָרְאוּ לָמוֹ   סוּרוּ סוּרוּ אַל־תִּגָּעוּ

↕

כִּי נָצוּ גַּם־נָעוּ   אָמְרוּ בַּגּוֹיִם   לֹא יוֹסִיפוּ לָגוּר

The scrapping of קָרְאוּ לָמוֹ[138] disrupts this structure and the parallel with אָמְרוּ בַּגּוֹיִם. The poets employed a longer strophe as a means of underlining the fate of the priests and the prophets. It is not necessary, therefore, to drop one of the imperatives סוּרוּ from the text as Robinson suggests in BHS. This is only motivated by a desire to restore the *qinah* metre. It is quite probable, however, that the poets have employed a change of metre here in order to render the voice of the public. The same phenomenon can be found in 2_{15c}. The repetitions in the first tricolon are also quite appropriate for a public declaration.

With respect to the delimitation of the text one must bear the possibility in mind that our canticle runs from 4_{13}–4_{16}. A couple of literary arguments support this position:

inclusion: כֹּהֲנֶיהָ (4_{13aB}) // כֹּהֲנִים (4_{16bA})
concatenation: דַּם (4_{13bB}) // בַּדָּם (4_{14aB})

Concatenation, however, is not always a reliable indicator of cohesion. Indeed, the same style figure can also serve to link larger literary units together (cf the concatenation between the canticles in the third song). Moreover, there are strong indications in support of establishing the limits

[138] Cf text critical apparatus BHS.

of the canticle between verses 4_{14}–4_{16}. There is evidence, for example, of a change of theme from the guilt of the priests and prophets in 4_{13} to the fate which is the result of their sins in 4_{14}. Further literary indications support our delimitation.

inclusions:	עִוְרִים (14aA) // פְּנֵי (16bA)
	עִוְרִים (14aA) // כֹּהֲנִים (16bA)
	...בְּלֹא (14bA) // ...לֹא (16aB)
	סוּרוּ (15aA) // לֹא יוֹסִיפוּ לָגוּר (15bC)
responses:	לֹא (15bB) // לֹא (16b) // בְּלֹא (14bA)
	עִוְרִים (14aA) // לְהַבִּיטָם ... לֹא (16aB)[139]
	לָגוּר ... לֹא (15bB) // לֹא נָשָׂאוּ (16bA)
ext par:	נָעוּ (14aA) // נָעוּ (15bA)
concatenations:	יִגְּעוּ (14bA) // תִּגָּעוּ (15aB)
	לֹא יוֹסִיפוּ (15bB) // לֹא יוֹסִיף (16aB)
	לֹא (14bA) // לֹא (15bB) // לֹא (16aB)

14aA *Blind, they falter through the streets,* נָעוּ עִוְרִים בַּחוּצוֹת

There is some difference of opinion with respect to the subject of נָעוּ. Ewald, Thenius and later Kraus and Brunet[140] maintain that the צַדִּיקִים from 4_{13bB} are intended. As a consequence of the practices of priests and prophets these צַדִּיקִים have been rejected as unclean individuals and condemned to live outside the city. Such a position is difficult to uphold. Since שָׁפַךְ דָּם 'to shed blood' literally has death as its result (cf 4_{13b}) it is difficult to see how the murdered צַדִּיקִים can still be living outside the city whether in misery or not. Thus the subject of נָעוּ must be the prophets and priests mentioned in 4_{13}. The root נוע means 'to shake' (cf 2_{15}). 4_{13} can be seen as a supplementary song-response to 2_{15} at the canticle level: those who pass by shake their heads at the decline of Jerusalem's once angelic beauty as well as that of her now halting cultic officials. In the present text, √נעו refers to the groping, stumbling progress (cf √כשל in 1_{14b}!) of someone who has (just) become blind; thus we translate with 'faltering' (cf Isa 59_{10}). This calls to mind associations with the prophecy of doom in Zeph 1_{17}, for example, in which the people are condemned to walk like the blind (כַּ)עִוְרִים on the day of YHWH's judgement on account of their sins (√חטא) against him.[141] According to Wächter "Blindheit und

[139] As cause.

[140] GBrunet, 'Les Lamentationes contre Jérémie', Bibliothèque de l'Ecole des hautes études. Sciences Religieuses 75, Paris 1968, 76f.

Orientierungslosigkeit kann als Folge der Strafe oder des Zornes Gottes aufgefaßt werden."[142] This explanation remains to some extent unsatisfactory. What precedes and what follows leads one to think in particular of the fate of the priests and the prophets and not of the people as a whole. In addition, the comparative particle (כְּ) found before עִוְרִים in Zeph 1_{17} is missing here in 4_{14}. For a variety of reasons, therefore, it would seem that the reference is focused here not so much on the faltering steps of the blind but rather on the fact of blindness itself. They do not walk as blind individuals; they falter blind through the streets. One might wonder how this blindness should be understood. Physical blindness does not appear to be intended nor is it a logical consequence of famine and starvation. The poets are referring here to a different kind of 'lack of sight', that of those who once 'saw' visions. Once again the parallel strophe in the second song leads the way to a sound interpretation. In 2_{14} the prophets are spoken of as seers, as men who saw visions. It is evident, therefore, that 'seeing' (חָזוּ) in 2_{14aA} is related to 'not seeing' or 'blindness' (עִוְרִים) here in 4_{14aA}. Indeed, such 'seeing' is not completely detached from the fact of blindness since the former is the very cause of the latter. The 'seeing' in question was deficient seeing, in this case worthless prophecy of salvation! A literal connection between נָבִיא, the verb עור I and/or עִוֵּר is not to be found in the OT although it is present at the level of content in Mic 3_{6f} and Isa 29_{9f}, texts in which the fate of false prophets is portrayed in the context of an announcement of doom. These 'seers' were likewise guilty of unjustifiably prophesying salvation. The judgement to come would uncover their lies, unmask them as frauds and make it impossible for them to continue to speak God's words.[143] They would thus find themselves in the darkness of the night (of YHWH's judgement; cf 1_{2a}) and no new prophetic inspiration would ever overcome them. Jer 23_{12}, in which prophet and priest are condemned to walk along dark and slippery paths, says much the same thing. They are doomed to lose their way and fall. Lam 2_{9c} gives witness to the actualisation of such prophecy of doom. In our exegesis of this bicolon we already spoke of the deep crisis of faith in which the prophets of Jerusalem found themsleves on account of the fall of the city. In spite of this, however, they were intent on continuing to receive divine revelation. The present text repeats that their efforts to this end were to no avail.

---

[141] Cf also Deut 28_{29} (= later, cf 1983, 30).

[142] Cf TWAT VI 1192.

[143] Cf ASvdWoude, *Micha*, Nijkerk 1976, 112–115 and HWWolff, *Dodekapropheton 4, Micha*, BKAT XIV/4, Neukirchen-Vluyn 1982, 73f.

The visionaries have become blind (cf Isa 56_{10}) and there is no new divine utterance to illumine the darkness in which they find themselves (\\ Ps 36_{10} and 119_{105}). This is the situation which we now see reflected in the physical condition of the prophets: spiritually broken, all their strength has been sapped from their bodies. Thus blind, they falter through the city streets.

The question remains as to whether the blindness of which we have been speaking refers to the prophets alone. In a certain sense there is a direct relationship with them via the root חזה. The picture of those stained with blood mentioned in the second colon, however, reminds one of the priests, even although it is presented as part of the fate of the blind. Moreover, both prophets and priests are mentioned together in 4_{13a} as responsible for the fall of the city. It would seem, therefore, that עִוְרִים includes both prophets and priests. Jeremiah's prophecy of doom concerning the prophets (23_{9-32}) also mentions both groups together (cf Jer 23_{11}). Furthermore, one can assume an inclusion in the present canticle between עִוְרִים (14aA) // כֹּהֲנִים + זְקֵנִים (16b). For the combination of priests and elders see 1_{19bc}, a text which says the same as is said here of 'the blind', namely that they wander round in the city grown weak to the point of death. The root גוע employed in 1_{19} reveals a degree of assonance / consonance with the verb employed here in 4_{14}. For more information on the relationship between priests and elders see $1_{16b,19b}$.

There are clear indications that the priests had charge over the preaching of the prophets. See Am 7_{10-17}, Jer $28_{1,5}$ [144] and 29_{26}. They were responsible, therefore, for what was permitted as prophetic preaching. In Jer 26 they are continually mentioned in their function as judges in this regard.[145] It is highly likely, moreover, that the same priests – as the individuals most directly involved in the temple and the liturgy – were fervent supporters of the now disavowed Zion theology. Their desperate state, therefore, was not only due to the collapse of temple and cult (cf $1_{4b,19bc}$) but also to their now disgraced faith.

Further connections with the remaining songs are also worthy of note. Lady Jerusalem in her 'night' (1_{2a}) and the גֶּבֶר in his 'darkness' (3_2) objectively experience this same moment of judgement. The poets refer thereby, however, to the effects of such judgement as they relate to the 'individuals' involved: Lady Jerusalem loses her status, lovers and mighty men;

[144] Cf JRenkema, 'A note on Jeremia xxviii 5', VT XLVII (1997), 253–255.
[145] Cf THAT II 10 (Jeremias).

the גֶּבֶר is confronted with the loss of his physical and spiritual strength; the prophets are cut to the very core of their existence: the cessation of divine utterance; the priests are bereft of the cult as well as their personal fitness to engage therein. A connection with the parallel strophe (3_{40-42}) in the third song is also evident. Whereas in the past, the גֶּבֶר and his own people no longer received divine guidance by way of the prophets,[146] they were forced thereby to look back to earlier prophetic voices which had in fact predicted the disaster confronting them and re-examine their ways in light of such complaints (see the explanation of 3_{42}). We already outlined the evident connection with 2_{14}. We conclude by noting that Lady Jerusalem's lament in 1_{14} also exhibits strong agreement with 4_{14}: because of her sin she stumbles as do her priests and prophets.

14aB *smearing themselves with blood.* נְגֹאֲלוּ בַּדָּם

The vocalisation of נְגֹאֲלוּ is unusual and suggestive of a mixed form incorporating *niph'al* pf and *pu'al* pf.[147] Albrektson presumes that the Masoretes did this on purpose in order to avoid confusion with √גאל I (to redeem). √גאל II constitutes a more recent spelling of √געל (cf HAL 162). Fuhs[148] notes that the verb גאל is frequently used in parallel with √מאס I (Lev $26_{15,43f}$, Jer 14_{19}) a verb which can indeed be found in the canticle parallel 3_{45}. The meaning is well established: the verb implies '(cultic) impurity'. In Mal $1_{7,12}$, Ezra 2_{62} and Neh 7_{64} the term is used with reference to a person's qualifications (or the lack thereof) for the priesthood, quite apart from the lifestyle and behaviour of the individuals involved. This is clearly not the case in the present text. The proximate re-use of the term דָּם makes it impossible to deny a connection with the spilled blood of the righteous, even although literal and metaphorical significance clearly alternates. Van Selms denies any concatenation via the term דָּם. He proposes that those who were physically blind in Jerusalem had stepped in the blood of those who had been slain which stood in pools on the ground. The blind to whom he refers, however, are not those intended here. Indeed, in light of what follows, we remain in the context of the fate of prophets and priests. The blood they spilled has brought guilt upon their heads. In fact, this very outrage has already made them ritually unclean (cf Ps 15 and 24_{3f}). Nevertheless, the undetermined use of דָּם here does not only refer to the blood of the צַדִּיקִים from the preceding strophe. The association runs much

[146] Cf I Sam $28_{6,15}$, I Kgs 14_{1ff}, 22_{5ff}, II Kgs 1_3, 19_{2ff}, Jer 37_{17}, 38_{14ff} etcetera.
[147] Cf GES-K § 51*h*.
[148] See TWAT II 49.

deeper: by being guilty of spilling the blood of the righteous, priests and prophets are responsible for the fall of Jerusalem and the blood of her slain inhabitants. The filth of decaying corpses (cf the following bicolon) which could be found scattered throughout the streets of the city both during and after the siege is a result of their sin. As they stagger and stumble throughout the city, they smear themsleves with such filth and thus make themselves unclean. Remarkably enough, the root גאל II (*hiph'il*) is used in Isa 63_3 with YHWH as subject. How is it possible, however, for YHWH to make himself ritually impure? In order to avoid such an association, the author of Isa 63 opted for an alternative term for blood, namely נֵצַח, a rare synonym of דָּם.[149]

14b *Things forbidden to them,* בְּלֹא יוּכְלוּ
they touch with their clothing. יִגְּעוּ בִּלְבֻשֵׁיהֶם

This bicolon is often translated 'so that no one was able to touch their garments' (NRSV; cf Peshitta, Löhr, Haller, Kraus, Gordis, Brandscheidt etcetera) but one is then left with the problem of making sense of such an expression. Although there is a close relationship between a person and his or her clothing in the OT[150] there is no evidence of a custom of touching a priest's garments or a prophet's mantle in order to receive blessing or healing of some kind.[151] To a certain extent, Ezek 44_{19} would appear to be in conflict with this analysis. In this text, priestly liturgical vestments are seen as a medium of holiness, although the priests themselves try to avoid letting their clothing be touched by the people.[152] Hag 2_{13} takes matters even further and makes it clear that a sacred garment does not transmit holiness to another but rather impurity.[153] Given these provisions, it is highly unlikely that our present text is referring to some sort of permissible touching of priestly attire. It seems more plausible in the context that we are dealing with a kind of touching which was not permitted, one which made the clergy ritually impure. At the same time, there is no need to insist that liturgical vestements were the object of soiling since the cultic purity of the priests also included their ordinary clothing. The translation offered here provides for further intense contrast: the very ones

[149] Cf HAL 676 sv נצח II (*hapax*).
[150] Cf I Sam 18_4, 24_5, I Kgs 19_{19}, II Kgs 2_{13f}.
[151] Cf, however, Mt 9_{20} and Strack-Billerbeck I, 520.
[152] Cf also Ezek 42_{14} and WZimmerli, *Ezechiel 25–48*, BKAT XIII/2, Neukirchen 1969, 1064.
[153] See JLKoole, *Haggaï*, Kampen 1965, 75–77 and Lev 15_{4ff}.

who are responsible for the purity of others and who ought to ensure their own purity are themselves unclean (cf Lev 21). Albrektson, followed by Gottlieb, Kaiser and others, rightly takes בְּלֹא יוּכְלוּ to be a relative clause governed by יָגְעוּ and thus supporting our translation; √נגע + בְּ means 'to touch' (cf Gen 3_{3}, Ex 19_{12}, Deut 14_{8} etcetera; for the division of this bicolon see the introduction to this canticle).

The poets draw our attention here to the necessary purity of those who minister to the cult in the sanctuary. Whoever would appear before the presence of God had to be purged of every impurity (cf II Chron 23_{19}). YHWH himself is pure and cannot even look upon evil / wrongdoing (Hab 1_{13}). Indeed, whatever is impure cannot be tolerated by either the Holy (One) or holy things.[154] Thus unclean shoes and unwashed clothing had to be disposed of or washed.[155] It is interesting to note that in the relevant cleanliness codes,[156] priestly clothing is referred to with the term בֶּגֶד or בְּגָדִים. The verb לבשׁ does not refer so much to individual pieces of clothing but rather to clothing as a whole or to a special piece of clothing. For the most part, √לבשׁ does not appear in the cleanliness codes, being chiefly employed for ceremonies of consecration. According to Gamberoni, this 'Sitz im Leben' is quite possibly the natural and original context in which √לבשׁ was used. "Dies dürfte ein bestätigendes Indiz dafür sein, daß P jeweils den ganzen kultischen Ornat ins Auge faßt und auch *lbš* durch sich selbst die Ganzheit konnotiert."[157] This notion is doubtless older than the later P redactions and thus significant for our explanation of the present text. It implies that not only part of the clothing in question (for example the hem, cf 1_{9a}) but all of it was defiled. Clearly, for a person who stumbles and falters as he walks through the dark and slippery streets the chances of falling are pretty high as is the likelihood of dirtying more than the hem of one's garment (Jer 23_{12}). Hence our interpretation fits well in the context.

Whose clothing is being spoken of here? Once again it seems logical to think of the priests although, given the cultic context in which the prophets of Jerusalem exercised their profession, we should not draw too sharp a division between the two groups (cf the explanation of 2_{20c}) In his commentary on Ezek 44_{19}, Zimmerli notes that the priestly head coverings

[154] Cf TWAT III 353 (André).

[155] See Ex 3_{5}, $19_{10,14}$; cf also RdVaux *Institutions II*, 353f and TWAT IV 480 (Gamberoni).

[156] Lev $11_{24f,28,32,40}$, 13_{58} etcetera

[157] See TWAT IV 481; cf II Kgs 10_{22}.

mentioned therein are prophetic garments in Ezek $24_{17,23}$.[158] Whatever the case, the prophets just like the priests also had to remain pure for the practice of their ministry. Indeed, given that the words (אֲמָרוֹת) of YHWH are pure words (אֲמָרוֹת טְהֹרוֹת)[159] it is unacceptable to limit impurity to the priests alone.[160] The prophets also must include it as part of their lot. What brings about impurity in this context? Blood – which has already been mentioned – does not as such make a person or thing impure and can in fact be used in a purification ceremony.[161] The context of blood flow is therefore determinative. Menstruation causes uncleanness[162] as does the blood lost in giving birth.[163] The present context is one of the spilling of blood and death,[164] and thus the fact that "Die rituelle Unreinheit ist oft mit der Todessphäre verbunden" is of the essence.[165] The association between impurity and death is evident in Num 19_{11-22}. It is striking that in only one of the provisions found in this text do we find a sanction against lack of attention to impurity: the person who enters the sanctuary in an impure state shall be cut off from Israel (Num $19_{13,20}$). One can determine from such texts as Lev $21_{1f,11}$, Num 5_{2f}, 6_{6-12}, 9_6, Deut 21_{23}, Hag 2_{14} (MT 2_{13}) that the high priest was to place his personal purity above all else. Although no explicit mention is made of touching the blood of the dead in such texts it is certainly implicitly prohibited in Num 19_{16}, a text from which we can conclude that every form of contact with the body or remains of a dead person resulted in impurity. As a matter of fact, the text in question actually mentions coming in contact with 'those pierced by the sword' (חַלְלֵי־חֶרֶב) which is reminiscent of Lam 1_{20c}, 2_{21b} and 4_{9a} where reference is made to those in the city who were slain by the sword. Lam 2_{21} even mentions the fact that such corpses were left lying in the streets. The present reference to the fact that the clothing of both priest and prophet is defiled with blood can be explained as follows: unable to see, the priests and prophets move falteringly through the streets of Jerusalem and are unable to avoid the corpes lying around them which they touch with their clothing (נָגַע בְּ). The formulation בְּלֹא יוּכְלוּ (literally 'with [which] not they may'), however, appears to imply more than just

[158] Cf WZimmerli, *Ezechiel 25–48*, BKAT XIII/2, Neukirchen 1969, 1133f.
[159] Ps 12_7; cf Isa 6_5, Jer 1_5.
[160] Cf, for example, Weiser and Gordis.
[161] Cf Lev $14_{14,49ff}$.
[162] Lev 15_{19ff}, 18_{19}.
[163] Lev 12_{22ff}; cf Ezek $16_{6,9}$. In Lev 12_{4f}, however, there is talk of בִּדְמֵי טָהֳרָה.
[164] Cf the preceding שָׁפַךְ דָּם; // in 3_{43}: הָרַגְתָּ and in 5_{15}: נֶהְפַּךְ לְאֵבֶל מְחֹלֵנוּ.
[165] See TWAT III 353 (Ringgren).

blood. In fact, they seem to be unable to avoid the very things they are not supposed to touch (see also the filth and rubbish mentioned in the song-response 3_{45}; cf Zeph 1_{17}). All that remains visible of what they have touched is the blood and grime of the corpses of the slain and the filth and muck of the ash heaps (cf 4_5).

15a *"Make way! Unclean!",* סוּרוּ טָמֵא
people give warning concerning them. קָרְאוּ לָמוֹ
"Make way! Make way! Do not touch!" סוּרוּ סוּרוּ אַל־תִּגָּעוּ

The *qal* imperative plural סוּרוּ of the root סור meaning 'to stand aside' has no specific 'Sitz im Leben' in the OT and appears to be used in a variety of contexts.[166] The reason for the use of the imperative can mostly be derived from the relevant context. Num 16_{26}, in which the people are told to make way for iniquitous Levites and avoid touching anything belonging to them, exhibits particular parallels with the present context. The avoidance of evildoers is mentioned with some frequency in the Psalms.[167] Given earlier references to the sins of the prophets and the priests, it is possible that a similar idea of avoidance is at work in the present tricolon. Nevertheless, a more significant motif appears to dominate here, namely the unclean status of the aforementioned prophets and priests indicated by the use of the term טָמֵא. As an exclamation, the adjective in question does have an established context, that of the leper who is obliged to inform those around him / her of his / her unclean status (cf Lev 13_{45}). The suggestion found in BHS that we read the plural טְמֵאִים ('the unclean') instead of טָמֵא, fails to appreciate the exclamatory character of the term and should be ignored in spite of the reading of the LXX: ἀπόστητε ἀκαθάρτων. Lev 13 unveils the tragic turn of events which has taken place here in portraying the priests in their capacity as guardians of purity. They themselves are now defiled. The very people who once commanded others to warn those around them of their unclean state are now confronted with warnings directed against their own impurity.

It is possible, of course, but highly unlikely, that the imperatives in this tricolon are from the lips of the priests themselves. As unclean indivuals, they constitute the point of reference of the entire strophe and not its speakers. Refer to the explanation of the following colon as well as Lam 4_{16} in the present canticle where loss of authority among the priests and prophets is specifically mentioned.

166 Cf Gen 19_2, I Sam 15_6, Isa 30_{11} etcetera.
167 See Ps 6_9, 119_{115} and 139_{19}.

As noted in the introduction to the present canticle, the colon קָרְאוּ לָמוֹ has been a source of difficulties among exegetes. Löhr, Albrektson, Kraus, Boecker and Westermann, among others, scrap it as redundant along with BHK and BHS, even although the reading of the LXX καλέσατε αὐτούς supports the correctness of the MT. What are the possible interpretations? While the reading of the LXX 'call out to them' is the usual rendering of the Hebrew expression קָרָא לְ, the present context demands a different interpretation (see below). It is possible to maintain the aorist imperative of the LXX and render the text as: 'call with respect to them', that is 'give warning concerning them'. Even although the Masoretic vocalisation reads a *qal* pf 3m pl instead of an imperative, the translation 'they call out' with prophets and priests as subject is precluded by the presence of the suffixed preposition לָמוֹ, unless, that is, one is willing to ascribe a reflexive meaning to the expression: 'they call out concerning themselves'.[168] The content of 4_{14} tends to rule out such an interpretation. As blind and faltering in 4_{14}, they cannot avoid touching what is unclean yet here it would seem that they are suddenly alert enough to be aware of their own impurity, see the approaching passers by and even warn them of their impurity. The formulation in 4_{15a} also deviates from the usual double exclamation of impurity 'Unclean! Unclean!'[169] Thus the idea here is not that the priests and the prophets utter the following imperatives and caution the passers by to get out of the way and not touch them as Gordis would have it: "Turn away, turn away, do not touch us!". The prohibitive אַל־תִּגָּעוּ (literally: 'you must not touch') does not include a prefix which would justify such a translation. Gordis wrongly assumes that the priests and the prophets are the speakers here.

What then are the possible meanings of קָרָא לְ? In the first place, the expression implies 'to call a person('s name)',[170] and always refers to other people. This provides us with a further indication that the priests and the prophets are not the subject of the sentence since they would hardly be calling upon themselves. An impersonal, collective subject seems to offer itself here: 'people call out', bystanders or passers-by.[171] It remains clear, however, that 'they' are not calling upon the (name of) the blind and faltering prophets and priests in order to bring them closer. The imperatives which follow are not proper nouns. One is impelled, therefore, to

[168] Cf GES-K § 135*i*.

[169] Cf Lev 13_{45}.

[170] Cf Gen 12_{18}, I Kgs $1_{28,32}$, II Kgs 4_{15} etcetera; cf also HAL 1053.

[171] See for this interpretation of the 3m pl form GES-K § 144*d*.

interpret the suffixed preposition לָמוֹ as 'concerning them'[172] and the entire expression as 'people give warning (cry out) concerning them'. Given the situation it seems logical that the imperatives and the prohibitive are directed against the unclean. Indeed, as Keil points out, these blind, unseeing individuals have already smeared themselves with unclean things and are now urged to make way for the passers-by so as to avoid touching them. The double imperative סוּרוּ סוּרוּ supports this interpretation and is quite appropriate as a public exclamation of warning. Unclean individuals themselves were expected to employ the double טָמֵא טָמֵא in order to warn those ahead of them of their unclean status. The blind and defiled individuals in the present context have neglected their duty in this regard and thus the passers-by are forced to exclaim a double סוּרוּ סוּרוּ in its place.

It is also possible that the passers-by are warning each other here that there are unclean people around and that they should avoid touching them. Both interpretations are not mutually exclusive. On the level of content, however, it seems less likely. The very countenance of the blind and defiled priests and prophets must have been enough in itself to elicit profound horror. Appeals to make way and avoid touching these people would have to be considered redundant.

15bA *Yes, they make way and wander around;* כִּי נָצוּ גַּם־נָעוּ

The meaning of the *hapax* √נוץ is unclear. HAL (645) suggests 'sich entfernen' on the basis of a possible identification with an Arabic verb with similar sounding consonants. Gottlieb points out that the meaning is provided by the following נָעוּ and that √נוץ must mean something like 'to flee'. His proposal remains unconvincing, however, especially when one is forced to understand the root נוע in the same way as in the preceding strophe (4_{14aA}), namely 'to stumble, falter'. Flight of any kind demands a level of speed and agility which would clearly not be appropriate in the context. At the same time, the verb נוע also has the broader meaning of 'roaming around' without a roof over one's head.[173] In Gen $4_{12,14}$ the verb in question stands in parallel with √נוד meaning 'to drift, wander', making Budde's suggestion[174] that we substitute נָדוּ for נָצוּ quite attractive. It would seem that the poets would like us to see the priests and the prophets as refugees and vagrants.

[172] Cf HAL 483 sv לְ (6); Gen 20_3 and Ps 3_3.

[173] Cf Ps 59_{16}, 109_{19}, Prov 5_6.

[174] Followed by Haller, KBL 629 and HAL 640.

Even if one takes the root נוד as one's point of departure one is left with more or less the same meaning. We are then confronted with the motif of being condemned to wander as a fugitive for the spilling of innocent blood (cf Cain in Gen 4_{11f}). The fugitive 'wanderer motif' is found in one other place in the OT, namely II Sam $16_{7,13}$. If we compare Gen 4_{11f} with II Sam $16_{7,13}$ on the one hand and Lam 4_{15} on the other then we see that all three texts speak of the spilling of innocent blood and subsequent wandering but that Lam 4_{15} is unique among the three in that it does not mention any kind of imprecation or curse. The idiom remains very close, nevertheless. In Jer $44_{8,12}$, for example, sword, hunger and abuse are placed on one and the same line with curse. Likewise, the horror of the fall of Judah is described in terms of imprecation and malediction in Deut 28.[175] Impurity can also be seen as an extension of imprecation. As Speyer notes: "Der Verfluchte und sein Eigentum sind körperlich unrein, damit aber tabu...".[176] Nevertheless, one is forced to honour the fact that the poets do not mention anything about the priests and the prophets being cursed. Perhaps such imprecation was too absolute and its realisation irreversible. In Jer 44_{12}, for example, the end of the exiles in Egypt is placed on a par with cursing.[177] Clearly such a state of affairs would be difficult to reconcile with the idea of hoped for restoration which the poets continue to cherish in spite of everything.[178]

The association between blood spilling and wandering lost, however, is clearly present. Being condemned to a life of fugitive wandering is a consequence of rejection by the community within which the original crime took place. Westermann notes in his commentary on Gen 4_{11f}: "Man muß dann vorsichtig sein mit dem Urteil, die Verstoßung sei eine geringere oder mildere Strafe als die Todesstrafe. Sie ist vielmehr die in sehr früher Zeit nachweisbare Strafe für Mord am Sippengenossen." [179] Expulsion from the family group still takes places among the Bedouin in the case of murder. The analogy is important for our interpretation of Lam 4_{15}. The expulsion of the priests and prophets has taken place on the initiative of their own countrymen. As was already apparent in 4_{15a}, this is the clear intention of the imperatives סוּרוּ סוּרוּ. It is not only a reaction against their unclean status but also against their shedding of blood.

---

175 Redacted for the most part in the post-exilic period; cf 1983, 30.

176 See RAC col 1165.

177 Cf, however, II Sam 16_{12}.

178 See the explanation of 3_{55-66} and 5_{21-22}.

179 CWestermann, *Genesis 1–11*, BKAT I/1, Neukirchen-Vluyn 1974, 416–419.

15b *it is said among the nations:* אָמְרוּ בַּגּוֹיִם
"they can no longer stay here!" לֹא יוֹסִיפוּ לָגוּר

In light of the 3_{45} (song-response), the almost universally held opinion that אָמְרוּ בַּגּוֹיִם is an explanatory gloss has to be rejected. The parallel between בַּגּוֹיִם and בְּקֶרֶב הָעַמִּים is too clear to procede otherwise. אָמְרוּ, moreover, is a literary song-response to 2_{15c}: (שֶׁ)יֹּאמְרוּ likewise with an impersonal subject. There is also a clear connection at the level of content: the disappearance of liturgy in Zion ultimately implies that there is no longer a place for her priests and prophets. Lam 3_{45}, where the גֶּבֶר laments that he and his people have been reduced to the status of filth and rubbish in the midst of the nations, offers a further clarification of 4_{15b}. As was the case with 1_{3bA} one need not infer that the poets had the exile in mind here. They refer, rather, to Lady Jerusalem's neighbours and former allies and lovers who now despise her because of the impurity that clings to her garments (cf the explanation of $1_{8,9}$). Lam 4_{15} interprets the גֶּבֶר's lament with specific reference to the fate of Jerusalem's priests and prophets.

The imperatives סוּרוּ סוּרוּ had their effect. It is reasonable to assume that after the fall of the city, the priests and the prophets sought refuge elsewhere. Indeed, from this point in Lamentations on they are no longer mentioned. Lam 5_7 states in fact that these 'fathers' have disappeared (cf Ps 74_9). It would seem that the prophets were held responsible in no small measure for the disaster confronting Judah and Jerusalem (cf 2_{14} and 4_{12f}). Laying the blame at their door and jeering at them would appear to be an attractive option, to say the least. Clearly their departure to safer territory would have been obvious, even if only to escape the turmoil of the city. Many others would have abandoned Judah for similar reasons in search of refuge in some foreign country.[180] Jer 40_{11f} reveals that many Judeans tried to escape the violence of war and the general upheaval by fleeing to Moab, Ammon and Edom. As is frequently the case, fellow nationals tend to find one another when forced to seek refuge in foreign lands but in the present case not everyone was equally pleased with the encounter. The enforced exile made things difficult enough but sudden confrontation with the very people who had caused the disaster in the first place must have been a bitter pill to swallow. The prophets had failed in their religious responsibilities and were guilty of the death of their kinsmen and countrymen. Their prophecies were mere deception. Indeed, YHWH had rejected them. Who could bear to have such people

[180] Cf the explanation of 5_6.

around them? They did not have the right to enjoy the relative safety of this foreign refuge. Thus the fate of priests and prophets is given an expanded treatment. They are not only unable to live in Judah or Jerusalem they are also hunted from the surrounding territories which offer them no refuge. They are condemned to wander without rest for the shedding of innocent blood.

The subject of אָמְרוּ should not be assumed to be the countrymen of the unclean priests and prophets alone. As foreigners in a strange land they had very little say in who could stay and who should be refused refuge. The local authorities alone had the right to expel the priests and prophets. It is in this sense that we must understand the final colon לֹא יוֹסִיפוּ לָגוּר. √גור I means here 'to reside as a foreigner'.[181] Foreign refugees, wherever and whenever they are found, are always treated with reticence and often suffer maltreatment. Certainly any criminal elements among them would be refused asylum. According to Speyer, their impurity would make them equally taboo in the land of their desired refuge: "Wer mit dem Verfluchten umgeht, wird angesteckt und selbst zum Verfluchten." [182] Thus the fugitive priests and the prophets are nowhere welcome and are condemned to wander as outcasts (cf Ezek 13_9).

16a *The countenance of* YHWH *scatters them;* פְּנֵי יְהוָה חִלְּקָם
he no longer regards them. לֹא יוֹסִיף לְהַבִּיטָם

This final strophe provides the fate of the priests and the prophets with theological foundation. Westermann suspects that 4_{16b} originally stood before 4_{14-15}, strophes which appear to offer an explanation thereof (cf also Kraus). This is highly unlikely, however, since an emendation along these lines would seriously disrupt the concentric structure of the present canto.[183] Moreover, as the canticle's closing strophe, one can ascribe a summarising character to 4_{16}, offering a theological perspective on what the preceding strophes have described.[184] The fate of the priests and elders does not have a human source. It comes, rather, from YHWH himself through the agency of compatriot and enemy alike. This is the significance of the expression 'countenance of YHWH' which underlines the fact that it is ultimately YHWH who brings about their fate. His countenance implies his regard as well as his actions.[185] Van der Woude is correct in refusing

[181] See Gen 19_9, Deut 26_5, Isa 23_7.
[182] In RAC col 1165.
[183] See 1988, 342.
[184] Cf also the cohesion between Lam 2_{16-17}.

to accept an indirect presence of YHWH here, as if reference were being made to his face as the subject of an action.[186] He is wrong, however, in leaving open the possibility of interpreting פְּנֵי יְהוָה as YHWH's raging gaze. This notion is indeed contained in an expression using the term פָּנִים, cf: √שִׂים/נָתַן פָּנִים בְּ,[187] but one cannot derive 'raging gaze' from פְּנֵי יְהוָה alone since it is also to be found in positive contexts (cf Num 6$_{26}$). Thus the emphasis falls on YHWH as subject.[188] The present strophe summarises what YHWH has done to the priests and the prophets (cf 4$_{14-15}$) with the term 'to scatter'. The relative rarity of this interpretation of √חלק II inclines Dahood[189] to propose a root חלק III meaning 'to die' based on the Ugaritic root *ḫlq* which is found as a synonym of *mt* 'death' (cf HAL 310). His proposal is without justification, however, since the interpretation 'to scatter' is confirmed by the appearance of √חלק II in parallel with √פוץ in Gen 49$_{7}$. The verb in question clearly has a place in the prophetic announcement of doom.[190] Without a shepherd the sheep are scattered and become prey to wild animals.[191] To scatter – or synonymously 'to put someone to flight' – implies the deprivation of power and protection (cf Gen 11$_{4}$). The very fact that YHWH treated Israel's enemies in this way in times gone by (Ps 68$_{2}$; cf Num 10$_{35}$) highlights the contrast hinted at by 4$_{16a}$: now the same YHWH scatters his own servants. This particular implication might explain why the poets used the rare √חלק II instead of √פוץ. After all, it was the Levites who confessed YHWH as their Portion (חֶלְקִי; cf the exegesis of 3$_{24a}$). Their Portion, however, has scattered them and thereby withdrawn their protection and livelihood.[192]

16b *The face of the priests they do not honour* פְּנֵי כֹהֲנִים לֹא נָשָׂאוּ
and for the elders they have no respect. זְקֵנִים לֹא חָנָנוּ

The combination פְּנֵי כֹהֲנִים is a construct relationship and refers to the 'face' of the priests. In Hebrew idiom one can 'lift up' someone's face (נָשָׂא פָּנִים) which means 'to treat someone as eminent' or 'to honour someone', but

185 Cf the explanation of 3$_{50}$.
186 Cf THAT II 446ff; see also Deut 4$_{37}$ and Isa 63$_{9}$.
187 Cf Lev 17$_{10}$, 20$_{3,6}$, Ezek 15$_{7}$ etcetera.
188 Cf also Simian–Yofre (TWAT VI 637) and 2$_{17a}$.
189 MDahood, in his review of: BAlbrektson, *Studies in the Text and Theology of the Book of Lamentations, with a Critical Edition of the Peshitta Text.* (Studia Theologica Lundensia 21) 1963; in: Biblica 44 (1963), 548.
190 See Jer 13$_{24}$, 18$_{17}$; cf Hab 3$_{14}$.
191 Cf Jer 10$_{21}$, Ezek 34$_{5}$ and Zech 13$_{7}$ with metaphorical usage.
192 Cf Jer 40$_{15}$ and see TWAT VI 545f (Ringgren).

this can only be done by people of superior social status with respect to those of a lesser social status.[193] The implicit presence of a relationship of authority is important for determining the subject of נָשָׂאוּ. Thus one cannot opt for the priests' fellow Israelites since they, as lay people, held an inferior position. The enemy would appear to be the most manifest option as subject given that their dominant position is indicated in 1_{5aA} (הָיוּ צָרֶיהָ לְרֹאשׁ). This probability is confirmed by song-responses 1_{16}, 2_{16} and 3_{46} in which the power of the enemy and their humiliation and destruction of the inhabitants of Judah is spoken of. Cohesion between 4_{15b} and 4_{16a} is clear and has been indicated by the poets on more than one occasion: the enemy only have free reign because of YHWH's agency ($2_{7,16-17}$). The present text applies the enemy's free reign to individuals: only because YHWH has withdrawn his protection are the enemy in a position to hold his servants in contempt. Thus the additional content of the present strophe becomes clear, since the implicit contempt of the inhabitants of Judah was already expressed in 4_{15a} in their attempts to dispel the priests and the prophets.

In our explanation of 1_{21b}, we noted that within the songs as a whole there is no mention of any recognition of YHWH by the enemy, a fact which is graphically expressed in their destruction of his temple (cf the explanation of 1_{4b}). It is evident from the present bicolon that they likewise do not have a grain of respect for his servants the priests. Lam 2_{20} is first to mention the fact that the priests and the prophets were being murdered in the temple precincts. Enemy disdain is now extended outside both temple and city. In spite of their official position, the priests who are forced to wander as fugitives are offered no respect. This too implies a further turn around in hitherto prevailing relationships. The same applies to the elders[194] whose position accustomed them to the honour and respect of the people. Now all of that has vanished. The NRSV translation (cf also NBG): "no favour (was shown) to the elders" is incorrect. Translation in the perfect gives the impression that the humiliation and contempt is a thing of the past while in fact it is still a very real and ongoing experience.[195] Moreover, placed in the context of human relationships, the expression 'no favour' has juridical associations and is reminiscent of an irreversible verdict. The root חנן I, on the other hand, tends more towards the notion of 'benevolence', 'goodwill',

---

193 Cf Gen 19_{21}, I Sam 25_{35} and Job 42_{8f}; cf also TWAT V 640 (Freedman – Willoughby).

194 For the relationship between the elders and the cult see the explanation of $1_{6b,19b}$.

195 For the present tense translations of the Hebrew perfect cf the explanation of 1_1 etcetera, and GES-K § 106g.

'friendliness' (cf Prov 22_{11}) and implies an active and positive attitude where human relations are concerned.[196] It constitutes a word-pair with the expression נָשָׂא פָּנִים.[197] The enemy clearly do not show benevolence or respect towards the elders. Thus, from the human perspective, we are not only confronted with an inversion at the level of relationships but also with the fact that the elders are consequently unable to exercise their usual leadership role because they lack the customary esteem. The explanation of 5_{12B} is also relevant here. 5_{14} states also that the elders have disappeared from the gates, the very places where they once exercised their authority.

Canticle III (Lam 4_{17})

Content / theme: *There is no help*

Literary argumentation:

The potential response גּוֹי (17bB) // בַּגּוֹיִם (20bB) hints at the possibility of a single canticle running from verses 17–20. The presence of the same בַּגּוֹיִם in 4_{15bB}, however, suggests that the expression functions at a higher level within the song. With respect to content, it would appear that there is no direct association with the preceding canticle. The change of subject (to 1st person pl) suggests that 4_{17} constitutes a new canticle, while the introduction of a new theme in 4_{18} likewise sugests that we should consider this strophe to be an independent small canticle. The macrostructure of the song supports this opinion, 4_{17} being placed opposite the other mini-canticle 4_6 in the diptych. In addition, and in like fashion to Lam III, both panels exhibit an identical layout in terms of canticle division.[198]

As before, the absence of literary and direct thematic associations do not imply that there is no relationship with the context. The second canto, like the first, exhibits a strongly concentric structure in which 4_{17} holds a central position. In contrast to 4_6, however, the present strophe does not present us with any fundamental formula which is further elaborated in the remainder of the canto. The relationship with the context (and also with 4_6) is complementary: in the present disaster (which is worse than that which overcame Sodom) there is no one to offer help.

---

196 Cf TWAT III 25f, 28ff (Freedman – Lundblom).

197 Cf Deut 28_{50}, Num 6_{25}, Mal 1_9.

198 Cf page 483 and 1988, 354.

17a *Our eyes yearn continually for help, (but) in vain.*

עוֹדֵינָה תִּכְלֶינָה עֵינֵינוּ
אֶל־עֶזְרָתֵנוּ הָבֶל

From the text critical perspective the *k^e tīḇ* עוֹדֵינָה has the strongest documentary support.[199] The 3f pl suffix can be associated with עֵינֵינוּ, 'our eyes' as can the verbal form תִּכְלֶינָה (= *qal* impf 3f pl of √כלה I). Thus the *k^e tīḇ* is preferred over the *q^e rē* עוֹדֵינוּ (1 pl suffix). The combination of עַיִן and √כלה I is also to be found in 2_{11a} where Lady Jerusalem's eyes can no longer see because of her unrelenting tears. The element of duration is contained in the term עוֹד which should be seen in the context as adverbial (cf Gen 46_{29}, Ps 84_{5}). The idea of 'pining' is translated here as 'longing'/'yearning'. Note, in addition, the combination כָּלָה אֶל, whereby the preposition אֶל "zäher an der räumlichen Grundbedeutung festhält." [200] Yearning for help suggests longingly looking out to the horizon.

Compared with what precedes it, the present canticle clearly has a different subject: 1st person plural. The poets are representing the hopes, fears and disappointments of the population. It is quite understandable that some translations (SV, NBG, NRSV) opt for a perfect tense here given the possible associations with help from Egypt mentioned in Jer 34_{21} and $37_{5,11}$. Thus certain commentators and translators have associated this bicolon with the hoped for intervention on the part of pharaoh which was prevalent just before the fall of Judah. The גֶּבֶר's change of heart described in Lam III, in which the last remnants of his belief in a good outcome now rest in YHWH alone, supports such an interpretation of the text. The poets are referring here to the bygone hopes of the people.

Such a 'one after the other' portrayal of events, however, is not evident in Lamentations as a whole. It is incorrect to suggest that the disaster came to an end once Jerusalem had been taken. On the contrary, many of the complaints described in the text are related to what happened precisely after that terrible event: hunger, devastation, arbitrary hostility, terror and carnage. It is certainly quite human to continue to hope against hope in such affliction, to long for help whoever that helper may be. Given the following bicolon, thoughts turn automatically to Egypt as a political ally. There had always been political movements in Judah who saw more profit in an alliance with Egypt at certain moments in history than loyalty with respect to Assyria at first and Babylon later. From the military perspective Egypt had raised Judah's expectations[201] and even proved

199 Compare 5QThr^b.
200 Brockelmann § 108.

her capacity by sending an army which successfully – if temporarily – broke the Babylonian siege of Jerusalem just before the fall of the city. This need not imply, however, that immediately after the fall of Judah all hope in Egypt was definitively abandoned. Via the combination עוֹד and √כלה I, the present text leads us to believe that people continued to hope for renewed intervention, a fact confirmed in its own way by the song-response 1_{17a} in which daughter Zion in desperation stretches out her hands for help. It is evident in both places, however, that there is no one to bring comfort and offer a helping hand (cf also the refrain אֵין מְנַחֵם לָהּ). Indeed, the song-response 2_{17a} reveals the theological origin of Zion's helplessness: it is ultimately YHWH's decision, yet the people have no one else to turn to but Him for salvation (cf $3_{49,50}$ [the 17th strophe!]). In our explanation of 1_{7c} we already noted that the root עזר I implied the provision of assistance between unequal parties in which the more powerful offered a helping hand to the less powerful. The term עֶזְרָה, therefore, means more than just the kind of every day assistance one person might offer another. The idea of military intervention and protection by the (relatively) powerful Egyptians fits well into the context and use of terminology. Those who held out for Egyptian help, however, did so to no avail. The Egyptian army did not appear! Associations with prophetic texts are evident. We already noted the connection between the present bicolon and Isa 30_{7a} (וּמִצְרַיִם הֶבֶל וָרִיק יַעְזֹרוּ: 'and Egypt – worthless and empty is her help'[202]). The prophecies of Isa 30_{1-5} and 31_{1-3} are directed against any form of alliance with Egypt and predict nothing but disappointment as a result.[203]

17b *On our vantage points we look out* בְּצִפִּיָּתֵנוּ צִפִּינוּ
for a nation that does not save. אֶל־גּוֹי לֹא יוֹשִׁעַ

Many exegetes[204] also translate this bicolon in the perfect tense and relate it to the temporary reprieve brought about by the Egyptian army in the siege of Jerusalem. Rudolph states in this regard: "Dieser »Wir« Abschnitt, der den Dichter als Mitbeteiligten verrät, führt zunächst wieder in die Zeit der Belagerung zurück...". Such an exegetical position considers the present text as retrospective: 'when we were in need we looked out in vain for...' but this does not harmonize with the meaning of the

201 Cf 1983, 108–135.
202 Cf 1983, 265
203 Cf Isa 20_6; see also the parallel verse Lam 2_{17}!
204 Cf Thenius, Löhr, Kraus, Plöger, Kaiser, Groß etcetera.

preceding bicolon where the emphasis was on the 'non-stop' character of the people's yearning for help. It is far from improbable that there was an ongoing hope that the Egyptians would intervene anew. In such profound affliction people tend to grasp at straws and rumours tend to abound. The use of the perfect צִפִּינוּ for the act of 'looking out' for help does nothing to alter this fact. Once again one must view this 'looking out for help' as an act which may have had its origins in the past but which continues in the present and thus warrants a present tense translation.[205] Moreover, given what follows, it would seem more appropriate to envisage a period immediately after the siege of the city when the situation had deteriorated because of the fact that the enemy had such a free hand. Every cherished expectation and every form of hope is ultimately doomed to frustration: there is no army of salvation waiting on the horizon. In this sense, the present complaint corresponds with 1_2 in which it is stated that none of Lady Jerusalem's lovers is there to assist her in her hour of need.

The *qal* of the root צפה I is normally employed for the act of 'looking out' as such. The *pi'el* employed here, however, indicates that this 'looking out' had no particular object in mind,[206] a fact underlined by the second colon. The act itself took place from a suitably high vantage point: the roof of the city gate in II Sam 18_{24} and a tower in II Kgs 9_{17}. Thus Dahood interprets the *hapax* צְפִיָּה as 'watchtowers'.[207] Jerusalem's gates, however, had already been destroyed (cf 1_{4b} and 2_{9a}) and even if they had remained intact they would have been useless for looking out for help from Egypt because the surrounding hills would have blocked the view. It would seem more appropriate, therefore, to think of nearby hilltops (cf HAL 981) which were used as natural vantage points or as intermediate stages for passing on signals.[208]

'A people that does not save' constitutes the object of the act of looking out (יוֹשִׁעַ = *hiph'il* impf 3m sg). Where the poets once employed the plural 'lovers' as a reference to Jerusalem's former allies (1_2), here they expressly mention one single people. Evidently they must have had Egypt in mind since this was the only nation with sufficient military potential to drive off the Babylonians. The text suggests that the people still hoped

---

[205] Cf the use of the present tense translation for the perfect יָשְׁבָה (1_{1aA}) etcetera, and GES-K § 106*g*.

[206] Cf TWAT VI 1088f (Steins).

[207] MDahood, 'Hebrew-Ugaritic Lexicography VIII', Biblica 51 (1970), 403; cf also Van Selms.

[208] Cf Lachish ostracon nr 4, TGI[3] 77.

for a liberating intervention on the part of the Egyptian army in the very midst of their present misfortune. The unusual subject of יוֹשִׁעַ stands out somewhat. Indeed, it is the name of YHWH which constitutes the most appropriate subject of Israel's liberation; his salvific intervention clearly demonstrates his divine superiority.[209] The liberation of Israel is the specific task of YHWH and cannot be performed by foreign gods.[210] When people appear as subject of √ישׁע they usually do so in a representative capacity, as the king might represent YHWH in the context of the administration of justice.[211] Of further importance for our understanding of the present text is Josh 10_6 where the identical combination of the root עזר (see the parallel עֶזְרָתֵנוּ in the preceding colon) and √ישׁע is to be found in an analogous context, namely the assistance of a city (Gibeon) against hostile forces. In light of his promise of protection, made in the context of the covenant with the Gibeonites, YHWH undertakes to save Gibeon. When salvation is rendered with a form of the root ישׁע, we are evidently dealing with an *opus proprium* of YHWH. When the present text speakes of a nation that cannot save, therefore, it means more than just 'they are of no help'. The statement clearly implies that the nation in question cannot do what YHWH alone is able to do. Thus, as the watchers turn their gaze south in expectation of a saviour, they experience the fulfilment of the prophecy: seeking shelter in the shadow of Egypt is and shall be their humiliation (Isa 30_2; cf Lam 5_1 [חֶרְפָּתֵנוּ] and the song-response 2_{17}: the fulfilment of the true prophetic word).

Such disappointment is partly responsible for making the people realise that they should look to YHWH who alone can save them. In this sense the גֶּבֶר leads the way. Indeed, in the parallel strophe of the third song (3_{50}) we are told that he will not cease his weeping until YHWH looks down from heaven and saves.

Canticle IV (Lam 4_{18-20})

Content / theme: *Routed and kingless*

Literary argumentation:

It is quite imaginable the one might call the cohesion between 4_{18-19} and 4_{20} into question, given that being hunted down by the enemy would

209 See, for example, Ex 14_{13}, Judg 7_2 and TWAT III 1045f (Sawyer); cf also the explanation of תְּשׁוּעַת יְהוָה in 3_{26B}.

210 Compare the irony and sarcasm of Judg 10_4.

211 Cf THAT I 786 (Stolz).

appear to constitute a different theme from that of the imprisonment of the king. Nevertheless, a connection is evident between both in the suffix of בְּשְׁחִיתוֹתָם (4_{20aB}), the antecedent of which has to be the pursuers of 4_{18-19}. If one does not make this connection then the suffix must remain unexplained. Closer analysis reveals that the themes of each section are not so different, the imprisonment of the king being among the consequences of the hostile pursuit of 4_{18-19} (cf II Kgs 25_5).

We were not yet able to mention any concrete or literary arguments based on homonyms or (supplementary) synonyms.[212] We now draw the reader's attention to the following:

inclusions:	כִּי־בָא קִצֵּינוּ (18bB) // נִלְכַּד בִּשְׁחִיתוֹתָם (20aB)
	צָדוּ צְעָדֵינוּ (18aA) \\ בְּצִלּוֹ (20bA)
responses:	צָדוּ (18aA) // נִלְכַּד בִּשְׁחִיתוֹתָם (20aB)
	מָלְאוּ יָמֵינוּ (18aB) \\ נִחְיֶה (20bB)
	בַּמִּדְבָּר (19bB) \\ בְּצִלּוֹ (20bA)
	רְדָפֻנוּ (19aA) // נִלְכַּד (20aB)

Additionally, 4_{18b} and 4_{20a} are both tricola and the 3m pl suffix is frequent in the canticle (10x) creating inclusions, responses and concatenation. If one reads the canticle out loud it becomes evident how such phonic repetition makes for a sense of literary unity (for further explanation of the content of the aforementioned inclusions and responses see the exegesis).

It is assumed on the basis of 4_{18-20} that the poets of Lamentations were among the company of king Zedekiah when the latter was superseded by the Babylonians. This need not be the case since the account of pursuit and imprisonment very probably spread like a rumour and would have quickly become familiar (cf the explanation of 4_{20a}).

18a *They hem us in with every step,* צָדוּ צְעָדֵינוּ
we cannot show ourselves in the open! מִלֶּכֶת בִּרְחֹבֹתֵינוּ

Van Selms finds the transition from 4_{17} to 4_{18ff} somewhat abrupt although it is not evident why he should think so! The text itself progresses with logical cohesion: since Egypt provides no assistance, the enemy have a free hand and can do what they want with the population unhindered.

The form צָדוּ can be derived from a number of verbal roots. HAL discusses it under √צדה I (939) and √צוד (947), the former, 'to lie in wait for'

[212] Cf 1988, 340.

being a frequent option among exegetes.[213] This too is often related to the siege and capture of Jerusalem. "Meist nimmt man an, daß hier von Belagerungstürmen die Rede ist, von denen aus die Feinde nicht nur in die Stadt hineinsehen, sondern die Menschen auch unter Beschuß nehmen konnten." (Boecker). Rudolph, followed by Gordis and Kaiser, emends the MT and derives the term from √צרר I, intransitive: "to drive someone into a corner" (cf Job 18_7). Hiller translates literally with 'to hunt' but upholds Rudolph's position in his commentary.

It is somewhat surprising that no one refers to the parallel צ-strophe in the third song, 3_{52-54}, a song-response in which the גֶּבֶר laments that his enemies have hunted him down like a bird and imprisoned him. The parallel is striking even at the level of content. A similar example of such close cohesion can be found between 2_{4f} and 3_{12f}. Supported by the LXX[214] and the Peshitta, we have reason, therefore, to derive צָדוּ from the root צוד employed in 3_{52}. The term אֹיְבַי in 3_{52} also helps us to identify the subject of the present bicolon: 'the enemy'. What follows similarly suggests that the same hunting imagery is being employed here and that the time being referred to is likewise after the capture of Jerusalem when the Babylonians hunted down those they considered dangerous among the prominent figures in the city.[215] While it is true that the object of the hunt may seem a little strange – literally "they hunted our steps" – it is not impossible: hunters always follow every trace of their prey (cf Peshitta). The noun צַעַד, 'step' has a solemn ring to it[216] while the equivalent verbal form 'to strut'/'parade' does not fit well with the idea of 'flight'. The term is perhaps intended to reveal something about the people fleeing, however. A glance at corresponding strophe (4_7) in the first panel provides a clue: we are dealing here with the nobility who were once to be found in all their finery 'parading' through the squares of the city.[217] Although they are now unrecognisable to their fellow citizens, they are still being hunted by the enemy and are fearful to show themselves in public. Thus we interpret מִלֶּכֶת בִּרְחֹבֹתֵינוּ – literally: 'without walking in our squares' – as the fear of showing oneself openly in the open places adjacent to the city gates where public life took its daily course.[218] The expression 'without walk-

---

213 Cf, for example, Keil, Albrektson, Kraus, Weiser, Haller, Groß, Westermann.
214 Cf Albrektson on the 1st person plur ἀπεσκοπεύσαμεν.
215 See II Kgs 25_{5-7} and 25_{18-21}.
216 Cf II Sam 6_{13}, 22_{37}.
217 Cf II Kgs 25_{18f}.
218 Cf 2_{11c}; 5_{14} and HAL 1131 sv רחב I.

ing / going' (מִלֶּכֶת, *qal* inf + preposition מִן) cannot refer to the enemy who were free to go wherever they desired. If the nobles dared to show themselves – driven by hunger – the enemy were waiting for them. Compare the already mentioned complaint of the גֶּבֶר in the parallel 3_{52}.

18b *Our end is near,* קָרַב קִצֵּינוּ
our days are running out, מָלְאוּ יָמֵינוּ
yes, our end has come! כִּי־בָא קִצֵּינוּ

Unhappy with the fact that the tricolon interrupts the sequence of bicola, Gordis considers the present text corrupt in some way and suggests that either A or C (which repeat each other) should be scrapped. In so doing he reveals his misunderstanding of the 'Sitz in Leben' of the exploited idiom, the style and terminology of which are most frequently found in the prophetic announcement of the day of YHWH. Zimmerli correctly points out the characteristic style-figure of repetition found therein: "Diese liebt die in ihrer Monotonie unheimliche Wiederholung (10mal עַל כָּל [יוֹם]) Jes 2^{2-16}, sechsmaliges יוֹם mit gen. Zeph 1^{15f}, viermaliges עַל (פקד) Zeph 1^{8f}, drei Sätze mit בְּטֶרֶם Zeph 2^{2}, zweimahl wiederholtes (יוֹם יְהוָה) קָרוֹב Zeph 1^{14}."[219] He does this on the basis of Ezek 7 where the prophet speaks of the approaching end of Israel in terms of the יוֹם יְהוָה. Although the discussion of this 'end' is more appropriate to Amos (Am 8_{1-3}) who influenced Ezekiel in this regard, the presence of the word combination √בוא + the noun קֵץ, which is only to be found in Ezekiel (Ezek $7_{2,6}$) and here in Lamentations, implies that the influence of Ezekiel is all we can establish.

As with Ezekiel, the word 'end' does not bear the later (apocalyptic) meaning of 'end-time',[220] but rather the idea of imminent 'destruction' (cf Gen 6_{13}). Even the adverb קָרוֹב suggests that the poets are referring to a moment which is 'about to break' in the actual history of the speaker or reader.[221] The said adverb is a standard expression in the terminology of the יוֹם יְהוָה.[222] Thus, although the present use of 'end' does not refer to the end of time as such, it does refer to the end of time for those involved in the present disaster (the end of their time) in the sense that for them there is no relevant 'after'. Furthermore, it would be a mistake to see קֵץ as the end-point of a temporal line but rather as the expiration of a period

219 WZimmerli, *Ezechiel 1–24*, BKAT XIII/1, Neukirchen 1979², 167.
220 Cf Dan 8_{17}, $11_{35,40}$, $12_{4,9}$ and THAT II 662 (Wagner).
221 Cf THAT II 676 (Kühlewein).
222 See, for example, Zeph $1_{7,14}$, Ezek 7_{7}; cf THAT II 680 (Kühlewein).

of time, the time of the end. During this time, all the things which go to make up the end of the collective – the events of the day of YHWH – play themselves out, even although they need not all happen or be experienced at one and the same time.

The meaning of the combination מָלְאוּ יָמֵינוּ takes us a step further, pointing to the end of a specific period of time such as the end of a pregnancy (Gen 25_{24}). A person's life can also be seen as a period of time which must inevitably run out when one's 'days' are complete, as it were.[223] The same, of course, can be understood in a figurative sense. Without speaking of death as such, one's life can be seen as 'expired' because it has been robbed of every form of joy and meaning. It is here that we touch on the precise meaning of the present text. For the city's prominent citizens time has run out! Their erstwhile joyful existence in Zion (cf song-response 5_{18}) with all its luxury[224] and precious adornment (1_{11bA}) has come to an end.

We consider the כִּי of כִּי־בָא קִצֵּינוּ to be emphatic: 'yes, our end has come!' With respect to the first colon of the present tricolon, the final colon suggests a degree of progress: 'our end is near – yes, our end has come!' The canticle's sequence of chase / hunt followed by imprisonment confirms this and supports the probability that it was intended by the poets. Enemy pursuit corresponds with the proximity of the end while the imprisonment of the king signifies the end as such. We can determine this from a somewhat hidden inclusion, namely between: כִּי־בָא קִצֵּינוּ (4_{18bC}) // מְשִׁיחַ יְהוָה נִלְכַּד בִּשְׁחִיתוֹתָם (4_{20aB}). The report of the kings imprisonment is heard and then confirmed. Only then is the end 'real'! Now it is over for the people also. As YHWH's annointed one, the Davidic king was the protector and divine guarantee of their existence.[225]

The end of individual lives is not the main focus here, although many had been and were to be killed throughout this period. The poets are primarily speaking of the beginning of the end of the period in which Israel existed as a people under the protection of YHWH and his king. The judgement announced in this regard has achieved its dreadful fulfilment: their time is at an end. This does not mean that there can be no life during this time of judgement. Life is possible but it is a life without joy, a threatened existence, a life without שָׁלוֹם (see $3_{17,22A}$ and the fifth song).

---

[223] Cf Ex 23_{26}, II Sam 7_{12}, I Chron 17_{11}.

[224] See $4_{5aA,bA}$ (inclusion at the song level).

[225] Cf the explanation of 4_{20}.

Note the lament of the people in Ezek 37_{11}: although they are alive, the exiles lament that they are completely cut off and that their hope is lost.

We already noted the quite close parallel at the level of content with the צ-strophe in the third song (3_{52-54}). There too the poets speak of pursuit and imprisonment and there too the גֶּבֶר in his cistern, with the water rising beyond his lips, imagines that his life is at an end.[226]

19a *Our pursuers are faster* קַלִּים הָיוּ רֹדְפֵינוּ
than eagles in the heavens! מִנִּשְׁרֵי שָׁמָיִם

Many commentators consider this and the following bicolon to be a unit, describing the attempted flight and imprisonment of king Zedekiah. Detailed information on these events can be found in II Kgs 25_{3-7}[227] (// Jer 52_{7-11}) as well as in the report of Ezek $12_{12,13}$. The question remains, however, whether the pursuit mentioned in the present verse is exclusively related to the aforementioned historical events. Elsewhere in the songs there is also mention of enemy pursuit, with respect to which – perhaps with the exception of 1_{6c} (cf 2_{9b}) – little if any association with the flight of the king can be discerned (cf 1_3 and 5_5). For this reason we translate here in the present tense although we include therein the imprisonment of the king as an event in the past. The capture of Zedekiah did not bring an end to the enemy pursuit. The hunt continues unabated!

The flight speed of an eagle is proverbial (cf II Sam 1_{23}). Jeremiah employs the image of the eagle as an unexpected attacker which strikes its prey in mid-flight.[228] The speed of these pursuers, however, goes beyond such a menace. Indeed, the inescapable speed of the enemy is a topos in the prophetic announcement of doom.[229] Jer 4_{13} even speaks of enemy horses being faster than eagles.

19b *Fired up, they hunt us on the mountains,* עַל־הֶהָרִים דְּלָקֻנוּ
in the wilderness they lie in wait for us. בַּמִּדְבָּר אָרְבוּ לָנוּ

The root דלק can be found in this sense in Gen 31_{36} and I Sam 17_{53}.[230] The verb itself has overtones of 'burning' and 'pursuit', both of which are found in the expression חִצֵּי דֹלְקִים 'burning arrows' (cf Ps 7_{14}). From

[226] See the song-response אָמַרְתִּי נִגְזָרְתִּי (3_{54B}) // כִּי־בָא קִצֵּינוּ (4_{18bB}).
[227] Cf the explanation of JGray, *I & II Kings*, London 1970², 765f.
[228] Jer 48_{30}, 49_{22}.
[229] Cf Hos 8_1, Isa 30_{16}, Hab 1_8.
[230] For the construction see Brockelmann § 97a.

the metaphorical perspective it can be used with reference to 'inflamed' individuals (cf Isa 5_{11}), which appears to be the poets' intention in the present text: the pursuit of the enemy is hard and intense, such that their starving and exhausted prey, unfamiliar as they are with the mountain terrain, do not stand the slightest chance of escape (cf Ezek 7_{16}). Even the heat of the desert is not shunned as a place to enslave the Judeans or to rob them of their possessions (cf 5_9). The root ארב is used in 3_{10} with YHWH as subject and the גֶּבֶר as object.

20aA *Our life's breath,* רוּחַ אַפֵּינוּ

Enemy pursuit ultimately leads to the imprisonment of the king. The present verse expresses the deep disappointment and sense of dismay accompanying this event. It is only here in this strophe that one can find a trace of the poets' intense faith expectations in association with the Davidic kingship. While these feelings are presented here 'in a nutshell', as it were, the charged language remains quite revealing.[231]

The poets begin by declaring the special qualities of the king: he is their 'life's breath'. The expression רוּחַ אַפֵּינוּ is not unique in the context of the Ancient Near East. The Egyptian pharaoh is portrayed as the life's breath of his subjects,[232] and is even graphically depicted as a sort of atmosphere which encompasses the earth in which people are able to breath.[233]

The expression in question, however, is only found here in the OT leaving us to question its specific meaning within the Hebrew idiom. The dual stands for the nostrils, as a reference to the organ with which humans breath in their life's breath. Where breath in the physical sense is intended then Hebrew tends to employ the noun נְשָׁמָה.[234] The term רוּחַ can also imply 'breath' but it clearly suggests an additional dimension which Albertz / Westermann locate in the vitality and spiritual energy of a human person.[235] It is possible for a person to breath without רוּחַ but beyond

231 Cf 1983, 288–294 on the Davidic kingship.

232 Cf JdSavignac, 'Théologie pharaonique et messianisme d'Israel', VT VII (1957), 82; cf also CGrave, 'On the use of an Egyptian Idiom in an Amarna Letter from Tyre in a Hymn to the Aten', OA XIX (1980), 212f.

233 See images 26 – 33 in OKeel, *Die Welt der altorientalischen Bildsymbolik und das Alte Testament*, Zürich-Einsiedeln-Köln-Neukirchen-Vluyn 1977², 26–30; for the relevant texts see page 22.

234 Cf Gen 2_7, 7_{22} and see CWestermann, *Genesis 1–11*, BKAT I/1, Neukirchen-Vluyn 1974, 281ff and 590; cf also I Kgs 17_7, Ps 104_{29}, Isa 2_{22} etcetera.

235 See THAT II 750f.

this there is nothing but complete apathy. A person can in fact lose his or her רוּחַ due to some insurmountable loss or setback.[236] This may have a physiological cause, such as exhaustion brought on by hunger or thirst.[237] The mortal apathy of the exiles in Ezek 37_{11} is reversed by the gift of רוּחַ which restores their will to live. Thus in the present colon, the poets are suggesting that the king was a source of inspiration which gave spirit and vitality to his subjects' existence.

20aB YHWH*'s annointed,* מְשִׁיחַ יְהוָה

The inspiration mentioned above does not find its source in just anyone, rather it is granted by the Davidic king. In contrast to $2_{6,8}$, the poets do not refer to the king with מֶלֶךְ but with the expression מְשִׁיחַ יְהוָה.[238] He, YHWH's annointed, was the driving רוּחַ in their lives. It is not without reason that they refer to the king with this profoundly theological concept at this point. Much of the poets' expectations and faith is expressed in this phrase, particularly the unique relationship between YHWH and the Davidic king which took shape in the covenant between them.[239] This ultimately had its roots in YHWH's choice of David and his house[240] of which 'annointing' was the sign.

One can determine from Ps 2 that the institution of the Davidic monarch as מְשִׁיחַ יְהוָה was based on YHWH's own decree (חֹק יְהוָה) and was to be further qualified as (an adoptive) sonship (Ps 2_{7f}). This implied, on the one hand, that God would protect the king against enemies and nations[241] while on the other, it meant that the appointed and protected Davidic king had to represent YHWH's dominion on earth as His 'regent'. The king's mandate, therefore, was directly related to his authentic exercise of justice and right.[242] As such, his reign would be a source of blessing and prosperity for the people.[243] People had the freedom to live and increase under the peace which the king established and preserved. Although many a Davidic king had been rather disappointing in this regard the people's

---

236 Cf Gen 45_{27} and I Kgs 21_5 (רוּחֲךָ סָרָה).

237 Cf Judg 15_{19} and I Sam 30_{12}.

238 See Seybold's detailed study in TWAT V 46–56 plus literature.

239 Cf II Sam $23_{1,5}$ and Ps $89_{4,29,35}$.

240 Cf I Sam 16_{12} and II Sam $7_{11,16}$.

241 See Ps 2_{4-6}; cf I Sam 2_{10}, Ps 18_{44-51}, 28_8.

242 Cf Ps 18_{21-25}, II Sam 7_{14}.

243 See the elaboration hereof in Ps 72 and 101 while 84_{10} and 89_{19} laud him as a protective shield.

expectations of him continued undiminished. Each new Davidic king had the potential to fulfill those expectations.

20aC *is imprisoned in their pits,* נִלְכַּד בִּשְׁחִיתוֹתָם

The translation of שְׁחִית as 'trap' or 'pit' is supported by Ps 107_{20} (cf HAL 1355). The theological position of the king outlined above explains the centuries long stability of the Davidic dynasty. It is only against this background that one can understand the enormity of the disappointment and dismay which is distinctly audible in this report of the king's capture and imprisonment. In the history of the Davidic monarchy there had been moments when the king had to be disciplined or hard pressed because of his disobedience. This may indeed have given rise to oppression and affliction (Ps 89_{31-52}) yet there had never been a time when the disruption of the dynasty was its result, not even when Nubuchadnezar occupied Jerusalem in 597 and carried off king Jehoiakin to Babylon; a new Davidic king was simply installed in his place.[244] The rejection of the king was already mentioned in 2_{6c} and his exile in 2_{9b}. Indeed, precedents, such as the aforementioned abduction of Jehoiakin, were not unknown (cf Ps 89_{39ff}) but a definitive rupture in the dynasty? Never! Things have changed. What the people are now experiencing has no historical parallel. With the destruction of gates, walls, palace and temple, it is hard for the poets to understand the situation as anything less than a definitive rupture. It is for this reason that they speak of the 'end' in 4_{18b} for it is evidently over between YHWH and their king. This fact has immediate consequences for the relationship between YHWH and themselves. For the poets and the people, the continuity of the Davidic dynasty was not simply a remarkable phenomenon nor had they any exalted emotional attachment to the human royal house: for Judah the Davidic king was visible theology. The prolonged continuity of Davidic monarchy was a sign that, in spite of the many failures and frequent disobedience of their kings, YHWH still remained mercifully closeby. Their present experience, however, appeared to be evidence that God's patience had reached its end. The contrast must have been unfathomable: YHWH's former protection of the king and superiority over the nations (cf Ps 2) versus the humiliation of imprisonment – YHWH's annointed hunted like an animal and captured in the nations' trap. Together with the destruction of the temple[245] this can have meant nothing less than the end. Although we noted above that

[244] For the continuity of the Davidic dynasty cf 1983, 90–145.
[245] Cf the explanation of 1_{4b}.

the use of בוא קֵץ in 4_{18a} pointed to the influence of Ezekiel, the present text reveals a distinction from the prophet in question. The imprisonment in Babylon of king Jehoiakin – under whose reign Ezekiel dates his prophecies – did not seem to pose a threat to the continuity of the Davidic dynasty, yet here the poets interpret the simple capture of their king as its end. Such radicality is also present in II Kgs 25_7 in contrast to the additional conclusion II Kgs 25_{27-10}.

The question might also be asked whether or not there is a relationship between the imprisonment of the גֶּבֶר in the third song and the imprisonment of the king.[246] A positive answer to this question would perhaps support Van Selm's hypothesis which considers the גֶּבֶר to be identical with the imprisoned Davidic monarch. The similarities between the two events do not, however, justify identification. The entire population was being hunted and pursued (cf 1_{3c} and 5_5) and as such the fate of the king was far from unique. Indeed, the terminology employed in 3_{46} refers to the entire population of which the גֶּבֶר considers himself a part.

This portion of the text has led some to draw conclusion as to the origin of the poet(s). Only someone who was closely involved with the attempted escape of king Zedekiah would have been able to describe the events in this way (Weiser). On the other hand, the lot of Zedekiah would certainly have been widely known and there is certainly no reason to follow Van Selms and identify the king in question with Jehoiakin. The imprisonment of Zedekiah is presented as a consequence of the persecution described in these texts, while the deportation of Jehoiakin to Babylon had taken place almost a decade earlier.

20b *he, of whom we thought:* אֲשֶׁר אָמַרְנוּ
in his shadow we shall live in the midst of the nations. בְּצִלּוֹ נִחְיֶה בַגּוֹיִם

The division of the cola in this text appears somewhat uneven. BHS associates בְּצִלּוֹ with the first colon but this makes little sense at the level of content. If one respects the Masoretic *zāqēf qāṭōn* attached to אָמַרְנוּ, however, one is then led to divide and translate the text as above.

Although there is no mention of a tree in the present bicolon it is clear that the king is being described metaphorically as a shadow-providing tree. The best explanation of this bicolon can be found in the messianic expectation of Ezek 17_{22-24} (cf Isa 32_2) where the Davidic king is presented as a cedar planted by YHWH, in the branches of which every sort

246 Compare the similar use of hunting terminology in $3_{47,52}$.

of bird can make its nest. It goes without saying that in the Middle Eastern heat, trees with their shadow and their (juicy) fruit were of great importance and were also given metaphorical significance. In Egypt, the goddesses Hathor and Nut were represented as tree goddesses.[247] Even the early Sumerian royal hymns liken the king to a magnificent tree (of life) which offers his people shadow and protection.[248] The OT gives evidence of the same metaphorical usage.[249] In harmony with the power and magnificence ascribed to him in Ezek 31, the pharaoh is compared to a tree of paradisiacal dimensions, in the protective shadow of which the great nations live.[250] It is hardly strange that Zion theology would have transferred this image to the Davidic king as the 'world king' appointed by YHWH[251] in whose shadow his own people would live in peace in the midst of the surrounding nations (בַגּוֹיִם). According to Keil, for example, there is no mention of the exile here: the poets are glancing back to the time of the fall of Jerusalem and Judah. The shelter and protection provided by the Davidic king was granted and guaranteed by YHWH himself, which explains the fact that there is often direct mention of the protective shadow of YHWH.[252]

In Hos 14_8, YHWH compares himself with an evergreen cyprus tree which provides its fruit for Israel.[253] Such interchangeability in the use of the image is important here since the loss of the Davidic king would mean that Israel had to fall back on YHWH himself, the true provider of justice and right judgement, shelter and protection. Evidence of this can be seen in Lamentations with respect to the גֶּבֶר who, in the absence of the king, turned directly to YHWH for liberation and protection.[254] Thus the portrayal of the poets' disappointment at the loss of YHWH's annointed is not out of place within the book as a whole (contra Westermann).

---

[247] Cf TWAT VI 285 (Ringgren) together with figures 253–255 in OKeel, *Die Welt der altorientalischen Bildsymbolik und das Alte Testament*, Zürich-Einsiedeln-Köln-Neukirchen-Vluyn1977², 165f.

[248] Cf GWidengren, *The King and the Tree of Life in Ancient Near Eastern Religion (King and Saviour IV)*, Uppsala 1951, 59 and WHPRömer, *Sumerische 'Königshymnen' der Isin-Zeit*, Leiden 1965, 21, 23f, 51f; cf also TWAT VI 286 (Ringgren).

[249] Compare Judg 9_{8ff}, Ezek 17, 19, 31; see also TWAT IV 467f (Mulder) and TWAT VI 293f (Nielsen).

[250] Ezek $31_{6,9}$; cf Isa 30_2.

[251] Cf Ps 2 and Widengren, 57f.

[252] Ps 91_1, Isa 25_4; cf TWAT VI 1040 (Schwab).

[253] Cf MCAKorpel, *A Rift in the Clouds*, Münster 1990, 593f.

[254] Cf the parallel strophe in the third song, 3_{55-57}.

A further connection with the third song is also evident in relation to the tree metaphor: the chopping down of the 'royal' tree implies the disappearence of the protection its branches offered to the birds. It is not without reason, therefore, that the גֶּבֶר laments that the enemy hunts him down like a bird as he does in 3_{52} which is parallel with 4_{18}. This song-response uncovers the presence of the antithetical inclusion: צָדוּ צְעָדֵינוּ (18aA) \\ בְּצִלּוֹ (20bA): hunted versus protected.

Canticle V (4_{21-22})

Content / theme: *Edom shall undergo the same punishment as Zion*

Literary argumentation:

inclusions:	בַּת־אֱדוֹם (21aA) // בַּת־אֱדוֹם (22bA)
	עוּץ (21aB) // בַּת־אֱדוֹם (21aA)
	הַגְלוֹתֵךְ (22aB) // תִּשְׁכְּרִי וְתִתְעָרִי (21bB)
responses:	עָלַיִךְ (21bA) // עַל (22bB)
	גַּם... (21bA) // פָּקַד עֲוֹנֵךְ (22bA)
	תִּשְׁכְּרִי וְתִתְעָרִי (21bB) // גִּלָּה עַל־חַטֹּאתָיִךְ (22bB)
allit / asson:	גַּם (21bA) // תַּם (22aA)
resp / concat:	via the 2f sg suffixes

As we already noted in the introduction, it is unusual that there is no mention of prayer to YHWH at the end of Lam IV when compared with the other songs. A degree of association is evident nevertheless: where YHWH is the object of prayer in 1_{20a} // 2_{20a} // 3_{58}, 4_{20} provides the actual reason behind the turn to YHWH: the king, whose function it was to protect and liberate in God's name, has been taken prisoner.

A further relationship can be determined at this level with the remaining songs. If one were to read the fourth song in isolation from the rest then the present canticle might come accross as rather strange at the level of content: after the mention of so much loss we are suddenly confronted with an outburst of confidence that the enemy also will be brought to justice and receive due punishment for her misdeeds. Read in isolation this sudden sense of reassurance might make little sense but – as the poets clearly intend – everything makes sense if we read the songs in context with one another. Thus the prayer we hear at the end of the first song: 'let them become like me' (1_{21c}) has become a conviction of faith for the גֶּבֶר who, after his change of heart, ultimately came to believe that YHWH would also punish the enemy for their misdeeds.[255] This same conviction is evident in the final canticle of the present song. In addition, there is a level of agreement with the final canticle of the second song (2_{22b}) via the day of YHWH and the mention of daughter Zion drinking the cup of judgement in the present canticle.

21a *Rejoice and be glad, daughter Edom,* שִׂישִׂי וְשִׂמְחִי בַּת־אֱדוֹם
you, inhabitant of the land of Uz! יוֹשֶׁבְתִּי בְּאֶרֶץ עוּץ

The transition to the present canticle turns out to be less abrupt than it might seem at first sight. Now that YHWH's protection via the Davidic king has disappeared, the enemy have a free hand in Judah. Clearly for the enemy this was something to shout and rejoice about. Indeed they had similarly profited from the misfortune of Lady Jerusalem portrayed in the song-response שָׂשׂוּ / רָעָתִי (1_{21bA}) (// שִׂישִׂי וְשִׂמְחִי).

The extent of the contrast between sadness and joy is made evident in the diptych structure in which enemy joy is placed opposite the grief of the women who are forced to eat their own dead children to feed their sorrow: 4_{10} \\ 4_{21}. The poets already spoke of the joy of the enemy in similar terms in 1_{21b} (שָׂשׂוּ) and 2_{17c} (וַיְשַׂמַּח), while the גֶּבֶר likewise lamented that he had become the mocking-song of his enemies (3_{63B}). For the precise meaning of √שׂושׂ and √שׂמח see the explanation of the relevant verses. While enemy rejoicing is clearly not a new theme, the specific jubilation of Edom is. For the first time in the book of Lamentations we find an enemy explicitly named.[256] Given the text's consistent vagueness with respect to the naming of hostile forces and even former allies the present mention of Edom is all the more striking. Its presence can only be explained by the fact that the actuality of Edom's hostile behaviour was likewise exceptional. This is supported by numerous texts throughout the OT which respond to the outrages performed by Edom at that time.[257] The historical context of Lamentations does not permit us to de-historicise this fact and treat Edom as a chiffre for the enemy in general. We already noted with respect to 3_{60A} that Edom had earned a terrible reputation in the history of Israel for its behaviour towards her, a reputation which was not easily pushed to one side. This amply explains why Edom experienced such immense joy at the downfall of their hated enemy Judah. Given what follows, however, it is evident that the poets trust that this joy will not last for long.

[255] Cf the explanation of 1_{21c} and 3_{64-66}.
[256] Cf, however, the hidden reference to the Babylonians in $3_{62,65}$ with לֵב קָמַי.
[257] Cf Ps 137_7, Ezek 25_{12-14}, $35_{5,10}$, Joel 4_{19}, Ob $_{10-14}$.

Their entreaty to daughter Edom is, therefore, full of irony: enjoy your victory while you can! Their hopeful expectations are clearly intended to encourage those fellow Israelites who had remained in Judah and who had been forced to endure the full intensity of Edom's campaign of terror (see below).

The personification of Edom as a woman is analogous with that of Judah.[258] The land of Edom was located to the east of the wadi Arabah and bordered to the south on Moab.[259] The second colon should be understood as a poetic repetition of בַּת־אֱדוֹם. The final י of יוֹשַׁבְתִּי is somewhat unexpected. Evidently the Masoretes felt the need to correct the text (cf *qᵉrē*) but Joüon-Muraoka § 93*o* illustrates the correctness of this ancient form while GES-K § 90*m* underlines its more solemn character. The extent to which we can identify Edom with the Land of Uz is unclear. Jer $25_{20,21}$ appears to distinguish the two and to use Uz as an indication of the more southerly regions below Edom.[260] It would seem that the present text is already making allusion to Edom's expansionist policies. The reference to Uz is absent from LXX but the reading with only ἐπὶ (τῆς) γῆς is a fair indication that the name Uz has fallen out (cf Rudolph).

21bA *To you also shall the cup pass* גַּם־עָלַיִךְ תַּעֲבָר־כּוֹס

The poets are clearly certain that Edom will also have to undergo YHWH's judgement. Kraus wrongly assumes, however, that the final canticle must therefore have been announced by a priest or a prophet to the assembled community in the form of a salvation oracle. His proposed liturgical setting, however, cannot be reconciled with 2_6 (cf introduction III.3) nor with what we have already heard with respect to the priests and the prophets who were either no longer active or had become fugitive.[261]

It is more probable here that the poets are expressing their recognition of those prophets who had predicted the end of Judah and Jerusalem. The accuracy of their predictions now becomes the basis of the poets' hope that their prophecies against Edom will also be fulfilled. After the fall of Judah, Ezekiel prophesied over Edom[262] and his voice was to be heard in Judah from far off Babylon. The Ezekelian 'vengefulness' evident in

258 See the explanation of 'daughter Judah' in 1_{4cB} together with TWAT I 868ff (Haag).
259 Cf BHH 366f.
260 Cf BHH 2070, Van Selms and JRBartlett, *Edom and the Edomites*, JSOT suppl series 77, Sheffield 1989, 40f.
261 Cf 2_9, 4_{14-16}.
262 Ezek 25_{12-14}, 35_{1-15}.

3_{60} might make reference thereto. It is also possible, however, that the present text stands primarily under the influence of Jeremiah since he is the only prophet who literally states (2x) that Edom must drink the cup of YHWH's judgement.[263] The prophecy against Edom in Isa 34_{1-17} appears to be post-exilic.[264]

The presence of the preposition עַל makes the combination עבר עַל somewhat ambiguous since the idea of 'direction' leads one to expect the preposition אֶל. The use of עַל, however, not only provides for direction in which the 'cup' is going but also its target or purpose.[265] It is no longer a question of 'going towards' but rather of 'overcoming'. YHWH's cup of judgement will overcome Edom. The conjunction גַּם indicates that daughter Edom is not alone. Of course, daughter Zion is also – first – among those who will drink the cup but in the summary found in Jer 25_{17-27} it is clear that many other (neighbouring) nations will follow suit, Edom among them.

כּוֹס stands for a drinking vessel or bowl shaped cup which was substantially larger than an ordinary wine glass. In Ezek 23_{32}, the cup of YHWH's judgement is descriped as deep and wide.[266]

The image of drinking a cup of (poisoned) wine to its dregs is used metaphorically in a number of pre-exilic and exilic prophetic texts for the endurance of YHWH's judgement,[267] the effects of the wine standing (also metaphorically) for the effects of YHWH's punitive judgement. Drunkenness brings a loss of physical and mental self-control and leads a person to behave like a fool, vomit, stagger, stumble and fall. Once a drunkard hits the ground he cannot get up again.[268] Increased body temperature brought on by drink can lead a person to strip naked[269] and expose him / herself to ridicule and ultimate vulnerability in the eyes of the enemy. Thus the enemy rejoice over Lady Jerusalem (// 1_{21}; cf 1_{8b}),

---

263 Cf Jer 25_{21}, 49_{12}; cf also 9_{24}.

264 Cf OKaiser, *Der Prophet Jesaja, Kapitel 13–39*, Göttingen 1973, 280.

265 Cf Gen $18_{3,5}$, I Kgs 9_8.

266 See the pictorial representations in OKeel, *Die Welt der altorientalischen Bildsymbolik und das Alte Testament*, Zürich-Einsiedeln-Köln-Neukirchen-Vluyn 1977², 176, 307f, 320 and ANEP 155 (cf TWAT IV 109 [Mayer]). For further information on (the possible origin of) YHWH's cup of wrath see HABrongers, 'Der Zornesbecher', OTS 15 (1969), 177–192 and excursus 10 following Jer 25_{15ff} in AvSelms, *Jeremia deel II*, Nijkerk 1974, 18f.

267 See Nah 3_{11}, Hab 2_{16}, Jer 49_{12}, 51_{17}, Ezek 23_{32-34}, Isa $51_{17,22}$; cf also Ps 75_9.

268 Jer $25_{16,27}$, 48_{26}, 51_7, Isa $51_{17,22}$; cf Nah 3_{11}.

269 Cf Gen 9_{21}, Hab $2_{15,16}$; cf also ASvdWoude, *Habakuk-Sefanja*, Nijkerk 1978, 47ff.

her children lie on the ground, slain by the sword (// 2_{21}) and the גֶּבֶר laments that he has become the laughing stock of his enemies (// $3_{62,63}$).

21bB *and you shall drink and uncover yourself!* תִּשְׁכְּרִי וְתִתְעָרִי

Daughter Edom will ultimately have to face her fate and confront the cup of YHWH's judgement.[270] She will be forced to drink the wine of YHWH's burning anger (Jer 25_{15}). Jeremiah's use of the term חֵמָה in this context fits well with the image of the cup since the basic meaning of חֵמָה has to do with 'heat' and alludes to a person's internal change of temperament when angry.[271] While it is true that the present strophe does not speak about YHWH's חֵמָה this can be found in the parallel concluding canticle of the first panel (4:11a) where the verb שׁפך first resounds and continues to resonate into the present verse. The wine of YHWH's wrath will cause daughter Edom to burst into flame (cf 4_{11bA}). Befuddled and inflamed with drink she will throw off her clothes.[272] Thus the same will happen to Edom as happened to Lady Jerusalem: her nakedness will be exposed with all the scandalous consequences thereof.[273]

22aA *Your iniquity has amplifed itself, daughter Zion!* תַּם־עֲוֹנֵךְ בַּת־צִיּוֹן

Kraus, for example, translates this colon as "Zu Ende ist deine Strafe", an approach which is consistent with his belief that these verses constitute an oracle of salvation which is being adressed to the people in YHWH's name. Van Selms has a similar understanding: God's anger has burnt itself out. In the same line: Calvin, Keil, Aalders, Haller, Wiesmann, Meek, Rudolph, Plöger, Gordis, Kaiser, Brandscheidt, Boecker, Groß, Westermann. In spite of the evident scholarly unanimity on this question, we are of the opinion that such an understanding of the text is incorrect. There is absolutely no evidence that Lady Zion's punishment is at an end. Indeed the parallel contexts offer powerful witness to the contrary. Thus, at the end of the first song Lady Zion complains that her heart is sick; at the end of the second song the poets describe the murder of her children; at the end of the third song, the humiliation and affliction of the גֶּבֶר is undiminished; the final song follows 4_{22} with the further portrayal of profound misfortune in the land. In addition, in all five songs, the ongoing

[270] Cf Jer 25_{21} and 49_{12}.

[271] See the explanation of 2_{4c}.

[272] Cf the meaning of the *pi'el* of √ערה in Gen 24_{20}, II Chron 24_{11}; cf also TWAT VI 370 (Niehr).

[273] Cf the explanation of 1_{8bB} for the complements of the nakedness metaphor.

affliction of the city and its inhabitants is rendered in the present tense (cf the introduction to the fourth song). A few exegetes do recognise this fact but they maintain their position in the case of 4_{22aA} by reading the verb as a prophetic perfect.[274]

The verb תמם does not mean the expiration of something but rather its complete execution: "Bei *tmm* ist nicht die Vorstellung eines Mannes leitend, der seinem Werk gegenüber steht und es vollendet, vielmehr geht es um einen Prozeß, der im betroffenen Gegenstand oder Menschen schon angelegt ist und durch immanente Notwendigkeit zu gutem oder bosem Ende führt."[275] While it is true that Koch is propounding his thesis of the 'Schicksalwirkende Tatsphäre' or immanent 'Tun-Ergehen Zusammenhang' here, he is nevertheless correct in pointing to the continuation of Jerusalem's עָוֹן to its bitter end with respect to this text: the guilt which she accrued on account of her עָוֹן ultimately results in her present fate. Koch incorrectly proposes the present text as proof of the immanent connection between sin and its consequence. Although God is not mentioned here, in the context of the five songs as a whole, the poets continue to see YHWH as The One who has permitted this great misfortune to afflict his people and turned them over to the power of their enemies.

Thus the present colon does not say that the punishment of daughter Zion has come to an end. At the same time, it has nothing to do with a salvation oracle proclaimed by some nameless prophetic figure. On the contrary, the poets clearly state that the destructive effects of the sin of daughter Zion have reached completion.[276] This can be verified quite simply from observable facts. The violation of covenant stipulations was punishable by sanctions which, in prophetic announcements of doom, were evocatively elaborated in the form of a gloomy future for Israel should her transgressions continue. A topical elaboration thereof, found among a variety of prophets, was the day of YHWH, the day upon which his judgement would take place. The poets are aware that all the elements of upheaval and affliction associated with that day are now present: hunger and thirst, sickness and death, powerful enemies, destruction of palace and temple, wall and city, loss of home and land, exile. All the threatening words of the earlier prophets have come true, their prediction of judgement is now a present reality for Israel. The poets experience it for themselves

274 Cf, for example, Keil, Aalders and Van Selms.

275 Koch in THAT II 1047.

276 Compare also the use and meaning of √תמם in Num 14_{33-35}.

and say as much: 'You have brought on the day which you announced", (1_{21} and passim in Lamentations).

22aB *He has completed your exposure!* לֹא יוֹסִיף לְהַגְלוֹתֵךְ

Misunderstanding of the preceding colon among commentators has been largely to blame for what they have assumed to be the content of the present colon. As far back LXX (οὐ προσθήσει ἔτι ἀποικίσαι σε), this colon has been widely translated as: 'you shall no longer go into exile' but questions remain as to the reasoning behind such an interpretation of the text. Besides the already mentioned prophetic salvation oracle, Kraus bases his translation on Jer 52_{28-30} where a deportation is mentioned for the last time in the OT, perhaps around 581. Kraus seems to assume that the reference in question pertains to the last actual deportation although this, of course, cannot be confirmed from the text. He thus dates Lam IV in the period immediately following 581, a fact upon which one can base the certainty of the poets. In addition, Kraus tacitly assumes that the phrase in question came into being immediately after 581. In our opinion, however, this remains highly improbable. The text of Jer 52_{28-30} gives the impression of having been written at a much greater chronological distance from these events. Although the exact figures call for further study, one is tempted to imagine a relationship with the lists which appear in Ezra 2. Real certainty concerning the end of the exile only emerges during the time of Deutero-Isaiah and the termination of Babylonian domination by the Persians. Details with respect to the intervening years are found precisely in Lamentations and these can scarcely be interpreted as suggesting that things had entered a period of greater calm. The preceding canticle complains unremittingly that the people are still being hunted like animals while the following song refers to ongoing oppression and persecution. No one can be sure of his or her life and for this reason very many in Judah continue to opt for a voluntary exile somewhere far from home.[277]

There is a further and more significant historical datum which would render the classical translation impossible. As was evident from 4_{21b}, the poets are convinced that YHWH's judgement will also be brought upon Edom. This implies that the expected events have not yet taken place and that Edom is still in good spirits and has the upper hand (cf 1_{5a}). Of course, this contented position was not to hold forever, brought to an end as it was during the time of the Babylonian domination. It was

[277] Cf the explanation of Lam 5_6.

not Nebuchadnezzar but one of his successors, Nabonidus (555–539 BCE), who attacked Edom during his military campagne of 552.[278] Ob $_{7}$ notes how Babylon, Edom's former ally (cf Ob $_{11}$), attacked the land and deported its inhabitants.[279] Evidently, the Babylonians still had the power to manoeuvre successfully in Southern Trans-Jordania and Northern Arabia up to the appearance of Cyrus. This territory was close to Juda and their actions would certainly not have created any degree of certainty that the possibility of exile had run its course. Such confidence only emerged during the time of Cyrus the Persian (550–530).

Of course, the translation which we dispute did not simply appear out of the blue. The *hiph'il* of the root גלה is normally used only with the meaning 'to force into exile'.[280] Given its present vocalisation (*hiph'il* infinitive) the Masoretes themselves understood the text in this sense and they have been followed in their interpretation up to now. Besides the already mentioned historical arguments, however, there remain a number of strong literary and substantive arguments against their reading of the text.

Thus Westermann and Albertz[281] point to the unconventional use of YHWH as the subject of the deportation of his people: "Wohl ist in der prophetischen Gerichtsankündigung fest verankert, daß das Exil Jahwes Gericht ist, doch eignet dem mit *glh* bezeichneten Vorgang die ganze Schwere eines konkreten politischen Geschehens, das sich gegen eine völlige Theologisierung sträubt". They further note that Ezekiel avoids making a connection between YHWH and √גלה II, preferring rather to speak of dispersion as is the case in Deuteronomy (cf also Jer 18_{17}). Lam 4_{22}, in contrast, would appear to make quite conspicuous connection between the two.

In 1988, 340 (note 20) we already outlined the concentric structure of the present canticle. Compare the strong inclusion בַּת־צִיּוֹן (21aA) // בַּת־אֱדוֹם (22bA) mentioned in the introduction. The two central bicola of the canticle also enjoy a close chiastic relationship at both the literary level and the level of content and both are qualified by the imagery of the cup of judgement. Via גַּם and the parallel texts in the other songs it became clear that daughter Zion had drained the cup of judgement and was now enduring

278 Cf ANET[3] 305 and KRVeenhof, 'De geschiedenis van het oude Nabije Oosten', in: Bijbels Handboek I, ed ASvdWoude, Kampen 1981, 426.

279 See JRBartlett, *Edom and the Edomites*, JSOT suppl series 77, Sheffield 1989, 159, 161.

280 See TWAT I 1021 (Zobel).

281 See THAT I 420f.

all the effects thereof, including the public exhibition of her nakedness (cf 4_{21bB} and 1_{8bB}). This is a well known image from the prophecy of judgement in which the capital city of the nation in question is always presented as a woman and her punishment as the exposure of her nakedness, the summit of humiliation and icon of destruction.[282] If the first colon (4_{22aA}) is stating that Zion's sin has achieved completion and if the sudden mention of an end to deportation seems out of place then it seems evident that – by analogy with the second colon of 4_{21b} (drinking and exposing one's nakedness) – the second colon (4_{22aB}) is introducing the same image of nakedness in a parallel text. This is quite possible if one does not read the form (ל)הגלות(ך) as a *hiph'il* infinitive (= הַגְלוֹתֵךְ) but rather as a *niph'al* infinitive (= הִגָּלוֹתֵךְ) whereby the consonantal text remains unaltered. Thus the term does not mean 'to go into exile' but 'to be stripped naked'.[283] Ezek 16_{39} reveals a still deeper connection in this regard: stripping includes the removal of jewels (תִּפְאֶרֶת), a detail reminiscent of Lam 2_1. We are thus confronted with an inclusion at the level of the entire book: בַּת־צִיּוֹן (2_{1aA}) // בַּת־צִיּוֹן (4_{22aA}) and הִשְׁלִיךְ ... תִּפְאֶרֶת (2_{1b}) // הִגָּלוֹתֵךְ (4_{22aB}). The removal of daughter Zion's jewellery by YHWH constitutes a component of her stripping and exposure; the infinitive construct should be understood as a noun.[284] We already noted that Israel's 'jewel' was her temple which explains why the destruction of the temple on Mount Zion is described at the end of the first panel in the parallel verse 4_{11} (sub-canto response). Our explanation of this part of the text pointed to the fact that the destruction of Zion also implied the laying bare of her foundations.

The parallel כ-strophe (4_{11} [sub-canto response]) is also useful in helping to clarify the present colon. Indeed, since YHWH has calmed his rage, the effects of daughter Zion's עֲוֹן are complete (כִּלָּה [4_{11aA}] // תַּם [4_{22aA}], the latter being the final ת of the last alphabetic acrostic in the book of Lamentations as a whole!). Furthermore, of all the disasters confronting the people, the destruction of the temple is the worst,[285] and at the same time the first and the final lament of the songs as a whole.[286] This is true

---

282 Cf Nineveh (Nah $3_{5,7}$), Jerusalem (Jer 13_{25}, Ezek 16_{37}), Babylon (Isa 47_{2f}); cf Israel in Hos 2_5; cf also Lam 1_{8b}.

283 Cf II Sam 6_{20}, Ezek 21_{24} (MT 21_{29}); cf also Isa 47_{2f}, Jer 13_{22}, Ezek $16_{36f,57}$, 23_{29} and our explanation of גָּלְתָה in 1_{3aA} as the stripping / exposure of Lady Judah.

284 Cf GES-K § 114a.

285 Cf the centre of canto I of the second song (2_{6a}).

286 See 1_4 and 5_{18}.

from a theological and faith perspective as well as a material one and likewise reveals the significance of לֹא יוֹסִיף in this colon: there is nothing more that can be added to daughter Zion's nakedness and shame. She has reached her deepest point, indeed her end has come (cf 4_{18b}). Everything predicted in the prophecy of doom has come about. The construction employed here is quite common. The *hiph'il* of √יסף as an auxiliary verb followed by an infinitive construct from a different verb means "fortfahren etwas zu tun", "etwas noch mehr oder weiter tun". The same holds for √יסף + לֹא.[287] The subject is of course YHWH. He has handed his people over to the power of the enemy. By withdrawing from them he has allowed this present misfortune to confront his people. The prophecy of doom is thereby fulfilled and YHWH has nothing more to add.

22bA *He shall visit your iniquity, daughter Edom!* פָּקַד עֲוֹנֵךְ בַּת־אֱדוֹם

√פקד with YHWH as subject often refers to God's direct intervention in response to the deeds of human persons as both judgement and its execution in one.[288] Secure in their belief in prophecy – cf the explanation of 4_{21bA} – the poets are convinced that Edom will also have to face YHWH's judgement. Jer 9_{25f} literally states that YHWH will visit Edom among others. It is worth noting that the idea of 'observing'/'seeing' is characteristic of the root פקד. Thus it can stand parallel with the *hiph'il* of √נבט[289] which is the (distant) case here with הַבִּיטָה in 3_{63} where the גֶּבֶר expresses his awareness that YHWH sees the very sitting and rising of the enemy, that is their every movement.[290]

22bB *Your sins he shall uncover!* גִּלָּה עַל־חַטֹּאתָיִךְ

By way of the expression גלה עַל (*pi'el*), this final colon of Lam IV is likewise reminiscent of 2_{14} and the exposure of the עָוֹן of Jerusalem. At the same time, however, there is a significant difference between the two. While the text in 2_{14} had to do with the exposure of deeds of injustice, the (punitive) consequences of which were not yet visible, the present text pictures the actual public exposure of the consequences of sin. This in turn is reminiscent of the central strophe 4_6 in the first sub-canto (4_{1-11}), with the

286 See 1_4 and 5_{18}.

287 53x, cf Deut 25_3, Josh 23_{13}, Ps 41_9 etcetera; cf also TWAT III 687 (André).

288 Cf Jer $5_{9,29}$, 9_8, 25_{12} etcetera; cf also THAT II 477–484 (Schottroff) and TWAT VI 716–718 (André). For the translation of the perfect as a present with a future significance see GES-K § 106*m,n*.

289 Cf TWAT VI 471 (André).

290 For the content of the term עָוֹן cf 2_{14b}.

same combination and in the same order: חַטָּאת and עָוֹן. Both concepts incorporate the notions of violation and its associated punishment although each can enjoy a different emphasis depending on the context (cf 2_{14} and 4_6). The use of עָוֹן in Lam 4_6 gives the impression that the emphasis is being placed on the transgression itself whereas the use of חַטָּאת seems to focus more on the consequences thereof.[291] The same is evident in the present colon: YHWH sees / examines the sins of Edom and He will effect the relevant punishment in a visible way. This is the sense in which one should understand the use of גלה (*pi'el* 3m sg pf) here. Indeed the literary concatenation which is established via הַגְלוֹתֵךְ in 4_{22aB} suggests an analogous interpretation of √גלה in the present text: 'to strip'/'to expose'. As a matter of fact, this and the previous colon offer a positive expectation with respect to the outcome of the prayer in 1_{21cB}: וְיִהְיוּ כָמוֹנִי 'let them become like me' and the elaboration thereof in the same final canticle of the first song: 1_{22ab}: 'deal with them as you have dealt with me because of all my transgressions'. Even the final canticle of Lam III (3_{64-66}) very strongly reflects the prophecy of the cup of judgement which YHWH will make the nations drink on account of their iniquities. This very parallel effectively supports our explanation of the text.

The question remains as to the substance of daughter Edom's עָוֹן and חַטָּאת which has brought upon her such a punishment. In the prophecy of Obadiah, Edom is accused of gloating, looting, cutting off refugees (cf Ezek 35_5), making slaves and assisting in the transportation of prisoners (Ob $_{11-14}$) but none of these transgressions can be derived from the present canticle.

What can we derive from the context? In the parallel colon in 1_{22aA} 'all their evildoing' (כָּל־רָעָתָם) is mentioned but this refers to the enemy in general and is of no real help here. In 2_{21f} mention is made of merciless massacres. Given the strong associations between the second and the fourth songs together with the reference to this crime in Obadiah it seems evident that texts in question point to the work of the Edomites.

The final canticle of the third song provides further information still. Our explanation of this canticle revealed that the deprivation of land and homes was assumed in 3_{65}. This is confirmed by 5_2. It is evident from Ezek 35_{10} and 36_6 that even the exiles were aware of this hostile policy and the horrendous problems it created for the population of Judah and Jerusalem.

[291] See the explanation of 1_{8a} for the particular accents of חַטָּאת.

Archaeological research has confirmed that Edom invaded the south of Judah after 587 at the latest and took partial possession of the land.[292] Beit-Arieh has recently reported on the excavation of a large Edomite sanctuary at Horvat Qitmit, ± 30 kilometers west of the southern tip of the Dead Sea, offering further proof of Edomite expansion into Judah.[293]

In conclusion, one particular text concerning the transgressions of Edom against Judah is particularly striking, III Ezra 4_{45}. This non-canonical text speaks of the Edomites as the ones who set fire to the temple in Jerusalem. In the light of II Kgs 25_{8f} one is tempted not to attach much value to this report. Nevertheless, III Ezra does have a great deal in common with the books of Chronicles, Ezra and Nehemia and the Greek offers a better translation of the relevent Hebrew and Aramaic portions than that of the canonical texts.[294] While it is true that 4_{45} occurs at the conclusion of an interpolation concerning the three courtiers of king Darius (III Ezra 3_1-4_{63}), it remains an extremely remarkable statement and one which cannot be easily derived from other well known data. Bartlett is incorrect in suggesting that the later power of the Edomites is being projected back here to 587.[295] The biblical authors did not deal with history in such a simple fashion. It would seem more reasonable to assume that a historical transmission process lies behind the text. Thus Ob $_{11}$ gives the impression that Edomite factions took part in the military engagements which ultimately brought about the fall of Jerusalem.[296] It is clear that the Babylonians exercised a supervising role in the destruction of the temple and that they had primary responsibility therefore (cf II Kgs 25_{8-10}). Indeed the Babylonians went down in history in this capacity and are mentioned as such not only in the canonical tradition – with strong connections to the prophecies of doom in Jeremiah and Ezekiel – but also in III Ezra itself (1_{55}). It is not unimaginable, however, that in destroying the temple, the Babylonians did not wish to risk incurring the wrath of the god who

---

292 Cf AAlt, 'Judas Gaue unter Josia', PJB 21 (1925), 100–115; MNoth, 'Die Einnahme von Jerusalem im Jahre 597 v. Chr.', ZDPV 74 (1958), 155f; SHerrmann, *Geschichte Israels*, München 1973, 388; JMMyers, 'Edom and Judah in the Sixth-Fifth Centuries B.C.', in: *Near Eastern Studies in Honor of WFAlbright*, ed HGoedicke, Baltimore 1971, 386–392; JRBartlett, *Edom and the Edomites*, JSOT suppl series 77, Sheffield 1989, 127f, 140–143.

293 IBeit-Arieh, 'New Light on the Edomites', BAR (1988), 28–41.

294 Cf OEissfeldt, *Einleitung in das Alte Testament*, 1964[3], 777–781.

295 Cf Bartlett, 156.

296 Cf HWWolff, *Dodekapropheton 4, Obadja, Jona*, BKAT XIV/3, Neukirchen–Vluyn 1977, 35f.

was being worshipped there so they handed the task to the self-confident Edomites. Strikingly enough, Ps 137_7 points in a similar direction, the Edomites being the very ones mentioned as the 'demolishers' of Zion. The literary structure of Lam IV confirms this in its own way. Our explanation of 4_{12} revealed an inclusion within the sub-canto (4_{12-22}) which established a relationship between the enemy within Jerusalem's gates and the Edomites: צַר וְאוֹיֵב (4_{12}) // בַּת־אֱדוֹם (4_{22b}). Furthermore, 4_1 and 4_{11} speak of the destruction of the temple, the א-strophe (4_1 [devastation]) forming an inclusion with the ת-strophe (4_{11} [the Edomites]) at the song level. Within Lam IV the כ-strophe (4_{11}) is responsively related to the ת-strophe (4_{22}): the כ-strophe speaks of the burning of the temple while Edom is explicitly named in the ת-strophe which constitutes a response thereto. It would be wrong to conclude, however, that Edom's sin was the burning of the temple since this does not fit well with the theological declaration in 4_{11} where YHWH himself is seen as the actual instigator of the fire.

The concluding sections of Lam I–III offer further (implied) interpretations of Edom's עָוֹן. Besides this, however, the destruction of the temple has to be seen as the most accurate reflection of Edomite hubris and recklessness. It is quite possible that this attitude was based on their theological evaluation of the situation. Indeed, the discovery of the Edomite temple at Horvat Qitmit reveals that their claim to the land (Ezek 35_{10} and 36_5) had religious pretensions at its base: YHWH did not posses the land but rather their own divinity who could equally well be worshipped on Judean territory! It is reasonable to assume that this attack on YHWH's sovereignty was more offensive than the attrocities they committed against the Judean population (cf Ezek $35_{10,13}$!). Indeed this very sin of hubris is mentioned in Ps 74 as the reason for YHWH's intervention (cf Ps $74_{18,22f}$).

Lamentations V

1. *Remember,* YHWH, *what is happening to us,*
   look and see our humiliation!

2. *Our inheritence is in the hands of strangers,*
   our houses in the hands of hostile foreigners!

3. *We have become orphans,*
   fatherless,
   our mothers as widows!

4. *To drink our own water costs money*
   and for our own wood we are forced to pay!

---

5. *Upon our neck we are persecuted,*
   we are exhausted,
   no one offers us rest!

6. *To Egypt we hold out a hand,*
   to Assyria for relief with bread!

7. *Our fathers have sinned;*
   they are no longer,
   but we, we shoulder their iniquities!

8. *Servants rule over us,*
   no one saves us from their hand!

9. *We must endanger our lives to get our bread,*
   because of the sword of the wilderness!

10. *Our skin has become as coarse as an oven(-wall)*
    because of the furies of famine.

---

11. *Women in Zion they rape,*
    girls in the cities of Judah!

12. *Princes are hung up at their hands,*
    the countenance of the elders is not honoured!

13. *Young men take up the millstone*
and boys stagger under the burden of wood!

14. *Elders stay away from the gate,*
young men from their music!

---

15. *It has ceased the joy of our heart,*
transformed into mourning our dance!

16. *Fallen is the crown of our head!*
Woe to us, for we have sinned!

17. *Because of this our heart is sick,*
because of these things our eyes have grown dark:

18. *because of the desolate Mount Zion,*
because of the jackals which range there!

---

19. *You,* YHWH, *you sit enthroned forever!*
Your throne is from generation to generation!

20. *Why do you forget us unremittingly,*
leave us alone as (our) days pass by?

21. *Bring us back,* YHWH, *to you,*
and we shall repent!
renew our days as of old!

22. *Or do you prefer to reject us forever,*
to rage against us without measure?

LITERARY STRUCTURE OF THE CANTO LAMENTATIONS V

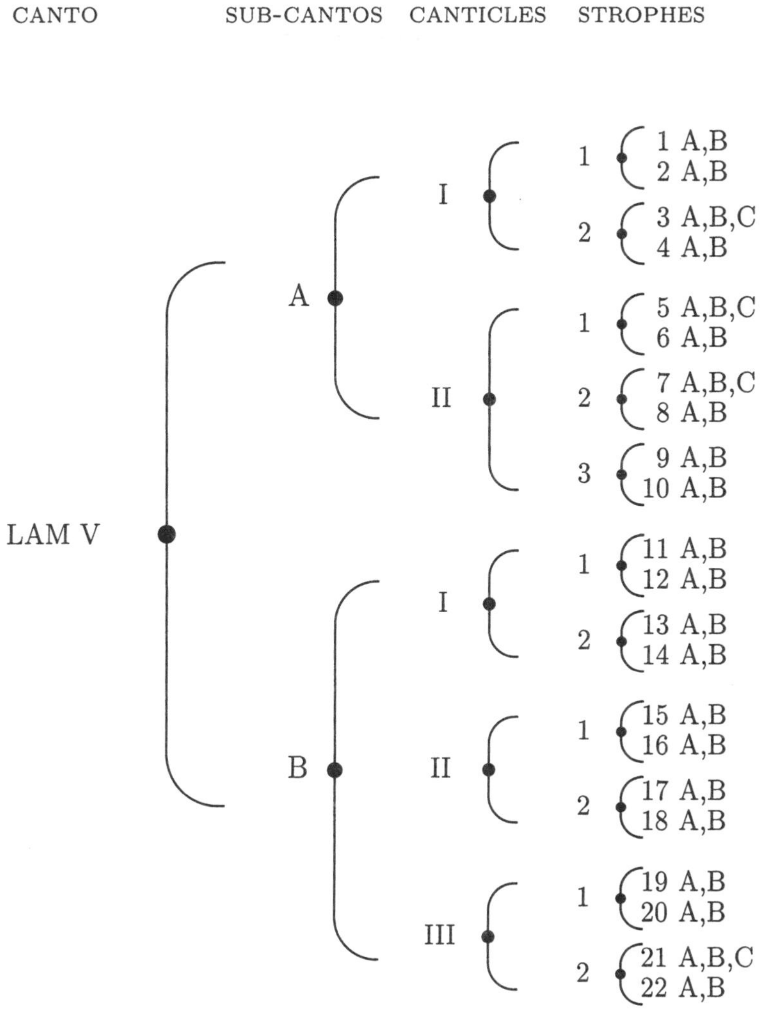

CANTO SUB-CANTOS CANTICLES STROPHES

- LAM V
  - A
    - I
      - 1
        - 1 A,B
        - 2 A,B
      - 2
        - 3 A,B,C
        - 4 A,B
    - II
      - 1
        - 5 A,B,C
        - 6 A,B
      - 2
        - 7 A,B,C
        - 8 A,B
      - 3
        - 9 A,B
        - 10 A,B
  - B
    - I
      - 1
        - 11 A,B
        - 12 A,B
      - 2
        - 13 A,B
        - 14 A,B
    - II
      - 1
        - 15 A,B
        - 16 A,B
      - 2
        - 17 A,B
        - 18 A,B
    - III
      - 1
        - 19 A,B
        - 20 A,B
      - 2
        - 21 A,B,C
        - 22 A,B

For literary argumentation see
1988, 347–360 and exegesis.

figure 5

Essentials and Perspectives

The fifth song departs most substantially from the characteristic features found in the other four. Perhaps the most striking difference is the opening words of the song which substitute the 'ah' of the lament for a unique accumulation of imperatives which articulate the most urgent appeal to YHWH known to the OT: 'Remember... look and see'. The significance of the three imperatives reveals the prayer character of Lam V. Compared with Lam I–III there is something of a reversal in this respect. The first three songs contain a variety of expressions of prayer spread more or less evenly throughout their portrayal of great affliction. The present song, however, places the same portrayal of affliction in the very midst of prayer, not only beginning with an appeal to YHWH but also ending with one. In association with this it is understandable that the form of the alphabetic acrostic is not employed in the composition of this last song. This acrostic form was an appropriate means for describing the disaster afflicting Judah and Jerusalem from A – Z but it is not fitting for unremitting prayer. While Judah continues in this dreadful situation such prayer must not cease (cf the explanation of 3_{50}). It is also striking that the plural forms no longer alternate with singular forms. This is a prayer of the community. The devout גֶּבֶר of the third song is joined by others around him and together they cry out to YHWH. The גֶּבֶר has found some allies to share in his renewed sense of turst and to hope with him that YHWH will intervene to liberate them.

In terms of structure, Lam V is similar to the first two songs: a concentric canto with two sub-cantos. The first sub-canto (5_{1-10}) begins with an appeal to YHWH. He is summoned to look upon the insults and humiliation the people have suffered made concrete in the description of the affliction in the land. The second sub-canto continues this but focuses primarily on the sorrow in and of Zion. It concludes with a prayer for release and restoration.

After the urgent opening appeal (5_1) the remainder of the first canticle (5_{1-4}) sets forth Judah's predicament before YHWH. The first concrete lament has to do with loss of inheritence, an essential loss since the land was the source of every good which came from YHWH. Loss of the land also had a direct effect on YHWH since he, as testator, had given it to Israel. Now he is confronted with the sight of foreigners running the land in place of its rightful possessors. The second lament further elaborates this theme. Together with the land, the cities and their houses have also been lost.

Hostile foreigners have taken the homes of the people of Judah for their own possession and the population is thus rootless. In 5_3 the poets place the emphasis on the people's defencelessness and vulnerability: Judah has no one to give her leadership and is forced to do without even the most essential necessities of life. Even their own water and wood have to be bought from the enemy.

The second canticle (5_{5-10}) of the first sub-canto (5_{1-10}) contains three strophes. The fourth strophe of Lam V stands in the centre of this canticle, a position which suggests a degree of accentuation. The sins of the now defunct and deported leaders are designated as the source of the present oppression. The same association is made in 2_{14} and 4_{12}. Although the speakers do not deny their own guilt, an emphasis on the primary responsibility of the 'fathers' creates a convincing impression that, to a significant extent, the affliction of the people has its roots in the guilt of others. This only makes the people's agony all the more acute, intense suffering which is further elaborated by way of references to the oppression of the people and the terrible famine. Following on from 5_7, 5_8 reports that the place of their deported leaders has been taken over by those who were once servants but who now have the authority. Such servants probably include the neighbouring nations who themselves were formerly subject to Judah. Their attitude towards their former enslavement is marked by viscious rancour. They simply exploit the population and force them into unremitting slave labour. This abuse goes hand in hand with great hunger. The people can no longer use their own fields to grow food (cf 4_9). There is little or no bread available and secret supplies of food hidden in the desert can only be drawn upon at extreme risk. The affliction is so great that many consider it pointless to remain in Judah and head for foreign territory in search of survival (5_6).

The second sub-canto (5_{11-22}) consists of three canticles: the first (5_{11-14}) is characterised by its concentration on the facts surrounding the actual situation of distress in Zion and in the land; the second (5_{15-18}) explains how ruin and destruction have robbed Zion of her *joie de vivre*; the third (5_{19-22}) rounds off the entire book of Lamentations with an urgent prayer for salvation and restoration.

The first canticle (5_{11-14}) continues the description of the distress, focusing particularly on Zion even though the dreadful situation in the other cities of Judah is also alluded to via concatenation. A number of the enemy's more degrading practices are mentioned. The absence (only here) of the 1st person plural suffix places emphasis on the fact of these events and not so much on the experience thereof. In harmony with the accentuation found elsewhere in the songs (cf the explanation of 3_{51}) the distress of the women is first to be named. They can find no safety and are forced to endure rape and humiliation as a consequence of the lack of even the most elementary protection. Authority's last remaining representatives – the princes and the elders – are either under threat themselves or already dead. The daily routine of the people has become impossible and any contentment they once found in it is gone. The complaints themselves serve to focus YHWH's attention on the violation of the way of life which he himself established and sanctioned.

It is striking that in the second canticle (5_{15-18}), which describes the sorrow of Zion, the poets do not engage in avoidance manoeuvres by placing the blame on the shoulders of the leadership. Zion's ruination is now blamed directly on her own sin. With the final prayer in mind, every possible excuse is avoided. The confession itself, however, does nothing to lessen Zion's sorrow. Zion's downfall is a death-blow to her people. Indeed, the once bustling temple mountain has become mound of corpses.

The final canticle (5_{19-22}) contains the final prayer of Lamentations expressed in compact but highly charged language. The direct address to 'YHWH' is extremely significant. The גֶּבֶר and his followers pray to him, to the one who ultimately permitted all this to happen. In spite of the facts, however, YHWH remains the God of Israel. He alone can bring about a reversal in their fortunes. The confession that YHWH is enthroned forever is not simply ornamental. It is as one enthroned that YHWH acts as judge and it is in this capacity that he is addressed here. YHWH is a God who brings about justice on behalf of the oppressed (cf the prayers at the end of the third song). The expression 'Your throne is from generation to generation!' is likewise far from being mere poetic embellishment. The fact that the poets – in spite of the destruction of Zion – continue to speak of YHWH's throne implies that they do not consider YHWH's enthronement to be bound to Zion. Thus, the tradition they once confessed remains true: the foundations of YHWH's throne are justice and righteousness. In mentioning the fact that the duration of YHWH's throne continues into the following generation, the poets focus our attention on a new generation, one which, while not guilty of the fall of Jerusalem and Judah is nevertheless forced to endure the terrible consequences thereof (cf 2_{18-19}).

The mention of YHWH's enthronement enduring from generation to generation thus constitutes an implicit prayer for justice and righteousness for the generation of Zion's downfall as well as for those which will follow it. While the poets continue to express the intense struggle involved in their experience of the conflict between bitter reality and the expectations of faith, they ultimately go on to confront YHWH with direct questions. Why does he not intervene? Why does he leave them to their fate when days of horror and despair pile up before them? After this the poets express their desires more explicitly, giving pride of place to an appeal to YHWH to make a new start with them. Their prayer for YHWH to bring them back to him is simultaneously an appeal for his renewed presence in Zion, a prayer for him to reside once again in his own city amongst his own people. He alone can make this happen. He alone can break the terrible silence between them. If he does return to them, then they will return to the practice of right relationship with him via the observance of the commandments and the liturgy. These latter thoughts are reminiscent of the good things of the past during the time of the monarchy under the protection of the Davidic kings. Thus the final prayer of the songs constitutes an appeal for the restoration of those years of prosperity.

The final words of Lamentations reveal that even renewed faith and trust do not provide absolute certainty. Only YHWH himself can provide such a thing. Will he hear their prayer? The poets express the possibility that he might refuse to listen their prayer with the most pregnant of terms. They speculate concerning the tension brought on by the gulf which stands between reality and God's heart. Will YHWH really reject those he once chose to be his own people, Israel? Will he really let his wrath go so far that survival will become impossible? The songs thus conclude with an open question, an implied appeal to God's mercy. He alone can save them and restore their lives.

Lamentations V

Scholarly Exposition

Introduction

At first sight it is hardly surprising that the history of research into the book of Lamentations has tended to consider the final song as a somewhat unusual literary unit. What strikes commentators immediately is the absence of the alphabetic acrostic[1] but differences in metre also set Lam v apart, the *qinah* rhythm of the first four songs making way for bicola with 3 + 3 or 4 + 3 measures. In addition, the final song is much shorter than the preceding four. An analysis of the argumentation which favours the literary isolation of Lam v, however, reveals that it has its roots in an obsession with form. Commentators only accept that the songs which belong together are those which share similar or even identical forms. We have already discussed the principle arguments for and against the isolation of Lam v in greater detail elsewhere.[2] Further research, however, has produced two extremely important arguments which tend to support the original unity of Lam i–v. Thus, it would seem that the poets themselves anticipated the question of the absence of the alphabetic acrostic with the expression אֵין אָב in 5_3 (see the exegesis). A stronger argument, however, is evident in the strong cohesion between all of the songs which is clear from the variety of song-responses. In our structural analysis we offered a survey of the various examples of external parallelism at the same level between the songs.[3] Closer examination of the text, however, has uncovered even more levels of association and this has prompted us to provide an updated survey in the present commentary (cf pp 636–641).

---

[1] Cf SBergler, 'Threni V – nur ein alphabetisierendes Lied? Versuch einer Deutung', VT XVII (1977), 311–313.

[2] Cf 1983, 59–77.

[3] See 1988, 392–394 and also introduction III.1.

The most important of the two aforementioned arguments in support of the original unity of Lam I–V deserves closer examination. Lam V has 22 verses which agrees numerically with the number of strophes in Lam I–IV. The absence of an alphabetic acrostic is intentional. The poets intially employed the acrostic form to render the idea of the totality of the disaster confronting the people: from A – Z.[4] This took place primarily in the form of laments interspersed with prayers. In the final song, however, the opposite is the case: the laments are now spread out in the primary context of prayer. Early in the songs it was stated that this prayer would continue until YHWH listened (cf 2_{18}, 3_{49f}), but the all-inclusive totality of the alpabetic acrostic was not in harmony with the ongoing character of the prayer and thus the poets opted to drop it in the final song. The distinction in size between this and the other songs is also intentional. The poets wanted to define the shape of the songs as a whole by the *qinah* metre with its 3 (long) + 2 (short) measures.[5]

A further new argument can now be supplied to the structural arguments explored above: without the fifth song the fourth song is like a tailless torso. The first three songs conclude with prayer but this is absent from the conclusion of Lam IV. If one were to take the fourth and the fifth songs together, however, then the fifth complements the fourth in terms of prayer. Furthermore, Lam IV and V taken together amount to practically the same dimensions as the first three songs taken separately. This is in harmony with the poetic style of the Hebrew in which the poets strove to establish a balance between the larger units.[6] What we find in 1_{20}, 2_{20} and 3_{58} as the introduction to prayer can be found in the fifth song at the very beginning: 'Look and see'. The extended prayer of Lam V is in fact an expansion of the concluding sections of the first three songs.

Unity and Structure

The above-mentioned responsive cohesion between the songs likewise implies the unity of Lam V. Such cohesion ultimately excludes the possibility that Lamentations as such consists of distinct and independently com-

---

4 See introduction III.5.

5 Cf WHShea, 'The qinah Structure of the Book of Lamentations', Biblica 60 (1979), 103–107. Further information on this matter can be found in the introduction (III.1).

6 Cf MCAKorpel – JCdMoor, 'Fundamentals of Ugaritic and Hebrew Poetry', in: *The Structural Analysis of Biblical and Canaanite Poetry*, (eds WvdMeer and JCdMoor) JSOT suppl series 74, Sheffield 1988, 52, 56; cf also 1988, 388.

posed poems which were later brought together into the collection we have before us, as Brunet suggests.[7] For Brunet, the composite character of the songs also relates to Lam V which he views as two independent poems, namely 5_{1-14} and 5_{15-22}. His decision to split Lam V in this way is based on a presumed distinction in style and content between the two parts. His primary argument focuses on a contradiction in the 'Letztgestalt' of the song which he proposes between 5_7: 'the fathers have sinned' and 5_{16}: 'we have sinned'. According to Brunet it is still basically possible to harmonise both expressions but he prefers to take it as evidence of two different poets.

At the level of content Brunet's argument remains unconvincing. The sin of one does not exclude the sin of another. From the literary perspective, there are a multitude of arguments to be found in the many inclusions and responses which serve to unite both 'hypothetical' parts of the song. Indeed, the inclusions betray a strongly concentric structure:

Literary argumentation:

inclusions (at strophe level):

(22A) כִּי אִם . . . \\ (1A) זְכֹר
(19A, 21A) יְהוָה // (1A) יְהוָה
(22B) קָצַפְתָּ // (1B) חֶרְפָּתֵנוּ[8]
(21B) חַדֵּשׁ יָמֵינוּ כְּקֶדֶם \\ (2B) בָּתֵּינוּ לְנָכְרִים
(21B) חַדֵּשׁ יָמֵינוּ כְּקֶדֶם \\ (2A) נַחֲלָתֵנוּ נֶהֶפְכָה לְזָרִים
(20) לָמָּה . . . תַּעַזְבֵנוּ // (3A) אֵין אָב
(18A) הַר־צִיּוֹן שֶׁשָּׁמֵם // (6) מִצְרַיִם . . . אַשּׁוּר
(16B) חָטָאנוּ // (7A) חָטְאוּ
(16A) נָפְלָה עֲטֶרֶת רֹאשֵׁנוּ // (8A) עֲבָדִים מָשְׁלוּ בָנוּ
(14A) זְקֵנִים מִשַּׁעַר שָׁבָתוּ // (9B) מִפְּנֵי חֶרֶב
(12A) שָׂרִים בְּיָדָם נִתְלוּ // (11A) נָשִׁים בְּצִיּוֹן עִנּוּ

responses:

(15B) נֶהְפַּךְ // (2A) נֶהֶפְכָה
(11B, 13) נְעָרִים/בַּחוּרִים/בְּתֻלֹת // (3A) יְתוֹמִים
(11) בְּתֻלֹת // נָשִׁים // (3B) אִמֹּתֵינוּ
(12A) שָׂרִים בְּיָדָם נִתְלוּ // (3A) אֵין אָב
(13B) בָּעֵץ // (4B) עֵצֵינוּ
(16A) רֹאשֵׁנוּ // (5A) צַוָּארֵנוּ
(17A) לִבֵּנוּ // (9A) בְּנַפְשֵׁנוּ

---

[7] GBrunet, 'La Cinquième Lamentation', VT XXXIII (1983), 149–170.

[8] cf Jer 24_9, 49_{13}, Ezek 5_{15} etcetera.

These responses are to be found primarily at the canticle level (see the exegesis for delimitation and argumentation). The many inclusions point to the song's evidently concentric structure which clearly could not have come into existence with the combination of two different songs, unless one is willing to accept further reworking after this point. If this were the case then one would be better to speak of a new song or poem which made use of existing material. I do not believe, however, that this is what we have in Lam V. The intertwining of this last song with those which precede it reveals that Lam V was part of the book of Lamentations from the start.

Strophic Division

While Lam V does not have the strophic, alphabetical acrostic form of the other four songs this does not imply that the verses simply follow one another in an unrelated fashion. Indeed, past commentators have already defended the existence of strophes in Lam V although there has been little agreement with respect to the boundaries thereof.[9] We understand the strophic division of Lam V as follows: as with the fourth song, each strophe consists of two consecutive verses. Although this is not immediately evident in the first six verses, the scheme becomes quite clear from verses 7–8 onwards:

STROPHE:	DISTINGUISHING AND BINDING ELEMENTS:
IV (5_{7-8})	אֵינָם (7A) // אֵין (8B); antithetical parallelism אֲבֹתֵינוּ (7B) \\ עֲבָדִים (8A).
V (5_{9-10})	מִפְּנֵי חֶרֶב הַמִּדְבָּר (9b) // מִפְּנֵי זַלְעֲפוֹת רָעָב (10B); see also the inclusion מִּדְבָּר (4_{3bB}) // רָעָב (4_{9aB}) between the second and fourth canticles of Lam IV. Furthermore, there is chiastic parallelism between לַחְמֵנוּ (9A) and רָעָב (10B).
VI (5_{11-12})	There is assonance/alliteration and formal parallelism between נָשִׁים בְּ (11A) and שָׂרִים בְּ (12B). With regard to the parallelism between בְּתֻלֹת (11B) and זְקֵנִים (12B) see Lam $2_{10,21}$.
VII (5_{13-14})	Chiastic parallelism is clearly evident beween בַּחוּרִים (13A) and בַּחוּרִים (14B) as well as between נְעָרִים (13B) and זְקֵנִים (14A). Cf also Lam 2_{21}.

[9] Cf 1988, 347f.

VIII (5_{15-16}) There is linear parallelism between לִבֵּנוּ (15A) and רֹאשֵׁנוּ (16B) as well as between אֲבֵל (15B) and אוֹי־נָא לָנוּ (16B).

IX (5_{17-18}) Linear parallelism is evident between עַל (17A) and עַל (18A). At the same time there is a disjunctive *petucha* after 5_{18}.

X (5_{19-20}) Linear parallelism is evident between לְעוֹלָם (19A) and לָנֶצַח (20A) and between לְדֹר וָדוֹר (19B) and לְאֹרֶךְ יָמִים (20B). Cf also the vocative יְהוָה at the beginning of 5_{19} which often indicates the beginning of a new strophe in the Psalms.[10] The same is true for the first word of 5_{19}, the personal pronoun אַתָּה.[11] In 5_{20}, the expression לָנֶצַח and the parallel לְאֹרֶךְ יָמִים indicates the end of this strophe.[12]

XI (5_{21-22}) The vocative יְהוָה is also present in 21A. In addition, there appears to be a formal parallelism between הֲשִׁיבֵנוּ...וְנָשׁוּב (21A) and מָאֹס מְאַסְתָּנוּ (22A) as well as antithetical parallelism between חַדֵּשׁ יָמֵינוּ כְּקֶדֶם (21B) and כִּי אִם...קָצַפְתָּ עָלֵינוּ עַד־מְאֹד (22B).

Given the fact that each of these strophes consists of two Masoretic verses, it seems reasonable to examine the first six verses for a similar strophic division: 1–2 / 3–4 / 5–6. Comparison with other strophes does indeed provide arguments in support of this division:

STROPHE: DISTINGUISHING AND BINDING ELEMENTS:

I (5_{1-2}) The beginning of the first strophe is marked by the vocative יְהוָה which corresponds with similar usage in the last two strophes. One argument in support of the end of this strophe – in conjunction with the evidence that each strophe consists of two verses – is the observation that the second strophe clearly begins with 5_3. Additional arguments can be found below. At the level of content, Joel 2_{17} supports the parallel between humiliation and lost inheritence

[10] Cf PvdLugt, *Strofische structuren in de bijbels-hebreeuwse poëzie*, Kampen 1980, 515f.

[11] See for this and other markers which (often) indicate the beginning of a strophe vdLugt, 510–517.

[12] See for this and other markers which (often) indicate the end of a strophe vdLugt, 519–524.

(cf also Ezek 36_{4f} and $35_{12,15}$). In Ps $74_{10,18}$, the root נאץ ('humiliate') employed here is parallel with √חרף II.

II (5_{3-4}) Here we can refer to the opening of the fourth strophe (5_{7-8}) which begins with the same words אַיִן and אָב. Via the loss of the leaders (see exegesis), this word combination offers a different accent at the level of content when compared with the first strophe. See below for indications of the end of this strophe.

III (5_{5-6}) In terms of content we are presented with a new theme at this point, namely that of oppression. The end of this strophe is evident from our analysis of the beginning of the fourth strophe. In 5_6 we find parallelism between מִצְרַיִם and אַשּׁוּר, which exhibits a degree of analogy with the parallelism in 5_2: זָרִים // נָכְרִים. This in turn indicates a response at the strophe level. The same is true for לֶחֶם (6B) at the end of this strophe which is parallel with מֵימֵינוּ and עֵצֵינוּ in 5_4. One has reason to assume, therefore, that 5_4 constitutes the end of the second strophe.

Higher level structuring is evident in the cohesion between strophes 5_{1-4}, 5_{5-10}, 5_{11-14}, 5_{15-18} and 5_{19-22} which ought to be considered as canticles. With respect to one another there is clear difference in their cohesion. From the literary perspective, the first two canticles appear to constitute a sub-canto (5_{1-10}) while the last three canticles (5_{11-22}) likewise constitute a second sub-canto, both from the literary perspective and from the perspective of content. Both sub-cantos combine to form one canto which is equivalent to Lam V.[13]

Thematically speaking, the first sub-canto is determined by the initial appeal to YHWH to look upon the humiliation his people have suffered because of the loss of their land. This loss constitutes the source of all their further afflictions, such as the loss of their cities and fields, enemy oppression, starvation and migration to foreign parts (cf the central strophe of this sub-canto: 5_{5-6}).

The second sub-canto continues with the description of Judah's misfortune but the focus of attention shifts from the land to the city and is typified by

[13] See page 575; for the literary argumentation: 1988, 355–357.

the mention of Zion in 5_{11}. The second canticle (5_{15-18}) is central to this sub-canto. It portrays the loss of joy which is associated with the destruction of the sanctuary – still the focus of Judah's loss. The two framing canticles continue this theme, each in its own fashion. The destruction of Zion signifies the end of YHWH's protection, thus permitting the enemy to commence their reign of terror (5_{11-14}). In the context of prayer, the final canticle (5_{19-22}) formulates the most essential prerequisite for the cessation of affliction and the restoration of former glory: the return to YHWH. The whole of Lam V exhibits a concentric structure. As the first sub-canto opens with prayer so the second ends with prayer. Introductory prayer and concluding prayer surround and include every lament.

Genre

Both opening and conclusion reveal the primary character of the last song: it is a prayer! The consistent first person plural suggests a collective prayer, often described by commentators as a complaint of the people.[14] At the same time, however, we are certainly not in the presence of a model example of this genre. In terms of 'Sitz im Leben', for example, there is clearly no mention of the sanctuary or the liturgy. A further important distinction lies in the unusual length of the lament as such in 5_{2-18}; "Die Klage ist hier über ihre Ufer geströmt und hat sich in klagende Schilderung ergossen."[15] Indeed, the concrete nature of the complaints themselves together with their unmistakable relationship to the events of 587 further distinguishes Lam V from the conventional CP. Westermann also misses the elements of retrospection and expression of trust.

If one is not inclined to view Lam V as an independent literary unit but rather as a constituent part of the larger composition of Lamentations then it is clear that the so-called missing elements of the CP can be found elsewhere in the songs. The גֶּבֶר's expressions of trust at the end of the third song together with the reminiscences of Lady Jerusalem in 1_7 are examples which immediately spring to mind. Thus it would appear that the poets did employ elements from well-known literary genres although in an imperfect and selective manner. Partly due to their different arrangement of the existing constituent elements of these genres, the poets were able to place at their service what for Israel was a new and unique poetic form.[16]

[14] A CP; cf HGunkel – JBegrich, *Einleitung in die Psalmen*, Göttingen 1975³, 125.

[15] Cf CWestermann, 'Struktur und Geschichte der Klage im Alten Testament', in: *Forschung am AT*, ThB 24, München 1964, 278.

[16] See also the general introduction III.2 and VI.2.1.

Exegesis

Canticle I (5_{1-4})

Content/theme: *Loss of inheritence*

Literary argumentation:

inclusions:
בָּתֵּינוּ (2B) // אִמֹּתֵינוּ (3B)
זָרִים / נָכְרִים (2) // אֵין אָב (3A)

responses:
מֶה־הָיָה לָנוּ (1A) // הָיִינוּ (3A)
חֶרְפָּתֵנוּ (1B) // כְּאַלְמָנוֹת (3B)
נַחֲלָתֵנוּ (2A) // מֵימֵינוּ (4A)[17]
בָּתֵּינוּ (2B) // עֵצֵינוּ (4B)

The canticle opens with a singularly urgent supplicatory prayer together with a thematic statement of the humiliation endured by the survivors and those remaining in Judah. A degree of imitation of the גֶּבֶר from Lam III is evident therein. In the prayers of lament which follow, the poets endeavour to articulate their belief in YHWH's involvement in all they have endured.

The first significant interpretation of the people's humiliation has to do with their loss of inheritence, the very basis of their existence as human beings and as a people. YHWH granted the land to his people as their inheritence and it is in the loss of the land that all their affliction has its roots, particularly the lack of elementary necessities of life and protection from hostile forces.

1A *Remember,* YHWH, *what is happening to us,* זְכֹר יְהוָה מֶה־הָיָה לָנוּ

The song begins with the usual vocative opening associated with the CP genre.[18] The same combination of imperative √זכר + יְהוָה can be found in Ps 132_1; comparable with Ps $74_{18,22}$ and 89_{51} in which the imperative זְכֹר is also combined with 'humiliation'. The opening words establish a significant shift in tone. In the third song we heard the individual voice of the גֶּבֶר exhorting his people to follow his lead and renew their faith in YHWH. The few places in the third song where we find mention of a first person plural ($3_{22A,40A,42A,46A}$) can be understood as either inclusive or adhortative. Characteristic of Lam III is the fact that it opens and closes with the personal pronoun ($3_{1A,63B}$). Things are quite different where the

[17] Cf Deut 8_7.
[18] Cf HGunkel – JBegrich, *Einleitung in die Psalmen*, Göttingen 1975[3], 117.

final song is concerned in which the first person plural is the only form used. The גֶּבֶר has gained something of a following, people who desire to share in his renewed faith and trust in God. This is apparent from the prayer they now direct to YHWH which was already implied, however, in the prayers of Lady Jerusalem in $1_{9c,11c,20-22}$ and 2_{20-22}. Thus, imitation of the גֶּבֶר in his renewed faith is also evident in Lam I and II but this should not tempt us to search for any kind of chronological order in the songs. In contrast to $1_{11,20}$ and 2_{20} (cf $3_{59A,60A}$) the present song does not open with רְאֵה and/or הַבִּיטָה but with the imperative זְכֹר.

The root זכר I 'to remember', does not only suggest the calling to mind of events which took place in the past, it can also refer to those aspects of reality which determine the current state of affairs.[19] One might render such a notion with the terms 'consider' or 'be aware of'. This appeal to 'remember' does not depart from the assumption that YHWH has forgotten the people's affliction, rather that those who call out to him in prayer cannot yet see whether he has turned to them or not (cf 2_9, 3_{44}) and they call upon him, therefore, to be aware of the intensity of their misfortune. This is not the only contribution of the imperative זְכֹר, however. Frequently it is used to move YHWH to live up to his word and keep his promises.[20] Thus the present text contains an implicit appeal for a renewal in the present of YHWH's past salvific deeds: "Dem Gedenken Jahwes an Israel korrespondiert Israels Gedenken an Jahwe und sein Heilshandelen."[21] By way of inclusion the final strophe concludes the song with a more or less similar request for YHWH to renew 'their days' as of old (זְכֹר [1A] // חַדֵּשׁ יָמֵינוּ [21B]). It is indeed evident that YHWH's active involvement in the life of his people lies concealed within his 'remembering'. In this regard Eising speaks of a 'Tatkomponente'.[22] The expression מֶה־הָיָה לָנוּ, to conclude, is parallel at the level of content with חֶרְפָּתֵנוּ in the following colon. Once again we have opted for a present tense translation since. Although it may have its roots in the past, the affliction confronting the people continues unabated (cf 1_{1aA} and passim in Lamentations).

1B *look and see our humiliation!* הַבֵּיט וּרְאֵה אֶת־חֶרְפָּתֵנוּ

If YHWH is to be aware of the misfortune and suffering of his people then he must turn his attention to them and look. This is evident from

[19] Cf 1_{7aA} and THAT I 511 (Schottroff).
[20] Cf Ex 32_{13}, Deut 9_7, Ps 25_6.
[21] Cf THAT I 516 (Schottroff).
[22] In TWAT II 578; cf also Gen 30_{22}, Judg 16_{28}.

the double imperative employed in this colon: הַבִּיט וּרְאֵה.[23] The unusually urgent character of the vocative YHWH combined with these imperatives as well as the fact that we are here confronted with a focal moment in Lamentations as a whole already became evident in our exegesis of 1_{9c} and 1_{11c}. The present imperatives together with זְכֹר from the preceding colon combine to make Lam 5_1 perhaps the most insistent prayer found in the Old Testament. The speakers beg YHWH to take note of their situation, to look and to see. For the significance of the imperatives הַבִּיט וּרְאֵה see the exegesis of $1_{9c,11c}$. The affliction he will observe when he 'looks' and 'sees' will move him, they hope, to intervene to save them. Once again there is a relationship with the primary theme of the songs which the poets formulated in $3_{17,50}$: the people's misfortune will only come to an end when YHWH turns his gaze upon them once again.[24]

The dreadful affliction portrayed throughout the songs is presented here in condensed fashion by the term חֶרְפָּתֵנוּ 'our humiliation'. חֶרְפָּה is derived from √חרף II which means 'to be sharp'/'to stab' and thus figuratively 'to humiliate'.[25] The Hebrew expression, however, contains a number of nuances which do not fully resonate in the translation 'humiliation'. First of all there is the nuance of the self-will and self-importance of those who engage in such acts of humiliation, a nuance which might be better rendered with the term 'pride' (cf Zeph $2_{8,10}$). Whenever the one humiliated is the stronger then he will be inclined to indignation and desire to have revenge (Judg 8_{15f}). Thus the scorn of the nations during the fall of Judah in 587 is used in the Psalms to confront YHWH with their insults: 'Where is their God?'[26] and spur him to action and intervention. At the same time, the noun חֶרְפָּה does not only signify 'humiliation' in the sense of the 'taunts' or 'jeers' of one's enemy, it also includes the subjective experience of the one humiliated. Indeed, the content of חֶרְפָּה varies according to the context. The experience of 'humiliation' is portrayed, for example, as contempt (I Sam 25_{29}), widowhood (Isa 4_1, 54_1), childlessness (Ezek 36_{15}) and, strikingly enough, famine (Ezek 36_{30}). The humilation of widowhood and famine appears to have a role to play in the verses which follow. While we already noted the response between חֶרְפָּתֵנוּ (1B) // כְּאַלְמָנוֹת (3B), there also appears to be a song-response with the metaphor of the 'sitting widow' in 1_{1bA}. This metaphor retains its significance as we

[23] Maintain the *k^etīḇ*, cf Ps 142_5 and BL 366*t*.
[24] Cf the exegesis of the core verse 3_{50}.
[25] Cf TWAT III 223f (Kutsch).
[26] See Ps $79_{10,12}$; cf also Ps $74_{10,18,22}$.

shall see below (cf 5_3). The first reading of Judah's humiliation, however, has to do with the loss of her inheritence.

2A *Our inheritence is in the hands of strangers,* נַחֲלָתֵנוּ נֶהֶפְכָה לְזָרִים

Humiliation as a result of loss of נַחֲלָה 'inheritence' is also mentioned in Ezek $35_{12,15}$; 36_{4f} and Joel 2_{17}. This lament alludes to the fulfilment of the prophetic announcement of doom in Mic 2_4. The placing of Judah's loss of inheritence at the forefront and its combining with 'humiliation' from the first strophe is not without significance. The land was literally the very 'ground' of Israel's existence and its giving embraced every good gift which YHWH desired for Israel (Deut $8_{7-10,12f}$). Thus the loss of the land was a source of every kind of misfortune and without it there could only be hunger and restless wandering (cf Jer 12_{7-13}). Loss of inheritence is rendered with the *niph'al* perfect 3rd person singular of the root הפך, the basic meaning of which is 'to overturn'. Based on the example of the shift from blessing to curse and from rejoicing to mourning (see 5_{15} below) Seybold suggests that the *niph'al* implies a complete turn about: "Vor allem im niph-Gebrauch ist die Tendenz zur abstrakten Vorstellung der Verwandlung in das Gegenteil zu beobachten." [27] In order to maintain this notion we have translated נֶהֶפְכָה in the present tense. Clearly we are confronted here with an enormous contrast: a nation's inheritence does not belong in the hands of foreigners. A variety of texts reveal the extent to which the people were attached to their forefathers' landed property on which the family grave was often located.[28] Thus it was only correct that such land should remain in the family (I Kgs 21_3).

The term נַחֲלָה, however, means more than inalienable property; the source of such property constitutes an essential dimension: "*nḥl* bezieht sich streng genommen nur auf einen zugeteilten Anteil, auf den man per Erbfolge ein Recht hat." [29] From whom then does the said inheritence originate? Clearly it is the land which YHWH granted as an inheritence to (Jacob) Israel (I Kgs 8_{36}). Behind this gift of land lies the notion of YHWH as Father of Israel,[30] a Father who treats Israel as his favourite child and grants her a magnificent inheritence (Ps 47_5, Jer 3_{19}). Of course, an inheritence need not be withheld until after the death of its donor. Such

[27] Cf TWAT II 456.

[28] Cf Jos $24_{30,32}$, I Sam 25_1, I Kgs 2_{34}.

[29] See TWAT V 345 (Lipiński).

[30] Cf Deut 32_6, Ex 4_{22f}, Isa 63_{13}, 64_7, Jer 3_4, 31_9, Hos 11_1, Mal 1_6; cf also MCAKorpel, *A Rift in the Clouds*, Münster 1990, 238.

a restriction would make the image employed here somewhat lame. Israel's tradition, rather, allowed for matters of inheritence to be settled during the life of the donor (II Sam 17_{23}, II Kgs 20_1), allowing him to pass on his possessions to his children as 'inalienable property'.[31] Clearly this was the case with respect to Israel's inheritence from YHWH, but such a situation implied that he was now forced to observe that his original intentions had been undermined and that the gift he had given to his children had found its way into the hands of strangers. Thus not only was the inheritence affected by the new circumstances but its donor also. The point of the present lament is all the more evident: can YHWH observe this situation and do nothing? The image is likewise more pressing if one realises that the metaphor of the land as an inheritence given by YHWH does not completely parallel the notion of human inheritence. Once an inheritence was given it became the legal property of the inheritor. In the relationship YHWH (donor), Israel (inheritor) and land (inheritence), however, this does not apply; YHWH maintained his right of ownership over the donated inheritence and could take it back as he pleased.[32] Thus whatever happens to the land continues to affect YHWH and the lament here is intended to draw his attention to the harrowing situation which has befallen Israel and underline his ongoing involvement.

This idea is also implicit in another metaphor associated with נַחֲלָה, namely 'the land as YHWH's inheritence'.[33] When Israel speaks of her inheritence she is unable to disassociate this from her awareness that she is speaking likewise of YHWH's inheritence (Lev 25_{23}). In fact, Israel is nothing more than an alien resident in a land which belongs to YHWH. Now that strangers have appropriated this inheritence against YHWH's original intentions, repercussions are inevitable with regard to the relationship between YHWH and his land as house of Israel. It is evident from Jer 12_{7-13} that the prophecy of doom had anticipated this situation and foreseen YHWH's anguish. It seems as if the authors of Lamentations have borrowed both terminologically and semantically from this passage. It expresses YHWH's sorrow concerning the sin of his people which has led him to abandon his inheritence with pain in his heart. The metaphor of the 'beloved of my heart' (יְדִדוּת נַפְשִׁי) is employed for the land (and the people),

---

[31] See Ezek 46_{16-18} and the later texts Sir 33_{20-24} and Lk 15_{12}; cf TWAT V 345f (Lipiński).

[32] Cf, for example, Jer 3_{12}, 12_{14f}, THAT II 57f (Wanke).

[33] Cf I Sam 26_{19}, II Sam 14_{16}, Jer 2_7, 12_7, 16_{18}, 50_{11}, Ps 68_{10}; for the background of this metaphor cf TWAT V 355ff (Lipiński) and Korpel, 304f.

an image associated with a much loved wife.[34] It can hardly be accidental that the song-response in 1_1 portrays Jerusalem as a woman abandoned by YHWH (cf also the explanation of 5_3).

The term נַחֲלָה most probably has even deeper significance. Zion itself is characterised as such in Ps 79_1 in which her desecration by pagans is presented.[35] The withdrawal of YHWH's presence in Zion makes it clear that he has abandoned his inheritence (cf 2_1). The first canticle of the fourth song (4_{1-2}) speaks of the destruction of both people and temple, thus providing evidence of a responsive relationship between the songs at this level. For the meaning of the term זָרִים see the explanation of the following colon.

2B *our houses in the hands of hostile foreigners!* בָּתֵּינוּ לְנָכְרִים

In the present context the phrase בָּתֵּינוּ has a broader meaning than 'our houses'. In this bicolon the term 'house' functions as a synonym for inheritence.[36] The idea of inheritence is likewise not restricted to land as such since it includes buildings, crops and wells.[37] The collective functioning of בָּתֵּינוּ is apparent from the fact that the verbal form נֶהֶפְכָה also governs the second colon,[38] making it unnecessary to introduce נִתְּנוּ (*niph'al* pf 3m pl of √נתן ['we must hand over']) as Robinson (BHK) suggests and Westermann actually does in his translation.

The poets lament the fact that land, houses and property now find themselves in the hands of foreigners. Hebrew has a number of words for 'foreigners', the most familiar of which being the גֵּר, a foreigner living within Israel's boundaries. The term found here is often employed by the prophets to refer to an enemy agressor or alien occupier. In contrast to גֵּרִים, the זָרִים are foreigners with a completely different background and without the slightest sensitivity for the way things are done in the land of Israel. Snijders[39] notes that such enemies turn everything upside down (with √הפך; cf the echoes with the Sodom tradition in $1_{13A,20bA}$, 2_{4c}, 4_6). Indeed, in Ezek 7_{21}, 11_9 and Ob $_{11}$, the זָרִים are not only foreigners of a

[34] Cf Korpel, 222.

[35] For the origins of the temple (mountain) as YHWH's inheritence cf THAT II 58 (Wanke) and TWAT V 358f (Lipiński).

[36] נַחֲלָתֵנוּ; cf parallels with Jer 12_7 – once again – as well as with Judg 11_{12}, Hos 8_1, 9_{15}, Zech 9_8.

[37] See TWAT I 637f (Hoffner) and Jos 15_{19}.

[38] Cf GES-K § 124a,s and Joüon-Muraoka § 136n.

[39] See TWAT II 559.

different disposition, they are the very זָרִים who destroyed Jerusalem, left the temple bereft of its magnificence and killed or imprisoned her inhabitants (thereby reconfirming the connection between 5_2 and $4_{1,2}$). The common translation 'foreigners' is thus far too insipid and as such justifies our addition of the adjective 'hostile'. The basic meaning of the term נָכְרִי used here in 5_{2B} bears a similarly hostile orientation.[40] In contrast to the גֵּרִים, the נָכְרִים remain outsiders.[41]

From the material perspective the present lament has to do with the situation which came into existence after the fall of Judah in 587. Defeat at the hands of the Babylonians and the deportations which followed meant that the land was no longer able to put up a fight. Neighbouring nations – especially Edom (concatenation with the preceding song) – made use of the opportunity to plunder Judah and enslave the population as well as to appropriate the land and its cities for themselves.[42]

3 *We have become orphans,*	יְתוֹמִים הָיִינוּ
fatherless,	אֵין אָב
our mothers as widows!	אִמֹּתֵינוּ כְּאַלְמָנוֹת

The laments here in 5_3 concerning fatherlessness and widowhood do not only indicate the height of defencelessness from an OT perspective. The status of the widow and the orphan stood for insecurety and vulnerability throughout Israel's 'Umwelt'.[43] This is evident in the OT from the fact that commandment not to oppress the widow and the orphan (Ex 22_{21}) are frequently repeated, as are ordinances to treat them justly (Deut 24_{17}, 27_{19}) and assist them by allowing them the gleanings after the harvest (Deut 24_{19ff}). Prophetic indictments make it clear, however, that the unprotected status of the widow and the orphan was abused nevertheless.[44] The word combination 'widow and orphan' can be found with considerable frequency throughout the OT,[45] a fact which has given rise to the question whether the meaning of the Hebrew word יָתוֹם is properly and fully embodied by our modern term 'orphan', in the sense of a child who has lost both mother and father.[46] On the basis of Job 24_9, one can as-

[40] Cf TWAT V 455 (Ringgren).

[41] See Deut 29_{10}, 31_{12}; cf also Ruth 2_{10}.

[42] Cf Ezek $35_{10,12,15}$, 36_{3f} and the explanation of 4_{22b}.

[43] Cf TWAT III 1075ff (Ringgren).

[44] See Isa $1_{17,23}$, 10_2, Jer 7_6, 22_3, Ezek 22_7; cf also Job 24_3.

[45] See texts in HAL 56.

[46] Cf also JRenkema, 'Does Hebrew *ytwm* really mean "fatherless"?', VT XLV (1995), 119–122.

sume that יָתוֹם-status had already been established with the loss of one's father, although the text is open to question. However, Ringgren notes on the basis of the present verse that the term יָתוֹם is to be rendered 'fatherless'.[47] Indeed, 5_3 clearly emphasises the fact that the fathers are no longer around while the very mention of the widow status of the mothers implies that they still are. If it is possible to refer to a child who has only lost his or her father as an orphan then we have come a long way to explaining the frequency of the combination 'widow and orphan'. The unprotected situation of both has its foundation in the death of the husband and father. In light of her weak (legal) position, the widow was unable to take the place of her husband as protector of her children.[48]

Of course, nothing of what we have said so far need imply that a יָתוֹם always had a mother. In spite of Ringgren's position, the question remains as to whether this was in fact the case after all. II Kgs 4_1 is quite significant in this regard since it speaks of a widow's children (יְלָדֶי) and not of her orphans. Widow + child seems to be the usual combination.[49] The only texts from which we can deduce that an orphan still had a mother are Ex 22_{23} and Job 24_9. The common interpretation of מִשֹּׁד in Job 24_9 as 'from the mother's breast',[50] however, refers in fact to the (premature) separation of a child from its female parent. The same is true for Ex 22_{23} (see below). Furthermore, there are several texts in which orphans are the subject but which do not contain the combination 'widow and orphan'.[51] It is also worth noting that while Hebrew only has one word for orphan, namely יָתוֹם, one can assume that there have always been children in Israel who had prematurely lost both parents. Indeed, children could still become orphans even when the mother was still alive, since, after the death of her husband, her debtors could satisfy their demands for repayment by taking them as slaves.[52] Something similar can also be determined from Ex 22_{23} and Job 24_9. The removal of children in this way would explain why widowhood frequently had the connotation of childlessness (cf Isa 47_{8f}). Similar echoes can be heard in the first song ($1_{1b,5c}$, and 1_{20c}). In its own way, every text which refers to יָתוֹם-status ultimately implies a definitive separation between children and their parents.

[47] Cf TWAT III 1077.
[48] Cf RdVaux, *Institutions I*, 67–69; cf II Kgs 4_1.
[49] Cf also Lev 22_{13}, II Sam 14_5, I Kgs 7_{14}, 11_{26}, $17_{9ff,20}$.
[50] Cf AvSelms, *Job deel II*, Nijkerk 1983, 28.
[51] Cf Ps $10_{14,18}$, 82_3, 109_{12} and Jer 5_{28}.
[52] Cf the aforementioned II Kgs 4_1.

These considerations are important for the exegesis of Lam 5_3. At first sight the text itself raises questions. Does it suggest that the mothers in Judah were, for the most part, widows and their children orphans, and thus both unprotected and helpless? What then is the significance of the comparative particle in the phrase כְּאַלְמָנוֹת? Furthermore, if orphans are speaking at this point in the text, how is it possible that they still have their mothers? If only their fathers have been lost, must orphanhood necessarily be assumed?! While we can speak of widowhood in such an event, we cannot yet speak of orphanhood. Thenius suggested long ago that the missing father should be understood as king Zedekiah and the widows as his destitute harem. It is difficult to accept, however, that such women could be referred to as 'our mothers'. More recent commentators suggest that many men were not killed but taken into captivity and deported and that their wives were left behind as widows.[53] From a historical perspective, however, this explanation is highly contestable. As far as we know, the number of men who died, were executed or imprisoned and sent into exile was in fact quite limited. It is reasonable to assume, therefore, that a significant portion of the population of Judah remained behind.[54]

The context of Lamentations itself, however, provides a much more attractive explanation. Almost every exegete neglects the evident parallel between 1_1 and 5_3 which contain the only examples of the combination of אַלְמָנוֹת/אַלְמָנָה with the preposition כְּ. One might term such an association as 'long distance distance parallelism'. In any event we are clearly dealing with a canticle response at the song level:

הָיְתָה כְּאַלְמָנָה (1_{1bA}) // אִמֹּתֵינוּ כְּאַלְמָנוֹת (הָיִינוּ) (5_{3B})

Rudolph is alone in recognising the connection with 1_{1b} although he is of the opinion that the expression has been taken up incorrectly by the last song. For Rudolph, 5_3 also refers to Jerusalem and this leads him to change the plural of 5_3 to a singular. In the first canticle of Lam I, however, the metaphor of the widow is also applied to Judah as a whole (cf the explanation of 1_{3b}). It seems clear, therefore, that the poets are not referring to human mothers in the present text but rather to the cities of Judah. Ewald was among the first to propose this interpretation: "Vaterlose waisen, weil ohne unsern rechtmäßigen könig 2,9 4,20 und ohne die Gottherrschaft; und da vater hier nicht im nächsten sinne gelten kann,

[53] Cf Kraus, Gordis, Kaiser, Brandscheidt, Boecker.

[54] Cf EJanssen, *Juda in der Exilszeit*, FRLANT NF 51, Göttingen 1956, 34–39.

so heißt es weiter unsre mütter d.i. gemeinden und städte sind wie witwen wie 1,1."[55] Sadly, this explanation appears either to have been unfamiliar to later exegetes or to have been unacceptable to them.[56] Not only has Jerusalem become like a widow but the other cities of Judah also find themselves in a similar position. As Gordis would have it, therefore, כְּ is evidently a comparative particle rather than an assurative one.[57] The image of the city as widow does not stand on its own. It is a metaphor derived from a so-called root metaphor, namely the presentation of the city as woman (cf the explanation of 1_{4cB}). A further metaphor derived from the same root is that of the city as mother, an image used by the poets in the present text. II Sam 20_{19} clearly refers to the city as a mother. By extension, we also find the presentation of an important city as mother with the surrounding smaller cities as her daughters. After reference to Zion, for example, Ps 97_8 refers to the cities of Judah as her daughters.[58]

As a consequence of the above interpretation we are also obliged to interpret the fathers mentioned in the second colon metaphorically (we uphold the *kᵉtīḇ* אֵין אָב). Two possibilities present themselves in this regard: we can take אָב to be a collective and interpret the fathers as the 'mayors' or chief officials of the cities of Judah. The idiom employed here does not stand in the way of such an interpretation.[59] In contrast to Rudolph, Gottwald correctly follows this line of thought.[60] The reference is to the priests, prophets, princes and king. From the spiritual and administrative perspective there is no longer any leadership or protection. Indeed, the songs state repeatedly that the leaders in question are no longer present. The priests and the prophets have been killed, 2_{19}, or expelled, 4_{15}; the king has been taken captive and forced to live abroad, 2_9, 4_{20}; the princes have likewise been taken into exile, 1_6, 2_9, or have been hanged, 5_{12}. As we noted earlier, it was a typical tactic of the Babylonians to deport the leading classes in order to prevent further resistance. The fathers (leaders) are gone, the mothers (their cities) remain and are portrayed metaphor-

55 In: HEwald, *Die Dichter des Alten Bundes I/2*, Göttingen 1866³, 346.

56 Cf Aalders, for example.

57 His translation: 'our mothers have truly become widows.'

58 Cf also Judg 1_{27} (בְּנוֹתֶיהָ [עִיר]), compare AAlt, *Kleine Schriften zur Geschichte des Volkes Israël I*, München 1959², 268; Hos 10_{14}, Ezek 16_{44-49} and MCAKorpel, *A Rift in the Clouds*, Münster 1990, 261, who refers, among other things, to Num 21_{15}, Jos 15_{47} and Jer 49_2.

59 For examples of this metaphorical understanding of אָב see Gen 45_8, Judg 17_{10}, 18_{19}, I Sam 24_{12}, II Kgs 2_{12}, 6_{21}, 13_{14}.

60 NKGottwald, *Studies in the Book of Lamentations*, London 1954, 67f.

ically as widows who, to add to their destitution, are childless because they have lost their inhabitants.[61] In their turn, the inhabitants in question are without leadership/fathers and have lost their cities/mothers (cf 5_2). Thus they have metaphorically become orphans. The comparative כְּ prior to אַלְמָנוֹת appears to work backwards to include יְתוֹמִים. We noted above that the status of orphanhood signified separation from the mother as well. As orphans they were vulnerable and without protection. They were bereft of their former rights and privileges and aliens now held sway in their stead. Our explanation reveals a strong degree of cohesion between the first and second strophe of Lam V, given literary visibility via the responses mentioned in the introduction.

Although a collective interpretation of אָב is clearly the authors' intention, and is confirmed as such by the inclusion with אֲבֹתֵינוּ ... אֵינָם in 5_7, the singular formulation remains somewhat unusual. Indeed, in order to express the intended theological dimension of אֵין אָב, the singular must have been used on purpose. The explanation of Lady Jerusalem being 'as a widow' in 1_{1b} revealed that the intended widowhood came about primarily as a result of YHWH's departure from her. Isa 54_{4ff} takes up the same image and YHWH comforts his people by stating that he will once again become the husband of Lady Zion. This is not the case in the present text since Lady Zion is still without her husband. As a consequence, both she and her children are without protection. The same applies with equal severity to the cities of Judah, however, which have likewise been abandoned by YHWH,[62] their inhabitants being left similary unprotected (cf the way the גֶּבֶר laments his captivity and his sense that YHWH is thereby spurning his prayer in the parallel verses 3_{7-9}).

At its core, the present verse laments that YHWH no longer exercises fatherhood over his people.[63] They have become like orphans and they have no one to help them.[64] The image becomes all the more painful when one realises that Israel has always confessed YHWH as pre-eminently the helper of the orphan.[65]

---

[61] Cf Korpel, 261: "A city, like a woman, also brings forth "children" namely its inhabitants."

[62] Cf 5_{20b} and the parallel strophe in Lam 2_{2f}: destruction of the fortified cities and the hacking off of the horns of Israel.

[63] For examples of the metaphorical usage of אָב for YHWH in the OT see Korpel, 235–239.

[64] See also the song-response: אֵין עוֹזֵר (1_{7c}) // אֲבֹתֵינוּ ... אֵינָם (5_7).

[65] Cf Ps $10_{14,18}$, 68_6, 146_9, Deut 10_{18} etcetera.

One final remark with respect to the expression אֵין אָב. It is quite possible that the question posed by many modern exegetes concerning the absence of the alphabetic acrostic in this final song was anticipated by the poets in the very composition of the song. It looks very much as if they are alluding to this fact via a pun based on the letters of the expression אֵין אָב. Thus, inspite of its collective significance, the singular still comes accross as somewhat strange in relation to the plural forms יְתוֹמִים and אִמֹּתֵינוּ. A plural formulation אֲבֹתֵינוּ ... אֵינָם – as we find in 5_7 – would evidently have been more appropriate. The first time the poets employ this metaphor, however, they clearly avoid a plural form and consciously opt for the singular:

אין אב

Evidently, אָב has a collective significance and the entire expression means that the fathers – in the sense of 'leaders' – are gone. At the same time, however, אָב is also a singular form which points to the fatherhood of YHWH. One might also postulate a third meaning, namely that is an abbreviation for the alphabet and its negation אֵין a reference to the missing alphabetic acrostic, that is no א, no ב, no ג etcetera. Obviously the first two interpretations remain dominant but this does not exclude the possibility that the third meaning is also part of the poets' intention. In this event we must consider the expression a somewhat hidden indication that the poets consciously abandoned the alphabetic acrostic when they came to the fifth song.

4 *To drink our own water costs money*	מֵימֵינוּ בְּכֶסֶף שָׁתִינוּ
and for our own wood we are forced to pay!	עֵצֵינוּ בִּמְחִיר יָבֹאוּ

Within the present canticle, 5_4 constitutes a response with 5_2. With the loss of נַחֲלָה, the properties and rights associated therewith have likewise been lost. Such a situation was diametrically opposed to the purpose of נַחֲלָה as inalienable landed property, flowing with milk and honey and marked off with boundary stones which on no account could be relocated.[66]

The provisions intended to maintain the inalienability of this נַחֲלָה go hand in hand with the function of the land as a means of subsistence. Society upheld the ideal of a portion of land for every family which they could use to support themselves and thereby live a carefree life amidst the vines

[66] Cf Deut 19_{14}, 27_{17}; cf also Job 24_2, Prov 22_{28}, 23_{10}.

and olive trees.[67] It was for this purpose that YHWH had given and ultimately blessed the land, which was his own possession.[68] As city culture developed, the significance of land ownership shifted towards the notion of inherited property in general.[69] Nevertheless, the accent in the present instance is clearly placed on the ownership of land. The prophets strongly condemned any efforts to alienate the land.[70]

In the present text we can clearly discern the tension between YHWH's desire for his נַחֲלָה and the actual situation, particularly as it touches on an issue so vital to Israel's existence, namely her water rights. Given the context, the reading of LXX: ἐξ ἡμερῶν ημῶν, which points to a different vocalisation of מֵימֵינוּ (5_{4A}) meaning 'of our days', provides a meaningless translation, according to Albrektson, "and another proof of the Greek translator's carelessness and lack of Judgement." We are clearly dealing with water here, a commodity essential for the lives of humans and animals alike. Indeed, it is not unusual to find disputes concerning water in the OT.[71]

Now that foreigners have appropriated the people's נַחֲלָה, their former rights to water are no longer respected. See the inclusion נַחֲלָתֵנוּ (5_{2A}) // מֵימֵינוּ (5_{4A}).[72] Foreign invaders now force the remaining population of Judah to pay a high price for their own water. The same is true for the wood which the land provided and which served for building and/or house repair (cf בָּתֵּינוּ [5_{2B}] // עֵצֵינוּ [5_{4B}]), as well as for cooking.[73]

The priceless character of the water is made clear in the parallel with 4_4 and 3_{15} which describe how the tongues of infants cleave to their palates from lack of water and how the גֶּבֶר is forced to drink poisonous plant juice to lessen his thirst. Added to the fact that there is already precious little to eat,[74] the people are now forced to pay dearly for the wood to cook what little they have. Where supplies and provisions are concerned life has become unbearable.

---

67 See I Kgs 5_5, Mic 4_4, Zech 3_{10}.

68 Cf Lev 25_{18ff} and GvRad, 'Verheißenes Land und Jahwes Land im Hexateuch', ZDPV (1943), 191–204. Reprint in: *Gesammelte Studien zum Alten Testament*, ThB 8, München 1958, 87–100.

69 Cf THAT II 56 (Wanke) and TWAT V 351 (Lipiński).

70 See Am 3_{10}, 4_1, Isa 5_8, Mic 2_2.

71 Cf Gen 21_{25}, 26_{15-33}, Ex 2_{16}, Judg 1_{15}, Prov 17_{14}.

72 For the construction see Brockelmann § 122*q*.

73 See also the explanation of 5_{13B}.

74 See 2_{20b} and 4_{11a}.

Canticle II (5_{5-10})

Content/theme: *Oppression and hunger*

Literary argumentation:

inclusions: צַוָּארֵנוּ (5A) // עוֹרֵנוּ (10A)
בְּנַפְשֵׁנוּ נָבִיא לַחְמֵנוּ (9A) \\ נָתַנּוּ יָד ... לִשְׂבֹּעַ לָחֶם (6A)

responses: סָבָלְנוּ (7B) // עַל צַוָּארֵנוּ (5A)
נַפְשֵׁנוּ (9A) // צַוָּארֵנוּ (5A)
יָדָם (8B) \\ יָד (6A)
עֲבָדִים (8A) \\ מִצְרַיִם/אַשּׁוּר (6)
מִפְּנֵי זַלְעֲפוֹת רָעָב (10B) // לִשְׂבֹּעַ לָחֶם (6B)

The third strophe (5_{7-8}) holds a central position in the present canticle, focusing on the 'missing fathers'. They are ultimately to blame for the fact that former servants now hold sway in the land and have plunged Judah into affliction. The remainder of the canticle focuses on two particular aspects of this affliction: oppression in $5_{5,8}$ and the dreadful famine in $5_{6,9-10}$ which much of the population has attempted to avoid by fleeing abroad. Given the fact that the famine is raised in the context of a number of song-responses (5_6 // 1_{6b} // 3_{16}; 5_9 // 4_9; 5_{10} // $3_{29,30}$ [יִשְׂבָּע][75] // 4_{10}), it is clearly the most prominent aspect of Judah's misfortune.

5 *Upon our neck we are persecuted,* עַל צַוָּארֵנוּ נִרְדָּפְנוּ
we are exhausted, יָגַעְנוּ
no one offers us rest! לֹא הוּנַח־לָנוּ

The Masoretic text (literally: 'on our neck we are persecuted') is considered by a number of exegetes to be corrupt. Proposed emendations to the text can be categorised into two groups. The first group emends צַוָּארֵנוּ ('our neck') to read אַרְצֵנוּ ('our land') thus allowing the persecution to take place 'in the land'. The second group changes the preposition עַל into the substantive עֹל ('yoke') and emends נִרְדָּפְנוּ to read הֲדַפְנוּ (qal 3m sg of √הדף + 3m pl suffix with 'yoke' as subject) rendering the text 'the yoke weighs heavy on our neck'. A number of objections may be raised to such emendations: one cannot flee, for example, with a yoke around one's neck (Gordis). The textual emendations themselves remain inexplicable. Together with Löhr, Aalders, Albrektson, Gordis and Van Selms, therefore, we maintain the MT, especially as the idiom is not quite as unusual as

[75] See 5_{1B} and Ezek 36_{30}.

some have suggested: "To say that the Israelites are chased or persecuted 'on their necks' is a way of expressing the imminence of the danger and the persistency of the persecutors; there are numerous parallels to this in other languages."[76] One might also add that in terms of content and terminology, agreement with the first song at this level favours the MT.

Although a new theme is evidently being broached in the present canticle – no longer the loss of land, home and leaders but rather the consequences thereof – the transition from the preceding canticle remains quite smooth. 5_5 deals with the consequences of the loss of protection. The population is now outlawed and persecuted with a vengeance. Clearly the neighbouring nations are the primary perpetrators of this relentless persecution, those who came to power in the region after the fall of Judah. A connection with $1_{3b,5a,6c}$ is evident here (cf at the same time כָּל־רֹדְפֶיהָ [1_{3cA}] // נִרְדָּפְנוּ [5_{5A}]) whereby emendation of the common √רדף in 5_{5A} is obviated. The present hostile attitude of Judah's former lovers is mentioned in 1_{2c}. At the same time, the response כָּל־רֵעֶיהָ (1_{2cA}) // כָּל־רֹדְפֶיהָ (1_{3cA}) makes it clear that one should not envisage persecution at the hands of the Babylonians here, even less the situation of the exile. The one-off disaster of persecution and deportation by the Babylonians is not the focus of the text but rather the ongoing affliction which followed Judah's downfall and which was marked by persecution of the population by neighbouring enemies.

Lam 1_3 offers further agreements. The עֲבֹדָה (1_{3aB}, cf מַס in 1_{1cB}) or slave labour imposed on the people clearly resonates in the expression יָגַעְנוּ employed here, literally: 'we are exhausted' (*qal* of √יגע). The following colon (לֹא הוּנַח־לָנוּ) indicates that this labour did not take place on a voluntary basis (הוּנַח = *hoph'al* pf of √נוח I, 'to let rest'). The same colon forms an external parallelism with 1_{3bB} : לֹא מָצְאָה מָנוֹחַ: the restlessness of 'widow' Judah being that of her inhabitants. The form מָנוֹחַ can have a locative meaning 'resting place'.[77] Widow Judah has not only lost her rest but also the place where she could enjoy that rest, namely her home (cf the explanation of 1_{3b}). This appears to be true of Judah's inhabitants in the present text (cf 5_2). The response with 1_{5a} is clear: her adversaries rule the roost and are not inclined to allow those who have remained behind even a modicum of space or a moments rest.

---

[76] BAlbrektson, *Studies in the Text and Theology of the Book of Lamentations, with a Critical Edition of the Peshitta Text*, STL 21, Lund 1963, 197.

[77] Cf Gen 8_9, Isa 34_{14}; TWAT V 306 (Preuß).

6 *To Egypt we hold out a hand,* מִצְרַיִם נָתַנּוּ יָד
to Assyria for relief with bread! אַשּׁוּר לִשְׂבֹּעַ לָחֶם

Most exegetes, among them Rudolph, Kraus, Van Selms, Hillers, Brandscheidt and Boecker, consider this verse to be a retrospective glance on behalf of the poets to Judah's former foreign policy. Lam 5_7, where it is stated that the fathers have sinned and 'are no longer', provides the basis of this interpretation. An additional argument rests on the expression נָתַן יָד employed here which is considered a *terminus technicus* for the establishment of a covenant. The fathers' foreign policy was continually criticised by the prophets as a sign of lack of faith in YHWH.[78] Thus the present text anticipates what will be said in the first colon of 5_7: 'our fathers have sinned'. The text turns our attention to the past where the ultimate source of the present affliction is to be found.

This understanding of the text is difficult to align with the 'present tense confessions' found in the songs (cf 1_{18}, 3_{42}). A small number of exegetes conclude, therefore, that these words do not refer to the past but to the present and to some sort of flight out of the country. Blaynes, Löhr, Haller and Meek follow this line of thought but with little supportive argumentation. What arguments can we find in the text itself? In the first instance there appear to be more questions than answers. Why are Egypt and Assyria mentioned together? How should we understand the expression נָתַן יָד? What is the precise meaning of the expression 'relief with bread'?
The combination 'Egypt – Asyria' appears in a variety of places in the OT, especially in Hosea,[79] and in a number of different contexts: a) political alliances with the lands in question;[80] b) exile thereto as judgement;[81] c) return therefrom in the form of salvific prophecy.[82] The texts give the impression that Assyria and Egypt constituted polar extremities with respect to foreign territories, as the expression 'from Dan to Beersheba' indicated the furthest boundaries of the land itself.

What might the expression נָתַן יָד mean in the context? Concordances list only three other occurences: I Chron 29_{24}, II Chron 30_8 and Ezek 17_{18}. The NRSV translates the first text as 'to pledge allegiance' and the second as 'to yield to the Lord' while the context in Ezek 17_{18} is one of confirming a

[78] Cf Isa 30_{17}, Hos 7_{11}, Jer $2_{16,18,36}$.
[79] 7_{11}, 9_3, $11_{5,11}$, 12_2; additionally in Mic 7_{12}, Jer $2_{18,36}$.
[80] Cf Hos 7_{12}, 12_2, Jer $2_{18,36}$; cf also II Kgs 21_{12ff}.
[81] Hos 9_3, 11_5.
[82] Hos 11_{11}, Mic7_{12}; cf also Isa 19_{23ff}.

covenant sealed with a handshake. Clearly the expression has to do with the act of entrusting oneself subjecting oneself to another. Fabry translates Lam 5_6 as follows: "Wir haben uns Ägypten und Assur unterworfen, um uns mit Brot zu sättigen." [83]

The expression 'to be satisfied with bread' (לִשְׂבֹּעַ לָחֶם) can be found in Ex $16_{8,12}$ (cf Ps 105_{40}: [NRSV: 'food in abundance']), Prov 20_{13} (NRSV: 'to have plenty of bread'), Prov 12_{11} and 28_{19}.[84] Of particular interest for our interpretation of Lam 5_6 is Jer 44_{17}.

A choice between past tense and present tense must constitute a necessary aspect of our explanation of the text. Understood as past tense, we are then faced with the explanation already mentioned, namely that the present generation is seen as one with its forefathers and that the text is speaking of inherited debt. In this case, the present bicolon functions in the prayer as a confession of guilt rather than a lament. What we have uncovered so far concerning the combination Egypt/Assyria and the expression נָתַן יָד does not contradict such an explanation. For two reasons, however, this exegesis must be viewed as questionable. Firstly, the content of Lam 5_3 refers to the affliction currently being endured by the Judeans and it would appear that reference to 'the fathers' is not to former generations but to recent leaders among the people. Secondly, given the context, the more inclusive interpretation of 'relief with bread' as 'care for Israel's economic existence' (Kraus) is not so evident. Such an interpretation is necessary, however, if one wishes to maintain the traditional explanation.

Nevertheless, if one bases oneself on the other OT texts which include the expression then the primary meaning has to be 'to receive a (generous) sufficiency of food'. The context reveals that this was certainly not the case for the people of Judah at that time, indeed the description of the dreadful famine shows that the very opposite was true (cf 5_{9-10}). Furthermore, the word לָחֶם (bread) occurs once again in 5_{9A}. Clearly it is unacceptable to interpret the present verse as a reference to some past event. It must, therefore, be a reference to a contemporary event. Given the people's extreme insecurity in their daily lives many had lost their faith in any form of continued existence in Judah. Their land and houses were gone, their leaders deported and their daily necessities severly curtailed. For many there was no reason left to stay in Judah so they turned to what seemed a better option abroad. Thus certain Judeans chose voluntary exile

[83] Cf TWAT V 698f.

[84] Cf also Ps 135_{15}, Prov 12_{14}, 18_{20} and 30_{22}!

and subjected themselves to a foreign authority in the hope that they might get enough food to satisfy their hunger. This process is expressed by way of the phrase 'to give the hand'. See Fabry's translation above where one need only change the perfect to a present tense. In this way, the antithetical inclusion noted in the introduction also becomes clear: נָתַנּוּ יָד ... לִשְׂבֹּעַ לָחֶם (6A) \\ בְּנַפְשֵׁנוּ נָבִיא לַחְמֵנוּ (9A).

A number of details serve to confirm this interpretation. Spurred on by Babylon's threatening actions, many people had already fled from Judah to the bordering lands of Moab, Ammon and Edom (cf Jer 40_{11f}). The desire for security and food is also mentioned in Jer 42_{14f} where Egypt is spoken of as the 'land of bread'. Jer 44_1 also notes that many Judeans fled to Egypt. With respect to voluntary exile in Assyria, however, nothing is known. From the geographical perspective such an exile seems unlikely since it would have taken the people a long way from home and into a territory which fell under Babylonian influence. It seems reasonable to assume, therefore, that the combination Egypt/Assyria was simply a traditional expression for foreign territory (cf Meek). The use of the perfect נָתַנּוּ might point to the fact that many had already fled Judah for foreign parts and that the poets are making reference to their departure. The present tense translation, however, intends to show that the migration is still underway. A turnabout is also evident in this event. Where earlier prophets considered the idea of seeking help in a foreign country to be evidence of a lack of faith in YHWH, now his very absence has turned such action into bitter necessity.

A few comments remain with respect to the cohesion between the songs at this level. The first song speaks of the departure from Zion of her starved and enfeebled princes (1_6) and this corresponds with 5_6 where the people depart from the famine stricken land. In 3_{16}, the גֶּבֶר states that YHWH has made him break his teeth on gravel while 4_5 speaks of Zion's children rooting around in the ashes in search of food, both reasons for leaving Zion and Judah. As 2_{5c} succinctly states: nothing more can be hoped for or expected from YHWH (cf 3_{18}). Misfortune and affliction are all that remains in Judah (תַּאֲנִיָּה וַאֲנִיָּה).

7 *Our fathers have sinned;* אֲבֹתֵינוּ חָטְאוּ
they are no longer, אֵינָם
but we, we shoulder their iniquities! אֲנַחְנוּ עֲוֹנֹתֵיהֶם סָבָלְנוּ

For the meaning of √חטא see the exegesis of 1_8 and for that of עָוֹן 2_{14b}. The almost literal response אֵין אָב (3A) // אֲבֹתֵינוּ ... אֵינָם (7A) within the first sub-canto (5_{1-10}) forces us to be consistent in our explanation and, in light of the plural form, understand the fathers mentioned here primarily as (spiritual) leaders among the people.[85] Attention to the use of terminology reveals that the songs would appear to have recent leaders in mind. Comparison with Ps 79 confirms this. The question in Ps 79_5 'how much longer?' shows that the psalm in question was written some time after the fall of Judah and Jerusalem. Questions concerning the long duration of the affliction are absent from Lamentations, however.[86] As Westermann points out "Die frage, "wie lange?" setzt schon eine Dauer der Not voraus; sie klagt nicht über eben erlittenen Schlag, sondern über einen andauernden Druck." [87] Ps 79_8, which would appear at first sight to correspond closely with Lam 5_7, supports this impression in its own way. While the psalm in question clearly speaks of the iniquities of the fathers, the latter are expressly designated with the term רִאשֹׁנִים 'forefathers' and not with אָבוֹת.

Lam 5_{7-8} functions as the core of the second canticle, designating the focus and source of Judah's misfortune. The almost parallel and likewise central verse 6 of the fourth song speaks of the terrible sins of the people using the terms עָוֹן and חַטָּאת which are placed on a level with the iniquities of the 'fathers'. The sins of the prophets and priests would appear to have been of determining importance for the realisation of the fall of the city and the land.[88] Our exegesis of 4_{15} already proved that these 'fathers' were no longer among the people.[89] The consequences of their sins, however, continue to be fully manifest, as is evident from the use of the verb סבל 'to burden/be burdened with'. The more common Hebrew expression for 'to bear iniquity' is נָשָׂא עָוֹן,[90] which suggests that the consequences of עָוֹן rest on those who perpetrate it. The present text, however, does not suggest that the 'fathers' are suffering the consequences of their own sins but rather their 'children'. Thus it is not a question of the transmission of guilt down through the generations but of the consequences of the much more recent failures of the leadership which have brought about this extraordinary burden which the people are now being forced to bear (cf

[85] This in contrast to our former explanation in 1983, 199.
[86] Cf 1983, 56.
[87] See CWestermann, 'Struktur und Geschichte der Klage im Alten Testament', in: *Forschung am AT*, ThB 24, München 1964, 276.
[88] Cf 2_{14}, 4_{13} together with Jeremiah's criticism thereof: 5_5, 10_{21}.
[89] Cf Brockelmann § 80*e*.
[90] Cf TWAT V 633–640 (Freedman – Willoughby).

Ezek 22_{30}). It is significant that the poets employ a different term – √סבל – for bearing this עָוֹן than the usual √נשׂא. The root סבל also means 'to bear' a burden but it is normally used for heavier loads: 'to shoulder',[91] and has the added connotation forced labour[92] and foreign domination.[93] All these elements are present in the song. Strikingly enough, the same word combination can also be found in Isa 53_{11}.[94] One question remains: what is the significance of mentioning the guilt of the leaders in this prayer? The purpose can only have been to underline the traumatic nature of the affliction. While personal guilt is not denied, the poets clearly insist that the present affliction was set in motion by others who once held positions of great responsiblity.

8 *Servants rule over us,* עֲבָדִים מָשְׁלוּ בָנוּ
no one saves us from their hand! פֹּרֵק אֵין מִיָּדָם

The shouldering of burdens is a result of the new political regime. The use of the root משׁל II 'to rule over' does not place the emphasis on the person but rather on the exercise of power,[95] in this case the political and military power being exercised in the land after its downfall. This domination is further elaborated by the mention of its perpetrators, עֲבָדִים 'servants', who now hold sway in Judah. Such a situation reflects the dreadful change of fortunes which the people have been forced to face, an echo of 1_{9b}: 'appallingly deep was her downfall'. Since these servants now hold the reigns of power, it is clear that we are not dealing with some independent terrorist groups but with the more constantly present domination of those who have filled the power vacuum created by the fall of Judah.

Who are these servants? Rudolph and Hillers are of the opinion that they are Babylonian occupiers, the 'servants of Nebuchadnezzar'.[96] It remains a question, however, whether the Babylonians actually stationed a permanent occupying force in Judah after their successful campaign against Jerusalem.[97] The extent of the change in the people's fortunes only becomes clear when one realises that the new rulers were once servants of

[91] Cf Gen 49_{15} and TWAT V 745f (Kellermann).
[92] Cf Ex 1_{11}, 2_{11}, 5_{5}.
[93] See Isa 9_{3}.
[94] See for the relationship between Lamentations and Deutero-Isaiah: 1983, 325–331.
[95] Cf TWAT V 74 (Groß).
[96] Cf II Kgs 24_{10f}, 25_{24}.
[97] Cf II Kgs 25_{22f}, Jer $40_{5,7,19}$.

Judah. עֶבֶד can be used to refer to the status of a weaker king with respect to his stronger foreign counterpart,[98] the sovereign of some neighbouring people which once endured servitude under Judah and longed to see the final end of her domination.[99] Once again the vindictive Edomites are the most likely candidates.[100] Slaves who become kings are the worst of all,[101] and it is to such as these that Judah has been handed over, former servants who now impose מַס and רֹב עֲבֹדָה upon their erstwhile masters.[102] The second colon emphasises the people's defencelessness: there is no one to save them from the power of their oppressors.

9 *We must endanger our lives to get our bread,* בְּנַפְשֵׁנוּ נָבִיא לַחְמֵנוּ
because of the sword of the wilderness! מִפְּנֵי חֶרֶב הַמִּדְבָּר

In light of the song-response with 4_9 (likewise with 'sword'), the frequently proposed emendation of חֶרֶב to read חֹרֶב, 'heat' instead of 'sword' (cf Gordis, for example) becomes unnescessary (cf also Gottlieb). In time of famine, food is the first priority to those who are starving and people are resourceful. In the Judean countryside outside Jerusalem some had managed to store provisions of wheat, barley, oil and honey hidden in the fields (cf Jer 41_8). If Judg 6_{11} is anything to go by, this was an ancient tactic. Obviously the enemy was aware of this fact and they would have tried to confiscate these provisions. Lam 4_{19} speaks of persecutors lying in wait in the desert, hostile forces who would have observed the Judeans if they tried to lay claim to their concealed food stores. Those who were caught would have been put to death immediately. בְּנַפְשֵׁנוּ with ב-*pretii* [103] literally means 'at the cost of our lives'. The parallel with 4_9 is really quite cynical: given the dreadful hunger, death by the sword actually meant one was better off.

10 *Our skin has become as coarse as an oven(-wall)* עוֹרֵנוּ כְּתַנּוּר נִכְמָרוּ
because of the furies of famine. מִפְּנֵי זַלְעֲפוֹת רָעָב

The canticle concludes with a reference to the appalling famine. The text is difficult. עוֹרֵנוּ is a singular with a 1st person plural suffix [104] but the verbal form is a *niph'al* 3rd person m pl.[105] One can, however, interpret as a

[98] II Kgs 16_7, 17_3, 24_1 and TWAT V 997 (Ringgren).
[99] See the explanation of 2_{16c}.
[100] Compare the exegesis of 3_{60}.
[101] Cf Prov 30_{22}.
[102] See the explanation of $1_{1c,3a}$.
[103] Cf Joüon–Muraoka § 133*c*.
[104] Cf LXX with τὸ δέρμα ἡμῶν.

collective, with the suffix corresponding to נִכְמָרוּ.[106] Of greater importance is the translation. Gordis renders the text "our skin is as hot as an oven." (cf also Kraus and Brandscheidt). Based on experience, Van Selms remarks with respect to this proposal that he cannot understand how hunger can make a person's skin glow. In line with the LXX, commentators such as Hillers, for example, translate 'our skin has grown dark'. See, however, our explanation of 4_{8aA}. Driver offers the most acceptable interpretation of the text. In his opinion the poets are comparing the skin of the starving people with the crackled inner walls of a תַּנּוּר or 'baking oven'. This consisted of a dug out fireplace upon which a ± 1 meter high clay pot was placed (like an upside down flower pot without its base). When the fire was aglow the baker would press handfulls of dough against the inside of the oven.[107] When the baking was complete and the bread was removed from the oven walls, some hardened dough remained in the cracks and groves of the clay thus causing a crackled surface. Dried out (cf כָּעֵץ in 4_{8b}) and wrinkled skin has similar appearance. The verb כמר can also be used for the wrinkling effect one can observe as fruit becomes over-ripe.[108] Such wrinkled and atrophied skin is a result of the זַלְעֲפוֹת רָעָב. זַלְעֲפוֹת is a construct plural of זַלְעָפָה, rendered in Ps 119_{53} as 'fury' (cf HAL 261). The plural here is thus appropriately rendered 'the furies of hunger'.

Sub-canto II (Lam 5_{11-22})

This sub-canto is formed by the last three canticles. Compared with the first sub-canto, the poets now turn their attention at the end of their work to a joyless and ruined Zion and round off their songs with an urgent prayer for deliverance and restoration.

Canticle I (5_{11-14})

Content/theme: *defilement and affliction, death and grief*

Literary argumentation:

105 LXX corrects this verbal form with the singular ἐπελειώθη (passive of πελῖ-όομαι, 'to become dark').

106 Cf also 3_{38}; PWernberg–Møller, Review of: BAlbrektson, *Studies in the Text and Theology of the Book of Lamentations, with a Critical Edition of the Peshitta Text*, (STL 21) 1963; in: JSS X (1955), 109f and Meek.

107 Cf Hos 7_4 and figure in BRL^2, 30.

108 Cf HAL 459 sv כמר I; cf likewise Albrektson.

inclusions: בְּעָרֵי (11B) // מִשַּׁעַר (14A)
בְּתֻלֹת (11B) // בַּחוּרִים (14B)
זְקֵנִים (12B) // נְעָרִים (13B)[109]

responses: נָשִׁים (11A) // בַּחוּרִים (13A)[110]
בְּתֻלֹת (11B) // נְעָרִים (13B)
זְקֵנִים (12B) // זְקֵנִים (14A)
זְקֵנִים (12B) // בַּחוּרִים (14B)

When compared with the other canticles, the first canticle of the second sub-canto (5_{11-22}), which is also the central canticle of the final song as a whole, is striking for its lack of use of the suffix נוּ. At the level of content, therefore, the canticle does not focus on subjectively experienced affliction but rather on the actual calamitous situation facing the country as a whole. It is worth noting that the poets avoid reference to material destruction in this concentrated summary, turning their attention exclusively to human misfortune. Their reason for doing so probably has to do with the fact that the various material disasters facing the population only have an indirect affect on their lives while the poets wish to speak only of direct human affliction at this point. While the theme of famine was dealt with in detail in the preceding canticle ($5_{6,9,10}$), it is not directly mentioned here and only enjoys a degree of indirect reference in 5_{13}. The emphasis is clearly and intentionally placed on the reign of terror being endured by the entire people: women and girls, princes and elders, men and boys. No one is spared its ravages.

11 *Women in Zion they rape,* נָשִׁים בְּצִיּוֹן עִנּוּ
girls in the cities of Judah! בְּתֻלֹת בְּעָרֵי יְהוּדָה

Van Selms points out that, without any transition, the poets now turn their attention to the crimes of the invading soldiers during the fall of Jerusalem and for this reason he translates the text as a perfect. As a lament before YHWH, however, a perfect tense interpretation would have the effect of emasculating the text. YHWH does not undo crimes which took place in the past but it is within his power to bring an end to the violence and injustice which is still taking place. Given the opening line 'look and see' in 5_1 we are obliged to translate this verse in the present tense, the Hebrew perfect being descriptive of the existing situation in the land.[111] In addition, the somewhat abrupt change of theme can be

---

109 Cf 2_{21aB}
110 See exegesis.

explained by the opening of the second sub-canto and the new canticle, even although the ongoing absence of protection maintains a degree of continuity with the preceding verses.

In line with levels of accentuation elsewhere in the songs, it is striking that the suffering of the women is first to be mentioned here. The rape of the women reveals the deeply humiliating and dreadful consequences of the lack of any form of protection. By placing this in the centre of the final song, the plight of the women, tormented by hunger and humiliated by rape, is thereby given centre stage.[112]

12A *Princes are hung up at their hands,* שָׂרִים בְּיָדָם נִתְלוּ

The princes' obvious abuse of power made them the target of considerable prophetic critique[113] and judgement was proclaimed over their outrages.[114] Ezekiel in particular predecited that the hands of strangers (בְּיַד־זָרִים) would execute judgement against such princes: Ezek 11_9. Hanging criminals by a noose was an unknown punishment in Israel. Normally, the corpses of criminals were hung on wooden stakes after stoning as a sign of shame.[115] Based on their reading of Gen 40_{19}, Aalders and Van Selms consider the present text to refer to impalement, but the Genesis text seems to speak of hanging rather than impaling on a stake (cf HAL 1601). The non-Israelite character of this sort of execution is further evidence of the work of hostile foreigners.

Kaiser's reading of the text is worthy of note. He considers it possible that the princes were hung up by their hands in a sort of crucifixion, but it seems more logical that בְּיָדָם should be understood as a reference back to 5_8 and the mention of the servants who now have dominion in the land (cf מִיָּדָם). It is true that a number of princes were deported to Babylon but it is likewise true that several important and prominent figures remained behind.[116] Such individuals became the victims of the terror attacks perpetrated by the 'servants' mentioned in 5_8. As a matter of fact, daily governance was often in the hands of the princes[117] and as

---

111 See Lam 1_1 and cf GES-K § 106*g*.

112 Cf the associations with 1_{10} as well as the explanation of 3_{51}.

113 Isa 1_{23}, Ezek $1_{1-3,6}$, 22_{27}.

114 Jer 24_8, 34_{21}.

115 Jos 10_{26}, II Sam 4_{12}; cf RdVaux, *Institutions I*, 244f.

116 Cf Jer 40_{7f}, 41_1.

117 Cf the explanation of 1_{6b}.

such they constituted a (potential) threat to the new order which could only benefit from defencelessness, chaos and the absence of law and order.

12B *the countenance of the elders is not honoured!* פְּנֵי זְקֵנִים לֹא נֶהְדָּרוּ

For the construction פְּנֵי זְקֵנִים see the exegesis of 4_{16}. In situations where the leadership was absent, at least the elders were still around to offer some degree of guidance.[118] Evidently the responsiblity for governance was transferred to their shoulders since "Der alte Mensch ist der Inbegriff langer Erfahrung (Deut 32,7; cf Ps 37,25) und der daraus resultierenden Fähigkeit zu besonnenem Rat in politischen Entscheidungen." [119] Esteem for the elderly was a duty, not only in the sense that they had to be cared for but also in the sense that their rights and authority as representatives of families had to be honoured (cf Lev 19_{32}). Family order in general and as a fundamental structure of human existence was thus maintained. From the social perspective, since it extended beyond the family circle, the influence of the elders' representative function led to them being held in high esteem throughout the land or at least being deserving of such. This kind of treatment was not specific to Israel but was reflected in similar traditions throughout her 'Umwelt'.[120] Thus the humiliation of the remaining elders by the new regime simply ran counter to any kind of human value system. Although this lament is almost identical to that in 4_{16B}, the context of prayer provides it with a different degree of pointedness. Indeed, the very hopelessness of the situation is now being explicitly brought before YHWH (5_1). What is happening in Israel is his business also. The widely held value of respect for one's elders had theological legitimation in Israel via the fifth commandment to honour one's parents.[121] In Lev 19_{32}, respect for the elders and the parallel concept of the fear of God were literally held up before Israel as Mosaic law: "You shall rise before the aged, and defer to the old; and you shall fear your God." Thus the humiliation of the elders by the enemy constituted an attack on the divine order sanctioned by YHWH.

13 *Young men take up the millstone* בַּחוּרִים טְחוֹן נָשָׂאוּ
and boys stagger under the burden of wood! וּנְעָרִים בָּעֵץ כָּשָׁלוּ

[118] Note how of the groups of persons mentioned in 2_{9-10} only daughter Zion's elders remain.
[119] Conrad in TWAT II 641f.
[120] Cf TWAT II 643 (Conrad).
[121] Cf JLKoole, *De tien geboden*, Baarn 1964, 85.

While interpretation of טְחוֹן as a 'millstone' is well established,[122] the verb נשׂא, however, seems to be a source of problems for a variety of commentators. What does the expression 'to carry a millstone' actually mean? Dalman interprets the text literally and sees in it a description of what happened on the journey to the land of the exile: "Es ist eine Schande, für Jünglinge, Mühle und Brennholz auf dem Zuge in die Fremde schleppen zu müssen." [123] Lam V, however, deals specifically and explicitly with the situation in Judah itself. Driver [124] suggests that נָשָׂאוּ should be read as 'to endure' in the sense of 'to put up with', that is the young men are forced to endure the work of milling normally reserved for women or female slaves.[125] It remains possible, nevertheless, to stay close to the more literal meaning of נשׂא in 'to take up'/'to raise'.[126] The object of the verb is clearly the grinding stone or millstone. A mill consisted of a large flat stone upon which different kinds of cereal were ground under a smaller millstone. The larger stone was fixed in place and was left unmoved while the millstone in contrast was moveable and quite easy to lift (cf Judg 9_{53}). Such ease of removal was necessary since the millstone had to be lifted each time to allow for a new sprinkling of cereal on the lower stone.[127]

Grinding cereal was woman's work and best left to servant girls or female slaves.[128] On this very aspect the present text seems unusual: not women but בַּחוּרִים are forced to mill the grain. One is reminded here of 1_{15b} where Lady Jerusalem laments the fact that her young men are being crushed like grains of wheat on the harvest festival which YHWH has proclaimed against her. The crushed בַּחוּרִים in their turn crush only grain in the mill. Why might this be so? Aalders, Kraus, Van Selms and Gordis interpret their work as the slave labour performed by prisoners on behalf of their captors (cf Judg 16_{21}). Gordis considers the second colon to be supplementary parallel with the first. At the same time, he interprets the wood mentioned in this colon as a sort of turnstile for a larger mill which was first brought to the desired location and then used for milling. Whatever the case the weight of their burden is too much for the בַּחוּרִים and they

122 Cf HAL 357; for the formation of the noun from √טחן see BL 473*h*.

123 GDalman, *Arbeit und Sitte in Palästina III*, 1933, 211f.

124 GRDriver, 'Hebrew Notes on "Song of Songs" and "Lamentations" ', Fs ABertholet, Tübingen 1950, 144.

125 For this understanding of √נשׂא see Isa 1_{14}, Mic 7_9, Job 21_3 and HAL 685 sv נשׂא (14).

126 Cf also LXX with ἀνέλαβον.

127 See Dalman, III, 207–210, the figures in BHH 1246f and BRL² 232f.

128 Ex 11_5 and Isa 47_2.

stumble beneath it. Gordis' interpretation appears to take no notice of the change of subject: one cannot place בַּחוּרִים on the same level as נְעָרִים. The response within the canticle נָשִׁים (11A) // בַּחוּרִים (13A) supports an alternative explanation: even within the cities the women and young girls were subject to rape (cf 5_{11}). Indeed, the terror was such that they lacked any kind of safe haven. The sound of the millstone grinding would have given away their location and thus the little grain that was left was milled by the younger men. The response בְּתֻלֹת (11B) // נְעָרִים (13B) points to a similar connection: since the young girls were no longer safe outside, the young boys had to take care of the wood necessary for cooking. The merism evident in this canticle (נְעָרִים – זְקֵנִים) suggests that the boys in question must have been quite young indeed, although the exact age group is difficult to determine.[129] Under normal circumstances such young boys would have been able to carry a certain amount of wood without difficulty but under the present famine the children are exhausted. Given the scarcity of wood it was necessary to travel further to find what little was left. In mentioning that these young men stumble from fatigue under their bundles of sticks, the poets offer a further elaboration of Lady Jerusalem's stumbling (הִכְשִׁיל כֹּחִי [1_{14B}] // כָּשָׁלוּ [5_{13B}]), since her lot is that of her people.

14A *Elders stay away from the gate,* זְקֵנִים מִשַּׁעַר שָׁבָתוּ

Under normal circumstances the area adjacent to the gate was the place par excellence where one might find the elders passing their day.[130] At the same time, the area around the gate was the forum of public life[131] as well as the place where matters of justice were dealt with.[132] Job 29_{7-17} provides a detailed illustration in this regard (cf also Prov 31_{23}). Aalders, who understands the verb שׁבת to mean 'rest', notes that the very place which was usually full of life "...is now deathly still." His interpretation wrongly introduces the flavour of sabbath rest to the scene, however. Given the fact that the verbal form שָׁבָתוּ also governs the second colon, in the present context the *qal* of the root must simply mean 'to cease (from)'. Silence would hardly be a characteristic of the gate at this point either. The literary structure shows the reason why the elders are no longer to be found in their usual place: it is stated in 5_{12} (response) that the occupiers do not treat them with the appropriate respect. At the same level it is

[129] Cf TWAT V 513f (Fuhs).

[130] Cf for זְקֵנִים $1_{6b,19b}$, 2_{10a}, 4_{16bB} and 5_{12}.

[131] Gen 19_1, I Kgs 21_{10}, Prov 1_{21}, 31_{31} etcetera.

[132] Cf Deut 21_{19}, Jos 20_4, Ruth 4_{1ff}.

noted in the fourth song (4_{12}, song-response) that the enemy have entered the gates of Jerusalem (cf Ob $_{11,13}$). The occupation of the gate was thus a demonstration of supremacy. In addition, the gates were evidently the most appropriate place from which the enemy might keep an eye on what was going on in the cities of Judah. Given that they were not inclined to show respect to those they encountered it was just as dangerous in the gate for the elders as it was for anyone else. Thus they stay away. Lam 4_{16bB} and 5_{12B} state categorically that the elders were not given due honour by the enemy.

14B *young men from their music!* בַּחוּרִים מִנְּגִינָתָם

One can observe that in every culture and in every period of history music making as a popular activity among the young. Clearly something serious must have been happening if it forced the בַּחוּרִים to lay down their instruments. The prophets place this in a theological framework: when the music stopped the time for judgement had come.[133] Isa 38_{20} and Ps 30_{12} present the opposite state of affairs. Why does the present text specifically mention the בַּחוּרִים? Once again we are reminded of the first song in which the poets tell us that YHWH has crushed Lady Jerusalem's young men (1_{15b}). Finally, the inclusion in the present strophe בַּחוּרִים (5_{13A}) // בַּחוּרִים (5_{14B}) suggests that the young men's fingers were not only too sore from milling but their pleasure in music making was spoiled by the fact that such work was humiliating for them.

Canticle II (5_{15-18})

Content/theme: *grief at Zion's devastation*

Literary argumentation:

inclusions:
מְשׂוֹשׂ לִבֵּנוּ (15A) // הַר־צִיּוֹן (18A)
רֹאשֵׁנוּ (16A) // לִבֵּנוּ (17A)

responses:
לִבֵּנוּ (15A) // לִבֵּנוּ (17A)
נֶהְפַּךְ לְאֵבֶל מְחֹלֵנוּ (15B) // חָשְׁכוּ עֵינֵינוּ (17B)
עֲטֶרֶת (16A) // הַר־צִיּוֹן (18A)
נָפְלָה (16A) // שֶׁשָּׁמֵם (18A)

The suffix נוּ returns once again and features in every colon of the present canticle except those of the concluding verse 18 (cf the *petucha*). Such concatenation is impressively consolidative. Based on this and other literary

[133] Cf Isa 16_{10}, Jer 7_{34}, 16_{9}, 25_{10}, 48_{33}, Ezek 26_{13}.

argumentation it is reasonable to assume, therefore, that both strophes (5_{15-16} and 5_{17-18}) constitute a single canticle. One additional characteristic worthy of note is the fact that the final canticle to speak of the current misfortune focuses entirely on the ruination of Zion and the despair it has caused.

15A *It has ceased the joy of our heart,* שָׁבַת מְשׂוֹשׂ לִבֵּנוּ

At first sight there appears to be no clear distinction between 5_{14} and the present verse, thus leaving our canticle division open to dispute. The lost joy mentioned here seems to be fully in line with the cessation of music making in 5_{14B}.[134] In spite of this fact, a significant difference between the two cola can be clearly discerned. One can assume that the string music referred to in 5_{14} was profane music, but the joy intended here has a cultic context: the מְשׂוֹשׂ לִבֵּנוּ is the jubilation experienced during the liturgy in Zion.[135]

Cohesion in terms of content is also telling at this level: 1_{15} (\\ feast for the enemy), 2_{15} (// destruction of Zion), 3_{43-45} (// shame without mercy or forgiveness), 4_{15} (// expulsion of priests and prophets). While Zion is not directly mentioned in 2_{15}, however, this is not the case in the present canticle (cf the inclusion מְשׂוֹשׂ לִבֵּנוּ [5_{15A}] // הַר־צִיּוֹן [5_{18A}]). This would appear to be of some significance since this final canticle in which Zion's misfortune is described ends with the mention of her destruction. The first canticle to speak of destruction was the second canticle of Lam I and the first destruction mentioned there was likewise that of Zion (cf 1_{4-6}).

So the last canticle but one and the second canticle in the entire book form an inclusion (at the book level). One can say, therefore, that the destruction of Zion must have been the greatest source of sadness the authors and population had to face. Zion's ruin included all the rest.[136] The present lament also contains an echo of prophetic announcement of doom, the word combination שבת מְשׂוֹשׂ being found in this context in Hosea.[137]

15B *transformed into mourning our dance!* נֶהְפַּךְ לְאֵבֶל מְחֹלֵנוּ

For the radicality of this transformation via נֶהְפַּךְ see the explanation of 5_{2A}. It is far from accidental that in the songs of Zion, reference is made to

---

134 Cf also the repetition of the verb שׁבת.

135 Cf the explanation of 2_{15C}.

136 For לֵב as the seat of human emotions see 1_{20bA}.

137 Cf Hos 2_{10} (MT 2_{13}): וְהִשְׁבַּתִּי כָּל־מְשׂוֹשָׂהּ.

to the dance as a form of liturgical expression.[138] Dance is an expression of joy and happiness[139] and in terms of emotional experience is diametrically opposite to sorrow and mourning. In Ps 30_{12} joy and sorrow are set in opposition to one another as extremes, but the same verse speaks of the reverse situation to that of our present colon: YHWH turns mourning into dancing.

This lament is reminiscent of the preaching of Amos (cf 8_{10}) in which darkness, sackcloth and ashes and bitterness are likewise presented as facets of YHWH's day of doom. The use of this kind of terminology here reveals the extent to which the poets experienced their present reality as the fulfilment of such prophetic judgement. The present colon also reveals the association between lament and mourning as we already noted with respect to the preceding songs.

16A *Fallen is the crown of our head!* נָפְלָה עֲטֶרֶת רֹאשֵׁנוּ

This colon is also difficult to understand outside the context of prophetic judgement, especially that of Isaiah concerning Samaria: Isa 28_{1-4}[140] and Jeremiah: Jer 13_{15-27}. Shared terminology with Isaiah includes עֲטָרָה and רֹאשׁ. See also הוֹי // אוֹי. Borrowing from Isaiah is also understandable, therefore, since this is the final colon in the book as a whole in which the fall of Jerusalem is mentioned. As a matter of fact, in Israel's history, the fall of Jerusalem had only one precedent: the fall of Samaria.[141] As a concluding description of the situation, the present colon may have a summary character but its language is far from inconsequential.

What is the meaning of עֲטֶרֶת רֹאשֵׁנוּ? In Isa 28_4 it is proposed that רֹאשׁ refers to the round, orb-like hill upon which the city of Samaria stood.[142] The crown was the city itself which capped the mountain. One can imagine the walls surrounding such a 'crown'-city looking something like a garland encircling a mountain/hill.[143] When such a 'capital' city fell into the hands of an enemy force then this also implied that the crown of the king within

---

[138] Cf Ps 87_7 and HJKraus, *Psalmen, 60–150*, BKAT XV/2, Neukirchen 1978[5], 768; Ps 149_3 and 150_4; cf also Ps 68_{26} and its use of the term תֹּף (tambourine), the preferred instrument for accompanying dance.

[139] Cf Ex 15_{20}, Judg 11_{34}, I Sam 18_6.

[140] See HWildberger, *Jesaja 28–39*, BKAT X/3, Neukirchen 1982, 1045f for authenticity.

[141] Cf also Ezek 23_{32f} where it is predicted that daughter Jerusalem would also be forced to drink the cup of sister Samaria.

[142] Cf I Kgs 16_{24} and Wildberger, 1049.

[143] Cf TWAT IV 29f (Kellermann).

the city had fallen, that is his authority had expired.[144] In such a context, the falling of the crown refers to the fall of Jerusalem.

Two other possibilties present themselves. Firstly, one might understand ראשׁ as Jerusalem itself, that is as the capital city.[145] As such, however, the significance of the crown becomes more obscure. Perhaps it refers to the walls of the city but this seems rather abrupt in the context. The second possibility is that the metaphor has to do with the temple mountain and ראשׁ stands for Zion (cf Isa 2_2). The crown could then be understood as a metaphor for the temple complex – a raised and thus distinctive feature of the city-scape – the walls of which might be understood as the outer circle of the crown itself. Viewed from this perspective an evident response emerges between עֲטֶרֶת ראשֵׁנוּ (5_{16A}) and הַר־צִיּוֹן (5_{18A}) and the fall in question is clearly that of Zion. Given this and other details, such as the inclusion (at book level) with the second canticle of the first song, this must have been the intended meaning of the present colon. The second canticle of Lam I describes the destruction of Zion('s gates) employing similar terminology: כָּל־שְׁעָרֶיהָ שׁוֹמֵמִין (1_{4bA}) // הַר־צִיּוֹן שֶׁשָּׁמֵם (5_{18A}) and cf אֲבֵלוֹת (1_{4aA}) // לְאֵבֶל (5_{15B}). One further important argument is the connection between תִּפְאֶרֶת (splendour) and עֲטָרָה (crown).[146] The תִּפְאֶרֶת in 2_{1bB} also appears to refer to the temple on Zion.

The poets baldy state that Zion has fallen, but in the present context there is an added negative condition: 'into the hands of enemies'.[147] This could only happen because the enemy had become לְראשׁ (cf 1_{5a}). At the level of content, Zion's fall is comparable with her destruction (cf the response נָפְלָה [16A] // שֶׁשָּׁמֵם [18A]). The root נפל is also a technical term in the context of mourning.[148]

16B *Woe to us, for we have sinned!* אוֹי־נָא לָנוּ כִּי חָטָאנוּ

The usual construction אוֹי לְ is strengthened here with the particle נָא, a combination only found elswhere in Jer 4_{31} and 45_3. A glance at Jer 4_{31}, however, shows the degree of agreement with the present text to be much greater than merely a shared literary figure. Jer 4_{31} is part of an early prophecy of Jeremiah in which the prophet hears and sees the affliction of daughter Zion which is the result of her sin. She suffers the

144 Cf the perspective of condemnation found in Jer 13_{18}.

145 For this interpretation of ראשׁ see Jos 11_{10}, Isa 7_8.

146 Cf Isa $28_{1,4}$, Jer 13_{18}, Ezek 16_{12}.

147 Cf Jer 51_8, Ezek 13_{14}.

148 Cf II Sam $1_{19,25,27}$, 3_{34}, Am 5_2.

anguish of a women in labour[149] who stretches out her hands for breath.[150] Jeremiah proposes the treachery of her allies as the political antecedent of her misfortune, lovers who instead of loving her sought her life and ultimately destroyed her (Jer 4_{30f}). The prophet envisages her stretching out her hands for help (cf Lam 1_{17aA}) and hears her painful cry of anguish: אוֹי־נָא לִי. By taking over this terminology the poets indicate how they and their fellow Israelites experience their present affliction as the fulfilment of Jeremiah's vision of doom. How real that vision has now become!

אוֹי is rightly qualified as an exclamation of angst[151] uttered in a context of retribution, destruction and ruin.[152] In combination with לְ + 1st person plural suffix it renders the 'angst' of the speaker(s). Where אוֹי is combined with a 2nd or 3rd person suffix then angst is anticipated for the addressee(s) in the face of impending doom. This is frequently the case with respect to prophetic announcements of judgement.

In the present text the speakers are referring to their own angst, although it is striking that no concrete misfortune is mentioned as its source which is frequently the case elsewhere.[153] In contrast to these occurences of the expression the present usage points to personal sin as the source of the speakers angst. Does this mean that they are afraid of their own deeds? An alternative and more acceptable interpretation becomes apparent when one examines the use of the more menacing אוֹי in prophetic announcements of doom where it is implicitly associated with the terrifying consequences of sin.[154] In order to demonstrate the fact their belief that they are experiencing the fulfilment of such prophecy, the poets use a contraction of the angst announced by the prophets. Their angst ultimately has its source in their concrete experience of the dreadful consquences of sin. For their sins Zion was destroyed and as a consequence they must now live with vulnerability and crippling fear (cf the response חָטָאנוּ [5_{16B}] // הַר־צִיּוֹן שֶׁשָּׁמֵם [5_{18A}]). For the present affliction as the fulfilment of prophecy see Mic 3_{12}, Jer 7_{14}, $26_{6,18}$, Ezek 24_{21}; see also the exegesis of Lam 2_{6a}.

Although it is evident that what follows focuses more on the consequences of sin, it is clear, nevertheless, that we are also dealing with a collective

---

149 Cf the use of the root אנח in $1_{4,8,11,21}$, אַנְחֹתַי in 1_{22} and the explanation of 1_{4bB}.

150 Cf also the parallel with 1_{17}: פֵּרְשָׂה צִיּוֹן בְּיָדֶיהָ.

151 Cf HWWolff, *Dodekapropheton 2, Joel und Amos*, BKAT XIV/2, Neukirchen–Vluyn 1969, 284.

152 Cf TWAT II 384 (Zobel).

153 Cf I Sam $4_{7,8}$, Isa 6_5, 24_{16}, Jer $4_{13,31}$, 6_4, 10_{19}, 15_{10}; cf also Prov 23_{29}.

154 Isa $3_{9,11}$, Ezek 16_{23}, $24_{6,9}$, Hos 7_{13}, 9_{12}.

admission that it was not only the fathers – the priests and the prophets – who sinned (5_7). While they may have had the lion's share of the responsibility (cf 2_{14}, 4_{13}), personal sin also had a role to play. In itself such iniquity was enough reason for the fall of the city and the land (cf 2_{14b}). Any explanation of the text must honour the fact that the priests and prophets, however guilty, are no longer mentioned here. In fact, the supplicants blame Zion's downfall on their own sin and guilt and rightly so since, with an eye to the final prayer, every form of excuse making has to be avoided.[155]

17A *Because of this our heart is sick,* עַל־זֶה הָיָה דָוֶה לִבֵּנוּ

Given the inclusion/response עַל // עַל within the ninth strophe (5_{17-18}) it would seem that עַל־זֶה in 5_{17A} refers to עַל in 5_{18A}: their heart is sick because of the destruction of Zion. As Brockelmann notes, "Weiterhin bezeichnet עַל die Grundlage einer Stimmung oder Handlung" (§ 110*e*). The fact that the loss of Zion is repeated here makes it clear just how much this event stands at the heart of the supplicants' 'sickness' of heart. This was already mentioned in 5_{15-16}. The emotion of angst (אוֹי) has physical consequences: a deathly malady of the heart. It should come as no surprise that the present lament is identical with that of Lady Jerusalem in 1_{13c} and 1_{22c}. Her lament is ultimately that of her inhabitants.

17B *because of these things our eyes have grown dark:* עַל־אֵלֶּה חָשְׁכוּ עֵינֵינוּ

The image of being blinded by one's tears can be found elsewhere in Lamentations: 1_{16aA}: עַל־אֵלֶּה אֲנִי בוֹכִיָּה // עַל־אֵלֶּה חָשְׁכוּ עֵינֵינוּ (5_{17B}; song-response). In 2_{11aA} it is once again Lady Jerusalem who has cried herself blind; in 3_{49} (song-response) it is the גֶּבֶר who weeps, lamenting the fact that YHWH has driven him into darkness (3_2). 4_{17} (song-response) speaks of 'failing eyes'. In each case the sorrow which leads to these blinding tears is different: in 1_{16a} the absence of a comforter and the desolation of the children; in 2_{11} the fall of Jerusalem and the suffering of the children; in 3_{49} the suffering of the women of Jerusalem and in 4_{17} the futile expectation of help. 5_{17} is alone in employing the combination עַיִן + √חשך, however, and is thus the most direct expression of this hopeless situation. The final lament focuses on the ultimate cause of their 'darkened eyes' (cf 5_{18}). The sequence of demonstrative pronouns זֶה (singular) and אֵלֶּה (plural) corresponds with the singular 'Zion' and the plural 'jackals' in 5_{18}.

155 For the significance of √חטא see 1_{8a}; cf also the explanation of 3_{40-42}.

18A *because of the desolate Mount Zion,* עַל הַר־צִיּוֹן שֶׁשָּׁמֵם

With respect to שֶׁשָּׁמֵם, the text critical apparatus of BHS refers to the *k^e^tīḇ occidentalis* (K^{Oc}) which has a *hiph'il* infinitive. This form is reminiscent of Mic 6_{13}, a rough matrix of the lament expressed in Lam $5_{17,18}$. The maintenance of the MT, however, deserves preference since it has the more common clause construction (adjective שָׁמֵם preceded by שֶׁ as a determinative pronoun). In any event, the meaning remains unaltered.[156]

The poets' final lament concerns the destruction of the mountain of Zion which, as a consequence, now lies abandoned. הַר־צִיּוֹן is identical with הַר קֹדֶשׁ, the holy temple mountain.[157] Of all the peoples' suffering, the destruction of Zion hurts the most. She has become a visible symbol of abandonment by YHWH. Her palaces no longer house God's annointed, the Davidic king. Such devastation spells the end (4_{18b}). YHWH's protection has been withdrawn and as a consequence she has been handed over to the capricious behaviour of the enemy (// 4_{18a}, 3_{52-54}), her children cry out in vain (// 2_{18a}) and her future has been taken captive, her young men and young women (// 1_{18c}).[158]

18B *because of the jackals which range there!* שׁוּעָלִים הִלְּכוּ־בוֹ

As Margalith points out[159] שׁוּעָלִים are most probably not to be identified with European foxes but rather with jackals (*canis aureus*; cf also HAL 1341). One argument in support of this is that foxes (*vulpes vulpes*) are shy animals which live a solitary life within their own territory whereas jackals hunt at night in groups, ravage mountainside and plain and even enter towns and villages in search of house pets to eat.[160] The plural employed here thus suggests jackals. We can determine from a number of sources that jackals rooted around in the ashes and ruins of once inhabited places.[161] The use of the verb הלך (*pi'el*) in association with these animals is also telling. It does not suggest a more or less fixed abode as is the case with the 'army of animals' in Jer 9_{10} and 10_{22}. Jackals are drifters.

Of all the animals which wander through ruins and ash-heaps why are the jackals singled out here? Prophetic announcements of doom do not include

156 Cf HAL 1448.
157 Cf Ps $48_{2,3}$ and THAT II 603 (Müller).
158 For the further implications of Zion's destruction see the exegesis of 1_{4b}, $2_{1,6,8}$, 4_{11}.
159 OMargalith, 'Samson's Foxes', VT XXXV (1985), 225.
160 Cf BHH 1682 (Feliks).
161 Song 2_{15}, Ezek 13_4 and Neh 3_{35}.

them by name in the same way as the wild animals and the ostrich. Jackals cannot thus serve as a sign of the fulfilment of such predicted judgement. An alternative association might shed some light on their appearance here. While it is true that jackals are not clearly mentioned elsewhere in the OT the same is not the case as far as ancient Egypt is concerned. There the jackals were the animal most closely associated with the necropolis.[162] The fact that jackals now roam freely in Zion is a sign that she has become a city of the dead.[163] Once again we have a further association between lament and mourning. It is striking that at the end of this penultimate canticle we should encounter an 'Egyptian motief', given that a similar motief was apparent at the penultimate canticle of the fourth song: 4_{20}.

Canticle III (5_{19-22})

Content/theme: *Final prayer for restoration*

Literary argumentation:

inclusions:
לְעוֹלָם (19A) // עַד־מְאֹד (22B)[164]
יָמִים (20B) // יָמֵינוּ (21B)

responses:
יְהוָה (19A) // יְהוָה (21A)[165]
לְדֹר וָדוֹר (19B) // קֶדֶם (21B)
כִּסְאֲךָ (19B) // כְּקֶדֶם (21B)
תִּשְׁכָּחֵנוּ (20A) // מְאַסְתָּנוּ (22A)
תַּעַזְבֵנוּ (20B) // מְאַסְתָּנוּ (22A)[166]
תַּעַזְבֵנוּ (20B) // קָצַפְתָּ עָלֵינוּ (22B)
לְאֹרֶךְ יָמִים (20B) // עַד־מְאֹד (22B)

alliteration: תֵּשֵׁב (19A) // וְנָשׁוּב and הֲשִׁיבֵנוּ (21A)

concatenation: as with the preceding canticle via the suffix נוּ

Having opened with a direct appeal to YHWH to look upon their affliction, followed by a detailed description thereof, the poets now conclude with a final prayer and direct address. At the level of content this prayer is of great importance since it provides a concise and concrete formulation of the poets' motivations and desires. It also becomes clear why they feel

[162] Cf OKeel, *Die Welt der altorientalischen Bildsymbolik und das Alte Testament*, Zürich-Einsiedeln-Köln-Neukirchen-Vluyn 1977[2], 33, 66f and possible Ps 63_{11}.

[163] Cf 2_{20c} and the explanation of $3_{16,17}$.

[164] Cf Ps 111_{8}, $145_{1,2,21}$, 148_{6}.

[165] Two vocatives.

[166] Cf Isa 54_{6}.

able to address this prayer to YHWH and what continues to be the basis of their faith. The present canticle reveals an essential aspect of the poets' theology, one which has survived the calamity confronting them.

19A *You,* YHWH, אַתָּה יְהוָה

The combination אַתָּה יְהוָה at the very beginning of a literary unit is relatively rare,[167] perhaps because writers experienced it as a little too direct. We noted a similar phenomenon with the imperative addressation of YHWH in $1_{9c,11c,20a}$, 2_{20a} and 5_1. Given the horrendous need, however, such urgency is now unavoidable. The use of the tetragrammaton is also significant: YHWH is Israel's God. The poets thus confess that as far as they are concerned YHWH is still their God. Nevertheless, their faith is rife with tension. One only has to ascertain the contexts in which the poets use the tetragrammaton. At such moments they are forced to mention the hard and bitter circumstances YHWH has allowed to befall them. As a matter of fact he alone is the enemy and the oppressor ($1_{5b,12c}$); he destroys, kills and is without mercy (2_{17}, 3_{42}); he is the enemy's great Leader (1_{17c}, 2_{22a}) and he alone, YHWH himself, is the one who has brought an end to Zion and the liturgy of her temple (2_{6-9}; 4_{16}). Now, in this perilous and distressful existence, the poets know of only One who has the power to reverse their fortunes: the very one who afflicted them in the first place, YHWH their god.

19B *you sit enthroned forever!* לְעוֹלָם תֵּשֵׁב

The present claim is likewise full of tension. Indeed, with devastated Zion in full view the poets now begin to speak of YHWH's enthronement,[168] that is his royal dominion.[169] √ישׁב is not static here in the sense that it only indicates YHWH's dwelling. Görg[170] speaks in this regard of a 'mansiver' element – that of 'dwelling' – and a 'sedativer' element – that of YHWH sitting on his throne of judgement, a very essential and active aspect in his kingship. It remains a question whether one can visualise both aspects in separation.[171] Görg is of the opinion that the present use of √ישׁב refers to its mansive component: " "Imperfektiven Aspekt" (...) mit "mansiver"

167 Ps 12_8, 40_{12}, Isa 63_{16}.
168 Cf the internal chiastic parallelism between תֵּשֵׁב and כִּסְאֲךָ.
169 Cf MMetzger, 'Himmlische und irdische Wohnstatt Jahwes', UF 2 (1970), 147 and THAT I 916 (Soggin).
170 See TWAT III 1025–1032.
171 Cf the parallelism in Ps 9_8.

Bedeutung bietet hingegen Kl 5,19: "In Ewigkeit thronst du!", wobei dieses Wohnen im Kontrast sum verwüsteten Zionsberg (v. 18) gesehen wird."[172] While this contrast is certainly present, the poets do not employ the usual participle in relation to YHWH's sitting 'enthroned'/'dwelling'.[173] They opt in the present context for the more unusual dynamic imperfect תֵּשֵׁב – only found elsewhere with YHWH as subject in the late text Ps 102_{13} – which is quite extraordinary and clearly points to the fact that the poets are not simply confessing their belief that YHWH still dwells in heaven (2_{1b}) in spite of the destruction of Zion. What good would that do them? The opening of the new canticle indicates that with the confession of his eternal enthronement (contra Görg) they have YHWH sitting on his royal throne of judgement in mind – and not his dwelling in the heavens – and that they still have hope that he will act with justice. On this very point there is a degree of cohesion with the conclusions of the other songs. Here too the poets appeal for YHWH's merciful intervention: 1_{22}, 2_{20}, 3_{64-66}; cf 4_{21b}. Thus the confession of YHWH's enthronement is simultaneously an implicit appeal to the Judge who is the Shepherd of Israel (cf Ps 80_1). The fact that the poets also speak of the eternity of YHWH's enthronement (לְעוֹלָם) should not be limited in its interpretation to long duration. The לְעוֹלָם of his enthronement equally implies the consistency of his kingship and thus the לְעוֹלָם of his divine justice.[174] So YHWH's חֶסֶד is also eternal.[175] In spite of the enormity of the tension – cf 3_{34-37} – this theological axiom has survived the crisis.

19B *Your throne is from generation to generation!* כִּסְאֲךָ לְדֹר וָדוֹר

Here too the tension brought about by the destruction of Zion is almost tangible. Zion herself is referred to throughout the OT as YHWH's throne.[176] Once again, however, the awareness that YHWH is not bound to the earthly Zion becomes apparent (cf Lam 2_1). His throne is in the heavens[177] and Zion is nothing more than an unnecessary extrapolation thereof: the merciful nearness of YHWH.[178] Jer 8_{19} offers an indication of the extent to which the kingship of YHWH on Zion is intended here. Fur-

[172] In TWAT III 1031.
[173] Cf, for example, I Sam 4_4, II Sam 6_2, II Kgs 9_{15}, Isa 6_1, 37_{16}, Ps 80_2; cf Ps 22_4 – he sits enthroned/he dwells there (but).
[174] Cf the explanation of 1_{22}.
[175] Cf Preuß (TWAT V 1154) and Ps 25_6 (with the imperative זְכֹר).
[176] Isa 8_{18}, Jer 14_{21}, 17_{12}, Ps 9_{12}; cf Ps 43_3, 48, 68_{17}, Jer 8_{19}, Ezek 43_7.
[177] Ps 2_4, 11_4, 123_1; cf Isa 66_1.
[178] Cf Isa 31_{4-5}, Jer 8_{19}.

thermore, according to Fabry, "Die Frage nach dem Thron JHWHs (...) is identisch mit der Frage nach JHWHs Königtum."[179] A review of the places where YHWH's throne is spoken of reveals statements of its facticity and its permanency,[180] as is the case with the present colon. Using a fixed formulation, Ps 89_{15} and 97_2 offer a striking definition of YHWH's throne as founded in justice (צֶדֶק) and righteousness (מִשְׁפָּט). This can be understood as an indication of the nature and character of YHWH's kingship and is thereby reminiscent of the statement in 1_{18aA}: צַדִּיק הוּא יְהוָה. Where this latter colon focused on the punitive aspect of YHWH's justice, the present colon turns to its other dimension: its salvific aspect. See the explanation of 1_{18a} as well as the parallel passage 3_{55ff} in which the גֶּבֶר calls upon YHWH to realise his redemptive salvation by treating him justly before the enemy.

The phrase 'from generation to generation' should not be understood as a standard expression but rather as having a quite concrete significance. The poets appear to be thinking specifically of the next generation which must suffer under the present situation of need even although they had no part in its cause. Lam 2_{19}, in which Lady Jerusalem must beg for the life of her children (עַל־נֶפֶשׁ עוֹלָלַיִךְ), ultimately deals with the same problem.[181] YHWH's dominion stretches out to include this new generation.

20A *Why do you forget us unremittingly,* לָמָּה לָנֶצַח תִּשְׁכָּחֵנוּ

The term 'why' (לָמָּה) is an expression of the absurdity of the situation which lies in the tension between YHWH's reign of righteousness and the people's ongoing affliction. In its durative aspect נֶצַח only refers to future time and can be applied to the continuation of an event or situation.[182] Mention of YHWH's 'forgetfulness' is typical of Israel's lament terminology: "In dieser Verwendung begegnet שׁכח in den für das isr. Klagelied typischen Fragen nach dem Grund und der Dauer der Abwendung Jahwes."[183] Such 'forgetfulness' does not imply any loss of memory, it is a statement rather of the fact that YHWH has not intervened to bring the affliction to an end.[184] In order to fully comprehend the extremity of the tension which the poets have presented to YHWH here one must first be aware of the cry

179 See TWAT IV 266; cf likewise THAT I 916 (Soggin) and, for example, Ps 103_{19}.
180 Ps 45_7, 93_2.
181 Cf the explanation of 2_{18aA} and 2_{19cB}.
182 Cf TWAT V 567 (Anderson).
183 See THAT II 901 (Schottroff).
184 Cf the explanation of 3_{17}.

of distress of the children in 2_{18} and Lady Jerusalem's prayer in response in 2_{20}. Indeed, based on experience, it was possible to confess that YHWH never 'forgot' the cry of the afflicted: לֹא־שָׁכַח צַעֲקַת עֲנִיִּים (Ps 9_{13}).[185] This positive confession also provides the words for the present lament: why does YHWH still forget?

20B *leave us alone...* תַּעַזְבֵנוּ

Most exegetes translate this term with 'to forsake/abandon' but in the present tense such a rendering has a hint of incompletion to it: one who abandons or forsakes is in the process of leaving. The present text suggests something more permanent: YHWH's abandonment is complete. One only has to refer to the words of Lady Jerusalem in 1_{16bA}, 'the comforter is far from me', to realise that YHWH has done nothing to expiate her loneliness.

In the Old Testament context, the term עזב 'to leave' – that is to establish a break in human relationships – is much more heavily laden than in our western, individualistic society. In Israel, the person who lost his or her bond with the collective was also in danger of losing his or her life. Life was only possible in society. "Das "Verlassen" des Sippenangehörigen, im Extremfall auch des Fremden oder gar des Feindes (Ex 23,5; Lev 19,10), ist ein Bruch elementarer Gemeinschaftsbindungen und stellt das Leben in Frage." [186]

The term can also be used for a rupture in the relationship between YHWH and his people; people can abandon YHWH and *vice versa*. Of course, the latter does not constitute a threat to YHWH but, with respect to humans, abandonment by YHWH does present a danger. The mortal horror of abandonment by human beings is given form in the image of the infant forgotten by its mother.[187] To be abandoned by YHWH implies the loss of his protection and solidarity. A person is thus thrown back on his or her own resources and abandoned to his or her misfortune and loneliness with all its deadly consequences.[188] One specific application of the term is found in the image of daughter Zion as the abandoned wife of YHWH.[189] As Gerstenberger points out: "Weibliche Verlassenheit bedeutet Witwenschaft (אַלְמָנָה)." [190] This is reminiscent of the beginning of Lamentations

[185] See also TWAT II 901 (Schottroff).
[186] So Gerstenberger in TWAT V 1202.
[187] Isa 49_{15}; cf Jer 14_5.
[188] See Ps $22_{2,12ff}$, 71_{11}.
[189] Cf Isa 54_6, 60_{15} and 62_4.
[190] In TWAT V 1203.

and the image of Lady Jerusalem as a widow sitting alone.[191] An inclusion is evident at the canticle level within the book as a whole: הָיְתָה כְּאַלְמָנָה (1_{1b}) // תַּעַזְבֵנוּ (5_{20B}). An inclusion is also evident in the final song: אִמֹּתֵינוּ כְּאַלְמָנוֹת (5_{3B}) // תַּעַזְבֵנוּ (5_{20B}) which likewise underlines the association with widowhood, all the more so since 'abandonment' is frequently used of ruined cities.[192] Clearly the tragedy of widowhood is wrapped up in the loneliness implied by the present colon.

20B *... as (our) days pass by?* לְאֹרֶךְ יָמִים

The combination לְאֹרֶךְ יָמִים with the preposition לְ is only to be found elsewhere in Ps 23_6 and 93_5. The NBG translates the text as a *potentialis*: 'Why should you forget us in the days to come?' but one might question whether this was really the possibility the poets had in mind. Indeed, the very idea that the current affliction would last for a very long time is unthinkable since it would have been too much to bear beyond its present severity. If one looks at other laments in the OT one can see that there is always a certain urgency in those who pray to YHWH in great need. If he does not come to their aid there is a chance they will not survive the misfortune facing them.[193]

The same objection can be raised, however, against a translation in the form of a lament: 'why do you abandon us for years to come?'[194] Such a translation understands לְאֹרֶךְ יָמִים to be a long period of time synonymous with a long life,[195] but this does not fit the present context. Calvin suggests, therefore, that the prophet (Jeremiah) is appealing here for the restoration of the generation now living. Indeed, the urgent imperatives at the beginning of the song are an indication that those offering this prayer desire YHWH's immediate intervention. In the meantime, however, there is no response to their prayer. On the contrary, their days pass by without any change for the good. Thus לְאֹרֶךְ יָמִים should not be understood as a reference to a long period of time but as the incessant sequence of days which the people experience one by one as days of unremitting affliction.[196]

---

191 Cf the exegesis of 1_{1bA}.

192 Cf Isa $17_{2,9}$, 32_{14}, 60_{15}, $62_{4,12}$, Jer 4_{29}, Ezek 36_4, Zeph 2_4.

193 Cf Ps 22_{20}, 38_{23}, 40_{14}, $70_{2,6}$, 71_{12}, 141_1.

194 Wambacq even translates "until the end of days"; cf Kraus and Groß.

195 See Deut 30_{20} and Job 12_{12}.

196 Cf לַבְּקָרִים in 3_{23A}: 'every morning'; cf also Prov 3_2 where the sequence of days is replaced by the sequence of years.

21A *Bring us back,* YHWH, *to you,* הֲשִׁיבֵנוּ יְהוָה אֵלֶיךָ

The *hiph'il* of √שׁוב means 'to bring back something/someone (to a point of departure)'.[197] In the present colon YHWH is the subject and the supplicants the object; they ask in prayer whether YHWH will bring them back. To which point do the supplicants wish to return? In other words, what is the exact meaning of אֵלֶיךָ here?

The combination √שׁוב + preposition לְ is used in a variety of contexts: to bring someone or something back to a particular place;[198] also figuratively: to the heart,[199] or to a person.[200] It is possible that the reference might be to a place, in which case the prayer would be that YHWH would bring the people back to the place where he is, that is to the ruins of Zion as God's ongoing and only real dwelling place. The prayer to be allowed to return to YHWH is a prayer to be allowed to return to Zion, a prayer which only makes sense from the situation of exile. If one interprets the final colon of this verse (5_{21B}) as a prayer for national restoration then internal parallelism clearly supports such an interpretation of the verse as a whole[201] but few exegetes support this perspective. In the context of Lamentations in its entirety, the topic of the exile is only a side discussion. Only the affliction in the land itself really counts. Moreover, the very ruination of Zion is a sign that YHWH no longer desires to dwell there.

With the actual destruction of Mount Zion in full view (5_{18A}), it is difficult to concieve that the poets are referring here to a return to Zion as the place of YHWH's dwelling. אֵלֶיךָ in this context can only have a personal meaning, pointing to the people's desire to be brought back by YHWH to YHWH. How then should we understand such a return? As a return to both person and place, the expression הֲשִׁיבֵנוּ יְהוָה אֵלֶיךָ contains both possibilities, especially if one imagines a renewed presence in Zion of the eternally enthroned YHWH, dwelling once more in the midst of his people (cf Thenius). This view creates the possibility that the people will be able once again to stand in the presence of their God. His renewed nearness will bring salvation and restoration.[202]

---

197 Cf MDijkstra – JCdMoor, 'Problematical Passages in the Ugaritic Legend of Aqhatu', UF 7 (1975), 190ff.

198 Gen 28_{15}, 48_{21}, Num 35_{25}, Jer 27_{22} etcetera.

199 See I Kgs 8_{47}, Lam 3_{21}.

200 Gen 37_{22}, 42_{37}, 44_{8}, Est $4_{13,15}$ etcetera.

201 Cf Ibn Ezra (see MZlotowitz, מגילת איכה, New York 1979[6], 140), Wambacq; cf also Aalders.

The question remains, however, as to whether such a restoration should be regarded as conversion (cf Kraus and Boecker). Conversion is a human action, although it might admit to a degree of divine guidance. In the present situation, however, it is the people's very inability to restore their relationship with God under their own steam which is the point of confession (echoes of the people's lament in Ezek 37_{11}; cf Ezek 33_{10}). Such powerlessness on the part of the supplicants is in harmony with a context in which YHWH, up to this point, has refused their prayer ($3_{8,44}$). YHWH alone, therefore, can break the great silence between himself and his people and create a new beginning. This is more a reflection of the prophetic mindset than that of the Deuteronomist. In the latter, the return to God is viewed as an 'Entscheidung' on the part of the people.[203] Jeremiah and Ezekiel, on the other hand, see the new beginning as only made possible by an initiative on YHWH's part.[204] As we shall see below, however, it is clear that any restoration by YHWH calls for an ultimately indispensible human response.

21A *and we shall repent!* וְנָשׁוּב

If the destruction of the temple is a sign of a broken relationship with YHWH[205] then any restoration of the temple must require the restoration of that relationship. The inseparability of both is evident in Jer 31_{18} in which the restoration of Ephraim follows upon his conversion. Likewise, in Neh $9_{26,29}$ the return to YHWH implies a return to the practice of his commandments.[206] It seems evident, therefore, that the present colon is a summarising contraction of 3_{40} and that (the *q^erē*) נָשׁוּבָה stands for וְנָשׁוּבָה עַד־יְהוָה, whereby the combination of √שׁוּב (*qal*) + preposition עַד refers to the people's intimate relationship with YHWH[207] The context of Lam 3_{40} together with that of the first canticle of Lamentations is reminiscent of the imagery in Hos 2_6 (MT 2_9): abandoned by her lovers, Lady Israel will return to her first husband: YHWH.

---

202 Cf Ps $80_{4-8,20}$ and the גֶּבֶר's confession of YHWH's closeness in $3_{61,63}$. This explanation also honours the parallelism with the second colon.

203 Cf THAT II 889f (Soggin), Deut 4_{30} and 30_2.

204 Cf Jer $24_{6,7}$, 31_{31-34}, Ezek 36_{26ff}, 37_{1-14}; cf also 1983, 190f and 198ff.

205 Cf Mic 3_{12}; Jer 7_{14} and the explanation of 2_{6-9} and 4_{11b}.

206 Cf also Jer 3_{14} and 4_{1ff}.

207 Cf HWWolff, 'Das Thema "Umkehr" in der alttestamentlichen Prophetie', in: *Gesammelte Studien zum Alten Testament*, ThB 22, München 1973², 154, and the explanation of 3_{40}.

21B *renew our days as of old!* חַדֵּשׁ יָמֵינוּ כְּקֶדֶם

Westermann notes: "Die Erfahrung des Neuen ist für den Israeliten auf ganz wenige Erfahrungskreise beschränkt; er redet sehr selten von Neuem." He goes on to point out that in God's history with Israel there is only talk of newness in the time of the exile.[208] North sees this, among other things, as a sign of effective interiorisation of the people's relationship with YHWH.[209] The renewal expected here lies contained within YHWH as subject: a hitherto unprecedented and new act of salvation is necessary on his part if Israel is to rise up from this terrible chaos and misfortune. With respect to the object of the longed for renewal, the 'eschatology' of Lamentations appears to imply a form of restoration, a return to the good old days.

When were the good old days? According to Wolff prophetic preaching together with the conversion of the people referred to a return to the first moments of their relationship with YHWH: "Das Thema "Umkehr" meint ursprünglich die "Rückkehr" Israels zu dem Anfang, den Jahwe mit seinem Volke als ganzem gemacht hat."[210] The questions still remains, however, whether the poets of Lamentations are referring here to this 'honeymoon' period in the people's relationship with YHWH.[211] The context of Lamentations suggests a less remote past. If one interprets the text from the perspective of 1_{7ab}: זָכְרָה יְרוּשָׁלַם... כֹּל מַחֲמֻדֶיהָ אֲשֶׁר הָיוּ מִימֵי קֶדֶם, then the point of reference is clearly not to the wilderness period but to the period of the kingdom, with Jerusalem as capital and temple city. The precious things with which Lady Jerusalem is preoccupied are the temple and the palace in their former splendour.[212] Thus, the appeal for restoration of the good old days implies an appeal for the restoration of Zion and we can then speak of a response within the present canticle: כִּסְאֲךָ לְדֹר וָדוֹר (19B) // כְּקֶדֶם (21B). This is not all, however. If one takes note of the final canticle of the third song then one can see that the גֶּבֶר has the return of the entire land in mind.[213] This is confirmed by the lament in 5_2 with which 5_{21} forms an inclusion: the people's lost inheritence has to be restored in its entirety also.

[208] See THAT II 526; cf also our explanation of 3_{23A}.
[209] Cf TWAT II 773f.
[210] Wolff, 183.
[211] Cf Hos 2_{13-22} (MT 2_{16-25}), Jer 2_2, Mic 7_{14-20}.
[212] See the explanation of 1_{7ab}.
[213] Cf the explanation of 3_{65}.

22A *Or do you prefer to reject us forever,* כִּי אִם־מָאֹס מְאַסְתָּנוּ

Gordis notes "The closing verse in Lamentations is crucial for the meaning and spirit of the entire poem." [214] Commentators do indeed provide this final verse of Lamentations with a variety of interpretations.[215] One has the impression that in the translation and exegesis of this text, grammatical and linguistic objectivity has been undermined by dogmatic considerations which have not always been equally explicit. The Jewish tradition, for example, was unwilling to conclude Lamentations with the negative possibilities of 5_{22} and simply repeated the conclusion of the penultimate verse.[216] This repetition is followed by Wiesmann. Among the more recent commentators, he alone considers a process of textual corruption to be at work whereby 5_{22} got separated from its original place and ended up as the final verse. His only argument in his own favour, however, is that the songs are thereby left with an unsatisfactory ending!

The most frequently chosen translation runs as follows: "or have you rejected us completely?" [217] Meek, Albrektson and Gordis point out, however, that כִּי אִם never means 'or'. Hillers understands כִּי אִם as a confirmation: "but you have abandoned us completely!" [218] Gordis is correct in noting that this interpretation does not fit well with the preceding prayer: one does not pray only to conclude with a statement that YHWH will not grant what one asks because he has completely abandoned the supplicant(s). Gordis' own position is hereby undermined, however. His point of departure is that the text is a confirmation of rejection: "renew our days as of old, even though you had despised us greatly." Westermann correctly point out here that YHWH's anger thus becomes past tense (perfect) while

[214] See RGordis, 'The Conclusion of the Book of Lamentations', JBL 93 (1974), 289; cf also Hillers.

[215] Cf the various translations mentioned in CWestermann, *Die Klagelieder*, Forschungsgeschichte und Auslegung, Neukirchen-Vluyn 1990, 178f.

[216] Cf Pesikta de Rab Kahana, R. Kahana's Compilation of Discourses for Sabbaths and Festal Days, translation of WGBraude & IJKapstein, London 1975, 265 note 40: "The Masorah, in line with its usual custom, prescribes the repetition of Lam. 5:21 after the concluding verse, in order to end the Book on a note of consolation." The text refers to a discussion between Rabbi Eleazar and Rabbi Johanan who had a difference of opinion with regard to the way the prophets concluded their prophecies: "(Returning to Jeremiah's concluding prophecy), is it not a fact that he says therein "But Thou hast utterly rejected us" (Lam. 5:22)? Yes, but directly after he says "Thou hast utterly rejected us", he goes on to say comfortingly, "Turn Thou us unto Thee" (Lam. 5:21)."

[217] See Westermann, 179.

[218] In line with ט, Luther, Calvin, KJV.

its results are still being experienced in full. The question remains as to whether there can still be talk of prayer if one assumes such an absolute degree of rejection. Kaiser translates: "Denn wenn du uns gänzlich verworfen hast, so zürnst du uns zu sehr." Such an approach, however, resounds with high-handed theological critique which cannot be reconciled with 1_{18a} and is certainly far from the poets' intentions.[219]

In our earlier work we followed Rudolph and opted for a translation of with 'unless'[220] but this translation has its weaknesses which call for a change of opinion. It is noteworthy that where כִּי אִם can be translated with 'unless', the protasis almost always contains or implies a negative.[221] One might present the syntax schematically as follows: *not x unless y*. Consistence in this regard prevented Albrektson from opting for this translation in 5_{22} since there is absolutely no question of a negative in the protasis (5_{21}). In our modern idiom the reverse of our schema is also possible: *x unless not y*, but as far as Hebrew is concerned, commentators have sought in vain for such a construction, in spite of the frequency of the combination כִּי אִם. The present text would in fact be the only example of its kind.

Two texts offer an alternative possibility for translation: Deut 10_{12} and Mic 6_8. The latter implicitly contains a question as to what YHWH desires. In the formulation of the verses one cannot detect any direct negation. Exclusivity, however, lies hidden in the כִּי אִם itself: 'YHWH desires nothing other than... '. While it is true that 5_{21} lacks an interrogative, nevertheless it clearly refers to what YHWH wants or desires. In the context of this prayer there are two possibilities: either YHWH will give ear to their prayerful imperative חַדֵּשׁ and renew their days or such renewal is not what he wants. It is this latter possibility which the poets are expressing in the present colon, as if they want to confront YHWH with the extreme consequences of such a response to their prayer: "or do you prefer to reject us forever?" The very use of the paranomastic construction with the verb מאס makes this clear.[222] It is evident from their fate thus far that rejection by YHWH is a fact (cf 3_{45}) but is it total and definitive or only temporary and partial? This is the burning question facing the poets at the end of their work. As in 3_{29}, an echo of 'perhaps' resonates in these final words also. There are signs of hope (cf $3_{22,23}$) but the final outcome is still uncertain.

[219] Cf also Boecker's objections.

[220] See 1983, 308ff.

[221] Cf Gen 32_{27}, Lev 22_6, Ruth 3_{18}, Isa 55_{10} etcetera.

[222] Cf GES-K § 113*l*–r.

Clearly the poets opt for the most compelling wording in order to secure YHWH's favour. We noted in our explanation of 3_{45} that rejection elicited an enormous tension in YHWH, that he was not inclined to reject what he had chosen. Indeed the poets' faith and trust was based on this very tension and rightly so. This was not only evident from the restoration after the exile but also from the fact that Israel had survived the period between fall and restoration! (cf 3_{22}). While the poets are aware of the factuality of rejection, it remains almost unthinkable for them that YHWH might have abandoned them for ever; witness texts such as Jer 31_{37}, $33_{24,26}$ and Isa 41_9. It is within this tension that the poets must live and work and pray. While the aforementioned Jeremiah texts may be post-exilic in style and expression,[223] an awareness of the incredibility of such a permanent rejection is certainly present in pre-exilic times.[224] The same awareness can be found elsewhere in Lamentations itself, in the structurally significant location at the end of the first canto of the third song: 'it is not according to God's heart'.[225] Wildberger, however, goes too far when he says: "Aber im Grunde steht der Beter der Klagelieder ungebrochen in der Kulttradition Jerusalems, er weiß, daß eine solche Verwerfung nicht Wirklichkeit sein kann." [226] Are the poets certain of this? Their mighty גֶּבֶר (3_1) is a broken man (3_8). At this point in their history, without a Davidic king in Jerusalem, with the temple destroyed, with YHWH silent (3_8) and hidden (3_{44}), the poets are far from certain. They have a degree of hope and their devout one might go as far as to say 'perhaps' (cf $3_{21,24,29}$) but certainty is not to be derived from their trust, only from the manifestation of a salvific and restorative intervention on the part of YHWH. Will that happen? Ultimately the poets realise that there is another possibility, one which they would prefer to avoid.

22B *to rage against us without measure?* קָצַפְתָּ עָלֵינוּ עַד־מְאֹד

According to Sauer "Nach dem Exil wird deutlich, daß der Zorn (Gottes) nicht ewig währt." [227] He suggests thereby that this insight could only have emerged in the light of a restored Israel. A few post-exilic texts can indeed be pointed out in favour of such a position [228] but the question

223 Cf WThiel, *Die deuteronomistische Redaktion von Jeremia 26–45*, WMANT 52, Neukirchen 1981, 37.
224 Cf Jer 14_{19} and THAT I 889 (Wildberger).
225 Cf the explanation of 3_{33}.
226 In THAT I 889.
227 See THAT II 665.
228 Cf Isa $54_{7,8}$ and Zech 1_{15}; cf also ASvdWoude, *Zacharia*, Nijkerk 1984, 39.

remains whether or not such a notion was already circulating in Israel at a much earlier period. As a matter of fact, short duration is already part and parcel of the metaphor of God's anger as such. This is much older than the exile.[229] The anger metaphor can only be understood by analogy with human anger as a short, furious burst of indignation brought on by disobedience and sin or, as Sauer himself formulates the meaning of the verb √קצף I which is found only here in Lamentations: "...eine rasch aufsteigende, heftige und bald auch wieder verklingende Gemütsbewegung...".[230] The results of human anger and wrath are retributive[231] and can even be deadly in nature.[232] The effects of divine anger are analogous: when unchecked it too can be retributive and deadly.[233]

It is to this possibility of unchecked divine anger that the poets turn their attention in the final words of their work. The adverbial expression עַד־מְאֹד suggests a culminating point and is often rendered as 'extreme' (I Kgs 1_4, Dan 11_{25}), 'complete' (Ps 38_9), 'total' (Ps 119_8), 'measureless' (Dan 8_8).[234] As we all know, such total, unbridled divine anger is deadly. At the same time, however, unrestrained wrath on the part of YHWH is in conflict with his nature, an *opus alienum*. See once again 3_{33}. God does not delight in the death of the godless (Ezek 18_{32}) nor is it according to his heart to take revenge against the people he created (cf Isa 57_{16}). Beuken's suggestion[235] that, based on Isa 57_{16}, we should understand God's anger as a reaction whereby he desires to make people 'humble of spirit' must be rejected on the basis of the other texts noted above. 'Humility of spirit' may be a consequence of divine punishment but not of divine wrath.[236]

Here at the very end of the songs, broken people confront YHWH with a question: will he turn against himself in order to repay them for their sins? It is a question for the divine conscience. What shall the outcome be: anger or mercy? Israel's confession of faith claimed that YHWH's anger was shortlived[237] and his mercy forever.[238] The supplicants of Lamentations

---

229 Cf MCAKorpel, *A Rift in the Clouds*, Münster 1990, 172–175; cf also Jer 3_{12}, Ps 30_6 and 103_9.

230 Sauer, THAT II 664.

231 Gen 40_2, Jer 37_{15}, Est $1_{12,19}$.

232 Cf Est 2_{21}.

233 Cf Jer 10_{10}, Deut $9_{8,19}$, Jos 22_{20}, Ps 38_2, Jer $21_{5,6}$, 50_{13}, Jonah 3_9; cf also Ps 90_7 and Korpel, 184.

234 Cf the similar sounding laments in Isa $64_{9,12}$ (MT $64_{8,11}$).

235 Cf WAMBeuken, *Jesaja deel IIIA*, Nijkerk 1989, 87.

236 Cf, for example, Judg 10_{7-14}.

237 Ps 30_6, 103_9, Jer 3_{12}.

hold fast to this faith. Once again, however, it is not their confession which will offer certainty, only YHWH's salvific intervention can bring them life and restore their faith.

*　　*　　*

[238] Ex 34_6, Ps 86_{15}, Jonah 4_2 etcetera.

Song-responses (a selection)

Lam I	Lam II	Lam III	Lam IV	Lam V
1–3	**1–3**	**1–9**	**1–3**	**1–3**
אֵיכָה	אֵיכָה	עָנִי	אֵיכָה	זָכֹר חֶרְפָּתֵנוּ ....
הָעִיר רַבָּתִי עָם	בַּת־צִיּוֹן	אֲנִי הַגֶּבֶר	בְּנֵי צִיּוֹן	לָנוּ ....
Js 54$_4$ כְּאַלְמָנָה	....	רָאָה עָנִי	....	רְאֵה אֶת־חֶרְפָּתֵנוּ ......
Ezek 16$_{39}$ כְּאַלְמָנָה	הִשְׁלִיךְ . . . תִּפְאֶרֶת			
לֵילָה	יָעִיב	חֹשֶׁךְ וְלֹא־אוֹר	יוּעַם	
	הִשְׁלִיךְ מִשָּׁמַיִם	יַהֲפֹךְ	תִּשְׁתַּפֵּכְנָה אַבְנֵי־קֹדֶשׁ ...	נֶהֶפְכָה ....
שָׂרָתִי בַּמְּדִינוֹת	תִּפְאֶרֶת יִשְׂרָאֵל	גֶּבֶר	הַיְקָרִים	בְּכֶסֶף/בִּמְחִיר\\ ....
	לֹא־זָכַר	....	....	זָכֹר ....
	הֲדֹם־רַגְלָיו	....	אַבְנֵי־קֹדֶשׁ	נַחֲלָתֵנוּ ....
	בְּעֶבְרָתוֹ	עֶבְרָתוֹ		
הָיוּ לָהּ	....	....	....	הָיָה לָנוּ ....
כְּאַלְמָנָה	....	....	....	כְּאַלְמָנוֹת ....
לֹא מָצְאָה מָנוֹחַ	....	....	....	כְּאַלְמָנוֹת ....
אֵין־לָהּ מְנַחֵם	לֹא חָמַל	לֹא־אוֹר	אֵין לָהֶם	אֵין אָב ....
גָּלְתָה יְהוּדָה	גָּדַע . . . יִשְׂרָאֵל	שִׁבַּר עַצְמוֹתָי	לְנִבְלֵי־חֶרֶשׂ	
4–6	**4–6**	**10–18**	**4–6**	**4–6**
שְׁעָרֶיהָ שׁוֹמֵמִין	וַיַּהֲרֹג . . . מַחֲמַדֵּי־עָיִן	שָׂמַנִי שֹׁמֵם	נָשַׁמּוּ בַחוּצוֹת	יְתוֹמִים ....
	כְּאוֹיֵב	דֹּב/אַרְיֵה		

	שָׁאֲלוּ . . . פֹּרֵשׂ אֵין לָהֶם.	שָׂתַם תְּפִלָּתִי		
			אֹהֶל . . .צִיּוֹן..........	דַּרְכֵי צִיּוֹן
	גּוּרֵיהֶן	אַרְיֵה בְּמִסְתָּרִים		
		דָּרַךְ קַשְׁתּוֹ........	דָּרַךְ קַשְׁתּוֹ...........	דַּרְכֵי (allit)
	נָשַׁמּוּ...........	בְּנֵי אַשְׁפָּתוֹ........	הָיָה אֲדֹנָי כְּאוֹיֵב.......	אֹיְבֶיהָ שָׁלוּ
לִשְׂבֹּעַ..............	....	הִשְׂבִּיעַנִי		
	עוֹלָלִים............	....	....	עוֹלָלֶיהָ
מֵימֵינוּ..............	דָּבַק לְשׁוֹן........	הִרְוַנִי לַעֲנָה		
	לְמַעֲדַנִּים \\	מְרוֹרִים/לַעֲנָה........	תַּאֲנִיָּה וַאֲנִיָּה.........	וְהִיא מַר־לָהּ
לִשְׂבֹּעַ לָחֶם..........	חִבְּקוּ אַשְׁפַּתּוֹת........	חָצָץ . . .אֵפֶר		
נָתַנּוּ יָד.............	....	אָבַד נִצְחִי וְתוֹחַלְתִּי.......	....	וַיֵּצֵא מִן־בַּת־צִיּוֹן . . .
	הָאֱמֻנִים עֲלֵי תוֹלָע.....	נָשִׁיתִי טוֹבָה..........	שִׁכַּח . . .בְּצִיּוֹן..........	וַיֵּצֵא מִן־בַּת־צִיּוֹן . . .
		אָבַד נִצְחִי..........	מֶלֶךְ וְכֹהֵן..........	שָׂרֶיהָ
נִרְדָּפְנוּ.............	....	....	....	רוֹדֵף
7–9	**7–9**	**19–27**	**7–9**	**7–9**
חָטְאוּ/עֲוֹנֹתֵיהֶם........	....	....	....	חֵטְא חָטְאָה
		זְכָר־עָנְיִי..........	....	זָכְרָה יְרוּשָׁלַםִ
סָבָלְנוּ............	....	עָנְיִי וּמְרוּדִי/לַעֲנָה וָרֹאשׁ		
פֹּרֵק אֵין מִיָּדָם........	....	וְתָשִׁיחַ עָלַי נַפְשִׁי........	בְּיַד־אוֹיֵב...........	בְּיַד־צָר
			בַּת־צִיּוֹן..........	יְרוּשָׁלָםִ
		חַסְדֵי יְהוָה \\	חָשַׁב יְהוָה . . .	
לַחְמֵנוּ/חֶרֶב..........	חֶרֶב/רָעָב			

אֵין מְנַחֵם לָהּ	.... אֵין תּוֹרָה	טוֹב . . . תִּדְרְשֻׁנּוּ \\		
		טוֹב	.... טוֹבִים	
אֵין עוֹזֵר	....	....	....	...... אֵינָם . . . אבֹתֵינוּ
רְאֵה יְהוָה . . .	....	...... לִתְשׁוּעַת יְהוָה . . .		
		לְנֶפֶשׁ	....	.... בְּנַפְשֵׁנוּ
10–11	**10–11**	**28–33**	**10–11**	**10–11**
מִקְדָּשָׁהּ	.... בַּת־צִיּוֹן/קִרְיָה	....	.... בְּצִיּוֹן	.... בְּצִיּוֹן
	יֵשְׁבוּ . . . יִדְּמוּ	.... יֵשֵׁב בָּדָד וְיִדֹּם		
	עָפָר עַל־רֹאשָׁם	.... יִתֵּן בֶּעָפָר פִּיהוּ	.... לְבָרוֹת . . .	.... זַלְעֲפוֹת רָעָב
	כָּלוּ	....	.... כִּלָּה יְהוָה	
כָּל־מַחֲמַדֶּיהָ	.... בְּתוּלֹת יְרוּשָׁלָם	....	.... נָשִׁים רַחֲמָנִיּוֹת	.... נָשִׁים בְּצִיּוֹן
	נִשְׁפַּךְ	....	.... שָׁפַךְ	
	שֶׁבֶר בַּת־עַמִּי	....	.... שֶׁבֶר בַּת־עַמִּי	
		לֹא יִזְנַח לְעוֹלָם אֲדֹנָי	.... כִּלָּה יְהוָה	
לְהָשִׁיב נָפֶשׁ	.... בֵּעָטֵף עוֹלֵל	....	.... תֹּאכַל/יַלְדֵיהֶן	.... רָעָב
לָחֶם	.... דָּגָן (12)	....	.... בִּשְׁלוּ/בָרוֹת	.... לחמו / רָעָב
רְאֵה יְהוָה	...... עוֹלֵל וְיוֹנֵק/שֶׁבֶר			
		לֹא עִנָּה מִלִּבּוֹ	....	.... נָשִׁים . . . עִנּוּ
12–13	**12–13**	**34–39**	**12–13**	**12–13**
וְרָאוּ	....	.... אֲדֹנָי לֹא רָאָה		
אִם־יֵשׁ . . . כְּמַכְאֹבִי	..... בֵּעָטֵף עוֹלֵל וְיוֹנֵק			

בְּיָדָם........	צַר וְאוֹיֵב........	תַּחַת רַגְלָיו........	....	לְרַגְלַי
זְקֵנִים לֹא נֶהְדָּרוּ........	צַר וְאוֹיֵב בְּשַׁעֲרֵי			
שָׂרִים בְּיָדָם נִתְלוּ........	בְּשַׁעֲרֵי........	לְעַוֵּת/לְהַטּוֹת		
	מֵחַטֹּאת........	מַה־יִּתְאוֹנֵן \\	מָה (3x)	אִם־יֵשׁ מַכְאוֹב
צִיּוֹן........	יְרוּשָׁלַםִ........	....	יְרוּשָׁלַםִ	
	נְבִיאֶיהָ/כֹּהֲנֶיהָ	מִי זֶה אָמַר........	נְבִיאַיִךְ (14)	
	מֵחַטֹּאת נְבִיאֶיהָ........	הָרָעוֹת........	מַשְׂאוֹת שָׁוְא (14)	
כִּי חָטָאנוּ (16)	מֵחַטֹּאת........	חָטְאוּ........	עֲוֹנֵךְ (14)	פְּשָׁעַי (14)
		יִתְאוֹנֵן... חָטְאוּ........	שִׁבְרֵךְ........	שֹׁמֵמָה
		אָדָם חָי \\	מִי יִרְפָּא־לָךְ........	כָּל־הַיּוֹם דָּוָה
14–16	**14–16**	**40–48**	**14–16**	**14–16**
...טְחוֹן נָשָׂאוּ........	....	....	....	עֹל...עַל־צַוָּארִי
כָּשְׁלוּ........	נָעוּ עִוְרִים........	....	....	הִכְשִׁיל
	עִוְרִים........	....	נְבִיאַיִךְ חָזוּ לָךְ שָׁוְא...	
		נַחְפְּשָׂה דְרָכֵינוּ........	לֹא־גִלּוּ עַל־עֲוֹנֵךְ	
	בְּלֹא יוּכְלוּ יִגְּעוּ........	פָּשַׁעְנוּ וּמָרִינוּ........	עֲוֹנֵךְ........	פְּשָׁעַי
נָפְלָה עֲטֶרֶת רֹאשֵׁנוּ....	נְגֹאֲלוּ/טָמֵא........	סְחִי וּמָאוֹס........	הֲזֹאת הָעִיר...כְּלִילַת יֹפִי	
	בַּגּוֹיִם........	בְּקֶרֶב הָעַמִּים........	כָּל־עֹבְרֵי דֶרֶךְ	
		הָרַגְתָּ........	....	לְשַׁבֹּר/גַּת דָּרַךְ
בַּחוּרִים........	....	....	....	בַּחוּרָי
			בַּת יְרוּשָׁלָםִ........	בַּת־יְהוּדָה
	סוּרוּ טָמֵא........	סְחִי וּמָאוֹס........	סָפְקוּ/שָׁרְקוּ	

	וַיָּנֻעוּ	....	נָעוּ........	
	שֶׁיֹּאמְרוּ	....	אָמְרוּ........	
	מָשׂוֹשׂ	סְחִי וּמָאוֹס \\.........	....	מְשׂוֹשׂ לִבֵּנוּ........
אוֹיֵב	אוֹיְבַיִךְ........	כָּל־אֹיְבֵינוּ........		
עֵינַי יָרְדָה מַּיִם	פָּצוּ עָלַיִךְ פִּיהֶם \\.....	מַיִם תֵּרַד עֵינִי........		
		עֵינִי נִגְּרָה	תִּכְלֶינָה עֵינֵינוּ........	חָשְׁכוּ עֵינֵינוּ........
	בִּלָּעְנוּ	הַשֵּׁאת וְהַשָּׁבֶר........	....	נָפְלָה עֲטֶרֶת........
עַל־אֵלֶּה	....	עַל־שֶׁבֶר בַּת־עַמִּי......	....	עַל־אֵלֶּה........
17–19	**17–19**	**49–57**	**17–19**	**17–19**
	אַל־תִּדֹּם	וְלֹא תִדְמֶה........		
	פוּגַת	הֲפֻגוֹת........		
אֵין מְנַחֵם לָהּ	לֹא חָמָל........	לֹא/אֵין........	לֹא יוֹשַׁע........	
צִוָּה יְהוָה	צִוָּה (יְהוָה)........	עַד־יַשְׁקִיף...יְהוָה....		
	בִּצַּע אֶמְרָתוֹ	....	עֶזְרָתֵנוּ הָבֶל........	
צִיּוֹן/יְרוּשָׁלַםִ	בַּת־צִיּוֹן........	עִירִי........	....	צִיּוֹן........
צָרָיו	אוֹיֵב/צָרָיִךְ........	אֹיְבַי........		
	צָעַק לִבָּם	....	....	דָּוֶה לִבֵּנוּ........
צַדִּיק הוּא יְהוָה	צָעַק לִבָּם אֶל־אֲדֹנָי....	....	....	אַתָּה יְהוָה........
צַדִּיק הוּא יְהוָה	פְּנֵי אֲדֹנָי........	יְהוָה........	....	כִּסְאֲךָ לְדֹר וָדוֹר......
הָלְכוּ בַשֶּׁבִי	....	....	מַלְכֻת/נִלְכַּד........	
		צוֹד צָו יְנִי	צָדוּ צְעָדֵינוּ........	

	מִנִּשְׁרֵי שָׁמָיִם..........	כַּצִּפּוֹר		
אַתָּה יְהוָה..........	....	קָרָאתִי שִׁמְךָ יְהוָה......	שִׁפְכִי... לִבֵּךְ........	\\ קָרָאתִי לַמְאַהֲבַי
	קָרַב קִצֵּינוּ \\.........	קָרַבְתָּ		
		לְרַוְחָתִי לְשַׁוְעָתִי.......	הָעֲטוּפִים בְּרָעָב........	בִּקְשׁוּ אֹכֶל לָמוֹ
צִיּוֹן שֻׁמָּמָה/שׁוּעָלִים....	כִּי־בָא קִצֵּינוּ..........	נִגְזָרְתִּי		
		נַפְשִׁי/חַיָּי.........	עַל־נֶפֶשׁ..........	אֶת־נַפְשָׁם
20–22	**20–22**	**55-66**	**20–22**	**20–22**
אַתָּה יְהוָה (19)........	מְשִׁיחַ יְהוָה..........	רָאִיתָה יְהוָה.........	רְאֵה יְהוָה..........	רְאֵה יְהוָה
		הַבִּיטָה..........	הַבִּיטָה	
	נִחְיֶה..........	גָּאַלְתָּ חַיָּי \\........	נָפְלוּ בֶחָרֶב.........	שִׁכְּלָה־חֶרֶב
	מְשִׁיחַ יְהוָה.........	....	כֹּהֵן וְנָבִיא	
		שָׁמַעְתָּ.........	....	שְׁמַע
יְהוָה..........	....	יְהוָה..........	....	אַתָּה עָשִׂיתָ
			לֹא חָמָלְתָּ..........	אֵין מְנַחֵם לִי
	שִׂישִׂי וְשִׂמְחִי.........	אֲנִי מַנְגִּינָתָם.........	....	שָׂשׂוּ
	כּוֹס..........	....	נָפְלוּ בֶחָרֶב	
לְאֹרֶךְ יָמִים..........	....	כָּל־הַיּוֹם..........	בְּיוֹם אַפֶּךָ..........	יוֹם־קָרָאתָ
	פָּקַד עֲוֹנֵךְ.........	תִּתֵּן לָהֶם מְגִנַּת־לֵב.....	....	עוֹלֵל לָמוֹ
	עֲוֹנֵךְ/חַטֹּאתָיִךְ.......	כְּמַעֲשֵׂה יְדֵיהֶם.......	....	כָּל־רָעָתָם
קָצַפְתָּ..........	....	בְּאַף..........	אַף־יְהוָה	
			רִבִּיתִי..........	רַבּוֹת
קָצַפְתָּ..........	כּוֹס..........	מְגִנַּת־לֵב..........	....	לִבִּי דַוָּי

HISTORICAL COMMENTARY ON THE OLD TESTAMENT

PUBLISHED VOLUMES

Exodus I: Exodus 1:1–7:13 (1993)	Cornelis Houtman, Kampen, The Netherlands
Exodus I: Exodus 7:14–19:25 (1996)	Cornelis Houtman, Kampen, The Netherlands
1 Kings I/1: 1 Kings 1–11 (1998)	Martin J. Mulder, Leiden, The Netherlands
Isaiah III/1: Isaiah 40–48 (1997)	Jan L. Koole, Kampen, The Netherlands
Lamentations (1998)	Johan Renkema, Kampen, The Netherlands
Nahum (1997)	Klaas Spronk, Kampen, The Netherlands

FORTHCOMING VOLUMES

Exodus III: Exodus 20-40	Cornelis Houtman, Kampen, The Netherlands
Isaiah 13-39	Willem A.M. Beuken, Louvain, Belgium
Isaiah III/2: Isaiah 49-55	Jan L. Koole, Kampen, The Netherlands
Isaiah III/3: Isaiah 56-66	Jan L. Koole, Kampen, The Netherlands
Zephaniah	Jan Vlaardingerbroek, Rotterdam, The Netherlands
Habakuk	Gert T.M. Prinsloo, Pretoria, South Africa

PROJECTED VOLUMES

Genesis	Erhard Blum, Augsburg, Germany
Leviticus	James W. Watts, Hastings, Nebraska U.S.A.
Numbers	F.A. Gosling, Sheffield, England
Deuteronomy	Cornelis Houtman, Kampen, The Netherlands
Joshua	Hartmut Rösel, Haifa, Israel
Judges	Klaas Spronk, Kampen, The Netherlands
Ruth	Marjo C.A. Korpel, Utrecht, The Netherlands
1 Samuel	Åke Viberg, Lund, Sweden
2 Samuel	Jichan Kim, Seoul, Korea
1 Kings 12-22	Jurie le Roux, Pretoria, South Africa
2 Kings	Kevin J. Cathcart, Dublin, Ireland
1 Chronicles	Peter B. Dirksen, Leiden, The Netherlands
2 Chronicles	Isaac Kalimi, Brookline, MA U.S.A.
Ezra	István Karasszon, Budapest, Hungary
Nehemiah	Edward Noort, Groningen, The Netherlands
Esther	Henk Jagersma, Brussels, Belgium

Job	Richard S. Hess, London, England
Psalms	Phil.J. Botha & Gert T.M. Prinsloo, Pretoria, South Africa
Proverbs	James A. Loader, Vienna, Austria
Ecclesiastes	Anton Schoors, Louvain, Belgium
Song of Songs	Wilfred G.E. Watson, New Castle, England
Isaiah 1-12	Hendrik Leene, Amsterdam, The Netherlands
Jeremiah	Ben J. Oosterhoff† & Erik Peels, Apeldoorn, The Netherlands
Ezekiel 1-24	Herrie F. van Rooy, Potchefstroom, South Africa
Ezekiel 25-48	Corrine Patton, Tallahassee, Florida, U.S.A.
Daniel	Tibor Marjovszki, Debrecen, Hungary
Hosea	Dwight R. Daniels, Glendale, CA U.S.A.
Joel	Willem van der Meer, Kampen, The Netherlands
Amos	Meindert Dijkstra, Utrecht, The Netherlands
Obadaiah	Johan Renkema, Kampen, The Netherlands
Jonah	Johannes H. Potgieter, Pretoria, South Africa
Micah	Johannes C. de Moor, Kampen, The Netherlands
Haggai	William Th. Koopmans, Peterborough, Ont. Canada
Zechariah	Al Wolters, Ancaster, Ont. Canada
Malachi	Raymond C. Van Leeuwen, Ardmore, PA U.S.A.